ROUTLEDGE HANDBOOK OF LATIN AMERICAN SECURITY

This new Handbook is a comprehensive collection of cutting-edge essays on all aspects of Latin American security by a mix of established and emerging scholars.

The *Routledge Handbook of Latin American Security* identifies the key contemporary topics of research and debate, taking into account that the study of Latin America's comparative and international politics has undergone dramatic changes since the end of the Cold War, the return of democracy, and the relegitimization and rearmament of the military against the background of low-level uses of force short of war.

Latin America's security issues have become an important topic in international relations and Latin American studies. This Handbook sets a rigorous agenda for future research and is organized into five key parts:

- The Evolution of Security in Latin America
- Theoretical Approaches to Security in Latin America
- Different 'Securities'
- Contemporary Regional Security Challenges
- Latin America and Contemporary International Security Challenges

With a focus on contemporary challenges and the failures of regional institutions to eliminate the threat of the use of force among Latin Americans, this Handbook will be of great interest to students of Latin American politics, security studies, war and conflict studies, and international relations in general.

David R. Mares holds the Institute of the Americas Chair for Inter-American Affairs, University of California, San Diego. He is author/editor of nine books, including most recently *Debating Civil-Military Relations in Latin America* (with Rafael Martínez, 2013).

Arie M. Kacowicz is the Chaim Weizmann Chair in International Relations and associate professor at the Hebrew University of Jerusalem, Israel. He is the author of four books, including most recently *Globalization and the Distribution of Wealth: The Latin American Experience, 1982–2008* (2013).

ROUTLEDGE HANDBOOK OF LATIN AMERICAN SECURITY

Edited by David R. Mares and Arie M. Kacowicz

Routledge
Taylor & Francis Group
LONDON AND NEW YORK

First published 2016
byRoutledge
2 Park Square, Milton Park, Abingdon, Oxon OX14 4RN

and by Routledge
52 Vanderbilt Avenue, New York, NY 10017

First issued in paperback 2020

Routledge is an imprint of the Taylor & Francis Group, an informa business

British Library Cataloguing in Publication Data
A catalogue record for this book is available from the British Library

Library of Congress Cataloging-in-Publication Data
Routledge handbook of Latin American security / edited by David R. Mares and Arie M. Kacowicz.
pages cm
Includes bibliographical references and index.
1. Security, International—LatinAmerica. 2. National security—Latin America. 3. Human security—Latin America. 4. Democracy—Latin America. 5. Latin America—Politics and government. I. Mares, David R. II. Kacowicz, Arie Marcelo.
JZ6009.L29N37 2015
355′.03308—dc23
2015003317

ISBN 13: 978-0-367-58174-9 (pbk)
ISBN 13: 978-0-415-71869-1 (hbk)

Typeset in Times New Roman
by Apex CoVantage, LLC

CONTENTS

LIST OF TABLES

PREFACE

John J. Mearsheimer

When most Americans think about international security, they focus mainly on events in Asia, Europe, and the Middle East. Little attention is paid to Latin America, or the Western Hemisphere more generally. And this is despite the fact that Latin America is of much greater strategic importance to the United States than those other three areas, primarily because of geographic proximity.

Not surprisingly, the leading academics who study Latin America tend to be comparativists, who focus most of their attention on what is happening inside particular states, rather than looking at international relations within the region. Even among those who focus on interactions between Latin American countries, few pay attention to security issues. They concentrate instead on matters relating to international political economy (IPE).

We benefit greatly from having a rich stable of comparativists and IPE scholars studying Latin America. But as the various chapters in this Handbook make clear, there are a host of important security issues related to that strategically significant region that need to be examined by first-rate researchers. This volume is a major step forward in remedying that problem.

This Handbook has another great virtue: its emphasis on theory. It is not an exaggeration to say that the political science discipline has become obsessed with empirical methods over the past three decades and in the process has lost sight of the manifest importance of theory for producing top-notch scholarship. This trend is reflected in the published works of most comparativists, who often pay theory little attention and trumpet their methodological skills instead. All too often, this is done to denigrate and marginalize "area specialists," who once dominated the study of comparative politics.

While it is imperative that scholars employ methods in sophisticated ways – be they qualitatively or quantitatively inclined – paying serious attention to theory is just as important. Methodologically driven work that concentrates on testing hypotheses, but does not carefully consider the theory that informs them, is bound to encounter serious problems. In other words, privileging methods over theory is a wrongheaded way of advancing knowledge.

Employing theory in a sophisticated way is critical to the development of cumulative knowledge, and efforts to test empirical hypotheses must be guided by a sophisticated understanding of theory. This is true, of course, whether one is studying comparative politics or international politics. Indeed, theory is indispensable for producing high-quality research in every field in the social sciences.

To the coeditors' great credit, this Handbook puts theory up in bright lights. Empirical methods are also paid ample attention by different authors, which makes eminently good sense. After all, creating theory and testing theory – which is what methods are ultimately all about – are both critical components of social science. Theory, however, is ultimately more important.

Although the Handbook places considerable emphasis on employing theory to examine security issues in Latin America, it does not try to make the case for any particular theory. On the contrary, different authors bring different theoretical approaches to bear, including constructivism, liberalism, Marxism, and realism. Thus, the reader acquires a good feel for how one can think about security in Latin America in distinct ways, depending on his or her chosen theory.

The volume is not only catholic regarding theoretical content; it also takes a pluralist approach toward methods, which is surely for the good. The kind of methods one employs in his or her work should depend on the question being asked and the available evidence. The coeditors went out of their way to convey this message, and with the help of the various authors, they have succeeded.

The Handbook is comprised of 28 chapters, which means it covers a broad range of subjects that fall under the rubric of international security. This wide selection of topics shows there is no shortage of security issues for students of Latin America to study in the years ahead. This is especially true when one considers there are a number of security issues relevant to the region that are not covered in this volume, simply due to space constraints.

In addition to the variety of security-related themes discussed in the Handbook, the various authors come from all over the planet, not just Latin America and the United States. There are experts from Europe and the Middle East as well, all of which help give the book an international perspective on this important region.

In essence, the Handbook makes the case for smartly employing theory and methods to study security issues in Latin America, a truly important subject that is somewhat neglected by social scientists. In pursuit of that goal, it exposes readers to a wide range of perspectives offered up by an impressive array of scholars.

For students just beginning to think about security in Latin America, this book will be invaluable. Not only does it provide an excellent guide on how to do social science research, it also offers useful insights on future research topics. There is no question the Handbook deserves to be widely read.

ACKNOWLEDGMENTS

This Handbook sets the research agenda for the study of 'security' in Latin America. As such, it is the result of the commitment, energy, and intellectual strengths of many people, even though the two editors are ultimately responsible for its content. We begin these acknowledgments by thanking the other 28 contributors to this volume for putting up with our demands, and for participating in a truly multinational effort to understand and explain the contemporary security landscape in Latin America. Owing to their spirit of collaboration, this complex and important endeavor to develop a comprehensive guide for scholarly research could become a reality.

Arie Kacowicz thanks the generous support of the Thyssen Foundation (Germany) for his research project on linking regional and global governance in the context of Latin America, as reflected in Chapter 28. He also thanks the precious research assistance and cooperation of Keren Sasson, Daniel Wajner, and Exequiel Lacovsky, as well as the insightful suggestions and comments of friends and colleagues, including Galia Press-Barnathan, Andrea Oelsner, Ruth Diamint, Carlos Escudé, and Andrea Feldmann.

David Mares thanks his two graduate students, Sofia Lana and Weijun Yuan, for research assistance and editing. Their willingness to turn things around quickly and work through holiday breaks was of enormous help and much appreciated by both editors.

We are particularly grateful to John J. Mearsheimer for writing the preface for this Handbook. John is a tireless advocate for understanding the causal logic of one's theory, and cares deeply about the appropriate use of methods and the importance of empirical support for an argument. He is, therefore, an especially appropriate scholar to introduce this Handbook.

Several authors presented their preliminary chapters at two panels of the International Studies Association (ISA) Annual Meeting in Toronto in March of 2014. We thank the ISA convention organizers for allocating space to our endeavor and the participants in the well-attended panels for their comments and suggestions.

Finally, our gratitude goes to Andrew Humphrys, our editor at Routledge, as well as Hannah Ferguson and the entire team for their guidance and assistance in bringing this project to a broad scholarly audience.

Jerusalem and San Diego

ABBREVIATIONS

ABACC	Brazilian-Argentine Agency for Accounting and Control of Nuclear Materials
ABC	Argentina, Brazil, and Chile
ALBA	Bolivarian Alliance for the Peoples of Our America
APEC	Asia-Pacific Economic Cooperation
ASEAN	Association of Southeast Asian Nations
AUC	United Self-Defense Forces of Colombia
BRICS	Brazil, Russia, India, China, and South Africa
CACM	Central American Common Market
CAN	Andean Community of Nations
CELAC	Community of Latin American and Caribbean States
CONAIE	Confederation of Indigenous Nationalities of Ecuador
CSBMs	Confidence- and Security-Building Measures
ECB	European Central Bank
ECLAC/CEPAL	Economic Commission for Latin America and the Caribbean
ECOWAS	Economic Community of West African States
ELN	*Ejército de Liberación Nacional*
EPP	Paraguayan People's Army
EPR	Mexico's *Ejército Popular Revolucionario*
EU	European Union
EZLN	Army of National Liberation of Emiliano Zapata
FARC	Revolutionary Armed Forces of Colombia
FMLN	Farabundo Martí National Liberation Front
FTA	Free Trade Area
FTAA	Free Trade Area of the Americas
IAEA	International Atomic Energy Agency
IBSA	India, Brazil, and South Africa
IMF	International Monetary Fund
IIRSA	Initiative for the Integration of the Regional South American Infrastructure

LAFTA	Latin American Free Trade Area
MERCOSUR/ MERCOSUL	Common Market of the South
MIDs	Militarized Interstate Disputes
MINUSTAH	United Nations Stabilization Mission in Haiti
MTCR	Missile Technology Control Regime
NAFTA	North American Free Trade Agreement
NATO	North Atlantic Treaty Organization
NPT	Non-Proliferation of Nuclear Weapons Treaty
NSG	Nuclear Suppliers Group
NWFZ	Nuclear-Weapons-Free Zone
OAS	Organization of American States
OECD	Organization of Economic Cooperation and Development
OPANAL	Agency for the Prohibition of Nuclear Weapons in Latin America and the Caribbean
OPEC	Organization of Petroleum Exporting Countries
SAFTA	South American Free Trade Area
SCO	Shanghai Cooperation Organization
SDC (UNASUR)	UNASUR Security and Defense Council
TBA	Tri-Border Area (Argentina, Brazil, Paraguay)
UNASUR	Union of South American Nations
UNCLOS	United Nations Convention on the Law of the Seas
UNMIH	United Nations Mission in Haiti
UNODOC	United Nations Office on Drugs and Crime
WSF	World Social Forum
ZOPACAS	Zone of Peace and Cooperation of the South Atlantic

NOTES ON CONTRIBUTORS

Jorge Battaglino is a tenured senior researcher at Argentina's Council of Scientific Research (CONICET) and professor in the Department of Political Science and International Relations at Torcuato Di Tella University, Buenos Aires, Argentina. He has been recently appointed as the director of the National Defense School. His research interests include civil-military relations, South American security, militarization, arms purchases, and defense policy. His publications have appeared in journals such as *Journal of Politics in Latin America*, *Defense and Security Analysis*, *Política y Gobierno*, *Iconos*, *Foreign Affairs Latinoamérica*, *Revista Brasileira de Política Internacional*, *Perfiles Latinoamericanos*, *Política Externa*, *Estudios Internacionales*, and *Conflict, Security and Development*.

Anne Clunan is associate professor of national security at the Naval Postgraduate School in Monterey, California and a visiting scholar at the Center for International Security and Cooperation at Stanford University. Her recent books include *Ungoverned Spaces? Alternatives to State Authority in an Era of Softened Sovereignty* (Stanford University Press, 2010) with Harold Trinkunas, *The Social Construction of Russia's Resurgence: Aspirations, Identity, and Security Interests* (Johns Hopkins University Press, 2009), and *Terrorism, War or Disease? Unraveling the Use of Biological Weapons* (Stanford University Press, 2008) with Peter R. Lavoy and Susan B. Martin.

Christopher Darnton is an assistant professor of politics at the Catholic University of America in Washington, DC, where he specializes in international security, inter-American relations, Brazilian and comparative foreign policy, and qualitative research methods. He is the author of *Rivalry and Alliance Politics in Cold War Latin America* (Johns Hopkins University Press, 2014), as well as articles in *International Studies Quarterly*, *Security Studies*, *Latin American Research Review*, and *The Journal of Cold War Studies*.

Marcela Donadio is the executive secretary of RESDAL – *Red de Seguridad y Defensa de América Latina* (Latin American Defense and Security Network). Dr. Donadio was a professor of international security between 1992 and 2005 at various universities in Argentina. She has been a fellow of the National Council of Scientific and Technical Research (CONICET) of Argentina, a country in which she also worked at the Ministry of Defense. She has received scholarships from the OAS, the Friedrich Naumann Foundation, the University of York (Summer Institute), and the International Council for Canadian Studies. Dr. Donadio directed a UNDP project on public security budget for the Security Council in Argentina and the Comparative Atlas of Defense in Latin America and the Caribbean since its first publication in 2005. She is responsible for RESDAL's Gender and Peace Operations program, which has covered the cases of Haiti, the Democratic Republic of Congo, and Lebanon, as well as the Public Safety Index, whose latest release was in October 2013.

R. Evan Ellis is a research professor of Latin American Studies at the Strategic Studies Institute, U.S. Army War College with a research focus on the region's relationships with China and other non-Western Hemisphere actors. He has presented his work in a broad range of business and governments in 25 countries on four continents. Dr. Ellis has published over 90 works, including *China in Latin America: The Whats and Wherefores* (2009), *The Strategic Dimension of Chinese Engagement with Latin America* (2013), and *China on the Ground in Latin America* (2014).

Carlos Escudé is a tenured senior researcher at Argentina's Council of Scientific Research (CONICET). He has been a Fullbright Fellow and a Guggenheim Fellow. In 1986 he was awarded the Order of Bernardo O'Higgins for his campaign in favor of the 1984 Treaty of Peace and Friendship between Argentina and Chile. During 1991–1992 he was a special advisor to Argentina's foreign minister, Guido Di Tella. Among his many books are *Foreign Policy Theory in Menem's Argentina* (University Press Florida, 1997) and *Principios de Realismo Periférico* (Lumiere, 2012). He also coedited a 15-volume work on the history of Argentine foreign relations – *Historica General de las Relaciones Internacionales de la República Argentina* (GEL, 1998–2003).

Daniel M. Goldstein is professor in the Department of Anthropology at Rutgers University. He is the author of the books *The Spectacular City: Violence and Performance in Urban Bolivia* (Duke University Press, 2004) and *Outlawed: Between Security and Rights in a Bolivian City* (Duke University Press, 2012). He is the coeditor (with Enrique D. Arias) of the collection *Violent Democracies in Latin America*. A political and legal anthropologist, Dr. Goldstein specializes in the anthropology of security; his current research examines undocumented migrants' use of the U.S. legal system in a context of securitized migration.

Caroline A. Hartzell is a professor of political science at Gettysburg College. Her publications include the books *Crafting Peace: Power Sharing Institutions and the Negotiated Resolution of Civil Wars* (coauthored with Matthew Hoddie), *Strengthening Peace in Post-Civil War States: Transforming Spoilers into Stakeholders*, and *Segment States in the Developing World: Conflict's Cause or Cure?* (the latter two coedited with Matthew Hoddie). Her research interests include a cross-national focus on the effects that the terms of civil war settlements have on the duration and quality of the peace and a regional focus on civil war in Latin America.

Arie M. Kacowicz is the Chaim Weizmann Chair in International Relations and associate professor in the Department of International Relations at the Hebrew University of Jerusalem, Israel. He is the author of *Peaceful Territorial Change* (University of South Carolina Press, 1994), *Zones of Peace in the Third World: South America and West Africa in Comparative Perspective* (SUNY, 1998), *The Impact of Norms in International Society: The Latin American Experience, 1881–2001* (University of Notre Dame Press, 2005), and *Globalization and the*

Distribution of Wealth: The Latin American Experience, 1982–2008 (Cambridge University Press, 2013). His areas of interest include international relations theory, peace studies, international relations of Latin America, globalization and global governance, and the Arab-Israeli conflict.

José Antonio Lucero is Chair of Latin American and Caribbean Studies and associate professor in the Henry M. Jackson School of International Studies at the University of Washington. He was born in El Paso, Texas and raised on both sides of the Mexico-U.S. border. In addition to numerous articles, Dr. Lucero is the author of *Struggles of Voice: The Politics of Indigenous Representation in the Andes* (University of Pittsburgh Press, 2008) and the coeditor of the *Oxford Handbook of Indigenous Peoples Politics* (Oxford University Press, forthcoming).

Andrés Malamud is a research fellow at the Institute of Social Sciences of the University of Lisbon. He has been visiting researcher at the Max Planck Institute in Heidelberg and the University of Maryland, College Park and is a recurring visiting professor at universities in Argentina, Brazil, Italy, Portugal, and Spain. His areas of interest include comparative regional integration, EU Studies, and Latin American politics. His work has been published in such journals such as *Latin American Research Review*, *Cambridge Review of International Affairs*, *Journal of European Integration*, *Latin American Politics and Society*, and *European Political Science*.

Gabriel Marcella is a retired professor of third world studies and former director of the Americas studies in the Department of National Security and Strategy at the U.S. Army War College. During his government career he served as International Affairs Advisor to the Commander in Chief, United States Southern Command and advisor to the Departments of State and Defense on Latin American security. Dr. Marcella has written extensively on Latin American security issues and U.S. policy. Recent publications include the monographs *American Grand Strategy for Latin America in the Age of Resentment*, *Affairs of State: The Interagency and National Security*, and *Teaching Strategy: Challenge and Response* (all published by the Strategic Studies Institute, U.S. Army War College) and the edited book (with Richard Downes) *Cooperation in the Western Hemisphere: Resolving the Ecuador-Peru Conflict* (Lynne Rienner, 1999). Dr. Marcella's current research focuses on the Colombian crisis and U.S. strategy, national security decision-making, and the teaching of strategy. Currently, he is an adjunct professor at the Army War College and consultant to the Project on National Security System Reform. His most recent publication, "The Transformation of Security in Latin America: A Cause for Common Action," appeared in the *Journal of International Affairs*, Spring–Summer 2013.

David R. Mares holds the Institute of the Americas Chair for Inter-American Affairs at the University of California, San Diego, where he is also director of the Center for Iberian and Latin American Studies, professor of political science, and adjunct professor at the Graduate School of International Relations and Pacific Studies. He is a member of the International Institute for Strategic Studies (IISS) and the Council on Foreign Relations. Mares was previously professor, El Colegio de México; Fulbright Professor, Universidad de Chile; visiting professor, FLACSO Ecuador; and a fellow at the Oxford Institute for Energy Studies, the Weatherhead Center for International Affairs at Harvard University, the Japan External Trade Research Organization, and the Center for Advanced Study in the Behavioral Sciences at Stanford University. Dr. Mares has prepared reports for the Carnegie Commission, Stockholm International Peace Research Institute, Netherlands Institute of International Relations, the Conflict Prevention

Network (Berlin), and the Arias Foundation for Peace and Human Progress (Costa Rica). He has written or edited nine books, as well as over 100 articles, chapters, and reports.

Federico Merke teaches international relations theory and international politics in the Department of Social Sciences and is the director of political science and international relations at the University of San Andrés, Argentina. He has been deputy director of academic affairs at the Argentine Council for International Relations (CARI) and lecturer at the Universidad del Salvador, Buenos Aires, Argentina. His research orientation lies somewhere between international relations and area studies, combining Latin American studies with international relations theory. His main research interests revolve around the political and security dimensions of Latin American international relations, with a particular interest in Argentina and Brazil's foreign policies. His articles were published in journals such as *Pensamiento Propio*, *Sociedad Global*, *Foro Internacional*.

Detlef Nolte is vice president of the German Institute of Global and Area Studies (GIGA), director of the GIGA Institute of Latin American Studies, and professor of political science at the University of Hamburg. Nolte has been the president of the German Latin American Studies Association (ADLF) since 2010. His recent articles were published in *Review of International Studies*, *International Area Studies Review*. His areas of interest include comparative regionalism, regional security governance, regional powers, and constitutional change in Latin America.

Deborah L. Norden is a professor of political science at Whittier College. Her research has focused on civil-military relations, democratization, and contentious politics in Latin America, particularly in Argentina and Venezuela. Her recent work explores various themes, including the causes of civilian and military challenges to democratic regimes in Latin America and government responses to those challenges, military roles in internal security, and the legacies of Hugo Chávez in Venezuela. Dr. Norden's publications include *Military Rebellion in Argentina: Between Coups and Consolidation* (University of Nebraska Press, 1996) and *Argentina and the United States: Changing Relations in a Changing World* (coauthored with Roberto Russell, Routledge, 2002), as well as articles in several journals and edited volumes and journals.

Andrea Oelsner is senior lecturer in politics and international relations at the University of Aberdeen. She is the author of *International Relations in Latin America: Peace and Security in the Southern Cone* (Routledge, 2005) and coeditor (with S. Koschut) of *Friendship and International Relations* (Palgrave, 2014). Her publications have appeared in *Critical Review of International and Social Political Philosophy*, *Security Dialogue*, *International Politics*, and *International Studies Quarterly*, among others.

Román D. Ortiz is director of Decisive Point, a consulting company specializing in security and defense. He has worked as an external adviser for counterterrorism and counternarcotics to different Colombian security and defense institutions, including the Ministry of Defense, the General Command of the Military Forces, the Navy, the Air Force, and the National Police. Previously, he worked as coordinator of the security studies area of *Fundación Ideas Para la Paz* in Bogotá, Colombia. He was also director of the Defense and Security Observatory of Latin America (OSAL) at the Ortega y Gasset University Institute in Madrid, Spain. Dr. Ortiz has taught and researched topics related to political violence and organized crime at Spanish and Latin American academic institutions, including the General Gutiérrez Mellado University Institute in Madrid, Los Andes University in Bogotá, and Externado University in Bogotá.

Gavin O'Toole holds a Ph.D. from Queen Mary, University of London, where he taught Latin American politics and democratic theory. He was a visiting postdoctoral fellow at the Institute for the Study of the Americas in London. He works as a writer, journalist, and consultant, and edits the *Latin American Review of Books*. He has published several books: *Politics Latin America* (Routledge, 2nd edition, 2014), *Environmental Politics in Latin America and the Caribbean* (Volumes I and II, Liverpool University Press, 2014), *The Reinvention of Mexico* (Liverpool University Press, 2010), and *Che in Verse* (Aflame Books, 2007). His main areas of interest are environmental politics and political ideas in Latin America.

Carlo Patti is an assistant professor in international relations at the Federal University of Goiás, Brazil. He received his Ph.D. in history of international relations from the University of Florence in 2012, and between 2012 and 2013 he has been a postdoctoral fellow at Getulio Vargas Foundation (Rio de Janeiro), the University of Brasilia, and the Institute of International Relations at the Pontifical Catholic University of Rio de Janeiro, Brazil. Since 2013, he has been teaching international history and international relations. He published *O Programa Nuclear Brasileiro: Uma História Oral* (CPDOC-FGV, 2014), as well as articles in *Revista Brasileira de Política Internacional*, *Cold War History*, *Il Politico*, *Limes*, and *Meridiano 47*. His research focuses on Brazil's foreign policy, Brazil's nuclear history, international history, nuclear diplomacy, and international security.

Luis L. Schenoni is an assistant professor at the Universidad Católica in Buenos Aires, Argentina. He has been visiting researcher at the German Institute of Global and Area Studies (Hamburg University, Germany), the Institute of International Relations (Sao Paulo University, Brazil), and the Center for Social Studies (Coimbra University, Portugal). His areas of interest include IR theory, international political economy, foreign policy analysis and comparative politics, with a special focus in South America. His work has been published in such journals as *Revista Brasileira de Política Internacional* and *Contexto Internacional*.

Andrés Serbin is an anthropologist who holds a doctorate in political science and is currently the president of the *Coordinadora Regional de Investigaciones Económicas y Sociales (CRIES)*, a Latin American and Caribbean network of NGOs and research centers. He is a founding member and former chair of the International Coalition for the Responsibility to Protect (ICRtoP) and of the Global Partnership for the Prevention of Armed Conflict (GPPAC). He retired as full professor of the Central University of Venezuela in 2001. He has been visiting professor at several universities in the United Kingdom, the United States, France, Brazil, and is currently teaching at FLACSO. He has authored several books, both in Spanish and English, and published more than 200 academic articles in Spanish, English, French, German, and Russian. His most recent book in Spanish is *Chávez, Venezuela y la Reconfiguración Política de América Latina y el Caribe* (Siglo XXI, 2011).

Andrei Serbin Pont attended the Argentine National Defense School and holds a Master's degree in international relations with specialization in peace, defense, and security from the San Thiago Dantas Program (Brazil). He is currently research coordinator for Coordinadora Regional de Investigaciones Económicas y Sociales (CRIES). He has published articles in *Foreign Affairs Latinoamericana*, *Pensamiento Propio*, *Foreign Policy*, and *Política Externa*. His current research interests focus on defense, security, regional integration, conflict prevention, mass atrocity prevention, defense policy, and defense industry.

Arturo C. Sotomayor is an associate professor in the Department of Political Science and Geography at the University of Texas, San Antonio. His areas of interest include civil-military relations in Latin America, UN peacekeeping participation by South American countries, Latin American comparative foreign policy, and nuclear policy in Argentina, Brazil, and Mexico. His publications have appeared in *Security Studies*, *International Peacekeeping*, *Journal of Latin American Politics and Society*, *Hemisphere*, *Nonproliferation Review*, and other edited volumes. He is the author of *The Myth of the Democratic Peacekeeper: Civil-Military Relations and the United Nations* (Johns Hopkins University Press, 2014) and coeditor of *Mexico's Security Failure* (Routledge, 2011). Sotomayor has held research fellowships from the Woodrow Wilson Center for International Scholars, Tulane University, and Centro de Investigación y Docencia Económica (CIDE) in Mexico City.

Cameron G. Thies is professor and director of the School of Politics and Global Studies at Arizona State University. Prior to joining ASU in 2013, he was the Harlan E. McGregor Faculty Fellow and chair of the Department of Political Science at the University of Iowa. His research interests include state building in the developing world, the political economy of conflict, and international relations theory. His most recent book is *Intra-Industry Trade: Cooperation and Conflict in the Global Political Economy* (Stanford University Press, forthcoming).

Arlene B. Tickner is a professor of international relations in the Political Science Department at the Universidad de los Andes, Bogotá, Colombia. Her main areas of research include sociology of IR knowledge in non-core settings, Latin American security, and Colombian foreign policy. She is the coeditor (with David L. Blaney) of *Claiming the International* (2013) and *Thinking International Relations Differently* (2012).

Harold Trinkunas is the Charles W. Robinson Chair and senior fellow and director of the Latin America Initiative in the Foreign Policy Program at the Brookings Institution in Washington, DC. His research focuses on Latin American politics, particularly on issues related to foreign policy, governance, and security. Dr. Trinkunas has also written on terrorism financing, borders, and ungoverned spaces. He previously served as an associate professor and chair of the Department of National Security Affairs at the Naval Postgraduate School in Monterey, California.

Maria Velez de Berliner is president of Latin Intelligence Corporation, professor of intelligence and strategic analysis at The George Washington University, and instructor on LATAM's security issues at the USAD SOC/SOS Hurlburt Field, Cannon USAFB, Davis-Monthan USAFB, Homestead Air Reserve Base, and Lackland USAFB/JIOWC. She published articles in *The Harvard Business Review Brasil*; *The Harvard Business Review América Latina; The Latin American Advisor*; *Transnational Organized Crime* (London); and *Temas de Reflexión* (Universidad EAFIT, Colombia).

Leslie E. Wehner is a senior lecturer in politics and international relations at the University of Bath, United Kingdom. Previously, he was a senior research fellow at the GIGA German Institute of Global and Area Studies, Hamburg. His research interests include foreign policy analysis, international relations theory, and international political economy, as well as regional cooperation and trade strategies of Latin American states. He is the author of *Explaining Free Trade Agreement Negotiations: Cases from Latin America* (2010), and his most recent articles have been published in *Foreign Policy Analysis*, *International Studies Review*, and *International Politics*.

Phil Williams is Wesley W. Posvar Professor and director of the Matthew B. Ridgway Center for International Security Studies at the University of Pittsburgh. Professor Williams has published extensively in the field of international security. He has written books on *Crisis Management*, *The U.S. Senate and Troops in Europe*, and *Superpower Détente*, and edited volumes on Russian organized crime, trafficking in women, and combating transnational crime. From 2007 to 2009 he was visiting professor at the Strategic Studies Institute, U.S. Army War College, where he published two monographs, entitled *From the New Middle Ages to a New Dark Age: The Decline of the State and U.S. Strategy* and *Criminals, Militias and Insurgents: Organized Crime in Iraq*.

INTRODUCTION

David R. Mares and Arie M. Kacowicz

Latin America's security issues have become an important topic in international relations and Latin American studies. The region has undergone significant change during the last 20 years, and its experience informs scholarly debates about war, regional peace, arms races, terrorism, peacekeeping operations, and even nuclear arms potential. There are more undergraduate and graduate students studying Latin America's security issues than ever before. Bolstering this trend is the greater relevance of regional security studies generally since the end of the Cold War due to the increased autonomy of the different regions of the world and the research focus on regionalism and the potential for regional security governance.

The topic of security in Latin America provides a variety of analytic puzzles for the social scientist. In addition to outstanding interstate issues, the conflicting dyads of societal mistrust and diplomatic cooperation, interstate threats, sporadic violence but reluctance to engage in large-scale violence, and norms of non-intervention but ideological proclivities to promote 'appropriate' change in fellow Latin American nations are all present in Latin America.

Beyond the traditional security concerns of interstate, insurgent, and terrorist violence, the topic of security studies in Latin America has undergone dramatic changes since the end of the Cold War, the return of democracy, and the relegitimization and rearmament of the military against the background of low-level uses of force short of war. Security studies is now understood to also encompass threats to personal security such as environmental degradation, organized crime, and threats to indigenous identity. With its comprehensive collection of cutting-edge essays by a mix of established and up-and-coming international scholars across the broad spectrum of security issues, this *Handbook of Latin American Security* offers a truly novel collection of texts on security studies.

In addition to addressing a broad spectrum of security studies, another important agenda of this volume is to encourage well-theorized, empirically grounded, and methodologically rigorous research on these topics. Too often the current study of Latin America's international relations, especially its interstate security relations, fails those standards. There is an inner contradiction in Latin American scholarship between tailoring one's scholarship based on what one desires to see in public policy and the elaboration of testable arguments that follow from the development and application of theory. The question of 'objective scholarship' vs. the 'responsibility' of a scholar to write in ways that cannot be misused by opposing groups may lie behind this selective scholarship. However understandable might be the motivation, the result is too often research that fails rigorous testing.

In an effort to strengthen the field going forward, this volume seeks to set a rigorous agenda for future research on the topic of security studies. Thus the chapters in this volume are not review essays. Each author writes about the analytic paradigm in which she works; in this way, experts on an approach are critiquing the state of knowledge in their preferred paradigm. That critique ranges across theoretical challenges, methodological shortcomings, and empirical lacunae in an effort to develop the research agenda for scholars and their graduate students working within that particular approach.

When Routledge approached David Mares with the idea for a handbook on Latin American security, he realized the potential for the Handbook to influence a new generation of scholars, but he knew that his own approach represented only a small part of the community studying the topic. To speak to the field as a whole, it would be important to partner with a social scientist who utilizes a different analytical approach, but is open to discussion, rigorous, and willing to engage in the time-consuming task of conceptualizing the volume, selecting appropriate authors, and keeping everyone focused on the social science purpose of the volume.

Arie Kacowicz has been an ideal collaborator in this endeavor, even when we disagree on the state of Latin American security and how to analyze it. We have written extensively about war and peace in Latin America, analyzing the same reality but sometimes drawing different and contradictory conclusions, coming from different theoretical perspectives. Yet, we are both committed to social science analysis and convinced that the next generation of scholars should continue developing social science answers to the questions that we have not yet answered, rather than fall into the descriptive or policy advocacy path that takes from social science analyses only what fits in with their view. The decision on what topics to include (unfortunately, there are far too many topics in the realm of Latin American security to include in a single volume) and who to invite to write chapters was discussed and debated until we reached agreement. As editors, both of us read each draft chapter, commented and suggested revisions that were sent to each author, and we both read again their revised versions, even several times.

This is not a Handbook designed for public policy-making, though research that builds on the agendas presented herein will undoubtedly influence political debates. The purpose of the Handbook is to help improve the scholarly content of work done on security in Latin America and to push the envelope. This is accomplished by critiquing what has been done, but most importantly by revealing the theoretical, methodological, and empirical challenges that must be part of the research agenda for security studies in Latin America. Each author briefly surveys the state of the discipline on her own subject, highlights emerging and cutting-edge themes, identifies key concerns, analytical perspectives, salient findings, and especially points toward avenues for future research on the topic. Thus, narration or description is limited to what is essential to buttress the analytical approach.

We expect the *Routledge Handbook of Latin American Security* to be a key reference work, since the authors are leading scholars on each topic and theoretical approach. Though we welcome all readers, we expect that most will be academics, including graduate students, whether focused on Latin American international relations or on Latin American domestic and comparative politics, and working in an area in which international relations is relevant. Yet others may be academics working in other regions that wish to learn about issues of converging interest. Thirty scholars from around the world have participated in this project. We hope it will become a genuinely and broadly shared effort from a community of scholars, diverse in their interests and approaches, but united in their desire to promote the use of social science in the study of Latin American security.

Plan and contents of the book

The volume comprises five sections. The first section (Chapter 1) reviews the historical roots of the study of Latin American security and the contributions to security studies. The second section (Chapters 2–8) looks at a wide variety of theoretical approaches to security in the region, including geopolitics, neoliberal institutionalism and neofunctionalism, peripheral realism, securitization, gender studies, English school and constructivism, and alternative governance. The third section (Chapters 9–14) focuses on different conceptions of security, including traditional (war and peace), cooperative and regional, citizen and human, cultural and alternative, military strategy, and pluralistic security communities. In the fourth section (Chapters 15–23) the volume addresses a number of contemporary regional security challenges, including civil wars, the rise of Brazil, guerrillas and terrorism, arms races, civic-military relations, interstate disputes, illicit threats, and environmental threats. Finally, the fifth section (Chapters 24–28) addresses Latin American security in the context of contemporary international security challenges, including those posed by China, the United States, the Middle East, peacekeeping operations, and the New World Security Architecture.

In Chapter 1 ("Security Studies and Security in Latin America: The First 200 Years"), Arie M. Kacowicz and David R. Mares consider the historical experience of Latin America from 1810 to roughly the turn of the 21st century. In the second part of the chapter we present our views on how studying security in the Latin American context can contribute to the field of security studies in general terms. The final section of the chapter teases out the themes embedded in the historical experience, in order to gain a deeper and clearer understanding of how security issues in contemporary Latin America are similar or different from those faced in the past.

Detlef Nolte and Leslie E. Wehner focus on major political and economic developments that have influenced geopolitical thinking, particularly in South America, in "Geopolitics in Latin America, Old and New" (Chapter 2). Moreover, they elucidate the constitutive and basic elements of existing geopolitical narratives.

In Chapter 3 ("Neoliberal Institutionalism and Neo-Functionalism in Latin American Security Studies"), Andrés Malamud and Luis L. Schenoni explore how the interaction between security dynamics and regional institutions has been studied so far. The first section of the chapter approaches the question from the vantage point of neoliberal institutionalism, and the second through neofunctionalist lenses.

Carlos Escudé provides an overview of his original theory of international relations, peripheral realism, in "Who Commands, Who Obeys, and Who Rebels: Latin American Security in a Peripheral-Realist Perspective" (Chapter 4). Escudé claims that socioeconomic development is the foremost national interest of a peripheral state, especially in the Latin American context. His theory attempts to demonstrate in both logical and empirical terms that mainstream realism's premises are diplomatically correct 'fantasies;' the world order, Escudé argues, is necessarily hierarchical and essentially undemocratic. As the cases of Argentina and Mexico demonstrate, political confrontation with a major rule-maker (such as the United States) is almost always counterproductive.

In Chapter 5 ("Securitization and the Limits of Democratic Security"), Arlene B. Tickner analyzes democratic security as a crucial stage of civilian-based security thinking that coincided with attempts to broaden the concept of security at the end of the Cold War. Moreover, she shows that democratic security is tied to both the policy challenges faced by governments following the transition from dictatorship to democracy and to dominant regional conceptions of knowledge rooted largely in the need to provide practical expertise and policy formulations.

Marcela Donadio addresses "Gender in Security Studies" in Chapter 6, suggesting how security studies in the region could benefit from the incorporation of a gender perspective, arguing that a 'strategic alliance' between the two is imperative for further development in both disciplines. She analyzes the existence of communication difficulties between both areas, the demands of the international community, and the influence of the incorporation of women into the armed forces and its relationship with the democratization process.

Writing on the "English School and Constructivism" in Chapter 7, Federico Merke argues that the English School and the Constructivist approach offer important insights into the transformation of state security interests from a nonmaterialist standpoint in the Latin American context. Merke explores how these theoretical contributions can illuminate security dynamics in the region and improve our understanding of regional security.

In Chapter 8 ("Alternative Governance in Latin America"), Harold Trinkunas and Anne Clunan assess the research agenda on alternatively governed spaces in Latin America, as well as the debate on when alternative governance modalities promote or impede human, national, and international security. In particular, they examine two areas where alternative governance has most commonly emerged in the region but where questions still remain: cities and borders.

Cameron G. Thies reviews the literature regarding the two dominant approaches to understanding war and peace in the region (type and prevalence of conflict vs. understanding the regional order) in "Traditional Security: War and Peace" (Chapter 9). He then suggests original ways to closely link the two approaches – such that explanations of both dyadic-level and regional-level phenomenon are captured within the same theoretical and empirical analysis.

In Chapter 10 ("Cooperative Security and Regional Governance"), Andrés Serbin and Andrei Serbin Point address the conceptual and empirical development of cooperative security and regional governance in Latin America. Their main argument is that different modalities of emerging regional security governance structures frame different approaches and policies in terms of cooperative security in particular, and with regards to security governance in the region in general, shaping a multilevel and multilayered complex dynamic.

Daniel M. Goldstein focuses on 'citizen security' and 'human security' as two frameworks within which security in Latin America is conceptualized. In "Citizen Security and Human Security in Latin America" (Chapter 11), the author calls attention to the idea of security as both a lived experience – that is, a routine part of daily life – for Latin American people and as an everyday program of state formation. Thus, unlike most of the other essays in the Handbook, this chapter is anthropologically oriented: It explores the conceptual bases of citizen security and human security, but grounds this exploration in the empirical reality of daily life.

In Chapter 12 ("Alterity and Security: Culture and Survival beyond the 'Indian Problem'"), José Antonio Lucero examines how security in Latin America has been entangled with the histories of racial difference and how racialized Others, especially indigenous movements and Afro-Latino peoples, have generated powerful challenges to dominant political and academic notions of security. Lucero provides three analytic lenses for thinking about security and identity: the 'coloniality of security,' 'recognition as security,' and a postliberal, post-positivist, and decolonial research agenda that takes seriously native ontologies and epistemologies.

In Chapter 13 ("Military Strategy in Latin America"), Gabriel Marcella explores various dimensions of military strategy and how they are developed and applied in Latin America. Marcella refers to the links between strategy and policy, defense strategies and *Libros Blancos*, the spectrum of conflict and military strategy, secondary military missions, security and insecurity dilemmas, and the differences between police and military. Many of the examples refer to the Colombian experience.

Andrea Oelsner discusses the possibilities and limitations of a pluralistic security community approach to the study of Latin American security in "Pluralistic Security Communities in Latin America" (Chapter 14). While some features of the region as a whole make it a good candidate to become a security community, a closer examination of historical intraregional relations and domestic practices may call this into question. In empirical terms, she focuses upon the cases of ALBA and the Southern Cone of Latin America.

In Chapter 15 ("Relative Peace and Emerging Fault Lines: Accounting for Trends in Intrastate Conflicts in Latin America"), Caroline A. Hartzell provides an overview of the landscape of civil wars in Latin America. Against the background of the near disappearance of civil wars in the region, Hartzell reviews the alternative explanations for the causes of civil war, assessing their relevance to the region's conflicts. Finally, she examines the implications of these factors for new or renewed civil wars in Latin America. Latin America constitutes a 'puzzle' regarding civil wars, since none appear to be on the horizon, yet the region still faces underlying problems that have produced civil wars in the past and elsewhere. In light of this puzzle, scholarship on civil war itself could benefit from a focus on the region.

In Chapter 16 ("The Rise of Brazil: Concepts and Comparisons"), Christopher Darnton critiques the conventional wisdom about Brazil as a rising power, discusses several alternative concepts in relation to Brazilian foreign policy, articulates problems with the reference groups in which policy analysts categorize contemporary Brazil, and suggest avenues for future comparative research on Brazilian decision-making and on broader regional and global security issues. Darnton concludes that in order to understand contemporary Brazilian foreign policy, we need to take into account more complexity than simply that associated with capabilities, while not losing sight of theory and focused comparison.

Román D. Ortiz argues in "Guerrillas, Terrorists, or Criminals? The New Face of Antistate Violence in Latin America" (Chapter 17) that the historical distinction between organized crime and political violence creates obstacles for analyzing the security challenges faced by Latin America and designing the strategies required to confront them. In Ortiz's view, the links between criminals and terrorists are progressively closer and their behavior remarkably similar. In addition to clarifying new concepts such as 'criminal insurgency,' it is fundamental to deepen our understanding of the dynamics that allow political and criminal violence to converge, detailing the causes that have led Latin American guerrillas to become criminalized, as well as how mafias and drug cartels have been able to acquire significant political roles.

In Chapter 18 ("Weapons of Mass Destruction: Will Latin America Backtrack?"), Carlo Patti deals with the possible change of Latin American attitudes towards nuclear nonproliferation through the analysis of two specific cases: Venezuela and Brazil. Patti also discusses the effectiveness of regional and subregional nuclear nonproliferation regimes. The chapter provides reasons to believe that the Latin American countries will not revise their attitudes towards weapons of mass destruction, especially in the nuclear realm. However, while Latin America is currently a region with a firm commitment towards nuclear nonproliferation, the criticism of crucial Latin American countries towards several measures for strengthening the international nonproliferation regime could weaken global efforts for curbing the spread of nuclear weapons.

Jorge Battaglino, in "The Politics of Arms Acquisitions in South America: Trends and Research Agenda" (Chapter 19), discusses methodological issues related to the research of arms purchases, while examining the state of the art of the literature on arms acquisitions. Battaglino assesses the central features of arms purchases in the region from 2005–2013, focusing upon the possible motivations of such acquisitions in the cases of Argentina, Brazil, Chile, and Venezuela. Battaglino demonstrates that a simple economic model to explain spending on defense and weapons is inadequate, and needs to be complemented by other, political variables.

He highlights some of these possible variables, and discusses the theoretical, methodological, and empirical challenges facing scholars who would incorporate them.

In Chapter 20 ("Latin American Militaries in the 21st Century: Civil-Military Relations in the Era of Disappearing Boundaries"), Deborah L. Norden examines the question of 'control' of the armed forces, by looking at the range from civilian autonomy, to domination, and finally to defense and security management. Norden assesses three significant challenges to civil-military relations: the political context, the security context, and the ways in which the composition and social bases of the armed forces may have shifted since the wave of democratic transitions. She concludes that, despite the apparent obsolescence of military regimes, civilian control remains limited and, in some ways, even precarious.

David R. Mares, in "Interstate Disputes: Militarized Coercion and 'Peaceful Settlement'" (Chapter 21), sets a research agenda for understanding why any use of force by one Latin American country against another continues to be considered a legitimate, if disagreeable, tool of foreign policy. He demonstrates the existence of an active record of contemporary militarization of interstate disputes and interstate coercion in Latin America from 2000 to 2011. Finally, Mares suggests a research agenda for the study of coercive diplomacy in intra–Latin American relations.

In Chapter 22 ("Illicit Threats: Organized Crime, Drugs, and Small Arms"), Phil Williams explores the contemporary manifestations of trafficking and organized crime in Latin America and its close association with violence. Williams examines the conditions in Latin America that have been so conducive to the rise of drug trafficking in particular, and why it constitutes a threat to different countries and subregions. His major concern is the need for a sustained analysis of how the deficiencies and weakness of governance mechanisms throughout much of Latin America can be overcome in ways that help to contain the security threats posed by drug trafficking, without reverting to past patterns of authoritarianism.

In Chapter 23 ("Environmental Security and Disasters in Latin America and the Caribbean: A Blind Spot in Research"), Gavin O'Toole addresses the theoretical and empirical lacuna regarding discussions on environmental and human security in the region. In his view, natural disasters are common in Latin America, which is exposed to a wide variety of hazards, and have had considerable impact upon the region's development. He finds that regional cooperation is increasing, and the armed forces have been engaging with ideas about environmental and human security.

In Chapter 24 ("The Impact of China on the Security Environment of Latin America and the Caribbean"), R. Evan Ellis analyzes the impact of Chinese engagement on the security environment of the region, including the indirect effects of economic engagement on political, social, and other dynamics that impact the security of the region and the United States. Thus, Ellis assesses ways in which, however inadvertently, the activities of the Popular Republic of China (PRC), Chinese companies, and other Chinese actors significantly impact the Latin American and Caribbean security environment.

David R. Mares discusses the different theoretical lenses that inform scholarship on U.S. relations with Latin America, including realism, liberal internationalism, constructivism, and Marxism in "The United States' Impact on Latin America's Security Environment: The Complexities of Power Disparity" (Chapter 25). He presents reasons to hypothesize that in the current international context in which U.S.–Latin American relations are taking place, Chinese, Russian, and Iranian relations with the region do not rise to the level of security concerns for the U.S. But, according to Mares, if Latin American countries cannot avoid recurring economic and political crises, the relative strength of the United States in economics, policing, institution-building, and even military mobilization can once again become attractive to Latin American governments and societies. Absent an extra-hemispheric threat, it is these situations that would increase both the interest and ability of the United States to have a more direct influence in the region.

In Chapter 26 ("The Middle East and Latin America: Implications for Latin America's Security"), Maria Velez de Berliner assesses the security implications for Latin America of its relations with the Middle East from the perspective of the long history of the Middle Eastern presence in the region. She focuses particularly on the case of Iran–Latin American relations. Velez de Berliner analyzes three general themes of concern: (1) foreign policy and diplomatic relations, (2) military and intelligence links, and (3) planning and abetting terrorist activities, with a particular reference to the terrorist attacks in Argentina in 1992 and 1994. In her analysis, scholars need to draw on the relevant international relations theories to understand how to conceptualize a trilateral relationship in which a great power (such as the United States) fears the use of neutral territory (Latin America) by nonconventional adversaries fighting the great power in their home territory.

Arturo C. Sotomayor, writing of "Latin America's Experience with Peace Support Operations: From Peacekeeping Recipients to Peace Exporters" (Chapter 27), explains the conditions and reasons for Latin America's increased role in peacekeeping operations, including democratization and impetus for military reform, international prestige and status, and evolving regional norms about intervention. Moreover, he identifies and discusses three problematic issue areas for Latin America's increased role in peacekeeping missions, including the erosion of regional organizations, failure in peace-building missions, and growing challenges in training practices. For Sotomayor, the so-called military diplomacy in Latin America is not necessarily a negative trend, provided the appropriate mechanisms for accountability are in place.

Completing the Handbook, in Chapter 28 ("Latin America in the New World Security Architecture"), Arie M. Kacowicz refers to the characteristics of the new World Security Architecture (WSA) since the end of the Cold War, and especially after 9/11. Kacowicz discusses the different roles that can be ascribed to Latin America in the WSA: (1) active and cooperative (in the form of peacekeeping operations and arms control agreements), (2) active and challenging (in the form of the revisionist approach adopted by ALBA), (3) active and subversive (in the form of transnational threats), (4) passive (through lack of intervention and rule-taking instead of rule-making), and (5) potential and ambiguous, as in the case of Brazil.

PART I

The evolution of security in Latin America

1

SECURITY STUDIES AND SECURITY IN LATIN AMERICA

The first 200 years

Arie M. Kacowicz and David R. Mares

Introduction

The ontology of security studies has become contested. A field that used to be the purview of military and diplomatic studies, which focused on the big questions of war and peace, has become democratized. Security studies now entails not only the traditional issues confronting states in their international relations, but also domestic challenges to regime stability. These include contestation of the state's monopoly of force in physical spaces of the country, cultural survival of minority groups within the nation, and the ability of individual citizens to live and work without fear of either criminals or an overbearing government. It is not that these topics only matter going forward; in addition, scholars in the field (historians, anthropologists, and sociologists have always taken a broader view of *security*) are looking back to reveal how those without a voice (i.e., 'subalterns') nevertheless resisted, mobilized, and called for justice and change.

In the context of contemporary Latin America, scholars are investigating multiple topics that have deep historical roots and significant manifestations in the region today. The Spanish 'conquest' of this part of the Americas, and even less so that of the Portuguese, was never completed, even after the independent states took up the mantle to subjugate and assimilate the indigenous polities. Though indigenous people do not reject the European defined boundaries, even when it cuts through their communities, they have mobilized around the idea that the survival of their communities (however scattered they may be) requires defending certain values and links to the land, even when the nation's ownership of subsoil resources is not contested.

The diplomacy of cooperation coexists with that of militarized coercion, just as in the past. Subversion of the political order continues to be of concern, now not by conservatives facing liberals as in the 19th century, or liberals confronting variants of Marxism in the 20th century, but rather by an amorphous group of 'socialists of the 21st century' challenging the liberal democratic and economic order. In addition, governments worry about international regimes defending human rights invading their purview today, just as they worried about property rights infringing upon state sovereignty throughout the last two centuries. For scholars addressing these issues, and the NGOs and citizens that follow their work, the topic of 'peace and security' is not limited to the discussion of whether 1,000 or more people died in a battlefield-related clash among polities recognized by the United Nations.

Of course, none of these contestations mean that traditional issues of military coercion and diplomacy, of interstate cooperation and conflict, do not matter. Scholars have defined the field of security studies in much broader terms, not rendering the old issues irrelevant. In that spirit of continuity and change, this first chapter of the *Handbook of Latin American Security* reviews the first two centuries of the study and discussion of relations among distinct polities that affect the security of those polities and the people living within them.

The chapter is organized into three parts. In the first, we consider the historical experience of Latin America, from independence beginning in 1810 to roughly the turn of the 21st century. We argue that the historical record has been read selectively, with the result that not only has richness been lost; we have also misunderstood security outcomes, and thus missed many of the empirical puzzles that drive contemporary research. It is important that we pursue our distinct research agendas based on a shared understanding of the facts. The second section presents our views on how studying security in the Latin American context can contribute to the field of security studies. The section discusses not only how non–Latin American security scholars can benefit from considering the experiences and puzzles in the Latin American case, but also how Latin American scholars have enriched the discipline. The final section teases out the themes embedded in the historical experience, in order to gain a deeper and clearer understanding of how security issues in contemporary Latin America are similar or different from those faced in the past.

Historical overview

Latin America was born into an ambiguous geographical reality. If one compares a map of post-independent Spanish America (1818–1823) with a map of Spanish America in 1883 (at the end of the War of the Pacific), one sees dramatic changes in the boundaries of the political units. In this time period, the United Provinces of Central America separates into five nations and Gran Colombia into three countries (Venezuela, Colombia, and Ecuador), whereas Guatemala separates from Mexico. Haiti conquers, and then loses the Dominican Republic, and Peru and Bolivia lose significant territory to Chile. To the east, the Spanish American states' claims to territory around Brazil, equivalent to the size of France, have not yet been settled in favor of Brazil. Further south, Patagonia is not yet divided between Chile and Argentina, while Uruguay, along with much of present-day Argentina, comprised the United Provinces of the Río de la Plata. The map continues to change in the 20th and 21st centuries, including Ecuador's loss of 40 per cent of what it claimed to Peru in 1941, and Nicaragua gaining maritime boundaries in the Caribbean.

In this process of territorial division, Latin American states most often appealed to pre-independence boundaries of the Spanish Empire. Because the Spanish Crown divided its empire into ecclesiastical, administrative, and military domains with overlapping boundaries, at the time of independence the new Spanish American states had legal and historical bases to disagree over the legitimate boundaries of their countries. Even if agreement could be reached on colonial boundaries, some Latin American states appealed to the principle of *uti possidetis de jure*, while others preferred *uti possidetis de facto* (the latter quite similar to European notions of 'effective occupation' at the 1884 Berlin Conference as a means of regulating competition in the division of Africa).

Even in cases where legitimate boundaries were not the issue, some Latin American states coveted their neighbors' territories, such as Chile in its northern border and Haiti in the island of Hispaniola. A masterful historical overview of how domestic politics, wealth, and an eye to balances of power affected South America in its first hundred years of independence is found in

Burr (1985). The book remains fundamental reading, but for international relations (IR) scholars the challenge is to convert that empirical richness into testable hypotheses about security policies and to bring these empirical cases into the discussion of contemporary security studies.

Wars of conquest among Latin American countries were part of their international relations, even without counting the myriad violent repressions of the indigenous peoples. Within months of claiming its independence from Spain and requesting incorporation into Gran Colombia, the Dominican Republic was conquered by Haiti in 1820 and only regained its independence in 1843. Chile fought its first war against Peru and Bolivia (1836–1839) simply to keep its neighbors weak. Chilean state-builder Diego Portales justified the war in balance of power terms:

> The Confederation must forever disappear from the American scene. By its geographical extent; by its larger white population; by the combined wealth of Peru and Bolivia, until now scarcely touched; by the rule that the new organization, taking it away from us, would . . . exercise on the Pacific . . . by the greater intelligence if indeed inferior character of its public men, the Confederation would soon smother Chile.
>
> *(Burr 1985: 38–43)*

Moreover, in the Pacific War among the three countries (1879–1883), Chile took territory from Bolivia and Peru, the defeated countries.

In the War of the Triple Alliance (1864–1870), Argentina, Brazil, and Uruguay fought a total war against Paraguay, causing the death of almost 90 per cent of the Paraguayan male population, up to 60 per cent of the total population, and requiring reparations from the vanquished people. The secret treaty among the three allies, which the British revealed at the time, stipulated that the victors would take possession of disputed parts of Paraguay and demand reparations (Brazil cancelled the remaining payments only in 1943!). Brazil enforced its maximum prewar territorial claims; Argentina, however, went beyond that. Initially, Argentina proposed to Brazil that Paraguay be divided between them; Brazil preferred another buffer state (Uruguay being the second) between itself and Argentina. Rebuffed, Argentina sought territory north of what it disputed before the war; only Bolivia's objection that these claims infringed on its own territorial disputes with Paraguay limited Argentina to its prewar claims. The punishment wrought on Paraguay led Chile to complain to the victors that a South American country should not be treated in the way that Europeans dealt with Poland. Interestingly enough, U.S. President Rutherford B. Hayes arbitrated one of the settlements, ruling in favor of Paraguay, which honored him by naming the province *Presidente Hayes*.

There were other wars of conquest. Bolivian Marshall Andrés de Santa Cruz sent his army into Peru to favor an internal rebellion led by those willing to become part of a confederation with Bolivia. Santa Cruz also favored the government's opponents in the Argentine Confederation. The Argentine dictator Juan Manuel de Rosas feared that Santa Cruz also wanted to bring his country into the Bolivian Confederation, and preemptively attacked Bolivia in 1837. Argentina and the Empire of Brazil fought two wars over control of the eastern bank of the Río de la Plata (Cisplatine War, 1825–1828, and Platine War (*La Guerra Grande)*, 1851–1852). The stalemate and Britain's mediation led to the creation of Uruguay as a buffer state in 1828. Peru invaded southern Ecuador in 1859, retreating only when Colombia and Chile protested Peru's efforts to alter the regional balance. Bolivia's invasion of Paraguay produced 100,000 deaths in the Chaco War (1932–1935), with Bolivia seeking more territory than it claimed under *uti possidetis de jure* and the final peace rewarding Paraguayan advances deep into the Chaco rather than based on legal arguments. Peru's invasion of undisputed territory in southern Ecuador in 1941 coerced Ecuador into withdrawing its claims on territory in the Amazon, which amounted to 40 per cent of Ecuadorian-claimed national territory. No Latin American country came to Ecuador's aid, and all were willing to accept Peru's condition that a withdrawal from occupied Ecuador required that country's recognition of Peruvian claims in the disputed Amazon. Argentina, Brazil, Chile, and the United States served as guarantors of the peace treaty, but the terms were those imposed upon Ecuador by Peru and recognized the reality of Peru's conquest, rather than resulting from a legal interpretation of historic rights (Burr 1985; Wood 1966).

As this brief overview begins to document, the wars of the first 70 years of independence had far-reaching consequences. States were created, confederations of states ceased to exist, and the position of states in the regional hierarchy was dramatically altered. The break up of the United Provinces of Central America led to four wars over 70 years to recreate it under either Guatemalan or Nicaraguan leadership. War also had implications for the regional distribution of power, as a Central America united under the auspices of one state would make it a more important player in regional politics. Perhaps the greatest impact of war on the regional hierarchy of states comes from the War of the Peru/Bolivia Confederation (1836–1839) and the War of the Triple Alliance (1864–1870). Those wars thwarted Bolivia and Paraguay, which had achieved domestic stability and were beginning to progress economically; their contemporary status as the poorest states by far in South America bears witness to the devastating impacts of the wars. By one estimate, 77 per cent of government budgets between 1820 and 1860 in Spanish America were spent on preparing for and defending against violent confrontations with neighboring countries, thereby limiting capital availability for economic development (Bates et al. 2006).

Many of these political units were also defining their internal boundaries, finishing the conquest begun by Spain 300 years earlier. These were the wars against the indigenous peoples in order to subjugate them to the European-descended Latin American elites, particularly against the Yaqui in Mexico (1867–1910) and the Mapuche in southern Chile (1861–1883) and Argentina (1879–1880). Given that these indigenous communities did not perceive themselves to be part of the particular Latin American country they were fighting, we can consider these to constitute extrasystemic wars and thus part of the region's international relations. This is a particularly apt classification for scholarship in a region that at least rhetorically seeks to contest Eurocentrism.

In the realm of ideational issues, the idea of a Western Hemisphere or Spanish American identity, with norms of behavior distinct from other regions, is not all that different from the European belief that Europe was distinct from the rest of the world – Christian, civilized, advanced – and therefore Europeans should get along with each other (i.e., the Peace of Westphalia, 1648, and the Congress of Vienna, 1814). Likewise, the tension between Pan-American or Spanish Americanism and national identity has also been present in Latin America. In short, Latin America behaved very much in line with its Western roots. As Burr notes, "South American statesmen accepted the axioms and techniques of European power politics. They used this jargon and did not hesitate to employ its forms of coercion in dealing with problems of intra-South American relations" (1985: 6).

The familiar narrative of 19th century Latin American interstate relations focuses on Simón Bolívar and José Martí and their desires for Spanish American unity, particularly against the United States, and laments that their visions for a united Spanish America had been consistently undermined by short-sighted leaders. But we do not often see alongside Bolívar's name those of his opponents and why they objected to his vision. For instance, Marshall Andrés de Santa Cruz in Bolivia and Diego Portales in Chile objected to Bolívar's plans for a lifelong presidency and a legislature that included a chamber of censors whose members served for life. There were also intellectuals and statesmen arguing that neighbors could not be trusted.

Brazil's great statesman, the Barón Rio Branco, distrusted Spanish America, but he believed it was necessary to get along with one's neighbors. Conversely, Rio Branco sustained that Brazil and the United States had significant commonalities and that there should be an informal alliance between the two countries (Bradford Burns 1966). Whereas Brazil perceived commonalities with the United States up to the 1970s, it would be difficult to read Peruvian or Bolivian history texts and conclude that those two societies found great commonalities with Chile.

Another prominent intellectual and politician with a distinctly anti-Bolívarian view was Estanislao Zeballos (1854–1923), twice president of the Argentine Chamber of Deputies, three times foreign minister, dean of the University of Buenos Aires Law School, founder of important scientific institutes, journals, and newspapers, and historian. Zeballos had a major impact on Argentine political science and history through his nationalist and racist writings regarding Brazil and Chile. The University of Buenos Aires republished his 1908–1910 essays in 1974, more than a half century later. In 1993 a member of the National Academy of History published a volume inspired by Zeballos's ideas, and in 2000 a major Argentine historian, Enrique Tandeter, edited the *Nueva Historia Argentina*, which promoted Zeballos's 1901 thesis that all of Patagonia belonged to the colonial unit of which Buenos Aires was leader (Viceroyalty of Rio de la Plata) (Lacoste 2003). Contemporary scholarship favoring a Latin American unity against the United States writes as if Augusto Sandino and Farabundo Martí had common visions that lead to the current 'Socialism of the 21st Century' movement. No one, however, seems to recall that Sandino rejected communism and expelled Farabundo Martí from his entourage because he was a communist (Macaulay 1985).

Other countries had their Zeballos and Sandinos as well, but a casual reader would think that Latin American intellectuals and leaders only thought about Latin American unity. They had a real impact on how governments and societies thought about each other and behaved towards each other (Escudé 1988). These are important factors in understanding the multiple failures to realize Bolívar's dream or José Vasconcelos's desire to create 'La Raza Cósmica,' and even for the development (or rather, underdevelopment) of the region.

The region's history reveals not just disunity, but at times Latin American countries even supporting extra-hemispheric powers fighting another Latin American country. During the war against Spain in the Pacific (1860s), the Atlantic states (Brazil, Uruguay, and Argentina) declared their neutrality, but sold provisions, including war material, to the Spanish fleet and would not permit Chilean ships to operate in their waters. Even though Argentine President Bartolomé Mitre ideologically favored Spanish American unity, he would not pass up the opportunity for Argentina to profit from the war nor to join the slave-holding, Portuguese-speaking Empire of Brazil in dismembering Paraguay (Burr 1985; Lacoste 1995–1996). During the *Baltimore* affair (1891) Argentina offered the United States navy support in case of a war with Chile (Lacoste 2003). Most recently, Chile provided aid to the British during their 1982 war with Argentina.

When territorial disputes in Latin America were resolved legally rather than through violence the United States, European nations, and other Latin American countries arbitrated. In fact, the United States was the country most often asked to provide a *laudo* (arbitration ruling) regarding boundary determinations. Latin American countries, however, also rejected arbitration that they had solicited at times (i.e., Ecuador in 1910 and Argentina in 1977) and at other times they refused arbitration (e.g., Peru after 1941 in its dispute with Ecuador and Chile in its dispute with Bolivia since 1883).

Similarly, between 1948 and 1959 the Organization of American States (OAS) dealt with seven cases of intra–Latin American conflict, all concluding without war and with general consensus. Moreover, in the entire period of the Cold War (1948–1989) the OAS dealt with

26 crises; only one (Honduras–El Salvador in 1969) resulted in war, and the OAS still played a key role in terminating the fighting (Shaw 2004; Stoetzer 1993: 273–291). One may disagree with the terms of settlements, but the OAS has an enviable record of dispute mitigation and resolution, despite the democratic deficit of most of its member-states.

In addition to interstate conflict, Latin American countries have historically intervened in the affairs of their neighbors even as they articulated doctrines that denounced Great Power assumptions of rights to intervene (Calvo and Drago Doctrines of 1896 and 1902). Uruguay and Bolivia suffered many interventions by Brazil and Argentina, each backing domestic factions, at times with money, arms, and even men, which favored one country or the other. Argentina's Mitre government accused Chile of providing money and men for the rebellion it faced in the 1860s. Mexico intervened covertly and overtly in Central American wars and civil conflicts from the 1860s to 1910. The Caribbean Legion of the 1940s and 1950s, centered in Guatemala, raised money and gathered men and weapons to fight dictators in the region and were instrumental in José Figueres's victory in Costa Rica's 1948 civil war. Castro's Cuba provided covert aid to revolutionaries throughout Latin America from the 1960s and into the 1980s.

Furthermore, Latin America's history is not free of ethnic cleansing or genocide. Ethnic cleansing is the forced removal of a people from a physical space; genocide is a controversial concept, but its essence is the destruction of a category of people in a particular space. There are at least two cases of ethnic cleansing apart from the forced relocation of indigenous peoples when they lost their wars against the Latin American states intruding into their homelands. In Mexico's Caste War of Yucatán (1847–1901) Mayans rebelled and massacred mestizos and whites, who retaliated as the fighting lasted decades (Reed 1964). In 1937 Dominicans slaughtered up to 12,000 Haitian migrants in their country. Brazil's Canudos War, which killed 15,000–30,000 people in a northeast community, might also fit in this category, though one could classify it as simply a secessionist movement that was brutally repressed (Levine 1995).

Many scholars accuse Latin American governments and the United States of genocide against indigenous peoples. By some definitions, the effort of leftist Latin American governments to turn indigenous peoples into 'peasants' can be considered genocide, since it would eliminate their identity as indigenous. The Argentine military government from 1976 to 1983 has been accused of genocide against its own people (*la guerra sucia*). There are also clearer cases. A month after achieving independence from France in 1804, Haitian President Jean-Jacques Dessalines ordered the massacre of 3,000–5,000 whites. Guatemala experienced a particularly brutal period in the 1980s that numerous international fora label genocide, and the dictator Efraín Rios Montt was found guilty in a Guatemalan court of genocide, though the country's supreme court has granted him a retrial.

The extreme violence in Latin American civil wars is also relevant to explain international relations. These wars were not simply military coups, followed by military repression, as in the cases of the brutal national security regimes of the Southern Cone in the late 1960s and 1970s. These civil wars are society-wide events, such as the Mexican Revolution (1910–1917) and the Cristero Rebellion of 1926–1929, in which over a million Mexicans perished, or Colombia's *La Violencia* (1948–1958), in which up to 200,000 deaths occurred. Since the 'democratic peace' model is based on the claim that citizens extrapolate to foreigners their experiences with fellow citizens at home, we can suspect a similar logic regarding extrapolating violence from within to abroad. Following that logic, in a society wracked by extreme violence citizens should be quite willing to fight their neighbors to a decisive and bloody victory, as they did in the War of the Triple Alliance from 1864 to 1870. If they can be that bloody against domestic opponents, why should one believe that they would be willing to follow international rules against foreign rivals? Internal violence can impact international relations in other ways as well. Colombia's

War of a Thousand Days (1899–1902), a civil war in which up to 130,000 people died, contributed to the government's inability to quickly suppress the revolt in 1903 in the Isthmus of Panama, which the United States exploited to protect a new nation, Panama, and to build the Panama Canal. For any discussion of the U.S. intervention in Panama, surely the violent domestic situation in Colombia at the time is very relevant.

This short overview demonstrates that Latin America's international history, as related to security issues, is rich and complicated and cannot be simply characterized as one in which wars rarely occurred and were inconsequential, conquest was never a goal, peaceful settlements the norm, and unity against the U.S. an underlying dynamic. As scholars of security studies we must challenge ourselves to understand how war and peace, cooperation and conflict, nationalism and Pan–Latin Americanism, and attraction and opposition to the United States can be explained and understood.

Latin American security and the field of security studies

In this second section we examine the place of Latin American security within the field of security studies. In terms of the discipline of international relations and its theoretical paradigms, the interpretation of Latin American security could follow predictable theoretical lines. Thus, realists and neorealists could look at geopolitics, to the hegemonic roles of Great Britain in the 19th century and of the United States since the turn of the 20th century, to regional balances of power and to the (ambiguous) role of Brazil in South America against a background of recurrent conflicts. Conversely, dependency and neo-Marxists see the security of the region as reflecting the current stages of global capitalism. Finally, liberals might focus upon domestic politics, cycles of authoritarianism and democratization, interdependence and integration, and the role of institutions (local, regional, and international) in bringing (or not) about cooperation (Hurrell 1998). We want, however, to emphasize particular experiences and puzzles that drew the attention of non–Latin American scholars interested in the region's security beyond the usual paradigmatic distinctions. Moreover, in the second half of this section we briefly refer to particular contribution of the Latin American scholarship, as well as the practice of Latin American security, to the general discipline of security studies.

Experiences and puzzles of Latin American security

The historical record yields a number of experiences and puzzles that are relevant and peculiar to the contemporary study of Latin American security. We select five of these to highlight in this subsection. The first concerns the issue of ungovernability that has plagued the region and led foreign governments to be concerned with the lives and property of their resident citizens. This leads directly to a second issue: how sovereignty and the principle of nonintervention could provide unstable governments with the opportunity to resolve their internal problems, as they believed proper. The links between economics and security, especially as they affect national development, is a third conundrum for the region that attracts scholars. The role of democracy in Latin America's security situation is another major puzzle for research. Latin America does not fit the liberal 'democratic peace' paradigm, but its experience with war and peace should reveal new insights about the conditions under which the occurrence of war can be eliminated and peace maintained, even while military force remains a foreign policy tool. Our final puzzle focuses on the ontology and epistemology of the study of Latin American security. Constructivists argue that ideas and facts are socially constructed, so an interesting question for the field to consider can be conceptualized as 'why Bolívar, and not Portales?'

The question of ungovernability

> Latin America is ungovernable, the man who serves a revolution plows the sea; this nation will fall inevitably into the hands of the unruly mob and then will pass into the hands of almost indistinguishable petty tyrants of every color and race.
>
> *(García Márquez 1989)*

This quote, attributed to Simón Bolívar, epitomizes the recurrent theme of ungovernability in the region during the 19th century and the early decades of the 20th century, with several lingering echoes until the present.

For the first half of the century after independence, Mexico, Central America, Hispaniola, Peru, and Argentina were beset by recurrent and widespread wars of state formation and nation-building, both international and civil wars. These long periods of civil war and political instability obstructed the process of state-building and consolidation, further contributing to a widespread climate of political violence and ungovernability. This presaged a pattern common to other postcolonial regions in the developing world in more recent times.

Yet Gran Colombia, Chile, and Brazil significantly avoided this trap, experiencing only short-lived bouts of internal conflict. Brazil was an important exception, although it witnessed the Farrapos War in 1835 and recurrent internal crises before and after the end of the monarchy in 1889. Bolivia and Paraguay seemed set to follow Chile's example shortly after independence, but international war not only cut short their nation-building, but also thrust them into long-term political and economic instability. Uruguay, partly with the protection of Great Britain, began its process of nation-building early, but Paraguay, Brazil, and Argentina fomented internal rebellion as each sought to dominate its politics, if not annex the country.

Ungovernability during the 19th and early 20th centuries resulted in numerous cases of external intervention and violation of international law by Europeans, the United States, and Latin Americans. Because European countries and the United States were mainly concerned with collecting debts and protecting the lives and property of their citizens residing in Latin America, even the stable Latin American nations would fear this behavior. The diplomatic and legal reaction of Latin American scholars and practitioners against Great Power intervention developed into legal doctrines that emphasized the norms of sovereignty and nonintervention. Latin Americans in general and Mexicans in particular feared the U.S. land expansion. Though Mexico suffered the most from its northern neighbor, it was Cuba's José Martí who best expressed the fear that the U.S. desire for new land might reveal itself in more subtle ways, through the Pan-American movement, for instance. Later on, such conception has been more than justified against the historical background of recurrent U.S. interventions in Mexico, the Caribbean, and Central America, especially between 1904 and 1938, and during the Cold War. Still, the heterogeneity of Latin American domestic politics meant that at times some Latin American governments wanted the United States to play an active role in defending their countries against other Latin American countries (i.e., Costa Rica against Nicaragua, and Peru against Chile). Moreover, some Latin American governments were also the source of instability vis-à-vis their neighbors, whether for ideological reasons or simply those of control (e.g., Guatemala and the Caribbean League, Argentina in Bolivia, and revolutionary Cuba after 1959).

The principles of sovereignty and nonintervention in Latin America

Latin American countries developed a strong rejection of overt external intervention, due to the significant record of European, U.S., and even Latin American involvement, so they developed a remarkable sensitivity to the issue. Moreover, Latin America as a region developed a distinctive juridical tradition of embedded principles of national sovereignty, nonintervention, and peaceful settlement of disputes among themselves, avoiding through legal mechanisms the involvement of extraregional powers (Kacowicz 2005). Unlike Europe, where the main threat to Westphalian sovereignty came from the same European states and the resulting solution was to modify the relationship among them, in Latin America, the principle of nonintervention has traditionally been enshrined as a legal antidote against foreign intervention. Therefore, the norms of sovereignty and equality of states have been deeply rooted in the tradition of Latin American and inter-American international law, despite their inconsistency with the actual practice of powerful states, first and foremost the United States, and even among the Latin American countries themselves. As a corollary, the principle of nonintervention has received special attention, reflecting the Latin American resistance to unilateral acts of intervention by the European powers and the United States. This principle was clearly exposed in the Calvo Doctrine of 1896 and the Drago Doctrine of 1902. Both doctrines stressed the absolute juridical equality of states and the inviolability of sovereignty, pointing out that foreign intervention was legally invalid.

Security, economics, and development

Since the end of the 19th century Latin American countries have been mainly concerned with issues of economic development and socioeconomic problems, essentially in their own domestic arenas. This overwhelming concern has been prioritized over 'traditional' security issues of war and peace. Hence, for the Latin American countries, economics has been usually securitized as 'high politics.' One interesting exception is the case of El Salvador, which in 1969 invaded Honduras in an effort to settle migration and border delimitation issues. The resulting war destroyed the Central American Common Market, of which El Salvador had been a major beneficiary. Bolivia's refusal to export natural gas to Chile until it receives some type of sovereign access to the Pacific is another case in which traditional security issues (the delimitation of national boundaries) trump economics.

Paradoxically, since economics might be more important for Latin American countries (and citizens) than traditional security issues, they have managed to successfully cooperate in security issues rather than economic ones; hence, there might be a 'spillover' from security to economics rather than the other way around, as in Europe and other regions of the world.

In the context of Latin America, the central political stake continues to be economic development, not power or interstate security. Moreover, in Latin America there is an intrinsic relationship between security and development, both in terms of violence as related to poverty and inequality, and in the relationship between developmentalism (*desarrollismo*) and security, as in the case of the Brazilian concern with national security and industrialization during the military regime of 1964–1985 (Sikkink 1991). Interestingly, Chile recognized this link back in the 1830s.

Security and democracy, and the relative irrelevance of the 'democratic peace'

Security in Latin America has also been related to the democratic civil control over the military, so it is closely linked to issues of democracy and political stability. In Latin America, traditional security has always been about national defense, restricted to the military, and lacking both civilian leadership or inputs from the academic sector until quite recently

(Diamint 2004). And yet, the focus on democratic civil control over the military and the issue of political stability are nowadays bumping up against the current violence of crime in Mexico, Guatemala, Honduras, El Salvador, Venezuela, and Brazil that brings back problems of ungovernability.

What is the specific link between security and democracy in general, and of peace and democracy in particular? As the historical record indicates, the law and theory of 'democratic peace' encounter many difficulties when applied to the region, since in the case of South America peace has preceded and anticipated democracy. Thus, democratic peace provides a very partial and often misleading guide to understand the history of interstate conflict and cooperation in the region. At best, it might explain the 'upgrade' in the level of peace and cooperation once the countries of the region, like those of the Southern Cone, moved towards liberal democracy in the 1980s (Kacowicz 1998; Mares 2001, 2012a; Battaglino 2012).

The ontology and epistemology of the study of Latin American security

From constructivism we learn that ideas and facts are socially constructed, whether in everyday life, politics, or academia. Latin America's history, as we have seen, is rich, complex, and even contradictory. Yet Bolívar stands out in scholarly claims about the region's international relations as the leader and intellectual who had the appropriate foresight to understand how the region could be successful. Bolívar, the Liberator (*Libertador*), was only one of the major generals who defeated the Spanish and achieved Latin American independence, but he is the one upon whom scholars focus, despite the fact that he failed in his efforts to create a united Latin American nation, as well as in his prescription for cooperative relations. An argument could be made that scholarship should focus on Diego Portales instead. The Chilean leader created a political structure that turned a population and resource-sparse country into a stable, prosperous, and powerful country that sought cooperative relations with its neighbors based on the primacy of sovereignty (a highly valued concept in the region). Neither man was a democrat, but Bolívar believed in the necessity for his direct and permanent control, while Portales believed that institutions could provide the necessary context, and never sought presidential office.

The focus on Bolívar by Latin American and Western scholars created a bias in the construction and historical reconstruction of the region in terms of its potential for regional unity that was never realized (at least until recently). Similarly, Bolívar became a trademark for contemporary politicians like the late Hugo Chávez, who used and misused the 'Bolivarian' discourse for his own political agenda. Might a 'Portalian' focus produce more domestic stability and regional unity sooner?

Contributions of Latin American scholarship and practice to the field of security studies

We briefly refer to the contributions of Latin American scholars and practitioners to the field of security studies. Due to space limitations, we address a partial list of contributions. We include: (1) diplomats, jurists, and international scholars in the early 20th century (Luis M. Drago and Barón de Rio Branco), (2) Raúl Prebisch and structuralism, (3) the South American dependency school, (4) Alfonso García Robles and nuclear nonproliferation, (5) Carlos Escudé and peripheral realism, (6) Arie M. Kacowicz and zones of peace, (7) David R. Mares and interstate, militarized disputes, and (8) Andrew Hurrell and theories of international relations.

Diplomats, jurists, and international scholars in the early 20th century: Luis María Drago and Barón de Rio Branco

On December 29, 1902, Luis M. Drago, Argentine minister of foreign affairs, sent a note to the Argentine minister in Washington, referring to the attempt being made by Great Britain, Germany, and Italy to collect claims against Venezuela by forcible means. In the note (which became known as the 'Drago doctrine') he suggested that "the public debt [of an American state] cannot occasion armed intervention, nor even the actual occupation of the territory of American nations by a European power" (Hershey 1907: 30). The doctrine set an important precedent against the right of a nation to intervene to protect the lives and property of its nationals in another state, enshrining the principle of sovereignty and nonintervention, and had an everlasting effect in terms of international security and peace (Drago 1907).

Another important practitioner and innovator of international security who set a world record of peaceful territorial changes in Latin America was the Barón de Rio Branco, Brazilian foreign minister from 1902 to 1912. The establishment of borders is always a crucial problem for the foreign policy of any nation. Brazil has 10 neighbors, and it was Rio Branco who managed to peacefully draw the Brazilian map, first as legal advisor and then as foreign minister. Thanks to his vast knowledge of South American history and geography, the 'Golden Chancellor' managed to delineate nearly 9,000 miles of borders and enlarge Brazil with about 342,000 square miles of territory, an area larger than France, by peaceful means. Thus, in terms of international security, Brazil stood out for its skillful diplomatic performance that translated into territorial gains from all of its neighbors. Brazilian diplomacy successfully combined implicit and explicit coercive threats, like in the case of Bolivia and the Acre region, with enticing offers of nonterritorial trade-offs, such as financial and military aid, economic compensations, and freedom of navigation through the Brazilian rivers. In sum, it is difficult to find in the history of international relations a negotiating performance and an exclusively peaceful pattern similar to the Brazilian one in the establishment of its national borders (Lafer 2000: 214; Kacowicz 1994: 65; Bradford Burns 1967: 196–197). The examples of Drago and Rio Branco illustrate a Grotian assessment of international reality, emphasizing the elements of diplomacy and international law in the Latin American regional international society.

Raúl Prebisch and 'developmentalism'

As a precursor of dependency theory, the Economic Commission for Latin America and the Caribbean (ECLAC) model of economic reform and integration had important security implications by establishing an intrinsic link between security and economic development. The ECLAC model was elaborated by the economists Raúl Prebisch and Celso Furtado; it inspired the evolution of 'developmentalism' (*desarrollismo*) and the establishment of the Latin American Free Trade Area (LAFTA) in 1960. Beyond its economic formulation, ECLAC argued in favor of the need for a strong, active Latin American state.

Prebisch and Furtado claimed that the postwar global trading environment did not provide a level playing field, but rather 'the terms of trade' widened the gap between rich and poor countries, whereas Latin America provided minerals and agricultural products (at cheap prices), and the former colonial powers exported manufactured end products. This creates asymmetrical relations and a lopsided power distribution, so the countries of the South, and Latin America in particular, should opt for autarky at both the national and regional levels (through policies of import-substitution industrialization [ISI] and regional integration) (Prebisch 1950, 1959, 1984; Furtado 1964). Today, the increasing economic success of China and Brazil has rendered

Prebisch's binary North-South divide anachronistic, but Latin America continues to search for the key to sustained development.

The South American dependency school

At the end of World War II, several Latin American countries seemed to be ready for industrialization and self-sustaining economic growth. Instead, they found that they had exchanged old forms of political and economic dependence for a new kind of dependency on the international capitalism of multinational corporations. Thus, the South American version of the dependency approach in the late 1960s and the 1970s emphasized the nefarious role of international structural factors, first and foremost the U.S. influence, the role of the international financial institutions, and the transnational presence of multinational corporations for the region's economics and politics. The South American dependency school expanded but criticized the thread of the argument as elaborated by Prebisch and his associates, demonstrating the limitations of the ISI and the reformist model of 'developmentalism.'

According to the *dependencia* argument, the processes of economic globalization have led to the incorporation of the countries of the region into the global economy, even allowing for some form of 'dependent development.' In this sense, Cardoso and Faletto (1979), alongside other South American scholars, developed an original theory of international relations that accounts for an alternative and nuanced vision of North-South relations and international political economy, with significant repercussions for security studies as well. Interestingly enough, when Cardoso became the president of Brazil in the 1990s he abandoned his theoretical tenets in favor of more pragmatic economic and foreign policies that inserted his country in the economic globalization.

Dependency and the reproduction of power relations unfavorable to Latin America has remained a central theme since the 1960s, usually tackled in terms similar to the realist theory of international relations, although there are different and contradictory versions in this approach. For instance, since the 1970s there has been an overwhelming concern with the issues of autonomy and heterodox autonomy, combining nationalism, developmentalism, and dependency analysis (Jaguaribe 1979; Puig 1980). Another original contribution to comparative politics and security studies is the formulation of Guillermo O'Donnell regarding the linkage between dependent economic modernization and industrialization in Latin America, the failure of the ISI, and the rise of political authoritarianism in the form of military regimes coined 'bureaucratic-authoritarian (BA)' in Brazil, Argentina, Peru, Chile, and Uruguay in the 1960s and 1970s (O'Donnell 1973, 1988), though the model later encountered significant challenges (Hirschman 1979).

Alfonso García Robles and nuclear nonproliferation: the signing of the Tlatelolco Treaty (1967)

The most important Latin American contribution to the implementation of norms of disarmament and nonproliferation has been the establishment of the Latin American nuclear-weapons-free zone (NWFZ) through the Treaty of Tlatelolco (Treaty for the Prohibition of Nuclear Weapons in Latin America), signed by 14 Latin American countries on February 14, 1967 (see Patti, this volume). The Treaty of Tlatelolco institutionalized a regional regime of nuclear nonproliferation that has been completed with the final accession of Argentina, Brazil, and Chile in 1994, and of Cuba in 1995. The Latin American NWFZ, the first of its sort in a populated region of the world, was conceived as a consequence of the Cuban missile crisis and as an effort to prevent further incursions by the nuclear superpowers.

Alfonso García Robles, then under-secretary of state in the Mexican Foreign Office, was the person responsible for urging the president of Mexico to take the initiative and raise the matter at the United Nations. Later on, as the Mexican representative at the United Nations, he was the chair of the Preparatory Commission for Drawing Up the Preliminary Draft of a Treaty on the Denuclearization of Latin America (COPREDAL), leading the negotiations in 1965, 1966, and 1967 that came to fruition at Tlatelolco. As a result of his patient and persistent efforts, it came into effect and became a model for the creation of all other nuclear-weapons-free zones in the world (Epstein 2001: 154; Kacowicz 2005: 139–145).

Carlos Escudé and peripheral realism

In the realm of security studies, scholars from the developing world such as Carlos Escudé and Mohammed Ayoob (2002) developed original theories of 'subordinated' or 'peripheral' realism to explain the asymmetrical and unequal security relations between the countries of the Global North and those of the Global South. Thus, the power structure of the international system is examined from the perspective of the South, with emphasis on its oligarchic and nondemocratic nature (Escudé 1997, 2012; see Escudé, this volume).

According to Escudé (1995), the goal of autonomy in the shaping of foreign policies for Latin American countries became an end in itself, ultimately competing with other important national goals, such as economic development. In his analysis, the two major fallacies of dependency thinking and subsequent writings on autonomy (heterodox or not) were to assume that autonomy was a prerequisite for development; and conversely, that dependency necessarily led to underdevelopment. Instead, 'peripheral realism' recognizes the division of labor between 'rule-makers' (of the North) and 'rule-takers' (of the South), advising the Latin American countries to cater to the hegemon (United States in the recent past, China in the possible future).

Arie M. Kacowicz and the South American 'zone of peace'

The term 'zone of peace' has been usually referred to in the context of the 'long peace' of the Cold War period in Europe (1945–1989), and the separate peace among the democracies developed progressively throughout the last 200 years. In 1998 Kacowicz moved beyond a European or Northern focus to consider the theoretical and historical significance of the term in the context of the Global South. In this context, he argued that there has been a 'long South American peace' since 1883, with the interruptions of the Chaco War (1932–1935) and the Peru-Ecuador conflict (limited wars in 1941, 1981, and 1995).

Kacowicz (1998) explains how regional peace has been maintained in South America, through the distilling of alternative explanations, including realism, liberalism, and satisfaction with the territorial status quo. The argument is that peace can indeed be maintained among nondemocratic states, although there is a direct relationship between the quality of the regional peace and the type of political regimes sustained by the countries in a given region.

With the end of the Cold War and the resolution of conflicts in Central America, Latin America has become progressively one of the most peaceful regions of the world in international relations, and not only South America. Major transformations have occurred in the relations among the countries of the region, which have for the most part improved the prospects for peace, in terms of the traditional concerns of international security and peace (Domínguez 1998: 4–11). At least in rhetorical terms, the 33 Latin American and Caribbean countries signed in Havana on January 31, 2014 a declaration pledging to make the region a 'zone of peace.'

David R. Mares and militarized interstate disputes in Latin America

While looking at the same empirical reality in the region, characterized by the absence of widespread, full-fledged wars, Mares asks different questions concerning coercion and violence, rather than peace: Why do we define 'peace' as any international behavior that results in fewer than 1,000 battlefield-related deaths? Why are Latin American states still using military force against each other, but short of war? What role do international institutions and norms play in a context in which governments continue to see the use of military force as a legitimate tool in relations with their Latin American neighbors? Thus, he develops the concept of 'violent peace,' refers to peace as an 'illusion,' and elaborates a theoretical model of 'militarized bargaining' to explain the 'violent peace' of Latin America (Mares 2001, 2012a).

Mares has also promoted a focus on the institutional design of security institutions in the region to understand how they might create a 'moral hazard' with regards to the use of force in interstate relations (Mares 1996/1997, 2012b, 2012c). Mares focuses attention upon the empirical record of the use of military force in Latin America's international relations. He has developed a database of militarized interstate disputes in the region that regularly precedes the publication of the Correlates of War (COW) Militarized Interstate Disputes (MIDs) database and includes MIDs missed by the global set, since his is regionally focused.

Andrew Hurrell and the relevance of international relations theories

In our assessment, the scholarship of Andrew Hurrell is among the best analyses of the international relations of the Americas (with a particular focus on Brazil), and represents one of the most important contributions and impacts on security studies worldwide. Stemming from a theoretical perspective that combines the English school version of international society, constructivism, and normative international theory, Hurrell brings a comparative regional perspective to the study of security in the region, by assessing relevant themes such as the potential emergence of a pluralistic security community in the Southern Cone, the relevance of regional frameworks, and most recently, the impact of emerging powers (such as Brazil) and the globalization of international society (Hurrell 1998, 2007, 2013).

Themes of Latin American security in its first 200 years

After reviewing the historical record of Latin American security we turn in this concluding section to trace recurring themes and patterns embedded in that rich history. We include the following subjects: (1) Latin Americanism vs. Pan-Americanism, (2) patterns of traditional security: war, peace, and conflict, (3) patterns of nontraditional security, and (4) change and continuity in Latin American security and security studies.

Latin Americanism vs. Pan-Americanism, and the prism of U.S.–Latin American relations

As a basic theme in the formation and evolution of Latin America as a regional international society, the supranational aspirations for regional unity have been developed by two overlapping and sometimes opposing ideological movements: Bolivarianism (or Latin Americanism) and Pan-Americanism. Bolivarianism has been expressed in the Latin American congresses of the 19th century, the regional efforts to resolve the Central American civil wars in the 1980s by the Contadora and Río Groups, and the current schemes for economic, political, and security integration throughout the region, from MERCOSUR to UNASUR to CELAC. Conversely, Pan-Americanism has been reflected in a series of inter-American conferences held since 1889, the work of the Rio Treaty since 1947 and the OAS since 1948, as well as numerous inter-American institutions, including the recent Presidential Summits of the Americas since 1994.

Pan-Americanism and Latin Americanism represent then the two axes in which security discussions have been historically articulated in the region. For instance, one might argue that the contemporary inter-American security system is the outcome of the often contradictory security policies undertaken by the hemispheric hegemon (the United States) in juxtaposition to those of the governments of Latin American and Caribbean countries, in order to guarantee their national security while simultaneously bolstering the collective security of the Americas (Hirst and Rico 1992: 2–3; Bagley and Horwitz 2007: 4).

Traditional security: war, peace, and conflict

The classic themes of strategic studies, particularly the discussion of national defense and strategy based on evaluations of state capacities and threats to the territorial integrity, constitute the majority of theories, ideas, and ideologies present in publications and public debates in the region regarding international and regional security (see Marcella, this volume). The peculiar reality of the region (a long international peace, but a violent and elusive one) has been reflected in the proliferation of territorial conflicts and interstate militarized disputes (Grabendorff 1982; Little 1987; Mares, this volume).

When we turn the focus of our analysis to South America, we find that a cluster of its security agenda consists of long-standing territorial conflicts and border disputes – 'traditional threats' (Domínguez 2003). The disputed territories and boundaries have been consistently the subject of diplomatic crises, or have even turned into arenas of military operations within the wars that took place in the region.

Despite the optimistic argument regarding the emergence of an incipient, pluralistic security community in the Southern Cone of South America (see Oelsner, this volume), there are still orthodox beliefs in South America about the primary object of security; namely, the survival of the nation-state (and/or the ruling regime) from either external attack or internal subversion. In both cases, the threat and use of force to deter and to defend against the so-called enemies of the state are still the primary means by which security is sought and maintained, to confront these traditional threats (see the various Defense White Papers [*Libros Blancos*] published by South American countries).

Nontraditional security: expanding 'security'

As in other parts of the world, the terms of the security debate in Latin America have shifted dramatically over the last 25 years. Since the end of the Cold War, the countries (and peoples) of the region confront new types of security challenges that they have been hard-pressed to tackle effectively, rendering traditional issues of war and peace irrelevant to cope with *intermestic* (international and domestic) problems of national and international security. Thus, by broadening the concept of security we might include issues such as increasing unemployment, inequality, and poverty; marginality of many sectors of the population; recurrent violations of human rights; environmental degradation; threats to democratic development and economic wellbeing; and political and economic stability.

The expanded concept of security allows for a focus on the so-called new security threats and risks emerging with the intensification of globalization processes. These threats transcend state borders and often derive from nonstate actors. For instance, according to the Managua Declaration of 2006, terrorism, drug trafficking, human trafficking, organized crime, money laundering, corruption, and the proliferation of small arms and light weapons all pose significant threats to Latin American security.

In sum, new and broader concepts of security such as 'common,' 'mutual,' 'comprehensive,' 'cooperative,' and 'human' have added a multidimensional character to traditional security relations in the region. A broader concept of security might include, in addition to the obvious military dimension, diplomatic, political, economic, and cultural aspects. The diplomatic dimension is subordinated to the idea of national sovereignty within the context of a regional vision of security. The political aspect refers to the type of political regime; for instance, a threat to democracy is regarded as a threat to regional security. With the structural economic reforms of the 1980s and 1990s and the plans for economic integration at the regional and subregional level in the new millennium, the economic dimension has also been incorporated into the general scheme of security. Finally, the cultural dimension refers to the normative dimension of potentially sharing common values at different levels of analysis, such as local, subnational, national, and regional.

Change and continuity in Latin American security and security studies

In the last 30 years we can identify academic studies of international security in Latin America done by Latin American scholars, in contrast with the previous military exclusivity regarding the relations between the use of force and foreign policy (Diamint 2004). Moreover, the expansion of the concept of security allowed Latin American scholars and analysts to refer to both traditional and nontraditional threats, including an increasing attention to socioeconomic factors (Diamint 2001; Grabendorff 2003; Mathieu and Rodríguez 2009; Mason and Tickner 2006; Tavares 2014).

Nowadays Latin America's security agenda demands the simultaneous management of domestic crises, interstate conflicts, and transnational threats. Though located at different levels of analysis – national or intrastate, regional (international) or interstate and transnational – the three conflict clusters are often interrelated and tend to overlap in the region's border areas (Jaskoski et al. 2015). Moreover, in the last two decades there has been an attempt of building regional structures to cope with these threats, though not always effectively (Flemes and Radseck 2009).

In sum, the reality of Latin American security reflects both conflict and cooperation, stable peace in the Southern Cone and (neorealist) mistrust and coercion in other subregions; a kind of what Battaglino (2012) defines as 'hybrid peace.' Moreover, the traditional security dilemma has been at times transcended by an 'insecurity dilemma' of intrastate security (or better, insecurity), especially in the cases of Mexico and Colombia (Feldmann 2014).

Conclusions

Looking back at the first 200 years of Latin American security we can agree that intrastate issues have always dominated the security agenda. At the same time, we are witnessing nowadays attempts to frame some of the security problems in regional and subregional terms (rather than inter-American), through ALBA, UNASUR, and CELAC. In between these two concerns with security (subnational and regional), the Latin American state remains both the problem and the solution to cope with many of the challenges of Latin American security in the 21st century.

Both the historical overview and the links between Latin American security and the field of security studies show the richness, complexity, and contradictions of Latin American security realities. Thus, in our view, Latin American security issues remain at a paramount place in order to understand Latin American politics, economics, and societies, both in international relations and in domestic terms. Moreover, Latin America serves as an empirical laboratory to explore and suggest hypotheses and theories to make sense of this complex reality. In addition, Latin American security can serve as a source of inspiration to offer genuine contributions to the general field of security studies, well beyond the Western Hemisphere.

References

Ayoob, M. (2002) 'Inequality and Theorizing in International Relations: The Case of Subaltern Realism', *International Studies Review*, 4(3): 27–48.

Bagley, B.M. and Horwitz, B. (2007) *Regional Security in the Americas: Past, Present, and Future*, Miami: Miami University.

Bates, R.H., Coatsworth, J.H. and Williamson, J.G. (2006) 'Lost Decades: Lessons from Post-Independence Latin America for Today's Africa', *NBER Working Paper Series*, 12610.

Battaglino, J.M. (2012) 'The Coexistence of Peace and Conflict in South America: Toward a New Conceptualization of Types of Peace', *Revista Brasileira de Política Internacional*, 55(2): 131–151.

Bradford Burns, E. (1966) *The Unwritten Alliance: Rio-Branco and Brazilian-American Relations*, New York: Columbia University Press.

——— (1967) 'Traditions and Variation in Brazilian Foreign Policy', *Journal of Inter-American Studies*, 9(2): 195–212.

Burr, R.N. (1985) *By Reason or Force: Chile and the Balancing of Power in South America*, Berkeley: University of California Press.

Cardoso, F.H. and Faletto, E. (1979) *Dependency and Development in Latin America*, Berkeley: University of California Press.

Diamint, R. (2001) *Seguridad y democracia en América Latina*, Buenos Aires: GEL.

——— (2004) 'Security Challenges in Latin America', *Bulletin of Latin American Research*, 23(1): 43–62.

Domínguez, J.I. (1998) 'Security, Peace, and Democracy in Latin America and the Caribbean: Challenges for the Post-Cold War Era' in J. I. Domínguez (ed) *International Security and Democracy: Latin America and the Caribbean in the Post-Cold War Era*, Pittsburgh: Pittsburgh University Press, pp. 3–28.

——— (2003) 'Boundary Disputes in Latin America', *Peaceworks*, 50: 1–45.

Drago, L.M. (1907) 'State Loans in Their Relations to International Policy', *The American Journal of International Law*, 1(3): 692–726.

Epstein, W. (2001) 'The Making of the Treaty of Tlatelolco', *Journal of the History of International Law*, 3: 153–179.

Escudé, C. (1988) 'Argentine Territorial Nationalism', *Journal of Latin American Studies*, 20(1): 139–165.

——— (1995) *El realismo de los estados débiles*, Buenos Aires: GEL.

——— (1997) *Foreign Policy Theory in Menem's Argentina*, Gainesville: University Press of Florida.

——— (2012) *Principios de realismo periférico: Una teoría Argentina y su vigencia ante el ascenso de China*, Buenos Aires: Lumiere.

Feldmann, A. (2014) 'Narcotics Insecurity and the Para-Militarization of Violence in Colombia and Mexico', Unpublished manuscript, pp. 1–33.

Flemes, D. and Radseck, M. (2009) 'Creating Multilevel Security Governance in South America', *GIGA Working Papers*, 117.

Furtado, C. (1964) *Development and Underdevelopment*, Los Angeles: University of California Press.

García Márquez, G. (1989) *El general en su laberinto*, Bogotá: Oveja Negra.

Grabendorff, W. (1982) 'Interstate Conflict Behavior and Regional Potential for Conflict in Latin America', *Journal of Interamerican Studies and World Affairs*, 24(3): 267–294.
——— (ed) (2003) *La seguridad en las Américas: Enfoques críticos y conceptos alternativos*, Bogotá: FESCOL-CEREC.
Hershey, A. S. (1907) 'The Calvo and Drago Doctrines', *The American Journal of International Law*, 1(1): 26–45.
Hirschman, A. O. (1979) 'The Turn Towards Authoritarianism in Latin America and the Search for Economic Determinants' in D. Collier (ed) *The New Authoritarianism in Latin America*, Princeton: Princeton University Press, pp. 61–98.
Hirst, M. and Rico, C. (1992) 'Regional Security Perceptions in Latin América', *Documentos e Informes de Investigación, FLACSO*, 129: 1–74.
Hurrell, A. (1998) 'Security in Latin America', *International Affairs*, 74(3): 529–546.
——— (2007) 'One World? Many Worlds? The Place of Regions in the Study of International Society', *International Affairs*, 83(1): 151–166.
——— (2013) 'Rising Powers and the Emerging Global Order' in J. Baylis, S. Smith and P. Owens (eds) *The Globalization of World Politics*, Oxford: Oxford University Press, pp. 80–97.
Jaguaribe, H. (1979) 'Autonomía periférica y hegemonía centrica', *Estudios Internacionales*, 46: 91–130.
Jaskoski, M., Trinkunas, H. and Sotomayor, A. (eds) (2015) *Border and Borderlands in the Americas: Conflict and Harmonies*, Baltimore: Johns Hopkins University Press.
Kacowicz, A. M. (1994) *Peaceful Territorial Change*, Columbia: University of South Carolina Press.
——— (1998) *Zones of Peace in the Third World: South America and West Africa in Comparative Perspective*, Albany: SUNY Press.
——— (2005) *The Impact of Norms in International Society: The Latin American Experience, 1881–2001*, Notre Dame: University of Notre Dame Press.
Lacoste, P. (1995–1996) 'Las guerras Hispanoamericana y de la Triple Alianza, la Revolución de los Colorados, y su impacto en las relaciones entre Argentina y Chile', *Historia*, 29: 125–158.
——— (2003) 'Estanislao Zeballos y la política exterior Argentina con Brasil y Chile', *Revista Confluencia*, 1: 107–118.
Lafer, C. (2000) 'Brazilian International Identity and Foreign Policy: Past, Present, and Future', *Daedalus*, 129(2): 207–238.
Levine, R. M. (1995) *Vale of Tears: Revisiting the Canudos Massacre in Northeast Brazil, 1893–1897*, Berkeley: University of California Press.
Little, W. (1987) 'International Conflict in Latin America', *International Affairs*, 63(4): 589–601.
Macaulay, N. (1985) *The Sandino Affair*, Durham: Duke University Press.
Mares, D. R. (1996/1997) 'Deterrence Bargaining in the Ecuador-Peru Enduring Rivalry: Designing Strategies Around Military Weakness', *Security Studies*, 6(2): 91–123.
——— (2001) *Violent Peace: Militarized Interstate Bargaining in Latin America*, New York: Columbia University Press.
——— (2012a) *Latin America and the Illusion of Peace*, London: Routledge.
——— (2012b) 'Por que os Latino-Americanos continuam a se ameaçarem o uso da força militar nas relações intra Latino-Americanas', *Varia Historia,* 28(48): 599–625.
——— (2012c) 'Constructing Real Peace and Security in Latin America: Minimizing the "Moral Hazard" Character of Security Institutions', *Pensamiento Propio*, 36/37: 157–174.
Mason, A. and Tickner, A. (2006) 'A Transregional Security Cartography of the Andes' in P. W. Drake and E. Hershberg (eds) *State and Society in Conflict: Comparative Perspectives on Andean Crises*, Pittsburgh: University of Pittsburgh Press, pp. 74–98.
Matthieu, H. and Rodríguez, P. (eds) (2009) *Seguridad regional en América Latina y el Caribe*, Bogotá: Friedrich Ebert Stiftung.
O'Donnell, G. (1973) *Modernization and Bureaucratic-Authoritarianism*, Berkeley: Institute of International Studies, University of California at Berkeley.
——— (1988) *Bureaucratic Authoritarianism: Argentina, 1966–1973, in Comparative Perspective*, Berkeley: University of California Press.
Prebisch, R. (1950) *The Economic Development of Latin America and its Principal Problems*, New York: United Nations.
——— (1959) 'Commercial Policy in the Underdeveloped Countries', *American Economic Review*, 49: 251–273.

——— (1984) 'Five Stages in My Thinking on Development' in G. M. Meier and D. Seers (eds) *Pioneers in Development*, New York: Oxford University Press, pp. 173–191.
Puig, J. C. (1980) *Doctrinas internacionales y autonomía Latinoamericana*, Caracas: Instituto de Altos Estudios de América Latina, Universidad Simón Bolívar.
Reed, N. (1964) *The Caste War of Yucatán*, Stanford: Stanford University Press.
Shaw, C. M. (2004) *Cooperation, Conflict, and Consensus in the Organization of American States*, New York: Palgrave.
Sikkink, K. (1991) *Ideas and Institutions: Developmentalism in Brazil and Argentina*, Ithaca: Cornell University Press.
Stoetzer, C. O. (1993) *The Organization of American States*, Westport: Praeger.
Tavares, R. (2014) *Security in South America: The Role of States and Regional Organizations*, Boulder: Lynne Rienner.
Wood, B. (1966) *The United States and Latin American Wars, 1932–1942*, New York: Columbia University Press.
Zeballos, E. (1901) 'Conferencia inaugural de la Liga Patriótica Nacional', dada en el Politeama Argentino de Buenos Aires la noche del 19 de diciembre de 1901. En Revista de Derecho, Historía y Letras. Año IV, Tomo XI, pp. 413–456.

PART II

Theoretical approaches to security in Latin America

2

GEOPOLITICS IN LATIN AMERICA, OLD AND NEW

Detlef Nolte and Leslie E. Wehner

Introduction

Geography can certainly influence politics, as the complicated topography of South America with its inaccessible rainforests, deserts, and high mountains illustrates. This topography has historically made the establishment of communication channels and contacts (including warfare) difficult, not only between neighboring countries but also between the center and the periphery within many countries. However, geographic obstacles are not as insurmountable as recent transcontinental infrastructure projects have demonstrated. Being endowed with natural resources creates opportunities for action to be taken in terms of exploitation, development of infrastructure, and securitization. However, political decisions must be made in order for changes related to geographic spaces and endowments to occur. Geopolitical thinking constructs narratives at the interplay of territory, geography, and politics, and with regards to how these elements should shape the interactions of states within a region (Cohen 2009; Kacowicz 2000; Kelly 1997).

Geopolitical thinking and policy-making may have waned in other regions of the world, but Latin America is still a fertile ground for the development of geopolitical ideas and doctrines. If we look at the maps included in the different defense White Books (*Libros Blancos*) of South American governments, they show the enduring importance of geopolitical markers – maps of the maritime boundaries, lost and/or reclaimed territories, and territorial projections into the Antarctic. In fact, the attempts of Latin American governments to construct identities based on territorial and maritime spaces are deeply rooted in geopolitical thinking (Dodds 1993), as demonstrated by the 'Blue Amazon' narrative promoted by the Brazilian navy since the first decade of the 2000s. The enduring importance of geopolitics in Latin America is also reflected in the high number of books, journals, and articles in print with the word 'geopolitics' in their title (whether in Spanish, Portuguese, or English), and in its being a salient component of the curricula of military academies in this region.

While geopolitics is still important in political discourses and foreign policy in Latin America, there are only few analyses of current geopolitical thinking. Moreover, most of these works are rather descriptive or adopt a historical perspective on the development of geopolitical ideas. While Latin America is a region in which geopolitical thinking is influential and pervasive, the avenue of 'critical geopolitics' – which seeks to unpack the different rationales and meanings of geopolitical discourses – is, paradoxically, rather underdeveloped (exceptions are Cairo et al. 2007; Preciado and Uc 2010; Cabrera 2011) when compared to mainstream geopolitics approaches focusing on cases outside of Latin America (Dodds et al. 2013). Critical geopolitics refers to the analysis of the spatializing of boundaries and dangers (the geopolitical map of the world), and of the geopolitical representations of self and other (the geopolitical imagination) (Mamadouh 1998: 244).

'Neoclassical geopolitics' (Guzzini 2014), however, is the dominant perspective in Latin America. It is a policy-oriented approach, which conceptualizes foreign policy challenges and the international politics of a state in light of its geographical features, or its position on the map. It formulates guidelines for conducting statecraft based on this analysis (van der Wusten and Dijkink 2002: 20). Therefore, neoclassical geopolitics gives explanatory primacy to physical and human geographical factors – for example, whether a country is landlocked or has a large coastline, or whether it is rich or poor with regard to raw materials – which tend to lead to environmental and structural determinism. This chapter focuses on both major political and economic developments that have influenced geopolitical thinking in South America. It also seeks to elucidate the constitutive and basic elements of existing geopolitical narratives.

Classical geopolitics in Latin America

The reference to geopolitical codes and maps (i.e., on postage stamps; Child 2008) is a pervasive element of political thinking in Latin America. Thus, the past still has a significant psychological impact on the current international relations of the region and present-day boundary disputes (Kacowicz 2000: 84–85).

Latin American geopolitics until the end of the Cold War era was characterized by a focus on the state – sometimes perceived as an organic entity – as the provider of territorial security in both its domestic and external dimensions. The state prioritized the need to exert control over its own territory by trying to provide space for population growth and economic expansion. However, few connections were made between the internal territorial geographies and topographies in the field of geopolitics in its old variant – that is, the study of sparsely populated areas as places from which nonconformist sectors of society (including criminal networks) can subvert and control the state (Cohen 2009: 36).

The centrality of the state in geopolitical thinking was related to the need to determine and defend its territorial boundaries. Border disputes are related to the very origins of the nation-state in Latin America (Parodi 2002). This explains why "territorial disputes embody the essence of South American geopolitics" (Kelly 1997: 135). South America has been referred to as a 'zone of negative peace' or a 'zone of violent peace;' both phrases reflect the reality of rivalry of South American states vis-à-vis territory and border disputes. However, these terms simultaneously attest to the lack of large-scale armed conflicts in the region, despite the existing rivalries (Kacowicz 1998; Mares 2001).

The authoritarian regimes of the 1960s and 1970s tended to emphasize nationalistic narratives in the face of territorial issues. The geopolitical thinking of the military governments was closely linked to national security doctrines (Kacowicz 2000). Moreover, geopolitical thinkers from the military became political protagonists who were able to shape relationships with other states in the region. A good example is General Augusto Pinochet, who was a professor of geopolitics but not an important geopolitical author. In contrast, General Golbery do Couto e Silva, another geopolitical thinker, was able to influence Brazil's foreign policy as advisor to different authoritarian presidents after 1964 (Child 1979; Kacowicz 2000). The predominance of the military sector in the field of geopolitics is related to the role played by the military geographical institutes that exist in most Latin American countries. These institutes' main duties were to control and elaborate the cartography of the state. However, the same institutes also played the role of academic centers for geopolitical and military training (Barton 1997: 63). They were closely linked to the respective national military academies.

While traditional geopolitics perceived the state as a unitary actor, geopolitical narratives and policies have always been contested. Geopolitics at the domestic level has remained under-researched in terms of actors, competing policies and narratives, and internal dilemmas regarding the implementation of one policy over another. The subfield of foreign policy analysis can illuminate this facet of geopolitics, as it has shown that even in authoritarian contexts policies can be contested domestically.

Traditional geopolitics in the 1960s and 1970s was influenced by the structural frame set by the systemic variable of bipolarity during the Cold War. The key point is that ideological and power structures had the upper hand in geopolitics in South America. Geopolitics in Latin America was thus reduced to Great Power politics management by the United States and the Soviet Union in developing regions. For instance, the dissemination of anticommunism of the United States was key for the development of the national security doctrines in Latin America (Cohen 2009; Child 1979; Kelly 1997).

Further, an overemphasis on border delimitations in the analysis of old geopolitics research may have influenced the lack of interest in geo-economic issues. While economic issues were present in existing studies of old geopolitics, they were nested in studies of disputes over territorial and maritime boundaries without being distinguished from the study of sovereignty issues. For instance, the maritime treaties signed by Chile, Ecuador, and Peru in 1952 and 1954 were not exclusively driven by the need to delimit sea borders. Rather, economic strategic reasons were fundamental for the signing of these accords, to exert economic control over those 200 miles, to protect national fishing industries, and to allow for national economic development as a whole and in specific geographical zones that could serve as economic poles. A reexamination of old geopolitics topics in Latin America could lead to new understandings of concepts and to new perspectives of research, such as the observed but neglected intrinsic relationship between security and development in this period.

New geopolitics in Latin America

The main factors influencing geopolitical thinking in Latin America since the 1990s can be summarized as follows: (1) Latin America has become geopolitically less marginalized in international politics, and as a side effect the geopolitical perspective and room to maneuver have become broader; (2) geopolitical thinking has moved from the national to the regional or continental level, giving room to geopolitics of integration; (3) as part of this development South America has been constructed as a new geopolitical region, with Brazil as its major regional power; (4) the United States has lost centrality in South America, and extra-hemispheric actors such as China have become major players in Latin America; (5) as a result of global power shifts and the new international positioning of Latin America both the Pacific Basin and the South Atlantic (including the Antarctic) have become more important in Latin American geopolitical narratives; and (6) natural resources have again turned out to be a central issue in Latin American geopolitical thinking, leading to their increasing securitization and to new territorial disputes, especially related to maritime borders.

Latin America as a geopolitical region

In the 1980s Latin America was a "zone of marginality within the world power structure," (Cohen 2009) and at the end of the 1990s geopolitical analysis still emphasized the peripheral role of South America in international politics (Kelly 1997: 183). A decade later, however, South America had become an independent geopolitical region with balanced ties to the United States, Europe, and Asia (Cohen 2009). There are now new interregional dialogue forums with Europe, Africa, Asia, and the Arab countries. As a result of this, Latin American countries have been able to take more independent positions – for example, as temporary members of the UN Security Council (as during the Iraq crisis of 2003 or with regard to Iran's nuclear program). Brazil is a constitutive part of the networks of rising powers like IBSA and BRICS. Mexico (1994) and Chile (2000) entered into the OECD, and Colombia is currently in the accession process. Moreover, Brazil, Mexico, and Argentina are part of the G-20 of leading economies. States from this region are also important partners in global governance forums such as climate summits; in this way, Latin American countries are increasingly shaping the global architecture.

Geopolitics of integration

The early 1990s represented a period of change characterized by a sequence of different regional cooperation projects. These projects were manifestations of divergent geo-economic and geopolitical interests. Historically there has been always an overlap of intraregional cooperation (Latin America) and inter-American or hemispheric cooperation (Hurrell 1992). In the 1990s the idea of the Americas as a political and economic geographical space was in vogue. The Americas project was a reaction to contemporary major global geopolitical and geo-economic trends, such as the fear of an exclusive regionalism in other parts of the world. Mexico, the United States, and Canada consolidated a common geo-economic space with the creation of the North American Free Trade Agreement (NAFTA) in 1994. At the same time, the U.S. government promoted the idea of a Free Trade Area of the Americas (FTAA) stretching from Alaska to Tierra del Fuego; the preparatory process started with the first Summit of the Americas in Miami in 1994, although it never materialized. For a short time, the so-called Washington Consensus unified the region behind the same economic model. Moreover, Canada joined the Organization of American States (OAS) in 1990 to convert it into a genuinely all-encompassing continental organization of the Americas.

Liberalization within the framework of the Washington Consensus facilitated economic cooperation projects in Latin America under the premise of open regionalism. Observers identified a positive transformation from geopolitics to geo-economics (Kacowicz 2000). However, the dream of creating the (neo)liberal Americas under benign U.S. leadership lasted only a decade; it crumbled in the face of other harsh geopolitical and geo-economic realities. The EU started to court Latin America, organizing regular European–Latin American and Caribbean summits (since 1998) – giving way to a competitive summitry (Legler 2013) – and offering free trade agreements to the Latin American countries. While extra-hemispheric actors have won influence, the United States has lost economic and political leverage in Latin America. Russia is displaying a renewed geostrategic interest in Latin America (Blank 2009). Other important newcomers in the region are China and, on a minor scale, India (Malamud and García 2014). From the U.S. perspective, the 'dragon in the backyard' is perceived as a threat to the geopolitical position of the United States in the Western Hemisphere. In fact, in some South American countries China has already displaced the United States as their most important trading partner.

In the shadow of declining U.S. influence and perceiving the FTAA as a threat to its own geostrategic interests, Brazil has been developing its own geopolitical project in South America. At the same time, in Venezuela, President Hugo Chávez (in office 1999–2013) used oil revenues to create his own Latin American networks from which to project power such as ALBA, Petrocaribe, and Petroamerica. The idea of trade in the Americas via the FTAA lost its appeal for a number of South American countries, illustrated by the fate of the Summit of the Americas (Legler 2013). The 2005 Mar del Plata summit completely buried the hemispheric project of the FTAA. In contrast to the previous three summits, there was no reference made to hemispheric integration in the summit declaration. Moreover, the next two summits in Port of Spain (2009) and Cartagena (2012) ended without the approval of a common declaration, revealing a rift between the United States and many Latin American governments.

The end of the 'Americas project' illustrates that Latin America has become more independent and self-confident. Yet, it has also become more heterogeneous and segmented, both economically and politically. In fact, in Latin America there is a proliferation of regional and subregional organizations that serve to delineate and consolidate geographic (sub)regions. While these organizations give the geographic regions an identity (or 'actorness'), as a social construct they can also lead to a drifting apart of countries belonging to different regional organizations. Thus, when Mexico, the United States, and Canada signed NAFTA, Mexico became more dependent on the United States and more separated from the rest of Latin America, especially South America.

Unlike Latin America, South America is a relatively new social construct – its creation was strongly influenced by Brazilian foreign policy strategies designed to demarcate that country's sphere of influence (Spektor 2010; Malamud 2012). Regional cooperation and integration was made possible by Argentine-Brazilian rapprochement, seen as a geopolitical turning point (Kelly 1997). The move from geopolitical rivalry to cooperation was fundamental for the creation of MERCOSUR in 1991 and the emergence of a security community in the Southern Cone (including Chile, Paraguay, and Uruguay) (Hurrell 1998).

From a geopolitical perspective, Brazil can be seen as a 'core state' that facilitates the deepening of integration (Rivarola 2011). As early as the 1990s, Brazil envisioned a free trade area focusing exclusively on South America (SAFTA), but it was not until 2000 that a first summit of South American presidents took place in Brasilia. Brazil also led the push to establish the South American Community of Nations (later renamed the Union of South American Nations, UNASUR) during the third presidential summit in Cuzco (Peru) in 2004, whose constitutive treaty was signed in 2008. UNASUR has since facilitated South America's becoming a political and economic entity with increasing international actorhood (Rivarola 2011). The creation of UNASUR is both a part of Brazil's strategy to consolidate a South American autonomy vis-à-vis the United States (Brands 2010) and an instrument for the integration – both physically and in terms of energy resources – of South America. Thus, the emergence of Brazil as a regional power with a global projection capacity has strengthened South America's role as an independent geopolitical region (Cohen 2009: 147).

The process of South American integration has been underpinned by a current of strategic thinking branded the 'geopolitics of integration,' which links geography, integration, and development thinking with the objective of creating and consolidating South America as a new continental geographic unit (Rivarola 2011). Moreover, the (re)construction of regions is also a topic of critical geopolitics (Preciado and Uc 2010), and it is linked to the idea of more 'geopolitical autonomy.'

From the beginning, the idea of expanding South America's physical and energy infrastructure was a central element of 'positive integration' in the region, as it encouraged political consensus-building, promoted regional interdependencies, and increased cooperation in non-trade issues (Sanahuja 2012). Consequently, one of the first concrete results of the 2000 South American presidential summit was the Initiative for the Integration of the Regional South American Infrastructure (IIRSA), which was later integrated into the UNASUR structure. IIRSA is a geopolitical project constructing a new regional territorial space in order to strengthen the interdependence of the South American countries (Perrier Buslé 2013).

The Pacific and South Atlantic as geopolitical markers

The economic promise and market projection into the Pacific Basin was already present in the traditional geopolitical thinking with regards to the Pacific Ocean. In these narratives the South American countries, which have a coastline on the Pacific, constituted a separate regional subsystem (Kelly 1997: 7–10, 30–31). However, for most of the 20th century Latin America's most important trading partner was the United States; second most important was Europe. So the 'Atlantic Triangle' was more important than the Pacific Basin. With the rise of Asian economies and especially China's upsurge in the 21st century the geo-economic parameters have changed, and the Pacific Rim (including the Western parts of the United States) have become more important.

As a manifestation of the emerging 'Pacific Consensus' – the movement in terms of trade and investment toward the Pacific geo-economic region (Vadell 2013) – three Latin American countries (Chile, Mexico, and Peru) became members of the Asia-Pacific Economic Cooperation (APEC) in the 1990s. Other countries such as Colombia, Costa Rica, Ecuador, and Panama are also interested in joining the organization. Moreover, Chile and Mexico – as APEC members and having multiple FTAs with Asian states – have cast narratives of being gateways for trade between both regions (Wehner and Thies 2014).

In 2012, Chile, Colombia, Peru, and Mexico created the Pacific Alliance, a regional project that seeks to create a free trade zone between its members and make connections to Asian economies. Later, Panama and Costa Rica also applied for membership. However, this economic project had additional, significant political consequences, furthering the fragmentation of Latin American economic integration, as the Pacific Alliance became a counterweight to a more statist MERCOSUR and the anti-neoliberal ALBA project (Briceño-Ruiz 2014).

The idea to link the Atlantic and Pacific through bi-oceanic corridors – as part of the IIRSA project – is both a recognition of the growing importance of the Pacific Basin and a reaction of Brazil to this development. IIRSA is thus an instrument to counter the centrifugal forces of a Pacific and an Atlantic South America by strengthening the South American core.

Moreover, from a Brazilian viewpoint, the 'wider Atlantic' is of strategic importance (Alcaro and Alessandri 2013), wherein the South Atlantic has become an area of strong geopolitical and strategic competition (Lesser 2010). Brazil, which has by far the longest South Atlantic coastline (4,350 miles), believes this border is vulnerable – especially following the discoveries of large oil and gas deposits within the pre-salt layers of Brazil's continental shelf. Moreover, the Brazilian government is promoting a redefinition and extension of its continental shelf by way of the United Nations Convention on the Law of the Seas (UNCLOS), which would expand Brazil's maritime space and exclusive economic zone.

More than 90 per cent of Brazilian trade is shipped via Atlantic sea routes, and the country has a major strategic interest related to the security of the main sea lines of communication (SLOCS) crossing the South Atlantic (Reis 2012) and any possible choke points therein. Of importance for sea transport (as mentioned in the 2012 *National Defense White Book*) are the 'Atlantic Gorge' between northeastern Brazilian and West Africa, the Strait of Magellan (as an alternative to the Panama Canal, especially for large ships), and the Cape of Good Hope, which links the Southern Atlantic and the Indian Ocean, as an alternative to the Suez Canal. There is also growing attention being given to new, nontraditional security threats related to the South Atlantic, such as smuggling, the transatlantic drug trade (especially with West African countries), illegal immigration, environmental crimes, terrorism, and piracy.

In this context the Brazilian government has securitized the South Atlantic and clearly defined its position both in the 2008 *National Strategy of Defense* and in the 2012 *National Defense White Book*. In the middle of the first decade of the 2000s the Brazilian navy launched the 'Blue Amazon' campaign – a new geopolitical concept whose objective is to foster the idea that South Atlantic resources within Brazil's exclusive economic zone (an area equal to 52 per cent of the country's continental land mass) are of vital interest to all Brazilians. The securitization of the South Atlantic is in line with the strategy taken up by other regional powers in the world to give 'their' region a maritime perimeter (Abdenur and Marcondes 2014a). As a consequence, Brazil started a naval modernization program that included the construction of nuclear-powered submarines (in cooperation with France), vessels that are particularly suited to long-distance patrols in the South Atlantic.

For the Brazilian military, the South Atlantic is an area of power projection (Reis 2012), whereas the African coast is perceived as part of the Brazilian defensive perimeter. Since 2007, Brazil has revitalized the 'zone of peace and cooperation of the South Atlantic' (ZOPACAS, following the Portuguese acronym) created by the UN General Assembly in 1986 as a multilateral negotiation mechanism between West African and South American countries. ZOPACAS (specially mentioned in the 2012 *National Defense White Book*) is comprised of three South American countries (Argentina, Brazil, and Uruguay) and 21 African countries. ZOPACAS seeks to address regional issues without outside interference and to keep the South Atlantic out of geostrategic Great Power games (Kornegay 2013). The main concern is that NATO will expand its influence to the South Atlantic and establish new partnerships beyond the North Atlantic. From the Brazilian perspective there is also a critical appraisal of British postcolonial possessions – a string of islands stretching from Ascension Island to Saint Helena and Tristan da Cunha, ending in the Falkland/Malvinas Islands – and military bases in the South Atlantic (Costa 2012). From these islands positioned between Brazil and Africa it might be possible to control maritime transport and sea-lanes in the South Atlantic. Moreover, there is the challenge of territorial claims and power projection by the United Kingdom into the Antarctic (Reis 2012), where Brazil and especially Argentina and Chile have their own geopolitical interests and cooperation mechanisms (Gómez 2005). Since 1982 Brazil has run an Antarctic program with a research station and sees its Antarctic policy as a way to legitimize its status as a major international player (Abdenur and Neto 2014b).

Thus, the geopolitics of the South Atlantic is closely linked to the geopolitics of the Antarctic, which will continue to be a contested area. There is no prospect in the foreseeable future that Argentina will renounce its claim to sovereignty over the Malvinas Islands (the Falklands), especially if substantial oil and gas resources are found in the surrounding waters. The Malvinas issue has also been framed as a struggle against European colonial practices (Benwell and Dodds 2011) and has been raised in regional forums like UNASUR or the newly created Community of Latin American and Caribbean States (CELAC).

From the British perspective, the Falkland Islands are considered a 'strategic gateway' to both the Antarctic (the British Antarctic Territory) and the South Atlantic (Dodds 2012). The Falkland Islands, as well as the South Georgia and the South Sandwich Islands, are along with the British Antarctic Territory (the southern part of which was named Queen Elizabeth Land in 2012) all part of the British Overseas Territories. After the Falklands War (1982), the United

Kingdom increased its economic stakes and its military presence on the islands. In this context, the Mount Pleasant Airbase in East Falkland is of geostrategic importance, where around 1,300 members of personnel are stationed and which is linked by an air bridge to the U.S.-British airbase (Wideawake Airfield) on Ascension Island. The British government created an exclusive fishery zone and a fishing-licensing regime in the late 1980s, which altered the economic livelihood of the islanders. Moreover, it is expected that gas and oil resources will be found in the seabed around the islands, which increases the importance of these territorial possessions for the British government.

Natural resources: protection and power projection

The abundance of natural resources has always been an important element in Latin American development and underdevelopment, continually attracting the interest of foreign companies and countries. The region is a major participant in the global production and reserves of copper, silver, selenium, gold, zinc, manganese, tin, boron, antimony, nickel, molybdenum, bauxite, lead, iron ore, niobium, and lithium (CEPAL and UNASUR 2013). Further, Latin America also boasts a rich biodiversity, as well as important freshwater reserves.

Since the turn of the century, natural resources have again become an important geopolitical and geo-economic factor. Both Latin American politicians and scientists use the concept of geopolitics in relation to natural resources. The rising demand for minerals – especially from Asia – along with increasing prices has recently made Latin America wealthier and more independent, and it gives the region strategic leverage (Bruckmann 2011). Some governments claim the right to exploit natural resources for national development (critics speak of neo-extractivism) and take a negative view of international NGOs, which are perceived as instruments of foreign interests that seek to undermine national sovereignty (García 2012). Other governments use the earnings from natural resources for regional power projection (as in the case of Venezuelan oil) or as a foreign policy instrument (as in the case of the Bolivian refusal to sell natural gas to Chile). Natural resources may change the economic and political weight of a country, as in the case of Bolivia (which is rich in gas and lithium), or of Brazil (which is becoming a net exporter of oil).

In Latin America, natural resources are both an aspect of integration (including infrastructure projects) and of conflict over territories where resources were expected to exist. Already in the 1990s, maritime geopolitics changed, turning away from sea-lanes and choke points to fishing resources and exploitation – which made the maritime frontiers a major concern of South American geopolitics (Kelly 1997: 45). Moreover, the change in international maritime law (the aforementioned UNCLOS of 1982), the extension of maritime economic and environmental jurisdiction out to 200 miles, and the discovery and development of new technologies to exploit marine and seabed resources raised the salience of many territorial disputes (Domínguez et al. 2003) – which, in contrast to other ongoing border disputes, are not a legacy from colonial times but rather linked to the more recent interest in drawing or redrawing maritime borders.

As a consequence of their importance to national development, most Latin American countries have securitized their natural resources – such as energy, water, the Amazon rainforest (as in the Brazilian *National Strategy of Defense*), and agricultural land (to prevent 'land-grabbing'). Natural resources were, from the beginning, part of the agenda of UNASUR. It is significant that the creation of UNASUR was announced during the first South American energy summit, held in Isla Margarita (Venezuela) in 2007. There is a growing consensus within UNASUR that regional cooperation is also a means of protecting natural resources from exploitation by external forces. Thus, the South American Defense Council assigns high priority to the safeguarding of biodiversity and strategic natural resources.

Conclusions

Latin America in general and South America in particular are fertile areas for neoclassical geopolitics. While geopolitical thinking no longer has the same prominence that it did during the era of military regimes in Latin America, it is still influential in the foreign and security policies of states in this region. While traditional geopolitics in the 1960s and 1970s was influenced by the structural frame set by the Cold War, new geopolitical thinking at first responded to the 'unipolar moment' and to the U.S. dominance regarding the Americas and the FTAA project in the 1990s, and later came to reflect the growing multipolarity and the waning of U.S. influence in the first decade of the 21st century. Territorial boundaries are still important in the relationships between Latin American states. However, new geopolitical narratives deal with border issues in a more nuanced way, as they are not an issue exclusive to security politics but are also of importance for geo-economic interests. In fact, maritime border conflicts have become more prominent in new geopolitics, because they are linked to economic interests such as the exploitation of natural resources. Geopolitical narratives have also become less nationalistic. For instance, Latin American and especially South American integration is now an integral part of geopolitical thinking. Traditional geopolitics was mainly limited to the continental space and its coastlines, whereas the horizon of geopolitical projections has become wider and even transregional in its new variant, as the inclusion of the South Atlantic and the Pacific Rim in geopolitical narratives demonstrates.

Geopolitical narratives construct links between geography and politics. Geopolitical analysis should unpack these narratives. In Latin America there is lack of critical geopolitical analysis. One may speculate that the lack of critical analysis of geopolitical discourses is related to their association with military thinking and a burdened past. However, geopolitical terms and narratives are also part of the vocabulary of analysts located on the left of the political spectrum in this region.

Most of the geopolitical writing is affirmative and follows a geographic determinism. However, certain geographical factors, such as whether a nation is landlocked or has a long coastline or a particular geographical endowment (such as prized resources), do not necessarily determine a specific foreign policy, as political actors still enjoy a high degree of latitude in making and advancing decisions and adopting geopolitical narratives to justify their policies.

This chapter's purpose was to present an overview of geopolitical thinking in Latin America that will hopefully inspire further research on geopolitical topics and narratives along the subsequently sketched-out thematic corridors. First, each country's geopolitical reality and narratives should be analyzed in order to compare their different historical trajectories. Second, a new geopolitical research agenda should also focus on the reasons why and when actors resort to geopolitical narratives and should study whether these are reactions to political crisis or whether they reflect an identity crisis over the foreign policy roles of a state. Third, further systematic research on geopolitics in Latin America should also consider the role of new geopolitical narratives as the result (or not) of a changing international status of states, as the case of Brazil indicates.

A future research agenda on geopolitics might also explore the reasons why geopolitical narratives are still so popular in Latin America. One aspect that should be dissected and analyzed surrounds the producers, propagators, and drivers of these narratives, as well as the existing types of audiences involved. Another course of investigation may focus on the mechanisms of dissemination of geopolitical narratives. Further, there is an academic void with regard to the study of the consequences and outcomes of existing geopolitical discourses on the foreign policy and behavior of different states. While geopolitical narratives may instigate interstate conflicts in Latin America, they may also function as a way to promote regional cooperation and integration.

References

Abdenur, A.E. and Neto, D.M. (2014a) 'Region-Building by Rising Powers: The South Atlantic and Indian Ocean Rims Compared', *Journal of Indian Ocean Region*, 10(1): 1–17.

——— (2014b) 'Rising Powers and Antarctica: Brazil's Changing Interest', *The Polar Journal*, 4(1): 1–16.

Alcaro, R. and Alessandri, E. (2013, February 5) 'A Deeper and Wider Atlantic', paper produced in the framework of the International Workshop Europe and the Americas Deepening and Widening the Atlantic Italian Ministry of Foreign Affairs, Rome. Retrieved from http://www.gmfus.org/wp-content/blogs.dir/1/files_mf/1360337936A_Deeper_and_Wider_Atlantic.pdf.

Barton, J. (1997) *A Political Geography of Latin America*, London: Routledge.

Benwell, M. and Dodds, K. (2011) 'Argentine Territorial Nationalism Revisited: The Malvinas/Falklands Dispute and Geographies of Everyday Nationalism', *Political Geography*, 30(8): 441–449.

Blank, S. (2009) 'Russia in Latin America: Geopolitical Games in the US's Neighborhood', *Russie.NEI. Visions*, 38, Paris: Russia/NIS Center.

Brands, H. (2010) *Dilemmas of Brazilian Grand Strategy*, Carlisle: Strategic Studies Institute, U.S. Army War College.

Briceño R. J. (2014) 'Regional Dynamics and External Influences in the Discussions about the Model of Economic Integration in Latin America', *EUI Working Paper*, RSCAS 2014/11, Florence: EUI.

Bruckmann, M. (2011) 'Recursos naturais e a geopolítica da integração sul-Americana' in A.R. Viana and P.S. Barros (eds) *Governança global e integração da América do sul*, Brasília: Ipea, pp. 197–246.

Cabrera T. L. (2011) 'La controversia por la delimitación marítima entre Chile y Perú: Construcción y aplicación de un discurso geopolítico', *CONfines*, 7(14): 101–128.

Cairo C. H., Preciado, J. and Rocha, V. A. (eds) (2007) *La construcción de una región: México y la geopolítica del plan Puebla-Panamá*, Madrid: Los Libros de la Catarata.

CEPAL and UNASUR (2013) *Recursos naturales en UNASUR. Situación y tendencias para una agenda de desarrollo regional*, Santiago de Chile: CEPAL.

Child, J. (1979) 'Geopolitical Thinking in Latin America', *Latin American Research Review*, 14(2): 89–111.

——— (2008) *Miniature Messages: The Semiotics and Politics of Latin American Postage Stamps*, Durham: Duke University Press.

Cohen, S.B. (2009) *Geopolitics. The Geography of International Relations* (2nd ed.), Lanham, MD: Rowman & Littlefield Publishers.

Costa, W.M.D. (2012) 'Projeção do Brasil no Atlântico sul: Geopolítica e estratégia', *REVISTA USP*, 95: 9–22.

Dodds, K. (1993) 'Geopolitics, Cartography and the State in South America', *Political Geography*, 12(4): 361–381.

——— (2012) 'The Falkland Islands as a "Strategic Gateway": Britain and the South Atlantic Overseas Territories', *The RUSI Journal*, 157(6): 18–25.

Dodds, K., Kuus, M. and Sharp, J. (eds) (2013) *The Ashgate Research Companion to Critical Geopolitics*, Farnham: Ashgate.

Domínguez, J.I. et al. (2003) *Boundary Disputes in Latin America*, Washington, DC: United States Institute of Peace.

García L. Á. (2012) *Geopolítica de la Amazonía. Poder hacendal-patrimonial y acumulación capitalista*, La Paz: Vicepresidencia del Estado Plurinacional.

Gómez G. M. (2005) 'Geopolítica Sudamericana y la Antárctica ¿Confrontación o cooperación?', *Revista de Marina*, 2: 138–157.

Guzzini, S. (ed) (2014) *The Return of Geopolitics in Europe? Social Mechanisms and Foreign Policy Identity Crises*, Cambridge: Cambridge University Press.

Hurrell, A. (1992) 'Latin America in the New World Order: A Regional Bloc of the Americas?', *International Affairs*, 74(3): 121–139.

——— (1998) 'An Emerging Security Community in Latin America?' in E. Adler and M. Barnett (eds) *Security Communities*, Cambridge: Cambridge University Press, pp. 228–264.

Kacowicz, A. (1998) *Zones of Peace in the Third World: South America and West Africa in a Comparative Perspective*, Albany: State University of New York Press.

——— (2000) 'Geopolitics and Territorial Issues: Relevance for South America', *Geopolitics*, 5(1): 81–100.

Kelly, P. (1997) *Checkerboards and Shatterbelts: The Geopolitics of South America*, Austin: University of Texas-Austin.

Kornegay, F.A. (2013) 'South Africa, The South Atlantic and the IBSA-BRICS Equation: The Transatlantic Space in Transition', *Austral: Brazilian Journal of Strategy & International Relations*, 2(3): 75–100.

Legler, T. (2013) 'The Rise and Decline of the Summit of the Americas', *Journal of Iberian and Latin American Research*, 19(2): 179–193.

Lesser, I. O. (2010) 'Southern Atlanticism. Geopolitics and Strategy for the Other Half of the Atlantic Rim', Working Paper, Washington, DC: The German Marshall Fund of the United States.

Malamud, A. (2012) 'Moving Regions: Brazil's Global Emergence and the Redefinition of Latin American Borders' in P. Riggirozzi and D. Tussie (eds) *The Rise of Post-Hegemonic Regionalism. The Case of Latin America*, Dordrech: Springer, pp. 167–182.

Malamud, C. and García, E. C. (2014) *El elefante Indio desembarca en América Latina*, Madrid: Real Instituto Elcano (Documento de Trabajo 6/2014).

Mamadouh, V. D. (1998) 'Geopolitics in the Nineties: One Flag, Many Meanings', *GeoJournal*, 46: 237–253.

Mares, D. (2001) *Violent Peace: Militarized Interstate Bargaining in Latin America*, New York: Columbia University Press.

Parodi, C. (2002) *The Politics of South American Boundaries*, Westport: Praeger.

Perrier Buslé, L. (2013) 'The Border as a Marker of Territoriality: Multi-Scalar Perspectives and Multi-Agent Processes in a South American Borderland Region', *Geopolitics*, 18(3): 584–611.

Preciado, C. J. and Uc, P. (2010) 'La construcción de una geopolítica crítica desde América Latina y el Caribe. Hacia una agenda de investigación regional', *Geopolítica(s). Revista de estudios sobre espacio y poder*, 1(1): 65–94.

Reis, R.G.G.D. (2012) 'Atlântico sul: Um desafio para o século XXI – As velhas ameaças se perpetuam nas "novas?" ' in L. Acioly and R. Fracalossi de Moraes (eds) *Prospectiva, estratégias e cenários globais: Visões de Atlântico sul, África lusófona, América do sul e Amazônia*, Brasília: IPEA, pp. 61–82.

Rivarola, A. (2011) 'Geopolitics of Integration and the Imagination of South America', *Geopolitics*, 14(4): 846–864.

Sanahuja, J.A. (2012) 'Post-Liberal Regionalism in South America: The Case of UNASUR', *EUI Working Paper RSCAS 2012/05*, Florence: EUI.

Spektor, M. (2010) 'Ideias de ativismo regional: A transformação das leituras Brasileiras da região', *Revista Brasileira de Política Internacional*, 53(1): 25–44.

Vadell, J.A. (2013) 'The North of the South: The Geopolitical Implications of "Pacific Consensus" in South America and the Brazilian Dilemma', *Latin American Policy*, 4(1): 36–56.

van der Wusten, H. and Dijkink, G. (2002) 'German British and French Geopolitics: The Enduring Differences', *Geopolitics*, 7(3): 19–38.

Wehner, L. and Thies, C. (2014) 'Role Theory, Narratives and Interpretation: The Domestic Contestation of Roles', *International Studies Review*, 16(3): 411–436.

3

NEOLIBERAL INSTITUTIONALISM AND NEOFUNCTIONALISM IN LATIN AMERICAN SECURITY STUDIES

Andrés Malamud and Luis L. Schenoni

Unlike realism – which posits survival and power as drivers and balance as mechanism – and constructivism – which posits ideas and identities as drivers and human interaction as mechanism – neoliberal institutionalism and neofunctionalism are two subsets of liberalism that focus on interests as drivers and institutions as mechanisms in determining preference formation and decision-making. In so doing, they offer a better explanation of international cooperation, integration processes, and institutional development than their theoretical alternatives. However, both theories differ in terms of level of analysis, key actors, and the causal mechanisms through which institutions are expected to condition policy outcomes.

The focus of neoliberal institutionalists is international cooperation. For them, *international* institutions – i.e., laws and customs, conventions, international regimes, and governmental and non-governmental organizations (Keohane 1989: 1–4) – enhance cooperation, by offering states a common arena in which direct interaction facilitates communication and confidence-building. In game-theoretical jargon, institutions provide long-term horizons (they extend the 'shadow of the future'), regularity of stakes, reliability of information, monitoring capacity, and instruments to punish defectors (Axelrod and Keohane 1985).

The central concern of neofunctionalists is integration, a subset of cooperation. They look beyond the state as a cohesive actor and give explanatory autonomy to the domestic, transnational, and supranational levels. On this view, *supranational* institutions, those possessing or demanding jurisdiction over preexisting nation-states (Haas 1961: 367), foster integration in two ways: by generating benefits and opportunities for domestic actors, who then push for deepening and widening the process, and by empowering supranational authorities and transnational technocrats. The concept of *spillover* synthesizes the incremental – and often unintended – effect of these strategies.

Security has played a central role in the motivation and formation of regional institutions in Latin America. It was the hazardous security context following the independence wars that prompted Simón Bolívar to organize the Panama Conference in 1826 (Domínguez 2006). Since then, security issues have rarely been absent from regional agreements. Yet, unlike other regions of the world, they usually have been downplayed or combined with other priorities. This calls for attention to context and history, as "where wars have been rare, power may have a softer meaning than elsewhere, and policy options may thus be framed differently" (Malamud 2011: 4).

Latin America's interstate system has particularities propitious for neoliberal explanations, and they are even more pronounced in South America (Merke 2013: 301). First, few states disappeared or emerged since the wars of independence. Second, the principle of *uti possidetis* ('as you possess, you may possess') was agreed upon even before independence from Portugal and Spain, allowing borders to be delimited more peacefully than in Europe. Third, Latin America is the region with the most bilateral and multilateral agreements for the peaceful settlement of conflicts (Holsti 1996; Kacowicz 2005), and that which holds the "world record of adjudication and arbitration" (Kacowicz 2004: 199; see also Simmons 1999: 213–214). Fourth, Latin America is a nuclear-weapons-free zone. In sum, since state survival has been virtually assured, wars have been rare, and the legal resolution of disputes has been the norm; the region "provides important grounds for doubting that regional 'anarchies' are everywhere alike" (Hurrell 1998a: 260).

This does not mean that international violence has been eradicated, but rather that "there has been a limited conception of force within a strong diplomatic culture" (Hurrell 1998b: 532; Mares 2001). Latin American international law embodies "a host of legal principles related to the right of self-determination, territorial inviolability, and non-intervention [that] were captured in juridical instruments such as the Calvo, Drago, and Estrada doctrines,[1] and enshrined in the OAS and UN Charters" (Legler 2013: 181). However, this dense legal framework has not always led to security cooperation. Institutions designed to avoid interstate conflict frequently have been trumped by mechanisms designed to protect sovereignty. Consequently, some territorial disputes remain unresolved (Domínguez et al. 2004), interstate rivalry has become a cornerstone of the region's strategic culture (Thies 2005), and the militarization of disputes has been recurrent (Mares 2012: 169–176). Yet, violence in Latin America has mostly developed within rather than across borders. Security has thus acquired a more domestic rather than international connotation, as the armed forces singled out internal enemies instead of confronting each other (Martin 2006). Even though the political landscape has been mostly peaceful since democratization in the 1980s, Latin America remains the most violent world region in terms of homicide rates (UNOCD 2013).

This chapter explores how the interaction between security dynamics and regional institutions has been studied so far. The first section approaches the question from the vantage point of neoliberal institutionalism, and the second through neofunctionalist lenses. The final section summarizes the findings.

Neoliberal institutionalism and security in Latin America

Liberal explanations of international cooperation are usually threefold (Keohane 1990): republican liberalism, which makes reference to the pacifying effects of democracy; commercial liberalism, which defends interdependence as the main driver of cooperation; and regulatory liberalism, which asserts the positive effects of institutions.

For neoliberal institutionalists, institutions are synonymous with international regimes; i.e., implicit or explicit principles, norms, rules, and decision-making procedures around which actors' expectations converge in a given area of international relations (Krasner 1983). Their central interest is in how such regimes increase the propensity to cooperate. They focus on the effect of different institutions and institutional designs: membership range, scope of issues, voting procedures, degree of centralization, or flexibility (Koremnos et al. 2003) on state compliance. Their research agenda is concerned with institutional creation, evolution and overlapping, and other regime-related phenomena (Stein 2008: 212–216). In Latin America, the implementation of institutional rules has tended to be lax (Domínguez 2006: 95) and security cooperation[2] has usually preceded the establishment of regional organizations (Alcañiz 2005), an inauspicious combination for those who emphasize the independent effect of regimes. Admittedly, institutions alone cannot explain long-term phenomena such as South America's "long lasting peace" (Martin 2006: 114). However, there is a general understanding that arms control agreements, cooperative verification schemes, confidence-building measures, dispute resolution clauses, and other security-related institutions at least have helped to prevent backsliding in security cooperation (Hurrell 1998b: 533). Since this consensus has rarely been based on the theoretical contributions of neoliberal institutionalism, there is still work to be done to understand which institutions have a political significance of their own, beyond being just a consequence of cooperation, and how they have enhanced it.

International security in Latin American regional organizations

There are many international organizations in Latin America, but only a few are preeminently security oriented. Built upon the spirit of the Pan-American Conferences of the 19th century, the OAS has been the main forum for Latin American countries to deal with defense and security (Hêrz 2008). However, since the Central American crisis in the 1980s, the inaction of the OAS and the United States' unilateralism led to the establishment of distinct Latin American fora – beginning with the Contadora Group, which was joined by the Support Group to form the Rio Group in 1986 and then turned into CELAC in 2011. More recently, UNASUR has emerged to contest the 'hemispheric' tradition in South America. Both the OAS and UNASUR involve security/defense regimes, the key difference being that the latter excludes the United States (Weiffen et al. 2013).

The inter-American security system

From its inception, the OAS has dealt with the peaceful settlement of emerging disputes in the hemisphere (Nye 1971; Zacher 1979). Between 1947 and 1982, inter-American conflict prevention mechanisms were activated on 33 occasions. In contrast, only six were deployed after 1970 (Van Walraven 1998: 38; Atkins 1997). In this context of declining performance,[3] the 1975 Protocol of Amendment to the Rio Treaty acknowledged that the OAS Treaty did not prevent states from resorting to the UN instead of the OAS, such that, from the Central American crisis onwards, inter-American mechanisms have fallen increasingly into disuse (Pellicer 1998; Shaw 2004). Because of the paucity of theoretically informed analyses, it is not possible to know whether this signals organizational adaptability or whether "by the mid-1980s the inter-American system was moribund" (Corrales and Feinberg 1999: 7).

Reforms proposed by the Committee on Hemispheric Security (1992) made the case for a flexible OAS, and for conflict prevention, collective defense, and collective security to give way to cooperative security – i.e., the construction of international regimes to promote transparency, communication, and socialization (Wallander and Keohane 1999). The purpose was to reorient hemispheric institutions towards threat prevention rather than conflict resolution (Varas 1998: 11). Alongside trade summitry, this strategy has been interpreted as a switch from unilateral to cooperative hegemony (Mace and Loiseau 2005). The focus was on developing confidence and security-building measures (CSBMs) to inhibit the use of force (Tulchin et al. 1998). However, CSBMs were mainly bilateral or subregional, and therefore only loosely associated with the inter-American system (Griffith 1998).

During the 1990s, the OAS also broadened its understanding of security to include issues ranging from cybernetic attacks to physical assaults on pedestrians, therefore diluting its defense focus (Pion-Berlin and Trinkunas 2007: 78). Two 'new threats' became particularly important: drug trafficking and terrorism. In both cases, the OAS sought institutional expansion. The Inter-American Drug Abuse Control Commission is deemed to have smoothed cooperation in spite of a bias towards Washington's prohibitionist preferences (Horwitz 2010). Similarly, the Inter-American Committee against Terrorism seems to have been successful in providing legislative assistance and training for crisis management (Kiernan 2011). However, the translation of this agenda into operational goals has languished due to great variations in threat perception, legal structures, and in the capacity of security forces (Trinkunas 2013: 94).

Most of our knowledge on the OAS comes from descriptive case studies, which do not provide solid ground for assessing the theoretical hypotheses advanced by neoliberal institutionalism. As it approaches its 70th anniversary, the OAS system has an impressive reservoir of unexplored data – resolutions, votes, and missions – that awaits systematization and analysis.

The South American security system

Neoliberal institutionalism is also concerned with institutional choice. States can choose between reforming existing institutions such as the OAS, a range of rival organizations, and creating new ones (Merke 2014). The establishment of the UNASUR Security and Defense Council (SDC) in 2009 – an officially complementary, but arguably alternative, security arrangement (Battaglino 2012; Weiffen et al. 2013) – exemplifies the latter choice.

Initially, UNASUR de facto assumed the conflict prevention role that the Rio Group had once had. During the 2008 Andean crisis, involving Colombia, Ecuador, and Venezuela, and the controversy caused by the 2009 agreement between Colombia and the United States on the use of military bases, UNASUR provided an arena for dialogue and negotiation when other channels were inactive, involving all actors within the cooperative scheme and allowing for quick feedback and access to reliable information. Subsequently, the organization expanded its functions by incorporating some of the roles played by the OAS in a process defined as institutional segmentation (Malamud and Gardini 2012) or institutional overlap (Weiffen et al. 2013). A series of CSBMs were implemented under the SDC, such as keeping record of defense expenditures, coordinating military exercises, communicating the commercialization and use of military equipment, visiting military facilities, notifying other members about military activities, creating a South American military inventory, and launching a Defense Strategic Studies Center (Bromley and Solmirano 2012; Teixeira and Sousa 2013; Saint-Pierre and Montoya 2014; Nolte and Wehner 2014). In parallel, UNASUR addressed 'multidimensional' security through organs such as the South American Council Against Drug Trafficking and the South American Council on Citizen Security, Justice and Transnational Organized Crime (Weiffen et al. 2013), although these initiatives suffered from the same shortcomings as their inter-American equivalents (Trinkunas 2013).

The brief existence of UNASUR and its SDC makes it difficult to evaluate their independent effect on security dynamics, but they constitute an interesting opportunity to understand processes of institutional creation, overlapping, and early evolution. Research agendas have yet to exploit the potential of comparison with similar organizations in other regions, and insert UNASUR into the broader theoretical debate.

The big picture: myriad security regimes

Apart from the OAS and UNASUR, a wide range of regional regimes has contributed to security and defense cooperation. The Agency for the Prohibition of Nuclear Weapons in Latin America and the Caribbean (OPANAL) has been a tool to build confidence in nuclear nonproliferation. Supporting other bilateral agencies, it accomplished the full ratification of the Tlatelolco Treaty (1995) and the Non-Proliferation of Nuclear Weapons Treaty (NPT) (1997) in the region. Although these institutions were not the main driving force behind cooperation (Solingen 1994), they successfully locked in previous commitments: To date, the Latin American nuclear regime, as well as its chemical and biological weapons conventions, have not been rolled back (Coutto 2013).

Latin American regional distinctiveness resides in the proliferation of agreements devoted to the peaceful settlement of disputes (Holsti 1996; Kacowicz 2004).[4] However, it has been argued that the effectiveness of dispute resolution clauses and the use of arbitration is not only due to neoliberal institutional factors – such as the existence of a broader regional normative framework, reciprocity, and reputation – but also to the structure of the international system, executive/legislative relations, and regime type, among other factors (Kacowicz 2004: 202–214). Paradoxically, effectiveness has acted like an insurance policy and created incentives not to solve persisting territorial disputes, therefore producing moral hazard in the defense realm (Domínguez et al. 2004).

There are additional agreements at the bilateral and subregional levels – i.e., on education and training of security forces, joint military exercises, and a wide range of CSBMs – whose design, effects, and evolution can be analyzed comparatively through the neoliberal institutionalist lenses. At the multilateral level, Latin American participation in joint command of UN peacekeeping operations, voting behavior in UN organs, and other security-related organizations for instance, provide raw material for understanding institutional choice and utilization. Finally, there are multiple ways through which economic organizations influence regional security dynamics: a type of explanation Keohane (1990) called 'sophisticated liberalism'.[5] Neofunctionalism is well equipped to address these causal mechanisms.

Neofunctionalism, Latin America, and regional security

The neofunctionalist approach to security is less direct and more complex than neoliberal institutionalism, as domestic, international, and transnational dynamics, as well as different agendas, interact. Moreover, it defines institutions more broadly than regimes because they can become supranational or be propelled by transnational actors. For neofunctionalists the question is how integration has affected Latin American security and defense and *vice-versa*.

Neofunctionalists posit that, under conditions of democracy and pluralistic representation, national governments will find themselves increasingly entangled in regional interactions and end up resolving conflicts by giving the organizations they create broader scope and authority. Over time, the expectations of citizens and social groups shift towards their region, and meeting those expectations increases the likelihood that functional and economic integration will 'spillover' into political integration (Haas 1958: 1964).

Spillover is the process whereby integration in one sector creates incentives for integration in other sectors. Neofunctionalism has identified two sorts of spillover: functional and political. The theory initially predicted that integration would become self-sustaining on the basis of an analysis of the European Communities. In order to test this hypothesis elsewhere, early neofunctionalists focused on the Central American Common Market (CACM).

Integration and peace: Central America and beyond

Established in 1960, the creation of CACM was economically as well as politically motivated. The perceived threat posed by the Cuban revolution was paramount and explains U.S. support for the nascent organization (Schmitter 1970). By the late 1960s it was widely recognized as "the underdeveloped world's most successful regional integration effort" (Wynia 1970: 319). By 1965 the level and scope of integration approximated that of a customs union. This progress was due to technical – as opposed to politicized – management, and to the low political and economic costs of integration: CACM did not threaten any powerful interests, and administrative costs were paid by foreign sources (Mattli 1999). However, the fragility of these achievements became apparent, with the task of holding together rather than expanding the integrative structure after the boom of the first years. The result was an expansion in the issue areas dealt with by an increasing number of regional institutions, without a concomitant increase in their decision-making authority. Schmitter (1970) called this mechanism *spill-around*, to distinguish it from the expected *spillover* effect. Eventually, the so-called Football War between El Salvador and Honduras in 1969 dealt a near terminal blow to the integration process. The ensuing stagnation lasted two decades, amidst civil wars and democratic breakdowns in its member-states.

In the early 1990s, pacification and democratization led to a CACM revival (Mattli 1999). Costa Rican President Oscar Arias and his counterparts crafted a plan "to pacify the region by democratizing its political regimes . . . This collective work of crisis resolution unintentionally reactivated the regional integration process" (Dabène 2009: 56). But this was a sluggish process dependent on foreign aid. The Central American experience taught neofunctionalists an important lesson: that peace and security are a precondition, at least as much as a goal, of integration (Malamud and Schmitter 2011: 153).

An analogous link between security and integration manifested itself in the Southern Cone. Expert bureaucrats rather than political leaders or civil society organizations were instrumental in building confidence and promoting cooperation in sensitive areas. For instance, epistemic communities and transgovernmental networks, two mechanisms akin to those highlighted by neofunctionalism, were at the root of nuclear cooperation between Argentina and Brazil (Alcañiz 2010). This process led to the creation of the Brazilian-Argentine Agency for Accounting and Control of Nuclear Materials (ABACC) in 1991. As stated on its website, ABACC "is the only bi-national safeguard organization in the world." Its operation is independent from member governments and depends on highly qualified technical staff and on a cooperative, treaty-based relationship with the International Atomic Energy Agency (IAEA). ABACC can be considered a case of neofunctionalist encapsulation, an isolated, supranational initiative that has neither spilled over nor spilled back. Although some studies support this interpretation (Milanese 2007), others argue that spillover between security and nonsecurity arenas has not only taken place but has been deliberately promoted (Alcañiz 2005). Further research is required to test the validity of these opposing claims.

Security coordination spilling around regionalization

Collective security challenges involve not only state threats but also domestic and transnational threats. Focusing exclusively on interstate cooperation may lead to an incomplete understanding of regional security governance, as policy coordination is equally relevant. Integration, when it occurs, produces even greater effects on the security environment.

Although Latin American efforts at integration have always emphasized a shared history and culture, neofunctionalism considers this irrelevant at best. Socioeconomic conditions and institutions, rather than culture, are at the root of joint governance. Malamud and Schmitter (2011) argue that democracy is a necessary condition for joint governance for three reasons. First, only nationally legitimate governments can make credible sovereignty sharing commitments. Second, the prevalence of democratic regimes increases the likelihood that governments will not resort to force to resolve disputes. Third, the formation of transnational interest associations and social movements, and their intervention in supranational policy-making, further contributes to the integration process. Thus, democratic peace and democratic integration reinforce each other. True, peace can be maintained among nondemocratic states, but there is a direct relationship between the quality of the regional peace and the type of political regimes that prevail in a given region (Kacowicz 1998). As integration requires more than negative peace, the presence of nondemocratic regimes hinders integration.

In a similar vein, an extensive literature suggests that regional integration was initially attempted to shield democratic regimes from domestic threats, and thereafter to lock in sweeping economic reforms. Through democratic density (Pevehouse 2005) or democratic clauses (Ribeiro-Hoffmann 2007), regional organizations could have intervened to preserve democracy and prevent political violence in member-states. However, recent studies found that the type of democracy in place also affects the kind of regional institutions that are created. Integration in Latin America is characterized by inter-presidentialism, an extreme type of intergovernmentalism (Malamud 2005). An outcome of combining an international strategy (presidential diplomacy) with a domestic institutional structure (presidential democracy), inter-presidentialism consists of direct negotiations between national presidents who, making use of their institutional and political capabilities, intervene in regional affairs whenever a crucial decision has to be made or a critical conflict needs to be solved. As a consequence, security regimes have rarely been promoted as a result of demand by domestic actors, but have been strictly a result of diplomatic initiatives. Organizations like UNASUR have been driven by presidential diplomacy or by foreign or defense ministers, who only respond to their presidents.

State capacity also affects regional institutions and has hindered neofunctionalist spillover. As Kelly argues, "weak-state regions [such as Latin America] actually generate international organizations that reinforce, not erode, sovereignty" (2007: 218). The same has been shown for other areas, such as trade, since "in countries where the rule of law is weak and infrastructure is insufficient . . . it is difficult to implement trade agreements . . . Domestic capacity – both physical and institutional – can explain the implementation gap between what agreements promise and what they deliver"[6] (Gray 2014: 55).

Security coordination in South America

Although international security is a precondition for regional integration, MERCOSUR shows how organizations primarily intended to regulate the economic realm can lead, if not to defense cooperation, at least to the coordination of domestic and transnational security practices.

Five years after the foundation of MERCOSUR, a semiannual Conference of Interior Ministries was set up to deal with citizen security. This institution played a central role in the creation of the Trilateral Federal Police Command in 1996 – a regional Argentine-Brazilian-Paraguayan intelligence center working on crime, drug trafficking, and terrorist activities – which promoted the exchange of sensitive information and the coordination of security operations (Oelsner 2014: 213). Since the 2001 agreement on police cooperation, coordination efforts have flourished in border areas (Flemes and Radseck 2009: 27). Although defense-related issues have rarely been addressed, coordination mechanisms have spilled around into issues such as drug and arms trafficking, terrorism, money laundering, and environmental crimes. In 1998 MERCOSUR signed a joint statement with associate members Bolivia and Chile declaring the region a zone of peace, free of weapons of mass destruction (Oelsner 2014). As successive South American countries have signed association agreements, all the countries in the subcontinent share most of the provisions of MERCOSUR (except those relating to customs and trade). This has led observers to claim that "a nascent security community" is developing (Flemes and Radseck 2009: 6), especially since the establishment of UNASUR's Defense Council. According to neofunctionalism, this process is unlikely to be rolled back for endogenous reasons, but an exogenous shock – such as military intervention by an extraregional power – could lead to its unraveling.

Conclusions

Compared to other regions of the world, Latin America is characterized by lower threats to state survival, fewer wars, a dense network of international treaties, and a higher level of judicialization of conflicts. Yet, it is neither as peaceful as North America nor as institutionally integrated as Western Europe. Thus, the region offers "much more than the realists would admit and much less than the liberals would prefer" (Merke 2013: 307). The resilience of regional institutions and the insistence of states in creating more of them in spite of their lackluster performance remain a puzzle for neoliberal institutionalists and neofunctionalists to solve (Dabène 2012).

Security is averse to positive sum games, but it is amenable to 'mixed-motive' cooperation, which suggests "institutionalist theory should be highly applicable to security issues because its arguments revolve around the role of institutions in providing *information*" (Keohane and Martin 1995: 43). This is particularly relevant in the Latin American case. Therefore, neoliberal institutionalist analyses of Latin America can be advanced in two ways. First, in methodological terms, we encourage research with a transition from descriptive to explanatory approaches, and from case studies to comparative and 'large n' studies. Second, in theoretical terms, we should promote the development of innovative concepts and theoretical approaches. The concept of "norm laxity" – the apparent oxymoron that rule-breaking may be a rule (Domínguez 2006: 97) – and the idea that effective conflict resolution mechanisms can create moral hazard are just two examples of how the region could enrich neoliberal institutionalist debates on the causes of state compliance.

In turn, neofunctionalism seems to offer a better explanation of the consequences of interstate conflicts or security improvements than of their causes, at least until epistemic communities and transnational networks entered the research agenda. The conditions under which integration and policy coordination bring about pacification or vice versa have yet to be specified. Encapsulation and spill-around rather than spillover should be studied further, as regional organizations have reproduced a pattern of either stagnation or increasing issue coverage and proliferating regional agencies without a concomitant upgrading of authority. National executives have been careful not to devolve power to domestic or transnational actors or to delegate to supranational institutions or technocratic elites. Consequently, regional organizations have multiplied, but by segmenting territories and overlapping functions rather than through greater coordination. Resilience, proliferation, segmentation, and overlap should therefore gain prominence in research agendas. Apart from the Inter-American Court of Human Rights and the Brazilian-Argentine Agency for Accounting and Control of Nuclear Materials, no significant supranationality has emerged in the security area; thus, a vigilant eye should be kept on any new developments in this regard.

In Latin America, national sovereignty is paramount, foreign policy takes precedence over region-centered interests, and state-centrism prevails. However, regional organizations are everywhere, and they multiply and persist. For the most part, the national and the regional levels have been articulated through inter-presidentialism (most visibly through executive summitry), a few international adjudication authorities, and inchoate transgovernmental networks. These mechanisms illustrate the complex but significant role of neoliberal institutionalism and neofunctionalism for the comprehension of the regional security dynamics.

Notes

1 The Drago Doctrine, named after an Argentine foreign minister, stated that no foreign power could use force against an American nation to collect debt. The Calvo Doctrine, which also originated in Argentina, holds that jurisdiction in international investment disputes lies with the country in which the investment is located. The Estrada Doctrine, named after a Mexican foreign minister, holds that states should not judge governments or changes in government in foreign nations.

2 Neoliberal institutionalism conceives security as 'national security,' focusing on the state as the foremost actor and threat and emphasizing interstate relations. Most Latin American countries prefer to call this *defense*, reserving the term *security* for police matters.

3 The MID3 data set shows that militarized interstate disputes increased during 1970–1982 (Ghosn et al. 2004).

4 "There have been some twenty-two instances of legally binding third-party arbitrations or adjudications with respect to sovereignty over territory in Latin America; similar rulings apply to only one small case in continental Europe; two among independent states in Africa; two in the Middle East; and three in Asia, the Far East, and the Pacific" (Simmons 1999: 6–7).

5 Hurrell warns that "economic regionalism can, however, be much more directly implicated in the *generation* of insecurity" (1998b: 540), facilitating illicit flows and reducing state capacity, among other factors.

6 There are exceptions though. The Inter-American Human Rights System helped to homogenize the regional understanding of what constitutes human rights violations and the illegitimate use of force by the state. The subnational origin of these demands and their reinforcement by a supranational judicial authority is an example of how institutions sometimes work as predicted by neofunctionalism, even against the will of the states that establish them (Keck and Sikkink 1998). Yet, given the attacks unleashed by Bolivarian Alliance for the Peoples of Our America (ALBA) in 2012 and the pulling out of Venezuela in 2013, the Inter-American Court might see its operations impaired, even if no formal changes take place.

References

Alcañiz, I. (2005) 'An Economic Road to Peace, a Peaceful Road for Growth: Regional Integration through the Side Door in Western Europe and South America', *CIES e-Working Paper* N° 3/2005.

——— (2010) 'Bureaucratic Networks and Government Spending: A Network Analysis of Nuclear Cooperation in Latin America', *Latin American Research Review*, 45(1): 148–172.

Atkins, P. (1997) *Encyclopedia of the Inter-American System*, Westport: Greenwood Press.

Axelrod, R. and Keohane, R. O. (1985) 'Achieving Cooperation under Anarchy: Strategies and Institutions', *World Politics*, 38(1): 226–254.

Battaglino, J. (2012) 'Defense in a Post Hegemonic Regional Agenda: The Case of the South American Defense Council' in P. Riggirozzi and D. Tussie (eds) *The Rise of Post-Hegemonic Regionalism: The Case of Latin America*, London: Springer.

Bromley, M. and Solmirano, C. (2012) 'Transparency in Military Spending and Arms Acquisitions in Latin America and the Caribbean', *SIPRI Policy Paper Series* 31.

Corrales, J. and Feinberg, R. (1999) 'Regimes of Cooperation in the Western Hemisphere: Power, Interests, and Intellectual Traditions', *International Studies Quarterly*, 43(1): 1–36.

Coutto, T. (2013) 'América del sur y la proliferación de armas biológicas', *Revista CIDOB d'Afers Internacionals*, 101: 81–106.

Dabène, O. (2009) *The Politics of Regional Integration in Latin America: Theoretical and Comparative Exploration*, New York: Palgrave MacMillan.

——— (2012) 'Consistency and Resilience through Cycles of Repolitization' in P. Riggirozzi and D. Tussie (eds) *The Rise of Post-Hegemonic Regionalism. The Case of Latin America*, London: Springer.

Domínguez, J. (2006) 'International Cooperation in Latin America: The Design of Regional Institutions by Slow Accretion' in A. Acharya and A. Johnston (eds) *Crafting Cooperation: Regional International Institutions in Comparative Perspective*, Cambridge: Cambridge University Press.

Domínguez, J., Mares, D., Orozco, M., Palmer, D. S., Rojas Aravena, F. and Serbin, A. (2004) 'Disputas fronterizas en América Latina', *Foro Internacional*, 177(3): 357–391.

Flemes, D. and Radseck, M. (2009) 'Creating Multilevel Security Governance in Latina America', *GIGA Working Papers*, 117.

Ghosn, F., Palmer, G. and Bremer, S. (2004) 'The MID3 Data Set, 1993–2001: Procedures, Coding Rules, and Description', *Conflict Management and Peace Science*, 21: 133–154.

Gray, J. (2014) 'Domestic Capacity and the Implementation Gap in Regional Trade Agreements', *Comparative Political Studies*, 47(1): 55–84.

Griffith, I. (1998) 'Security Collaboration and Confidence Building in the Americas' in J. Domínguez (ed) *International Security and Democracy: Latin America and the Caribbean in the Post-Cold War Era*, Pittsburgh: University of Pittsburgh Press.

Haas, E. B. (1958) *The Uniting of Europe*, Stanford: Stanford University Press.

——— (1961) 'European and Universal Integration', *International Organization*, 15(3): 366–392.

Hêrz, M. (2008) 'Does the Organisation of American States Matter?', *Crisis States Research Centre, Working Paper*, 34.

Holsti, K. J. (1996) *War, the State, and the State of War*, Cambridge: Cambridge University Press.

Horwitz, B. (2010) 'The Role of the Inter-American Drug Abuse Control Commission (CICAD): Confronting the Problem of Illegal Drugs in the Americas', *Latin American Politics and Society*, 52(2): 139–165.

Hurrell, A. (1998a) 'An Emerging Security Community in Latin America?' in E. Adler and M. Barnett (eds) *Security Communities*, Cambridge: Cambridge University Press.

——— (1998b) 'Security in Latin America', *International Affairs*, 74(3): 529–546.

Kacowicz, A. M. (1998) *Zones of Peace in the Third World: South America and West Africa in Comparative Perspective*, New York: State University of New York Press.

——— (2004) 'Compliance and Non-Compliance with International Norms in Territorial Disputes: The Latin American Record of Arbitrations' in E. Benvenisti and M. Hirsch (eds) *The Impact of International Law on International Cooperation*, Cambridge: Cambridge University Press.

——— (2005) *The Impact of Norms in International Society: The Latin American Experience, 1881–2001*, Notre Dame: University of Notre Dame Press.

Keck, M. and Sikkink, K. (1998) *Activists Beyond Borders*, Ithaca: Cornell University Press.

Kelly, R.E. (2007) 'Security Theory in the "New Regionalism"', *International Studies Review*, 9(2): 197–229.

Keohane, R.O. (1989) *International Institutions and State Power: Essays in International Relations Theory*, Boulder: Westview Press.

——— (1990) 'International Liberalism Reconsidered' in J. Dunn (ed) *The Economic Limits to Modern Politics*, Cambridge: Cambridge University Press.

Keohane, R.O. and Martin, L. (1995) 'The Promise of Institutionalist Theory', *International Security*, 20(1): 39–51.

Kiernan, J. (2011) 'Multidimensional Security in the Americas', *Americas*, 63(3): 28–35.

Koremnos, B., Lipson, C. and Snidal, D. (eds) (2003) *The Rational Design of International Institutions*, Cambridge: Cambridge University Press.

Krasner, S. (1983) 'Structural Causes and Regime Consequences: Regimes as Intervening Variables' in S. Krasner (ed) *International Regimes*, Ithaca: Cornell University Press.

Legler, T. (2013) 'Post-Hegemonic Regionalism and Sovereignty in Latin America: Optimists, Skeptics, and an Emerging Research Agenda', *Contexto Internacional*, 35(2): 181–208.

Mace, G. and Loiseau, H. (2005) 'Cooperative Hegemony and Summitry in the Americas', *Latin American Politics and Society*, 47(4): 107–134.

Malamud, A. (2005) 'Presidential Diplomacy and the Institutional Underpinnings of Mercosur. An Empirical Examination', *Latin American Research Review*, 40(1): 138–164.

——— (2011) 'A Leader Without Followers? The Growing Divergence Between the Regional and Global Performance of Brazilian Foreign Policy', *Latin American Politics and Society*, 53(3): 1–24.
Malamud, A. and Gardini. G. L. (2012) 'Has Regionalism Peaked? The Latin American Quagmire and its Lessons', *The International Spectator*, 47(1): 116–133.
Malamud, A. and Schmitter, P. C. (2011) 'The Experience of European Integration and the Potential for Integration in South America' in A. Warleigh-Lack, N. Robinson and B. Rosamond (eds) *New Regionalism and the European Union. Dialogues, Comparisons and New Research Directions*, London: Routledge.
Mares, D. (2001) *Violent Peace: Militarized Interstate Bargaining in Latin America*, New York: Columbia University Press.
——— (2012) *Latin America and the Illusion of Peace*, London: Routledge.
Martin, F. (2006) *Militarist Peace in South America: Conditions for War and Peace*, New York: Palgrave.
Mattli, W. (1999) *The Logic of Regional Integration. Europe and Beyond*, Cambridge: Cambridge University Press.
Merke, F. (2013) 'Neither Balance nor Bandwagon: South America Meets Brazil's Rising Power', *6th Regional Powers Network Conference*, Rio de Janeiro: PUC-Rio.
——— (2014) 'Política exterior Argentina y elección institucional: La OEA en el espejo de la UNASUR y el Mercosur', *Pensamiento Propio*, 19(39): 353–381.
Milanese, J. P. (2007) 'A "Nuclear Integration": Constructing Supranationality in the South American Southern Cone', *Hiroshima Peace Science*, 29: 109–136.
Nolte, D. and Wehner, L. (2014) 'UNASUR and Regional Security in South America' in S. Aris and A. Wenger (eds) *Regional Organizations and Security*, London: Routledge.
Nye, J. (1971) *Peace in Parts: Integration and Conflict in Regional Organization*, Boston: Little Brown.
Oelsner, A. (2014) 'Articulating Mercosur's Security Conceptions and Practices' in S. Aris and A. Wenger (eds) *Regional Organizations and Security*, London: Routledge.
Pellicer, O. (1998) *Regional Mechanisms and International Security in Latin America*, Tokyo: United Nations University Press.
Pevehouse, J. C. (2005) *Democracy from Above. Regional Organizations and Democratization*, Cambridge: Cambridge University Press.
Pion-Berlin, D. and Trinkunas, H. (2007) 'Attention Deficits: Why Politicians Ignore Defense Policy in Latin America', *Latin American Research Review*, 42(3): 76–100.
Ribeiro-Hoffmann, A. (2007) 'Political Conditionality and Democratic Clauses in the EU and Mercosur' in A. Ribeiro Hoffmann and A. van der Vleuten (eds) *Closing or Widening the Gap? Legitimacy and Democracy of Regional International Organizations*, Hampshire: Ashgate.
Saint-Pierre, H. and Montoya, A. (2014) 'As medidas de confiança no conselho de defesa sul-Americano (CDS)', *Revista Brasileira de Politica Internacional*, 57(1): 22–39.
Schmitter, P. C. (1970) 'Central American Integration: Spill-Over, Spill-Around or Encapsulation?', *Journal of Common Market Studies*, 9(1): 1–48.
Shaw, C. (2004) *Cooperation, Conflict, and Consensus in the Organization of American States*, New York: Palgrave Macmillan.
Simmons, B. (1999) 'See You in "Court"? The Appeal to Quasi-Judicial Legal Processes in the Settlement of Territorial Disputes' in P. Diehl (ed) *A Roadmap to War: Territorial Dimensions of International Conflict*, Nashville: Vanderbilt University Press.
Solingen, E. (1994) 'The Political Economy of Nuclear Restraint', *International Security*, 19(2): 126–159.
Stein, A. (2008) 'Neoliberal Institutionalism' in C. Reus-Smit and D. Snidal (eds) *Oxford Handbook on International Relations*, New York: Oxford University Press.
Teixeira, A. and Sousa, V. (2013) 'O desafio do uso da força e a evolução das medidas de confiança mútua no conselho de defesa sul-Americano da UNASUL', *Boletim Meridiano*, 14(140): 42–48.
Thies, C. G. (2005) 'War, Rivalry, and State Building in Latin America', *American Journal of Political Science*, 49(3): 451–465.
Trinkunas, H. (2013) 'Reordering Regional Security in Latin America', *Journal of International Affairs*, 66(2): 83–99.
Tulchin, J., Rojas Aravena, F. and Espach, R. (eds) (1998) *Strategic Balance and Confidence Building Measures in the Americas*, Stanford: Stanford University Press.
UNOCD (2013) 'United Nations Office on Drugs and Crime Online Database'. Retrieved from http://www.unodc.org/unodc/en/data-and-analysis/Research-Database.html.

Van Walraven, K. (1998) 'Inter-Governmental Organizations and Preventing Conflicts: Political Practice Since the End of the Cold War' in K. van Walraven (ed) *Early Warning and Conflict Prevention, Limitations and Possibilities*, Cambridge: Kluwer Law International.

Varas, A. (1998) 'Cooperative Hemispheric Security after the Cold War' in O. Pellicer (ed) *Regional Mechanisms and International Security in Latin America*, Tokyo: United Nations University Press.

Wallander, C. and Keohane, R. O. (1999) 'Risk, Threat, and Security Institutions' in H. Haftendorn, R. O. Keohane and C. Wallander (eds) *Imperfect Unions. Security Institutions over Time and Space*, Oxford: Oxford University Press.

Weiffen, B., Wehner, L. and Nolte, D. (2013) 'Overlapping Regional Security Institutions in South America: The Case of OAS and UNASUR', *International Area Studies Review*, 16(4): 370–389.

Wynia, G. (1970) 'Central American Integration: The Paradox of Success', *International Organization*, 24(2): 319–332.

Zacher, M. (1979) *International Conflicts and Collective Security, 1946–1977: The United Nations, Organization of American States, Organization of African Unity, and Arab League*, New York: Praeger.

4

WHO COMMANDS, WHO OBEYS, AND WHO REBELS

Latin American security in a peripheral-realist perspective

Carlos Escudé

Introduction

"The strong do what they can; the weak suffer what they must." In this brief and brilliant formula, the interstate hierarchy often ignored by mainstream, Anglo-American international relations (IR) theory was encapsulated two and a half millennia ago by a Greek genius, Thucydides.

Peripheral realism (RP, from the Spanish original) is a Latin American theoretical construct inspired by his work. First presented in the United States in 1997, it attempts to correct some of the main concepts of the realist and neorealist schools of international relations theory, contesting the idea that the international system has an anarchic structure, famously proposed by Hedley Bull and Kenneth Waltz, among others. It also claims that, because so-called rogue Third World states sometimes have a strong impact on world politics, it is absurd to coin an IR theory that ignores the periphery (Escudé 1997).

RP logically and empirically demonstrates that although Great Powers interact under conditions of anarchy, the world order as a whole is hierarchical, and in this it converges with David A. Lake's (2009: 33–34) much more recent work on hierarchy. According to Stephanie Neuman (2009: 85), Douglas Lemke (2002: 203), and Ira Straus (2004: 67), RP is a correction to realist IR theory that was badly overdue. Notwithstanding, it has been largely overlooked by most mainstream theorists, at least partly for the structural reasons studied by Arlene B. Tickner (2013) – as in other endeavors, the academic mainstream stems from the center, not the periphery.

Because normative suggestions flow from its explanatory platform, RP has developed tentative policy guidelines for peripheral states, which are logically derived from its understanding of an imperfectly hierarchical world order. And because, in conjunction with this understanding, it claims that socioeconomic development is the foremost national interest of a peripheral state, especially in the Latin American context, RP advocates for a greater 'butter' component in the expenditures of peripheral countries that do not suffer from obvious external security threats.

RP borrows its main analytical category, center-periphery, from the Raúl Prebisch/ECLAC tradition of development studies, importing it into international studies. Indeed, during the late 1940s and early 1950s, ECLAC studied the unequal role of central and peripheral countries in the generation of economic cycles (Pinto and Kn̂akal 1973). Although an analogous inequality of functions is at work in political and diplomatic issues, mainstream IR theory has obscured this fact, and this flaw is especially visible in the neorealist concept of anarchy as coined by Waltz (1979: 98), who claims that states are "like units" with similar functions in the interstate system, even if there are enormous power differentials between them.

RP amends this error, introducing a conception of the structure of the interstate system that includes three functionally differentiated types of states: rule-makers (which forge both the written and unwritten rules of world order), rule-takers, and rebel states (Escudé 1997).

The rule-makers, which are also the principal rule-breakers, are the five permanent members of the UN Security Council, plus an economic Great Power, Germany. The permanent members are considered rule-makers because they have the capacity to destroy the world. This is what made it possible for Russia to capture Crimea in 2014, breaching fundamental norms without fear of a major war.

Germany is also a rule-maker because of its tutelage over the Eurozone and the European Central Bank. The size of its economy determines the value of the euro, making it easy to export German machinery but difficult to export agricultural products with little value added. Combined with European Union rules, this mechanism has turned the Eurozone into a virtually captive market for Germany.

Contrariwise to such rule-makers, so-called rogue states like North Korea and a few others belong to the category of rebel states. And the remaining members of the international community, including most advanced industrial countries, are essentially rule-takers. Together with the rebels, they are operationally defined in RP as 'peripheral states.'

For a peripheral state, rebellion is costly. Imagine the harm that would befall rule-taking Italy if its government decided to develop its own atomic weapons free of international safeguards, arguing that if London, Paris, and Washington can do it, so can Rome. In contrast, if under a new Hitler, rule-making Germany were to attempt this, it is likely that its economic and technological prowess would make it possible for it to rapidly achieve its objective, making it a *fait accompli* long before being ruined by international sanctions.

With respect to Latin America, these assertions are neither assumptions nor speculations, but the offshoot of empirical historiographical research conducted mainly in the late 1970s and 1980s (Simonoff 2003). These studies, based on declassified U.S. and British documents, revealed the costs of systematic confrontations with the United States, the power that at least since World War II (and in most cases, long before) has been the most important extraregional constraint to their development. Notwithstanding, even if it emerges from the study of Latin American cases vis-à-vis the United States, as an explanatory theory RP purports to be relevant for our understanding of the world order as a whole.

The epistemological origin of the dangerous myth of interstate anarchy

The juridical equality of states was only a diplomatic fiction until the ratification of the United Nations Charter. After that it is not even a fiction insofar as, for security issues, its Chapter 7 formally awards intervention powers to the oligopolic Security Council. The same dissimilarity of functions is present in regimes such as the NPT. When Brazil ratified the NPT in 1998, it was acknowledging that it is not the equal of France.

Indeed, states are neither formally nor informally equal. Yet Waltz (1979: 88) asserts with confidence that no state "is entitled to command; none is required to obey," and other prominent scholars have endorsed this claim. This is an error that tends to legitimize brinkmanship. Where does it come from?

Unlike the idealist critique of state equality formulated by Lake (2009), which hinges on the legitimate command of a supposedly beneficial leader-state, RP's critique is structural. It argues that there is a fallacy built into the central nucleus of realist and neorealist IR theories. It had its origins in the pioneering work of Hans Morgenthau, who proposed that power be considered "an autonomous sphere of action and understanding," as compared to other allegedly autonomous spheres, such as "interest defined as wealth" (Morgenthau 1948: 5).

From a peripheral perspective this was the worst possible way of building theory, because the link between military and economic capabilities is stronger, or at least more visible, the poorer a country is. If peripheral countries had been included from the start in the building of IR theory, Morgenthau's error would not have been committed, and the concept of anarchy probably would not have taken roots. The president of the United States can make abstraction of the economic sources of his/her country's military might when s/he moves fleets across the oceans. But the same is not true for a country that would run out of ammunition in a week if a war with a neighboring state broke out, as would happen if Argentina and Paraguay had an armed conflict. Once we rid theory of this fallacy, hierarchy replaces anarchy as the structuring principle of the interstate system. Thus, *the natural function of a Great Power that can move fleets around without worrying about the costs of fuel is to rule over those who cannot.*

Consequently, given that wealth and power are not autonomous spheres but rather interdependent, we must disagree with Morgenthau when he claims that the "main signpost that helps political realism to find its way through the landscape of international politics is the concept of interest defined in terms of power" (1948: 4–5). At least from a peripheral perspective, the main signpost is the concept of interest defined in terms of socioeconomic development, without which there is no real power in the long term (Escudé 1997: 54).

If the main principle of political realism is thus redefined, then the dismantlement of Argentina's confrontational policies of the 1980s, with which we will deal later on, was the normative consequence of a realist analysis of the situation once account was taken of the probability of U.S. sanctions and of the vulnerability of Argentina. Saddam Hussein did not have this foresight, and his state's infrastructure and institutions were obliterated, while Kim Jong-un and the Iranian ayatollahs continue to gamble their countries' very existence, aggressively defying the interstate order as if this were the sport of despots.

Conversely, the cases of Japan and Germany show that the interstate order is not crystallized but that there is room for upward mobility. Devastated after their defeat in World War II, they became docile rule-takers in most political and military affairs, while doggedly defending their economic interests. They confronted only when it was required for their continued socioeconomic ascent.

Indeed, the Japanese and German strategy for escaping from the periphery, into which they had fallen as a consequence of utter destruction, is one of the best examples of applied RP. In our times, theirs is probably the only way to transit from the periphery to the core. Germany especially is a truly revisionist state, inasmuch as through the Eurozone and the ECB it has reshaped part of the world order, although not necessarily for the better.

Thus, RP inverts the traditional distinction between high and low politics. And because it raises socioeconomic development to the level of high politics, it is much more in tune to the interests of citizens than mainstream IR theory, which is unabashedly state-centric. Mainstream theory unwittingly introduces authoritarian values. Contrariwise, RP is citizen-centric and thus domestically more democratic.

All roads lead to interstate hierarchy

In the ultimate instance, state-centric theory (which is not to be confused with a state-centric policy rationale) leads to fallacious anthropomorphisms, insofar as it assumes that the state is to the interstate system what the individual is to the state.

This analogy is flawed, but few authors are aware of its fallacy. State freedom and individual freedom, for example, are fundamentally at odds with each other simply because if the state is to have full freedom to maneuver in the interstate order, it must be able to subject its population to whatever sacrifices are necessary to achieve its ends, sometimes with brutal limitations of individual freedom, which becomes subordinated to the *raison d'état*. In other words:

TOTAL STATE FREEDOM = ABSOLUTE DOMESTIC TYRANNY

This equation is a cornerstone of peripheral realism, because *the weaker a country is, the lower the threshold beyond which the exercise of state freedom leads to limitations of individual welfare and freedom*.

This reasoning converges with RP's dismantling of Morgenthau's mistaken postulation of an "autonomy of the political sphere of action and understanding" seen in the previous section. There we showed that *the weaker a country is, the lower the threshold beyond which the falsehood of this alleged autonomy becomes visible*.

It is interesting to note that these two complementary analyses have exactly the same structure, and both lead to unveiling the unwelcome fact of the hierarchical structure of interstate order. Furthermore, *they both reveal the even more disturbing reality that the interstate order can never be democratic*.

The corollary of autocratic power

Moreover, our equation resembles a two-sided coin in which the obverse is more relevant for peripheral states, whilst the reverse is of greater significance for powerful rule-makers. If it is true that, *ceteris paribus*, the poorer a country is, the greater the domestic authoritarianism it will have to recur to in order to compete politically and militarily with stronger states, it is no less true that, *all other things being equal*, among the rule-makers the more authoritarian state will tend to be the more powerful one. This is postulated as a tendency, not an absolute rule. Put graphically:

LESS DOMESTIC FREEDOM → MORE FREEDOM VIS-À-VIS THE WORLD

This corollary is easily verified empirically, Russia being one of the best examples. During a great part of its history it has had more interstate power than would be expected from its economic development because, given the characteristics of its social structure and/or political culture, it has been able to sacrifice the welfare and freedom of its population. This is one of the reasons why during the Napoleonic invasions it was able to defeat France, and during World War II it could defeat Germany. And it is also why, although today's Germany is financially much stronger, militarily Moscow is much more powerful than Berlin. Indeed, Moscow spends twice as much on its defense than Berlin and three times as much as a percentage of its GDP (SIPRI Yearbook 2013).

Although many political scientists have postulated that the overwhelming power of Great Britain and the United States during the last 200 years has stemmed from the fact that free citizens generate more wealth and willingly give it to governments that they create and limit, this line of thinking omits the fact that the British power was built with a combination of absolutism and mercantilism.

The United States seems to be the only major empirical exception to our corollary, and its star may be waning. Chinese firms, both private and public, follow their government's guidelines when investing abroad and in return receive official favors. The government's strategy is not very different from the British one in the 17th century. Indeed, Sergio Garbrielli, chief executive of Brazilian oil giant Petrobras, noted that "the United States has a problem. There isn't someone in the U.S. government that we can sit down with and have the kinds of discussions we're having with the Chinese" (Lyons 2009).

Mercantilist China has a strategy. Market-oriented United States is like a mindless giant. When concerned with their profits, U.S. telecommunications firms withdrew from Argentina in 2001, and China's Huawei and ZTE rapidly moved in, encouraged by their government. This generated concern in Washington, inasmuch as Huawei and ZTE were suspected of intelligence activities and cyberwar capabilities. If it is true that Brazil and China have already cooperated in the development of spy satellites, as the Heritage Foundation's *Backgrounder* of October 24, 2005 claims, then the United States really has a problem.

Thus, our equation and its corollary summarize the predicament of what Robert Cox (1986) called "state/society complexes" – the true actors of the interstate system. Because economic development is the only way out of the periphery, citizen-centric foreign and security policies are usually advisable for peripheral states. But for the rule-makers, which are usually not vulnerable to the penalties of breaking the rules, choices are not so simple. Citizen-centric policies can lead, in the long term, to subordination vis-à-vis less democratic peers, whilst state-centric policies designed to compete more effectively with their rivals can lead to authoritarianism.

This predicament is a harsh one. Interstate order is not perfectly hierarchical. The oligopoly of rule-makers is subject to no binding rules and therefore lives under conditions of anarchy. Does the U.S. leadership find it acceptable to fall behind China in terms of power, simply because it is deemed immoral for Washington to resort to the illiberal policies that Beijing habitually practices?

The rule-making oligopoly and its systematic rule-breaking: the case of the United States, 1979–2013

Offhand, the answer seems to be 'no.' Among other decisions, President Barack Obama's 2010 order to assassinate a U.S. citizen abroad suggests it. Anwar al-Awlaki was murdered in 2011 without a trial and without the disclosure of the evidence or even the legal reasoning that made him suspect of being an al-Qaeda combatant (Editorial 2011).

The deed seems no less infamous than the Operation Cóndor of the Southern Cone dictatorships during the late 1970s and early 1980s, when, with partial U.S. complicity, the regimes of these countries agreed to give each other a green light for the assassination of their own citizens on foreign soil (Dinges 2004: 156–174). But although the White House has been criticized for the assassination of al-Awlaki, the crime has never been compared to Operation Cóndor. This double standard originates in the seldom confessed fact that, as Lake (2009) also argues through a different logic, Washington has 'rights' that Latin American governments are denied. The data suggest that while Obama has the 'right' to order the murder of U.S.-born citizens abroad, Pinochet had no such 'right' vis-à-vis Orlando Letelier in Washington.

Another example lies in the supposed war that the United States wages against drugs and terror. It is a proven fact that Washington played a role in the rise of Islamist terrorism.

Beginning early in the Cold War, Islam was used as a bulwark against the Soviet Union, and after the Soviet invasion of Afghanistan the paradigm was 'Islam-as-sword.' Among several proxies, the CIA used the jihadist network that eventually gave birth to al-Qaeda (Dreyfuss 2006: 245, 265).

Escalating, in February 1982, little after President Ronald Reagan authorized the CIA's undercover support for the *Contras* in Nicaragua, Attorney General William French Smith signed a secret memo waiving the CIA's obligation to inform on drug smuggling operations undertaken by its operatives (Cooley 2002: 111). Thus, the CIA had access to funds that did not need to be accounted for, and fed this drug money to its terrorist proxies in Afghanistan and Nicaragua.

Under the administration of George H. W. Bush there was further escalation through 'Operation Cyclone,' which led to the training of tens of thousands of Islamist militants by the CIA, MI6, and SAS. Some were trained in a CIA camp located in Virginia, and in the al-Kifah center of Brooklyn, New York, part of the so-called MaK network (Scott 2007: 115, 123). According to *Jane's Intelligence Review* of August 1, 2001, MaK channeled billions of Western dollars to the Afghan jihad through the CIA and MI6.

Obviously, if Mexico or Brazil were to engage in such policies on their own they would soon face a reality as grim as Iraq's in 2003. But the rule-maker can break its own rules. This is how interstate hierarchy works.

From rule-breaking rebel to ruined rule-taker: the changing policies of Argentina, 1889–2013

Having looked at the behavior of the leading rule-maker, let us now take a glimpse at the possibilities of members of the periphery. The first case chosen, Argentina, is interesting because of the diversity of polices it has adopted through the decades.

Until the advent of the Menem administration in 1989, and ever since the first Pan-American Conference in 1889, Argentina and the United States had relations that, with few exceptions, were antagonistic. Argentina systematically confronted the United States in diplomatic fora and was neutral during both world wars. Notwithstanding, until World War II it was under the British sphere of influence, and the complementarity of the Argentine and UK economies had generated a per capita income that by 1940 placed it among the most prosperous countries in the world. By 1970, however, it was an increasingly backward member of the Third World (Escudé 1983: 13).

Attempts at explaining this 'reversal of development' ranged from dependency theory to hypotheses based on political culture, but they failed to explain Argentina's success prior to 1940. With the declassification of U.S. and UK archives, however, it became possible to understand the consequences of Argentine neutrality, in terms of a Washington-led policy of economic boycott and political destabilization that was coupled to the military and economic promotion of Brazil.

To be sure, this was not the only variable underlying Argentina's decline, but it is a fact to consider when understanding the process. Conversely, it is important to note that the issue with Argentine neutrality was not the breaking of written rules, but rather that Buenos Aires took its sovereign right to neutrality seriously, and exercised it. It broke unwritten rules, behaving as if international law were really applicable to all (Escudé 1983: 23–83, 223–248).

Once U.S. hegemony was established, the consequences of this legalistic attitude were devastating. Suffice to say that, in January 1944, President Franklin D. Roosevelt wrote to Secretary of State Cordell Hull instructing him "to give Brazil an effective fighting force near the

Argentine border such as two or three divisions of motorized regiments" (Frank 1979: 65), and that by February 1945, U.S. Export Policy towards Argentina read: "Export of capital goods should be kept at present minimums. It is essential not to permit the expansion of Argentine heavy industry" (Escudé 1983: 270).

But Argentina did not learn the lesson, and its challenge did not end there. Come the nuclear age, under successive governments and regardless of the type of domestic regime, the Argentine state refused to sign the NPT, did not ratify the Tlatelolco Treaty of 1967 for the prohibition of nuclear weapons in Latin America, devoted its scarce resources to the enrichment of uranium, and under the democratic administration of Raúl Alfonsín (1983–1989) undertook a joint venture with Egypt, Iraq, and Libya for the development of an intermediate-range guided missile, the Cóndor II, which could have destabilized the Middle East. Conversely, until 1979 relations with Brazil were tense, while war almost broke out with Chile in 1978.

Furthermore, in 1982 Argentina invaded the British-held Falkland/Malvinas Islands. Unlike Argentine neutrality during the world wars, this went beyond the breaking of unwritten rules: Argentina attacked a major rule-making state. While not intervening directly, the United States sided with its ally, and Argentina was defeated. Diplomatic relations with Britain were not reestablished until 1990. By then, Argentina had the fourth most anti-U.S. voting profile in the United Nations General Assembly.

But by the time the Menem Administration (1989–1999) was inaugurated, the historiographical research regarding the U.S. boycott of the World War II era had been understood by part of the political leadership. The new government realized that Argentina's profile vis-à-vis the world was dangerous only to itself and that, if Buenos Aires continued to be perceived as a potential destabilizer and proliferator, another U.S. boycott of devastating consequences could be unleashed. Hence, it set out to reform its foreign and security policies.

Among other measures, it reestablished relations with Great Britain, dismantled the Cóndor II project, became a member of the Missile Technology Control Regime (MTCR), and signed and ratified the nuclear treaties. This reform, which essentially followed RP normative guidelines, is still largely in place. Today, Brazil and Chile spend billions of dollars per year in arms procurement, while Argentina spends nearly nothing. In 2012, Argentina's military expenditure as a percentage of GDP was 0.9%, the lowest in South America (SIPRI Yearbook 2013). Despite the anti-U.S. rhetoric of presidents Néstor Kirchner (2003–2007) and Cristina Fernández (2007–2015), Argentina has not denounced the nuclear treaties or the MTCR. And despite anti-British rhetoric, diplomatic relations with the United Kingdom are normal, and Argentines can travel to Britain without a visa.

Moreover, starting in 2006, Argentina consistently denounced Iran for a 1994 terrorist bombing in Buenos Aires and for human rights violations, converging with the United States on these key global problems. Indeed, although since 2013 Argentina holds talks with Iran over the bombing (as does the United States over other issues), it has not ceased to criticize Tehran in the General Assembly.

But this post-1990 reaction vis-à-vis its previous excesses may have come too late. The Falkland/Malvinas War meant not only a humiliating defeat but also the beginning of a major military debacle. It was the worst possible end for the military dictatorship, because unlike the Brazilian and Chilean cases, after defeat at war the Argentine military lost the domestic bargaining power needed to preserve an appropriate part of the national budget. The neoliberal dismantling of the arms industry in the 1990s, plus successive economic crises, did the rest.

Because of the rarity of interstate war in South America, which ranks as one of the greatest zones of peace of the world (Kacowicz 1998), it is unlikely that Argentina's present situation will imperil its territorial integrity. Notwithstanding that fact, normative RP only advocates for a moderation of confrontations, not for unilateral disarmament. Because rule-makers are rule-breakers, they cannot be trusted to punish perpetrators (Neuman 2009: 81–82). Argentina's territorial integrity depends more on a Brasilia-Santiago consensus than on a U.S. security umbrella. Hence, this is one of the most radical pacifist experiments of all time. It is a Russian roulette that unwittingly tests the hypotheses of classical realism in the South American context.

Some may argue that the unilateral disarmament of Argentina is the product of an excessive dose of normative RP. I do not agree. If RP's guidelines had prevailed in the long term of Argentina's foreign and security policies, the Falkland/Malvinas War would never have taken place, Argentina's military corporation would not have lost its bargaining power vis-à-vis the professional politicians any more than its Chilean and Brazilian counterparts, and Buenos Aires would continue to be master of its own defense vis-à-vis its neighbors.

But such is no longer the case. For peripheral states, engaging in major rule-breaking can lead not only to severe external sanctions but also to the breaking of the country's very backbone.

Rule-taking Mexico's shift to applied RP, 1992–2012

As Varun Sahni (2001) noted in his discussion of RP, Mexico's confrontational policies vis-à-vis the United States can be traced at least to 1848, when it was forced to cede half of its territory to its neighbor. Although relations improved during the regime of Porfirio Díaz (1876–1880), the Mexican Revolution (1910–1920) was a blow to bilateral cooperation, leaving a legacy of opposition to Washington's interests. Mexico's good relations with Havana after the Cuban Revolution (1959) were an eloquent symbol of this long-lasting opposition to its northern neighbor. Although it was never an outright rebel, as was Argentina in 1982, Mexico accepted rules grudgingly.

Things changed dramatically, however, with Mexico's accession to the North American Free Trade Agreement (NAFTA) in 1994. Regardless of official rhetoric, it shifted Mexican policy in the direction of RP's normative guidelines.

In terms of diplomatic gestures, Vicente Fox (2000–2006) went further in this direction, attempting to please Washington by supporting the ill-fated Free Trade Area of the Americas (FTAA) and successfully campaigning to keep Venezuela's Chávez regime out of the Security Council. In ideological terms, foreign minister Jorge G. Castañeda went a long way when he postulated that Mexico should turn its "foreign policy into an instrument of socioeconomic development" (as quoted and translated in Domínguez 2006: 5). Knowingly or not, he was quoting RP normative guidelines.

Notwithstanding, while words come and go, the substantive and long-lasting structural change in Mexico took place with its previous accession to NAFTA. Largely thanks to the treaty, by December 2012 it had become the United States' third most important trading partner, after Canada and China. According to the U.S. Bureau of the Census, its total trade with the United States is slightly higher than the sum of that of Japan, Germany, and the United Kingdom, which are fourth, fifth, and sixth in the ranking.

Thus, regardless of its changing foreign policy rhetoric, out of necessity Mexico adopted the most extreme brand of applied RP. The United States buys 78 per cent of its exports and sells 50.5 per cent of its imports (CIA 2014).

Such trade dependence is not alarming if we consider that it was even higher in the 1970s. Moreover, thanks to NAFTA, the percentage of manufacturing exports in total exports has increased, and extreme poverty has diminished. This is, essentially, RP's normative objective; so if we limit ourselves to these data we must conclude that Mexico's RP has been a success.

However, if we look beyond socioeconomic data and analyze the impact of RP upon Mexican domestic violence, we might have second thoughts. After all, RP focuses on socioeconomic development because it is an important indicator of the 'good society;' so other factors needed for a good society should also count.

The overriding negative consequence of Mexico's shift towards RP is causally linked to the domestic weakness of its state. As Mohammed Ayoob (1998) has observed, this is a common trait of the Global South that impinges upon international relations. In the case of Mexico, trade integration with a superpower neighbor had, out of necessity, led to increased cooperation with Washington's so-called war on drugs. And this, in turn, led to self-destructive domestic conflicts.

Indeed, the Mexican state has not been able to cope with the contradictory drives that emerge from the United States' state/society complex. On the one hand, the United States market demands narcotics, but on the other the United States government forbids their supply. Notwithstanding, no matter how forbidden, if the production or acquisition of the outlawed goods is feasible, a high demand generates a supply. And this is all the more valid for a country with huge masses of poor people ready to brave the risks (Buxton 2006: 101–102).

Indeed, because they are the product of United States demand, Mexico's illegal exports of narcotics to the United States seem impossible to interrupt without increasing violence. Hence, the greater the cooperation between both states, the greater the violence in the weaker of the two is bound to be.

The toll on Mexico has been huge. This was indicated by the surge in the rule-taker's domestic violence when, under Felipe Calderón's administration (2006–2012), the will to cooperate with the rule-maker reached a peak. Apparently, the main result of Calderón's strong military offensive against the cartels was that the rate of intentional homicides per 100,000 people soared from 8.1 in 2007 to 23.7 in 2011 (UNODC 2014). The data suggest that the Mexican state/society complex could not bear the type of cooperation that came together with its brand of applied RP, and burst into criminal violence.

In contrast, the United States' rate of intentional homicides in 2011 was 4.8, while remote Southern Cone countries like Chile, Argentina, and Uruguay were in the same league as the superpower, with 3.7, 5.5, and 5.9, respectively.

Of course, domestic violence in Latin America does not come solely from cooperation with the United States' war on drugs. For example, Brazil's high level of domestic violence, which with 21.8 homicides per 100,000 inhabitants is not far below Mexico's (UNODC 2013), cannot be attributed to its relationship with the United States. But there can be little doubt that, in the case of Mexico, the increase in violence was due to Calderón's extreme brand of RP.

These costs, however, can be mitigated. Overall, considering the successes in poverty reduction and trade intensification, it would appear that the results of applied RP in Mexico are at least marginally positive. Since RP has generated stakeholders in the further development of the partnership with the United States, we should expect to see future increases in benefits and reductions in costs.

Conclusions

The moral for the Mexican, Argentine, and U.S. stories told here is a simple one. It can be summarized in Thucydides' dictum about the weak and the strong, with which we began. However, this is not to say that relevant IR theory such as RP generates easy policy recipes for peripheral states. It is not simply a question of acquiescing to the will of the rule-makers. Both the Argentine and the Mexican cases teach that many deadly paradoxes lurk in the labyrinthine alleyways of theory and practice. The interplay between foreign policy and state/society complexes can generate unpredictable phenomena, such as Argentina's unilateral disarmament and Mexico's increasing domestic violence.

Indeed, applied RP does not always work as we expect it to. What experience does corroborate, however, is that extreme political confrontation with a major rule-maker is almost always counterproductive. It is hard to contest that, despite its short-term achievements' reducing of poverty levels, the Chávez regime has eroded the very foundations of the Venezuelan people's long-term welfare. And it seems clear that Salvador Allende's idealistic but radical challenge to capitalism in Chile generated a reaction from the U.S. rule-maker that culminated in a despotic, right-wing dictatorship lasting 17 years (not very different from what happened to Czechoslovakia in 1968 vis-à-vis the Soviet Union). An RP research agenda will require looking into these cases, as well as into even more puzzling ones, such as the Cuban Revolution's challenge to its northerly Goliath, and the (probably positive) cost-benefit equation of Colombia's RP (1998–2010), Plan Colombia included.

Nevertheless, Thucydides works, as does RP theory, which stands on a much firmer ground than RP as a normative doctrine. The Greek historian's precept was lost to mainstream IR theory largely because of the methodological errors analyzed in our first section, which converged with the complacent diplomatic rhetoric of sovereignty. This is how the myth of interstate anarchy was engendered.

Furthermore, the mistaken separation of the political and economic spheres led to the formulation of a security-obsessed, state-centric realist theory that did not find it easy to cope with the fact that, being the only way out of the periphery, socioeconomic development is the national interest par excellence of all peripheral states. Thus, true high politics came to be considered low politics and vice versa.

For the vast majority of peripheral states, no valid normative conclusions could derive from such a theory, which encouraged brinkmanship. This is why, in the 1990s, I attempted to develop sketchy RP foreign policy guidelines. Indeed, Argentina's past sovereignty-obsessed behavior would be at least partially justifiable if one were to take the fictions of mainstream IR seriously.

Notwithstanding, as RP shows, it is logically and empirically demonstrable that mainstream realism's premises are diplomatically correct fantasies, and that world order is necessarily hierarchical and essentially undemocratic. Hence, rebel states not only fail to serve their people. They tend to be self-destructive.

References

Ayoob, M. (1998) 'Subaltern Realism: International Relations Theory Meets the Third World' in S. G. Neuman (ed) *International Relations Theory and the Third World*, New York: St. Martin's Press, pp. 31–54.

Buxton, J. (2006) *The Political Economy of Narcotics: Production, Consumption and Global Markets*, New York: Zed Books.

Central Intelligence Agency (CIA) (2014) 'The World Factbook'. Retrieved from https://www.cia.gov/library/publications/resources/the-word-factbook/.

Cooley, J. (2002*) Unholy Wars: Afghanistan, America and International Terrorism*, London: Pluto Press.

Cox, R. W. (1986) 'Social Forces, States, and World Orders: Beyond International Relations Theory' in R. O. Keohane (ed) *Neorealism and its Critics*, New York: Columbia University Press, pp. 204–254.

Dinges, J. (2004) *The Condor Years: How Pinochet and His Allies Brought Terrorism to Three Continents*, New York: The New Press.

Domínguez, R. (2006) Mexican Foreign Policy: the limits of democratic transformation. Retrieved from http://larc.ucalgary.ca/sites/larc.ucalgary.ca/files/CALACS/Paperstwo/dominguez.pdf

Dreyfuss, R. (2006) *Devil's Game: How the United States Helped Unleash Fundamentalist Islam*, New York: Dell Publishing.
Editorial (2011, October 2) 'Anwar Awlaki: Targeted for Death', *Los Angeles Times*. Retrieved from http://articles.latimes.com/2011/oct/02/opinion/la-ed-1001-awlaki-20111002.
Escudé, C. (1983) *Gran Bretaña, Estados Unidos y la declinación Argentina, 1942–49*, Buenos Aires: Editorial de Belgrano.
——— (1997) *Foreign Policy Theory in Menem's Argentina*, Gainesville: University Press of Florida.
Frank, G. (1979) *Struggle for Hegemony: Argentina, Brazil and the United States During the Second World War Era*, Coral Gables: University of Miami.
Kacowicz, A. M. (1998) *Zones of Peace in the Third World: South America and West Africa in Comparative Perspective*, Albany, NY: State University of New York Press.
Lake, D. A. (2009) *Hierarchy in International Relations*, Ithaca: Cornell University Press.
Lemke, D. (2002) *Regions of War and Peace*, Cambridge: Cambridge University Press.
Lyons, J. (2009, May 18) 'Brazil Turns to China to Help Finance Oil Projects', *The Wall Street Journal*. Retrieved from http://www.wsj.com/articles/SB124259318084927919.
Morgenthau, H. J. (1948) *Politics Among Nations: The Struggle for Power and Peace*, New York: A.A. Knopf.
Neuman, S. G. (2009) 'Power, Influence and Hierarchy: Defense Industries in a Unipolar World' in R.A. Bitzinger (ed) *The Modern Defense Industry*, Santa Barbara: Praeger Security, pp. 60–94.
Pinto, A. and Kñakal, J. (1973) 'The Centre-Periphery System Twenty Years Later', *Social and Economic Studies*, 22(1): 34–89.
Sahni, V. (2001) 'Peripheric Realism Versus Complex Interdependence: Analyzing Argentine and Mexican Foreign Policies since 1988', *International Studies*, 38: 1.
Scott, P. D. (2007) *The Road to 9/11: Wealth, Empire and the Future of America*, Berkeley: University of California Press.
Simonoff, A. (2003) 'La interpretación del pasado como eje de la disputa de la política exterior actual: De Puig a Escudé', *Relaciones Internacionales*, 12(25): 129–148.
Stockholm International Peace Research Institute (SIPRI) (2013) *SIPRI Yearbook 2013: Armaments, Disarmaments and International Security*.
Straus, I. (2004) 'Reversing Proliferation', *The National Interest*, 74: 63–70.
Tickner, A. B. (2013) 'Core, Periphery and (Neo)imperialist International Relations', *European Journal of International Relations*, 19: 627–646.
Waltz, K. N. (1979) *Theory of International Politics*, Reading: Addison-Wesley.

5

SECURITIZATION AND THE LIMITS OF DEMOCRATIC SECURITY

Arlene B. Tickner

From independence in the 19th century until the 1980s, when a wave of democracy took hold in much of Latin America and violent armed conflict in Central America was nearing an end, security thinking and policy was almost exclusively the domain of the military. During the Cold War in particular, the leading mode of thought, national security doctrine (NSD), legitimated authoritarian rule and widespread repression of leftist dissent, based upon the idea that domestic 'Communist' movements constituted the region's largest security threat. For the last 30 years, however, Latin American scholars and practitioners have challenged traditional, militarized readings of security, and developed new and alternative conceptions following democratization.

Within both the global policy world and the academic fields of international relations and security studies, a debate has simmered during this same period over the very concept of security. While previous use of the term was commonly restricted to external military threats posed to states, critical scholars have argued that it should be widened to include nonmilitary problems and other referent objects (most importantly, individuals) (Krause and Williams 1997). At the international level, this discussion has revolved mainly around 'human security,' whereas in Latin America, it was originally coined in terms of 'democratic security' (DS) and has focused more recently on 'multidimensional' and 'citizen security' (see Serbin and Serbin; Goldstein, this volume). Conversely, proponents of the so-called Copenhagen school (Wæver 1995; Buzan et al. 1998; Buzan and Wæver 2003) have expressed skepticism towards the widening of 'security,' given the potentially negative consequences of securitization.[1]

In Latin America, little scholarly attention has been paid to the processes through which the meaning of security has changed or to the political implications of such shifts. In this chapter I analyze democratic security as a crucial stage of civilian-based security thinking that coincided with attempts to broaden the concept at the Cold War's end, but that is also unique to the region's historical and political landscape.[2] To this latter end, I show that democratic security is tied to both the policy challenges faced by governments following the transition from dictatorship to democracy – namely, removing the military from the political realm and designing a security and defense architecture characterized by civilian control and respect for democracy – and to dominant regional conceptions of knowledge rooted largely in the need to provide practical expertise susceptible to being translated into public policy formulae (Tickner 2008).

Following a brief discussion of securitization theory, I review the academic literature on both national security doctrine and democratic security in order to show that security-based analyses of democratization, demilitarization, and cooperation have regularly overlooked the potential political risks of securitization, including the empowerment of the state to enact emergency measures, the adoption of a 'friend-enemy' mentality, the removal of topics from public debate, and ultimately the undermining of the democratic process. Although the democratic security concept constituted a reaction to the most noxious effects of NSD – authoritarianism, militarization, and repression – the securitization of democracy entails analogous risks that security scholars would be well advised to examine. I identify several in the chapter's final section and point to potential areas of future research that could possibly address this gap.

Securitization

The Copenhagen school revolves around three main ideas: securitization, the distinction between security discourses taking place in diverse sectors (military, political, economic, societal, and environmental), and regional processes or security complexes (Wæver 1995; Buzan et al. 1998; Wæver 2012). Although academic debate has centered largely on securitization, which is ultimately what defines the school metatheoretically, the study of sectors and regional security complexes offers additional lenses for analyzing specific empirical cases, as I will suggest in my discussion of Latin American security scholarship.

Securitization is rooted in a post-positivist reading of reality in which 'security' cannot be understood as an objective condition, but rather is a subjective (and intersubjective) social construct. Namely, through discursive practice or speech acts, diverse issues *become* security threats. According to Wæver, "[b]y uttering 'security' a state-representative moves a particular development into a specific area, and thereby claims a special right to do use whatever means are necessary to block it" (1995: 55). When issues are defined successfully as security threats, elites can circumvent ordinary rules of the political game with greater ease, public debate tends to stop, and citizens are more likely to accept state decisions without much questioning. Equally important for my discussion, securitization is often adverse to democracy, given that it bypasses key mechanisms and institutions of the democratic process, leading in extreme instances to militarization. In contrast, desecuritization involves "the shifting of issues out of the emergency mode into the normal bargaining processes of the political sphere" (Buzan et al. 1998: 4).

Therefore, the main focus of securitization is not the identification and classification of different security problems, given that there are no objective threats, but how elites label specific issues as security threats and to what effect (Eriksson 1999). The 'how possible' questions typical of securitization normally require dense empirical description to account for this process, including: the specific political dynamics that lead to securitization and desecuritization, the discourses used to construct securitizing moves, the specific actors that perform them, the diverse referent objects identified as being threatened, their respective threats, and the audiences to which securitizing moves are directed. In this sense, securitization might be considered a causal mechanism of an interpretative kind: ". . . why certain moves can be expected in given national security discourses, why some of them may find a receptive audience . . . and indeed why certain action-complexes can then follow. But such 'why' is always a 'how causality' " (Guzzini 2011: 338).

Although securitization processes are at the core of both national security doctrine and democratic security, two of the main lenses through which security has been practiced and analyzed in Latin America, they have not been adequately scrutinized in the scholarly literature, as will be illustrated in the sections that follow.

National security doctrine

National security doctrine constituted a "conceptual system" (Cavagnari and Lesbat 1994: 52), adopted region-wide during the 1960s, which was highly influenced by French and U.S. strategic thinking (Stepan 1971; Comblin 1978; Lowenthal and Fitch 1986; Pion-Berlin 1989; Leal 1994). Following the onset of the Cold War, U.S. security interests in Latin America and the Caribbean grew, with which regional security dynamics became largely entwined with the bipolar conflict. Institutional arrangements such as the Inter-American Reciprocal Defense Treaty (Rio Treaty of 1947) and bilateral military assistance agreements provided channels for hemispheric defense cooperation, while the School of the Americas (SOA) provided the main venue through which knowledge transfer took place and ideological bonds were formed. Between 1946 and 2001, the SOA trained over 60,000 members of the Latin American military in counterinsurgency theory and tactics (Gill 2004: 6). The level of collusion was such that it lent itself to joint anticommunist efforts, as occurred with Operation Cóndor, a South American intelligence network created to combat the leftist opposition with U.S. assistance (McSherry 2005).

The Cuban Revolution (1959) and the mushrooming of guerilla movements throughout Latin America confirmed an elite-based reading of instability and insecurity as rooted in a communist threat deriving from national armed insurgencies and leftist governments, thus hastening the adoption of NSD. Notwithstanding slight national variations, regional security policies exhibited a series of shared assumptions concerning security, its relation to development, the state, and the definition of threat. Independently of regime type, NSD validated the large-scale involvement of the armed forces in politics. In addition to traditional defense matters and the preservation of domestic order, Latin American militaries came to see their mission as exercising control over the state. Historically, the military has been one of the main institutions in Latin America, along with the state and the church, and its self-conception has been rooted largely in the idea that it embodies order, the 'nation,' and even "Christianity" (Mares 2008: 390). As a caretaker of the 'state' and 'nation,' the military thus came to see itself as 'above' civilian rule and answerable only to the 'nation.'

Among the military's goals in penetrating the state, 'securing' the social order became a key objective. To the extent that individual security and freedom were deemed at odds with national security, the prevailing view espoused by NSD was that these needed to be sacrificed in the name of the 'greater good.' This tendency was common both in countries that succumbed to authoritarianism and in formal democracies in which states of exception were declared permanently in order to bypass laws or rules that might impair the state's self-defense (Loveman 1994).

The main source of communist threat identified by NSD was local in origin, and not the Soviet Union, with which the 'internal enemy' became the central target of security policies. The resulting 'friend-enemy' logic led to generalized persecution and repression of both armed insurgencies and any other opposition group deemed to obstruct state objectives. In the more extreme cases of authoritarian rule this amorphous 'enemy' was regularly portrayed as a 'tumor' or 'cancer' that needed to be extracted from an organic body politic (O'Donnell 1978; Pion-Berlin 1989).

In addition to a militarized, reductionist reading of security, NSD also reinforced a particular conception of the Latin American state (O'Donnell 1975, 1978; Maira 1990; Mares 2008). Guillermo O'Donnell refers to this 'national security state,' as it evolved in Brazil and the Southern Cone (and Mexico, under the PRI), with the adjective *bureaucratic-authoritarian* (BA), but many of its core traits are observable throughout the region. The catalysts for this model included rapid economic modernization, industrialization, and social change largely associated with the rise of the middle and popular classes. BA regimes set out to restimulate economic growth and development, for which domestic order was considered a necessary precondition. Distinct measures were adopted to achieve these goals, including: the use of extensive repression; the reversal of political and economic gains of recently enfranchised popular classes;[3] the depoliticization of economic, social, and political life; the division of distinct leadership tasks between the armed forces and civilian technocrats; and the renewal of strategic alliances with foreign capital (O'Donnell 1975, 1978; Maira 1990; see Collier 1980 for a critique and reformulation of bureaucratic-authoritarianism).

NSD was functional to this state model in that it offered an interpretation of instability and threat that meshed well with bureaucratic-authoritarianism's objectives; namely, that political, economic, and social crisis, under the guise of communism or popular upheaval, inhibited national development. Given that both the military and political elites viewed the latter as the driving force of the nation, national development and national security became a mutually reinforcing duo around which the Latin American state, as well as security policy and thinking, gravitated.

Democratic security

The end of the Cold War, the transition to democracy in South America, the peaceful settlement of the civil wars in Central America, and liberal economic reform all led to a re-visioning of security in the late 1980s. The main challenge during this period was to create a post-authoritarian, postconflict, post–Cold War blueprint for security and defense policies in which the armed forces were placed firmly under civilian control. At the same time, Latin American states were concerned with designing region-wide institutional frameworks, given the shared assumption that economic liberalization and integration were crucial to both democratization and to hemispheric stability and security (Hurrell 1998; Tulchin and Espach 1998; Oelsner 2009; Herz 2010). Although the bipolar conflict and NSD had in fact provided a common framework for cooperative action, understandably it was deemed antithetical to these goals in the new post–Cold War era.

The drivers of this specific Latin American mode of security-widening by association with democracy hailed from several corners of the hemisphere and from abroad. Initially, the South American Peace, Security, and Democracy Commission, created in 1987 by a group of ex-presidents, politicians, clergy members, private sector representatives, and academics, conceived the term 'democratic security' (DS) as an alternative to national security doctrine (Comisión Sudamericana de Paz 1988; Somavía and Insulza 1990). President Oscar Arias, the architect of the Arias Peace Plan, picked up this thinking through Costa Rica's interaction with the Contadora Support Group (created in 1985), and via direct dialogue with the Commission. Foreign governments too, especially from Europe, where scholars and peace activists were involved in their own widening debates (Wæver 2012), influenced regional discussions through their involvement in both the transition to democracy and the Central American peace process.

DS might also be viewed as a by-product of what I have described elsewhere as Latin America's stab at independent thinking in international relations (Tickner 2008, 2009), in which the problem of autonomy figured prominently. Given that debates on security, defense, and public order were monopolized by the armed forces, developments within regional IR did not spread to the security realm until the late 1980s. Augusto Varas (1987: 9) suggests that the subordinate relations that characterized Latin America's post-independence history applied to the military sector as well, in the guise of strategic doctrines, concepts, and technological transfers supplied by foreign actors. However, 'new' security thinking sought to assert itself both conceptually and politically via civilian autonomy and control over the military; autonomy from NSD, identified as the source of the armed forces' encroachment upon the state; and autonomy from the main author of national security thinking and policy, the United States.

Democratic security was thus a neologism developed largely in opposition to the widely accepted concepts of national security and defense, both of which highlight the independence, territorial integrity, and sovereign rights of the state against external (or internal) threats. In contrast, as employed in both South and Central America, DS was conceived as an integral, ". . . more encompassing and positive concept that prioritizes the needs of individuals to live in peace and to have access to the economic, political and environmental resources required for a dignified existence" (Somavía and Insulza 1990: 7). Security was thus envisioned as a *human* need rooted in the absence of economic, social, political, military, cultural, judicial, and ecological threat (Comisión Sudamericana de Paz 1988: 10), while national security doctrine placed the security of the *state* and the *nation* (narrowly defined) above that of Latin American citizens, justifying systematic repression and exclusion, and the political tutelage of the armed forces. Institutional development, democracy, respect for human rights, civilian control over the military, and economies geared towards the satisfaction of basic needs were therefore highlighted as the main domestic ingredients of DS.

On paper at least, democratic security as developed in Latin America seems quite similar to the now popular idea of human security, and was actually coined earlier. The first and most widely cited definition of the latter, developed by the United Nations Development Program (UNDP) in 1994, highlights the safety of individuals from all-encompassing chronic threats and needs, both physical and other (Paris 2001: 89–90). However, human security was never embraced by regional security scholars (see Rojas and Gaucha 2002, for one exception). As I will discuss subsequently, this apparent misfit underscores the fact that DS, notwithstanding its supposed emphasis on people, operates within the same state-centrism characteristic of traditional definitions of security.

Furthermore, the tendency to view the state as the main referent object to be protected, and the principal agent responsible for providing security to individuals (Rial 1990), points to an important ambiguity in Latin American thinking. Perhaps better than any other policy document of this period, the Framework Treaty on Democratic Security in Central America, signed in 1995, embodies this tension by incorporating state-based provisions such as the separation of military and police matters, civilian control of the armed forces and the police, free and democratic elections, *and* individual freedoms and social development as prerequisites of security (Urgell 2006/2007).

Another key offshoot of the democratic security concept was the shared perception that regional cooperation, integration, and institutionalization were critical instruments of democratization and security. The Contadora group, created originally by Mexico, Venezuela, Colombia, and Panama to seek a negotiated settlement to armed conflicts in Central America, was the first to assert this link, and was followed shortly thereafter by the Rio Group (in which democracy became a prerequisite for membership) and the OAS, which adopted a 'democratic security clause' via the Santiago Declaration and Resolution 1080 (1991), the Washington Protocol (1992), and the Democratic Charter (2001) (Oeslner 2009; Herz 2010). Other regional organizations, including MERCOSUR (Common Market of the South), CAN (Andean Community of Nations), and UNASUR (Union of South American Nations), followed suit by internalizing formal democracy as the sole legitimate form of government.

DS was thus a multipronged concept geared towards ". . . assuring development with social justice at the domestic level, deepening peace, cooperation and integration at the regional level, and autonomy and independence internationally" (Comisión Sudamericana de Paz 1998: 33). However, Latin American scholarship on democratic security focused almost exclusively on providing knowledge relevant to regional policy processes, which in practice translated into state-centric studies on civil-military relations (Rial 1990; Oliveira 1994; Diamint 2001), the differentiation between security and defense, and the development of confidence-building measures (Varas 1987; Palma 1990; Tulchin and Rojas 1998; Domínguez 1998). In the minds of civilian policy-makers and academics alike, constraining the role of the military and subjecting it to democratic control, on the one hand, and reducing high levels of interstate mistrust, on the other, constituted two of the main challenges faced by the majority of Latin American countries. Both were rooted in the need to reclaim security and defense from the hands of the armed forces, to design civilian-led policies, and to replace regional power balancing, rivalry, and conflict preparedness – relational patterns that would eventually prompt greater military involvement – with cooperative security (see Serbin and Serbin, this volume).

As a result of the above, the requisite measures for enhancing security cooperation, in particular transparency, confidence-building, and institutional strengthening, came to the fore of the regional research agenda, given their role in administering civil-military relations locally. According to Jorge I. Domínguez (1998:12), "[u]ltimately, the goal might be to create what Karl Deutsch . . . called pluralistic security communities" in which member countries agree that ". . . common social problems must and can be resolved . . . without resort to large-scale physical force." Despite the existence of shared interests and identities rooted in a common commitment to democratization, and ultimately conducive to cooperative relations, up until the late 1990s authors such as Domínguez (1998) and Andrew Hurrell (1998) observed that the norms and rules, mature institutions, and 'we-feeling' characteristic of security communities were still missing in Latin America, even in the Central and South American subregional contexts in which DS was most firmly established.

Notwithstanding its unquestionable contribution to peace, cooperation, integration, and democratization in Latin America, as well as to more recent debates on multidimensional and citizen security, the democratic security concept is beset by a paradox that regional security studies have yet to disentangle. Although borne out of an acute sensitivity to the ways in which national security had been deployed by the military in the past in support of antidemocratic and repressive purposes, the widened definition developed by DS did not produce nearly the same degree of wariness towards securitization, underlining the lack of scholarly attention to the performative effects of security discourse. Instead, once security policy and thinking was 'demilitarized' and switched hands from the armed forces to civilians, many of the concerns aired previously with the undesirable effects of security became less palpable and more subdued.

Securitization as a research agenda

To securitize or not, and the dangers of securitization, have been common features of the Latin American security lexicon since the transition to democracy (Oelsner 2009; Herz 2010). Although the risk of widening was recognized early on, precisely given the history of authoritarianism and military domination over the security realm, frequent use of the term in public discourse and academic debate has been largely empty of much of securitization's theoretical and epistemological content (Tickner and Herz 2012: 108). Two silences are especially noteworthy in Latin American security studies. First, little actual research has been conducted on the political effects of security 'speech acts' in terms of militarization and de-democratization. Second, the controversy over 'what' or 'who' is to be secured, which is central to securitization theory, has been relatively inexistent. As mentioned previously, regional security thinking continues to be state-centric (Herz 2010: 606), even though on paper at least, democratic security places the individual squarely at its center.

Basically, DS widened security by including issues of political regime. My discussion of the democratic security literature suggests that this entailed three distinct but related objectives: (1) state protection of the democratic rights, broadly defined, of *individuals*; (2) protection of newly democratized, civilian-run *states* from military encroachment; and (3) strengthening of *regional* integration and institutions. In the first meaning, the democratic rights of the citizens are the referent object that is under threat, whereas in the second and third, the democratic state is in danger (and is threatened by the military). As highlighted previously, one of the main questions raised by securitizing moves such as these is related to the political dynamics that they set into play.

According to Andrea Oelsner (2009: 197), one of the few, if not the only, Latin American scholars to examine democratic security from a securitization perspective, in the 1980s in South America "[t]here was a convergent perception . . . that failing to secure stable democratic systems and equitable economic conditions could endanger the very viability of the region's states." Therefore, 'democracy' and 'development' were securitized by civilian elites, while the emergency measures required to block the single largest threat to them – namely, the military – included overcoming animosity with regional neighbors and strengthening regional cooperative institutions. Not surprisingly, Latin American citizens were nowhere to be seen in this equation. Oelsner views securitization in a positive light, as according to her it provided the groundwork for a regional security architecture that reflected consensus among member countries concerning what the main threats were. More significantly, as democracy stabilized, in no small measure due to its securitization, it ". . . was progressively moved out of the regional security agenda and began to be dealt with through regular political procedures" (Oelsner 2009: 203).

The logic described runs counter to the Copenhagen school's expectation that securitization puts into play processes and outcomes that may ultimately undermine democracy, including emergency politics, militarization, and a national security mindset (Wæver 1995; Buzan et al. 1998), and thus points to an interesting area of future research. No less important, in their treatment of security complexes, Buzan and Wæver (2003) predict that the transition from regional 'conflict formation,' characteristic of Latin America before democratization, to one of 'security community' entails both the replacement of patterns of enmity with amity and a process of desecuritization. However, as the authors themselves note in the case of MERCOSUR, once it was deemed that democracy was no longer under threat in the subregion, the institution lost its main source of cohesion and its sense of urgency (Buzan and Wæver 2003: 325).

What this suggests is that securitization also provides salience to specific issues that run the risk of becoming unimportant or irrelevant when they are desecuritized and thus returned to normal and routine procedures (Booth 2007: 165). Therefore, the harmful implications of widening security need to be weighed more systematically against the potential benefits of such a bid. Two negatives that stand out in the case of the DS concept include its state-centrism and its awkward relation to militarization.

State-centrism

International relations and security studies in Latin America, in keeping with dominant global trends, have focused largely upon matters of the state (Tickner 2009). Notwithstanding its battle against national security doctrine, DS targeted the state as its main referent object, given the identification of a certain political regime type (namely, authoritarianism) as the main threat to both national and regional insecurity. In doing so, democratic security became a powerful discourse for talking about the affairs of the state and the duties of democratic regimes towards their citizens. Contrary to academic work on human security, however, Latin American analysts of DS never made individuals their main object of study, nor have regional security studies in general interrogated their own tendency towards state-centrism.

Although the distinctiveness of the Latin American state is implicit in concepts such as democratic security, and has been addressed in significant depth by the dependency school, among others, rarely do security scholars engage with the conceptual implications of such difference. Even less has the modern Westphalian state model and its implications for thinking about security in the region been questioned. According to Mohammed Ayoob (1995: 11), the 'Third World' security problematique is closely linked to the state formation process. In particular, postcolonial states are characterized by insufficient levels of 'stateness,' described by the author as a combination of coercive capacities, infrastructural power and efficiency, and legitimacy. Therefore, insecurity is largely the by-product of a lack of unconditional legitimacy of state borders, institutions and representatives, and low levels of consensus concerning fundamental political, economic, and social themes (Ayoob 1995: 28).

Given the centrality of state strengthening in the political life of Latin American countries and the fact that most activities associated with this process carry the name 'security,' the logical conclusion to Ayoob's argument is that Latin American states securitize in specific ways and that a fundamental portion of elite behavior revolves around the securitization of those issues deemed to endanger the effectiveness and survival of the state (Tickner 2004). Viewing the state as a site of contestation and tracing shifts in the salience of distinct security sectors (military, political, economic, societal, and environmental) constitutes just one way in which the securitizing moves of regional elites might be analyzed.

A second avenue of promising inquiry relates precisely to 'who' performs securitization. In contexts of incomplete state-building and democratization especially, such as those that characterize much of Latin America, 'security' is performed exclusively by elites, and rarely by citizens writ large or even specific social groups. As Lene Hansen (2000) argues in the case of gender, securitization theory presupposes the existence of situations in which speech, and thus securitizing moves, are in fact possible. However, in cases of marginalized actors, including but not limited to women, insecurities cannot be voiced due to both a lack of access to political channels and to the potentially counterproductive effects of securitizing given issues, such as sexual or drug-related violence in Latin America.

Securitization and militarization

The DS debate in Latin America also highlights the fact that articulating alternative security concerns outside the domain of the military is at once an attractive and dangerous option. Regional efforts to demilitarize security policy and thinking following the transition to democracy have yet to be matched by systematic reflection on the affinity between securitization and militarization. Admittedly, the two terms are not synonymous. Although securitization often works in favor of the use of military solutions to existential threats so-defined, military means are not necessarily the automatic strategy of choice when a securitizing move is made.

As highlighted previously, the historical legacy of dictatorship and military involvement in the political sphere in Latin America led to concerted efforts to demilitarize the security domain at both the national and the regional levels. The implicit assumption of regional scholarship on DS seems indeed to be that by replacing the adjective 'military' with 'civilian,' 'security' could be broadened to include nontraditional issues, such as democracy, thus correcting the reductionist nature of national security doctrine, while at the same time keeping the military and militarization at bay.

Securitization theory points to the faulty nature of this argument, first by highlighting the risk of aggrandizing state power, even when in civilian hands, and second by showing that establishing civilian control over the military, however urgent, is not tantamount to demilitarization or desecuritization. Militarization can be described as a process by which societal acceptance of military participation and militaristic means for solving distinct problems becomes normalized (Enloe 2004: 217–219). In securitizing democracy, it could be argued that DS put into play a contradictory logic in which, at the same time that military participation in the security realm was eschewed, the declaration of an existential threat to democracy called for extraordinary and eventually militarized measures. In other words, among its undesired effects, securitization begets militarization. Therefore, and paradoxically, securitizing moves such as DS may lead to (re)militarization, even though their intended objective is just the opposite. Identifying how and when this occurs constitutes a key item on the securitization research agenda. In particular, more rigorous empirical description is called for in order to gain greater insight into the different discursive repertoires employed by Latin American states and the distinct securitization processes that are produced therein.

Conclusions

Since the 1980s, when security was first linked to democracy and regional integration via the DS concept, Latin American security scholars have gone to great lengths debating the desired scope of 'security' and the types of issues that it should and should not envelop. Nevertheless, scant debate has taken place over what security *does*. My discussion of securitization theory suggests that moving issues to the security agenda, as occurred in the case of democracy security, is an essentially conflicted decision. While successfully focusing national and regional attention and energies on democratization, the logic of urgency/emergency introduced by securitization runs the risk of undermining the very democratic process that DS was intended to strengthen, and reinforces the centrality of the state, thus reducing the importance of citizens and individuals in general.

Despite fears that a broad, multidimensional definition of security might produce unwanted militarization of distinct regional issues, a critical interrogation of security as a speech act and a political process has yet to be conducted. In the case of DS, rather than leading to a wider theorization on the links between security, democracy, the state, and regional integration, and on the political implications of securitization, the 'new' security thinking introduced by this concept morphed into applied analyses on civil-military relations and confidence-building measures. Hence, while DS may have underwritten innovative and democratic security strategies in Latin America, it failed to produce a solid conceptual framework within which to understand security in the region.

In addition to offering a novel research agenda, securitization theory points to the responsibility of analysts (and not only practitioners) to reflect critically on what is at stake politically when specific issues are identified as dangers and threats. Both democratic security thinking and its contemporary successor, citizen security, underscore the lack of attention to date in Latin American scholarship to the performative effects of security discourse, especially when practiced by civilians.

Notes

1 Securitization is a discursive process (or speech act) by which an actor states that a referent object 'x' is threatened, claims the right to take extraordinary measures to deal with the threat, and convinces an audience that such action, which bypasses public debate and democratic procedures, is justified. See Buzan et al. (1998: 23–26).

2 My analysis draws from both general accounts of international relations in Latin America developed previously (Tickner 2003, 2009) and a more recent examination of regional security thinking (Tickner and Herz 2012).

3 Other Latin American countries that did not succumb to authoritarianism also enacted elite pacts in order to dismantle popular demands.

References

Ayoob, M. (1995) *The Third World Security Predicament*, Boulder: Lynne Rienner Publishers.

Booth, K. (2007) *Theory of World Security*, Cambridge: University of Cambridge Press.

Buzan, B., de Wilde, J. and Wæver, O. (1998) *Security: A New Framework for Analysis*, Boulder: Lynne Rienner Publishers.

Buzan, B. and Wæver, O. (2003) *Regions and Powers*, Cambridge: Cambridge University Press.

Cavagnari, F. and Lesbat, G. (1994) 'América del Sur: Algunos elementos para la definición de la seguridad nacional' in F. Leal Buitrago and J. G. Tokatlian (eds) *Orden mundial y seguridad. Nuevos desafíos para Colombia y América Latina*, Bogotá: TM Editores-SID-IEPRI.

Collier, D. (ed) (1980) *The New Authoritarianism in Latin America*, Princeton: Princeton University Press.

Comblin, J. (1978) *A ideologia da Segurança Nacional: O poder militar na América Latina*, Rio de Janeiro: Civilização Brasileira.

Comisión Sudamericana para la paz, la seguridad regional y la democracia (1988) *Second Plenary Session, June 8–10, 1988*, Santiago de Chile: Instituto Latinoamericano de Estudios Transnacionales.

Diamint, R. (2001) *Seguridad y democracia en América Latina*, Buenos Aires: GEL-Nuevohacer-Universidad Torcuato Di Tella.

Domínguez, J. I. (ed) (1998) *International Security and Democracy. Latin America and the Caribbean in the Post-Cold War Era*, Pittsburgh: University of Pittsburgh Press.

Enloe, C. (2004) *The Curious Feminist: Searching for Women in a New Age of Empire*, Berkeley: University of California Press.

Eriksson, J. (1999) 'Observers or Analysts? On the Political Role of Security Analysts', *Cooperation and Conflict*, 3(3): 311–330.

Gill, L. (2004) *The School of the Americas, Military Training and Political Violence in the Americas*, Durham: Duke University Press.

Guzzini, S. (2011) 'Securitization as a Causal Mechanism', *Security Dialogue*, 42(4–5): 329–341.

Hansen, L. (2000) 'The Little Mermaid's Silent Security Dilemma and the Absence of Gender in the Copenhagen School', *Milennium*, 29(2): 285–306.

Herz, M. (2010) 'Concepts of Security in South America', *International Peacekeeping*, 17(5): 598–612.

Hurrell, A. (1998) 'An Emerging Security Community in South America?' in E. Adler and M. Barnett (eds) *Security Communities*, Cambridge: University of Cambridge Press, pp. 228–264.

Krause, K. and Williams, M. C. (eds) (1997) *Critical Security Studies*, Minneapolis: University of Minnesota Press.

Leal Buitrago, F. (1994) *El oficio de la guerra. La seguridad nacional en Colombia*, Bogotá: TM Editores-IEPRI.

Loveman, B. (1994) *The Constitution of Tyranny. Regimes of Exception in South America*, Pittsburgh: University of Pittsburgh Press.

Lowenthal, A. F. and Fitch, J. S. (eds) (1986) *Armies and Politics in Latin America*, New York: Holmes & Meier.

Maira, L. (1990) 'El estado de la seguridad nacional en América Latina' in P. González Casanova (ed) *El Estado en América Latina. Teoría y práctica*, Mexico: Siglo XXI Editores-Universidad de la ONU, pp. 108–131.

Mares, D. (2008) 'The National Security State' in T. H. Holloway (ed) *A Companion to Latin American History*, Oxford: Wiley-Blackwell, pp. 386–405.

McSherry, J. P. (2005) *Predatory States: Operation Condor and Covert War in Latin America*, Boulder: Rowman & Littlefield Publishers.
O'Donnell, G. (1975) 'Reflexiones sobre las tendencias generales de cambio en el Estado burocrático-autoritario', *Documento CEDES-CLACSO*, 1.
——— (1978) 'Tensiones en el Estado burocrático-autoritario y la cuestión de la democracia', *Documento CEDES-CLACSO*, 11.
Oelsner, A. (2009) 'Consensus and Governance in Mercosur: The Evolution of the South American Security Agenda', *Security Dialogue*, 40(2): 191–212.
Oliveira, F.E.B. (1994) *Social Security Systems in Latin America*, Washington, DC: Inter-American Development Bank.
Palma, H. (1990) 'Medidas de confianza recíproca' in J. Somavía and J. M. Insulza (eds) *Seguridad democrática regional. Una concepción alternativa*, Santiago: Comisión Sudamericana de Paz-Nueva Sociedad, pp. 283–319.
Paris, R. (2001) 'Human Security. Paradigm Shift or Hot Air?', *International Security*, 26(2): 87–102.
Pion-Berlin, D. (1989) 'Latin American National Security Doctrines: Hard and Softline Themes', *Armed Forces & Society*, 15(3): 411–429.
Rial, J. (1990) 'Relaciones cívico-militares: Diálogo para el fortalecimiento de la democracia' in J. Somavía and J. M. Insulza (eds) *Seguridad democrática regional. Una concepción alternativa*, Santiago: Comisión Sudamericana de Paz-Nueva Sociedad, pp. 253–264.
Rojas Aravena, F. and Gaucha, M. (2002) *Seguridad humana, prevención de conflictos y paz*, Santiago: UNESCO-FLACSO.
Somavía, J. and Insulza, J. M. (eds) (1990) *Seguridad democrática regional. Una concepción alternativa*, Santiago: Comisión Sudamericana de Paz-Nueva Sociedad.
Stepan, A. (1971) *The Military in Politics. Changing Patterns in Brazil*, Princeton: Princeton University Press.
Tickner, A. B. (2003, January 1). 'Seeing IR Differently: Notes from the Third World', *Millennium/London School of Economics*, 322: 295–324.
——— (2004) 'La securitización de la crisis colombiana: Bases conceptuales y tendencias generales', *Colombia Internacional*, 60: 13–35.
——— (2008) 'Latin American IR and the Primacy of *lo práctico*', *International Studies Review*, 10(4): 735–748.
——— (2009) 'Latin America. Still Policy Dependent after all these Years?' in A. B. Tickner and O. Wæver (eds) *International Relations Scholarship around the World*, London: Routledge, pp. 32–52.
Tickner, A. B. and Herz, M. (2012) 'No Place for Theory? Security Studies in Latin America' in A. B. Tickner and D. L. Blaney (eds) *Thinking International Relations Differently*, London: Routledge, pp. 92–114.
Tulchin, J. S. and Espach, R. H. (1998) 'Confidence Building in the Americas: A Conclusion' in J. S. Tulchin and F. Rojas Aravena (eds) *Strategic Balance and Confidence Building Measures in the Americas*, Washington, DC: Woodrow Wilson Center Press-Stanford University Press, pp. 172–178.
Tulchin, J. S. and Rojas Aravena, F. (eds) (1998) *Strategic Balance and Confidence Building Measures in the Americas*, Washington, DC: Woodrow Wilson Center Press-Stanford University Press.
Urgell García, J. (2006/2007) 'La seguridad (humana) en Centroamérica: ¿Retomo al pasado?', *Revista CIDOB D'Afers Internacionals*, 76: 143–158.
Varas, A. (1987) 'De la competencia a la cooperación militar en América Latina' in A. Varas (ed) *Paz, desarme y desarrollo en América Latina*, Buenos Aires: GEL-RIAL, pp. 9–21.
Wæver, O. (1995) 'Securitization and Desecuritization' in R. D. Lipschutz (ed) *On Security*, New York: Columbia University Press, pp. 46–86.
——— (2012) 'Aberystwyth, Paris, Copenhagen: The Europeanness of New "Schools" of Security Theory in an American Field' in A. B. Tickner and D. L. Blaney (eds) *Thinking International Relations Differently*, London: Routledge, pp. 48–71.

6
GENDER IN SECURITY STUDIES

Marcela Donadio

A look at global discourse over the past two decades corroborates the assumption that gender and security are linked: One can observe this link in debates and sometimes in policies, as well as in multilateral initiatives such as those of the United Nations Security Council through its resolutions on Women, Peace, and Security.[1] Also – referring now to the Latin American context – several countries have modified their policies in order to open up space for the issue of gender within the armed forces and, to a lesser extent, within police institutions. The need to consider the issue of gender has become the norm in both academic and political contexts, especially since the adoption of Security Council Resolution 1325 in 2000.

Yet, there has been little reflection on the linkage between security and gender at the conceptual level. The security field still seems to be centered on historical deliberations regarding concepts such as human security, national security, and complex security issues without opening itself up much to a discussion of how they impact theoretical and practical developments in the areas of economics, politics, and gender.

In this chapter I suggest how security studies in Latin America could benefit from the incorporation of a gender perspective, arguing that a strategic alliance between the fields of security and gender is an imperative for further development in both disciplines. I analyze the existence of communication difficulties between both areas, the demands of the international community, and the influence of the incorporation of women into the armed forces and its relationship with the process of democratization. I conclude that a concept of security adjusted to contemporary challenges must incorporate the gender dimension.

The link between gender and security

We understand security as the situation in which states are capable of dissuading and/or facing up to threats to their vital interests, so that their citizens are able to develop individual lives freely and in peace. Similarly, we understand gender according to the definition used by the United Nations: "Gender refers to the socially constructed roles as ascribed to women and men, as opposed to biological and physical characteristics. Gender roles vary according to socio-economic, political and cultural contexts, and are affected by other factors, including age, race, class, and ethnicity" (United Nations 2002: 12). 'Gender' is not thus solely about women and sex.

An important debate has focused on the very object of security: Should the *state* or the *individual* be the principal object of security? This issue remains highly controversial in Latin America. The experiences of the military dictatorships generated certain hostility towards the category of 'national security' (see Tickner, this volume), and in turn, it opened the way for a broader understanding of security, such as that proposed by then secretary general of the United Nations: ". . . a new understanding of the concept of security is evolving. Once synonymous with the defense of territory from external attack, the requirements of security today have come to embrace the protection of communities and individuals from internal violence" (Annan 2001: 43). But neither regionally nor globally is a gender perspective present in security analysis. An example of this is suggested by Sjoberg and Martin in an interesting analysis of the relationship between these fields: "Less than forty out of more than 5,000 articles in the top five security studies journals over the last twenty years explicitly address gender issues as a major substantive theme" (Sjoberg and Martin 2007: 2). In 2013, of the articles published in leading journals, such as *International Security* and *Security Studies*, only 12 per cent of authors were women.

Thus, theoretical developments in the fields of security and gender have advanced along separate lines, with no clear connection between the two. While political developments encourage a linkage between the two concepts (as suggested by the increasing vulnerability of women in armed conflicts and resulting societal and media demands, both locally and internationally), it is difficult to find theoretical works that explain this link.

Security analysts have been reluctant to incorporate gender issues into the discipline. The same cannot be said about specialists in gender studies, especially within feminism; both in North America and Europe there have been numerous works about 'security in gender studies.' Academic efforts to bring security analysts into the field of gender have been intense in both regions, but not in Latin America, where not even an approach from gender towards security has been produced. Maybe this is due to the resistance that the military issue still generates in countries with a painful history in this respect. In addition, the claim by security experts that "technical knowledge about the military is necessary" hinders opening up a discipline that struggles to communicate not just with gender studies, but also with economics and anthropology.

The level of theoretical abstraction that tends to be presented in gender studies may also complicate the linkage between the two. As one of the most frequently cited pieces of work on the issue notes, "to scholars trained in conventional scientific methodologies, feminist approaches appear to be atheoretical" (Tickner 1996: 612–614). My own experience over the last six years giving conferences and interviewing security actors, seeking to introduce a gender perspective into security discussions, is revealing. The first 20 minutes of any activity are a test in which it is necessary to gain the other's trust, as if the very introduction of the topic was a threat. In fact, the mere mention of the word 'gender' implies an immediate barrier in theoretical debates and their derivatives. It gives birth to attitudes such as "it ought to be like this," "political correctness," and the thought of "again this topic? What else do they want?" – or more unconsciously, "they are talking about gender but really what they want to discuss is sexual abuse" – all feelings and impressions that are contained within the overall 'obligation' to listen to things that "have nothing to do with my daily job." In short, students of international relations do not believe that gender is related to international politics.

The fact that introducing this perspective is vital to the very survival of the discipline is often ignored. Would security analysis renounce the economic or ideological dimensions? Few would respond affirmatively, and it is certainly the fact that we would not even ask the question. The prejudices that we carry about gender, sometimes culturally ingrained, mean that we will ask ourselves things that would not even occur to us in relation to other fields of the social sciences. The gender dimension in human relations is inescapable. And given that not only states are the subject of study within the field of security, but individuals also, the discipline must stop referring to the issue simply because it is the politically correct thing to do, and begin to analyze and study it as something that is inherent to our human condition.

The cryptic language used in feminist studies does not help to link the two disciplines either, nor does the tendency to employ hypotheses without corroborations. Gender studies also have their own demons, one of which is the debate around the fact that gender not only refers to women, but also to men. Opportunities to introduce the topic (for example, in the hour and a half often allocated within predeployment courses for peacekeepers) are usually spent on presentations covering the differences between gender and sex, an abstract topic that lacks any sense if not translated into its significance for our daily life.

Finally, as various feminist studies underline, we should emphasize the fact that security has tended to be a topic dominated by a masculine presence, undermining the effort to bring the two areas together. Although the experience of the Latin American Security and Defense Network (RESDAL) with security actors has not revealed a significant difference in the reactions of men and women to the security topic, the impact of generations of socialization has made it difficult for feminist views to influence the thinking of people who have made successful careers in the security field.

The academic field of security studies has lagged behind the political developments made in regional and international politics, where the link between gender, peace, and security is now commonplace. But it is not the only area facing difficulties in adapting to changing realities: The same applies to many other topics, such as youth, religion, and rural/urban divide. The state-centered vision still predominates in a field that can consider such abstract and incommensurable topics as the strategic balance of power, yet at the same time ignores what are supposedly marginal issues, which in reality directly impact the discipline.[2] Among these is gender.

Impact on policies and security sector reforms

Gender issues are essential to security analysis with regard to at least three objects of study: society, armed institutions and security sector reform, and the types of conflicts. The world's population is almost exactly equally divided between men and women (50.4 per cent and 49.6 per cent, respectively, according to the World Bank). If the actions, ideas, and perceptions of these actors are immersed in any security context, it should be hypothesized that these actors have a gender perspective that impacts their individual perceptions, just as analysts do in the case of race, social class, or even national origin.

Turning to security sector reform and its analysis in Latin America, a number of relevant questions should be investigated. Does insecurity affect men and women equally? Are women more inclined to turn to peace than men? Does a feminine presence in a police operation help bring the institution closer to society? Do female and male soldiers respond differently in conflict situations? Do psychological vulnerabilities among soldiers vary by gender? Why is it that sexual violence as a weapon of war has spread across civil wars? These are among the issues that ought to be incorporated into security studies from a gender perspective.

Public policy reforms throughout Latin America have been followed by a gradual inclusion of gender discussions, acceptance of the gender equity paradigm, and prohibition of gender-based discrimination – as presented in international conventions, and even in the sanctioning of a regional convention on violence against women (Bélem do Pará 1994). The focus on gender in domestic security has been principally on intrafamily violence, although in the last two decades the phenomenon of femicide/feminicide[3] has begun to take a prominent place on the agenda, understood as a "phenomenon of gender-based violence related to social and political violence of unprecedented scope" (Cruz 2007: 45).

The mobilization of women has meant that in various countries acts that were once considered private or even shameful for the victims themselves are now considered public, providing new meanings to public security (Villalba 2006). The data on violence against women across the region are shocking. So is the invisibility of violence against women in public security discussions, and the case of Central America illustrates this. There is an overriding focus on homicide rates, yet the figures related to gender-based violence are telling of more complex social realities and structural forms of violence (see Table 6.1).

The formidable nature of these figures is further amplified when the larger context of the phenomenon is taken into account: The quantity of reports is just the tip of the iceberg, and it is estimated that many numbers of cases go unreported. Table 6.1 also suggests that significant cross-national variations may exist and need to be understood, including that some countries may underreport cases.

The debates on public security and the role of armed personnel representing the state in internal or external conflict situations raise two aspects that are central to the relationship between gender and security reform. One is the incorporation of female personnel into armed and police forces. Another concerns the training of all personnel regarding the impact and importance of gender in their institutional roles and interactions with society.

Generally speaking, the incorporation of women into police forces in Latin America was slow and related to the formation of national police institutions. Operational necessities led to their incorporation, especially with regard to functions related to social problems. These employment reforms were based on the idea that a female police officer can better approach the community and, as such, play the role of mediator and protector. Nevertheless, within the security forces, groups initially developed separately – all-female brigades, detachments, or auxiliary groups – and they were only gradually integrated into the rest of the police forces (Donadio and Mazzotta 2009: 82). In the context of democratization, the incorporation of females was accentuated by the desire of police institutions to build closer links with the population; the police's image, stained by the dictatorships during which the police forces became part of the military apparatus and, as such, of its abuses, needed to be linked in new ways to society. In Brazil, for example, human rights courses in the police training programs were introduced, and community policing was initiated (Soares and Musumeci 2005: 16).

Table 6.1 Homicides/gender-based violence in Central American countries, 2012

Country	*Homicides per 100,000 inhabitants*	*Per day*	*Cases of domestic violence reported per 100,000 inhabitants*	*Per day*
Costa Rica	8.8	1.1	104	13.4
El Salvador	41.5	7.1	20.4	3.5
Guatemala	34.3	14.1	33.3	13.7
Honduras	85.5	19.6	36.1	8.5
Nicaragua	11	1.8	170.9	28.4
Panama	17.8	1.8	94.5	9.8

Source: Public Security Index: Central America: Costa Rica, El Salvador, Guatemala, Honduras, Nicaragua and Panama, Buenos Aires: RESDAL, 2013.

The incorporation of women as a means of approaching society was important in the case of the armed forces as well. As with the police, there were bodies and sections that historically assigned certain positions to women – positions for which they were considered 'qualified,' such as assistants, doctors, lawyers, or nurses. However, the key to their full insertion is their incorporation into the officer ranks and into the officer academies.

The debates in Latin America about female incorporation into the security forces have not been so different from those in North America and Europe. Although there were differences in timing, and while in the latter cases the participation of women as uniformed personnel goes without saying, in Latin America it is a more recent theme, and there are very few female officers that have reached senior command positions – as of 2014, there is only one female general, in charge of a regiment in Bolivia. In the security field, the true challenge of incorporating women into the armed forces is to overcome the numerous clichés that surround the issue. The impulse to be politically correct impedes a true discussion on the role of military personnel (both women and men). Meanwhile, in diverse scenarios, such as peacekeeping operations, tokenism dominates. This term alludes to the practice in institutions and organizations of showing 'antidiscriminatory policies' through the inclusion of minorities, which are the 'token' to publicize, a display of what the minority in question can do. At the same time, it supposes a continuous observation of past practices by other employees or institutional actors, and several difficulties in the workplace (for example, when some perceive that minorities receive privileges that the majority do not) (Kanter 1977).

Photos appearing in newspapers every time a new female icon graduates, persistent discourses on women, and appointments 'due to being a woman' hide a deeper reality. It is rare for women to leave the barracks, given that they have purely administrative functions. Female military units deployed on peacekeeping missions generally have no direct contact with the local population. Senior male officers systematically send women to international events on gender. There is little real participation of women in the more coveted positions (for instance, the composition of military staff in the headquarters of international peace missions), and female soldiers are hindered by the famous 'glass ceilings.' Moreover, Latin American militaries might actually experience, in the future, a 'glass cliff' (Ryan and Haslam 2005: 81–90), whereby women are promoted to senior positions that are deliberately precarious.

Across the world the background to discussions on the integration of women into the military forces has been their combat capacity. Associated with this are questions related to the physical abilities that supposedly distinguish men from women, as well as a supposed emotional barrier that impedes women from expressing the aggressive impulses necessary for combat. However, the reasons why the military has remained masculinized over centuries allow for a questioning of its very role. Nowadays, military forces around the world experience serious debates – due both to the introduction of new technologies and to the centrality that logistics have acquired – over what type of personnel they require. The personnel question becomes more complex when one considers noncombat missions that militaries are increasingly performing today – support to local populations (especially in cases of disasters) and peacekeeping. As DeGroot argued in 2001, the new role that the military plays stimulates great debate regarding the integration of women, and notes that "the gender stereotypes which previously acted as a barrier to female participation in war might actually enhance the potential for women in the military of today" (DeGroot 2001: 24). A significant pending question for military sociological studies thus revolves around the actual and relevant differences between men and women in perceptions and in the execution of tasks.

Cultural institutional resistance to the incorporation of a gender perspective can also be resistance to a paradigm shift. Military leaderships may be unable to react to a process for which they have provided little planning. Consequently, security studies should also consider gender within a context of personnel policies. As in the case of any organization, entrance into the institution implies winning a competition for salaries and social benefits. While there is a need to analyze 'glass ceilings' that exist in career development, issues surrounding the entrance of women into military institutions may sometimes simply relate to additional competition for posts, command positions, and other possibilities.

Additionally, security studies could benefit from organizational analysis on gender. One of the most interesting contributions made by feminism is that organizations are not gender neutral, but instead represent the behaviors and perspectives of those within them (Acker 1990: 139–158). Thus, when the masculine attribute is prevalent, it tends to be assumed that these are institutional behaviors, when in reality they simply reflect the people that make up the institution. In these cases, the influx of women must overcome personnel policies and infrastructure that have been designed by, and for, males, thereby contributing to a perception that gender issues represent an annoyance within a neutral structure. A very clear example is found in arguments that the inclusion of women in a company, battalion, or ship requires particular analysis because "we must make bathrooms especially for them." Another curious case is that of female officers who are housed with noncommissioned officers (NCOs) and soldiers "because it would be necessary to build another bedroom for just a few," when within the culture of officers sharing accommodation outside officialdom is virtually unthinkable.[4]

Types of conflict, security, and gender

The second major issue that security must address from a gender perspective refers to the type of conflict; the relationship between women, peace, and security; and the systematic use of sexual violence as a weapon of war. The international community, and especially the United Nations Security Council, has promoted certain positions on the subject that have been accepted by civil society organizations across the world in their case studies and policy recommendations. Two Security Council Resolutions constitute the basis of this international regime: SCR 1325 of 2000, and SCR 1820 of 2008.

The year 2000 evidenced a questioning of the context of the rights of women at the international level, which joined with another, far-reaching reformulation regarding forms of contemporary conflict and the utility and possibilities of operations under a UN mandate. The cases of Somalia, the ex-Yugoslavia, and Rwanda left the international system facing deep burdens that were difficult to overcome. Violence against civilians, especially women, surpassed the usual invisibility of the issue, placing directly before the eyes of the international community the worst examples of human behavior within conflict settings.

UN Resolution 1325 was a historical turning point regarding the role of women in peace and international security. Its principal points directly link women, peace, and security, and establish that states must increase the representation of women in decision-making and operational personnel. Although the number of women in peacekeeping operations has not increased significantly (1.84 per cent in August 2006 to 2.84 per cent in May 2014), the creation of gender focal points in all missions and the formulation of national action plans to incorporate a gender perspective into security was accomplished in various countries around the world (Chile is the only Latin American case as of 2014). This implies, especially with regard to the military function, that the right to gender equality between men and women is understood as women being subjects and not just objects of action. Latin America has made more progress here. In Bolivia, for example, women have reached the rank of colonel and even of army general, as was previously cited, in what constitutes a unique case of female command in the region. In

Chile, Ecuador, Argentina, Uruguay, and Venezuela women have also held the position of ministers of defense. Internal gender policies within the armed forces in Argentina have led female officers to occupy positions such as military attachés, and even within the Inter-American Defense Board. Another example of women who want to be subjects and not objects is the recent opening-up to women of entrance into the Brazilian Army's officer academy: in 2013, 34 per cent of aspiring officers entering the Brazilian Army were women (RESDAL 2014: 59).

Moreover, advances in gender legislation across the region in general have been accompanied by specific norms within military institutions. Nevertheless, while the entrance of female personnel is almost now generalized across the entire region, regulatory modifications for the performance of female personnel are still under discussion, and there is a lack of general consensus with regard to whether or not there should be differences or special conditions in place for women. For example, pregnancy creates new issues for the institutions. While many argue that a pregnant cadet should abandon the career, others postulate that she should be given the option to interrupt her studies and return later on (Argentina, for instance, recently adopted leave policies for pregnant cadets).

Contemporary conflicts such as that experienced in the Democratic Republic of Congo have converted the local population into the battlefield and thus the target of action. Recent studies have shown how this targeting seeks to break the identity of the victim (which has been not only women, but also men) and is considered an effective way to displace a particular group from a disputed territory (Skjelsbæk 2010: 27–30). The International Criminal Tribunals for the former Yugoslavia (ICTY) and Rwanda (ICTR) ruled that sexual crimes in conflict situations were crimes against humanity and a form of torture. In the ICTY case, the definition of genocide included, among other considerations, causing serious physical or mental harm to members of the attacked group. Unlike common crimes – and an issue that has also formed part of the difficulties in attaining proof in both tribunals – consideration of rape and torture as crimes against humanity requires that they form part of a broader systematic plan, which in many cases is the most difficult aspect to prove. Despite this, the verdicts of the tribunals recognized that in the aforementioned cases rape can be considered as a war crime and a crime against humanity and can form part of genocide, and torture through rape is a particularly serious form of torture (UN 2010: 26).

While sexual violence has, throughout history, been part of war, it is only recently that it has been made visible and become a security issue, and SCR 1820 has had a lot to do with this. One must be aware of the temptation to perpetuate gender roles and "change so that nothing changes" even in these efforts. Referring to SCR 1325, Puechguirbal suggests that in UN texts "women are primarily represented in a narrow essentialist definition that allows male decision-makers to keep them in the subordinated position of victim, thus removing their agency" (2010: 173). Sexual violence is a security problem in two dimensions: the protection of human rights and its use as a weapon of war, as a means to achieve the objective of the struggle (for example, when it was part of the 'counterinsurgency' torture methods in the 1970s, as in the case of the last Argentine military dictatorship).

In the absence of in-depth security studies, it is difficult to know up until what point these phenomena are representative of a systematic plan. What is known is that in conflict zones the rape and murder of women, men, and children have multiplied; that these events occur in an organized manner; that force is used to oblige them to deliver food and provide other services; and that housing and community settings such as schools or churches are destroyed. The occupation by the enemy does not need to be physical; it is sufficient that the population is believed to be a basis of support or that that it sympathizes with the enemy. In the case of international forces, the victims' role in prevention and protection from these abuses occupies the center of the debate; while the media and public opinion tend to focus on what they see as unjustifiable inaction, interviews in missions (Donadio and Rial 2013) show that for international actors it is not clear that Security Council mandates cover their involvement in direct actions (see also Sotomayor, this volume).

In Latin America sexual violence has been part of internal conflicts, and there exist testimonies in Argentina, Colombia, El Salvador, Guatemala, Honduras, Mexico, Nicaragua, and Peru regarding rapes perpetrated in the context of their internal conflicts. Attacks on women due to being women reach aberrant levels in cases such as Ciudad Juárez in Mexico, where other phenomena such as the complicities of the state and the vulnerability of those that investigate and fight against this calamity are also at play. Although the scarcity of data from the 1970s and 1980s impedes understanding of how generalized this phenomenon was in these conflicts, studies of Colombia and Peru speak of the use of rape by various groups as a form of terrorizing the population, and of inhibiting their support for insurgent groups. Even truth commissions established by the state itself have analyzed this. Despite these efforts by researchers and legal teams, the theme continues to be largely invisible and even thought of as something that occurs in other, distant parts of the world, far detached from the circumstances of this region (Cabrera 2010: 14).

Feminists focused on the Latin American experiences have sought to carry out studies and create some perspective of historical registry of the cases. The variable of intersectionalism (whose simplest meaning refers to the intersection of simultaneous structures of oppression) also intervenes in Latin American studies. In this view, violence against women is part of a broader scheme of oppression and one that requires comprehensive attention by the state, academia, and civil society.

Conclusions: the need for a gender perspective in security

The issues that have been analyzed pose challenges to the security sector, and especially with regard to the composition, training, and mentality of military and police forces. These institutions continue to be seen as 'gender neutral.' In fact, their structures, education, and socialization processes need to incorporate a less neutral perspective that is more suited to the type of society that they represent. Three general areas of study need to be addressed.

First, the specifics of a gender perspective within the police and armed forces and their relationship to democratization in Latin America need to be theorized and developed. This is especially the case in the military. The inclusion and advancement of women clashes with the heroic images of military professionals that continue to prevail and is often a cliché representative of a tokenism that must be overcome. The opportunities that this topic has for advancing the democratic culture of armed and police forces need to be investigated and promoted.

Second, the contemporary experience of women in security-focused institutions presents a wealth of data that needs to be collected, analyzed, and understood. Women present in the security field, whether state or academic, may be at a crossroads: "I am a woman, a mother, and a peacekeeper," declared a woman who was interviewed about her experience in the armed forces. The way in which a complex sociocultural structure frames the subject's action is worth further analysis.

Third, with regard to public security, an enormous field opens itself up: How does security/insecurity affect men and women, what is the role of one or the other with regard to protection frameworks? Similarly, the need for systematic, serious, and gender-based criminal statistics is noteworthy, since most Latin American countries do not possess any. The statistics produced by governments are delayed and with scarce, or sometimes inexistent, construction of series over time. The last Regional Human Development Report 2013/2014 for Latin America, published by the UNDP on the topic of citizen security, presented approximate rates when data were not available. In statistical reports on Central America, to cite another example, do disparities between the countries show the lack of registers or underreporting for sexual violence in some of the cases? This is a basic problem that affects not only gender studies, but also security in general.

Finally, and in terms of international security, the production of historical and current analysis from a security perspective of the types of conflicts and the use of sexual violence as weapon of war is a type of study that has to be further developed not only in Latin America but globally.

Latin America is a region that has changed its image in the last decades in a positive direction. Democratization, human rights, and economic growth are some of the characteristics that can be highlighted. Regarding security, on the one hand, it is a region that has worked to overcome interstate conflicts through the strengthening of mutual trust. But, on the other hand, there is a lingering scenario of internal violence and public security problems that affect all the countries of the region. The gender policies developed at the social and political level also stand out as one of the regional advances, and have just begun to take a hold in state security institutions such as the police and armed forces. As a whole, it is necessary for the security sector to open itself up to a strategic alliance with academics studying gender and security, and also with state institutions and civil society.

Notes

1 There exists a body of resolutions from the year 2000: S/RES/1325, October 31, 2000; S/RES/1820, June 19, 2008; S/RES/1888, September 18, 2009; S/RES/1889, October 5, 2009; S/RES/1960, December 16, 2010; S/RES/2106, June 24, 2013; S/RES/2122, October 18, 2013.

2 For example, in one of the major academic congresses on Latin American studies (LASA), it is more likely to find talks on gender and security in the gender section than in the security section, in which they are not usually considered.

3 The first known definition emanated from North American academia and declared that: "I first encountered the term *femicide* when an acquaintance told me in 1974 that American writer Carol Orlock was preparing an anthology on femicide. . . . it resonated powerfully with me as one that might refer to the killing of women by men *because* they are women. We have long needed such a term as an alternative to the gender-neutral *homicide*" (Radford and Russell 1992: xiv). In Latin America, this definition was brought forward by the pioneering Mexican academia (especially the anthropologist Marcela Lagarde), to the point that in 2014 the term was included in the Real Spanish Academy Dictionary. The term 'feminicide' allows for the analysis of the social construction of violence and of the state's role.

4 I have heard directly of two Latin American cases in UN missions. In one, the senior officer did not seem to be concerned. In the other, the designated person made an official complaint that should have been addressed.

References

Acker, J. (1990) 'Hierarchies, Jobs, Bodies: A Theory of Gendered Organizations', *Gender & Society*, 4: 139–158.

Annan, K.A. (2001) *We the Peoples: The Role of the United Nations in the 21st Century*, New York: Department of Public Information, United Nations.

Organization of American States, *Inter-American Convention on the Prevention, Punishment and Eradication of Violence Against Women 'Convention of Belem Do Para'* http://www.oas.org/juridico/english/treaties/a-61.html

Cabrera, P. M. (2010) *Intersecting Inequalities. A Review of Feminist Theories and Debates on Violence against Women and Poverty in Latin America*, London: Central America Women's Network.

Cruz, C.D.L. (2007) *Género, derechos y desarrollo humano*. San Salvador: Programa de las Naciones Unidas para el Desarrollo.
Degroot, G. J. (2001) 'A Few Good Women: Gender Stereotypes, the Military and Peacekeeping', *Women and International Peacekeeping*, 4(2): 23–38.
Donadio, M. and Mazzotta, C. (2009) *La mujer en las instituciones armadas y policiales: Resolución 1325 y operaciones de paz en América Latina*, Buenos Aires: Red de Seguridad y Defensa de America Latina.
Donadio, M. and Rial, J. (2013) *Engendering Peacekeeping: The Cases of Haiti and Democratic Republic of Congo. A Gender and Security Analysis from a Latin American Perspective*, Buenos Aires: Resdal.
Kanter, R. M. (1977) *Men and Women of the Corporation*, New York: Basic Books.
Puechguirbal, N. (2010) 'Discourses on Gender, Patriarchy and Resolution 1325: A Textual Analysis of UN Documents', *International Peacekeeping*, 17: 172–187.
Radford, J., and Russell, D.E.H. (1992) *Femicide: The Politics of Woman Killing*, New York: Twayne.
RESDAL (2013) *Atlas comparativo de la defensa en América Latina*. Buenos Aires: RESDAL, Red de Seguridad y Defensa de América Latina.
——— (2014) *Atlas comparativo de la defensa en América Latina*, Buenos Aires: RESDAL, Red de Seguridad y Defensa de América Latina.
Ryan, M. K. and Haslam, S.A. (2005) 'The Glass Cliff: Evidence that Women are Over-Represented in Precarious Leadership Positions', *British Journal of Management*, 16: 81–90.
Sjoberg, L and Martin, J. (2007) 'Feminist Security Studies: Conversations and Introductions' https://www.academia.edu/292413/Feminist_Security_Studies_Conversations_and_Introductions
Soares, B. M. and Musumeci, L. (2005) *Mulheres policiais: Presença feminina na Polícia Militar do Rio de Janeiro*, Rio de Janeiro: Civilização Brasileira.
Tickner, J.A. (1996) *You Just Don't Understand: Troubled Engagements Between Feminists and IR Theorists*, Canberra, AU: Research School of Pacific Studies, Australian National University.
United Nations (2002) *Women, Peace and Security: Study Submitted by the Secretary-General Pursuant to Security Council Resolution 1325* (2000).
——— DPKO (2010) *Review of the Sexual Violence Elements of the Judgments of the International Criminal Tribunal for the Former Yugoslavia, the International Criminal Tribunal for Rwanda, and the Special Court for Sierra Leone in the light of Security Council Resolution 1820*, New York.
Villalba, M. S. (2006) 'La violencia de género: ¿Un asunto de seguridad ciudadana?' *Ciudad Segura* 9. Quito: Flacso Ecuador.

7
ENGLISH SCHOOL AND CONSTRUCTIVISM

Federico Merke

Introduction[1]

Scholars of international security have increasingly recognized the importance of ideational factors, such as beliefs, norms, and culture, in explaining a variety of security outcomes. This recognition appears to challenge traditional conceptions of security and power politics. Against this background, English school and constructivism have emerged as two prominent social approaches. In this chapter, I argue that these theories offer important insights into the transformation of state security interests from a nonmaterialist standpoint in the context of Latin America.

The structure of the chapter is as follows. In the first part I introduce the core elements of the English school and constructivism and examine their contributions to the study of regional security. I then move on to explore how these contributions can illuminate security dynamics in Latin America. The last section concludes by summarizing the arguments and evaluating how the English school and constructivism can improve our understanding of regional security in the region.

Between power and norms: English school and security

The richness of English school lies in the fundamental observation that international politics "resembles a game that is partly distributive but also partly productive" (Bull 1977: 26), and so it entails a complex relationship between law and norms on the one hand, and power and interests on the other. This game can hardly be reduced to a unique pattern of interactions, but rather it works on three arenas, empirically connected yet analytically distinguishable.

The *international system* assumes a mechanical and material view of international politics where states are the central units and base their moves on strategic logics of national interest. Its understanding in classical English school comes close to that in realism, whereas the world is depicted as a kind of Hobbesian international anarchy inhabited by selfish states wanting to survive and increase power. *International society* is a socially constructed vision of international politics where states remain the central units but base their moves on normative arrangements and the logic of common interest. Therefore, international society plays a significant role in pushing states towards more socialized forms of diplomatic intercourse. Finally, *world society* or *community* is a vision that transcends the state as an actor and considers individuals and human groups as key players, which base their moves on humanitarian and cosmopolitan principles.

International society is about institutions and norms. In the English school usage, institutions are understood as constitutive of both states and society. Barry Buzan (2004) calls them 'primary institutions,' among which sovereignty, territoriality, diplomacy, international law, balance of power, and war are salient. These institutions allow for the creation of 'secondary institutions' that are concrete intergovernmental bodies such as the UN, NATO, or the World Bank. These institutions, in turn, are subject to normative debates. English school distinguishes two normative standpoints, namely 'pluralism' and 'solidarism.' Pluralism has a skeptical view of progress in the international order. It is based on a communitarian standpoint that supports a plurality of self-contained values along Westphalian lines. Its aim is put on survival and coexistence and advocates an international law based on interaction rules. Solidarism has a more positive view on the potential for progress at the global level. It is based more on a cosmopolitan spirit, and it is centered on progress and domestic convergence. Although initially conceived as mutually exclusive positions, pluralism and solidarism can be examined as "positions on a spectrum representing, respectively, thin and thick sets of shared norms, rules and institutions" (Buzan 2004: 139).

Based on this instrumental view of society, norms, and institutions, Buzan (2010) put forward a way to conceptualize regional societies based on what type of institutions lead regional interactions. Thus, a *power political* interstate society is rather thin in terms of primary institutions. Rivalry, enmity, and war prevail over diplomacy, law, and the market. Survival is the main driver, and sovereignty among equals as an organizing principle is rather unstable. A *coexistence* interstate society is the typical, pluralist, Westphalian order in which sovereignty, balance of power, diplomacy, Great Power management, war, and international law hang together to form an ordered, stable society. A *cooperative* interstate society goes beyond pluralism to incorporate more solidarist values, such as democracy and human rights or the *umma* for the Islamic world. It can also lead to more market openness and integration. In this type of society, secondary institutions abound, war becomes improbable, and international law gets more sophisticated with more elaborated concepts of membership. Finally, a *convergence* interstate society has to do with "shared values within a set of states to make them adopt similar political, legal and economic forms" (Buzan 2010: 36).

Upon this elaboration, it becomes apparent that "what type of international society one is in has huge consequences for what the agenda of international security will look like" (Buzan 2010: 36). As we move from power political towards the convergence end of the spectrum, for instance, "security concerns move away from the traditional military one toward economic, social and environmental ones, and the human security agenda" (Buzan 2010: 36). Buzan (2012: 12) observes that this typology of interstate society overlaps comfortably with the regional security complex theory typology of security orders. Thus, power political and some coexistence interstate societies fall into *conflict formation* in which mutual securitization becomes the dominant pattern. At some point between coexistence and cooperative interstate society are *security regimes*, in which states have agreed principles and codes of conduct in order to mitigate security dilemmas, build trust, and ensure peaceful change. Lastly, bridging between cooperative and convergence interstate society is a *security community*, in which states have abandoned mutual fears and so do not prepare to use force among each other.

Given this elaboration, security cooperation is less of a puzzle than for some other IR theories. International society is a social structure in which cooperation becomes a fundamental mode of interaction. Thus, English school moves the security problematique from the 'logic of anarchy' to the 'logic of society.' Realism depicts international politics as a highly asocial domain composed by rational egoist states seeking to survive. Security in this domain is mostly the result of balance of power, alliance, hegemony, or strategic deterrence. By contrast, English school examines states as being embedded in a structure that is both material and social. Security in this realm is more driven by a societal balance of power, norms, diplomacy, and international law than by brute material capabilities. The presence of institutions and a common culture shared by the major states is a social condition that facilitates contrivance and cooperation among states. Thus, the interplay among international law, diplomacy, and balance of power both defines and frames the whole concept of security.

To sum up, the English school understands security as a process shaped both by the structure and the character of the international system. While realists view the structure of the international system as a determinant feature upon which security evolves along material lines, English school considers that the character (i.e., the type of international society) of the system is a fundamental dimension in which norms can trump power. It then follows that security problems will exhibit variations depending on the type of society we have and where it is placed along the pluralist-solidarist spectrum.

Ideas all the way down: constructivism and security

The fundamental observation of constructivism to understand international politics is that states live in a "world of our making" (Onuf 1989). Thus, the international system is the result of a historical process that is constantly in flux. Constructivism challenges the significance of anarchy in defining the conditions of international relations. It claims that "anarchy is what states make of it" (Wendt 1992). This means that anarchy does not exist separate from the interaction among states. It is not some externally created constraint, but rather an intersubjective process.

Wendt elaborates a cultural theory of international politics in which power and interests are themselves the effect of shared ideas. For Wendt, the character of international politics "is determined by the beliefs and expectations that states have about each other, and these are constituted largely by social rather than material structures" (Wendt 1999: 20). Social structures have constitutive effects, such as norms. Norms are "collective expectations about proper behavior for a given identity" (Jepperson et al. 1996: 54). As such, norms have both behavioral and constitutive effects ('a good state does *X*'). This is also the case of identity, another type of idea. Wendt defines identity as "a property of intentional actors that generates motivational and behavioral dispositions" (1999: 224). Identity, therefore, provides an interpretive framework that allows governments to make sense of the world they live in. Thus, interests are the outcome of an identity-building process that is part of larger cognitive structures. What states want depends on what they think they are (e.g., a 'world police,' 'the center of Europe,' a 'normative power,' a 'trading state,' and so on).

Wendt presents three different types of cultures of anarchy; namely Hobbesian, Lockean, and Kantian. Each culture has its own logic and responds to distinct distributions of knowledge. Constructivism holds that the prevailing interests and identity of states determine whether they interact on the basis of enmity, rivalry, or friendship. According to which culture dominates world affairs, sharply contrasted outcomes can be expected. A bipolar structure in a Hobbesian culture is quite different from a bipolar structure in a Kantian culture. Each culture has a specific role relationship; namely enemy, rival, or friend. These roles are defined by the actor's interaction with and relationship to others. These interactions, in turn, shape the identity of each actor, which is reinforced by mutual expectations and cognitive structures.

Although "the extent to which constructivists have developed a theory of international security is limited" (McDonald 2008: 60), constructivism has advanced a number of general propositions and empirical analysis on different security problems. In this sense, constructivism may not be a theory of security per se, but it does serve as a broader social approach that informs how we might understand security dynamics from nonmaterialist lenses.

Constructivism posits that the fundamental dynamics of international security are socially constituted through intersubjective interaction. Indeed, from a constructivist standpoint, security and identity unfold in a similar manner – namely, that no state's security is self-contained, but is about other states, and thus inherently relational. Constructivism highlights the role of intersubjective understandings in giving meaning to security issues. In other words, meanings of security are not given outside social interaction or simply deduced from structural, material constraints. They arise from ideational factors. Therefore, it follows that ideational factors "are central to the construction and practices of security in world politics" (McDonald 2008: 61). Simply put, threats are not objective facts waiting to be addressed by state officers but brought into being by intersubjective understandings of what constitutes a threat. Security, therefore, can be understood as a "thick signifier" (Huysmans 1998) that concentrates on the wider order of meaning that security articulates. Thus, security becomes a site of negotiation and contestation between leaders and audiences and between different political actors competing for alternative visions of security and identity (McDonald 2008: 64). This entails a significant ideological labor to make sure that a specific understanding of security prevails (see Tickner, this volume).

The constructivist literature in IR has made central the role of ideas and the socialization of practices between international actors. In the security field, constructivism posits an intimate relation between identity and security. It argues that security transformation arises not only from shifting material interests but also from changing intersubjective understandings. It also claims that states are undergoing a growing process of socialization into international standards, including those related to peace and security. Thus constructivism examines in particular how states internalize norms and how these norms shape foreign policy and security interests. These security interests are neither universal nor self-explanatory, since much depends on which game the states are involved in.

Although constructivism and English school share the ontology of mutual constitution of agents and structures, both traditions tend to focus on the structural side of the agent-structure relationship and how structure reinforces prevailing behaviors and roles. English school examines international security as an endogenous process of international society that is subject to the institutions of diplomacy, international law, balance of power, Great Power management, and war, among others. Constructivism goes beyond institutions and pays attention to the culture of anarchy that prevails, be it Hobbesian, Lockean, or Kantian. In order to examine these societal trends in regional settings we could analyze, for instance, how meanings (e.g., state sovereignty) stabilize into rules (e.g., nonintervention); how sets of rules (e.g., nonintervention, peaceful conflict resolution, and multilateralism) constitute institutions (e.g., OAS, Rio Group); and how a cluster of institutions (e.g., OAS, Rio Group, UNASUR, CELAC) constitutes social structures (e.g., a Grotian or Lockean interstate culture).

The next section identifies puzzles that emerge when we examine Latin America's security dynamics from both English school and constructivism. It does so through a dialogue, albeit with some tensions, between both research traditions. Although each tradition exhibits its own assumptions and forms of theorizing, both English school and Constructivism (a) offer a systemic approach to international politics, (b) consider states as intentional or purposive actors, (c) agree in their claim that realists discount the role of norms and ideas upon state behavior, and (d) structure their reasoning upon triads, suggesting that there is not just one logic of anarchy, but several. On this account, the exploration of how the English school and constructivism could engage with regional security in Latin America is, therefore, a welcome one, and invites a fruitful interaction between theory and regional studies of security.

The social construction of Latin American security

Although Latin America offers a rich array of cases to examine regional security, the theoretical landscape to understand security dynamics in Latin America has been rather narrow, with realism being the dominant perspective and thus still serving as "the basis for discussion on security in Latin America" (Herz 2013: 133). This realist reading affirms that "the cold peace between states in Latin America endures" (Trinkunas 2013: 95), and thus a "violent peace" (Mares 2001) continues to be the main feature of the region. Yes, realists recognize that the region has witnessed few interstate wars. Yet, "historical conflicts over boundary definition persist and anxieties over past territorial losses are still fresh and intense" (Chipman and Lockhart Smith 2009: 81). More in particular, realism emphasizes the failure of democracy and regional integration in overcoming traditional geopolitical tensions. These tensions are apparent in the conflictive dyadic interactions (e.g., Chile/Bolivia, Chile/Peru, Peru/Ecuador, Colombia/Venezuela, Costa Rica/Nicaragua) that are subject to frequent disruption and militarized disputes. They are also apparent in the many difficulties to build a sound regional security regime. As a result, "some old security problems persist, others of a newer generation have arisen" (Chipman and Lockhart Smith 2009: 99), and there is "no coherent regional vision of security which integrates the inter-state security threats" (Mares 2012: 22).

English school and constructivism have another story to tell; one that offers a more nuanced perspective than realism. This story suggests that Latin America goes beyond power politics, yet it stops short of institutionalized cooperation. Yes, there are subtle strategic rivalries working on, but a purely realist world is not active today in South America. Governments in South America conduct their foreign policy as if the most serious long-term threat they face is neither war nor domination by an aspiring regional hegemon but rather domestic failure and external marginalization.

Given space considerations, this section aims to flesh out the essential contours of how a societal approach might look. This approach, I suggest, opens up a promising venue for understanding how power politics and security dynamics in Latin America are tempered by a social structure made up of social institutions and normative arrangements.

A good starting point is to examine the role norms play in shaping interstate security in Latin America, a role largely ignored by realist studies. In contrast, English school has made few but important inroads in this field. This is the case of Arie M. Kacowicz, a leading expert who has examined Latin America from a broad interpretive approach combining English school and constructivism. Kacowicz (2005) explores Latin American regional transformation from a system to society through the adoption of security norms – namely, arms control, denuclearization, conflict resolution mechanisms, and confidence-building measures, among others. Kacowicz traces the evolution of these regional norms in Latin America and how they shaped security cooperation in Central America, the Andes, and especially the Southern Cone. The overall argument is that regional norms have shaped interactions in two ways. First, norms made of war an expensive option in diplomatic and legal terms, without mentioning the costs that this would imply to states with limited capabilities. Second, norms have reshaped state interests in foreign policy. Regional norms, says Kacowicz, have been "both regulative and constitutive, both shaping interests and identities and reflecting them" (Kacowicz 2005: 12). As a result, regional norms have helped to maintain the long peace in South America (at least since 1883), have reshaped state interests in line with regional norms, and have helped to upgrade peaceful relations after democratization in the direction of a pluralistic security community (Kacowicz 2005: 166).

The presence of norms in Latin America led different authors to depict the region alternatively as a "regional society of states" (Hurrell 1998: 229), a "Grotian society" (Kacowicz 2005), a "Lockean interstate culture" (Thies 2008), or a "microcosm" (Jones 2007) with its memories, institutions, and *habitus*. Although this rendition comes with its own nuances, the overall idea is that the region has shown, and continues to show, an inclination toward peaceful conflict resolution. Thus, depicting Latin America as a regional *society* has important consequences for how we understand regional security. It means that the Latin American regional interstate society has evolved beyond the typical dynamics of balance of power – namely, arms races, alliances, and war (Kacowicz 1998; Holsti 1996). It also suggests that social rather than material factors may also contribute to smooth conflict among states that conceive themselves attached to a common set of rules.

Since the end of the Cold War regional order and security have increasingly come to be defined in terms of the collective defense of democracy and the promotion of liberal economic reforms and regional integration. This move seemed to place the region somewhere between coexistence and a cooperative interstate society. Yet the working of regional rules and institutions does not seem to push the region towards more liberal understanding of how institutions work. The region remains a pluralist international society that is still pretty much attached to Westphalian norms of sovereignty and nonintervention. Simply put, Latin America contains much more than the realists would admit and much less than the liberals would prefer. This observation opens up a theoretical space to introduce a middle ground concept – namely, *concertación*.

From a societal approach, *concertación* can be presented as a unique Latin American institution that has managed interstate security in the region. *Concertación* can be defined as a loose form of international institution based on consensus-seeking and peaceful settlement of disputes. Its normative instrumental follows predictable lines – namely, *uti possidetis*, nonaggression, nonintervention, and arbitration. As an institution, *concertación* does not advocate the need for transcending sovereignty and the nation-state, nor does it rely on a strong state nationalism. It has been, and continues to be, one of the most significant mechanisms for conducting interstate conflicts within a framework of settled rules. As a practice, *concertación* is embedded in a deep-seated social construction of Latin America as a *Patria Grande* – namely, a nation split into 22 republics. *Concertación* depicts Latin America as *Gemeinschaft*, a community sharing a language, a religion, and a homogeneous cultural trait. *Concertación*, according to Arie Kacowicz, has limited the recourse to interstate war and explains "the relatively peaceful settlement of disputes that has characterized the international relations of the region, especially in South America, since 1883" (2005: 63). "In sum," says Kacowicz, "the Latin American countries have reached a high degree of civility in their international relations" (2005).

If *concertación* speaks for the relatively peaceful character of South America, how do we account of the conflicts that took place, and continue to take place, in the region? Jorge Domínguez (2003: 29) argues that the distribution of power, the regional institutional structure, and regional norms may generate very few incentives to go to war, but they maintain high incentives to start military disputes. Thus, assuming that *concertación* is a sound interstate institution for conflict resolution, English school needs to address cases that do not conform to its predictions. Take the recurrent militarized interstate disputes (MIDs) that have so much plagued Latin America. David Mares holds that MIDs are "part of a strategy of inter-state bargaining" wherein one state rationally decides that "some level of use of military force would be advantageous in its dealings with a rival" (2012: 10). While wars of aggression are for many reasons excluded from the strategic menu of Latin American governments, Mares affirms that "neither international nor domestic constraints are sufficient to keep Latin American countries from militarizing disagreements they perceive to be important to national sovereignty, defense or security" (Mares 2012: 13). In other words, the "long-standing pattern in Latin America is for leaders to avoid major war, while still using military force to influence their relations with other states in the region" (Mares 2012: 63).

Mares's rendition seems to paint a different picture to the one of *concertación*. Yet *concertación* can be posited as an institution that has avoided, not militarized conflicts, but escalation thereof. Said otherwise, English school could explore the extent to which militarization may be examined as a regional institution somehow replacing war. Put differently, militarization, when it is the work of a rational plan, may not point in the direction of war but in the direction of forcing the state and the region under threat to go back and negotiate under new terms. In Andrew Hurrell's view, the use of force in Latin America has not had much to do with the idea of winning in the Clausewitzian sense, but was more considered "a diplomatic instrument to push the matter at issue back on the agenda and to facilitate the winning of concessions at the diplomatic negotiations that, as both sides knew, would inevitably follow" (Hurrell 1998: 532). In sum, when it comes to interstate conflict, English school may contribute to a dialogue with realism, each one pointing to the different sources of conflict and how they may evolve, or not, into more stable orders.

Beyond norms, role identities may also play a crucial role in explaining Latin American patterns of interstate security. However, there is still much to be done to understand security in Latin America from the perspective that highlights the influence of role identity in shaping security interests. From a constructivist standpoint, for instance, UNASUR's South American Defence Council cannot be examined without studying the rise of a South American identity; namely, a geopolitical zone which should be protected. Upon this reasoning, South America can exist only if it has a common defense identity, and it is recognized as a distinctive actor in world affairs. Thus, 'region-making' and 'institution-making' are intertwined processes that connect identity to security and vice versa (see Oelsner, this volume).

Furthermore, in South America, state security is very much about identity (Barletta and Trinkunas 2004) *and* integration (Oelsner 2009). Thus, these three dimensions form three sides of a triangle where typically two sides converge at the expense of another; namely, from security to integration (e.g., Argentina, Brazil, and Chile via MERCOSUR), from identity to integration (ALBA states), and from identity to security – and back to identity (e.g., Chile/Bolivia, Chile/Peru, Peru/Ecuador). In these moves, it is clear that the interaction between identity and security presents a crucial challenge: The 'Other' ends up in the dual role of being necessary for my identity and the one who prevents me from being fully myself.

Upon this reasoning, constructivism may shed some light on enduring rivalries in Latin America and how territorial conflicts become embedded in symbolic conflicts that cut to the heart of national identity. In other words, the analytical challenge is to demonstrate that even the most power-driven interstate relations are also to some degree socially constructed. Take the case of Chile and Bolivia. Recent constructivist research has examined how the two countries form part of a "culture of rivalry" (Wehner 2010) or how Chile's international identity, based on neoliberalism and legality, was portrayed by Bolivia and Peru "as an imperialist and aggressive actor and as an enemy of the Bolivian and Peruvian people" (van der Ree 2010: 213).

Although the case of Chile and Bolivia may not be a representative one, it makes more apparent notwithstanding that the region is far from becoming a Kantian culture of anarchy.

Cameron Thies (2008) examined Latin American interstate culture based on a large *N* of dyadic observations. He found that "the rival role identity has come to dominate the structure or culture of Latin American interstate politics" (Thies 2008: 237). Thus, Thies identifies a Lockean interstate culture in Latin America, a finding that comes close to what Kacowicz referred as a "zone of negative peace."

Yet, the move from geopolitical rivalry to economic and political cooperation between Argentina and Brazil is a fascinating case that suggests how shifting political identities may lead to more convergent policies around security and economic integration (Russell and Tokatlian 2003). Upon this understanding, Oelsner and Vion (2011) examine the role of friendship in international politics, exploring the case of bilateral relations between Argentina and Brazil. The authors see friendship as a cumulative process made up of speech acts and institutional facts. In this sense, the bilateral relation between Argentina and Brazil exhibits a fascinating case in which evolving diplomatic dialogue, formal agreements, political promises, and proofs of engagement "helped to construct a common frame of revised values that accumulated in the form of political friendship" (Oelsner and Vion 2011: 143). This reasoning could also be extended to the rest of the MERCOSUR members; namely, Paraguay, Venezuela, and Uruguay, wherein politics, economics, and security have become intertwined dimensions which reinforce each other through institutionalized cooperation.

These shifting patterns opened up the question of whether South America was on the way to become a security community (see Oelsner, this volume). The concept of 'security community' was first introduced by Karl Deutsch but later on revisited from a constructivist standpoint in a collective volume edited by Adler and Barnett (1998). Adler and Barnett define a security community as a "transnational region comprised of sovereign states whose people maintain dependable expectations of peaceful change" (1998: 30). This definition comes close to a Kantian culture of anarchy in which war has been excluded from the options menu. Working upon this framework, Andrew Hurrell explored the Southern Cone as a potential security community and concluded that "a loosely coupled, if still imperfect, security community can be identified within MERCOSUR, built around the changes that have taken place in the core relationship between Brazil and Argentina" (1998: 260). Hurrell cautioned, however, that Argentina and Brazil still face many constraints in order to create a Kantian culture of anarchy. He also claimed that the rest of Latin America is still too anchored in traditional power politics to be understood as a security community.

With all these interesting findings, however, much of the identity cleavages in Latin America have not been international but domestic. Latin American states, says Kacowicz, "have been more concerned with their own domestic political problem than with confronting external security threats" (2005: 126). Barletta and Trinkunas agree with Kacowicz in saying that in Latin America "the competition for power among states is less pervasive, less important, and typically less lethal than the competition among internal factions within states" (2004: 335). Therefore, for constructivism, security discourses about the 'Other' have been typically more radical and violent *within* Latin American states than *among* them. "Historically," says Hurrell, "Latin America is distinctive in that high levels of domestic violence and social conflict have coexisted with a relatively low level of interstate wars" (1998: 544).

When internal security threats prevail, however, the central question becomes who controls the state. As Wendt and Barnett posit, the Sandinistas "were a threat to 'Nicaraguan' security during the Somoza regime, but not after coming to power." Similarly, "the United Sates threatened 'Nicaraguan' security during Sandinista rule, but not since" (1993: 329). What we have here is that particular understandings of security are shaped by particular constructions of identities. This has crucial implications for security, since security is always about a 'self' to be preserved. Yet, a key question in constructivist security analysis is: Who can do security in the name of what? Thus, security means different things to different actors, so constructivists examine how specific meanings of security become accepted. In Latin America, for instance, much of the debate about state security has been actually about regime survival, which in turn becomes a question of identity. This is most apparent in today's Venezuela, where Bolivarian identity became a security issue. It became high politics. But it has also been a recurrent theme in Bolivia, Ecuador, or Peru, where 'state security' has often been window dressing for 'regime security' ("we are threatened").

This domestic debate leads us to another interesting area of exploration – that of strategic culture. The concept of strategic culture is less related to interstate relations and more connected to foreign policy-making. There are already three generations of strategic culture scholars, and this is not the place to review its evolution. A useful and simple definition is that of Iain Johnston – namely, "an ideational milieu which limits behavior choices" (1995: 46). This ideational approach, according to Johnston, challenges the ahistorical, noncultural, materialist framework for analyzing security policies. Instead, the concept of strategic culture suggests that each state evaluates its foreign and security choices against a backdrop of domestic cognitive dispositions and social habits that emanates from the state's formative years and critical experiences.

To date, the most elaborate, comprehensive, and thought-provoking research on strategic culture in Latin American has been done by the Florida International University's Applied Research Center (FIU ARC). As a collaborative project, the FIU ARC has produced reports on 10 countries and their respective political, strategic, and cultural dimensions of state behavior and foreign policy. A central finding of this project is that different Latin American states have diverse strategic preferences which are rooted in the formative experiences of the state, and are shaped to some degree by the political and social structures of the state and its elites.

Interestingly, this concept of strategic culture resembles Bull's notion of "diplomatic culture" – namely, the "common stock of ideas and values possessed by the official representatives of states" (Bull 1977: 316). In South America, the study of diplomatic culture has been "rather limited," and yet it offers a potential avenue for historical and conceptual exploration in South America, a region which is often portrayed as having a "distinctive diplomatic culture," which, in turn, "has often been viewed as central to explaining particular patterns of conflict and cooperation" (Hurrell 2004: 1; see also Holsti 1996). Kacowicz's work finds that a common 'diplomatic culture' and normative consensus has reduced border disputes in South America, as states adopted the norm of *uti possidetis* with regard to inherited colonial borders. Other aspects of this consensus include the principle of *convivencia*, or peaceful international coexistence, nonintervention and mutual respect for state sovereignty, and peaceful settlement of disputes, including use of arbitration and mediation (Holsti 1996; Kacowicz 2005).

A forward vision for security studies in Latin America

The aim of this chapter has been to bring to the surface two complementary perspectives on regional security. English school and constructivism argue that the fundamental structure of international politics is social rather than strictly material. Social structures are made up of institutions, ideas, and practices. Thus, power politics is a social structure which can evolve into a security regime or a security community. Yet neither English school nor constructivism has an impressive record when it comes to theorizing about this evolution in Latin America. In sum, there is still a long way to go before English school and constructivism can claim a prominent place in the literature on regional security in Latin America. This chapter presented, however, few but important observations that suggest the potential research significance exhibited by these two theories. These observations, contentious and contestable as they surely are, nevertheless highlight a number of important points in our analytical understanding of regional security in general, and the Latin American case in particular.

First, we need more empirical studies to assess the validity of English school and constructivism. In particular, we need to gain better understanding of how norms, institutions, and ideas shape security interests. The strength of the English school lies in providing explanations of macrolevel, complex historical events, but it exhibits serious difficulties when it comes to explaining specific security crises or bilateral conflicts. Instead, constructivism seems to be more prepared to explain bilateral 'Othering' processes to assess role identities.

Second, both the English school and constructivism exhibit the same analytical problem; namely, that a wide range of behavior among states (from enmity to friendship) may be equally consistent with their assumptions. In addition, both traditions tend to place their eyes where it is most likely to confirm their strengths. Typically, constructivists examine normative or identity changes, while English school scholars study socialization processes that alter state behavior. Thus, in order to strengthen their analytical rigor, English school and constructivism should examine more difficult terrains to test their hypotheses. To overcome these shortcomings, English school and constructivism need to rely on a richer array of methods and to unearth the interplay between structure and agency in Latin American security studies. Particularly, the field could benefit much from research designs including comparable cases, most and least likely cases, deviant cases, and process tracing, among others, for the purpose of hypothesis testing.

Third, a regional turn within the English school and other IR theories such as constructivism offers a theoretical space to examine regions in the mirror of universal conceptualizations, such as international system or international society. Yet this approach, to be fruitful, should work with a multiplicity of sources, including raw data, theoretical works, and the literature on the region. Given its sensitivity for history and culture, English school stands itself as a useful heuristic device to combine international theory with area studies.

And fourth, much of the literature reviewed here examined mainly interstate security dynamics. Since the end of the Cold War, however, the Latin American security agenda has become primarily internal and transnational, and secondarily international/regional. Studies on narcoterrorism, organized international crime, arms smuggling, insurgencies, and security crises derived from large-scale migration have been rather absent from the discussion in societal approaches. Thus, a turn to domestic and transnational security issues offers new avenues of research which may reinvigorate constructivism and the English school.

Note

1 I would like to thank Arie M. Kacowicz and David R. Mares for their helpful comments.

References

Adler, E. and Barnett, M. (1998) 'Security Communities in Theoretical Perspectives' in E. Adler and M. Barnett (eds) *Security Communities*, Cambridge: Cambridge University Press, pp. 3–28.

Barletta, M. and Trinkunas, H. (2004) 'Regime Type and Regional Security in Latin America: Towards a Balance of Identity Theory' in T. V. Paul et al. (eds) *Balance of Power: Theory and Practice in the 21st Century*, Stanford: Stanford University Press, pp. 334–356.

Bull, H. (1977) *The Anarchical Society*, London: Macmillan

Buzan, B. (2004) *From International to World Society?*, Cambridge: Cambridge University Press.

——— (2010) 'The English School and International Security' in M. D. Cavelty and V. Mauer (eds) *The Routledge Handbook of Security Studies*, London: Routledge, pp. 34–44.
——— (2012) 'How Regions were Made and the Legacies of World Politics: An English School Reconnaissance' in T. V. Paul (ed) *International Relations Theory and Regional Transformation*, Cambridge: Cambridge University Press, pp. 22–48.
Chipman, J. and Smith, J. L. (2009) 'South America: Framing Regional Security', *Survival*, 51(6): 77–104.
Domínguez, J. (2003) 'Boundary Disputes in Latin America', *Peaceworks*, 50.
Herz, M. (2013) 'Seguridad', in T. Legler, A. S. Cruz and L. Z. González (eds) *Introducción a las relaciones internacionales: América Latina y la política global*, México, DF: Oxford University Press, pp. 123–133.
Holsti, K. J. (1996) *War, the State, and the State of War*, Cambridge: Cambridge University Press.
Hurrell, A. (1998) 'An Emerging Security Community in South America?' in E. Adler and M. Barnett (eds) *Security Communities*, Cambridge: Cambridge University Press, pp. 228–264.
——— (2004, March) 'Working with Diplomatic Culture: Some Latin American and Brazilian Questions', Paper prepared for ISA Meeting, Montreal.
Huysmans, J. (1998) 'Security! What Do You Mean? From Concept to Thick Signifier', *European Journal of International Relations*, 4(2): 226–255.
Jepperson, R., Wendt, A. and Katzenstein, P. (1996) 'Norms, Identity, and Culture in National Security' in P. Katzenstein (ed) *The Culture of National Security*, New York: Columbia, pp. 33–65.
Johnston, A. (1995) 'Thinking About Strategic Culture', *International Security*, 19(4): 32–64.
Jones, C. (2007) *American Civilization*, London: Institute for the Study of the Americas.
Kacowicz, A. (1998) *Zones of Peace in the Third World: South America and West Africa in Comparative Perspective*, New York: State University of New York Press.
——— (2005) *The Impact of Norms in International Society: The Latin American Experience, 1881–2001*, Notre Dame, IN: University of Notre Dame Press.
Mares, D. R. (2001) *Violent Peace: Militarized Interstate Bargaining in Latin America*, New York: Columbia University Press.
——— (2012) *Latin America and the Illusion of Peace*, Abingdon, UK: International Institute for Strategic Studies and Routledge Press.
McDonald, M. (2008) 'Constructivism' in P. D. Williams (ed) *Security Studies: An Introduction*, New York: Routledge, pp. 59–72.
Oelsner, A. (2009) 'Consensus and Governance in Mercosur: The Evolution of the South American Security Agenda', *Security Dialogue*, 40(2): 191–212.
Oelsner, A. and Vion, A. (2011) 'Friends in the Region: A Comparative Study on Friendship Building in Regional Integration', *International Politics*, 48(1): 129–151.
Onuf, N. (1989) *World of Our Making*, Columbia: University of South California Press.
Russell, R. and Tokatlian, J. G. (2003) 'From Antagonistic Autonomy to Relational Autonomy: A Theoretical Reflection from the Southern Cone', *Latin American Politics and Society*, 45(1): 1–24.
Thies, C. (2008) 'The Construction of a Latin American Interstate Culture of Rivalry', *International Interactions*, 34(3): 231–257.
Trinkunas, H. (2013) 'Reordering Regional Security in Latin America', *Journal of International Affairs*, 66(2): 83–99.
van der Ree, G. (2010) 'Chile's (Inter)National Identities: Framing the Relations with Bolivia and Peru', *Bulletin of Latin American Research*, 29(2): 208–223.
Wehner, L. (2010) 'From Rivalry to Mutual Trust: The Othering Process between Bolivia and Chile', *GIGA Working Paper*, No 135.
Wendt, A. (1992) 'Anarchy is What States Make of It: The Social Construction of Power Politics', *International Organization*, 46(2): 391–425.
——— (1999) *Social Theory of International Politics*, Cambridge: Cambridge University Press.
Wendt, A. and Barnett, M. (1993) 'Dependent State Formation and Third World Militarization', *Review of International Studies*, 19(4): 321–347.

8

ALTERNATIVE GOVERNANCE IN LATIN AMERICA

Harold Trinkunas and Anne Clunan

Who governs in Latin America when the state does not? State strength and capacity is notoriously variable across the region, yet human beings still make collective decisions with binding outcomes that govern the allocation of resources, establish rules of behavior, and enforce agreements. Alternative governance providers in the region span violent and nonviolent state actors, nongovernmental, licit, and illicit business organizations, physical and online activist communities, and formal and informal networks among them. This chapter assesses the research agenda on alternatively governed spaces in Latin America and the debate on when alternative governance modalities promote or impede human, national, and international security. When and why do actors govern with, against, or around the state? The chapter first takes a brief look at the history of alternative governance in Latin America. Next, it provides a theoretical overview of the origins of alternatively governed spaces and the policy responses these have provoked. It will then examine two zones where alternative governance has most commonly emerged in the region but where questions still remain: cities and borders. It concludes by identifying an agenda for studying how state and nonstate actors attempt to influence security outcomes in ungoverned spaces.

A brief history of alternative governance in Latin America

Latin America is a region that historically combined both zones of high state presence and zones of alternative governance, often coexisting alongside each other. The region's states are the product of an early effort to graft still evolving European conceptions of sovereignty, governance, and rule of law onto traditional New World societies that emerged from the encounter of cultures in 1492. By its very nature, the colonization process in Latin America was marked by the establishment of formal European settlements, constituted under legal systems imported from the metropolis. These were set down within a vast territory where traditional forms of social organization persisted, even after a demographic collapse among indigenous Americans that followed the colonial encounter (Restall 2003).

After independence in the 19th century, Latin American states featured complex constitutions and legal systems that made high claims for state power alongside persistent fiscal, military, and industrial weakness that hindered state consolidation. Societal, cultural, and linguistic integration eventually shrank the space occupied by alternative indigenous governance systems (although these persist to the present in some parts of the Andes and Central America). However, these were not necessarily replaced by the state, but rather by other private actors, such as landowners, mining companies, foreign investors, and insurgents. The late 19th and 20th centuries witnessed efforts to build up higher levels of state authority, either by professionalizing the armed forces, through state-led import substitution industrialization, or through expansion of state responsibilities for social welfare. These attempts were accompanied by extended periods of political instability that eventually produced enduring military authoritarian regimes in the 1960s and 1970s (Rouquié 1987; López-Alves 2000).

Today, the paradox of high state governance coexisting with its alternatives in Latin America persists. The wave of democratization that swept the region in the 1980s dismantled authoritarian state structures, but the regimes that followed did not necessarily build up state capacity. In large part, democratization was accompanied by economic crisis, and the prescription of the international financial institutions and aid donors for Latin America during this period was further dismantling of the state through liberalization of its economies. The withdrawal of the state from the economy and the military from governance considerably shrank the space for which the state was responsible. Advocates for liberalization believed that civil society and the private sector would be freed to take the place of the state, and in some cases that was true. But in many others, illicit economies and actors filled a vacuum and provided governance functions. Trafficking networks carrying drugs, cash, and migrants connected South and North America ever more intimately. The profits generated by these networks supported and attracted armed actors, nearly overwhelming some states, as occurred in Peru and Colombia during the 1990s.

The Latin American commodity export boom of the 2000s only partially redressed the shortcomings in state capacity governance across the region. In countries benefiting from the boom, largely in South America, governments expanded their functions, providing direct assistance to previously excluded populations in Venezuela and Bolivia, implementing conditional cash transfer programs in Brazil, and increasing the state role in the economy across the continent (Bouillon and Tejerina 2006). Peru and Colombia increased spending on their armed forces and police, established greater state presence in the countryside, and managed to beat back their insurgencies, partially displacing the illicit networks and the violence associated with them. Conversely, alternatively governed spaces persist in the informal, unplanned areas of major cities, such as Rio de Janeiro and Medellin (Arias 2010). Latin America's borders remain quite porous, and they became even more so as free trade pacts expanded the area of free transit of goods (Kacowicz 1998; Jaskoski et al. 2015). Central America and the Caribbean, which benefited much less from commodity exports, experienced worsening levels of state control relative to the criminal organizations associated with the illicit networks that transit their territories. The response in these areas has been the expansion of private security across Latin America, the formation of informal militias in Mexico and Brazil, the privatization of justice by the business sector through the use of arbitration, and governance provided by insurgents and drug trafficking organizations in the regions they control.

Alternative governance in theory

Governance has become a central concern in the policy and scholarly communities over the past 30 years. This is a response to the perceived erosion of state capacity and sovereignty in light of globalization and technological diffusion (Cerny 1995), and to increased concern about the relationship between instability and 'failing' and 'fragile' states (Rotberg 2003; Patrick 2006; Fukuyama 2004; Krasner and Pascual 2005). Illicit networks carrying people, goods, money, and ideas permeate the globe (Naím 2005). Rapid urbanization has raised the specter of 'feral' cities (Norton 2003), and with projections that by 2030 about two billion people worldwide will live in slums (UN-Habitat 2006), some argue that future insurgencies are likely to take place in urban areas that are "crowded, complex and coastal" (Kilcullen 2013). Increased concern about the inability of fragile states to effectively control their borders and provide minimal public goods and post-9/11 emphasis on transnational terrorism combined to produce policy interest in 'ungoverned' spaces as havens for all manner of violent, nonstate actors (Clunan and Trinkunas 2010).

These converging trends have produced a controversial securitization of development and of governance (Andreas and Price 2001), and an equally contentious expansion of security studies from a traditional emphasis on interstate conflict to nontraditional issues, such as militancy, crime, environment, poverty, urbanization, human rights and civil liberties, public health, and illicit markets. The United Nations (2004) captured this logic when it highlighted the "mutual vulnerability" of states and humans to terrorism, weapons proliferation, transnational crime, disease, and poverty (Bourne 2011). Today, ungoverned and undergoverned spaces join failing, failed, and fragile states as security problems for advanced countries in the West.

The capabilities of nonstate actors to mobilize, exercise influence, and provide governance outside the state has risen with globalization and technological innovation. States find themselves embedded in a web of international obligations, norms, laws, and institutions that have progressively raised the cost of using coercive mechanisms to impose governance; at the same time, their ability to use incentives to shape nonstate actors' preferences has shrunk under the impact of liberalization and crisis. Even governments as authoritarian as those in Syria and Tunisia – with abysmal human rights records – have found themselves peculiarly at a loss when it comes to attempting to successfully coerce their own rebellious populations. Taken together, it means that when states choose to govern, they find it ever more costly and difficult to do so, as they operate under conditions of softened sovereignty (Clunan and Trinkunas 2010).

Policy responses to such governance gaps tend in a top-down direction, with varying degrees of external intervention to produce conformity to Western 'best practices.' At one end are establishment of standards for 'good governance,' followed by efforts to increase sovereign states' capacity for governance and/or provision of human rights, public goods, or transparent business climates (Risse 2008; UN 2013). Others, drawing insight from the juxtaposition of hierarchies and markets (Williamson 1975) and networks (Powell 1990), promote a neoliberal 'best practice' to change in the organizational structure of the state. At the other end are direct interventions to provide governance, whether in calls for renewing a trusteeship system for failed and failing states (Lake 2007), or in armed interventions to eliminate bad governors through regime change (Nichols 2003). In between there are all manner of official and public-private assistance and train-and-equip programs to assist states in fighting poverty, disease, trafficking, and transnational criminal and terrorist organizations. But at heart, these policy perspectives stubbornly cling to a conceptualization of governance founded on the Western welfare state as the prototypical and optimal form of governance (Clunan and Trinkunas 2010).

Scholars, ourselves included, have responded to talk of ungoverned spaces and state failure by pointing out that we are witnessing a different phenomenon: not ungovernability or undergovernance, but alternative governance (Clunan and Trinkunas 2010; Scott 2009; Andreas 2013). Scholars highlighted the fact of "governance without government" (Rosenau and Czempiel 1992). They demonstrated the increased importance of nonstate actors and novel, nongovernmental mechanisms in establishing and implementing international authoritative rules, ranging from banning landmines (Price 1998), to preventing deforestation (Cashore 2002), to corporate responsibility for human rights (UN 2008; Ruggie 2008), to business arbitration (Cutler 2003), to produce what Rosenau (1990) terms "multiple spheres of authority" and Kobrin (1998) terms "neomedievalism." Domestically and internationally, scholars find a variety of alternative governance structures at work. These can take the form of cooperation between governmental and nongovernmental actors in what is called "multi-level governance" (Marks 1992; Bache and Flinders 2004) or "governance with government" (Risse 2011). Other alternative structures display overlap and blending of state and nonstate institutions and actors in providing governance. These can be "hybrid political orders," where distinctions between state and nonstate, public, private, or civil spaces and actors blur (Boege et al. 2009; Arias 2009); "twilight institutions" (Lund 2009), which exercise public authority but are neither public nor private; or "mediated states" (Menkhaus 2007), where states are mutually dependent with private institutions in enacting authority.

This chapter focuses on the motivations of and means by which nonstate and international actors influence governance and security outcomes in Latin American ungoverned spaces, ranging from dense urban areas to thinly populated border zones. In contrast to the state-building, failed states, and global governance literatures, this chapter takes a deliberately non-normative approach to governance, the better to understand what factors contribute to it. Expanding on Risse, this chapter defines governance as "*institutionalized modes of social coordination to produce and implement collectively binding rules and outcomes*" (2011).[1] In the following sections, the chapter examines alternative governance structures in borderlands and in urban areas.

Alternative governance in the borders and borderlands of the Americas

Traditional research on border governance draws on European and North American cases, and as such, it emphasizes strong states. Classic strong states with high levels of effective sovereignty and capacity are relatively rare in Latin America, and even states that are quite strong in some areas, such as Brazil, have vast and difficult interior borders where state presence is sparse. Historically, many borders, particularly in South America, were remote from the centers of power and economic activity, and so they received little *de facto* attention from the state. At the same time, states in Latin America were highly attentive to protecting their *de jure* borders, proposing the principle of *uti possidetis juris* that enshrined in international law the inviolability of the borders inherited from the colonial period. Border disputes were not a matter of actual territorial control, but rather legal disputes among teams of lawyers and diplomats arguing about what the borders had been prior to independence (Domínguez et al. 2003). This intersection between *de jure* borders and states that lack *de facto* presence or capacity to control them produced opportunities for nonstate actors to step in and pursue their own interests. In some cases, this has led to the provision of governance functions, such as policing, economic regulation, and other public goods in borderlands (Jaskoski et al. 2015).

Globalization and regionalization have more recently affected Latin American state capacity and interest in border control through the pressure to facilitate flows of trade and people across borderlands. Globalization, understood as the growing range of connections among individuals and the acceleration of economic, material, and informational transactions between them, tends to put pressure on state regulatory and border policing functions. Regionalization, defined as the progressive economic and political integration among states for the purposes of development, tends to weaken state border controls in the pursuit of accelerated growth. Latin America has experienced a wide range of regionalization projects, and the most significant ones under way today are the North American Free Trade Agreement (NAFTA), Common Market of the South (MERCOSUR, consisting of Argentina, Brazil, Uruguay, Paraguay, and Venezuela), and the Pacific Alliance (Colombia, Mexico, Chile, and Peru). The overall effect of globalization and regionalization is to empower nonstate actors relative to state actors and erode the rationale for a strong border (Kacowicz 1998).

Differences in capacity and commitment to governing borderlands and borderlines between adjacent states, as is the case along the U.S.-Mexico, Mexico-Guatemala, and Brazil-Paraguay borders, create a risk for securitizing interstate relations. The presence of alternatively governed areas on one side of a border limit and state-governed ones on the other side creates another dynamic in which borderland, nonstate actors may use their local knowledge and capacity to insert themselves into the provision of governance goods. This may extend to the provision of security by militias, gangs, or local warlords. It may also attract economic enterprises that benefit from arbitrage between the degree of governance on the two sides of borders, such as traffickers in illicit goods and migrants. This creates the temptation for the high capacity state to intervene, either directly – through pressure or assistance to the lower capacity neighboring state – or indirectly – through its interactions with nonstate actors providing governance functions in the borderlands (Clunan and Trinkunas 2010). Here, the *de jure* borderline and sovereignty under international law of the weaker state may be an obstacle to the ability of the more capable state to intervene overtly to protect its interests. In such cases, the securitization of the border and borderlands is a strong temptation for the more capable state.

Two kinds of ungoverned or alternatively governed spaces exist along borders in the Americas, each with its own risks for security: borders that are remote from state centers of power, and highly transited borders between suppliers and consumers of illicit goods, labor, and capital. Remote borders are principally problematic insofar as the weakness of state presence encourages local power holders, such as land holders, mining companies, traffickers, and insurgents, to pursue their own interests in ways that are predatory or damaging to the human security of less powerful inhabitants of the borderlands. Conversely, in heavily trafficked borders, the sheer volume of flows, of which the U.S.-Mexico border is a good example, allows illicit actors to hide smuggled goods and persons within the licit cross-border traffic. Highly transited borders that cut off suppliers from consumers of illicit substances, migration, or financial flows create their own competitive and conflictive dynamic. Conflict occurs not just between the state and illicit actors attempting to cross these borders, but among illicit actors for territorial control of the best transit routes (Rios-Contreras 2012). Moreover, territorial control by illicit actors can also be a way to limit access to markets by others located further from the border. Border control by illicit actors allows them to function as gatekeepers to the consumer markets beyond. Revenues associated with illicit flows fuel the capabilities of nonstate, armed actors relative to the states on both sides of the border (Jaskoski et al. 2015).

Paradoxically, it is the essential characteristic of borders as a delimiting line of sovereignty and jurisdictional authority between states that attracts illicit actors. The borderline provides opportunities to those who can navigate through and around the border. These include illicit armed actors, such as rebels, insurgents, and criminal organizations who shield themselves from pursuit by taking advantage of the continuing importance of *de jure* sovereignty among even the weakest states of Latin America. State agents are very reluctant to violate international law by pursuing illicit actors into the sovereignty of even very weak neighbors. Differences between states in jurisdictional authority, regulatory structures, and, consequently, markets are another driver for illicit actors, particularly smugglers and transnational criminal organizations. These actors seek to use special skills and knowledge to cross borders carrying illicit goods, persons, and capital, taking advantage of the higher rewards and/or lower risks available in other sovereign jurisdictions. In practice, illicit armed actors along the frontier can take advantage of both dimensions of borders – sovereignty and jurisdictional differences – to enable their activities (Andreas 2003).

The question then becomes: When do nonstate actors provide governance in place of the state along the border? The main incentive for illicit actors to provide governance is to reduce risk for their activities or maximize rewards by deterring or excluding competitors. Governance in such situations can have a territorial dimension and/or a regulatory dimension. Does it make a difference for human security if nonstate actors focus on regulating flows or controlling space? Does one approach produce more predatory behavior than the other?

The negative impact of alternatively governed spaces on security typically receives a great deal of attention, but there are also instances where these actors actually reduce violence and threats to human security. This principally occurs when they collude with other actors to reduce costs and risks. Collusive strategies, such as cartelization among drug traffickers in Mexico and Colombia, are frequently accompanied by patronage to local communities to build support and shield illicit organizations from the occasional interest of the state. This quasi–state-like behavior can be welfare improving and benefit local communities through access to resources in areas where the state has withdrawn or it is otherwise not present. However, since the ability to impose binding governance outcomes is often associated with the use of force, it is important to keep in mind that armed, nonstate actors feel little obligation to (and frequently do not) adhere to international norms and laws on democracy and human rights (Schneckener 2006).

Nonstate actors operating in alternatively governed border spaces are consequential for national and international security, even if they otherwise have a positive effect on some aspects of human security. Weakly governed borders are used for refuge by transnational criminal networks or insurgents. In 1992 and 1994, Islamist terrorists attacked Israeli and Jewish targets in Buenos Aires, Argentina. Their base of operations was Ciudad del Este, a border city in Paraguay (Lombardi and Sanchez 2007: 231–246). Given that illicit actors shield themselves behind sovereignty, the states that are targets of their activities have the temptation to securitize the relationship with neighbors, pressuring them to adopt harder-line security measures against border actors. This can produce greatly increased violence and a public opinion backlash, as occurred in Mexico during the Calderón administration's war on drug cartels in the 2000s. Another outcome of cross-border threats can be militarization, leading to a threat of interstate-armed conflict. The juxtaposition of alternatively governed spaces and borders, a defining characteristic of states, is what creates opportunities for nonstate actors and risks for governments. The underlying dynamic is one of asymmetry: Alternatively governed spaces arise because of differences in capacity of state and nonstate actors in a borderland, between state regulatory, legal, and police frameworks on either side of the border, and between supply and demand for labor, goods, and capital in neighboring countries. These asymmetries create opportunities that nonstate actors can exploit to their advantage. Governance is a by-product of a desire to maximize rewards and reduce risks. The consequences for human, national, and international security are greatest when competition between states and armed actors – as well as among the armed actors themselves – produces conflict.

Alternative governance in Latin America's urban areas

Latin America is a highly urbanized region, one where rapid migration from rural areas to cities during the 20th century frequently outstripped the ability of states to plan or manage. Urban migration was driven most often by the search for improved economic opportunities available in cities. It was also occasionally the product of dislocation produced by civil conflict, as occurred in Central America during the 1980s and in Colombia during the 1990s. The rise of informal urban settlements, variously termed *barrios*, *favelas*, and *ciudades jovenes* depending on the country, has created a juxtaposition of governed and alternatively governed spaces in close proximity to one another. Even in relatively strong states such as Brazil, Argentina, and Chile, informal communities exist within the larger planned urban areas, often providing shelter for marginalized or working-class citizens (Arias 2010).

Marginalization among dwellers of informal settlements, associated with poverty, lack of education, race, or rural background, is paralleled by an absence of state resources for governance in these communities. This also leads to a lack of police presence, which tends to concentrate on the protection of property and wealthier and more politically influential citizens in the governed parts of urban areas. Although some states in the region have recently made a greater commitment to social inclusion, such as Brazil, by and large the effect of the 1980s debt crisis and neoliberal economic reforms during the 1990s was a reduction in state presence in informal settlements within urban areas. States made choices on where to concentrate their remaining governance resources, and these tended to focus on the most politically and economically influential segments of society (Schuberth 2013). This generates a marked governance gap within urban spaces, with wealthy, well-governed enclaves amidst alternatively governed areas of urban exclusion.

Alternatively governed spaces in cities have both a spatial and a temporal dimension. Spatially, pockets of unplanned urban settlements can be found in the less desirable section within cities, such as gullies or hillsides, and in rings around fast-growing cities where the unplanned settlements have spilled over the planned urban boundaries. Where armed actors such as criminal gangs or militia have taken hold, these communities may become 'no go' zones for the police. Temporally, often the night is a time when state governance is weakest in a number of large cities where growth has outstripped the capacity of state security forces to maintain order. The state concentrates its efforts on securing the daylight hours, which are most economically productive. But the consequence is that the night in unplanned communities is a time of especially low levels of state governance (Williams 2010).

Within this governance gap emerged nonstate actors, particularly armed ones, which began to provide governance functions. This behavior was instrumental, a means to maximize utility by minimizing risk and increasing the rewards of engaging in illicit activities within these spaces (Arias 2009).

It is the very proximity of alternatively and formally governed spaces that attracts illicit, nonstate actors, since they exploit the boundary between what is governed and ungoverned for their own benefit for the same reasons that operate in formal border zones. In addition to providing opportunities, proximity to governed space is also a threat to illicit actors. Even weak states are capable of projecting power at such close range to their power base in cities, even if they cannot sustain that presence across time. Illicit actors thus have an additional incentive to engage in governance activities to build legitimacy and authority in informal communities in order to minimize visible, politically disruptive disorder that attracts the intervention of state forces (Felbab-Brown 2011). In some cases, proximity to governed spaces is a two-way street, since it provides illicit actors with the ability to influence governance through the threat of generating disorder (Misse 2011).

The interaction between governed and alternatively governed spaces in urban areas produces political, social, and human security effects on governance that extend across both realms. Because most of Latin America is governed by democracies, politicians have an interest in voters in alternatively governed spaces, creating the temptation to negotiate with illicit actors for access.

National and international security effects of urban, ungoverned spaces in Latin America are subtler. Across the region insurgencies are no longer common, whereas Colombia is negotiating with the FARC an end to the last major domestic conflict in the region. This diminishes the likelihood that urban, ungoverned spaces will be sites for political conflict. At the same time, illicit trafficking networks use cities as waypoints in international networks, because they provide access to air travel, and ports, for access to shipping. Cities in Brazil and Argentina are major transshipment sites for cocaine and manufactured drugs flowing to Europe. However, because ports and airports tend to be sites of high state presence, the concern raised by some analysts has been 'hybrid governance,' collusion amongst illicit traffickers and state officials to enable illicit flows, rather than the ungoverned spaces in cities themselves. On another front, international terrorism has been an issue in some parts of the region, but with the exception of 1992 and 1994 in Buenos Aires, Latin America seems to be part of logistics and fundraising networks for Islamist and Basque terrorist organizations outside the region rather than an operational base (Lombardi and Sanchez 2007; Domínguez 2011).

Conclusions

Latin America's alternatively governed spaces have existed since the state system was formally introduced into the region. In the 19th century, elites in the newly independent countries of the Americas had few resources, and governance focused – as it still does today – on the most economically and politically important sectors, particularly those associated with the export sector. Attempts to build up the state in the 20th century produced governing structures with grand scopes of responsibility, but with uneven capacity to act effectively and efficiently. The retreat from the 20th century social welfare state in the 1990s compounded the shortage of state capacity and created new potential for ungoverned spaces.

As this chapter suggests, all ungoverned spaces are actually governed, but by nonstate actors. The alternative providers of governance in so-called ungoverned spaces are usually pursuing their own interests – maximizing rewards and minimizing risks. Governance provision secures support from the local populations, reduces the likelihood of external threats or competition, provides intelligence on other actors operating in the space, and helps to shield them from the gaze of the state. Governance in such spaces is not an altruistic objective but a by-product of the activities of (mostly) illicit actors.

Alternative providers of governance in ungoverned spaces are almost invariably those with the coercive capacity to enforce binding outcomes. This means that while their actions may be welfare-improving to the extent they provide employment or patronage, it raises questions about the increased risk of abusive practices in the areas governed. Illicit, armed actors are not automatically predatory, since local popular support and legitimacy can both facilitate their rule and minimize the cost of providing governance goods. However, threats to human security become most acute where there is contestation and competition among armed actors.

There is still a rich research agenda to explore the degree to which ungoverned spaces produce a threat to the national security of states in Latin America. One of the principal effects of alternative governance, from the point of view of state institutions, is that it obscures observation of the activities taking place in parts of their territory. This activity could be inconsequential for state security, or it could provide cover for significant emerging threats, as occurred in the Huallaga Valley in Peru in the 1980s and in Ciudad del Este in the 1990s. The other possible risk alternative governance creates is when violence and other negative by-products of the operations of illicit actors spill over into governed spaces. Given perennially limited resources, what should states do to identify which areas of lack of governance are most threatening?

From an international security perspective, the main concern with alternatively governed spaces in Latin America today is their connection with the vast web of flows of information, goods, and people around the globe. Globalization has linked Latin America to other continents in an ever-greater number of ways. This interconnectivity has broadened during the 2000s as a result of Latin America's expanded trade with Asia and Africa. This means that actors operating in alternatively governed spaces in Latin America may potentially be able to have a significant impact on security in other parts of the world. And if *de jure* states have trouble observing the actions of illicit actors in alternatively governed spaces on their own territory, the problem is compounded for international actors attempting to assess threat levels at an additional remove. This leads external actors, particularly the major powers, to press Latin American states to fill in their ungoverned spaces, particularly those viewed as most closely linked to terrorism, illicit goods, and migration.

Responding to alternatively governed spaces is both a matter of resources and strategy, and there are still many questions to be answered on how to define and how to produce success. Given the resource constraints some Latin American states face, particularly in Central America and the Caribbean, the top-down, state-led strategies preferred by the international community remain difficult to implement. Despite the persistence of ungoverned spaces, Latin America is now seen by intergovernmental organizations and multilateral development banks as an upper-middle income region. As a result, many foreign and international aid agencies no longer make the region a priority for assistance, further diminishing the prospects for success of top-down development approaches to fill in governance gaps. Even security assistance, once readily available from the United States in the region, has dwindled in recent years. What remains is highly focused on a few key U.S. partners, such as Colombia and Mexico. The limited availability of overseas development assistance means that the ability for small states in the region to implement strategies successfully, whether they focus on security or development, is highly constrained. Such limited ability is of concern because it is precisely these countries that are most vulnerable to illicit, armed actors.

As a result, civil society and private sector bottom-up contributions to governance outcomes in alternatively governed Latin American spaces will become increasingly important in the coming decades. There are still many questions about their capacity to do so effectively. Their ability to achieve positive outcomes appears to rely mainly on moral suasion or economic incentives, unless they act in cooperation with the state, which has the coercive capacity, even if limited, to challenge illicit, armed actors. In Latin America, it is these licit, nonstate actors who will need to bring the state back in. They can do so through public-private partnerships that both send a demand signal to politicians to extend formal governance into alternatively governed areas and provide the resources needed to complement limited state capacity available and crowd out corrupt hybrid governance in many parts of the region. How to achieve a positive contribution by civil society and private sector actors to governance remains the ultimate unanswered question about ungoverned spaces.

Note

1 Emphasis is in the original. In contrast to Risse, we do not equate governance with the provision of collective goods, as this imports normative judgments into the concept of governance. Governance may produce what are normatively collective 'bads' (such as slavery or racial or gender discrimination) even as it provides stability and predictability in social life.

References

Andreas, P. (2003) 'Redrawing the Line: Borders and Security in the Twenty-first Century', *International Security*, 28(2): 78–111.

——— (2013). *Smuggler Nation: How Illicit Trade Made America*, Oxford: Oxford University Press.

Andreas, P. and Price, R. (2001) 'From War Fighting to Crime Fighting: Transforming the American National Security State', *International Studies Review*, 3(3): 31–52.

Arias, E. D. (2009) *Drugs and Democracy in Rio de Janeiro: Trafficking, Social Networks, and Public Security*, Chapel Hill: University of North Carolina Press.

——— (2010) 'Understanding Criminal Networks, Political Order, and Politics in Latin America' in A. L. Clunan and H. A. Trinkunas (eds) *Ungoverned Spaces: Alternatives to State Authority in an Era of Softened Sovereignty*, Stanford, CA: Stanford University Press, pp. 115–135.

Bache, I. and Flinders, M. (eds) (2004) *Multi-level Governance*, Oxford: Oxford University Press.

Boege, V., Brown, M. and Clements, K. (2009) 'Hybrid Political Orders, Not Fragile States', *Peace Review: A Journal of Social Justice*, 21(1): 13–21.

Bouillon, C. P. and Tejerina, L. (2006) *Do We Know What Works? A Systematic Review of Impact Evaluations of Social Programs in Latin America and the Caribbean*, Washington, DC: Inter-American Development Bank (IDB) Publications.

Bourne, M. (2011) 'Netwar Geopolitics: Security, Failed States and Illicit Flows', *British Journal of Politics and International Relations*, 13: 490–513.

Cashore, B. (2002) 'Legitimacy and the Privatization of Environmental Governance: How Non–State Market–Driven (NSMD) Systems Gain Rule-Making Authority', *Governance*, 15(4): 503–529.

Cerny, P. G. (1995) 'Globalization and the Changing Logic of Collective Action', *International Organization*, 49(4): 595–625.

Clunan, A. L. and Trinkunas, H. A. (eds) (2010) *Ungoverned Spaces: Alternatives to State Authority in an Era of Softened Sovereignty*, Stanford: Stanford University Press.

Cutler, A. C. (2003) *Private Power and Global Authority: Transnational Merchant Law in the Global Political Economy*, New York: Cambridge University Press.

Domínguez, F. (2011) 'Venezuela, el ultimo refugio de ETA', *Cuadernos de Pensamiento Político*, June: 31–40.

Domínguez, J. I. et al. (2003) *Boundary Disputes in Latin America*, Washington, DC: United States Institute of Peace.

Felbab-Brown, V. (2011) *Bringing the State to the Slum: Confronting Organized Crime and Urban Violence in Latin America*, Washington, DC: Brookings Institution.

Fukuyama, F. (2004) *State-Building: Governance and World Order in the 21st Century*, Ithaca, NY: Cornell University Press.

Jaskoski, M., Sotomayor, A. C. and Trinkunas, H. A. (forthcoming 2015) *American Crossings: Border Politics in the Western Hemisphere*, Baltimore, MD: Johns Hopkins University Press.

Kacowicz, A. M. (1998) 'Regionalization, Globalization, and Nationalism: Convergent, Divergent, or Overlapping?', Working Paper, No. 262, Notre Dame, IN: Helen Kellogg Institute for International Studies.

Kilcullen, D. (2013) *Out of the Mountains: The Coming Age of the Urban Guerrilla*, Oxford: Oxford University Press.

Kobrin, S. J. (1998) 'Back to the Future: Neomedievalism and the Postmodern Digital World Economy', *Journal of International Affairs*, 51(2): 361–387.

Krasner, S. D. and Pascual, C. (2005) 'Addressing State Failure: The Danger of Failed States', *Foreign Affairs*, 84(4): 153–163.

Lake, D. A. (2007, April 17) 'Building Legitimate States After Civil Wars: Order, Authority, and International Trusteeship', Unpublished manuscript.

Lombardi, J. and Sanchez, D. (2007) 'Terrorist Financing and the Tri-Border Area of South America: The Challenge of Effective Government Response in a Permissive Environment' in J. K. Giraldo and H. A. Trinkunas (eds) *Terrorism Financing and State Responses: A Comparative Perspective*, Stanford: Stanford University Press.

López-Alves, F. (2000) *State Formation and Democracy in Latin America, 1810–1900*, Durham, NC: Duke University Press.

Lund, C. (2009) 'Twilight Institutions: Public Authority and Local Politics in Africa', *Development and Change*, 37: 685–705.

Marks, G. (1992) 'Structural Policy in the European Community' in A. Sbragia (ed) *Euro-Politics: Institutions and Policymaking in the "New" European Community*, Washington, DC: The Brookings Institution, pp. 191–224.

Menkhaus, K. (2007) 'Governance without Government in Somalia. Spoilers, State Building, and the Politics of Coping', *International Security*, 31(3): 74–106.

Misse, M. (2011) 'Crime organizado e crime comum no Rio de Janeiro: Diferenças e afinidades', *Revista de Sociologia E Política*, 19(40): 13–25.
Naím, M. (2005) *Illicit: How Smugglers, Traffickers, and Copycats Are Hijacking the Global Economy*, New York: Doubleday.
Nichols, T. M. (2003) 'Just War, Not Prevention', *Ethics & International Affairs*, 17(1): 25–29.
Norton, R. J. (2003) 'Feral Cities', *Naval War College Review*, LVI(4): 97–106.
Patrick, S. (2006) 'Weak States and Global Threats: Fact or Fiction?', *The Washington Quarterly*, 29(2): 27–53.
Powell, W. W. (1990) 'Neither Market nor Hierarchy: Network Forms of Organization', *Research in Organizational Behavior*, 12: 295–336.
Price, R. (1998) 'Reversing the Gun Sights: Transnational Civil Society Targets Land Mines', *International Organization*, 52(3): 613–644.
Restall, M. (2003) *Seven Myths of the Spanish Conquest*, Oxford: Oxford University Press.
Rios-Contreras, V. (2012) 'How Government Structure Encourages Criminal Violence: The Causes of Mexico's Drug War', Ph.D. thesis, Harvard University.
Risse, T. (2008, March 26–30) 'Governance in Areas of Limited Statehood: How Far Do Concepts Travel?' Paper presented at the International Studies Association Annual Convention, San Francisco, CA.
——— (ed) (2011) *Governance Without a State? Policies and Politics in Areas of Limited Statehood*, New York: Columbia University Press.
Rosenau, J. N. (1990) *Turbulence in World Politics: A Theory of Change and Continuity*, Princeton, NJ: Princeton University Press.
Rosenau, J. N. and Czempiel, E. O. (1992) *Governance without Government: Order and Change in World Politics*, Cambridge, UK: Cambridge University Press.
Rotberg, R. I. (2003) 'Failed States, Collapsed States, Weak States: Causes and Indicators' in R. I. Rotberg (ed) *When States Fail: Causes and Consequences*, Princeton, NJ: Princeton University Press, pp. 1–25.
Rouquié, A. (1987) *The Military and the State in Latin America*, Berkeley, CA: University of California Press.
Ruggie, J. G. (2008) 'Taking Embedded Liberalism Global: The Corporate Connection' in J. G. Ruggie (ed.) *Embedding Global Markets: The Enduring Challenge*, Aldershot, UK: Ashgate, pp. 231–254.
Schneckener, U. (2006) 'Fragile Statehood, Armed Non-State Actors and Security Governance' in A. Bryden and M. Caparini (eds) *Private Actors and Security Governance*, Geneva: Centre for Democratic Control of Armed Forces (DCAF), pp. 23–40.
Schuberth, M. (2013, April) 'Challenging the Weak States Hypothesis: Vigilantism in South Africa and Brazil', *Journal of Peace, Conflict & Development*, 20: 38–51.
Scott, J. C. (2009) *The Art of Not Being Governed: An Anarchist History of Upland Southeast Asia*, New Haven: Yale University Press.
UN (2004) *A More Secure World: Our Shared Responsibility: Report of the High Level Panel on Threats, Challenges, and Change*, New York: United Nations.
——— (2008, April 7) *Protect, Respect and Remedy: A Framework for Business and Human Rights* (A/HRC/8/5).
——— (2013) 'Governance', *Global Issues*, United Nations. Retrieved from http://www.un.org/en/globalissues/governance/.
UN-Habitat (2006) *State of the World's Cities 2006/7*, London: Earthscan.
Williams, P., National Defense University Press and National Defense University (2010) *Enhancing Civilian Protection in Peace Operations: Insights from Africa*, Washington, DC: National Defense University Press.
Williamson, O. E. (1975) *Markets and Hierarchies: Analysis and Antitrust Implications*, New York: Free Press.

PART III

Different ‘securities’

9

TRADITIONAL SECURITY

War and peace

Cameron G. Thies

Introduction

Why continue to study traditional security in Latin America? Today the region is full of democracies, and there are a variety of international institutions in place designed to facilitate trade and resolve conflicts. Surely, militarized conflict and war are a thing of the past? Yet, as Mares notes in his recent book, *Latin America and the Illusion of Peace*, "we ignore the signs of potential militarized conflict in Latin America at our peril" (2012: 25). Unfortunately, the issuance of threats between countries, and the aggressive display and use of force has not disappeared. Since 2001, there have been over a dozen militarized interstate disputes (MIDs) in the region. We do not have to look too far back in time to find a full-fledged interstate war between Ecuador and Peru (1995's Cenapa Valley War that claimed 1,500 lives). Even joint democracy could not prevent this war, nor has it prevented a variety of MIDs in the region (Domínguez et al. 2003: 29; Simmons 1999). The use of force is not off the table in Latin America, and the sources of potential conflicts in the region have not been tamed; thus it is worthwhile to continue to engage in theoretical and empirical analyses regarding peace and security in the region.

There are two dominant approaches to understanding war and peace in Latin America. The first attempts to explain specific classes of conflict: war, rivalry, militarized interstate disputes (MIDs), and civil wars as phenomena in their own right. The second approach tries to explain the type of regional order (e.g., zone of peace) that prevails at any given time, and is mostly oriented toward the explanation of relatively peaceful regional relations. The two approaches to war and peace are not unrelated; indeed, the type and prevalence of conflict are important constitutive aspects of most approaches to understanding regional order. The causes of most forms of conflict are also often hypothesized to be the causes of most forms of regional order. In this chapter I briefly review the literature in both approaches, then suggest a way to more closely link the two approaches – such that explanations of both dyadic-level and regional-level phenomenon are captured within the same theoretical and empirical analysis.

Explaining conflict in Latin America

The first approach to understanding war and peace in Latin America is to study the specific forms of interstate and intrastate conflict that are prevalent in the contemporary interstate system. These forms include interstate conflicts short of war (MIDs), traditional interstate war, and interstate rivalry. The hypothesized sources of interstate conflict in its various forms are largely the same: boundary and territorial issues; riparian and maritime issues; ideology; natural resources; and the porosity of borders (e.g., transnational crime, cross-border insurgency, drug trade, arms trade, and migration).[1] None of these issues must necessarily become militarized, but they often do. Once they escalate, it can be hard to predict the overall hostility and severity associated with a conflict.[2] Some approaches move beyond specific issues to consider larger structural sources of conflict, such as the effect of regional balances of power or regional hegemony, as well as the nature and amount of trade flows. Great Power interventions have often served both as a source and potential resolution of some conflicts. Domestically, there is evidence for the use of diversionary force by leaders to take attention off of poor government performance at home, especially of an economic nature. Regime type seems largely unrelated to interstate conflict in Latin America – as democracy is certainly no guarantee of peace (Domínguez et al. 2003: 29; Simmons 1999).

Interstate conflicts short of war

Most studies of interstate conflicts short of war in Latin America are interested in their dynamics, rather than predicting or explaining the specific conflict. These dynamics can include intraconflict and interconflict changes. Mares (2001, 2012: 64–85) proposes a general model of intraconflict dynamics that helps to explain when a leader chooses to militarize a dispute. According to the model, a leader may choose to use force when the costs associated with a given political-military strategy, the strategic balance, and the characteristics of force are acceptable to the leader's constituency. Political-military strategies could include achieving a military conquest,[3] diverting attention from domestic problems,[4] keeping the issue in a dispute at the forefront of attention, affecting bilateral negotiations, defending the status quo, attracting the support of third parties, and imposing a solution. Strategic balance refers to "the factors which influence the likely costs produced by the strategies each actor can use in particular disputes, rather than in its more narrow military sense" (Mares 2012: 70). This would include the costs associated with anticipated diplomatic, economic, and military responses to militarization. Yet, because of both incomplete and private information held by either side, the strategic balance is never perfectly clear to both parties. The characteristics of force include the force alternatives and mobilization requirements related to military capabilities and the match to the specific context for which they will be used.

In addition to these three factors, Mares (2012: 86) also considers the costs that the leader's constituency is willing to bear. These are affected by political polarization, which produces the tendency to define issues in terms of the national interest, thus increasing their value, and the costs the constituency is willing to pay for their defense. The costs are also affected by the willingness of constituencies to use state power to address threats. Finally, Mares (2012: 88) argues that the accountability of a leader to a constituency can either impede or enhance militarization. A leader that is accountable to the constituency may choose to militarize a dispute based on the constituency's desires, though one that is not accountable will choose for her/himself. Mares (2001, 2012) tested this model against cases using narrative analysis and data on the conflict. As he notes, the implications of this model could be tested with quantitative methods as well, something future work in this area should consider.

Hensel (1994) proposes a model of interconflict dynamics that explains recurrent interstate conflict in Latin America. By recurrent interstate conflict, he means when the same two states engage in a series of two or more MIDs (Hensel 1994: 287). He focuses on territory as a contentious issue between states that is a likely culprit to link multiple MIDs across time. He finds that MIDs in which territory was at stake are more likely to be followed by further MIDs than other types of issues. Further, the outcome of MIDs over territory (i.e., decisive, stalemate, compromise) affects recurrent conflict, with compromise reducing the likelihood of future conflict, though not completely eliminating it. Compromise outcomes on territorial disputes produced the longest period of post-dispute stability (nearly 11 years on average), with decisive outcomes of somewhat shorter periods (nine years), and stalemates yielding the shortest stability, at only around four years. Combining this type of quantitative work with qualitative analyses of norms, institutional interventions, and the outcomes of conflict could be a very promising avenue for future research.

Table 9.1 documents MIDs in Latin America from 1826 to 2010, reflecting the most recent update to the MID project.[5] The overall number and yearly rate of MIDs during the 19th century is relatively low, reflecting the fact that states in the region were more typically engaging in war. The two 20th century periods reflect an increase in the overall numbers and rates of MIDs per year. One can see that Great Power intervention has declined over time in the region.[6] Finally, the table also documents the persistence of territorial issues across the periods at around 35 per cent of the total MIDs, with even a slight uptick in the post–World War II era.

The persistence of boundary and territorial disputes is frequently noted by scholars in the region (e.g., Domínguez et al. 2003; Mares 2012). While many of the stickiest boundary disputes have been settled in recent years, such as Argentina-Chile, Ecuador-Peru, and Chile-Peru, others are outstanding and generate 'hot spots' for conflict in Central America and the northern tier of South America. While arbitration and mediation have been successfully used for such disputes, there are a number of reasons why they persist. Domínguez et al. (2003: 26–28) suggest that geography has made it difficult to demarcate boundaries in many places, processes that might have led to permanent settlements have been interrupted by external interventions, international mediations may have cooled conflicts without resolving them, and the use of techniques of dispute management, such as freezing claims by treaty, may only put off conflicts until later dates. Moral hazards are introduced by the variety of inter-American peacekeeping institutions as well, as states know they can militarize a conflict relying on institutions to prevent it from escalating to war, and states that do not wish to compromise may use such institutions to prevent others from imposing a settlement. Future work should engage in additional qualitative and quantitative tests of territorial vs. other types of MIDs, the effect of Great Power interventions on conflict, and the stability of various forms of settlement. There are a variety of methods and approaches that have been developed in the general conflict literature that could usefully be harnessed to Latin America's MIDs, including geocoding and spatial analyses.

Table 9.1 Militarized interstate disputes (MIDs) in Latin America, 1826–2010

Time Period	*All MIDs*	*Territorial MIDs*	*Great Power MIDs*
1826–1899	122 (1.6 per year)	39 (33% of total)	77 (63% of total)
1900–1945	164 (3.6 per year)	56 (34% of total)	82 (50% of total)
1946–2010	205 (3.2 per year)	75 (37% of total)	69 (34% of total)
Totals	491 (2.7 per year)	170 (35% of total)	228 (47% of total)

Source: Correlates of War Project, http://www.correlatesofwar.org/.

Interstate war

Latin America has seen 15 wars between sovereign states in its history.[7] Most of these wars were fought in the 19th century in South America and at the turn of the 20th century in Central America. The list of interstate wars does not fully exhaust large-scale political violence between state-like entities, as 13 nonstate wars occurred between entities vying to organize and create modern states in the region in the early 19th century.[8] The Chaco War (1932–1935) was the last interstate war with large numbers of casualties. The last war in Central America was the Football War (1969), the last war in the Southern Cone was Argentina's war with the United Kingdom over the Falklands/Malvinas (1982), and the last war in the Andean subregion was also the entire region's last war between Ecuador and Peru (1995) in the Cenepa Valley. In general, Latin America displays a pattern that is to be expected given its historical emergence from colonialism with nonstate wars giving rise to sovereign states in the 19th century that went on to consolidate and fight other sovereign states over a variety of issues, followed by a general decline in the use of interstate war as a political instrument after World War II.[9] Scholars now refer to a "norm against conquest" (Fazal 2007), a "norm of territorial integrity" (Zacher 2001), or a "norm of fixed borders" (Atzili 2007) to explain the general decline in interstate war's acceptability and the belief that "force should not be used to alter interstate boundaries" (Zacher 2001: 215).

Domínguez et al. (2003: 20–22) also suggest three other factors that have reduced the likelihood of war to a rarity. The first is the structure of the international system in South and Central America. South America saw the rise of an effective balance of power system that prevented major war after the 1880s, while the U.S. occupation of Nicaragua put a temporary stop to Central American wars. The second factor is the relative insulation of Latin America from the international system. The third factor is the legal principle of *uti possidetis juris*, in which states kept the territory that the previous colonial power occupied. Though this principle was imperfect, it became a focal point for most territorial management, and there have only been six major exceptions to it over time. Related to this legal principle was the ideological principle that Spanish American elites felt they were part of a larger cultural (and possibly political) entity; thus, they should not go to war with each other. Both contributed to the prevalence of the use of mediation and arbitration in territorial disputes in Latin America.

It might still be premature to completely eliminate the idea of interstate war from our understanding of Latin American conflict. The strategic triangle formed by Colombia, Ecuador, and Venezuela has recently been to the brink of war in 2008, after the Colombian military attacked a guerrilla camp in Ecuador. Ecuador mobilized its military in response to the incursion, and Venezuela sent 6,000 troops to the border with a warning that war would ensue if Colombia violated its territorial sovereignty. A week later, the three presidents ended the crisis at a meeting of the Rio Group in the Dominican Republic, though Colombia and Ecuador did not reestablish diplomatic relations until 2010. This particular crisis escalated to the brink of war, though it was part of a chain of militarized disputes extending back to 2003 that drew in the three states over Colombia's continued fight against rebels and paramilitaries who move between the three. The interlinked nature of many of these militarized conflicts has led to the study of interstate rivalries in the region.

Rivalry

Interstate rivalries are a commonly noted feature of the Latin American regional system, according to regional specialists (Grabendorff 1994; Mares 2012). Conflict scholars also took note of Hensel's (1994) work on recurrent conflict, which was developed around the same time as early empirical work on enduring rivalries in international relations (e.g., Goertz and Diehl 1992). The empirical identification of rivalries largely outpaced the conceptualization of rivalry, though the seeds were clearly contained in Hensel's work on Latin America. The identification of contentious issues that gave rise to serial conflict became one of the major approaches to conceptualizing and operationalizing interstate rivalries. Mitchell and Thies (2011) develop several approaches to interstate rivalry grounded in the identification of contentious issues. Table 9.2 lists the Latin American rivalries from their approaches. For our purposes, we are likely interested in those rivalries that are listed in bold (experiencing two or more MIDs), or those in the third column labeled militarized rivalries. In both cases, the rivalries identified have featured the militarization of foreign policy surrounding an issue. The issues under contention in this list include territory, maritime, and riparian disputes. A total of 43 rivalries are identified for Latin America; 17 of these include Great Powers, such as the United States, Great Britain, France, Spain, and Russia. The importance of rivalries to the region is thus beyond dispute, but exactly how are they important other than as a representation of recurrent interstate conflict?

I have argued elsewhere that territory has been incorporated into the nation-building project of a number of Latin American states (Thies 2001). Drawing upon work by Escudé (1984, 1988), Ugarte (1925), and Calvert and Calvert (1989), I have documented the manner in which territorial conflicts gave rise to a form of territorial nationalism in the Argentina-Chile rivalry. In both Argentina and Chile, elite discourse over boundaries and territorial claims often initiated the process, such as debate over the title deeds of Patagonia in which both Argentines and Chileans attempted to marshal Crown documents to claim the entire southern region on both sides of the Andes – a case where *uti possidetis* was not particularly helpful. Elite discourse then wound its way through educational institutions, the press, public opinion, and the military to create a form of territorial nationalism that emphasized great territorial losses for both Argentina and Chile. Territorial nationalism therefore formed the glue that held together a series of 27 territorial conflicts, such that an interstate rivalry was formed between the two countries. The interstate rivalry therefore became an institutional feature of interstate relations, in which unresolved territorial conflicts shaped both national identity and foreign policy decision-making. Even periods of joint democratic governance did not constrain the militarization of territorial conflicts, as proponents of the democratic peace would have us believe, and public opinion often pushed for war when governments urged restraint (cf. Russett and Oneal 2001). Future research should identify other likely candidates where territorial conflict may give rise to territorial nationalism and form the heart of a rivalry. Ecuador-Peru seems a likely candidate based on previous work by Simmons (1999) and Herz and Noguiera (2002), as are many of the aforementioned rivalries between neighbors presented in bold print in Table 9.2.

According to Thies (2005, 2006) rivalries produced by such a process also helped to strengthen states in the region. Unlike Centeno's (2002) approach to classic bellicist theory, in which interstate wars are thought to improve state capacity, Thies argued that the declining utility of interstate war meant that other forms of conflict, such as rivalry, may be serving a similar feature in the contemporary interstate system. Centeno (2002) suggested that most Latin American wars were too limited in scope and fought at the wrong times in order to produce state-building. Thies's (2005, 2006) statistical analyses demonstrated that Centeno was largely correct – interstate wars reduced state capacity over time.[10] Conversely, interstate rivalries produce a small but robust improvement in the state's ability to extract taxes. This effect held even controlling for the ability to take on debt to fund conflicts. Thies suggested that rivalries helped to producer stronger, but not 'strong,' states in Latin America – strong enough to pursue

Table 9.2 Interstate rivalries in Latin America

Interstate Rivalry[1]	*Issue*[2]	*Militarized*[3]
United States–Haiti	1859–	
United States–Mexico	1831–2001	1831–48
United States–Honduras	1899–1972	
United States–Nicaragua	1900–28, 1965–	
United States–Panama	1923–95	
United States–Colombia	1890–1972	
United States–Ecuador		1952–
United States–Peru		1947–
Haiti–Dominican Republic	1894–1935	
Trinidad & Tobago–Venezuela		1962–
Belize–Guatemala	1981–	1981–
Belize–Honduras	1981–	
Guatemala–Honduras		1899–1933
Guatemala–United Kingdom	1868–1981	1868–1981
Honduras–El Salvador	1899–	1899–1992
Honduras–Nicaragua	1900–	1912–61, 1912–, 1999
Honduras–Colombia	1982–86	
Honduras–United Kingdom	1981	
Nicaragua–Colombia	1900–30, 1979–	1979–
Colombia–Venezuela	1951–	1951–, 1955–
Colombia–Peru	1839–1935	1839–1922, 1932–35
Venezuela–Guyana	1966–	1966–
Venezuela–United Kingdom	1841–1966	1841–99
Venezuela–Netherlands	1850–66	1854–66
Guyana–Suriname	1975–	1975–
Guyana–Netherlands	1966–75	
Ecuador–Peru	1854–1998	1854–1945, 1947–98
Ecuador–Brazil	1854–1922	
Peru–Bolivia	1848–1936	1848–1912
Peru–Chile	1879–1929	1879–84, 1884–1929
Peru–Spain	1864–66	
Brazil–Paraguay	1846–1929	1846–74
Brazil–Argentina	1972–98	
Brazil–United Kingdom	1826–1926	1838–1926
Brazil–France		1826–1900
Bolivia–Paraguay		1878–1938
Bolivia–Chile	1848–	1848–84, 1884–
Paraguay–Argentina	1941–83	
Chile–Argentina	1841–1998	1841–1903, 1904–85, 1900–85
Chile–United Kingdom	1940–	
Argentina–Uruguay	1882–1973	1882–1973, 1900–73
Argentina–United Kingdom	1841–	1841–, 1940–, 1966–
Argentina–Russia		1967–86

Note

[1]Rivalries in bold are those that experience two or more militarized disputes over the contested issues.

[2]An issue rivalry exists if the dyad experienced two or more territorial, maritime, or river claims simultaneously. The rivalry starts when the first issue claim begins and ends when the last issue claim is resolved.

[3] A militarized rivalry exists if the dyad experienced two or more MIDs over a specific issue. The rivalry begins when the issue claim begins and ends when the issue claim is resolved.

Source: Adapted from Mitchell and Thies (2011).

internal conflicts, but not strong enough to engage in anything other than serialized, low-level conflicts over territory and other salient issues. Future research should also further explore how domestic and interstate conflicts shape and constrain the capacity of the state as it encounters subsequent issues and has to decide whether and how to militarize them.

Civil wars

Intrastate or civil wars, while they are not generally a form of interstate conflict, can affect relations between states nonetheless (see Hartzell, this volume). In Latin America, the presence of civil conflicts within states has probably had an overall effect of dampening interstate conflict. According to Grabendorff (1994: 244), the emphasis placed on internal security problems contributed to the general lack of interstate conflict between 1948 and 1965. Table 9.3 identifies the number of intrastate conflicts, their years, and the estimated fatalities from each for Latin American countries. Thies's (2005, 2006) analysis indicated very few cases in which interstate and civil wars were fought simultaneously by a state. Thus, more civil war has had the effect of reducing interstate war. Andreski (1980) supplies the rationale for this, since he argues there is a fundamental incompatibility between internal and external uses of force, such that increased frequency of the internal use of force diminishes the capability of the military to wage war

Table 9.3 Intrastate wars in Latin America

State	*# Civil War*	*Civil War Years*	*Total Deaths*
Argentina	10	1841–42, 1861, 1863, 1866–67, 1870–71, 1874, 1879–80, 1880, 1955, 1975–77	10050+
Bolivia	3	1862, 1870–71, 1952	?
Brazil	7	1835–37, 1835–45, 1837–38, 1893–94, 1893–94, 1896–97, 1932	8500+
Chile	3	1851, 1891, 1973	9100+
Colombia	8	1840–42, 1860–61, 1876–77, 1884–85, 1895, 1899–1902, 1948–58, 1989–	164031+
Costa Rica	1	1948	2000
Cuba	2	1912, 1958–59	4050
Dominican Rep.	1	1965	2500+
Ecuador	2	1895, 1912–14	1000+
El Salvador	2	1932, 1979–92	3500+
Guatemala	3	1966–68, 1970–71, 1978–84	8000
Honduras	1	1924	?
Mexico	14	1832, 1835–36, 1841, 1848–55, 1855–56, 1858–61, 1867, 1876, 1899–1900, 1910–14, 1914–20, 1923–24, 1926–29, 1929	148800+
Nicaragua	2	1978–79, 1982–90	36200
Paraguay	2	1911–12, 1947	5000+
Peru	6	1853–55, 1856–58, 1885, 1894–95, 1932, 1982–92	?
Uruguay	1	1904	?
Venezuela	5	1848–49, 1859–63, 1868, 1899, 1901–03	27600+

Note: There are 74 total intrastate wars in Latin America out of a total of 334 for the entire world through 2007.
Source: Correlates of War Project, http://www.correlatesofwar.org/.

externally. This is because time, equipment, and organization directed toward the pursuit of internal threats detract from the pursuit of external threats. Thies (2005, 2006) found that civil wars reduce state fiscal capacity in Latin America, and Murdoch and Sandler (2002) show that they depress economic growth as well.

Civil conflict in Latin America also runs the risk of becoming internationalized, which may bring states into conflict with each other over their differing, domestic, political processes. For example, Colombia's long-running battle with the FARC and its uses of camps in neighboring Ecuador was a contributing factor in the 2008 incident described above that brought Colombia, Ecuador, and Venezuela to the brink of war. Gleditsch and Beardsley (2004) conducted an analysis of event data for three Central American civil wars (El Salvador, Guatemala, and Nicaragua) from 1984 to 2001 to show that existing third-party interveners affected the level of cooperation among competing groups.

Explaining peace in Latin America

Regional order

The second approach to studying war and peace in Latin America is largely focused on the regional level of analysis. The late 1990s saw a renewed interest in the idea of variation in regional international orders, such that some were more peaceful and others more conflict-prone for relatively long periods of time. Each of the general approaches to regional order revolves around the amount and type of the aforementioned interstate conflicts, and draws on many of their purported causes as causes of regional outcomes. Buzan and Waever (2003: 320) describe the Cold War South American regional security complex as a conflict formation significantly penetrated, but not superseded, by the United States. In the post–Cold War, they see South America split into two regional subcomplexes: a Southern Cone that is transforming into something approaching a pluralistic security community, and the Andean North that is still a traditional conflict formation.[11] Using the Adler and Barnett (1998) approach, Hurrell (1998: 260) suggests that a "loosely coupled, if still imperfect, security community can be identified within Mercosur" built largely around the changes in the Argentine-Brazilian relationship since the late 1970s. Miller (2007) describes South America in the 19th century as a zone of war due to state weakness that emerged into a "normal peace" in the 20th century as states consolidated. According to Kacowicz (1998), South America was a zone of conflict from 1810 to 1881, then emerged as a zone of negative peace during 1883–1919, which was interrupted by the interwar period, then renewed until the 1980s when a stable peace began to emerge in the Southern Cone. Mares (2001) referred more generally to the "violent peace" of the region, which connotes something similar to negative peace.

Thies (2008) merges Kacowicz's (1998) approach to zones of negative peace with Wendt's (1999) Lockean culture of anarchy to try and synthesize dyadic and regional theorizing and empirical analysis. I use Thies (2008) as an extended example of one way to usefully combine more traditional, dyadic conflict studies with the emerging interest in regional order in Latin America. Kacowicz (1998) proposes a number of hypotheses responsible for the maintenance of the negative peace of a region, which he groups into realist, liberal, and neo-Grotian categories. Thies (2008) matches these to Wendt's (1999: 285–290) three degrees of the institutionalization of sovereignty norms: coercion, self-interest, and legitimacy. The first degree is the realist path to a Lockean culture of anarchy based on coercion, which suggests that states are forced to respect sovereignty norms by others who are more powerful. Kacowicz includes the presence of a hegemon (regional or extraregional); a regional balance of power; an external threat to the states in the region; and geographical isolation, irrelevance, and impotence to wage wars as potential realist explanations of the zone of negative peace. The second degree is the liberal path to a Lockean culture of anarchy based on self-interest, which suggests that states respect sovereignty norms because of their self-interest in achieving other goals, like increased trade. The presence of liberal democratic regimes, high levels of economic development and prosperity, economic interdependence, and integration and transnational links are expected by Kacowicz to support the negative peace.[12] The third degree is what Wendt refers to as the constructivist path to a Lockean culture of anarchy based on legitimacy. This path suggests that states respect sovereignty norms because they are seen as legitimate, unquestioned parts of the interstate order. The related neo-Grotian explanation offered by Kacowicz (1998: 39) is that a common cultural framework and normative consensus about conflict management and resolution helps to keep the negative peace.

Rivalry becomes the linchpin of Thies's analyses, since Wendt argues that the dominance of the rival role identity should produce the Lockean culture of anarchy (also known as a zone of negative peace). Thies uses an existing measure of rivalry to conduct simultaneous equation modeling, where one equation predicts the Lockean culture of anarchy operationalized as the number of rivalries present in the region in a year. The second equation models the existence of a rivalry within a state dyad. Thus we have two equations, one predicting the Lockean culture of anarchy and one predicting rivalry, even as they both predict each other. What is particularly helpful about this statistical technique is that it allows us to capture the simultaneous constitution of agents and structures. The regional culture should result from previous regional and dyadic interactions, just as the dyadic role relationship is a result of previous dyadic and regional characteristics.

The Lockean culture of anarchy is predicted in this model by variables representing the nine realist, liberal, and neo-Grotian hypotheses from Kacowicz (1998), as well as the presence of a rival role relationship in the dyad. The rival role relationship is predicted by typical measures associated with rivalry, as well as the size of the Lockean culture of anarchy.

The analysis demonstrates that the formation of a rivalry and the size of the Lockean culture of anarchy mutually increase each other. This is some evidence of a mutual constitution of agents and structures, and that the rival role identity works empirically in the way that Wendt describes in his purely theoretical account. The other variables and their relationship to the three zones of peace/cultures of anarchy are presented in Table 9.4. In the center column is the zone of negative peace/Lockean culture of anarchy and the three paths that potentially support it (realist, liberal, and constructivist). The realist path to a Lockean culture of anarchy based on coercion is supported in the statistical model. For example, hegemonic presence and activity by the United States in Latin America supports the zone of negative peace, though cumulative intervention and the perception of overwhelming U.S. capabilities have the opposite effect. The later finding indicates that the United States sometimes acts as an overly intrusive *caudillo*, which would suggest movement toward a zone of conflict. The regional balance of power did not support the negative peace when it was in operation, but instead may have moved the region toward a zone of conflict. Domestic shocks (like civil wars) and distance maintain the negative peace. The liberal path based on self-interest finds that higher levels of democracy move the region away from a negative peace (possibly toward a stable peace), while regional trade agreements and regional economic development support a negative peace. Finally, the constructivist path based on legitimacy demonstrates that higher levels of regional satisfaction and negotiations to settle territorial issues in Latin America move the region away from negative peace (and possibly toward stable peace).

Table 9.4 Factors supporting zones of peace/cultures of anarchy

Zone of Conflict (Hobbesian Culture)	*Negative Peace (Lockean Culture)*	*Positive/Stable Peace (Kantian Culture)*
	Realist Path	
	U.S. Hegemonic Role	
U.S. Relative Capabilities		
	U.S. Intervention	
U.S. Cumulative Intervention		
Regional BOP		
System Shocks		
	Domestic Shocks	
	Distance	
	Liberal Path	
		Regional Polity Average
	Regional Economic Development	
	Regional Trade Agreements	
	Constructivist Path	
		Joint Satisfaction
		Negotiated Territorial Issues

Source: Based on Thies (2008).

Overall, the results both support and go beyond Kacowicz's qualitative analysis, as we have much more precise information about the effects of realist, liberal, and constructivist paths to a zone of negative peace/Lockean culture of anarchy. We can say with much more confidence which of these paths support the regional order and which seem to move the order away from negative peace. The statistical findings about the neo-Grotian/constructivist path are actually more in line with Kacowicz (2005), who focuses on the independent effect of norms on regional order. Such norms include *uti possidetis*, peaceful settlement of international disputes, respect for sovereignty and territorial integrity, nonintervention, self-determination, *convivencia*, *concertación*, arms control and disarmament, nonproliferation and confidence-building measures, and so on. He examines 11 cases from 1881 to the present to demonstrate the conditions under which norms succeeded/failed to facilitate peaceful outcomes. In general, he concludes that these norms helped to produce the 'long peace' in South America since 1883, reshaped how states pursue their interests via foreign relations, and moved the region toward a more pluralistic security community (Kacowicz 2005: 11). Kacowicz's (2005) approach to analyzing the region as an international society is thus in line with Thies (2008) and Merke (2011), both in terms of theoretical orientation and empirical findings.

Future work should continue to develop an understanding of the society of states in Latin America (see Merke, this volume). Latin America is not an easy case for off-the-shelf typologies, since its mix of conflicts short of war (and even the occasional war) is unusual, given the age of the states,[13] their common culture with widely accepted norms designed to mitigate conflict, and the prevalence of democratic political institutions, as well as institutions designed to facilitate trade and manage interstate conflict. Battaglino (2012) has recently advanced the concept of a 'hybrid peace' as a category between negative and positive peace to try and account for the persistence of conflicts short of war in South America between 1990 and 2010. The potential emergence of Brazil as a regional power that reorganizes the region's security away from the United States also deserves further research (e.g., Trinkunas 2013). More explicit attempts to incorporate the English school or constructivism may be useful for theoretical purposes, especially if they allow for the joining of regional- and dyadic-level empirical analyses (see Merke, this volume).

Conclusions

This chapter has reviewed the two basic approaches to understanding war and peace in Latin America: (1) explanations of particular forms of conflict (i.e., MIDs, interstate war, rivalry, civil war), and (2) explanations of regional order. I have highlighted areas in which both approaches might move forward separately, but I think a larger case should be made to combine them theoretically and empirically. I have noted that many of the hypothesized causes of the conflict are also thought to cause the particular forms of regional order, even as regional orders are constituted in part by the types and prevalence of conflict. How, then, can we best connect dyadic theorizing about the source of conflict with systemic theorizing about the sources of regional order? I used Thies's (2008) work uniting Kacowicz's (1998) zone of negative peace argument with Wendt's (1999) Lockean culture of anarchy as one example. Yet, there must be other ways to better theorize and empirically analyze the cross-level variation in dyadic conflict and regional order. Latin American states have, for most of their history, existed in some form of international society that conditions both the regional culture and the foreign policy behavior of the separate states in the region. I look forward to more work that marries the two into theoretically sophisticated, historically informed, and empirically rich analyses.

Notes

1 For useful reviews of the sources of conflict, see Mares (2012) and Grabendorff (1994).
2 For example, Moul (2013) finds that a bare majority of the wars in Latin America from 1816 until 1989 were fought between equal sides, and equal disputants were 13 times more likely to escalate to war than nonequals were.
3 Mares notes that contemporary Latin American states are unlikely to pursue military conquest, even when they claim significant portions of their neighbor's territory.
4 Mares suggests that diversion is rarely chosen on its own in Latin America, but it may be a result of increased tensions in a dispute. Miller and Elgün (2011) find that diversion conceptualized as increased coup risk is associated with increased likelihood of MID initiation in Latin America.
5 A militarized interstate dispute (MID) refers to "cases in which the threat, display or use of military force short of war by one member state is explicitly directed towards the government, official representatives, official forces, property, or territory of another state" (Jones et al. 1996: 168).
6 As a comparison, Pickering and Kisangani's (2009) data on international military interventions (IMIs) finds 45 Cold War and 25 post–Cold War IMIs, with yearly rates of around 1 and 1.5, respectively. Since World War II, Latin America has experienced only about six per cent of total IMIs, which makes it the least subject to such interventions of all of major regions in the world.

7 An interstate war is defined as "sustained combat, involving organized armed forces, resulting in a minimum of 1,000 battle-related fatalities" within a 12-month period between members of the interstate system (Sarkees and Wayman 2010). Interstate wars include the Mexican American (1846–1847), La Plata (1851–1852), Franco-Mexican (1862–1867), Ecuadorian–Colombian (1863), Lopez/War of the Triple Alliance (1864–1870), Naval/Guano (1865–1866), First Central American (1876), War of the Pacific (1879–1883), Second Central American (1885), Third Central American (1906), Fourth Central American (1907), Chaco (1932–1935), Brazilian participation in World War II (1944–1945), Colombian participation in Korean War (1951–1953), Football (1969), Falklands/Malvinas (1982), and Cenepa Valley (1995).

8 Nonstate wars meet the same operational definition as interstate wars, with the exception that at least one of the participants is not a sovereign state. Nonstate wars include Buenos Aires War (1820), Mexico–Yaqui Indian War (1825–1827), Central American Confederation War (1826–1829), Peru–Gran Colombia War (1828–1829), Argentine War for Unity (1829–1831), Argentina–Ranqueles Indian War (1833–1834), Bolivia Conquest of Peru (1835–1836), Dissolution of the Bolivia–Peru Confederation (1837–1839), Anti-Rosas War (1839–1840), First Haiti–Santo Domingo War (1844–1845), Second Haiti–Santo Domingo War (1855–1856), Central American War (1863), and Uruguay Colorados–Blancos War (1883–1884).

9 While the pattern may be similar to other regions, this does not mean that Latin America is necessarily as conflict-prone as other regions.

10 It is also possible that low levels of state capacity were responsible for the reduced probability for war, and the "limited" form of warfare that was prevalent in the region (Thies 2008: 246). Future research should examine the endogenous nature of this relationship for Latin America. See Thies and Sobek (2010) for such an attempt with a global sample.

11 Mares (1997) uses the regional security complex framework to argue that Latin America is still dominated by traditional conflict concerns. Wallensteen and Sollenberg's (1998) more inductive approach defines Central America as a regional conflict complex from 1989–1997.

12 Ripsman's (2005) analysis, however, suggests that these liberal factors would move regions away from a zone of negative peace and toward a zone of stable peace, if sufficiently present, since he considers some of these 'liberal' factors to be 'constructivist,' such as democratic regimes and IGOs.

13 European and North American states (the closest regions in terms of the age of states) do not engage in the same mix of militarized foreign policy with their neighbors that Latin American states continue to use. While MIDs may periodically occur in both regions, the likelihood of war is remote, and anything beyond threats and display of force over fishing disputes is rare (Mitchell and Prins 1999).

References

Adler, E. and Barnett, M. (eds) (1998) *Security Communities*, New York: Cambridge.

Andreski, S. (1980) 'On the Peaceful Disposition of Military Dictatorships', *Journal of Strategic Studies*, 3(3): 3–10.

Atzili, B. (2007) 'When Good Fences Make Bad Neighbors: Fixed Borders, State Weakness, and International Conflict', *International Security*, 31(3): 139–173.

Battaglino, J. M. (2012) 'The Coexistence of Peace and Conflict in South America: Toward a New Conceptualization of Types of Peace', *Revista Brasileira de Política Internacional*, 55(2): 131–151.

Buzan, B. and Waever, O (2003) *Regions and Powers: The Structure of International Security*, Cambridge: Cambridge University Press.

Calvert, S. and Calvert, P. (1989) *Argentina: Political Culture and Instability*, Pittsburgh, PA: University of Pittsburgh Press.

Centeno, M.A. (2002) *Blood and Debt: War and the Nation-State in Latin America*, University Park: Pennsylvania State University Press.

Domínguez, J. I., et al (2003) *Boundary Disputes in Latin America*, Washington, DC: United States Institute of Peace.

Escudé, C. (1984) *The Argentine Eclipse: The International Factor in Argentina's Post World War II Decline*, Ph.D. dissertation, Yale University.

——— (1988) 'Argentine Territorial Nationalism', *Journal of Latin American Studies* 20(1): 139–165.

Fazal, T. M. (2007) *State Death: The Politics and Geography of Conquest, Occupation, and Annexation*, Princeton: Princeton University Press.

Gleditsch, K. S. and Beardsley, K. (2004) 'Nosy Neighbors: Third-Party Actors in Central American Conflicts', *Journal of Conflict Resolution*, 46: 379–402.
Goertz, G. and Diehl, P. F. (1992) 'The Empirical Importance of Enduring Rivalries', *International Interactions*, 18(2): 151–163.
Grabendorff, W. (1994) 'Interstate Conflict Behavior and Regional Potential for Conflict in Latin America' in J. I. Domínguez (ed) *Latin America's International Relations and Their Domestic Consequences: War and Peace, Dependence and Autonomy*, New York: Routledge, pp. 239–263.
Hensel, P. R. (1994) 'One Thing Leads to Another: Recurrent Militarized Disputes in Latin America, 1816–1986', *Journal of Peace Research*, 31(1994): 281–297.
Herz, M. and Noguiera, J. P. (2002) *Ecuador vs. Peru: Peacemaking Amid Rivalry*, Boulder: Lynne Rienner.
Hurrell, A. (1998) 'An Emerging Security Community in South America?' in E. Adler and M. Barnett (eds) *Security Communities*, New York: Cambridge, pp. 228–264.
Jones, D. M., Bremer, S. A. and Singer, J. D. (1996) 'Militarized Interstate Disputes, 1816–1992: Rationale, Coding Rules, and Empirical Patterns', *Conflict Management and Peace Science*, 15(2): 163–213.
Kacowicz, A. M. (1998) *Zones of Peace in the Third World: South America and West Africa in Comparative Perspective*, Albany, NY: SUNY Press.
——— (2005) *The Impact of Norms in International Society: The Latin American Experience, 1881–2001*, Notre Dame, IN: University of Notre Dame Press.
Mares, D. R. (1997) 'Regional Conflict Management in Latin America: Power Complemented by Diplomacy' in D. A. Lake and P. M. Morgan (eds) *Regional Orders: Building Security in a New World*, University Park: Pennsylvania State University Press.
——— (2001) *Violent Peace: Militarized Interstate Bargaining in Latin America*, New York: Columbia University Press.
——— (2012) *Latin America and the Illusion of Peace*, London: The International Institute for Strategic Studies, Routledge.
Merke, F. (2011) 'The Primary Institutions of the Latin American Regional Interstate Society', Paper presented at the IDEAS Latin America Programme, London School of Economics, London, UK.
Miller, B. (2007) *States, Nations, and the Great Powers: The Source of Regional War and Peace*, New York: Cambridge.
Miller, R. A. and Elgün, Ö. (2011) 'Diversion and Political Survival in Latin America', *Journal of Conflict Resolution*, 55(2): 192–219.
Mitchell, S. and Thies, C. G. (2011) 'Issue Rivalries', *Conflict Management and Peace Science*, 28: 230–260.
Mitchell, S. M. and Prins, B. C. (1999) 'Beyond Territorial Contiguity: Issues at Stake in Democratic Militarized Interstate Disputes', *International Studies Quarterly*, 43: 169–183.
Moul, W. B. (2013) 'Balances without Great Powers: Some Evidence on War and Peace in the Americas, 1816–1989', *International Interactions*, 39(1): 30–53.
Murdoch, J. and Sandler, T. (2002) 'Civil Wars and Economic Growth: A Regional Comparison', *Defence and Peace Economics*, 13(6): 451–454.
Pickering, J. and Kisangani, E. F. (2009) 'The International Military Intervention Dataset: An Updated Resource for Conflict Scholars', *Journal of Peace Research*, 46: 589–599.
Ripsman, N. M. (2005) 'Two Stages of Transition from a Region of War to a Region of Peace: Realist Transition and Liberal Endurance', *International Studies Quarterly*, 49: 669–693.
Russett, B. M. and Oneal, J. R. (2001) *Triangulating Peace: Democracy, Interdependence, and International Organizations*, New York: Norton.
Sarkees, M. R. and Wayman, F. W. (2010) *Resort to War: A Data Guide to Inter-State, Extra-State, Intra-State, and Non-State Wars, 1816–2007*, Washington, DC: CQ Press.
Simmons, B. (1999) 'Territorial Disputes and Their Resolution: The Case of Ecuador and Peru', *Peaceworks*, 27, Washington, DC: United States Institute of Peace.
Thies, C. G. (2001) 'Territorial Nationalism in Spatial Rivalries: An Institutionalist Account of the Argentine-Chilean Rivalry', *International Interactions*, 27: 399–431.
——— (2005) 'War, Rivalry, and State Building in Latin America', *American Journal of Political Science*, 49: 451–465.
——— (2006) 'Public Violence and State Building in Central America', *Comparative Political Studies*, 39: 1263–1282.
——— (2008) 'The Construction of a Latin American Interstate Culture of Rivalry', *International Interactions*, 34: 231–257.

Thies, C. G. and Sobek, D. (2010) 'War, Economic and Political Development in the Contemporary International System', *International Studies Quarterly*, 54(1): 267–287.
Trinkunas, H. (2013) 'Reordering Regional Security in Latin America', *Journal of International Affairs*, 66(2): 83–99.
Ugarte, M. (1925) *Visiones de España: (Apuntes de un viajero argentino)*, Valencia: Prometeo.
Wallensteen, P. and Sollenberg, M. (1998) 'Armed Conflict and Regional Conflict Complexes', *Journal of Peace Research*, 35(5): 631–634.
Wendt, A. (1999) *Social Theory of International Politics*, Cambridge: Cambridge University Press.
Zacher, M. W. (2001) 'The Territorial Integrity Norm: International Boundaries and the Use of Force', *International Organization*, 55(2): 215–250.

10

COOPERATIVE SECURITY AND REGIONAL GOVERNANCE

Andrés Serbin and Andrei Serbin Pont

Introduction

This chapter addresses the conceptual and empirical development of cooperative security and regional governance in Latin America. It uses as a background the main experiences of security arrangements that can be characterized as cooperative and that have contributed to the building of regional security governance. Other important concepts are introduced briefly to better clarify the current state of the debate in the region and the conceptual framework of some of the existing regional security regimes and organizations.

The discussion of current cooperative security arrangements and regional governance in Latin America and the Caribbean should be addressed within the framework of three different problematiques. First of all, as the concept of security and cooperative security evolved in Latin America through different phases of the regionalization process, it is important to contextualize this evolution accordingly (Hänggi 2005: 9). Different phases and different approaches to the regionalization process imply distinct priorities and treatments of the security issues within diverse conceptual frames during the process of building regional governance, while facing threats and challenges from the external environment. This is particularly relevant in the case of Latin America, since different stages in the regionalization process led to alternative approaches to some basic schemes of regional security governance. In this regard, regionalization, reestablishment and consolidation of democracy, and cooperative security have been closely intertwined in the region. However, the changing role of the United States as a regional hegemon should be not underestimated when addressing those issues.

Second, this evolution opened a debate linked to different theories and conceptualizations of *security* in the regional context. This debate is associated with the differences among national security, cooperative security, collective security, democratic security, and human and multidimensional security, as anchoring notions for different modalities of regional security governance, and to the shift from predominantly realist approaches through neoliberal institutionalist to constructivist ones (Acharya 2011; Horowitz 2011). All these conceptualizations are related to the understanding of how cooperative security fits into the process of building regional governance security architecture in the different Latin America and Caribbean subregions. It is also relevant for the understanding of the prevalence of different approaches in terms of security communities, security complexes, and security governance, as Hurrell's (1998) argument about the emergence of a security community in South America was oriented by realist assumptions about balance of power, whereas more recent approaches related to security governance clearly reflect constructivist conceptualizations linked to the development of new ideas and identities and the creation of new regional norms and arrangements (Newman 2001; Fabbri 2005; Rynning 2011, see also Oelsen, this volume).

Third, and finally, it is important to underscore the ways that these conceptualizations materialize in the currently developing and fragmented regional governance structures, and particularly in hemispheric, regional, and subregional organizations such as the Organization of American States (OAS), the Union of South American Nations (UNASUR), the Central American Democratic Security Framework Treaty, and the Community of Latin American and Caribbean States (CELAC) (Serbin 2011, 2014).

Nevertheless, the three related problematiques show, both in the sphere of regional dynamics and in the regional literature, different levels of development. This is particularly relevant both on a conceptual and on a policy level, as different actors show different theoretical and policy approaches to the concept of security, and to the building of regional security governance structures.

Cooperative security in Latin America: genesis and current debate

The development of the concept of cooperative security in Latin America has its roots in the re-democratization and democratic consolidation phase in the region in the 1980s, when prevailing geopolitical conceptions and conflict hypotheses were put into question after the demise of the military regimes, even if some analysts argue that several cooperative measures emerged during the last stages of those regimes (Flemes 2005; Carreras 2007).

Within this context, cooperative security is understood as the set of actions aimed to the prevention of war, and avoiding the setting of means necessary for aggression through the cooperative commitment of the states involved (Carter et al. 1992). On a regional level it basically implies the development of a series of arrangements among neighboring countries to create a common approach to regional security issues and to build trust amongst them. These arrangements are generally part of a broader architecture of regional governance within regional integration processes. Within this framework, cooperative security implies a change of attitudes and perceptions among countries – from hostility to cooperation, and from coercion to prevention (Fontana 1996).

The concept of cooperative security was originally associated to the concept of 'preventive diplomacy' introduced by the United Nations as it attempted to combine the tendency towards international cooperation with the current realities in defense policies, such as the persistence of territorial disputes that maintained the traditional interstate threat perceptions and sustained preexisting conflict hypotheses.

Cooperative security relies on information exchange, transparency, and communication by means of collaboration in international organizations or within regional arrangements or treaties. Cooperative security, then, encompasses confidence-building measures (CBMs) to mitigate latent tensions and rivalries. Confidence- and security-building measures are considered as agreed military or nonmilitary measures to enhance mutual understanding and communication, convey nonhostile intentions, define acceptable norms and behavior, and reduce excessive fears and suspicions. Hence, they are reciprocated measures that reduce the potential for military surprise among the involved states (Gottwald, Hasenclever, and Kamis 2009).

It should be noted, however, that at the domestic level, the instability of political regimes constitutes another risk that can be addressed by a cooperative security strategy. This approach therefore also includes instruments that promote democracy and the respect for human rights and contribute to state-building, the establishment of the rule of law, and the reorganization of civil-military relations in former dictatorships (Weiffen 2010).

The concept of cooperative security took root in the Southern Cone before the end of the military regimes and the return to democracy in the 1980s. Thus, there were the agreements advanced between Argentina and Brazil restricting the development of nuclear power and the process of dilution of conflict hypotheses between these two countries in the 1980s that gradually forged a rapprochement between them that finally contributed to the creation of MERCOSUR in 1991. Similarly, the tensions which led to the verge of a war between Argentina and Chile in 1978 were finally overcome in the 1990s, after a series of cooperative security initiatives between the two nations.

In fact, in the South American context, from the beginning of the 1990s, there has been a trend in the convergence on security and integration matters led by Brazil and Argentina. After the 'lost decade' of the 1980s, this convergence was rooted in the idea that economic integration could not be sustainable in the long run if it did not reach agreements at the strategic and security levels as well (see Malamud and Schenoni, this volume). Under such circumstances, it is clear that MERCOSUR was created for strategic reasons that went beyond commercial purposes. Therefore, regional integration was not only merely interpreted on economic and commercial terms, but it also implied that the political element was decisive (Riquelme Rivera 2013), for which the previous steps in terms of cooperative security were crucial.

The decade of the 1990s was a period of multilateralism and convergence of Latin American and U.S. foreign policy priorities creating the conditions for the renewal of the inter-American system, a revision of the concept of security toward a more cooperative version, and a commitment to defending democracy (Weiffen et al. 2013: 382). In the aftermath of the Cold War and changes in the U.S. policy towards the region, particularly after September 11, 2001, the debate was nonetheless reflected in the reconceptualization of security notions both within the Western Hemisphere and within the different, Latin American, subregional processes. New security arrangements arose, particularly in the Southern Cone, with the creation of MERCOSUR in 1991 and the establishment of UNASUR and its South American Defense Council (SADC) in 2008. However, "after the turn of the millennium, the reassertion of U.S. unilateral projects (e.g., War on Terror) and the emergence of regional powers in South America made hemispheric cooperation more difficult again and led to an increasing South American disaffection with hemispheric institutions"[1] (Weiffen et al. 2013: 382), as well as the creation of its own regional governance structures (Serbin 2009, 2010a, 2010b). In this regard, several researchers point to the differences between the experience of the Organization of American States (OAS) at the hemispheric level and the Union of South American Nations (UNASUR) at the subregional level, both drawing on the concept of multidimensional security (Weiffen et al. 2013: 377), but at the same time building on different regional identities.

Within this framework, new security concepts emerged and developed in the region, as other important concepts and subregional experiences contributed also to broaden the debate around cooperative security. For instance, the peace processes and the democratic consolidation in Central America after the 1980s allowed for the development of a broader concept – democratic security – conceived as the "application of the principles and values of democracy at the level of the security problems of the states, therefore considering as security all those conditions that favor the welfare of the citizens – the development of representative mechanisms in political life, the absence of physical threats or risks, the creation of minimal conditions of income, housing, health, education, etcetera" (Arévalo 2002a: 38), as it was outlined in the Framework Treaty on Democratic Security in Central America.[2] Therefore, its importance lies in that it combines both the perspectives of citizen and human security, as well as states' security, especially in the framework of regional security, linked to or incorporating notions of cooperative or shared security (Jácome 2004; Arévalo 2002b).

Yet, the definitions of democratic security have faced strong criticism, due to the fact that they are so broad and encompassing that they cease to be operational, as they include diverse dimensions specifically by superposing the development and security agendas.

The democratic security concept is related to other previous conceptual developments. As a response to changes in the world scenario and its effects on domestic dynamics after the Cold War, the introduction of a broader perspective proposed a radical reconceptualization of security. In this sense, one of the most important reference documents has been the Report on Human Development presented by UNDP in 1994, which introduced the concept of human security (UNDP 1993).

Human security aims at identifying a group of threats to security that go beyond the threat to peace, and includes other dimensions that may affect the state, as well as society and individuals, leading to the discussion of a new security agenda that incorporates additional issues to the traditional ones of defense and military affairs, such as economic, political, and social conflicts, migrations, environmental issues, and drug trafficking.

The concept of human security influenced decisively the debates on security in the region in the early 1990s, a period which also witnessed the rise and development of the concept of multidimensional security in the framework of the inter-American system. At the XXXII General Assembly of the OAS in Bridgetown, Barbados in June 2002, the concept of 'multidimensional focus of hemispheric security' was introduced. This concept established that hemispheric security includes political, economic, social, health, and environmental aspects.

Multidimensional security represents a doctrinal and practical advancement from the broad human security concept to a specific framework for addressing issues on a regional level. Multidimensional security recognizes the persistence of traditional security threats and establishes a flexible architecture for each country to define its own security structure. As a concept, multidimensional security attempted to generate an alternative to the United States' unilateralism that aimed at assimilating security and defense, as well as prioritizing the war on terror after September 11, 2001. Yet, it has allowed for the expansion of security into the areas of economic and social policies, influencing a potential militarization of state answers to diverse areas or a securitization of the economic and social agendas. At the same time, both economic aspects (particularly those referring to trade and cooperation agreements amongst countries, and regional and subregional integration processes) and political and social aspects (especially those linked to democracy and democratic governance in the region) acquired an increasingly relevant role in the regional security agenda.

Within this framework it is relevant to point out that there is no common, regional perception on the priority of these new threats. While the countries in the region do tend to coincide on the priorities regarding drug trafficking and terrorism, the prioritization of other threats in the subregional and national agendas vary from subregion to subregion, and also from country to country. Yet we find that the background created by the ABC and the MERCOSUR experiences led to the creation of UNASUR, which is increasingly showing coordinated efforts oriented towards building and strengthening regional mechanisms to cope with some of these threats. The most recent examples are the creation of the councils for dealing with drug-related issues (*Consejo Suramericano de Lucha contra el Narcotráfico* and the *Consejo Suramericano sobre el Problema Mundial de Drogas*) that seek to coordinate policies at the regional level, as an important component of the new South American regional architecture. These efforts are supported by the common approach by regional governments to prioritize this issue, yet it faces the obstacle of contentious positions regarding how to deal with this problem, especially regarding the traditionally U.S.-supported 'war on drugs' approach vs. the recent pro-legalization initiatives led by several Latin American governments. However, notwithstanding the existing differences, the background for these recent cooperative efforts lies in the previous cooperative security measures implemented in the 1990s.

The evolution of cooperative security and regional governance in the hemisphere

Notwithstanding the cooperative security arrangements featured since the early 1990s by the OAS and the Southern Cone countries, and lately by UNASUR, in a move from collective defense towards cooperative security, at the conceptual level this trend was expressed through the conceptualization and use of the concept of multidimensional security, particularly after the Mexico conference on this issue in 2003.[3] Both the OAS and UNASUR dealt simultaneously with collective and cooperative security, and both resorted to the concept of multidimensional security to address traditional and nontraditional security issues, to the point that both organizations overlap to a large extent in their security conceptions (Weiffen et al. 2013: 378–379). While in the course of its restructuring in 2005, the OAS general secretariat created the secretariat for multidimensional security as one of its subunits and established in 2006 a formal link with the Inter-American Defense Board (IADB) originally created in 1942 and the oldest mechanism for security cooperation in the region (Serbin 2010a). UNASUR's main security institution is the South American Defense Council (SADC), focused on fostering, on an intergovernmental level, a closer cooperation in traditional defense matters among the member-states.[4]

At the same time, while UNASUR security practices are still under construction, to a large extent it emulates the OAS regarding specific security institutions and instruments, including the concept of multidimensional security as the main conceptual framework for the implementation of cooperative security measures (Weiffen et al. 2013: 380–381). However, there is a clear distinction in the reach and in the strategic discourses of both organizations as regional governance structures.

In this regard, even if regional security governance appears as a useful perspective to approach 'new' security issues, the first point to be underlined is that there is a scarcity of current Latin American literature on regional governance, and particularly on regional security governance. As pointed out by Mayorga and Cordova (2007: 2, 7), regional literature, particularly after the reestablishment of democracies in Latin America, was focused on issues linked more to governability related with political stability and the role of domestic actors than to the development of the concept of regional governance. However, governance went gradually from referring exclusively to the actions of government or the exercise of government in the region to "a set of rules, institutions and established practices that delineate boundaries and incentives for the behavior of individuals, organizations and enterprises" (Loyo 2002: 2). In general terms, this explains the diffusion in the management of the notion of governance,[5] as there is still no developed Latin American scholarly literature that summarizes and systematizes the use of the concept, which is usually conditioned by the particularities of each case studied (Legler 2013).

The consequences of this shift from government to governance are also reflected in the domain of security studies. It is suggested that part of the shift of transatlantic security policy from a state-centered focus towards an approach aimed at complex networks of state and non-state actors could be recognized as an emerging shift from *security government* to *security governance*. There also have been diverse theoretical and empirical findings showing that a transformation of *security government* to *security governance* is emerging as an alternative framework to address the security problems from the global to the regional and individual levels, and from traditional military security to the newly rising nonmilitary security management (Krahmann 2003).

Even if these distinctions are valid, the current trend in regional studies is to combine different conceptions, such as regional security governance, including regime complexity, security community, and multilevel security governance,[6] with mixed results. As a process, this regional trend is at an early stage, where new concepts are being assimilated and incorporated into the debate, in a similar manner to what is happening within the framework of broader governance, where a debate regarding multilevel governance is beginning to develop (Pastrana and Betancourt 2014).

The United States, the OAS, and UNASUR: recent developments in cooperative security and regional security governance

In sum, whereas during the Cold War there was a prevalence in the hemisphere of the collective defense approach fostered by the clear predominance of a hegemonic power (the United States), the external threat was defined according to the Cold War and the struggle against communism. Concomitantly, this legitimization of U.S. interventions in the region by the rationale of fighting the international communist threat contradicted and hampered a collective security approach that was developed in previous years on a hemispheric level: Aggressions by the United States against other OAS member-states were not addressed by this institution, and, due to fear of hegemonic interference, other conflicts within the region were often managed by alternative *ad hoc* security coalitions, such as the Contadora and later the Rio Group, which was recently fused into CELAC's structure, within a weak and flexible institutional framework (Serbin 2014).

Nevertheless, since the late 1990s, OAS security governance has been, more than ever before, guided by the interests of the Latin American countries. After the demise of communism, there was no need for collective defense arrangements, and even the TIAR (Rio Treaty) was contested by several Latin American countries, particularly after the conflict between Argentina and Britain over the Malvinas/Falkland Islands. Within this context collective security tasks were not usually addressed by the OAS, but by subregional organizations and coalitions or, in the face of more serious security threats, by the United Nations. The OAS consequently focused on the consolidation and defense of democracy, as well as on confidence-building.

After 2001, we can observe a somewhat odd coexistence of the continuity of the policy programs established in the 1990s and a reemergence of certain dynamics familiar to the Cold War era. In the aftermath of 9/11, fighting terrorism became the central objective of the U.S. government's approach. The focus of the United States shifted back to collective defense (although in fact the new threat of terrorism lay at the intersection of cooperative security – countering new 'intermestic' security challenges – and collective defense against an external, albeit unknown, enemy). Yet, for the majority of Latin American countries, international terrorism was not perceived as posing an imminent threat. However, in compliance with the collective defense paradigm, most states chose to collaborate with the United States in order to address their concerns, as in the case of the triple frontier between Argentina, Brazil, and Paraguay, especially following the terrorist attacks in Buenos Aires in 1992 and 1994.

At the same time, the Latin American countries maintained and further expanded their cooperative security and security management programs, as evidenced by the discussions on the new multidimensional security concept, the creation of the Inter-American Democratic Charter, new initiatives in CSBMs, such as the ones introduced by the SADC and by the creation of the *Centro de Estudios Estratégicos de Defensa*, which also serves as a mechanism for the measurement of defense expenditures in the region, and the multiplication of information activities. During the 1990s, the U.S.–Latin American policy had emphasized political liberalization, and in spite of its recent shift of attention, it still endorses this goal and hence has no incentive to hinder the cooperative security activities in the region. In addition to the security management activities, hemispheric institutions increasingly fulfill collective security tasks, if needed (Weiffen 2010: 21–22). It is relevant to point out that the United States' focus on the Central American and Caribbean region in terms of security and the weakening of the political influence of both the United States and the OAS have allowed the development of the already mentioned independent cooperative security initiatives in South America, which have also reinforced the existence of diverging perspectives on security at the hemispheric level. Therefore, the inter-American security system exhibits simultaneously elements of collective security, collective defense, and cooperative security arrangements. However, the focus of its mission shifts over time, and this shift is intrinsically linked to the power dynamics among its member-states (Wieffen 2010: 21).

The changes in the United States' interest in the region increased the autonomy of the Latin American countries, including issues related to the security realm. This autonomy is clearly illustrated at the subregional level, with the creation of UNASUR and the SADC in South America and with the still uncertain evolution, in terms of regional security governance at the Latin American and Caribbean level, of CELAC. In addition to the idea of promoting a zone of peace (Battaglino 2013), basically founded on the previous building of cooperative security by these two subregional organizations, the SADC materialized the previous Southern Cone and MERCOSUR process of building a South American security governance mechanism (Oelsner 2009). The SADC is the result of a long process of regional integration, in terms of defense, towards cooperative and multidimensional security. This process was partially influenced, in its first stages, by the United States and lately by Brazil, within the developments since the 1990s in the Southern Cone and, more recently, in South America as a whole (Heegaard 2010: 166).

However, it is important to underline that within the framework of the increasing degree of fragmentation and complexity of the contemporary international security system traditional models of security relations such as military alliances (Wohlforth 1999), security regimes (Krasner 1983), and security communities (Adler and Barnett 1998), according to Flemes and Radseck (2012), should be complemented by a more promissory concept such as security governance. In this regard, Adler and Greve (2009: 59) have conceptualized the different mentioned models as different "systems of security governance," which can coexist in time and space, applying Ruggie's (1993) multiple approaches to regional security governance. In this regard, Flemes and Radseck (2012: 206) suggest that different security governance systems overlap and coexist in South America, a suggestion that eventually could be extended to the rest of Latin America. A wide spectrum of bilateral and multilateral initiatives reflect the main traits of an emergent security community, as in the case of the SACD under the umbrella of UNASUR, while at the same time key regional players such as Brazil, Colombia, and Venezuela develop military alliances with extraregional powers as a result of power balances, which eventually could stimulate regional conflicts. Within this framework, according to those authors, neither the traditional models of power balance and alliance creation nor the security community approach suffices to explain the current security dynamics in South America. In addition, this happens in a region where national sovereignty still holds as a relevant principle in regional politics (Serbin 2012; Legler 2013). As a consequence, the emergent regional security governance in the region is mostly state-centric and excludes other relevant actors usually associated with this approach, such as civil society organizations and other, relevant nonstate actors.

Conclusions

The emerging regional security governance in Latin America is a complex social construct because of the multilevel agenda of security in the region, though it is still mostly state-centric, with a strong bias towards the role of executive governmental authorities (and particularly to the presidential role), with limited inputs from parliamentary and nonstate actors. The current regional security governance mechanisms confirm also the propensity to adopt *ad hoc* procedures when addressing interstate and domestic crisis; the principles of national sovereignty and nonintervention will hinder real progress towards a more institutionalized regional security governance in the case of transnational threats. Authority is not necessarily condensed in multilateral bodies and is eventually open to the preeminence of unilateral structures of authority (Brazil being the most relevant actor in this regard), a situation that demands the improvement and the development of a stronger regional multilateralism. Finally, even if regional stability should be the common aim of regional and extraregional state actors, the divergences among the interests of key actors and the predominance of power dimensions over the functional dimension could impose serious limitations to the effectiveness and legitimacy of regional governance schemes, conditioned by changes of the evolving environment (Flemes and Radseck 2012: 233–234).

In this regard, empirical analysis confirms the idea of the coexistence, particularly in South America, of different incipient security governance structures, as well of different security practices notwithstanding the development and the advancement of cooperative security mechanisms, for instance, in the case of UNASUR.

Thus, the main argument of this chapter is that different modalities of emerging regional security governance structures frame different approaches and policies in terms of cooperative security in particular, and with regards to security governance in the region in general, shaping a multilevel and multilayered complex dynamic. Accordingly, the three problematiques that we pointed out at the beginning of the chapter suggest several paths to follow in terms of new fields and topics to be researched, with regards to cooperative security and regional security governance in Latin America. From a policy point of view, one of the questions that should be addressed is whether the weight of national sovereignty and nonintervention principles embedded in the juridical tradition of the region can be channeled towards the building of regional security governance mechanisms that beg for supranational norms and regimes and stronger institutions, overcoming the often divergent national interest priorities. This question is related both to the changing, overlapping, and multilayered current regional environment of multiple and diverse institutions and organizations, and to the challenges posed by an uncertain and rapidly changing global environment, characterized by the emergence of new risks and threats. Finally, from a theoretical perspective, one of the main research venues seems to be related to the need for the search of a coherent and perhaps eclectic combination of the contributions of traditional theoretical approaches with the doctrinal and conceptual developments emerging in a region (with several subregions) that claims to be a zone of peace, while the traditional and the new threats and risks in this changing environment eventually challenge both the realist and the constructivist approaches. Therefore, the introduction of the concept of governance disputes the state-centric and ideological trends prevailing in the region, asking for a deeper understanding of transnational flows of goods, people, and ideas, which might impact upon the reality and the research on security studies.

Notes

1 Namely, the OAS and its related institutions, agencies, and treaties.
2 See *Tratado Marco de Seguridad Democrática en Centroamérica*. Retrieved from http://www.sicanet.org.sv/documentos/tratados.
3 "The OAS originally defined itself as a system of collective security and envisioned the creation of means for the pacific settlement of disputes in both its Charter (OAS, 1948: chapter V and VI) and the American Treaty on Pacific Settlement or Pact of Bogotá, signed in 1948 along with the Charter. With the Inter-American Treaty of Reciprocal Assistance (Río Treaty or TIAR, according to its Spanish acronym), it also featured a collective defense component to deal with military aggressions originating from outside the region" (Weiffen et al. 2013: 378).
4 Also, the Center for Strategic Defense Studies (CEED, according to its Spanish acronym) created in 2011 is supposed to become a think tank on regional defense and security studies, which will contribute to the conceptual development of the new notions of security and the building of regional security governance in South America.
5 Nevertheless, as pointed out by Liao, for the last decade, *governance* has been increasingly deemed as a superior framework of explaining the changing structure in the fields of public administration and security management. *Security governance* is therefore suggested "as an alternative theoretical *paradigm* for looking at national, regional, and global security practices" (Liao 2011).
6 As Krahmann argues for the cases of Europe and North America, "governance has been characterized by features and problems which might affect the emerging system of security governance. . . . These characteristics and problems are quite distinct from those addressed by balance of power theory, security regimes and security communities. Specifically, the analysis of security governance raises the questions of how the shift from government to governance affects our understanding of security and what consequences the fragmentation of power and authority has for the making and implementation of security policies in the region" (Krahmann 2003: 20).

References

Acharya, A. (2011) 'Norm Subsidiarity and Regional Orders: Sovereignty, Regionalism, and Rule-Making in the Third World', *International Studies Quarterly*, 55: 95–123.
Adler, E. and Barnett, M. (eds) (1998) *Security Communities*, Cambridge: Cambridge University Press.
Adler, E. and Greve, P. (2009) 'When Security Community Meets Balance of Power: Overlapping Regional Mechanisms of Security Governance', *Review of International Studies*, 35(1): 59–84.
Arévalo de León, B. (2002a) 'De la teoría a la práctica: Reflexiones sobre la seguridad democrática' in B. Arévalo de León (ed) *Seguridad democrática en Guatemala: Desafíos de la transformación*, Guatemala: Facultad Latinoamericana de Ciencias Sociales, pp. 19–85.
——— (ed) (2002b) *Hacia una política de seguridad para la democracia*, Guatemala: Facultad Latinoamericana de Ciencias Sociales.
Battaglino, J. (2013) 'La evolución de la zona de paz Sudamericana', *Documentos de Trabajo*, 12, Argentina: Escuela de Defensa Nacional, Ministerio de Defensa.
Carreras, M. (2007) 'The Southern Cone: An Imagined Security Community'. Retrieved from http//:www.miguelcarreras.com/documents/paper_sec_carreras.pdf.
Carter, A. E., Perry, W. J. and Steinbruner, J. D. (1992) *A New Concept of Cooperative Security*, Washington, DC: The Brookings Institution.
Fabbri, C. (2005, November) 'The Constructivist Promise and Regional Integration: An Answer to "Old" and "New" Puzzles. The South American Case', CSGR Working Paper No. 182/05, Department of Politics and International Relations, University of Warwick.

Flemes, D. (2005, December) 'Creating a Regional Security Community in Southern Latin America: The Institutionalisation of the Regional Defence and Security Policies', German Overseas Institute (DÜI), Research Program: Violence and Security Cooperation, No. 13.

Flemes, D. and Radseck, M. (2012) 'Governanza multinivel de seguridad en América del Sur', *Papel Político* (Bogotá), 17(1): 203–238.

Fontana, A. (1996). 'Seguridad cooperativa: Tendencias globales y el continente americano', *Serie Documentos de Trabajo*, No. 16, Buenos Aires: Instituto del Servicio Exterior de la Nación.

Gottwald, E., Hasenclever, A. and Kamis, B. (2009, February 15–18) 'Confidence-Building Measures, Joint Democracy and Disputes among (Former) Rivals', Paper presented at the International Studies Association Annual Meeting, New York.

Hänggi, H. (2005) 'Approaching peacebuilding from a security governance perspective', in H. Hänggi *Security governance in post-conflict peacebuilding*, Münster: LIT Verlag, pp. 3–19.

Heegaard, W. (2010) 'El camino largo de integración regional de defensa y seguridad: Desafíos y potencialidades del consejo de defensa Suramericano', *Independent Study Project (ISP) Collection*, Paper 1238. Retrieved from http://digitalcollections.sit.edu/isp_collection/1238.

Horowitz, B. (2011) *The Transformation of the Organization of American States. A Multilateral Framework for Regional Governance*, London: Anthem Press.

Hurrell, A. (1998) 'An Emerging Security Community in South America' in E. Adler and M. N. Barnett (eds) *Security Communities*, New York: Cambridge University Press, pp. 228–264.

Jácome, F. (coord) (2004) *Seguridad democrática en Centroamérica: Logros y limitaciones en Costa Rica, Panamá, Guatemala y El Salvador*, Caracas: Coordinación Regional de institutos de Investigación Económico y Social.

Krahmann, E. (2003) 'Conceptualizing Security Governance', *Cooperation and Conflict: Journal of the Nordic International Studies Association*, 38(1): 5–26.

Krasner, S. D. (ed) (1983) *International Regimes*, Ithaca, NY: Cornell University Press.

Legler, T. (2013) 'The Rise and Decline of the Summit of the Americas' *Journal of Iberian and Latin American Research 19*(2), 179–193

Liao, D. (2011) 'Security Governance: An Alternative Paradigm?', Working Paper, pp. 1–7. Retrieved from www.ijssh.org/papers/62-HO75.

Loyo Hernández, J.C. (2002) 'La arquitectura de gobernanza y la gobernabilidad del sistema politico venezolano: una explicación de la estabilidad y del cambio de la democracia en Venezuela', Paper presented to the VII Congreso Internacional del CLAD sobre la reforma del estado y el cambio de la democracia venezolana, Lisboa, Portugal, October 8–10, 2002. Retrieved from: http://www.un-pan1.un.org/intradoz/groups/public/documents/CLAD/clad00434.pdf.

Mayorga, F. y Cordova, E. (2007) 'Gobernabilidad y gobernanza en América Latina', *Working Paper NCCR Norte-Sur* IP8, Ginebra, unpublished.

Newman, E. (2001) 'Human Security and Constructivism', *International Studies Perspectives*, 2: 239–251.

Oelsner, A. (2009) 'Consensus and Governance in Mercosur: The Evolution of the South American Agenda', *Security Dialogue*, 40(2): 191–212.

Pastrana Buelvas, E. and Betancourt, R. (2014) 'Regionalización, regionalidad y gobernanza multinivel en Suramérica' in E. Pastrana Buelvas and H. Gehring (eds) *Suramérica en el escenario global: Gobernanza multinivel y birregionalismo*, Bogotá: Pontificia Universidad Javeriana-Konrad Adenauer Stiftung-Universidad Santiago de Cali, pp. 85–125.

Riquelme Rivera, J. (2013) 'La relación entre integración y seguridad en el MERCOSUR y sus proyecciones hacia Sudamérica', *Revista de relaciones internacionales, Estrategia y Seguridad*, Bogotá, 8(1): 279–308.

Ruggie, J. G. (1993) 'Territoriality and Beyond. Problematizing Modernity in International Relations', *International Organization*, 47(1): 139–174.

Rynning, S. (2011) 'Realism and the Common Security and Defence Policy', *Journal of Common Market Studies*, 49(1): 23–42.

Serbin, A. (2009) 'América del Sur en un mundo multipolar: ¿es la UNASUR la Alternativa?', *Nueva Sociedad* (Caracas), 219: 145–156.

——— (2010a) 'OEA y UNASUR: Seguridad regional y sociedad civil en América Latina', *Documentos CRIES*, Buenos Aires: CRIES.

——— (2010b) 'América Latina: ¿Un multilateralismo sui-géneris?' in A. Serbin, L. Martinez and H. Ramanzini (eds) *Anuario de la integración de América Latina y el Gran Caribe*, Buenos Aires: CRIES.

——— (coord) (2011) *De la ONU al ALBA: Prevención de conflictos y espacios de participación ciudadana*, Buenos Aires-Barcelona: CRIES/Editorial Icaria.
——— (2012) 'Globalización. Integración regional y sociedad civil', in Oliva C. and A. Serbin (eds.), *América Latina, el Caribe y Cuba en el context global*, Aráraquera: Laboratorio Editorial do DVL, pp. 19–86.
——— (2014) 'Los nuevos regionalismos y la CELAC' in A. Bonilla and I. Álvarez (eds) *Desafíos estratégicos del regionalismo contemporáneo: CELAC e Iberoamérica*, San José: FLACSO/AECID, pp. 47–78.
UNDP (1993) *Human Development Report*, Oxford: Oxford University Press.
Weiffen, B. (2010, September) 'Analyzing Regional Security Governance: The Example of the Organization of American States', Paper presented at the SGIR 7th, Pan-European International Relations Conference, Stockholm.
Weiffen. B., Wehner, L. and Nolte, D. (2013) 'Overlapping Regional Security Institutions in South America: The Case of the OAS and UNASUR', *International Area Studies Review*, 16(4): 376–389.
Wohlforth, W. C. (1999) 'The Stability of a Unipolar World', *International Security*, 21(1): 5–41.

11

CITIZEN SECURITY AND HUMAN SECURITY IN LATIN AMERICA

Daniel M. Goldstein

As the chapters of this Handbook make abundantly clear, *security* in all its forms is now, and has long been, a central preoccupation of states, citizens, and other actors in Latin America. In this chapter, I focus on *citizen security* and *human security* as two frameworks within which security in Latin America is conceptualized; I call attention to the idea of security as both a lived experience – that is, as a routine part of daily life – for Latin American people, and as an everyday program of state formation. Citizen security and human security are understood in this analysis as two powerful discourses, sets of policies, and regimes of governance around which much political contestation in Latin America is centered, as people, states, and nonstate actors (which might include private corporations, criminal gangs, paramilitaries, and local community organizations, among many others) negotiate the meaning of security and the appropriate means of attaining it in their societies. The chapter is thus anthropologically oriented: It explores the conceptual bases of citizen security and human security, but grounds this exploration in the empirical reality of daily life in Latin American societies, where people struggle every day to enhance their own security, nonstate actors take on new and variable roles in security provision, and states work to position themselves as the best and only providers of security for their citizens.[1]

There are two reasons for discussing citizen security and human security in the same analytical framework. For one, as political discourses and policy frameworks, both citizen security and human security aim to broaden the public understanding of what security is thought to entail. As security studies scholars have shown us, the academic and policy approach to security was long governed by those whom Buzan, Waever, and Wilde (1998) call the "traditionalists," for whom security pertains strictly to questions of military affairs and defense of the state against internal and external threats (e.g., Chipman 1992). Opposing the traditionalists, from this perspective, are the so-called wideners, those with a much broader view of security. These scholars reject the traditionalists' insistence on a military or interstate dimension, including security dilemmas and the prospect of an international nuclear war, as the sole criteria for identifying security threats (Waever et al. 1993). This broader perspective understands that security is a response to anything that can be persuasively identified as threatening to the state or society, and that this identification is a cultural and political process that varies across contexts. In keeping with this rough division of perspectives, citizen security and human security can be seen as efforts to widen public understanding of security. Both of these discourses represent ways of thinking and talking about security that locate the beneficiaries of security outside the state (i.e., as citizens or human beings), and identify a broadly inclusive range of possible threats to that security. Both of these discourses thus represent important departures from more traditional understandings of security in the Americas, which served to bolster the so-called national security state during the long years of authoritarianism and the Cold War. However, despite this broadening effect, in practice citizen security focuses almost exclusively on threats posed by criminality; it demonizes criminals, authorizes state and popular violence, and undermines citizens' basic rights in exchange for a promised security. Citizen security, then, like national security before it, narrows security to a focus on a particular perceived threat to public order and safety, while continuing to privilege the state as the only actor capable of producing and providing security. Therefore, this chapter contends that citizen security represents a new iteration of longstanding approaches to security: old wine in new bottles, if you will.

If, in their attempts to broaden the meaning of security, citizen security and human security seem fairly indistinguishable from one another, the second reason to discuss them within the same analytical frame is because of their fundamental differences. Chief among these is the distinction between what anthropologists would call 'emic' and 'etic' knowledge. Anthropologists use these terms to distinguish forms of knowledge or ways of conceptualizing the world that are empirically grounded in human social awareness and behavior (the emic approach) vs. knowledge or conceptualizations formulated by outsiders as instruments for interpreting ethnographic reality (the etic approach) (Pike 1967; Goodenough 1970). Drawing on this distinction, and through ethnographic study, one can conclude that despite their conceptual similarities, citizen security has emerged in Latin American societies as an emic category, while human security has remained a purely etic one. Attention to this difference highlights the changing nature of security in Latin America, particularly in popular communities, where the demand for citizen security has become a powerful rallying cry for people protesting state corruption and neglect of their security needs. Human security, by contrast, is a conceptual category restricted to scholars, analysts, and some transnational political actors, but has gained little traction as an instrument for social reform in the region. Recognition of this distinction emerges primarily from participant observation and other techniques of direct, qualitative investigation, and so points to the utility of an ethnographic methodology for the study of security.

In what follows I lay out a brief history of citizen security and human security as discourses that have emerged from a longer concern with security, more traditionally understood, in Latin America. I then go on to elaborate my critique of citizen security as an apparently progressive doctrine that in practice returns us to the authoritarian logic of the national security state, and of human security as an appealing framework that has not achieved popular recognition in the region. I conclude by discussing the ways in which ethnography and an attention to (in)security as a lived social reality can help to broaden and further the aims of security studies, with some brief suggestions for future research.

From national security to citizen security

In the decades following World War II, 'national security' became a paramount concern of many nation-states, framed within the logic of a clash between totalitarianism and freedom. National security, understood as the safety and stability of the nation-state in the face of an ever-threatening communist menace, emerged in the West as a predominant ideology justifying a range of repressive techniques of rule and interventionist foreign policies. The authoritarian states that governed much of Latin America from the 1960s through the 1980s derived their authority from a national security doctrine that advocated defending democracy against world communism and its destabilizing aims (Leal Buitrago 2003). Though part of a broader Cold War standoff between the Western and Soviet blocs, in Latin America the national security doctrine authorized the violation of human and civil rights in the name of winning the war against the 'internal enemies' of communist subversion (Mares 2007). The military, under this doctrine, assumed the tasks of domestic policing and maintaining 'public order,' with few limits placed on its ability to act in the name of national security. U.S. political and economic support for authoritarian regimes was also justified in terms of the effort to hold off the communist threat to Latin America and hence to hemispheric stability. Security by this logic was reduced to national security, which itself stood for a particular kind of social order that brooked no dissent and disregarded citizens' rights in the interests of maintaining social order.

With the end of the Cold War and the global rise of neoliberal democracy, the official understanding of security in Latin America remained bound to the political, particularly as the communist threat of the Cold War era came to be replaced by the terrorist threat of the Global War on Terror in the aftermath of September 11, 2001. Even as daily lives became more precarious throughout the region as a result of the steady institutionalization of neoliberal political economy (which led to rising income inequality, mounting poverty and unemployment, reduction of social services, and higher levels of violent crime [Gledhill 2004; Arias and Goldstein 2010]), 'security' in Latin America continued to be framed largely in terms of public order, with protection against external attacks or internal destabilization remaining the central preoccupations of state policies. Elsewhere (Goldstein 2005), I have argued that the 'security state,' whose principal focus is on maintaining public order and fighting terrorism, represents the extension of the neoliberal logic of privatization, part of a broader effort to charge civil institutions, communities, and individuals with tasks of governance once considered duties of the state. Relying on individualizing techniques of governmentality, the neoliberal state disobliges itself from the various responsibilities of maintaining its citizens, conferring on citizens themselves the daily obligations of self-reproduction and self-regulation. At the same time, the state claims for itself the exclusive right to define security and to implement it (maintaining, of course, the prerogative to subcontract that responsibility to nonstate actors, for example to private security firms and proxy armies [Ramírez 2011; on the rise of private security in Latin America, see Ungar 2007–2008]). The state authorizes itself to determine the existence of threats and to decide on an appropriate response, justifying extreme secrecy, the suspension of citizens' rights, and the control of popular dissent in the interests of security, identified as the "care and moral duty" of the state to its citizens (Hay and Andrejevic 2006; on the risk society, see Beck 1992; Giddens 1999). Under this model of the security society, the neoliberal subject is expected to be perpetually alert and prepared, continually on guard against the emergence of possible threats (Elmer and Opel 2006; Goldstein 2012). Individuals are encouraged to be suspicious and responsible, to assume a habitually anxious, cautious engagement with anyone or anything deemed unfamiliar and potentially threatening (O'Malley 1996).[2]

The 'security crisis' that began in the late 1990s marked another shift in perspective, as the terrorist threat now morphed into the threat of the common criminal. With the return to democracy, crimes against persons and property began to rise throughout the region (Ungar 2011), and violent crime worsened, with Latin America exhibiting the world's highest regional average for homicides (Carranza 2004; Moser et al. 2003; World Health Organization 2002). Simultaneously, public fear of crime mounted, motivated by stories, rumor, and gossip (Caldeira 2000), and exacerbated by media reports that sensationalized violence, often without correlation to its actual frequency (Briceño-Leon and Zubilaga 2002; Jusionyte 2013). The resulting climate of fear produced a pervasive sense of anxiety and uncertainty, augmented by the absence of a reliable authority operating according to a rule of law, to which people could turn to report crimes. In countries throughout the region, the neoliberal state demonstrated its inability or unwillingness to provide responsive police and judicial services to its citizens, leading to a declining sense of security in daily life and a frustration with perceived official corruption, at times calling into question the ruling legitimacy of the state itself.

It was in this context that the idea of 'citizen security' (*seguridad ciudadana*) emerged across Latin America. Dating to the late 1990s, citizen security became a discourse for conceptualizing the vulnerability to which ordinary people were exposed by criminal threat, and for coordinating efforts to counter it (Marquardt 2012). Introduced by a range of governments and nongovernmental organizations, citizen security was understood in its broadest sense to encompass "a movement away from security debates whose primary concern was threats to the state or regime toward a concern with threats to public, social and political order posed by rising common crime and public fear of crime" (Neild 1999: 1). The language of citizen security, representing a clear broadening of the security concept, was quickly adopted by policy-makers, politicians, academic analysts, and average citizens alike to describe the struggle for personal and social security within a democratic rule of law. Since the early 2000s, for example, Argentina, Brazil, and Colombia, among other nations, have initiated efforts in police reform (Frühling 2003), Peruvians have become engaged in a broad range of state-sponsored programs to promote "participatory security" (Marquardt 2012), and states from Bolivia to Chile have attempted to modernize their justice systems (Dammert 2006), all in the name of improving 'citizen security.' The more expansive conception contained in this new "security paradigm" (Agamben 2002) invokes the defense of basic rights and democracy, defining citizen security as "the protection of the normal functioning of democratic institutions, the defense of the citizenry from criminality in all of its facets and typologies, [and] the defense of citizens against corruption and other asocial acts that impede or problematize the normal development and enjoyment of the fundamental rights of persons" (Delgado Aguado and Guardia Maduell 1994: 20). This definition implies that citizens have the right to a safe and secure life, and demands that the state respect and guarantee this right (del Olmo 2000). So, unlike earlier understandings that opposed rights to security, citizen security acknowledges security to be a right that any state must guarantee its citizens.

Ideally, citizen security seems to offer a platform for the realization of other rights of citizens, including the extension of economic, political, and social rights to poor and marginalized groups (Bobea 2003). With that aim, the enhancement of citizen security became a major development goal in Latin America, promoted by states and nonstate actors, such as transnational institutions at work in the region. Particularly after September 11, 2001, when security became a focus of international donor attention, international development organizations (including the United Nations Development Program, the World Bank, and the US Agency for International Development [USAID]) offered grants to Latin American states to heighten citizen security.[3] That the new campaign against crime and promotion of the rule of law was also linked to the ongoing Global War on Terror was evident from the interest that the United States government once again showed in Latin American security: In the words of a USAID report, in which the agency quotes its own congressional budget justification for 2005,

> establishing the rule of law also helps to fight crime more effectively, and in the process improve security in those countries and throughout the region. In the new environment of security concerns and the War on Terror, the stability of the hemisphere is a high priority for the United States, especially as it recognizes that, in the post–Cold War environment, 'the greatest threats to U.S. interests at home and abroad stem not from conquering states, but from failing ones.'
>
> *(USAID 2005)*

Given this international interest in citizen security and the funding that often accompanied efforts to improve it, the language of *seguridad ciudadana* was written into some Latin American national constitutions (e.g., in Peru and Venezuela) and incorporated into a number of hemispheric pacts and programs of transnational cooperation (Gabaldón 2004). The Inter-American Development Bank, for example, has been engaged since the early 1990s in efforts to promote judicial and police reform, enhance the rule of law, and support crime prevention programs throughout the region, but only began to talk about these efforts in terms of citizen security in 2003 (IDB 2013). The UN Development Program (UNDP), similarly, is a major sponsor of a variety of reforms in most Latin American nations, in a concerted effort to combat what it now identifies as regional 'citizen insecurity' (UNDP 2013: 1).

Citizen security has become the dominant paradigm for conceptualizing the ongoing problems of crime and violence in Latin America, a language deployed by states, citizens, nonstate actors, and academics alike. Less widespread in usage is the concept of human security, a foreign import that began to be used in Latin America during the 2000s as another framework for broadening the traditional understanding of what security entails. Defined by the United Nations as freedom from want and freedom from fear (Human Security Unit 2009), human security represented an even broader, more abstract notion of security, incorporating an even greater range of rights than the idea of citizen security, and moving further from the notion of crime as the single most important threat to individual and collective security in the region. As the founding statement of the UN Commission on Human Security (CHS) put it, the goal of human security is

> to protect the vital core of all human lives in ways that enhance human freedoms and human fulfillment. Human security means protecting fundamental freedoms – freedoms that are the essence of life. It means protecting people from critical (severe) and pervasive (widespread) threats and situations. It means using processes that build on people's strengths and aspirations. It means creating political, social, environmental, economic, military and cultural systems that together give people the building blocks of survival, livelihood and dignity.
>
> *(CHS 2003: 4)*

Elaborating on these ideas, some scholars have advocated for a human security approach that explicitly links security to human rights and human development, arguing that in the contemporary world these must be understood as inseparable, and domestic and foreign security policies as inextricably linked (Kaldor 2007; Sen 2003).

The concept of human security (even more so than its counterpart, citizen security) has clearly pushed the boundaries of what are ordinarily considered to be security threats, and seeks to empower agents outside the state (including individual actors and communities) to respond to those threats. However, the breadth and ambition of the human security concept has limited its utility for many scholars of security in Latin America and elsewhere. Again, the old question of broadening or narrowing security continues to haunt the discussion, with the issue of violence being particularly problematic. Should human security limit its focus to violent threats to individual security, those with "identifiable human agents" (Bajpai 2000)? Or can it usefully be understood to include a much wider range of threats and agents of human suffering, thus moving beyond the state as the "referent object of security" (Mack 2004: 366; see also Svensson 2007)? Do such uncertainties make human security in general a "normatively attractive but analytically weak concept" (Newman 2004)? While these questions remain unresolved for human security scholarship (Owen 2004), the concept has received relatively little attention outside the realm of academics and NGOs, and is not widely used by Latin American states and citizens. This is in direct contrast to citizen security, which, despite its failures, and as the following section illustrates, has become a powerful discourse across a range of circumstances in Latin America.

Citizen security and human security in practice

Citizen security, though in many ways a progressive discourse of rights that broadens security beyond the state, has become something quite different in the daily practice of security-making in Latin American societies. In a context of pervasive crime and violence, ineffective and corrupt policing and judicial systems, and a climate of fear and suspicion surrounding daily life, understandings of security show a marked regression to older authoritarian conceptions (Dammert and Malone 2003; Neild 2002). Despite its broadening impulse, citizen security as a discourse of contemporary insecurity reproduces a narrowing of the security concept, to focus now on crime and criminality as fundamental threats. As such, citizen security demonizes criminals and potential criminals, often young, poor and working-class, black or indigenous men, who emerge as the new 'internal enemies' of the 'good' people of society. Criminals, like communists and terrorists before them, in the language of citizen security embody the insecurity that people feel as a general condition of their lives, and become the targets of repressive police campaigns; in official statements, the media and popular talk are made to bear full responsibility for pervasive insecurity. Citizen security, which had promised a movement away from equations of security with state stability, in the context of criminality and fear trends back to older meanings, so that it now comes to stand once again for the maintenance of public order, and permits the state to suspend rights and use force in creating security.

My research in Bolivia provides one example of how this retreat to older understandings of security works in practice, revealing both the ways in which citizen security is understood and deployed in everyday life, and the trend toward authoritarianism that it authorizes. In Bolivia, as elsewhere in the region, citizen security refers to defending people against crime. As crime rates have risen in the country following the introduction of neoliberal reforms (Bailey and Dammert 2006; Mollericona n.d.), the Bolivian state has adopted the language of citizen security to shift attention away from security as protection of the state (*orden público*, or public order) towards security as protection of the population (Comisión Andina de Juristas 1999). Beginning in the mid-1990s, the Bolivian state created a range of policies and programs to enhance citizen security – defined exclusively as protection from crime, against broader conceptions of what security might include. Most of this work consisted of institutional reorganization, of which the expressed goal was to increase cooperation and communication between different policing entities, without challenging those entities' historically centralized and hierarchical structure. And while little additional investment has been made in the daily work of policing, a neoliberal rhetoric of participation and individual responsibility has become widely used in public discussions of security (Arias and Ungar 2009).

The urban poor in Bolivia face a host of challenges to what scholars might term their human security – including poverty, disease, racism, precarious housing, lack of access to quality health care and education – but, like the Bolivian state, their principal preoccupation is crime and criminal violence. Among the people with whom I have lived and worked, the poor and indigenous residents of a 'marginal barrio' on the far southern fringe of the city of Cochabamba, citizen security is the language used by residents themselves to characterize their vulnerability to crime, and to demand better access to justice and honest, reliable police protection. Many barrio residents equate citizen security with police protection, effectively narrowing the meanings of this term and so echoing the rhetoric of the state. For example, Silvio Lopez, a barrio resident and local political leader, told me that "there used to be police here, three, four, now there are none, they've locked up the station and withdrawn . . . The southern zone is completely abandoned in terms of security, we don't have any citizen security."[4] As is evident in don Silvio's remarks, however, the discourse of citizen security also provides barrio residents with the tools to criticize the neoliberal state for its failure to provide security to its citizens.[5] If the state narrows citizen security to mean policing and protection from crime, barrio residents can use this same language to challenge the state to do more to live up to its expressed aims in this area. Furthermore, the perceived need to create citizen security seems to authorize people to take often violent measures to deal with crime in their neighborhoods. Feeling that they have been 'abandoned' by the state and the police, some barrio residents participate in or at least condone acts of vigilante lynching of criminal suspects, seen by many as the only way to make security in their communities. Said my friend Josias, effectively rearticulating the demonization of the criminal commonly found in Bolivian media, government, and popular talk, "I would do it personally, I would burn him [the criminal] with my own hands . . . I think that these people have to be killed, because they are beyond hope."[6]

As this statement indicates, the rights of criminal suspects are considered forfeit within the logic of citizen security. From this perspective, security can only be attained if the forces of insecurity and delinquency are opposed by the superior force of violence, either popular or state, and basic rights are considered as obstacles to the creation of law and public order. For the state, this logic enables a space of exception (Agamben 2005) in which the realization of citizens' or human rights can be indefinitely postponed, until such time as threats to social order can be subdued. This approach authorizes the remilitarizing of policing, reversing human rights groups' hard-won gains in excluding the armed forces from the work of domestic security provision (Machillanda 2005), allowing broader latitude for the police to use violent force in dealing with crime, adopting harsher criminal penalties, including the death penalty, increasingly popular in many Latin American societies (Dammert and Malone 2003), and prosecuting minors as adults. These official practices are reflected in more popular forms of security-making, including extralegal violence, which is similarly justified as a means to create citizen security. It is rather terrifying to note that under a discourse that authorizes greater citizen responsibility and 'participation' in making security, this should find expression in the form of a lynch mob. And ironically, as the rights of criminal suspects are ignored and the rights of citizens subordinated to the enhanced policing powers of the state, the 'right to security' emerges as the paramount right in local people's perceptions. The right to security trumps all other rights, and justifies violence – state, collective, or private – as a way to attain it.[7]

Conclusions

As the preceding discussion demonstrates, citizen security is a discourse, conceptual framework, and set of programs and policies initiated in the name of broadening security beyond the traditional defense of the state, but with the ultimate effect of reauthorizing state and popular forms of violence to produce a very narrowly understood set of security objectives. At the same time, citizen security is not just a set of government or transnational initiatives; it is a language for thinking and talking about security that has achieved widespread usage among citizens themselves, both as a way of conceptualizing their own insecure situations and of making claims against a negligent and inefficient state that has largely failed to provide any kind of enduring security for its people. In this sense, citizen security is what we might call an emic approach to security – one that is fully emergent from, and useful in, framing the lived experience of people in insecure settings.

The same cannot be said for human security, which remains an etic concept largely exterior to the daily lives of Latin American people. The broadening tendencies of human security, while welcome antidotes to the narrowing effects of citizen security and its antecedents, nevertheless fail to conform to local experience. Additionally, as Lemanski's work in South Africa demonstrates, while human security advocates may speak of empowering local citizens to face their everyday security problems, human security remains a top-down enterprise, focused more on global concerns and collective human needs, with little connection to the lived realities and specific situations of ordinary people. Human security approaches, concerned with state-led efforts, neglect the empirical reality in which "experiences of everyday human (in)security are frequently addressed by citizen-led informal and formal strategies, often explicitly avoiding reliance on a state perceived as distant and uninterested" (Lemanski 2012: 73; see also Hudson 2005). This observation conforms to my own example from Bolivia, where citizen security provides logic for both state and popular security-making approaches.

My emphasis in this chapter on the emic/etic distinction contains suggestions for future research on security, grounded in an interdisciplinary methodology and adopting a flexible conceptual approach. The analysis offered here points to the utility of focused ethnographic study for understanding the lived conditions of insecurity facing Latin American citizens, and the ways in which they go about confronting these on a daily basis. At the same time, these insights must be situated within the broader national, transnational, and policy-oriented perspectives that necessarily frame the daily experience of life in a context of insecurity. Studies of security and insecurity in Latin America, whether academic or from an applied, development-oriented approach, can employ an anthropological perspective, one that attends to citizen and human security not only as national and regional problems, but as problems that ordinary people must face in their daily lives. Such an approach can better illuminate the real causes and consequences of citizen insecurity in Latin America, revealing how global issues are experienced and managed in the local spaces of everyday life.

Notes

1 Anthropologists have not been the most robust contributors to security studies, broadly understood, though I would argue (and have; see Goldstein 2010) that a critical anthropological approach to security offers a distinct perspective on security as an increasingly significant lived experience and site of contestation in contemporary societies.

2 The most obvious examples of this neoliberal disposition in the United States can be found in the 'see something, say something' campaigns launched by a variety of state and civil institutions, including the U.S. Department of Homeland Security, the New York City Metropolitan Transportation Authority, and Walmart (CNN 2010).

3 For example, in 2004 USAID provided nearly $50,000,000 to strengthen democratic institutions and improve access to justice in Bolivia (USAID 2004).

4 Personal interview, June 30, 2007, Cochabamba.

5 Although the government of President Evo Morales is explicitly anti-neoliberal, the Bolivian state under Morales continued to exhibit distinct neoliberal tendencies, particularly in the area of security provision (see Goldstein 2012).

6 Personal interview, March 25, 2007, Loma Pampa, Cochabamba.

7 Other examples of the contradiction between rights and security abound in studies of other Latin American countries. In Colombia, President Uribe's policy of democratic security (close kin to citizen security) has been responsible for the reduced expression of citizens' rights and the perpetuation of state violence in the name of security (Hunt 2012; Idler 2012; Rojas 2009). In Chile, Dammert (2006) has described the transition from public security to citizen security in ways that echo many of the

themes mentioned here. Other studies from the Dominican Republic (Bobea 2011), Guatemala (Burrell 2010; Godoy 2004), and Venezuela (Rosales 2010) make similar contributions.

References

Agamben, G. (2002) 'Security and Terror', *Theory and Event*, 5(4): 5–6.

——— (2005) *State of Exception*, K. Atell (trans), Chicago: University of Chicago Press.

Arias, E. D. and Goldstein, D. M. (eds) (2010) *Violent Democracies in Latin America*, Durham: Duke University Press.

Arias, E. D. and Ungar, M. (2009) 'Community Policing and Latin America's Citizen Security Crisis', *Comparative Politics*, 41(4): 409–429.

Bailey, J. and Dammert, L. (2006) 'Public Security and Police Reform in the Americas' in J. Bailey and L. Dammert (eds) *Public Security and Police Reform in the Americas*, Pittsburgh: University of Pittsburgh Press.

Bajpai, K. (2000) 'Human Security: Concept and Measurement', Kroc Institute Occasional Paper 19, Notre Dame, IN: Joan B. Kroc Institute for International Peace Studies.

Beck, U. (1992) *Risk Society: Towards a New Modernity*, London: Sage.

Bobea, L. (ed) (2003) *Entre el crimen y el castigo: Seguridad ciudadana y control democrático en América Latina y el Caribe*, Caracas: Editorial Nueva Sociedad.

——— (2011) 'The Emergence of the Democratic Citizen Security Policy in the Dominican Republic', *Policing and Society: An International Journal of Research and Policy*, 22(1): 57–75.

Briceño-Leon, R. and Zubilaga, V. (2002) 'Violence and Globalization in Latin America', *Current Sociology*, 50(1): 19–37.

Burrell, J. (2010) 'In and Out of Rights: Security, Migration, and Human Rights Talk in Postwar Guatemala', *Journal of Latin American and Caribbean Anthropology*, 15(1): 90–115.

Buzan, B., Waever, O. and de Wilde, J. (1998) *Security: A New Framework for Analysis*, Boulder: Lynne Rienner.

Caldeira, T.P.R. (2000) *City of Walls: Crime, Segregation, and Citizenship in São Paulo*, Berkeley: University of California Press.

Carranza, E. (2004) 'Políticas públicas en materia de seguridad de los habitantes ante el delito en América Latina', *Nueva Sociedad*, 191: 52–64.

Chipman, J. (1992) 'The Future of Strategic Studies: Beyond Grand Strategy', *Survival*, 34(1): 109–131.

CNN (2010) 'Homeland Security Teams up with Walmart for Safety'. Retrieved from http://www.cnn.com/2010/US/12/06/washington.dhs.walmart/.

Comisión Andina de Juristas (1999) *Seguridad ciudadana: Cambios necesarios*, Lima.

Commission on Human Security (CHS) (2003) *Human Security Now*, New York.

Dammert, L. (2006) 'From Public Security to Citizen Security in Chile' in J. Bailey and L. Dammert (eds) *Public Security and Police Reform in the Americas*, Pittsburgh: University of Pittsburgh Press.

Dammert, L. and Malone, M.F.T. (2003) 'Fear of Crime or Fear of Life? Public Insecurities in Chile', *Bulletin of Latin American Research*, 22(1): 79–101.

del Olmo, R. (2000) 'Ciudades duras y violencia urbana', *Nueva Sociedad*, 167: 74–86.

Delgado Aguado, J. and Guardia Maduell, J. (1994) *Seguridad ciudadana y función policial: Una aproximación al análisis de entornos concretos*, Barcelona: Unión de Ciudades Capitales Iberoamericanas.

Elmer, G. and Opel, A. (2006) 'Surviving the Inevitable Future', *Cultural Studies*, 20(4): 477–492.

Frühling, H. (2003) 'Police Reform and the Process of Democratization' in H. Frühling, J. S. Tulchin and H. A. Golding (eds) *Crime and Violence in Latin America: Citizen Security, Democracy, and the State*, Washington, DC: Woodrow Wilson Center Press.

Gabaldón, L. G. (2004) 'Seguridad ciudadana y control del delito en América Latina', *Nueva Sociedad*, September: 1–10.

Giddens, A. (1999) 'Risk and Responsibility', *The Modern Law Review*, 62(1): 1–10.

Gledhill, J. (2004) 'Neoliberalism' in D. Nugent and J. Vincent (eds) *Companion to the Anthropology of Politics*, London: Blackwell.

Godoy, A. S. (2004) 'When "Justice" is Criminal: Lynchings in Contemporary Latin America', *Theory and Society*, 33(6): 621–651.

Goldstein, D. M. (2005) 'Flexible Justice: Neoliberal Violence and Self-help Security in Bolivia', *Critique of Anthropology*, 25: 389–411.

——— (2010) 'Toward a Critical Anthropology of Security', *Current Anthropology*, 51(4): 487–517.
——— (2012) *Outlawed: Between Security and Rights in a Bolivian City*, Durham: Duke University Press.
Goodenough, W. (1970) *Description and Comparison in Cultural Anthropology*, Cambridge, UK: Cambridge University Press.
Hay, J. and Andrejevic, M. (2006) 'Introduction: Toward an Analytic of Governmental Experiments in These Times: Homeland Security as the New Social Security', *Cultural Studies*, 20(4–5): 331–348.
Hudson, H. (2005) ' "Doing" Security as Though Humans Matter: A Feminist Perspective on Gender and the Politics of Human Security', *Security Dialogue*, 36(2): 155–174.
Human Security Unit (2009) *Human Security in Theory and Practice*, New York: Office for the Coordination of Humanitarian Affairs, United Nations.
Hunt, S. L. (2012) 'Everyday Engagement in Spectacular Situations: Popular Participation in Colombian Security Provision', *Third World Quarterly*, 33(7): 1305–1321.
Idler, A. (2012) 'Arrangements of Convenience in Colombia's Borderlands: An Invisible Threat to Citizen Security?', *St. Anthony's International Review*, 7(2): 93–119.
Inter-American Development Bank (IDB) (2013) *Citizen Security in Latin America and the Caribbean: IDB's Comparative Advantage*, Washington, DC.
Jusionyte, I. (2013) 'On and Off the Record: The Production of Legitimacy in an Argentine Border Town', *PoLAR: Political and Legal Anthropology Review*, 36(2): 231–248.
Kaldor, M. (2007) *Human Security*, Cambridge: Polity.
Leal Buitrago, F. (2003) 'La doctrina de seguridad nacional: Materialización de la Guerra Fría en América del Sur', *Revista de Estudios Sociales*, 15: 74–87.
Lemanski, C. (2012) 'Everyday Human (In)Security: Rescaling for the Southern City', *Security Dialogue*, 43(1): 61–78.
Machillanda, J. (2005) 'La remilitarización de la seguridad en América Latina', *Nueva Sociedad*, 198: 130–144.
Mack, A. (2004) 'A Signifier of Shared Values', *Security Dialogue*, 35(3): 366–367.
Mares, D. R. (2007) 'The National Security State' in T. Holloway (ed) *A Companion to Latin American History*, London: Blackwell.
Marquardt, K. M. (2012) 'Participatory Security: Citizen Security, Participation, and the Inequities of Citizenship in Urban Peru', *Bulletin of Latin American Research*, 31(2): 174–189.
Mollericona, J. Y. (n.d.) 'Políticas de seguridad ciudadana en Bolivia'. Retrieved from http://www.comunidadyprevencion.org/opinion_13.html.
Moser, C., Winton, A. and Moser, A. (2003) 'Violence, Fear and Insecurity and the Urban Poor in Latin America' in *World Bank LAC Regional Study of Urban Poverty*, Washington, DC: World Bank.
Neild, R. (1999) 'From National Security to Citizen Security: Civil Society and the Evolution of Public Order Debates', Paper written for the International Center for Human Rights and Democratic Development, Montreal, CA.
——— (2002) 'The New Face of Impunity', *Human Rights Dialogue*, 2(8): 1–2.
Newman, E. (2004) 'A Normatively Attractive but Analytically Weak Concept', *Security Dialogue*, 35(3): 358–359.
O'Malley, P. (1996) 'Risk and Responsibility' in A. Barry, R. Osborne and N. Rose (eds) *Foucault and Political Reason*, Chicago: University of Chicago Press.
Owen, T. (2004) 'Human Security – Conflict, Critique and Consensus: Colloquium Remarks and a Proposal for a Threshold-Based Definition', *Security Dialogue*, 35(3): 373–387.
Pike, K. L. (ed) (1967) *Language in Relation to a Unified Theory of the Structure of Human Behavior* (2nd ed.), The Hague: Mouton de Gruyter.
Ramírez, M. C. (2011) *Between the Guerrillas and the State: The Cocalero Movement, Citizenship, and Identity in the Colombian Amazon*, Durham: Duke University Press.
Rojas, C. (2009) 'Securing the State and Developing Social Insecurities: The Securitisation of Citizenship in Contemporary Colombia', *Third World Quarterly*, 30(1): 227–245.
Rosales, E. (2010) 'Sistema penal, seguridad ciudadana y policía en las metrópolis (Venezuela y el contexto regional)', *Espacio Abierto Cuaderno Venezolano de Sociología*, 19(2): 273–295.
Sen, A. (2003) 'Development, Rights, and Human Security, in Commission on Human Security' in *Human Security Now*, New York: CHS.
Svensson, K. (2007) 'Human Security as Inclusive Security – Gender, Epistemology and Equality', *African Security Review*, 16(2): 1–13.

Ungar, M. (2007–2008) 'The Privatization of Citizen Security in Latin America: From Elite Guards to Neighborhood Vigilantes', *Social Justice*, 34(3–4): 20–37.

——— (2011) *Policing Democracy: Overcoming Obstacles to Citizen Security in Latin America*, Baltimore: Johns Hopkins University Press.

United Nations Development Program (UNDP) (2013) *Citizen Security with a Human Face: Evidence and Proposals for Latin America, Regional Human Development Report 2013–14*, New York.

United States Agency for International Development (USAID) (2004) *FY 2005 Congressional Budget Justification, Bolivia*, Washington, DC. Retrieved from http://www.usaid.gov/policy/budget/cbj2005/lac/bo.html.

——— (2005) *USAID Promotes the Rule of Law in Latin America and Caribbean Democracies*, Washington, DC.

Waever, O., Buzan, B., Kelstrup, M. and Lemaitre, P. (1993) *Identity, Migration and the New Security Order in Europe*, London: Pinter.

World Health Organization (WHO) (2002) *World Report on Violence and Health*, Geneva: WHO.

12

ALTERITY AND SECURITY

Culture and survival beyond the 'Indian problem'

José Antonio Lucero

In the U.S.-Mexico borderlands I have seen a popular T-shirt that shows an iconic, late 19th-century photograph of four rifle-carrying Apache warriors, including Geronimo (Goyahkl), standing defiantly in northern Mexico. The following words (penned by a Navajo intellectual and activist named Matthew Tafoya) appear above the image: 'Homeland Security: Fighting Terrorism since 1492.'[1] This phrase and image raise an important question for the academic study of security in the Americas: "security for whom?"

Security and insecurity have been tightly intertwined with the histories of racial domination and resistance in the region. As this volume demonstrates, there is no one single notion of security. Nevertheless, in its conventional, state-centered formulation and even in some critical alternative formulations like 'human security' and 'societal security,' knowledge is produced from an unmarked vantage point regarding the proper subject of security: a 'we' (or an essentialized version of 'society') that should be protected.[2] Such ideas of 'we' and generic 'society' – as they have been institutionalized in the political systems and reproduced in the imaginaries of the Americas – have often invoked a dangerous, racialized Other that is a threat to 'us.' This chapter examines how security in Latin America has been entangled with the histories of racial difference and how racialized Others, especially indigenous movements and Afro-Latino peoples, have generated powerful challenges to dominant political and academic notions of security.

Though indigenous peoples and peoples of African descent are connected in many ways by histories of colonialism and slavery, this recognizes that these peoples occupy different locations in what Peter Wade (1997) calls "structures of alterity." During the formal colonial period, 'indigenous' was not only a racial designation but also a fiscal, administrative, and spatial category. Indigenous communities provided tribute, were tracked by censuses, and occupied certain spaces collectively. In other words, "[I]ndian was an institutionalized identity. Nothing comparable can be said for Blacks" (Wade 1996: 28). After slavery was abolished in the late 19th century, blackness took various directions in the Americas, but most countries in the region avoided the rigid Jim Crow racial orders of the United States. Ideologies of mixture, *mulataje*, and 'racial democracy' served to make blackness a more elusive and evasive social category than 'indigenous.' As indigenous collective identities in Latin America have generally been more coherent, more politicized, mobilized, and securitized than Afro-Latino ones, this chapter will focus largely on native peoples, with some comparative glances at other experiences.

This chapter proceeds by providing three analytic lenses for thinking about security and identity. First, by examining colonial legacies that have shaped a state-centered view of security and an orientalizing understanding of identity (Said 1979), I critically review a perspective I term the coloniality of security. Second, I review more 'people-centered' views of security and constructivist notions of identity that I will call 'recognition as security.' Finally, the chapter examines a postliberal, post-positivist, and decolonial research agenda that takes seriously native ontologies and epistemologies.[3] The chapter concludes by reviewing how these three perspectives differ in terms of their understandings of security and subaltern identities, and how they each call for different kinds of policy approaches.

The coloniality of security

The wave of rebellions in the Andes led by Tupac Amarú and Tupaj Katari in the 1780s in what are today the states of Peru and Bolivia, respectively, left a lasting impression on Creole (European descendant) political elites in the region. Similarly, the Haitian Revolution of the 1790s created something almost unthinkable in a slave-holding Atlantic world: a successful slave uprising. These popular insurrections were political tsunamis felt throughout the region.

For example, the writings of the great *Libertador* Simón Bolívar reflect deep racial anxieties about black and brown popular masses. After receiving crucial assistance from Haiti, the slave-owning Bolívar declared for the first time his support for the abolition of slavery; something that went along with the republican desire to do away with colonial distinctions, including the tributes that indigenous communities had paid the colonial state. His support of measures that moved toward formal equality, however, was tempered by his belief that political power should be in the hands of white creole elites, producing what Aline Helg has called a "double-edged" view of citizenship: "an active citizenship restricted to a tiny literate and skilled minority and an inactive citizenship for the immense majority of (mostly nonwhite) men" (Helg 2012: 21).

In many ways this double-edged notion of political membership lives on in the Americas and has become a constituent element of what Quijano (2000) calls the "coloniality of power," shorthand for the enduring patterns of racialized inequality, connected to global, national, and local constellations of power. For much of the 19th and 20th centuries, the goals of settler-colonial states across the Americas were at odds with the interests of native and Afro-Latino peoples. Indeed, indigenous peoples and their ways of knowing and political practices have often been placed in stark opposition to notions of national progress and modernity. Peruvian novelist and politician Mario Vargas Llosa puts this view quite clearly: "It is tragic to destroy what is still living, still a driving cultural possibility, even if it is archaic; but I am afraid we shall have to make a choice. . . . [W]here there is such an economic and social gap, modernization is possible only with the sacrifice of the Indian cultures" (Vargas Llosa 1990: 53).

In this view, the interests of the 'modern' nation are more important than the survival of 'archaic' cultures. This view has been challenged, most powerfully by native peoples themselves who refuse the premise that indigeneity is synonymous with backwardness or incompatible with modernity. Nevertheless, from this view, security concerns serve as an extension of the long struggle between what 19th-century Argentine President and intellectual Domingo Sarmiento called "civilization and barbarism" (Sarmiento 2003 [1845]). Native peoples have long been in the crosshairs of colonial and republican states. Tupac Amarú's rebellion in 18th-century Peru and Geronimo's (Goyahkl) raids in 19th-century Mexico and Texas provide variations of the "barbarous Indian" that had to be defeated for the sake of the ideals of the nation and civilization (Walker 2014; Saldaña Portillo forthcoming). Peruvian and Guatemalan militaries pursued scorched-earth policies in wars with leftist guerillas and often targeted indigenous peoples, who paid the deadliest price for those wars (García 2005; CVR 2003). Literally and figuratively, Indians have been killable bodies. It is revealing that the U.S. military operation that assassinated Osama Bin Laden was famously reported to President Obama with the following message: "Geronimo EKIA" [Enemy Killed In Action]" (Westcott 2011). 'Indian wars' echo from the past.

Beginning in the 1990s, powerful indigenous social movements emerged across the Americas. While these movements were largely peaceful and part of a larger democratizing trend in the region, there were many voices of alarm coming especially from some of the policy-oriented worlds of think tanks and security studies. Michael Radu of the Foreign Policy Research Institute describes the rise of indigenous movements in these terms:

> What is new, however, is the radicalization of Amerindians in the Andean region of South America and their adoption of anti-modern, anti-democratic, reactionary and strikingly fascistic attitudes. This trend is increasingly powerful in Bolivia, Ecuador, and Peru, and if not dealt with quickly, will lead to the region's collapsing into a political, economic, and social Stone Age – and it's becoming a danger to everyone, including the United States.
>
> *(Radu 2005)*

What evidence is there for such claims? In Radu's case, there is almost none, and his 2005 warnings about the chaos of potential victories by candidates Ollanta Humala in Peru and Evo Morales in Bolivia have not been borne out, as both Humala and Evo, as presidents of their respective countries, have pursued surprisingly centrist macroeconomic policies. Even with high profile " 'nationalizations' of the hydrocarbon sector, not a single foreign oil and gas company has pulled out of Bolivia and 'the firms' annual profits have remained about the same in dollar terms ($824 million)" (Acthenberg 2012).[4]

Security analysts like Radu produce more heat than light. Based on long-distance readings of indigenous critics, these authors' claims are not particularly compelling. It is harder to dismiss concerns raised by Julio Cotler, a leading Peruvian social scientist. Consider the following answer Cotler gave to a reporter's question about the 'danger' of indigenous movements in the Andes:

> Increasingly, these ethnic groups or the leaders of these groups begin to make demands based on ethnic or racial problems. Now, what is the danger that this can lead to? We already know the dangers; it can end in divided countries, in civil wars, in massacres. The Balkans is a good example. There are Bolivian leaders who want to eliminate all the whites.
>
> *(Cotler 2005)*

In a subsequent interview in his Lima office, I asked Cotler about his views, and he explained that he, as a long-time critic of internal colonialism, was not against indigenous movements ("that would be absurd," he said). Instead, he was reacting to a few extreme voices that spoke of expelling non-indigenous people and had threatened him personally. To put his comments in perspective, it is useful to recall that much of Cotler's own scholarship provides a different approach to understanding the dangers of national fragmentation.

In thinking about the dangers of disunity, one must first ask how 'unified' Latin American states are to begin with. Many Amazonian and Andean communities are situated precariously at the margins of the nation-state; often the only state institution with a significant presence in indigenous territories is the military. Yashar (2005) notes that one of the great lessons of indigenous politics has been to disabuse analysts and policy-makers of the idea that the Latin American state is a Weberian homogenous whole.

Moreover, most contemporary indigenous movements are not asking for separate republics. Rather, indigenous movements have been exploring new ways to decolonize nations and states without undoing them. Consider the names of well-known indigenous organizations like the Army of National Liberation of Emiliano Zapata (EZLN), where the 'Z' stands for Zapata – perhaps the greatest symbol of Mexican nationalism – or the Confederation of Indigenous Nationalities of Ecuador (CONAIE), where the 'E' stands for Ecuador. These are remarkably 'national' political actors. Indigenous peoples make claims not only about 'ethnic' or 'cultural' matters that are particular to them, but about broad economic issues that affect indigenous and non-indigenous peoples alike (Lucero 2008, 2011).

To return once more to the case of Bolivia, it is remarkable that indigenous political actors are emphasizing national sovereignty in the management of hydrocarbons and other natural resources, while neoliberal and regional elites are adopting *anti*national position in emphasizing their concern for regional autonomies and foreign investment. Indeed, Santa Cruz elites deployed ethnonational language in support of a *camba* or *cruceño* identity at the very moment that President Morales used the language of 'nationalization' in renegotiating contracts with foreign oil and gas firms and the discourse of 'refounding' the nation through the process of constitutional reform (Gustafson 2009: 994).

Let us review the analytic frame I have called the coloniality of security. Through this lens, security is seen in conventional, state-centric terms and indigenous identity in essentialist and orientalist ways. Native peoples encompass challenges to the national order of things not only because of their mobilizations but also more fundamentally because of their very existence. *Latin* America – in this colonialist view of security – must solve the Indian problem. It is important to note that as indigenous social movements became more influential and legitimate in the eyes of national and international publics, solutions to the Indian problem have shifted from old ideas of extermination or assimilation (though those approaches still have advocates) to new legislative and constitutional reforms that seek to create new regimes of inclusion. Those multicultural reforms require us to think about security and identity in different terms.

Recognition as security

Security is not simply understood from the view of the state or from the top down. Since the 1990s, the idea of human security has been championed by development agencies and scholars alike (UNDP 1994; Newman 2010). While there is great variety in the human security scholarship, generally speaking it is the view "that there is an ethical responsibility to re-orient security around the individual in line with internationally recognized standards of human rights and governance" (Newman 2010: 78). This concern with human rights and development is a welcome alternative and corrective view to state-centered views of security. One might certainly see native issues in a more favorable light, in what the UN Development Program (UNDP) calls a 'people-centered' view of development and security. Nevertheless, it is important to point out that 'people-centered' is an idea that works largely with the individual as the main unit of analysis and practice, a very different idea of what we might call *peoples*-centered notions of development that are concerned not only with individual flourishing, but the survival of peoples like the Asháninka, Purépecha, Maya, Quechua, Guaraní, and hundreds of other linguistically and politically differentiated peoples in the Americas.

Thus, if human security is too general and liberal a term for thinking about native and Afro-Latino peoples, perhaps it is worth thinking about a kind of multicultural 'societal security' and asking how policies of recognition can function as tools to manage difference. The goals of recognition policies certainly overlap with human security agendas in the sense of being concerned with the welfare and livelihoods of communities, yet their unit of analysis and action is a collective, not individual actor (Roe 2004). This view also marks a break with the colonialist conception of identity in that it moves from essentialist views of 'savagery' to more constructivist views of peoplehood. That is, even as it recognizes the existence of indigenous nationalities and peoples, it participates in shaping the very political subjects it recognizes. This view acknowledges that indigenous political subjectivities have been constructed with help from a transnational cast of actors, including NGOs, churches, and development agencies (Brysk 2000; Lucero 2008; Andolina et al. 2009).

Quickly reviewing the arc of managing difference in the Americas, the region has gone from periods of political ventriloquism (when state and other elites spoke on behalf of indigenous peoples), to the emergence of indigenous political voice (when states negotiated with powerful social movements), to a multicultural moment (when states passed legal and constitutional changes that recognized the importance of native and Afro-Latino voices within the political sphere). Space constraints prevent a full discussion of this arc (but see Lucero 2008), so we will examine all too briefly the rise of indigenous movements and multicultural regimes of recognition.

Oil shocks, debt crises, and other economic shocks during the 1980s set the stage for structural adjustment policies that shattered corporatist states in Latin America – states that tried to "rebaptize Indians as peasants," as Albó (1991) puts it. These crises led to the rise of "neoliberal citizenship regimes" throughout the region that changed state-society dynamics (Yashar 2005). In material terms, the end of agrarian reform made life in the countryside harder. In political and cultural terms, the democratic transitions of the 1980s offered more room for local communities to reconstitute themselves. Political opportunity structures became more permissive at the very moment that economic pressures were getting more oppressive. No longer part of corporatist mediating structures, indigenous people were able to move beyond what Andrés Guerrero calls 'ventriloquist' forms of representation and find their own national political voice, with the help of transnational allies like progressive churches and nongovernmental organizations (Guerrero 1994). These changes in the structures of interest mediation and the models of economic development thus allow us to understand the dramatic eruption of indigenous politics during the 1990s (Yashar 2005).

In several states, this marked the beginning of a decade-long series of confrontations and negotiations with national governments. These mobilizations often forced governments to halt or reverse economic policies and to pay greater attention to indigenous demands. These confrontations created unprecedented political openings for indigenous people. CONAIE, for example, negotiated with the Ecuadorian government and the World Bank for the creation of new agencies for indigenous development and intercultural bilingual education, agencies that were controlled by leaders from CONAIE. Additionally, indigenous movements also pushed for the inclusion of a set of collective rights that would form part of the constitutional reforms in the 1990s and early 2000s (Lucero 2008, 2011).

By the dawn of the 21st century, generations of indigenous struggle and negotiation transformed their political environment. By 2000, constitutions in virtually every Latin American country recognized indigenous collective rights, languages, and territories. Several countries grant indigenous territorial autonomy for particular regions of the country, and some (Bolivia, Colombia, Venezuela) reserve seats in elected office for indigenous representatives. In 2007, after decades of debate, the United Nations approved a Declaration on the Rights of Indigenous Peoples with the support of almost every country in the hemisphere. Beyond prohibiting discrimination and recognizing the "right to remain distinct," the Declaration enshrines the rights of indigenous peoples "to maintain and strengthen their own institutions, cultures and traditions, and to pursue their development in keeping with their own needs and aspirations."

It has been a slightly different story for Afro–Latin Americans. As mentioned above, blacks and Indians occupy different positions in Latin American 'structures of alterity.' Arguably, most multicultural policies have been designed more with indigenous peoples in mind than Afro-descendants. Afro–Latin Americans gain cultural rights 'when Afro becomes like indigenous.' Garifuna in Honduras (Anderson 2007) and quilombo communities in Brazil (French 2009) are examples of Afro-descendants who have 'indigenized' their claims for special recognition, usually by invoking what Greene has termed the "holy trinity of multicultural peoplehood: Culture + Language + Territory" (2007: 345). Multiculturalism, then, if it challenges the exclusion of indigenous people, seems to fall into the trap of reproducing the exclusion of Afro–Latin Americans (Hooker 2005).

For indigenous people, though, there is an unprecedented moment of official state recognition for government policies. But those policies are not without their contradictions. Take the very striking case of Bolivia, where an indigenous president has made 'decolonization' a state policy, declared the end of neoliberalism, and officially recognized indigenous autonomy. Yet, even here, the state has found itself the target of indigenous protests and discovered that very few indigenous communities have actually gone through the trouble of getting the official recognition as 'autonomous.' Tockman and Cameron explain why even this robust experiment in plurinationalism has been thwarted by two commitments of Morales's ruling party, the Movement toward Socialism (MAS):

> A commitment to expand the conventional economic development model based on the export of natural resources, which directly affects many would-be autonomous indigenous territories; and the MAS party's highly partisan pursuit of political power at all levels of politics, including in indigenous territories. As a consequence, beyond the notable yet underfinanced efforts of the Ministry of Autonomy, Bolivian government officials and policy serve principally to constrain the exercise of indigenous autonomy, allowing it to function only on a restricted scale and with limited jurisdiction for largely symbolic purposes.
>
> *(2014: 48)*

Even in Bolivia, the language of security and national development has been used to counter indigenous mobilization. When indigenous people protested the construction of a road that would run through a protected indigenous territory in order to link Bolivia with its powerful neighbor, Brazil, Morales was quick to blame NGOs, his right-wing critics, and the United States. Morales stated that anyone who was against the road was an "enemy of Bolivia" (quoted in Achtenberg 2011). Morales was forced to back down from this rhetoric, but has not totally abandoned the Isiboro-Sécure Indigenous Territory and National Park (TIPNIS) road project and other development projects. Moreover, in addition to expelling U.S. diplomats and agencies, he has also expelled European NGOs like Education for Development (IBIS) (Denmark) for supposed manipulation of indigenous organizations (Achtenberg 2011, 2012). It is an ironically familiar claim: If indigenous people are protesting, they must be led and/or manipulated by outsiders.

We have, perhaps surprisingly, come full circle. The coloniality of security yielded to the policies of official multiculturalism, only to find some surprising enclaves of coloniality within these policies of recognition. Yet, perhaps it is not so surprising. Progress, even in the decolonizing times of Evo Morales, is still measured in terms that are legible to the IMF, the World Bank, and Brazilian investors. Neoliberal multiculturalism, read most cynically, uses recognition selectively and strategically, disarticulating indigenous subjects into moderate and radical categories so that the state can coopt and repress more effectively (Hale 2002).

Decolonizing security?

So how does one go beyond state-centered and colonial views of security, or neoliberal forms of recognition? The most obvious answer is to have a strong view of self-determination, in which indigenous and Afro-Latino communities have the power to define their relationship to the broader polity and to the nonhuman worlds that are also seen as relevant political beings. Communities across the Americas have indeed not waited for states to recognize their ability to govern themselves, but have simply begun doing the work of providing security and welfare, often because the state does not. Thus in a strong empirical, if not legal, sense, *de facto* self-determination is being practiced because of the resilience and dynamism of indigenous and Afro-Latino Communities.

Yet, a crucial analytical question arises as we examine security from below. Borrowing from Roxanne Lynn Doty, are community security practices an example of "statecraft from below" or alternatively examples of "anti-statecraft" (2001)? This is another way of asking if community practices in essence continue the work of the state, in informal or 'vernacular' ways (Colloredo-Mansfeld 2009), or do they disrupt state geographies, logics, and ontologies? Let us consider some concrete examples.

Guerrero, Mexico offers one surprising example of how state projects of security can converge with indigenous self-governance. Since the late 1990s, Mixtec and Tlapeneco communities have organized and sustained a volunteer community police force, known as the *Comunitaria*. The *Comunitaria* has reduced crime and insecurity and shown the promise of indigenous forms of justice. Though the state initially saw the body as illegal, the *Comunitaria* had great local support in over 100 communities. State officials recognize that the *Comunitaria* has reduced crime by as much as 90 per cent. The achievements of the *Comunitaria* were perhaps even more surprising as the state of Guerrero, unlike Oaxaca or Chiapas, did not offer any legal recognition of indigenous rights or autonomy. Also unlike Chiapas, the *Comunitaria* does not directly confront the state, but rather operates at the edges of state and civil society in the effort to create a local political order within a broader crisis of citizen insecurity (Sierra 2010).

In 2014, the state made a change that formally recognized the self-determination of indigenous and Afro-Mexican communities and the importance of communitarian police forces. Yet, it also declared the following: "These police will have tight connection and collaboration with the State System of Public Security in terms of its registration, oversight, consultation, training and evaluation" (Gómez 2014). Thus, self-determination often seems to crash on the sharp rocks of statecraft (Maaka and Fleras 2008).

While the Guerrero indigenous police force may seem unique, it shares many elements with indigenous communities across the Americas. Like the self-defense *rondas campesinas* that emerged in response to the violence of the Shining Path in Peru or the Afro-Colombian and indigenous self-determination movements that also came out of the context of political violence in Colombia, there are many examples of communities trying to take matters into their own hands. As Latin American national states are often weakly present beyond major cities, local institutions often function as the authorities of first and last resort. Nevertheless, rather than being cases of state failure, these vernacular forms of statecraft are often tightly linked with official state powers.

There are other examples, though, that are closer to the anti-statecraft that Doty describes. The frustrating experience of the EZLN with the Mexican federal government prompted it to change the scale of its politics, moving from national to local levels, and ruling through institutions like the *Juntas de Buen Gobierno* (Good Government Councils). On this level, indigenous people are able to innovate and create new spaces for inclusion, as has been evidenced by the gains indigenous women have secured in many local settings. The Revolutionary Women's Law of the EZLN, which defends the rights of women to work, be educated, participate politically, and decide the number of children they want, is one of the better known examples of how indigenous women have been able to challenge racial discrimination and patriarchy (Speed 2007).

A more radical example requires us to move beyond political structures and to matters of epistemology and ontology. Following Marisol de la Cadena and Mario Blaser, I explore how "indigenous cosmopolitics" offers a sharp break with state-centered and even society-centered notions of security (de la Cadena 2010; Blaser 2010). Immediately, we must clarify a potential confusion. Unlike European notions of cosmopolitanism that seek to welcome many forms of difference into one world, *cosmopolitics* embraces the possibility that differences may be evidence of multiple worlds. To change terms slightly, this is a way of taking seriously non-Western ontologies. Ontology is usefully defined by sociologists Scott and Marshall as an inventory of "assumptions . . . about what kinds of things do or can exist, and what might be their conditions of existence, relations of dependency and so on" (2009: 531). Anthropologist Mario Blaser, building on this and other insights, suggests that ontologies are thus about enactments of worlds and "entail questions about what counts as knowledge" (2010: 3).

Thus, when Andean Quechua–speaking peoples speak of *apus*, or mountain deities, as living beings or Awajún Amazonians speak of rivers as brothers and the mutual obligations that exist between them, they are describing worlds that have a partial connection to the world of Western modernity. Those partial connections also involve serious conflicts, as they tend to emerge in the context of extractive industry. Conflicts over mining and oil exploration are not only environmental ones, but ones between different worlds. De la Cadena (2010) notes that some of her co-thinkers in Cusco worry about mining in the Ausangate Mountain because it will anger Ausangate, inviting a violent retaliation from this 'earth being.' When native peoples bring glaciers, mountains, or rivers into the public debates over extractivism, their views are often dismissed as hocus-pocus. Peruvian President Alan García mocked indigenous invocations of sacred earth beings as the fantasies of "old anti-capitalist communists of the nineteenth century who changed into protectionists in the twentieth century and have again changed into environmentalists in the twenty first century" (quoted in de la Cadena 2010: 340).

Thus it is not surprising that in the face of protests over extractive industry in 2009, García chose to view things through the lens of coloniality and used police forces to repress indigenous protestors who were obstacles to the modernization of the jungle. Yet, as de la Cadena notes, the challenge of indigeneity is much more radical than just opposition to government policies. "This appearance of indigeneities may inaugurate a different politics, plural not because they are enacted by bodies marked by gender, race, ethnicity, or sexuality demanding rights, or by environmentalists representing nature, but because they bring earth-beings to the political, and force into visibility the antagonism that proscribes their worlds" (de la Cadena 2010: 346).

Such antagonisms do not come just from right-leaning presidents like Alan García, but also from the left.

Blaser (2010) offers a helpful example when he describes a trip he took with an Yshiro leader from Paraguay to the World Social Forum (WSF) in Porto Alegre, Brazil. The motto of the WSF is familiar: "Another World is Possible." Blaser, however, observed many leftists reluctant to see that indigenous delegations at the WSF already represented 'other worlds.' Indeed, the marginalization of indigenous peoples in WSF spaces prompted Blaser to note pessimistically that the Otherness of native peoples seemed valuable to the WSF only for its symbolism.

A crucial question of securitization then emerges: What counts as security from an indigenous cosmopolitical perspective? What are the threats and what is being protected? Indigenous cosmopolitics calls for the protection of the earth or *pachamama*, though not for the reasons environmentalists and leftists often give. Indeed, native ways of knowing are sometimes incommensurable with Western science and politics. Moreover, what is being protected is not a discrete actor or community, but rather a set of sacred relations. Native peoples throughout the world stress the importance of relations, not only with each other, but also with all human and nonhuman kin. This is simultaneously a spiritual, political, and epistemological principle.[5]

A decolonial understanding of security requires several moves. The first is the provincialization of the state, to open up the possibility for other yardsticks of security. This at minimum means taking terms like 'self-determination' and 'autonomy' seriously as indigenous projects, rather than extensions of state projects of control. This goes against Weberian ideas of state sovereignty, but if indigenous sovereignty is to ever be anything but a slogan, other forms of political community must be imagined. More radically, there must be a move away from modernist insistences on universality and toward embracing the possibility of ontological, axiological, and epistemological multiplicity. This is not a call for 'anything goes' relativism, in which all views are valid. Instead, it is a call to be open and attentive to other, actually existing ways of thinking and being in the world, ones that reject a world always ordered by binaries and hierarchies and provide new ways of envisioning webs of relations and responsibilities.

All this might seem impossibly utopian and even naïve by the light of realist views of politics. Viewed from another perspective though, if one examines the vibrant existence of indigenous peoples, languages, and epistemologies in the Americas and beyond, one sees not only the effects of colonial violence, but also its limits. Despite over 500 years of coloniality and assimilation there still persist more kinds of difference than even the most imaginative political scientist could envision.

Conclusions

Briefly, I would like to review the three analytical lenses used to think about security and difference, and suggest some items for a research agenda that might connect them. The analytic lens of coloniality regards difference as dangerous. Indigenous communities, understood in essentialist and ahistorical ways, are seen as a threat to state projects of integration, stability, resource extraction, or to certain visions of national culture. In this view, difference must be neutralized either through assimilation or by force. Schools and police forces have been the policy tools most often used.

An alternative analytic and policy approach rejects the violence of assimilation and repression and makes appeals to a form of liberal inclusion that embraces multiculturalism. Homogeneity – even in its mestizo form – is no longer a national goal, and subaltern identities are respected. Though cultures are often seen as discrete and historical, multicultural inclusion is premised on a constructivist understanding that identities are shaped by situation and context. Programs of ethnodevelopment, intercultural bilingual education, and local autonomy seek to change the terms of recognition between the constituent parts of a plural society. Yet, the goal remains the management of difference. Thus, 'recognition' is deployed as an explicit security policy.

Finally, and most radically, a decolonial analytic lens seeks to drastically reframe security from a discourse and tactic of governmentality to a way of protecting native lands, ways of knowing, and webs of life. This analytic framework recognizes vast differences within the category of indigenous, but more importantly, and unlike neoliberal multiculturalism, does not shy away from the incommensurability of native and Western worlds. Without seeking to understand the world 'through native eyes,' it recognizes that native epistemologies open up more than different ways of seeing the world; they open up the possibility of seeing how different worlds exist and are partially connected. A policy approach to those partial connections means more radically robust regimes of autonomy, a rethinking of extractivist economic models, and an acceptance of indigenous ways of government, even if they seem to represent forms of anti-statecraft.

For researchers, these analytical lenses suggest that we must find new ways to understand how securitization empirically affects native lands and peoples, how forms of multiculturalism and plurinationalism are enabling and/or constraining indigenous politics, and finally how native ways of knowing provide new ways to unsettle understandings of nature, culture, and politics. Native perspectives can productively destabilize and invigorate a critical security studies that is aware of the ongoing work of colonialism, the dynamism of indigenous identities, and the limitations of the existing metrics of security and science.

Notes

1 While his original Chiricahua name was Goyaałé or Goyahkl, 'Geronimo' is how he has mostly been remembered in U.S. history (Hixon 2013). For more on Tafoya and the ideas behind the image, see Corman (2004).

2 For helpful and contrasting views of societal security as it related to identity, see Buzan (1993), Roe (2004), and Jutila (2006).

3 I use decolonial, rather than postcolonial, advisedly. Theorized by scholars like Linda Tuhiwai Smith (2012) and Arturo Escobar, decolonial projects recognize that coloniality is not past (post), and must be challenged by alternative ways of knowing that make 'worlds otherwise.'

4 For a surprisingly positive report card on Bolivia from the World Bank and IMF, see Neuman (2014).

5 The 'new materialism' of Latour (2005) and Bennett (2010) has provided another source for taking seriously nonhuman agency in politics. Yet, as Dakota scholar Kim TallBear (2013) argues, theorists of the 'new materialisms' are rediscovering what indigenous metaphysics revealed long ago.

References

Achtenberg, W. (2011) 'Bolivia: Indigenous Groups to March Against TIPNIS Highway,' *Rebel Currents*, August 12, Online. Available at: <https://nacla.org/blog/2011/8/12/bolivia-indigenous-groups-march-against-tipnis-highway> [Accessed 21 June 2014].

——— (2012) 'Nationalization, Bolivian Style: Morales Seizes Electric Grid, Boosts Oil Incentives', *Rebel Currents.* May 10, Online. Available at: <https://nacla.org/blog/2012/5/10/nationalization-bolivian-style-morales-seizes-electric-grid-boosts-oil-incentives> [Accessed 21 June 2014].

Albó, X. (1991) 'El retorno del indio,' *Revista Andina*, 9(2): 299–366.

Anderson, M. (2007) *Black and Indigenous: Garifuna Activism and Consumer Culture in Honduras*, Minnesota: University of Minnesota Press.

Andolina, R. et al. (2009) *Indigenous Development in the Andes: Culture, Power, and Transnationalism.* Durham: Duke University Press.
Bennett, J. (2010) *Vibrant Matter: A Political Ecology of Things*. Durham: Duke University Press.
Blaser, M. (2010) *Storytelling Globalization from the Chaco and Beyond.* Durham: Duke University Press.
Brysk, A. (2000) *From Tribal Village to Global Village: Indian Rights and International Relations in Latin America.* Stanford: Stanford University Press.
Buzan, B. (1993) 'Societal Security, State Security and Internationalisation', in O. Wæver, B. Buzan, M. Kelstrup & P. Lemaitre, *Identity, Migration and the New Security Agenda in Europe.* London: Pinter .
Colloredo-Mansfeld, R. (2009) *Fighting Like a Community: Andean Civil Society in an Era of Indian Uprisings*. Chicago: University of Chicago Press.
Corman, C. A. (2004, October 5) '9/11 and Acoma Pueblo Homeland Security in Indian Country', *Common-Place*, 1. Online. Available at: <www.common-place.org> [Accessed 21 June 2014].
Cotler, J. (2005, July 4) 'Existen grupos de interés muy fuertes alrededor del tema minero', Interviewed by Cecilia Valenzuela. Retrieved from http://agenciaperu.com/entrevistas/2005/jul/cotler.htm.
CVR (2003) *Informe final*, Lima: Comisión de la Verdad. Retrieved from http://www.cverdad.org.pe/ifinal/.
de la Cadena, M. (2010) 'Indigenous Cosmopolitics: In the Andes: Conceptual Reflections Beyond "Politics"', *Cultural Anthropology*, 25(2): 334–370.
French, J. H. (2009) *Legalizing Identities: Becoming Black or Indian in Brazil's Northeast*, Chapel Hill: University of North Carolina Press.
García, M. E. (2005) *Making Indigenous Citizens: Identities, Education, and Multicultural Development in Peru*, Stanford: Stanford University Press.
Gómez M. (2014, April 4) 'Crisis en la policía comunitaria en guerrero', *La Jornada*. Retrieved from http://www.jornada.unam.mx/2014/04/08/opinion/016a2pol.
Greene, S. (2007) 'Entre lo indio, lo negro, y lo incaico: The Spatial Hierarchies of Difference behind Peru's Multicultural Curtain', *Journal of Latin American and Caribbean Anthropology*, 12(2): 441–474.
Guerrero, A. (1994) 'Una imagen ventrílocua: El discurso liberal de la "desgraciada raza indígena" a fines del siglo XIX' in B. Muratorio (ed) *Imágenes e imagineros: Representaciones de los indígenas ecuatorianos, siglos XIX y XX*, Quito: Flacso, pp. 197–224.
Gustafson, B. (2009, Fall) 'Manipulating Cartographies: Plurinationalism, Autonomy, and Indigenous Resurgence in Bolivia', *Anthropological Quarterly*, 82: 985–1016.
Hale, C. (2002) 'Does Multicularalism Menace? Governance, Cultural Rights, and the Politics of Identity in Guatemala', *Journal of Latin American Studies*, 34: 485–524.
Helg, A. (2012) 'Simón Bolívar's Republic: A Bulwark Against the "Tyranny" of the Majority', *Revista de Sociologia e Política*, 20(42): 21–37. Online. Available at: http://www.scielo.br/scielo.php?script=sci_arttext&pid=S0104–44782012000200004&lng=en&tlng=en.10.1590/S0104–44782012000200004 [Accessed 21 June 2014].
Hixon, W. (2013) *American Settler Colonialism: A History*, New York: Palgrave-Macmillan.
Hooker, J. (2005) 'Indigenous Inclusion/Black Exclusion: Race, Ethnicity and Multicultural Citizenship in Latin America', *Journal of Latin American Studies*, 37(2): 285–310.
Jutila, M. (2006) 'Desecuritizing Minority Rights: Against Determinism', *Security Dialogue*, 37(2): 167–185.
Latour, B. (2005) *Reassembling the Social: An Introduction to Actor-Network-Theory*, Oxford: Oxford University Press
Lucero, J. A. (2011) 'Paradoxes of Indigenous Politics', *Americas Quarterly*, 5(3): 44–48.
——— (2008) *Struggles of Voice: The Politics of Indigenous Representation in the Andes*, Pittsburgh, PA: University of Pittsburgh Press.
Lynn Doty, R. (2001) 'Desert Tracts: Statecraft in Remote Places', *Alternatives: Global, Local, Political*, 26(4): 523–543.
Maaka, R. and Fleras, A. (2008) 'Contesting Indigenous Peoples Governance: The Politics of State-Determination vs. Self-Determining Autonomy' in Y. Belanger (ed) *Aboriginal Self-government in Canada: Current Trends and Issues*, Saskatoon, SA: Purich, pp. 69–104.
Neuman, W. (2014, February 17) 'Turnabout in Bolivia as Economy Rises From Instability', *New York Times*. Online. Available at: <http://www.nytimes.com/2014/02/17/world/americas/turnabout-in-bolivia-as-economy-rises-from-instability.html?_r=0> [Accessed 21 June 2014].

Newman, E. (2010) 'Critical Human Security Studies', *Review of International Studies*, 36: 77–94.
Quijano, A. (2000) 'Coloniality of Power, Eurocentrism, and Latin America', *Nepantla: Views From the South*, 1(3): 533–580.
Radu, M. (2005, February 9) 'Andean Stormtroopers', Foreign Policy Research Institute. Retrieved from http://archive.frontpagemag.com/readArticle.aspx?ARTID=9736.
Roe, P. (2004) 'Securitization of Minority Rights: Conditions of Desecuritization', *Security Dialogue*, 35(3): 279–294.
Said, E. (1979) *Orientalism*, New York: Vintage.
Saldaña Portillo, M. J. (forthcoming) *Indian Given: The Racial Geographies of Mexico, the United States and Aztlán*, Durham: Duke University Press.
Sarmiento, D. (2003 [1845]) *Facundo*, K. Ross (trans), Berkeley: University of California Press.
Scott, J. and Marshall, G. (2009). *A Dictionary of Sociology*, Oxford: Oxford University Press.
Sierra, M. T. (2010, September–October) 'Indigenous Justice Faces the State: The Community Police Force in Guerrero, Mexico', *NACLA Report on the Americas*, pp. 34–38.
Smith, L. T. (2012) *Decolonizing Methodologies: Research and Indigenous People*, London: Zed Books.
Speed, S. (2007) *Rights in Rebellion: Indigenous Struggle and Human Rights in Chiapas*, Stanford: Stanford University Press.
TallBear, K. (2013, May 23) 'An Indigenous Approach to Critical Animal Studies, Interspecies Thinking, and the New Materialisms', Lecture, Seattle, WA: University of Washington.
Tockman, J. and Cameron, J. (2014), 'Indigenous Autonomy and the Contradictions of Plurinationalism in Bolivia', *Latin American Politics and Society*, 56: 46–69.
UNDP (1994) *Human Development Report*, New York: Oxford University Press.
Vargas Llosa, M. (1990, December) 'Questions of Conquest: What Columbus Wrought and What He Did Not', *Harpers*: 45–54.
Wade, P. (1996) 'Reflections on Passivity and Activity in Teaching and Learning', *Anthropology in Action*, 3(2): 28–29.
——— (1997) *Race and Ethnicity in Latin America*, London: Pluto Press.
Walker, C. (2014) *The Tupac Amaru Rebellion*, Cambridge: Belknap Press.
Westcott, K. (2011, May 3) 'Osama Bin Laden: Why Geronimo?', *BBC News*. Online. Available at: <http://www.bbc.co.uk/news/world-us-canada-13265069> [Accessed 21 June 2014].
Yashar, D. J. (2005) *Contesting Citizenship: Indigenous Movements and the Post-Liberal Challenge in Latin America*, Cambridge: Cambridge University Press.

13

MILITARY STRATEGY IN LATIN AMERICA

*Gabriel Marcella**

Introduction

Strategy exists at various levels, from grand to military, theater, and campaign. Grand strategy is the use of the aggregate power of the state to promote its national interests. These are defense, economic prosperity, international order, and promoting certain values. Military strategy is a scheme to employ military means to achieve the objectives of policy. Strategy is most effective when guided by policy, which defines the goals and sets the parameters for permissible actions and the limits on 'blood and butter' that can be used. The subordination of policy to military strategy, the domination of ends by means, is a prescription for disaster of the kind seen in World War I, when railroad timetables determined the initiation of war and military officers told civilian leaders what to do. Disaster can take another form, where military operations are conducted in the absence of strategy.

In a frequently cited work, Richard K. Betts asserts that strategy is "a plan for using military means to achieve political ends . . . a value added to power." He expands: "Without strategy there is no rationale for how force will achieve purposes worth the price in blood and treasure. Without strategy, power is a loose cannon and war is mindless. Mindless killing can only be criminal" (Betts 2000: 5). Betts provides a clarion call for the effective and ethical use of force, lest the dogs of war are unleashed and lead to unacceptable consequences.

Making and implementing strategy involves the vicissitudes of interaction among civilians and military, and among military services. Because of the multidimensional nature of modern conflict, militaries are driven in the direction of joint strategy and operations – integrating land, air, and naval power into a cohesive effort. Modern military strategy also requires that it be combined with the whole of government, what in Latin America is called inter-institutional integration of military with nonmilitary elements, such as economic. These considerations underscore that military strategy is affected by many variables, some of which cannot be anticipated or controlled (Dorff 2011: 9).

Military strategy remains important in Latin America because militaries exist throughout, with the exception of Costa Rica and Haiti, indicating that political systems continue to see the relevance of military force (see Mares's chapter on military coercion, this volume.) The military establishments of Latin America range from the advanced capabilities of Brazil to the less sophisticated and small forces of countries like Nicaragua, Suriname, and Panama. Though armies dominate the defense sector, some countries have sizable and very professional navies and air forces as well. Moreover, Brazil, Argentina, Chile, Colombia, Mexico, and Peru possess military industrial capabilities that they export to the global market. Military institutions justify their slice of the national budgets by providing defense against threats to national security. To do so, they must develop a certain strategy to utilize the nation's military capabilities. Thus, this chapter explores various dimensions of military strategy, and how it is developed and applied. It should be noted that Latin America is the second least militarized region of the world, with four per cent of the global defense budget. There are approximately 1.7 million personnel under arms, not including police and reserves (International Institute for Strategic Studies [IISS] 2014: 357–410).

Strategy and policy

Strategy is the calculated relationship between ends and means. Military strategy is an art. It is complex, given the large number of variables that must be controlled. It is also dynamic, since conditions change, and the unplanned can occur when military power is applied. Consequently, strategy should be calibrated as conditions evolve and as the opponent adapts her strategy. The strategist must be attentive to balancing policy ends and the sufficiency of military means, and to the reality that implementation is not risk free. Strategic planning must include risk assessment, expressed as the ability of assigned resources to achieve objectives. Adjustments are made when the political objective is either unattainable or requires a different force mix. To reduce uncertainty in outcomes the strategist applies these criteria:

1. Is the military strategy suitable for attaining the objective?
2. Can the objective be achieved by the means available?
3. Are the costs acceptable?

(Yarger 2010: 50)

Classical thinkers – Clausewitz, Beaufre, Sun Tzu, and Liddell Hart – grace the curriculum of military schools in Latin America. Carl von Clausewitz's *On War* defined strategy parsimoniously as the art of the use of battles to achieve the purpose of the war, and he enunciated the famous dictum that war is policy by other means (Clausewitz 1989: 87, 605–610). The Prussian strategist added other critical concepts, such as the trinitarian relationship that should link the people, government, and armed forces in a common effort – i.e., attacking the enemy's army – which he defined as the center of gravity, and the uncertainties of war called friction (Clausewitz 1989: 80, 89, 119–121, 595–596). *On War* is full of cautions about the imperative of thinking through war before undertaking it. Clausewitz argued that in "war the result is never final," meaning that the way a war ends may determine how the next one begins (Clausewitz 1989: 80). Michael I. Handel, a modern student of Clausewitz, asserts that other factors can limit rationality in war – e.g., chance and uncertainty, uncontrollable passions, incompetence, and irrational behavior (Handel 2002: xviii).

André Beaufre, the French strategist, stated that "strategy is the art of the dialectic of two opposing wills using force to resolve their dispute" (Beaufre 1985: 16). This definition approximates Clausewitz's notion that "war is nothing but a duel on a larger scale . . . if you want to overcome your enemy you must match your effort against his power of resistance, which can be expressed as the product of two inseparable factors, viz. the total means at his disposal and the strength of his will" (Clausewitz 1989: 75, 77). Beaufre had influence in Argentina, Brazil, and Chile. He lectured on revolutionary warfare at the *Escuela Superior de Guerra* in Argentina, where French Army colonels taught and guided research from the 1950s into the 1970s. Beaufre's influence indicates that the United States was not the only foreign country that taught counterinsurgency in Latin America.

Because of the nature of modern conflict, what some call 'post-heroic war,' today's military strategist must have more than a passing acquaintance with international relations, foreign languages, foreign policy, law, economics, cultural anthropology, psychology, and civil-military relations. In essence, although formerly trained almost exclusively in military science, the modern strategist will also need social science. Military officer education in Latin America is moving in this direction. In 2014, for example, President Ollanta Humala of Peru stated that military officers would learn two foreign languages. Moreover, many senior officer development programs in Latin America now include master's degrees.

Since Latin American militaries are guided by a Clausewitzian perspective, it is relevant to ask how they have performed. There is a crucial difference between exercises within war colleges and planning staffs and the implementation of strategy. Clausewitz codified learning by witnessing the revolutionary nature of Napoleonic warfare, whereas Latin American militaries seldom see the application of military strategy in combat. The record is mixed.

Among the failures, Argentina's performance in the Malvinas/Falklands War (Operation Rosario 1982) stands out. Though the air force and certain units, such as the Fifth Marine Battalion, and elements of the army fought well, Argentina failed because of miscalculations in strategic planning. Argentina could not match Britain's NATO high-tech military power, which Buenos Aires thought they would not deploy to retake the islands. To be sure, Argentina's plans expected a bloodless taking of the islands, followed by diplomatic negotiations to secure the military success. Consequently, there were no plans for military occupation (Friedman and Gamba 1991: 103–110). Thus Argentina violated the Clausewitzian admonition about thinking through the consequences of war, especially the notion that the result is never final.

Among the successes of implementing Clausewitzian principles is Colombia after 2000. Given a massive increment of military power through more resources, reorganization, and better leadership, Colombian armed forces mounted a comprehensive counterinsurgency where they targeted legitimacy as the center of gravity of the Revolutionary Armed Forces of Colombia (FARC) and the Army of National Liberation (Ospina 2014). At the same time they reduced the maneuver space and financial base of the opposing forces, so much so that by 2014 negotiations to end the conflict were underway in Havana between the government and the FARC. The illegal paramilitary forces had already demobilized. The Colombian military's strategy for confronting the guerrillas after 2000 permitted President Manuel Santos's policy to negotiate an end to the conflict to move forward.

In the Ecuador-Peru War (1995) in the Upper Cenepa River of the Amazon jungle the two countries mobilized some 150,000 troops to dispute jurisdiction over a border disputed since the Rio Protocol of 1942. Ecuadorean troops prepared an excellent defense and acquitted themselves well. Peru's military strategy was based on its successful rout of an unprepared Ecuadorian incursion in 1981, but had not been adjusted to account for an improved Ecuadorian military capability. Peru's armed forces overcame initial weaknesses and counterattacked, with the confrontation ending in a temporary stalemate. After three years of negotiations mediated by the Four Guarantors (the United States, Brazil, Argentina, and Chile) and a fear that the Peruvian military was ready to embark on a full-scale war to impose a settlement, the governments of Ecuador and Peru agreed to a binding arbitration by the Guarantors. The Presidential Act of Brasilia of 1998 secured the peace, with provisions for the demarcation of the border, programs for economic development, along with the granting of rights to Ecuador to access a square kilometer of Peruvian territory to erect a monument and bury its war dead. The war termination demonstrated that the results in modern war can be ambiguous (Marcella and Downes 1999: 234–235).

After Colombia attacked a FARC camp across the border in Ecuador in 2008, Venezuelan President Hugo Chávez made a public denunciation of that attack and ordered a mechanized brigade to the border, ostensibly to deter Colombia from engaging in similar behavior on their common border. But the poor readiness of Venezuelan forces prevented the mobilization. Accordingly, the lack of military confrontation between the two countries could not be attributed to any deterrent strategy on the part of the Venezuelan military.

Defense strategies and *Libros Blancos*

Latin American countries are producing increasingly sophisticated strategy documents: Prominent examples are Brazil's *Estratégia Nacional de Defesa* of 2012 and Ecuador's *Agenda Política de la Defensa* in 2011. Colombia has produced a cascade of documents, beginning with *Plan Colombia: Plan for Peace, Prosperity, and the Strengthening of the State*. Published in 1999, *Plan Colombia* provided the framework for the strategic planning and impressive integrated state action that has brought greater security and economic progress. *Plan Colombia* was followed by *Democratic Security Policy* (2003), and the *Política Integral de Seguridad y Defensa para la Prosperidad* and the *Guía de Planeamiento Estratégico* in 2011.

Latin American strategy documents include the White Books, the *Libros Blancos*, which are statements of grand strategy, such as Chile's *Libro de Defensa Nacional de Chile 2010*. The country's third since 1999, the latest version portrays Chile's international role and the broad contours of defense planning and military resources. Argentina, Bolivia, Brazil, Dominican Republic, Ecuador, El Salvador, Honduras, Guatemala, Mexico, Peru, and Nicaragua also published them. Brazil's *Livro Branco de Defesa Nacional* of 2012 carries the assertion by President Dilma Rousseff about a strong defense:

> The elevation of Brazil to international stature in the 21st century is already a reality. A Brazil fully developed and with growing external presence will need adequate deterrent capability. And committed to the construction of a more peaceful and prosperous world order, Brazil cannot ignore defense.
>
> *(Brazil Ministry of Defense 2012: 11)*

Though *Libros Blancos* intend to serve a number of purposes, such as confidence-building, security cooperation, civil-military education, and communication between civil society and government, they share some weaknesses. The format varies from country to country; some countries have detailed content while others less so. Moreover, the impact of civil society is not as robust as it should be. They are nonetheless an intellectual foundation for developing military strategy. In the past military strategy was the domain of the armed forces, but since the 1990s civilians have become increasingly involved, both at the ministries of defense and within civil society. Some countries are developing capability-based strategic planning under the guidance of presidential policy. This means that military forces are organized, trained, and equipped to deal with the most serious threats facing the country, as defined by the civilian leadership.

Security vs. defense

Latin American militaries face the dilemma of balancing their principal mission of deterrence against conventional external threats with contributing to public security and socio-economic development. Defense documents are suffused with the mandate that the military assist in national development because it possesses fungible administrative and logistical capabilities. In the 1950s the Brazilian and Peruvian militaries enunciated that national security depended on social and economic development (Miguel 2002: 40–46; Masterson 1991: 243–298). The equation was elaborated by civilian and military intellectuals concerned that poverty would impede the accumulation of national power while international communism threatened to exploit the poverty and inequality. Underdevelopment, which the Peruvian strategist General Edgardo Mercado Jarrín termed 'latent insurgency,' was the real enemy (Mercado Jarrin 1982). Structural reforms and state action were imperative, with the military in the vanguard. Accordingly, in Peru the Revolutionary Government of the Armed Forces (1968–1975) instituted a sweeping, but incomplete, land reform and sought to develop the country as a means to avoid having to face a communist insurgency again, as in 1965. This did not prevent the emergence of the Shining Path. Brazilians, by contrast, implemented a strategy in the midst of rural insurgency. Their focus on national development was on a much larger scale and is epitomized by the rise of state-owned firms like EMBRAER. The Brazilian approach to the insurgency was enemy-centric counterinsurgency, with less regard for reforms. All the militaries of Latin America support national development. Yet the debate rages as to whether such missions detract from the central strategic value of military institutions, which is deterrence against foreign threats. The search for the appropriate balance between development and defense continues.

The spectrum of conflict and military strategy

Latin America has high levels of crime, ranging from drug-related violence to the proliferation of gangs, contraband, illegal logging, and trafficking in people (Marcella 2013). The insecurity is the result of internal and external factors, such as poor governance and ineffective public security, all multiplied by the international market for illegal drugs and the proliferation of small weapons. The cyber threat is stimulating defense planning throughout the region, and the militaries are integrating such planning into their strategies.

Military strategists search for frameworks that aid planning. One of the tools used is called the spectrum of conflict, a concept that incorporates the levels of the potential use of military power during peace and the various levels of conflict, from low (such as terrorism and insurgency) to high intensity (conventional war). Such frameworks provide a lexicon shared by the epistemic communities of military institutions and defense intellectuals. Military professionals maintain currency in strategic thinking by tapping into foreign education, professional military journals, and the world of blogs, as well as the formal and informal exchange of information among armed forces. Latin American militaries organize and train for national defense and secondary missions like humanitarian assistance, counterterrorism, peacekeeping, environmental operations, and support to civil authority for public security and for counterdrug activities. Given their missions, military officers are keen students and authors of military and strategic writings. Accordingly, they follow doctrinal developments in other countries. For example, former Commander of the Colombian Army, General Carlos Ospina, critiqued American military doctrine as inapplicable to his country's conflict:

> We were using American doctrine, where we conceptualized the continuum as "war" and "other than war." This was absolutely incorrect. There is only war, with the enemy fielding different mixes of the elements of war.
>
> *(Ospina 2006: 29)*

The region has seen its share of wars and militarized disputes and conflict (Mares 2001: 28–51). Border disputes occasionally roil the waters, such as the Argentine–United Kingdom dispute over the Falklands/Malvinas Islands, where the British maintain a deterrent force of 1,200 personnel (vs. 70 before Operation Rosario in 1982), plus naval and aircraft (BBC 2012). In addition, Guyana and Venezuela dispute the Essequibo region. Bolivia seeks a territorial adjustment which Chile rejects, while Colombia and Nicaragua dispute jurisdiction in the San Andrés–Providencia Archipelago.

The disagreements are not likely to generate wars. Six reasons combine to support this assessment. First, aside from Argentina and Venezuela, most states are 'geopolitically satisfied,' a term used to describe acceptance of national boundaries and level of international influence. Second, the conditions for interstate war in the region are rare. Third, Latin American military power projection and logistical capabilities are insufficient to operate for long. Difficult geography affects military calculations. Chile is like an island protected by mountains and the Atacama. One Chilean retired brigadier remarked that "all we have to do is maneuver tanks in the desert, we don't need strategy." Argentina has depth, the ocean, and the Andes. Brazil is protected by the vast Amazon Basin and the Atlantic. Colombia and Venezuela have natural defenses. Fourth, states are more likely to resolve disputes via international mediation, such as the verdict of the World Court on the Chile-Peru maritime border, though Colombia rejected the verdict of the International Court of Justice that awarded to Nicaragua territory in the Caribbean (Paterson and Flynn 2013: 5–6). The fifth reason is the emergence of cooperative security as a principle of foreign policy. Militaries are more likely to conduct peaceful military exercises with neighbors, such as the Argentine and Brazilian *Operação Guaraní* in August 2014, which was designed to "develop institutional cooperation and strengthen the bonds of friendship between the land forces of neighboring countries" (Folha Militar 2014). Argentina and Chile have developed a joint and combined brigade-size peacekeeping force, *Cruz del Sur*, composed of land, naval, and air forces (Mani 2013: 8). In 2014 Brazil announced its interest in joining the force. These developments reflect the reality that geopolitical competition between Argentina, Brazil, and Chile belongs to the past and yields to the benefits of cooperation and economic development. Other countries are undertaking similar initiatives with neighbors. And sixth, modern war is expensive.

Secondary military missions

Though interstate conflict appears remote, Latin America is a zone of violence. According to the United Nations there were 134,519 homicides in 2012, representing 31 per cent of the world's total. Most of the violence is criminal in nature. To deal with this challenge civilian governments draw the military into providing support to civil authority in public security, despite the fact that defense planning for the external threat remains the priority mission of the military. Such externally focused planning derives from the realist security dilemma that posits, paradoxically, that one state's defensive preparations may offend another state and that states must always be prepared to confront external threats. Accordingly, most Latin American military forces continue to perform their classical mission of deterrence against foreign threats.

The military's deterrence capacity provides assets (transportation, communication, security, medical service, intelligence, and administration) that are adaptable for a variety of secondary missions at home and abroad, especially humanitarian and peacekeeping. The capabilities required for counterinsurgency are adaptable for counterterrorism. Examples include Colombia's struggle against the Revolutionary Armed Forces of Colombia (FARC), the National Liberation Army, and the paramilitaries; Peru against the Shining Path; and Paraguay confronting the Paraguayan People's Army. In each of these cases the armed forces employ a mix of operational principles, with success in Peru and Colombia, while the Paraguayan case awaits judgment.

Secondary missions include counternarcotics support, humanitarian activities, support to public security, and a variety of activities in support of the civilian authority. The counternarcotics mission engages 76 per cent of the armies of Latin America, in addition to portions of the navies and air forces (Tibiletti 2014). The restructuring and downsizing of the Ecuadorean armed forces include these missions: support for national police in internal security, broadened responsibilities for the army corps of engineers, forest development, risk management in protected areas, and assistance in security and development on the northern border. Analysts and military officers alike fear that by taking on so many secondary missions the militaries will become politicized, as well as lose their professionalism. In Ecuador there is concern that the military will become a militarized police (Jarrín 2013, 2014).

Externally, Latin American militaries participate in United Nations–mandated peacekeeping missions (see Sotomayor, this volume). One of the largest, the United Nations Stabilization Mission to Haiti, has contributions from Argentina, Bolivia, Brazil, Chile, Ecuador, El Salvador, Guatemala, Honduras, Paraguay, Peru, and Uruguay. Brazil provides 1,700 troops, command and control, as well as logistical support. For Brazil, the payoff is global prestige and the opportunity to modernize the army.

Security and insecurity dilemmas

The security dilemma in Latin America is not driven by asymmetry in power between states, though power imbalance continues to concern military officers. It is rather the insecurity dilemma of states with weak institutional and governance capabilities, and notably ineffective judicial systems and public security. This means that the armed forces provide state presence and critical services in vast ungoverned spaces and borders that are often exploited by an assortment of delinquents who compete with the state over the monopoly of force, control of territory, and the hearts and minds of people caught between the difficult choices of *plata o plomo* (money or lead). Complicating matters is the fact that at the end of the Cold War intelligence and defense capabilities were cut back, while globalization empowered criminal actors to move narcotics, dirty money, guns, and contraband across borders. The asymmetric balance between state power and market power created opportunities for the illicit markets to thrive, as demand increased for many goods, while police, judiciary, and intelligence capabilities weakened. The paradigm of this process is the institutional collapse and violence in Honduras (Malone 2012: 70–78).

The challenge of defending large areas and unguarded borders is most readily appreciated in Brazil's nearly 17,000 kilometers of land borders, which are penetrated by criminals trafficking in drugs, precursor chemicals, guns, money, people, valuable flora and fauna, and stolen cars and electronics. The Brazilian Army's Amazon Military Command in Manaus is responsible for the defense of this vast and difficult region. There are 27,000 troops deployed in the Amazon. To assist in the surveillance and monitoring, the Integrated System for Monitoring Borders is expected to provide coverage and costs six billion dollars. According to Brazilian analysts, it will increase state presence, protect biodiversity, promote military cooperation with neighboring countries, combat illicit traffic, and assist indigenous populations.

The strategic significance of Angostura

An example of the challenge that military institutions face with respect to insecure borders is Operation Phoenix. On March 1, 2008, Colombian air, army, and police forces launched Operation Phoenix against the camp of Raúl Reyes, a senior commander of the Revolutionary Armed Forces of Colombia (FARC), at Angostura, Ecuador. Reyes had established this clandestine camp in the tropical forest of Ecuador's northeast, 1,800 meters from Colombia (Marcella 2008). The Colombian attack killed Reyes and other FARC members. The event caused celebration in Bogotá, but exposed the vulnerabilities of Ecuador and led the Correa government to break diplomatic relations with Colombia. Phoenix was an intelligence coup, as Colombian troops captured a trove of information in FARC computers (IISS 2012). The information detailed the linkages of international crime, terrorism, and drug trafficking with the alleged connivance of officials from the Ecuadorean and Venezuelan governments, and the participation of the international radical left.

Angostura laid bare the new threat: the nexus of insecure borders and ungoverned space, and crime (see Trinkunas and Clunan, this volume). Neither Ecuador nor Colombia controlled the border, which allowed the narcotics-funded FARC to rest and reequip inside Ecuador, and then wage war in Colombia. Colombia's borders with Panama, Ecuador, Peru, Brazil, and Venezuela are far from secure. In the aftermath Ecuador increased its defense effort on the border, deploying a better-equipped force of 12,000 troops, supplemented by logistics, radars, and drones. In 2012, the force conducted 48 operations and captured thousands of munitions (El Comercio 2013).

The Ecuador-Colombia distemper shows that military operations alone are not enough to reduce crime and integrate the population into the national polity. The strategy for such operations must integrate economic development, physical infrastructure, the rule of law, and effective institutions of the state and civil society.

Police vs. military

Besides the classical mission of deterrence, militaries are being asked to assist in public security. The police are often poorly equipped, trained, and paid, while judicial systems lack resources and are easily intimidated and corrupted. It is therefore tempting for governments to deploy troops for such as purposes as assisting the police in 'pacification' of the *favelas* of Río de Janeiro, dealing with the *maras* (gangs) in Honduras, or securing the road from the airport to San Salvador. Since they need to know how to perform the mission, however reluctant they are to do so, military institutions are establishing training programs, such as the Brazilian Army's Center of Instruction for Operations in Law Enforcement and Order located in Campinas and subordinated to the 11th Light Infantry Brigade.

There is a critical distinction between police and military approaches to the use of force: The police are trained and equipped to deter crime, use minimum force, and gather evidence, the military to use overwhelming force and not be concerned about evidence. Some fear that such deployments can lead to the de-professionalization of the military. Despite this risk, a number of countries have been implementing policies that blur the institutional boundaries between the police and the armed forces. Expressing a U.S. perspective on the distinction between police and military, Secretary of Defense Leon Panetta expressed this concern to Latin American ministers of defense: "In some cases, countries have turned to their defense forces to support civilian authorities . . . the use of the military to perform civil law enforcement cannot be a long-term solution" (Baldor 2012).

The Colombian experience

The greatest contemporary mobilization and application of military power and the other instruments of the state has occurred in Colombia. This was done in order to establish territorial control, extend governance to marginalized areas, and defeat the cocaine-fueled violence and terrorism. Colombia's experience deserves the attention of those seeking effective strategies to deal with the complex problems of insurgency, terrorism, narco-trafficking, and illegal paramilitary activities. This witch's brew was exacerbated by ungoverned space, weak to ineffective ministries of government, and military forces that did not have adequate personnel, intelligence, logistical, combat, and maneuver capabilities. In the late 1990s Colombia was hailed as a failing state, headed towards a narco-state in the form of an independent Farclandia in the southeast. Such forebodings did not materialize because the successive governments of Andrés Pastrana, Alvaro Uribe, and Juan Manuel Santos effectively mobilized national power, especially military, and implemented a comprehensive strategy. By 2014 the FARC's forces were greatly reduced in number and were on the defensive.

Key was generating more military power. Forces grew to 341,300 personnel by 2014, accompanied by a dramatic transformation of doctrine, strategy, leadership, intelligence, firepower, equipment, medical service, special operations, and joint operations. In 1998 the Colombian Army deployed a mere 35,000 troops for combat. The army lacked mobility, joint operations, logistical support, and intelligence to cover a country the size of Texas and California combined, in one of the world's most difficult geographies. Though considered experienced in counterinsurgency, the army was small, defensive minded, and accustomed to not getting enough money in the defense budget. Consequently, it was suffering humiliating battalion-sized defeats inflicted by the FARC, and losing territorial control to illegal paramilitaries. Moreover, support from civil society was weak. Alvaro Valencia Tovar, general of the Colombian Army and one of the few military strategists Latin America has produced (who died in 2014), said that one of the mistaken beliefs that contributed to the national tragedy was that winning the war was the responsibility solely of the armed forces, without societal support (Valencia Tovar 1997). Colombia's success would not have been possible without significant mobilization of support from civil society, underscoring the value of Clausewitz's trinitarian relationship between the people, government, and armed forces.

The transformation of the Colombian Army began in the late 1990s. Focus included the gamut of needs: education, personnel, leadership, values, health, manpower strength, organization, doctrine, training, intelligence, logistics, joint operations, civil-military relations, inter-institutional integrated action, and a new strategy of offensive action designed to deprive the FARC of operational space and legitimacy.

The expansion of military power was linked to the new grand strategy called 'Democratic Security and Defense Policy.' The derivative military strategy focused on weakening the illegal armed groups by attacking their economic and logistical infrastructures, protecting the civilian population and its resources, while maintaining deterrence to defend national territory from external threats. A Colombian colonel, who became vice-chief of the army, stated in 2006: "Legitimacy gives the armed forces support, recognition and credibility among the national and international community" (Giraldo 2006: 3). The development of the new military professionalism and capabilities changed the organizational culture. This attribute is seen in the high quality of the policies of division commanders, the *políticas de commando* (command policies) (Nieto n.d.). Aspects of Colombia's approach can be implemented in countries faced with institutional weakness and violence, such as Mexico. It implies professionalization and expansion of the police and military, better integration of intelligence, more resources for defense and security, territorial control, effective judicial system, and support from civil society.

A final fact about the Colombian experience is the civilian-headed Ministry of Defense, the only wartime defense ministry in today's Latin America. Because of many years of warfare and repeated iterations of planning the employment of military resources, it has become more effective in developing strategy, in the face of reluctance by the army, which historically dominated the process, to yield such authority to civilians. Much has been learned and applied, thanks in part to a strong investment in civilian talent (some of whom studied under Richard K. Betts). For example, the minister of defense has civilian strategists on his staff. Proud of its accomplishments, Colombia exports security advice to Mexico and to Central American, Caribbean, and West African countries. In view of these achievements, Colombia and NATO signed an agreement in 2014 to share information about counterterrorism and counternarcotics.

Conclusions

Scholars can make a significant contribution to sound strategy and democratic civil-military relations by exploring the following areas and drawing comparative conclusions. The research will enhance cooperative civil-military relations and shared responsibility for national defense:

1 The relationship between grand strategy and military strategy.
2 The role of defense ministries, and their level of control of and interaction with the military.
3 How military strategy is made.
4 The level of civilian participation in developing military strategy.
5 What universities and military schools teach about military strategy.
6 How the officer corps is educated to work in the complex security environment of the 21st century.
7 The balance between the primary mission and secondary missions.
8 The role of civil society in national defense.
9 Lessons learned from Colombia for military strategy.

Note

* I am indebted to Oswaldo Jarrín, John Fishel, John Cope, and David Mares for helpful comments.

References

Baldor, L.C. (2012, October 8) 'Panetta to Latin American Nations: Use Police, Not Military, for Enforcement', *Washington Times*. Retrieved from www.washingtontimes/com/news/2012/oct/8/panetta-use-police-not-military-enforcement.

BBC (2012, February 27) 'Could the UK Still Defend the Falklands?' Retrieved from www.bbc.com/news/magazine-17157373.

Beaufre, A. (1985) *Introduction a la strategie*, Paris: Economica.

Betts, R. (2000, Fall) 'Is Strategy an Illusion?', *International Security*, 25(2): 5–50.

Brazil Ministry of Defense (2012) *Estratégia nacional do Brasil*.

Clausewitz, C. (1989) *On War*, M. Howard and P. Paret (eds and trans), Princeton, NJ: Princeton University Press.

Dorff, R. H. (2011, December) 'Understanding and Teaching Strategy at the U.S. Army War College', *MilitaertTidsskrift*: 281–291.

El Comercio (2013, January 1) '48 operaciones militares en la frontera norte durante el 2012'. Retrieved from elcomercio.com.

Folha Militar (2014, August 8) 'Exércitos do Brasil e Argentina realizam operação conjunta no oeste gaúcho'. Retrieved from http://folhamilitaronline.com.br/.

Friedman, L. and Gamba-Stonehouse, V. (1991) *Signals of War: the Falklands Conflict of 1982*, Princeton, NJ: Princeton University Press.

Giraldo, C.G. (2006) 'Transforming the Colombian Army during the War on Terrorism', Carlisle: United States Army War College.

Handel, M.I. (2002) *Masters of War: Classical Strategic Thought*, London: Frank Cass.

International Institute for Strategic Studies (IISS) (2012) *The FARC Files: Venezuela, Ecuador, and the Secret Archives of 'Raúl Reyes'*, London: IISS.

——— (2014) *The Military Balance 2014*, London, UK: Routledge.

Jarrín, O. (2013, January 28) 'Paramilitares en Ecuador?'. Retreieved from elcomercio.com.

——— (2014, May 6) 'Ejércitos revolucionarios'. Retrieved from elcomercio.com.

Malone, M.F. (2012) 'Crimen y gobernabilidad de una Honduras contemporánea', *Air and Space Power Journal*, 23(4): 63–81.

Mani, K. (2013) 'Contributor Profile: Chile'. Retrieved from http://www.providingforpeacekeeping.org/wp-content/uploads/2013/09/Chile-Mani-16-Sept-2013.pdf.

Marcella, G. (2008) *War Without Borders: The Colombia–Ecuador Crisis of 2008*, U.S. Army War College, Strategic Studies Institute.

——— (2013, Spring–Summer) 'The Transformation of Security in Latin America: A Cause for Common Action', *Journal of International Affairs*, 66(2): 67–111.

Marcella, G. and Downes R. (eds) (1999) *Security Cooperation in the Western Hemisphere: Resolving the Ecuador–Peru Conflict*, Miami: North–South Center Press.

Mares, D. (2001) *Violent Peace: Militarized Interstate Bargaining in Latin America*, New York: Columbia University Press.

Masterson, D.M. (1991) *Militarism and Politics in Latin America: Peru from Sanchez Cerro to Sendero Luminoso*, New York: Greenwood.

Mercado Jarrín, E. (1982) *Política y defensa nacional*, Lima: Comisión Nacional de Gobierno.

Miguel, L.F. (2002) 'Segurança e desenvolvimento: Peculiaridades da ideología da segurança nacional no Brasil', *Diálogos Latinoamericanos*, 5: 1–18.

Nieto, G., Major General Ricardo, Army of Colombia, Commander of the Eighth Division (n.d.) 'Políticas de comando'. Retrieved from http://www.octavadivision.mil.co/?idcategoria=357716.

Ospina, C. (2006, Fall) 'Insights from Colombia's "Long War": Counterinsurgency Lessons Learned', *Counterterrorism*, 12(3): 26–33.

——— (2014, April) *La estratégia en Colombia: Variaciones del centro de gravedad*, Washington, DC: William Perry J. Center.

Paterson, P. and Flynn, R. (2013) *Border Disputes in Latin America*, Washington, DC: William Perry Center.
Tibiletti, P. (2014) *La lucha contra el narcotráfico involucra al 76% de ejércitos de América Latina*, Mexico, DF: Instituto Mexicano de la Radio.
Valencia Tovar, A. (1997) *Inseguridad y violencia en Colombia*, Bogotá: Universidad Sergio Arboleda.
Yarger, R. H. (2010) 'Toward a Theory of Strategy: Art Lykke and the U.S. Army War College Strategy Model', in B. Bartholomees *The U.S. Army War College Guide to National Security Issues*, Carlisle: U.S. Army War College, pp. 45–52.

14

PLURALISTIC SECURITY COMMUNITIES IN LATIN AMERICA

Andrea Oelsner

Introduction

In the aftermath of World War II Karl Deutsch and his colleagues (1957) published a thorough study on the use of large-scale physical force, or rather the absence thereof, in political communities. The goal was to establish the conditions and processes required for the achievement of long-term or permanent peace within a region in order to identify "possible ways in which men someday might abolish war" (Deutsch et al. 1957: 3). The authors concentrated upon the formation of security communities – that is, political communities that have eliminated war and the expectation of war within their boundaries – in a number of historical cases. They then examined the application of the conditions they found to be relevant for the constitution of pluralistic security community to the case of the North Atlantic area.

Eclipsed by the more successful neofunctionalist approach in the late 1950s and early 1960s, Deutsch's study fell short of making an impact on the scholarly debate of its time. It was not until the aftermath of another global conflict, the Cold War, that Emanuel Adler and Michael Barnett (1998b) recovered and redefined the concept of pluralistic security community, creating a new theoretical framework for its study from a social constructivist perspective.

In what follows, this chapter is divided into two main parts. The first part focuses on some theoretical and methodological matters, briefly reviewing Deutsch's original contribution to the study of security communities, and discussing Adler and Barnett's approach. The second part discusses the possibilities and limitations of a pluralistic security community approach to the study of Latin American security. Some features of the region as a whole make it a good candidate to become a security community. However, a closer examination of historical intraregional relations and domestic practices may call this into question. The focus thus moves to the subregions of ALBA and the Southern Cone of Latin America to assess if they can be considered pluralistic security communities. In the conclusion, the utility of using a pluralistic security community approach to the study of security in Latin America will be evaluated.

Pluralistic security communities in the study of international security

Karl Deutsch's pluralistic security communities

When Deutsch and his collaborators set out to study historical instances of the attainment of durable peace between political groups through what they called 'integration,' their subject matter fitted squarely into preoccupations of international and regional security. World War II had finished just over a decade earlier, and the Cold War was in full swing. Therefore, determining the conditions that would allow for the elimination of war was crucial. It was also controversial – while for Hans Morgenthau (1993: 389) "there can be no permanent peace without a world state," Deutsch et al. claimed that under the right conditions, regional, long-term peace was possible because the populations of the groups involved would develop a sense of community that would ensure that any changes to the status quo would not entail violence. In addition, this notion was also original: For the first time the concept of 'community' was applied not only to domestic or intrastate groups, but rather to international and even transnational relations.

The key elements in the Deutschian definition of security community are 'sense of community,' and 'peaceful change.' Integration is important because it provides a group of people with a sense of community and with "institutions and practices strong enough and widespread enough to assure, for a long time, dependable expectations of 'peaceful change' among its population" (Deutsch et al. 1957: 5). The sense of community is given by an understanding that common social problems will be resolved by processes of peaceful change, which in turn refers to institutionalized procedures.

Deutsch et al. discerned two types of security community: amalgamated and pluralistic. In *amalgamated* security communities, previously independent political units formally merge into a large state under a single government, like the United States. In *pluralistic* security communities, separate governments retain their legal independence, like in the case of the area formed by the United States and Canada. Contrary to the authors' own expectations, they found that *pluralistic* security communities are easier to achieve and preserve, as well as more durable than, and at least as effective in maintaining peace as, *amalgamated* security communities. Given that pluralistic integration is also more frequent than amalgamation, these findings suggested a promising road to eliminating international war. Their historical survey identified essential, and helpful but not essential, conditions for pluralistic security communities (Deutsch et al. 1957: 117–161). Interestingly, the authors found that in their test case, the North Atlantic area covering 19 states, most conditions were met, but one of the essential conditions – mutual responsiveness – appeared only weakly.

Deutsch was one of the pioneers of the social sciences' scientific revolution. Employing behavioral science techniques and quantitative methods, his transactionalist approach contended that expanding communication, interaction, and transactions between groups gives rise to a 'we feeling' that helps prevent war. Revolutionary as it was, Deutsch's theory failed to make an impact on its contemporaneous research. It was only in the 1990s that Adler and Barnett rediscovered the concept of pluralistic security community and used it to advance their own theoretical framework.

Adler and Barnett's security communities

In contrast to Deutsch et al.'s volume, Adler and Barnett's *Security Communities* (1998b) inspired a large number of studies using, sometimes loosely, the security community framework (see, among others, Acharya 2001; Bodemer 2002; Collins 2012; Cross et al. 2013; Davies 2004; Garofano 2002; Haacke 2005; Kavalski 2007; Möller 2006; Mouritzen 2001; Oelsner 2003; Pervez 2013; Pouliot 2006; Tusicisny 2007; Williams and Neumann 2000). In this second version of security communities, two main Deutschian elements remain central: the 'we feeling' and shared identities, and 'dependable expectations of peaceful change.' For Adler and Barnett, in a security community "a stable peace is tied to the existence of a transnational community" (1998a: 30–31).

But post-Deutschian security communities entail more than this. In true social constructivist fashion, security communities are socially constructed spaces of shared identities, values, and meanings; many-sided and direct relations; and reciprocal, long-term interest (Adler and Barnett 1998a: 31). Therefore, security communities exhibit not just *behavior* suggesting the avoidance of violent force to resolve disputes, but also deeply entrenched *habits and practices* of peaceful resolution of conflicts, basing these habits and practices themselves on shared, normative structures (Adler and Barnett 1998a: 35). International institutions and organizations help too, as they encourage interaction between states, open new areas of mutual interest, shape norms, and contribute to the construction of common identity among states and societies.

Security Communities presents nine case studies, including Andrew Hurrell's (1998) chapter on South America. For Hurrell, a loosely coupled security community is emerging within the area of the Common Market of the South (MERCOSUR), centered upon the core Argentine-Brazilian relationship. Hurrell (1998: 254–255) notes, however, three important limits to the idea of security community in the Southern Cone: first, modest progress towards a positive cooperative security agenda; second, weak institutionalization of regional governance; and third, diverging foreign policies and conflicting underpinning identities.

However limited it may be, this weak security community fails to extend to the rest of the Latin American region. For Hurrell (1998: 259–260), although there have been important, positive developments in the 1980s and 1990s, these have been insufficient to overturn a trend of increased social and economic heterogeneity and instability within the region, including the persistence of interstate territorial disputes and high levels of intrastate violence. As a result, the rest of Latin America is "still beset by a range of traditional and non-traditional security challenges" (Hurrell 1998: 260).

This perspective focuses predominantly on the view of elites, whereas other scholars find that trust and shared identity must emerge *also* between societies for security communities to be in place (see, for instance, Holsti 1996; Kacowicz 1998; Oelsner 2005). The remainder of this chapter explores the utility of a security community approach to Latin America, by briefly discussing the presence (or otherwise) of trust and common identity in the region.

Pluralistic security community in the study of Latin America

Latin America: a noncase of security community

At first glance, Latin America appears to make a good candidate for the application of the security community approach. From a low incidence of interstate war that most analysts highlight (see, among others, Desch 1998; Domínguez 2003b; Kacowicz 1998, 2005), to the presence of what may look like an overwhelming number of often overlapping regional organizations (Gómez Mera 2012; Naím 2014), the region minimally responds to the requirement of non-violence. Add to that common language (except for Brazil, although Portuguese and Spanish share a common Latin root), a common dominant religion, and a shared Iberian heritage, and the requirement of compatible values and principles could be easily fulfilled too.

In the 1980s, with the debt crisis and the so-called Latin American lost decade, a shared sense of financial vulnerability arose. In the Southern Cone, in particular, exposure to military dictatorships between the 1960s and the 1980s, followed by difficult processes of democratization, further added to the countries' shared experiences and a sense of mutual understanding. In short, there are also historical institutional reasons that could lead one to believe that constructing a security community with shared identity is possible. However, a number of factors have made this task more difficult. What follows is not an exhaustive list, but rather a sketch of some historical, economic, ideological, and political factors that have contributed to the contemporary structure of regional relations, in contraposition to the logic of security communities.

First, Latin America has historically been a region of low transnational societal links. Most states developed around strong metropolises – politically and economically dominant within their territories, but far apart from one another. Borders of these already sparsely populated countries ran through uninhabited and inhospitable areas – deserts, mountains, and jungles – making contacts and communications across societies difficult. Second, as the independence and civil wars scaled down, leaders became aware of the fact that their countries' external borders were far from clearly demarcated. This opened the door to the many territorial and maritime boundary disputes in the region, some of which escalated to military conflict and (although more infrequently) even war, and some of which still remain unresolved (see Domínguez 2003a; and Mares's chapter on interstate disputes, this volume).

A third factor explaining low regional interaction is economic in nature. Latin American economies developed a mostly competitive rather than complementary structure. The result has been that states often trade more with Europe and the United States than among themselves. In turn, a fourth, ideological factor presented a further obstacle to integration. Decades of nationalist, chauvinist, and militaristic discourse moved countries and societies even farther apart, discouraging cooperation. Still today, with most states under democratic rule, ideological rhetoric plays a divisive role in the region. The split between a vociferous left and a more moderate center surfaced again in the positions taken by the different Latin American governments regarding the governance crisis unfolding in Venezuela in 2014, rendering the OAS increasingly irrelevant, unable to uphold the principles embodied in the Democratic Charter or even guarantee open, transparent debate within its forum (see Malamud and Schenoni, this volume).

A fifth factor relates to the government system. The prevalent tradition of presidentialism across the region has effectively strengthened the Executive – whether civilian or military – making it the dominant power. This explains that most cases of South American rapprochement and integration have been centralized political decisions originating from the top level of government and then expanding to the middle level of bureaucracy, but hardly reaching far beyond.

Yet in security communities, the empirical observation of absence of organized, interstate violence actually reflects *internalized societal* practices, implying that "a region in which states are internally violent and unstable can hardly be meaningfully called a security community" (Väyrynen 2000: 118). Furthermore, Andrej Tusicisny emphasizes that Deutsch's definition of security community as a group of people necessarily includes "the values of societies, not only the attitudes of their elites" (2007: 429). However, historical and even contemporary levels of domestic violence make the region as a whole a doubtful candidate. Cold War examples include ideology-driven violence, which led to massive and well-documented human rights abuses, whereas post–Cold War examples involve cases of unresolved civil conflicts (Colombia), recurrent violent political mass protests and concomitant repression (Venezuela), and proliferation of street gangs/*maras* (Central America) and vast and powerful networks of organized crime (Mexico).

In what follows, the focus zooms in to two more geographically confined cases within Latin America in an attempt to test the applicability of the security community approach to the region. The first case is the *Alianza Bolivariana para los Pueblos de Nuestra América* – or the Bolivarian Alliance for the Peoples of Our America (ALBA). Given its strong and explicit emphasis on shared ideology, principles, and values, ALBA appears as a suitable region in which to find an emerging common identity that would explain high levels of mutual trust and dependable expectations of peaceful change. The second case under examination is the Southern Cone, which successfully moved from being a zone of unstable peace to one of stable peace in the 1980s. Here, the use or threat of force has been ruled out in interstate (and, to a more limited extent, intrastate) relations.

ALBA: a false positive

In December 2004 Presidents Fidel Castro (Cuba) and Hugo Chávez (Venezuela) founded ALBA. In 2009, though retaining the acronym, the association's name was changed from *Asociación* to *Alianza Bolivariana para los Pueblos de Nuestra América*, or Bolivarian Alliance for the Peoples of Our America, signaling "its mission to be an alliance of people to fulfil the dreams of Bolivar and Martí for a united and sovereign Latin America" (Girvan 2011: 161).

ALBA was envisaged as a reaction to the Washington Consensus and the then projected (and since failed) Free Trade Area of the Americas (FTAA) – a hemispheric integration plan led by the United States and aiming to create a free trade bloc. In contrast, from the start ALBA has sought integration guided by the principles of "solidarity, genuine cooperation, and complementarity."[1] Rather than a zone of free trade, ALBA claims to work towards a "zone free of hunger and poverty," as Ecuadorian President Correa (cited in Núñez 2013) put it. Briceño-Ruiz argues that ALBA could be labelled "social regionalism;" based on the notion of endogenous development, "social development is given a central position . . . with state-sponsored social projects run and equipped by regionally pooled resources, targeting specific areas such as education, health or sanitation deficiencies" (2014: 12–13).

Rather than geography (vicinity) or economic interdependence, as is the case of other integration schemes, what has sustained ALBA and united its members has been vocal Bolivarian and anti-American rhetoric, thus placing converging ideology at its core. Briceño-Ruiz goes further by claiming that "ALBA is an anti-capitalist and anti-imperialist integration model, at least according to the documents and speeches of their leaders" (2014: 2). This explains how its membership has expanded: Bolivia gained membership in 2006 soon after socialist coca growers' leader Evo Morales's electoral victory. Nicaragua joined in 2007, following the election of Sandinista leader Daniel Ortega. In 2008 Honduras adhered to ALBA when President Manuel Zelaya's government took a turn to the left, although the country was suspended after the 2009 coup d'état, and a year later it formally withdrew. Additionally, 2009 saw ALBA's expansion to "modern socialist" Rafael Correa's Ecuador.[2]

Between 2008 and 2013, the Caribbean islands of Dominica, St Vincent and the Grenadines, Antigua and Barbuda, and St Lucia also became ALBA members, after strengthening social and economic cooperation with Venezuela through Petrocaribe (see Altmann Borbón 2009; Girvan 2011). Founded in 2005, Petrocaribe is an initiative related to and complementary of ALBA, guided by the same spirit of solidarity, union, and cooperation, as well as complementarity, energy security, and socioeconomic development.[3] Through it, Venezuela offers Caribbean partners energy resources under advantageous conditions, while taking goods and services at preferential rates as part of payment.[4]

The association's change of name to 'Alliance' emphasizes the construction of solidarity and strong community in the face of the perceived threat of capitalism. This threat comes not only directly from the United States, but also from its regional proxies like Colombia, as well as from domestic elites responding to foreign interests, like the separatist movement in eastern Bolivia (Mares 2012: 35, 72), and the *golpista* factions in Honduras and Ecuador (Raby 2011). Although the dominant logic of alliance strengthens intra-ALBA cohesion, it also accentuates Latin American political polarization, leaving an unpleasant 'security aftertaste.' As Gian Luca Gardini observes,

> on the one hand, only those countries strictly adhering to the Bolivarian ideology are welcome to join, while on the other, a confrontational stance toward those not sharing these principles is almost inevitable. . . . [ALBA] is also potentially divisive as it exacerbates the dichotomy between supporters and non-supporters of the project. *(2011: 240)*

However, even within ALBA, this proclaimed shared anti-imperialist ideology and construction of community has limits. Girvan (2011) highlights the material benefits of ALBA membership to Caribbean Community states, demonstrating that rather than common identity and shared values, rational calculations may play a decisive role. For instance, in terms of development funds, ALBA and Petrocaribe have left the European Union far behind as a source of aid programs in the Caribbean. Josette Altmann Borbón (2009: 138) exposes a similar situation in Central America, where according to Costa Rican former President Oscar Arias (cited in Altmann Borbón 2009: 11) the assistance provided by Venezuela exceeds by four or five times that of the United States. For Altmann Borbón (2009: 144), while ALBA's politico-ideological agenda has not been echoed in Central America, its cooperation proposals are considered valuable opportunities.

Also, Diana Raby demonstrates that, despite the primacy of ideology in ALBA, the project contains a significant degree of "highly inventive, pragmatic, and strategic flexibility" (2011: 160). Raby further argues that pragmatism prevails in the case of Venezuela, the core and most radical of the ALBA states, as "some 60 percent of Venezuelan oil exports continue to be destined to the U.S. market . . . and U.S. corporations continue (or continued until the onset of the global recession) to invest in Venezuela" (2011: 164). Similarly, Venezuela seems to prioritize its commercial relationship with Colombia, even if that means seeking to reduce tensions with the U.S. favorite in the region (Raby 2011: 167). Also, David R. Mares (2012: 58) highlights the limits of ideology by pointing to Nicaraguan Daniel Ortega's swift move away from his Sandinista past and *Chavista* agenda towards new political alliances with right-wing sectors and the Catholic Church.

In addition to common values and principles resulting from a shared ideology, in a security community we would expect a shared identity to emerge, ideally between societies. For this, the participation of social and grassroots movements in the integration process is key. ALBA indeed puts great emphasis on its being an alternative model of integration, by having constituted, for instance, a Peoples' Trade Agreement (ALBA-TCP), as opposed to a Free Trade Agreement. However, as do most integration and cooperation projects in the region, ALBA depends too heavily on presidential initiatives.

The frequent reference in documents and discourse to an increasingly relevant social agenda is not necessarily followed by effective citizen participation in the integration process (Serbin 2007–2008: 199–206). This fact transpires from the language used in the ALBA Social Movements Summits' declarations. There, the movements' role appears mostly limited to "encouraging our governments," "supporting our countries' initiatives," "congratulating their strategic vision," and the like.[5] At the 2012 XI Summit, the first Meeting of Political Parties and Progressive and Revolutionary Movements of ALBA–TCP took place, where a Working Group coordinating Political Parties and Movements of ALBA–TCP was created – however, at the time of writing there is no evidence of its implementation.[6] Neither have there been plans for setting up parliamentary organisms either at the national or regional-institutional level. In short, ALBA is primarily "an interstate and, more concretely, inter-presidential initiative, where the same limitations and a similar 'democratic deficit' of other integration processes persist" (Serbin 2007–2008: 205).

Finally, some ALBA states – especially Venezuela, Bolivia, and Nicaragua – have been prone to resorting to violence, repression, corruption, and fraud when confronting domestic discontent. They have also exhibited revisionist inclinations, potentially triggering Latin American militarization (Mares 2012). Taken into consideration, the analytical applicability of the pluralistic security community approach to the ALBA subregion becomes further undermined.

Southern cone: a cautious positive

The Southern Cone is another logical candidate to the security community classification. Since the late 1970s, the two main dyads in the region – Argentina/Brazil and Argentina/Chile – have transformed their bilateral relations, moving away from hostility and instability, towards building partnerships and increasing trust (see Kacowicz 1998; Oelsner 2005). While this has not been a linear process, and the participation of society has been far from the ideal type of security community, one of Deutsch's requirements is clearly fulfilled: "People on both sides do not fear war and do not prepare for it" (1957: 6). In the remainder of this section, the Argentine-Brazilian dyad is analyzed first, followed by an exploration of the Chilean-Argentine case.

After decades of competition over regional prestige and leadership – which acquired even a nuclear dimension – and a concrete dispute over water resources, in 1979 Argentina and Brazil, along with Paraguay, signed the Itaipú Treaty, effectively unblocking rapid bilateral rapprochement. By the mid-1980s rapprochement gained momentum, with democratic transitions under way in both countries. Argentine and Brazilian leaders understood that if they could firmly rule out armed conflict and instead build partnership, they would be able to weaken domestic, antidemocratic, nationalist factions while simultaneously strengthening their frail democracies. In a clear top-down process, Presidents Raúl Alfonsín (Argentina) and José Sarney (Brazil) embarked on a series of frequent summits (at least eight between April 1985 and November 1988) and treaty signings to promote political cooperation, increase mutual trust, and install a sense of 'regional common destiny.' The references to common norms, mutual dialogue, and joint yearnings for Latin America in the text of the 1986 Argentine-Brazilian Friendship Act are revealing.[7] Also important due to their sensitive nature are the nuclear cooperation treaties and protocols signed between 1986 and 1988, as well as mutual presidential visits to each other's nuclear facilities (Oelsner 2005: 159).

Equally telling of their mutual commitment and engagement is the language chosen in the presidents' speeches during their frequent visits. One example of this is the opening of Alfonsín's speech on the occasion of the signing of the Treaty of Integration, Co-operation and Development: "The Argentines, and with them, their President, are honored to have with us once more the Head of State of Brazil. We welcome a friend and . . . the representative of a people who are friends with our people" (1988). He made further references to the "sincere and profound, uninterrupted dialogue" and the "climate of confidence that has no precedent in the history of our relations," reassuring his guest that "borders are not there to separate friends who share the same problems and destiny." For his part, Sarney gave equally strong signals of engagement by asserting, for instance, "never, in our common history, have we been so far away from divergences. Never has the dialogue between our governments been so frank and friendly" (1988).

With new administrations in both countries, the emerging security community continued to evolve, although with more ambiguous traits. Bilateral and regional organizations were created, contributing to further increasing mutual confidence, enabling more channels of communication, and establishing dynamics of interdependence. In 1991, Presidents Carlos Menem (Argentina) and Fernando Collor (Brazil) institutionalized nuclear transparency through the creation of the Argentine-Brazilian Agency of Control and Accountability. The security community was additionally expanded by the decision to speed up the establishment of a common market in the region – MERCOSUR – which was officially founded by Argentina, Brazil, Uruguay, and Paraguay in 1991.

MERCOSUR helped increase exchange, interaction, and interdependence among member states, bringing business communities closer together, enhancing communication, and making dialogue more fluid. In addition, as MERCOSUR consolidated an external agenda, a shared sense of regional bloc matured. The incorporation of Chile and Bolivia as MERCOSUR associated members (1996), and the decision to play as one single actor in international negotiations – especially those on the FTAA and on economic cooperation with the EU – reinforced this 'bloc' sense (Oelsner 2013).

However, contemporaneous to MERCOSUR, so-called Washington Consensus recipes were introduced throughout the region, including unilateral, neoliberal economic programs. With this, the thick fabric of politics and its dense language became diluted, thinned down, and displaced from the center of bilateral and regional integration agendas by more rational and technical-economic and trade issues. This is clearly apparent in the 1991 MERCOSUR founding treaty, which is a strictly economic and trade agreement with no reference to the political principles underpinning the project. The level of integration achieved between Argentina and Brazil, and within MERCOSUR, is still far behind the full common market projected in 1991. The sense of mutual political engagement has weakened since the turn of the millennium, and MERCOSUR's original ambition of becoming the European Union of the South has progressed only very slowly, to the point of being halted. Without overlooking positive transformations in the region, the thicker security community dynamics that had begun to emerge in the 1985–1995 period failed to fully mature and trickle down to the societal level. This should not take away from the fact, though, that military and security rapprochement in this formerly unstable subregion has reached unthinkable levels.

The second case in this section is the Argentine-Chilean relationship. With a history of abundant territorial disagreements, these states approached the brink of war on numerous occasions, the latest in December 1978. Papal mediation and democratic transition in Argentina first and in Chile later helped to transform their fragile peace in the late 1970s into stable peace by the mid-1990s. While this too was, on the whole, a top-down process led mostly by the Executives, the parliaments became deeply involved and contributed to expanding the reach of this emerging security community.

Twenty-four border disputes had lingered since the 1881 Border Treaty, which laid out demarcation criteria that subsequently proved inadequate and difficult to implement. Resolving these became a priority for Presidents Menem – elected in 1989 in Argentina – and Aylwin – who initiated the Chilean democratic transition in 1990. Within one year, technical teams successfully resolved 22 territorial issues. Of the last two remaining disputes, one was settled in 1994 by arbitration, the outcome of which Chile promptly accepted, despite being adverse to its interests. The final one proved more challenging. After seven years of failed negotiations and proposals, in 1998 a binational commission, made up by members of the two countries' parliaments, publicized an arrangement agreed upon in reserved meetings. Following the signing of the resulting treaty by the presidents, both congresses ratified it in simultaneous sessions in June 1999 – itself an act charged with symbolism.

Although admittedly not reaching beyond a few sections of bureaucracy, emblematically it has been the area of defense that has developed the deepest sense of security community, as Justin D. Vogler (2013) demonstrates. As in the previous cases, this one too was the result of a presidential initiative – the creation in the mid-1990s of the joint Permanent Security Committee (COMPERSEG). However, the ensuing routine of frequent meetings of middle-level officials, an increasingly busy schedule of combined practices and exercises, including the deployment of troops and equipment in border areas previously under dispute (see Sain 1999), and concrete joint policy decisions emanating from COMPERSEG have all contributed to creating a symbolic shared space of trust and engagement. Through this, the armed forces of both states have cultivated close and even personal links since the mid-1990s, allowing for the emergence of "affective cultural ties" (Vogler 2013: 261). Chilean Undersecretary for Defense García Pino contends that these bilateral practices constitute "the Decalogue of peaceful relations . . . clearly built from COMPERSEG" (quoted in Vogler 2013: 128).

In addition to COMPERSEG, Argentina and Chile are engaged in a dense web of institutionalized commitments, including military industrial cooperation, education exchanges, an 'inter-consultation mechanism' of commanders in chief and military staff, the 2+2 meetings between foreign and defense ministers, and bilateral communication channels of each of the individual forces, among others. Of these, the most representative of security community practice has been the establishment of the permanent joint peacekeeping force *Cruz del Sur*, or Southern Cross, whose name makes reference to a constellation clearly visible only from the Southern Hemisphere. *Cruz del Sur* represents a unique, binational force operating under a common flag, doctrine, command structure, and operational practices. Noteworthy, whereas COMPERSEG was a presidential initiative, *Cruz del Sur* was first envisaged at a meeting of commanders in chief and military staff (Vogler 2013: 144–152).

The developments in the area of Argentine-Chilean defense symbolize like no other the existence of a shared space of cooperation, mutual commitment, and trust. They provide concrete examples of not just leading elites, but middle-level bureaucracy coming into regular face-to-face contact in various settings and becoming part of a common initiative. As Lino Sarmiento indicates, confidence-building measures "are needed when there is no trust, but integration is possible when there is trust between the parties" (cited in Vogler, 2013: 148).

Conclusions

It is clear that the concept of pluralistic security community has limited explanatory value to analyze security conditions in Latin America as a whole. The features of security community include reassurance of absence of use or threat of interstate and intrastate violence, which is incompatible with a political culture in which aggression and polarizing rhetoric are acceptable. Moreover, differences in geographic, demographic, geopolitical, economic, and even ideological structures of the Latin American states have also prevented rapprochement between societies.

Two subregions were more closely scrutinized to assess the applicability of security community analysis: ALBA and the Southern Cone. Studying these subregions through the security community lens does highlight trends that point to understanding, cooperation, solidarity, and integration. In ALBA, however, there is little evidence that Deutsch's essential conditions (mutual compatibility of major values, mutual political responsiveness, and mutual predictability of behavior) apply beyond the most restricted definition of political leadership – and even then, Central American and Caribbean states' participation in ALBA appears to respond to material benefits rather than common values.

In turn, the Southern Cone does appear to have moved closer to pluralistic security community. The numerous Argentine-Brazilian and MERCOSUR organisms, coupled with institutionalized Argentine-Chilean political and military cooperation and integration, render the Southern Cone interconnected in a dense network of frequent and regular meetings and communication. This has ensured the emergence of confidence and trust among political elites and middle-level bureaucracy. It has further resulted in dependable expectations of peaceful change arising among societies. However, while employing the notion of community draws our attention to these positive transformations, it also highlights the low involvement of the grassroots and the rigidity of societal identities. Ultimately, Hurrell's assertion is as valid today as it was then: "Constructivism, then, helps us understand both the ways in which more expansive notions of community may emerge, but also the ways in which historically embedded identities constitute important obstacles to cooperation" (1998: 257).

Notes

1 ALBA (n.d.) '¿Qué es el ALBA–TPC?' Retrieved from http://www.alianzabolivariana.org/que_es_el_alba.php.
2 This is the characterization of President Correa himself in: (2014, April 15) 'Ecuador President Rafael Correa', *Bloomberg Businessweek*. Retrieved from http://www.businessweek.com/videos/2014–04–15/ecuador-pres-dot-rafael-correa-charlie-rose-04–15.
3 Petrocaribe (n.d.) 'Acerca de Petrocaribe: Principios'. Retrieved from http://www.petrocaribe.org/index.php?tpl=interface.sp/design/union/readmenu_acerca2.tpl.html&newsid_obj_id=627&newsid_temas=4.
4 Petróleos de Venezuela S.A. (2005, June 29) 'Acuerdo de cooperación energética Petrocaribe'. Retrieved from http://www.pdvsa.com/index.php?tpl=interface.sp/design/biblioteca/ readdoc.tpl.html&newsid_obj_id=1349&newsid_temas=111.
5 'Declaraciones y Resoluciones Cumbres'. Retrieved from http://alba-tcp.org/content/declaraciones-y-resoluciones-cumbres.
6 See 'Declaración de la I Reunión de Partidos Políticos, Movimientos Progresistas y Revolucionarios del ALBA-TCP'. Retrieved from http://alba-tcp.org/contenido/declaracion-de-la-i-reunion-de-partidos-politicos-movimientos-progresistas-y-revolucionari.
7 For the text of the Argentine-Brazilian Friendship Act, see http://www.iadb.org/Intal/intalcdi/integracion_latinoamericana/documentos/122-Documentacion.pdf.

References

Acharya, A. (2001) *Constructing a Security Community in Southeast Asia: ASEAN and the Problem of Regional Order*, Oxon: Routledge.

Adler, E., and Barnett, M.N. (1998a) 'A Framework for the Study of Security Communities' in E. Adler and M.N. Barnett (eds) *Security Communities*, Cambridge: Cambridge University Press, pp. 29–65.

——— (1998b) *Security Communities*, Cambridge: Cambridge University Press.

Alfonsín, R. (1988, November 29) *Discurso del presidente de la república Argentina, Raúl Alfonsín, en ocasión de la firma del tratado de integración, cooperación y desarrollo entre Argentina y Brasil*, Buenos Aires. Retrieved from http://www.iadb.org/intal/intalcdi/integracion_latinoamericana/documentos/142-Documentacion.pdf.

Altmann Borbón, J. (2009) 'El ALBA, petrocaribe y centroamérica: ¿Intereses comunes?', *Nueva Sociedad*, 219: pp. 127–144.

Bodemer, K. (2002) 'The Mercosur on the Way to a Cooperative Security Community?' in P. Giodano (ed) *An Integrated Approach to the EU–Mercosur Association*, Paris: Chaire Mercosur de Sciences Po, pp. 403–417.
Briceño-Ruiz, J. (2014) 'Regional Dynamics and External Influences in the Discussions About the Model of Economic Integration in Latin America', *EUI Working Papers*, RSCAS 2014/11.
Collins, A. (2012) *Building a People-Oriented Security Community the ASEAN Way*, London: Routledge.
Cross, S., Kentera, S., Vukadinovic, R. and Nation, R.C. (eds) (2013) *Shaping South East Europe's Security Community for the Twenty-First Century: Trust, Partnership, Integration*, Basingstoke: Palgrave Macmillan.
Davies, S.J. (2004) 'Community Versus Deterrence: Managing Security and Nuclear Proliferation in Latin America and South Asia', *International Relations*, 18(1): 55–72.
Desch, M.C. (1998) 'Why Latin America May Miss the Cold War? The United States and the Future of Inter-American Security Relations' in J. I. Domínguez (ed) *International Security and Democracy: Latin America and the Caribbean in the Post-Cold War Era*, Pittsburgh: Pittsburgh University Press, pp. 245–265.
Deutsch, K.W. (1957) *Political Community and the North Atlantic Area: International Organization in the Light of Historical Experience*, Princeton: Princeton University Press.
Domínguez, J. I. (2003a) *Boundary Disputes in Latin America*, Washington, DC: United States Institute of Peace.
——— (ed) (2003b) *Conflictos territoriales y democracia en América Latina*, Buenos Aires: Siglo XXI, Universidad de Belgrano, Flacso.
Gardini, G.L. (2011) 'Unity and Diversity in Latin American Visions of Regional Integration' in G.L. Gardini and P. Lambert (eds) *Latin American Foreign Policies: Between Ideology and Pragmatism*, New York: Palgrave Macmillan, pp. 235–254.
Garofano, J. (2002) 'Power, Institutions, and the ASEAN Regional Forum: A Security Community for Asia?', *Asian Survey*, 42(3): 502–521.
Girvan, N. (2011) 'Is ALBA a New Model of Integration? Reflections on the Caricom Experience', *International Journal of Cuban Studies*, 3: 157–180.
Gómez Mera, L. (2012) 'Latin American Economic Cooperation: Causes and Consequences of Regime Complexity' in A. Najam and R. Thrasher (eds) *The Future of South-South Economic Relations*, London: Zed Books, pp. 11–33.
Haacke, J. (2005) 'Enhanced Interaction with Myanmar and the Project of a Security Community: Is ASEAN Refining or Breaking with its Diplomatic and Security Culture?', *Contemporary Southeast Asia*, 27(2): 188–216.
Holsti, K. (1996) *The State, War, and the State of War*, Cambridge: Cambridge University Press.
Hurrell, A. (1998) 'An Emerging Security Community in South America?' in E. Adler and M. Barnett (eds) *Security Communities*, Cambridge: Cambridge University Press, pp. 228–264.
Kacowicz, A. M. (1998) *Zones of Peace in the Third World: South America and West Africa in Comparative Perspective*, Albany, NY: State University of New York Press.
——— (2005) *The Impact of Norms in International Society: The Latin American Experience, 1881–2001*, Notre Dame: University of Notre Dame.
Kavalski, E. (2007) *Extending the European Security Community: Constructing Peace in the Balkans*, London: I.B. Taurus.
Mares, D.R. (2012) *Latin America and the Illusion of Peace*, London: The International Institute for Strategic Studies, Routledge.
Möller, F. (2006) *Thinking Peaceful Change: Baltic Security Policies Security Community Building*, Syracuse: Syracuse University Press.
Morgenthau, H.J. (1993) *Politics Among Nations: The Struggle for Power and Peace*, New York: McGraw-Hill.
Mouritzen, H. (2001). 'Security Communities in the Baltic Sea Region: Real and Imagined', *Security Dialogue*, 3(3): 297–310.
Naím, M. (2014, 17 February) 'The Most Important Alliance You've Never Heard Of', *The Atlantic*. Retrieved from http://www.theatlantic.com/international/archive/2014/02/the-most-important-alliance-youve-never-heard-of/283877/
Núñez, R. (2013) 'El ALBA declara la guerra a la alianza del pacífico'. Retrieved from http://www.infolatam.com/2013/08/04/el-alba-declara-la-guerra-a-la-alianza-del-pacifico/.

Oelsner, A. (2003) 'The Two Sides of the Coin: Mutual Perceptions and Security Community in the Case of Argentina and Brazil' in F. Laursen (ed) *Comparative Regional Integration: Theoretical Perspectives*, Aldershot: Ashgate, pp. 185–206.
——— (2005) *International Relations in Latin America: Peace and Security in the Southern Cone*, New York: Routledge.
——— (2013) 'The Institutional Identity of Regional Organizations; or Mercosur's Identity Crisis', *International Studies Quarterly*, 57(1): 115–127.
Pervez, M. S. (2013) *Security Community in South Asia: India–Pakistan*, London: Routledge.
Pouliot, V. (2006) 'The Alive and Well Transatlantic Security Community: A Theoretical Reply to Michael Cox', *European Journal of International Relations*, 12(1): 119–127.
Raby, D. (2011) 'Venezuelan Foreign Policy Under Chávez, 1999–2010: The Pragmatic Success of Revolutionary Ideology?' in G. L. Gardini and P. Lambert (eds) *Latin American Foreign Policies: Between Ideology and Pragmatism*, New York: Palgrave Macmillan, pp. 159–177.
Sain, M. F. (1999) 'Seguridad regional, defensa nacional y relaciones cívico–militares en Argentina' in F. Rojas Aravena (ed) *Argentina, and Brasil y Chile: Integración y seguridad*, Caracas, VE: FLACSO, Chile and Editorial Nueva Sociedad, pp. 125–162.
Sarney, J. (1988, November 29) *Discurso del presidente de la república federativa del Brasil, José Sarney, en ocasión de la firma del tratado de integración, cooperación y desarrollo entre Argentina y Brasil*, Buenos Aires. Retrieved from http://www.iadb.org/intal/intalcdi/integracion_latinoamericana/documentos/142-Documentacion.pdf.
Serbin, A. (2007–2008) 'Entre UNASUR y ALBA: ¿Otra integración (ciudadana) es posible?', *Anuario CEIPAZ*, 1: 183–288.
Tusicisny, A. (2007) 'Security Communities and Their Values: Taking Masses Seriously', *International Political Science Review*, 28(4): 425–449.
Väyrynen, R. (2000) 'Stable Peace Through Security Communities? Steps Towards Theory-Building' in A. M. Kacowicz (ed) *Stable Peace Among Nations*, Lanham: Rowman & Littlefield Publishers, pp. 108–129.
Vogler, J. D. (2013) 'In the Shadow of the Condor: The Politics of Southern Cone Defence Integration', Unpublished manuscript.
Williams, M. C. and Neumann, I. B. (2000) 'From Alliance to Security Community: NATO, Russia and the Power of Identity', *Millennium: Journal of International Studies*, 29(2): 603–624.

PART IV

Contemporary regional security challenges

15

RELATIVE PEACE AND EMERGING FAULT LINES

Accounting for trends in intrastate conflict in Latin America

Caroline A. Hartzell

Although Latin America historically has experienced significantly less intrastate conflict than many other regions of the world, 14 civil wars were fought in the region during the Cold War period. Today, there is only one active intrastate conflict in Latin America: Colombia's long-lived conflict with the Fuerzas Armadas Revolucionarias de Colombia (FARC) and the Ejército de Liberación Nacional (ELN). If one were to categorize regions using the number of ongoing civil wars as a means of determining their proclivity for conflict, Latin America would currently rank as one of the most peaceful areas in the world, second only to North America.[1]

What accounts for the near disappearance of civil war in Latin America? Is it conceivable that the region soon could achieve the status of a civil war–free zone?[2] If so, is such a condition sustainable – or are there fault lines that signal the potential for renewed intrastate conflict? This chapter seeks to provide answers to these questions by drawing on the conflict studies literature. In what follows I first provide a brief overview of the landscape of civil war in Latin America. I next review explanations for the causes of civil war, assessing their relevance to the region's conflicts. I then seek to analyze what these factors imply for the potential for new or renewed civil wars in Latin America. I conclude with suggestions regarding avenues for further research on this topic.

Civil war in Latin America[3]

Although every civil war is unique, one goal of those who analyze intrastate conflict is to identify criteria that make it possible to compare and contrast conflicts of this nature in some systematic manner.[4] To that end, I begin by describing some of the characteristics shared by Latin America's civil wars. One feature that the region's civil wars have in common is that they have involved class struggles in countries that, by the latter half of the 20th century, were well embarked on a process of capitalist development. Another is that intrastate conflicts in Latin America generally have been nonethnic in nature. Only two civil wars in the region – Guatemala (1963–1996) and Nicaragua (1981–1989) – are classified as ethnic conflicts in the *Ethnic Armed Conflict Dataset* (Cederman et al. 2008).[5] These two attributes, it should be noted, distinguish Latin America's conflicts from those fought in many other regions of the world. A third characteristic Latin America's intrastate conflicts have in common is the stated incompatibility, or issue that the civil war adversaries have (or claim to have) contested; all civil wars in Latin America have been fought over control of the government rather than control of disputed territory.[6] In contrast to other regions of the world, none of Latin America's intrastate conflicts have involved secessionist attempts.

As Table 15.1 makes clear, Latin America's civil wars also differ from each other in some respects.[7] Civil wars in the region have varied in duration, intensity, and the means by which they have been ended. Latin America has been the site of some of the world's longest civil wars, as well as some of the shortest-lived armed intrastate conflicts. Although the number of battle deaths associated with some of the conflicts in the region has been staggeringly high, Latin America's civil wars have not been as intense in this respect as those in other regions of the world. Latin America's civil wars do resemble those in the rest of the world, however, in the growing proportion of conflicts that have been ended via negotiated settlement since the Cold War came to an end (Hartzell 2006).

Latin America has not experienced any new civil war onsets in the years since the end of the Cold War.[8] This sets the region apart from other areas of the world, all of which have seen one or more civil wars begin during the last two and a half decades. Latin America also seems, by and large, to have escaped the "conflict trap," in which countries that end a civil

Table 15.1 Latin America's civil wars: Duration, intensity, and means of resolution

	Duration (In weeks)	*Intensity (Number dead)*	*How the war ended*
Argentina (1955)	< 1 week	3,000	military victory by challenger (traditional elites)
Bolivia (1951)	< 1 week	3,000	military victory by challenger (subordinate social actors)
Colombia (1948–1957)	472 weeks	280,000	negotiated settlement (compromise among elites)
Colombia (1984–ongoing)			
Costa Rica (1948)	5 weeks	2,000	negotiated settlement (compromise among elites)
Cuba (1958–1959)	28 weeks	5,000	military victory by challenger (subordinate social actors)
Dominican Republic (1965)	18 weeks	3000	negotiated settlement (compromise among elites)
El Salvador (1979–1992)	652 weeks	75,000	negotiated settlement (elites/subordinate actors)
Guatemala (1954)	< 2 weeks	1,000	military victory by challenger (traditional elites)
Guatemala (1963–1996)	1,759 weeks	140,000	negotiated settlement (elites/subordinate actors)
Nicaragua (1978–1979)	44 weeks	50,000	military victory by challenger (subordinate social actors)
Nicaragua (1981–1989)	400 weeks	30,000	negotiated settlement (elites/subordinate actors)
Paraguay (1947)	22 weeks	1,000	military victory by government
Peru (1980–1992)	641 weeks	28,000	military victory by government

Source: Hartzell, Caroline A. (Forthcoming).

war have a high risk of lapsing back into conflict in the decade following the end of the war (Collier et al. 2003: 104). These apparently exceptional trends raise a number of questions. Are the factors that have put Latin America at risk of experiencing civil war the same as those in other areas of the world? If so, have their effects become attenuated where Latin America is concerned? Or do factors unique to the region help to explain the absence of any new civil war in Latin America? I turn to the literature on civil war in an effort to answer these questions.

The causes of civil war: implications for Latin America

Research on the causes of civil war, much of it quantitative and cross-national in nature, has burgeoned in the past 15 years. The theories seeking to address this issue "come from a variety of perspectives, including economic, political, psychological, rational choice, and constructivism" (Salehyan and Thyne 2012: 192). Although the types of explanations that have emerged for the occurrence of civil war vary in nature, the dominant ones center on nonstate actors' *motivations* for challenging the state, *opportunity* factors that make it possible for groups to mount such a challenge, and the role of *third-party actors*. I provide an overview of these explanations below, focusing on their relevance as explanations for civil war – as well as its current near-absence – in Latin America.

Motivation. Civil war is a social group activity. Challenging the state through force of arms requires an ability to mobilize would-be rebels for collective action. A shared sense of grievance on the part of a group has been theorized to provide the motive that makes such collective action possible (Collier and Hoeffler 2004). Two types of grievances in particular have been discussed in relation to civil war onset – discrimination and inequality.

Discrimination by the state against groups can take a variety of forms. Political discrimination that results in the exclusion from access to power at the political center, for example, has been linked to civil war onset (Cederman et al. 2010). States can also discriminate against groups on the basis of economic, cultural, and social factors. Most of the research that has focused on discrimination as a motive for civil war has focused on its implications for ethnic groups. One reason for this is that civil war "is more likely to be initiated by an ethnic group than any other type of group," an outcome which is hypothesized to occur because ethnic groups are believed to have more grievances against the state than nonethnic groups (Denny and Walter 2014: 199).

How relevant is discrimination as an explanation for civil war in Latin America? Discrimination against ethnic groups has long been a fact of life in the region. The recent use of arson by Mapuche indigenes in Chile voicing frustration with their lack of economic and political enfranchisement indicates that it continues to be an ongoing problem (*The Economist* 2010). Yet the fact that so few civil wars in Latin America have been classified as ethnic in nature suggests that the concept of discrimination, at least as linked to ethnicity, may not be that useful as a means of accounting for civil war in the region. One reason this may be the case is that "ethnic identities in the region are characterized by a great deal of fluidity and ambiguity," thus making it difficult to mobilize groups on the basis of a common sense of discrimination (Madrid 2009: 200).[9] Additionally, the emergence of ethnic (principally indigenous) parties in Latin America during the last two to three decades has provided groups that have suffered discrimination with a means of seeking redress for their grievances. If this has had the effect of reducing ethnic groups' perception that an armed challenge to the state is the only means they have for improving their situation, it could help to explain why there has been no new outbreak of civil war in Latin America during this period.[10]

Although discrimination along ethnic lines thus may not constitute the impetus for civil war in Latin America that it has in other regions of the world, that could change if groups, once organized, find themselves frustrated in their efforts to address their grievances. A case in point concerns the popular protests and massive uprisings ethnically identified political parties like Ecuador's Pachakutik, for example, have helped to organize following instances in which they have failed in their competition for power (Rice 2011). In cases in which the play of political forces results in the continued exclusion of indigenous or other group demands from the political agenda, discrimination could come to have more traction as a source of intrastate conflict in Latin America.

Inequality has been identified as a factor that may motivate actors to engage in violence if it results in relative deprivation, a sense on the part of some actors that they are less well off, comparatively speaking, than others in society (Gurr 1970). Research on the relationship between economic inequality, as measured by the Gini Index, and violent conflict has long produced inconsistent results. As Østby (2008) points out, this is not surprising, given that these tests have focused on vertical inequality, or inequality among individuals. Since civil war requires action by a group, scholars have suggested that it is horizontal inequality, or inequality among groups, which is more likely to be associated with the potential for conflict (Stewart 2008). Cross-national research on horizontal inequalities and ethnic conflict has provided support for this proposition (Østby 2008; Cederman et al. 2011).

Inequality has the potential to be an important source of grievance where Latin America is concerned. After all, the region has long been one of the most unequal in the world. Has inequality played a role in igniting the region's civil wars? Given the small number of ethnic civil wars in the region, a focus on horizontal inequalities among ethnic groups is unlikely to provide much traction on this issue. New research on popular rebellions, a type of conflict more characteristic of the civil wars in Latin America than is ethnic conflict, finds that high levels of vertical inequality in income and education have been associated with the onset of civil war (Bartusevičius 2014). The author suggests that social class, an important social category in Latin America, plays the same sort of role that ethnicity plays in other contexts, in that it serves as a means of mobilizing individuals for the type of collective action civil war requires. The linkage of vertical inequality with class-based conflict thus appears to have a good deal of explanatory power where Latin America's civil wars are concerned.

Do high levels of vertical inequality in Latin America pose a continued risk of civil war for the region? The region has made significant progress in reducing income inequality in the last decade and a half, a period which has seen "the unprecedented growth of the middle class" (Cord et al. 2013). This outcome has been attributed, in no small measure, to government transfer programs and the expansion of basic education (Lustig and Lopez-Calva 2010). Achievements in this area suggest that if inequality continues to trend downward and citizens give governments credit for the public policies that have helped to achieve this outcome, Latin America (or at least the countries in which this type of progress has been made) could have a diminished risk of experiencing civil war where this source of intrastate conflict is concerned.

There are reasons to believe, however, that inequality could again become a relevant source of conflict in Latin America. First, there is evidence that public education's ability to contribute to a narrowing of inequality may have reached its limit, given the low quality of education received by the poor in Latin America (Lustig and Lopez-Calva 2010). Additionally, research by the UN Economic Commission for Latin America and the Caribbean indicating that "distrust of the state's political institutions and a perception of unfairness in the relations between the state and its citizens are high, and that both [these] factors are associated with objectively measured inequality" casts some doubt on the extent to which the public credits government with playing a role in reducing inequality (ECLAC finding cited in Panizza 2013: 1). Finally, another factor that bears mentioning is that other types of vertical inequality, such as land inequality, that have proved more difficult to address through public policy in Latin America continue to be sources of contention, as the ongoing conflict in Colombia makes clear (Albertus and Kaplan 2013).[11]

Opportunity. Civil wars do not break out solely because a group of people has one or more grievances. Would-be rebels also require an opportunity to mount an armed challenge to the state. Research on civil wars has suggested that there are three factors whose presence increases the likelihood that such a challenge will be feasible: (1) a means of overcoming collective action problems, (2) resources, and (3) a weak state (Fearon and Laitin 2003; Collier and Hoeffler 2004; Denny and Walter 2014).

Collective action problems must be surmounted in order for a rebellion to take place. Fighters must be recruited and persuaded to employ violence against the state. Perhaps one of the most contested claims regarding the means by which the collective action problem is most likely to be overcome is that individuals join a rebellion in response to economic incentives. The 'greed' thesis stipulates that individuals whose incomes are low will be more likely to join a rebellion than individuals with higher incomes, as the opportunity costs are lower for the former group. Cross-national tests indicating that there is a relationship between low levels of income (proxied by GDP per capita) and civil war onset have been claimed to provide support for this hypothesis (Collier and Hoeffler 2004).[12]

It is the case that a number of civil wars in Latin America have been fought in some of the poorest countries in the region. However, case studies of conflicts in the region provide little evidence that rebels reap significant economic benefits in return for their participation in a civil war. Citing work by Gutiérrez Sanín on Colombia, Gray (2008) notes that before joining the FARC, an action that entailed a commitment to harsh discipline and difficult living conditions, the majority of the guerrilla group's members worked for wages that were higher than the national average. This suggests that something other than greed or material incentives has served as a means of overcoming collective action problems in Latin America.[13] One factor which may have a great deal of explanatory power in the Latin American context but which has yet to be explored in any systematic manner in cross-national studies of civil war is the role of ideology.[14] As Gutiérrez Sanín and Wood (2014) illustrate by drawing on the case of El Salvador's Frente Farabundo Martí para la Liberación Nacional (FMLN), armed groups can employ ideology in an instrumental fashion to aid with recruitment, socialization, and coordination, as well as to help construct strategies and institutions.

Rebel groups also require *resources* in order to wage a civil war. A variety of potential sources of finance are available to nonstate actors, including access to the sale of natural resources (both legal and illegal), trade in agricultural products, and funds or aid from third parties (Le Billon 2001; Buhaug and Gates 2002; de Soysa and Neumayer 2007). Although a number of studies have found linkages between rebel groups' ability to extract and sell a variety of natural resources and civil war, as Ross (2004) points out, those studies are not always clear about the causal mechanisms linking resources to conflict.[15] Ross's in-depth examination of the cases of Colombia (oil, gold, coca) and Peru (coca), for example, indicates that resource wealth in those two countries did not play a role in the onset of civil war, although it did contribute to the duration of conflict in each country and to the intensity of the conflict in Peru (2004).

State weakness has also been identified as a factor that facilitates rebellion (Fearon and Laitin 2003; Buhaug 2006). A number of characteristics have been ascribed to weak states, including an inability to extend control over their territories, a failure to penetrate society, and a lack of capacity to deliver core political goods, including security, rule of law, and public goods, to the majority of their populations. Plagued by a shortage of resources necessary to effectively practice counterinsurgency and lacking legitimacy, weak states are posited to lower the costs to nonstate actors of organizing rebellion.

Just how useful is the weak state concept for analyzing the risk of civil war in Latin America? A number of the features that have been attributed to weak states can be found in several Latin American countries. What is not clear, however, is whether some of these characteristics matter more than others where civil war onset is concerned, what the threshold is at which a rebel group considers a state weak enough to make it feasible to mount a violent challenge, and how state weakness is best measured.[16] Colombia, for example, has failed to exercise control over parts of its territory, as well as to deliver political goods to the population of those areas. Given that these factors are characteristic of a number of other countries in the region that are not currently experiencing civil war, it is not clear how or why they serve to lower the costs of insurgency in some instances, but not others.

Third-party actors. A growing body of research has established that the actions of third parties can have an impact on the likelihood and duration of intrastate conflict (Regan 2002; Gleditsch 2007; Salehyan 2009). This observation is likely to come as little surprise to students of Latin America familiar with the history of the United States' intervention in the region. The United States has provided rhetorical, financial, and military support to governments seeking to put down challenges by rebel groups, as well as to counterrevolutionary forces in the region. Focusing on Colombia, Gray (2008: 69) states that "some U.S. policies have supported war, strengthened certain belligerents, or inadvertently aggravated problems that fuel violence," a statement that equally well could be applied to other countries in the region.

The end of the Cold War, coupled with the U.S. preoccupation with the wars in Afghanistan and Iraq since 9/11, has meant that, for better or for worse, the United States has focused less attention on events in the region for the last decade. During that same time Latin American countries, in the words of one analyst, have become "more confident and more autonomous from the USA" (Panizza 2013: 15). What implications, if any, this degree of autonomy has for the potential for civil war onset in the region has yet to be systematically explored.

A region free of civil war?

The absence of any new civil war onsets in Latin America during the last 30 years and the end of all ongoing conflicts but one makes for an interesting puzzle for scholars of civil war. What accounts for this phenomenon? Although not all of the motive and opportunity factors identified by the literature on civil war appear to be relevant to the Latin American context, others clearly have played a role in the region's civil wars. Some of those sources of conflict, as I have suggested above, no longer appear to pose the same level of risk they once did. Income inequality in the region has been reduced. Low state capacity, which continues to be a fact of life for many countries in the region, may have reached its nadir during the externally enforced period of neoliberal retrenchment in the 1980s, reversing course to some extent since then. Finally, one factor not discussed above – democratic consolidation and the dominance of electoral politics in Latin America – must also be considered an important part of the explanation for the downward trend in civil wars in the region.[17] Whereas some groups may once have found it necessary to turn to violence in order to seek redress for their grievances, democratic institutions now provide a peaceful means of seeking change.

What does all of this augur for the future of civil war in Latin America? Could the region become a civil war–free zone? Answering this question requires returning to the analytical structure laid out above. Generally speaking, although a number of countries in the region still present actors with *opportunity* factors that facilitate mounting a rebellion against the state, grievances or *motivations* for challenging the state do not appear to be a high risk factor. Slower economic growth could make it more difficult for states to continue to move ahead with some of the policies (e.g., conditional cash transfers) that have helped to narrow inequality in the region. Unless inequality widens again, though, this factor seems unlikely to become an imminent source of grievance in the region.

The effect that third-party actors will have on future conflict trends in the region is less clear. Although the United States has been less focused on Latin America than it was during the Cold War period, it has remained fixated on the drug war, a policy that has been blamed for undermining state institutions in Bolivia, Colombia, Mexico, and Peru (Eaton 2012). If implemented, the Obama administration's recently announced shift in policy from a focus on the drug war to economics in its relations with Latin American countries could provide governments in the region with some breathing room they can use to strengthen state institutions in ways that are meaningful to their constituents (Shear and Archibold 2013).

Perhaps the most worrying fault lines in Latin America center on the region's democratic institutions. If democracy has played a role in reducing the likelihood of civil war onset in the region, dissatisfaction with democracy could signal a potential willingness on the part of actors to resort to some other means of dealing with grievances. Survey data from both the Americas' Barometer and the Project of Parliamentary Elites in Latin America focusing on citizens and political elites suggest there may be reason for concern on this front in some countries of the region. Legislators in Ecuador, Mexico, and Peru expressed some of the lowest levels of satisfaction with democracy in the region (less than 50 points on a 100-point scale), whereas citizens in El Salvador, Honduras, Paraguay, and Peru registered levels of satisfaction below the 50-point mark (Corral 2011).

If this assessment of an emerging fault line is correct, it suggests that certain countries in Latin America may bear careful monitoring for potential signs of civil war onset. Prominent among these are Honduras and Paraguay, where institutional coups carried out against democratically elected presidents may have sent supporters of the two men the message that victory is not always assured, even when one plays by the rules of the democratic game. And, although the election to the presidency of FMLN candidates in 2009 and 2014 in El Salvador augers well for the consolidation of democracy in that country, high rates of violent crime and gang activity signal a degree of state weakness that has become a source of concern to many.

Conclusions

As far as civil war is concerned, Latin America has become a relatively peaceful region during the last two decades. Perhaps as a consequence, little scholarly attention has been paid to the topic of civil war in Latin America. That neglect is to be regretted for a number of reasons. First, understanding how Latin America got to the point it is currently at could help countries in the region focus their energies and resources on policies and initiatives that foster peace. Second, it may be that other regions of the world that have continued to experience civil war onsets could learn something from the Latin American experience. Finally, given that Latin America constitutes a puzzle where the absence of any new civil wars is concerned, scholarship on civil war itself could benefit from a focus on Latin America.

Notes

1 For purposes of this chapter, I include Mexico as part of Latin America. North America thus consists of Canada and the United States.
2 The Colombian government and the FARC had reached agreement on three of the six items on their negotiating agenda for a peace process by mid-2014. Although exploratory contacts have been made between the Colombian government and the ELN, the latter group had not joined the peace process as of August 2014.
3 Because the focus of most of the conflict studies literature is on civil wars in the post–World War II period, I limit my attention to civil wars in Latin America during same time frame.
4 I classify intrastate conflicts as civil war if they meet the criteria employed by Small and Singer (1982) in the Correlates of War project: (1) The conflict produced at least 1,000 battle deaths per year, (2) the central government was one of the parties to the conflict, (3) there was effective resistance on the part of both the national government and its adversaries during the course of the conflict, and (4) the conflict occurred within a defined political unit.
5 Cederman, Min, and Wimmer (2008) define ethnic civil wars as "conflicts over ethnonational self-determination, the ethnic balance of power in government, ethnoregional autonomy, ethnic and racial discrimination (whether alleged or real), and language and other cultural rights" (page 1 of coding rules). Other scholars, it should be noted, have not classified these as ethnic conflicts (see, for example, work by Bartusevičius [2014], referenced below).
6 I rely on the UCDP/PRIO Armed Conflict Dataset's coding of the incompatibility for each conflict (Gleditsch et al. 2002; Themnér and Wallensteen 2013).
7 This section of the chapter draws on material from Hartzell (2009).
8 This does not mean that there have not been any armed challenges to the state in Latin America in the post–Cold War period. However, conflicts such as the one in Chiapas, Mexico have not rose beyond the level the UCDP/PRIO Armed Conflict Dataset codes as a "minor armed conflict."
9 The fluidity of ethnic identity in Latin America has been attributed, in part, to the prevalence of mestizos in many Latin American countries, a factor that "has helped blur the lines between ethnic categories" (Madrid 2009: 200). Additionally, individuals in Latin America have often made choices regarding whether or not to identify themselves as members of certain ethnic groups in response to incentives or tactics employed by the state (see, for example, Yashar 1999).
10 Although the level of conflict is too low to constitute a civil war, the Zapatista uprising by indigenous groups in the Mexican state of Chiapas constitutes one potential exception to this observation.
11 The importance that land ownership bears in relation to conflict in Latin America is attested to by the fact that land and rural development was the first item on the negotiating agenda in the current Colombian peace process on which the FARC and the government sought to reach an accord.
12 Many scholars have questioned whether GDP per capita, the indicator Collier and Hoeffler (2004) employ as a proxy for opportunity cost, adequately measures that concept. Additionally, Bartusevičius's (2014) finding that once one controls for level of income inequality GDP per capita is no longer a significant predictor of popular rebellion casts further doubt on the greed thesis.
13 Ethnicity has been identified as a potential tool for overcoming collective action problems. The previously discussed fluidity of ethnic identity in the Latin American context means that ethnicity is unlikely to serve as a very useful means of organizing groups for an armed challenge to states within the region.
14 Ideology was, of course, a prevalent factor during the Cold War but may have played a role more important as a means of obtaining support and resources from international audiences than in helping to surmount collective action problems. The absence of well-designed and systematic cross-national studies on this topic makes it difficult to assess exactly what role Cold War ideology played in Latin America's civil wars.
15 In addition to potentially impacting the opportunity structure for civil war, natural resources could also serve as a source of grievance as shown by socioenvironmental conflicts between the state and communities affected by the exploitation of oil resources in Ecuador (Godnick et al. 2008).
16 See Fjelde and de Soysa (2009) for a critique of the use of GDP per capita as a measure of state capacity and a more sophisticated effort to measure the three means by which a state avoids armed challenges to its authority. For a promising effort to measure state capacity in the Latin American context, see Soifer (2012).

17 Evidence regarding the relationship between democracy and civil war onset has been mixed. Some scholars have found evidence of a linear relationship between the two variables, others have found support for a curvilinear relationship, and other researchers have found no evidence of a relationship between these two factors.

References

Albertus, M. and Kaplan, O. (2013) 'Land Reform as a Counterinsurgency Policy: Evidence from Colombia', *Journal of Conflict Resolution*, 57(2): 198–231.

Bartusevičius, H. (2014) 'The Inequality-Conflict Nexus Re-examined: Income, Education and Popular Rebellions', *Journal of Peace Research*, 51(1): 35–50.

Buhaug, H. (2006) 'Rebel Capability and Rebel Objective in Civil War', *Journal of Peace Research*, 43(6): 691–708.

Buhaug, H. and Gates, S. (2002) 'The Geography of Civil War', *Journal of Peace Research*, 39(4): 417–433.

Cederman, L., Min, B. and Wimmer, A. (2008) 'Ethnic Armed Conflict Dataset'. Retrieved from http://hdl.handle.net/1902.1/11797 V1 [Version].

Cederman, L., Weidmann, N. B. and Gleditsch, K. S. (2011) 'Horizontal Inequalities and Ethno-nationalist Civil War: A Global Comparison', *American Political Science Review*, 105(3): 478–495.

Cederman, L., Wimmer, A. and Min, B. (2010) 'Why Do Ethnic Groups Rebel? New Data and Analysis', *World Politics*, 62(1): 87–119.

Collier, P., Elliot, V. L., Hegre, H., Hoeffler, A., Reynal-Querol, M. and Sambanis, N. (2003) *Breaking the Conflict Trap: Civil War and Development Policy*, Washington, DC: The World Bank.

Collier, P. and Hoeffler, A. (2004) 'Greed and Grievance in Civil War', *Oxford Economic Papers*, 56(4): 563–595.

Cord, L., Lucchetti, L., Castelán, C. R. and Ratzlaff, A. (2013, December 23) 'Prosperity and Poverty in Latin America and the Caribbean'. *Vox* Retrieved from http://www.voxeu.org/article/prosperity-and-poverty-latin-america-and-caribbean.

Corral, M. (2011) 'The State of Democracy in Latin America: A Comparative Analysis of the Attitudes of Elites and Citizens', *Boletín PNUD and Instituto de Iberoamérica*. Retrieved from http://www.vanderbilt.edu/lapop/insights/030711.PNUD_PELA_Report.pdf.

de Soysa, I., and Neumayer, E. (2007) 'Resource Wealth and the Risk of Civil War Onset: Results from a New Dataset of Natural Resource Rents, 1970–1999', *Conflict Management and Peace Science*, 24(3): 201–218.

Denny, E. K. and Walter, B. F. (2014) 'Ethnicity and Civil War', *Journal of Peace Research*, 51(2): 199–212.

Eaton, K. (2012) 'The State of the State in Latin America: Challenges, Challengers, Responses and Deficits', *Revista de Ciencia Política*, 32(3): 643–657.

Fearon, J. D. and Laitin, D. D. (2003) 'Ethnicity, Insurgency, and Civil War', *American Political Science Review*, 97(1): 75–90.

Fjelde, H. and de Soysa, I. (2009) 'Coercion, Co-optation, or Cooperation? State Capacity and the Risk of Civil War, 1961–2004', *Conflict Management and Peace Science*, 26(1): 5–25.

Gleditsch, K. S. (2007) 'Transnational Dimensions of Civil War', *Journal of Peace Research*, 44(3): 293–309.

Gleditsch, N., Wallensteen, P., Erikson, M., Sollenberg, M. and Strand, H. (2002) 'Armed Conflict 1946–2001: A New Dataset', *Journal of Peace Research*, 39(5): 615–637.

Godnick, W., Klein, D., Gonzalez-Posso, C., Mendoza, I. and Meneses, S. (2008) 'The Andean Region of South America: Conflict, Economy, International Cooperation, and Non-Renewable Natural Resources', Brussels: Initiative for Peacebuilding. Retrieved from http://www.initiativeforpeacebuilding.eu/pdf/Conflict_Economy_International_Cooperation_and_Non_Renewable_Natural_Resources.pdf.

Gray, V. J. (2008) 'The New Research on Civil Wars: Does It Help Us Understand the Colombian Conflict?', *Latin American Politics and Society*, 50(3): 63–91.

Gurr, T. R. (1970) *Why Men Rebel*, Princeton, NJ: Princeton University Press.

Gutiérrez Sanín, F. and Wood, E. J. (2014) 'Ideology in Civil War: Instrumental Adoption and Beyond', *Journal of Peace Research*, 51(2): 213–226.

Hartzell, C.A. (2006) 'Structuring the Peace: Negotiated Settlements and the Construction of Conflict Management Institutions' in T. D. Mason and J. D. Meernik (eds) *Conflict Prevention and Peacebuilding in Post-War Societies*, London: Routledge, pp. 31–52.

——— (2009, September 4) 'Intrastate Violence and Institutional Change in Latin America: Civil Wars as Critical Junctures', Keynote speech delivered for conference on *Communities in Conflict: Civil Wars and Their Legacies*, organized by Swansea School of Humanities and the German Historical Institute.

——— Forthcoming. 'Intrastate violence and institutional change in Latin America: Civil wars as critical junctures.' In Regina Portner and Andreas Gestrich, eds. *Communities in Conflict: Civil Wars and Their Legacies.* Leiden, NL: Brill Publishing.

Le Billon, P. (2001) 'Angola's Political Economy of War: The Role of Oil and Diamonds, 1975-2000', *African Affairs: The Journal of the Royal African Society*, 100(398): 55–80.

Lustig, N. and Lopez-Calva, L. (2010, June 6) 'Declining Latin American Inequality: Market Forces or State Action?', *Vox*. Retrieved from http://www.voxeu.org/article/declining-latin-american-inequality-market-forces-or-state-action.

Madrid, R.L. (2009) 'Indigenous Parties and Democracy in Latin America' in W. C. Smith (ed) *Latin American Democratic Transformations: Institutions, Actors, and Processes*, Chichester, UK: John Wiley & Sons, pp. 199–212.

Østby, G. (2008) 'Polarization, Horizontal Inequalities and Violent Civil Conflict', *Journal of Peace Research*, 45(2): 143–162.

Panizza, F. (2013) 'Stability and Change in Latin America', *Europa World Online*, London: Routledge. Retrieved from http://www.europaworld.com/entry/sac.essay.15.

Regan, P. (2002) 'Third Party Interventions and the Duration of Intrastate Conflicts', *Journal of Conflict Resolution*, 46(1): 55–73.

Rice, R. (2011) 'From the Ground Up: The Challenge of Indigenous Party Consolidation in Latin America', *Party Politics*, 17(2): 171–188.

Ross, M.L. (2004) 'How Do Natural Resources Influence Civil War? Evidence from Thirteen Cases', *International Organization*, 58(1): 35–67.

Salehyan, I. (2009) *Rebels Without Borders: Transnational Insurgencies In World Politics*, Ithaca, NY: Cornell University Press.

Salehyan, I. and Thyne, C.L. (2012) 'Civil Wars' in S. M. Mitchell, P. F. Diehl and J. D. Morrow (eds) *Guide to the Scientific Study of International Processes*, Oxford: Wiley-Blackwell, pp. 189–207.

Shear, M.D. and Archibold, R.C. (2013, May 5) 'In Latin America, U.S. Focus Shifts from Drug War to Economy', *The New York Times*. Retrieved from http://www.nytimes.com/2013/05/05/world/americas/in-latin-america-us-shifts-focus-from-drug-war-to-economy.html?_r=0.

Small, M. and Singer, J.D. (1982) *Resort to Arms: International and Civil Wars, 1816–1980*, Beverly Hills: Sage.

Soifer, H.D. (2012) 'Measuring State Capacity in Contemporary Latin America', *Revista de Ciencia Política*, 32(3): 585–598.

Stewart, F. (ed) (2008) *Horizontal Inequalities and Conflict: Understanding Group Violence in Multiethnic Societies*, London: Palgrave Macmillan.

The Economist (2010, October 7) 'Chile's Mapuches: Trying Violence'. Retrieved from http://www.economist.com/node/17209615.

Themnér, L. and Wallensteen, P. (2013) 'Armed Conflict, 1946–2012', *Journal of Peace Research*, 50(4): 509–521.

Yashar, D.J. (1999) 'Democracy, Indigenous Movements, and the Postliberal Challenge in Latin America', *World Politics*, 52(1): 76–104.

16

THE RISE OF BRAZIL

Concepts and comparisons

Christopher Darnton

As Brazil expands its capabilities, how will it act towards neighboring countries, the United States, and extraregional powers, and how do we know?[1] How valuable are security studies concepts, such as 'rising powers,' as templates for analyzing Brazilian foreign relations? This chapter critiques the conventional wisdom about Brazil as a rising power, discusses nine alternative concepts in relation to Brazilian foreign policy, articulates problems with the reference groups in which policy analysts categorize contemporary Brazil, and suggests avenues for future comparative research on Brazilian decision-making and on broader regional and global security issues.

The dominant narrative on Brazil in the new millennium frames the country as a rising power, and assumes that this change of status heralds a period of uncertainty about Brazil's objectives and actions in foreign affairs. In this view, Brazil, historically a backwater behemoth, has successfully established itself as a continental power and has triumphantly begun to march onto the world stage. While transitioning from a local to a regional to a global player, Brazil has marked its progress by building new bilateral partnerships and new institutions, changing not only the distribution of power but also the channels of interaction on economic and defense issues. Broadly, if the 1980s were years of economic crisis and of increasing regional partnership with Argentina (bookended by the 1991 creation of MERCOSUR), and the 1990s involved economic stability and hemispheric engagement and competition with the United States (concluded by the first South American summit, in Brasília in 2000, which eventually led to the creation of UNASUR), then the 2000s witnessed robust economic growth, the creation of new international (and, importantly, cross-regional) organizations such as IBSA and the BRICS, and regular involvement with countries beyond the Americas (a milestone at decade's end was the May 2010 Turkey-Iran-Brazil nuclear fuel swap accord). As of 2011, as Brazilian President Dilma Rousseff declared at the United Nations General Assembly, "Brazil is ready to take on its responsibilities as a permanent member" of the UN Security Council (Fundação Alexandre de Gusmão 2013).

That story has several authors. For Juan de Onis (2008), a longtime journalist of inter-American affairs, the image is one of an awakening giant, one with massive and newly discovered offshore petroleum deposits. For Larry Rohter, it is one of "Brazil on the rise" (2010). Two volumes by Samuel Pinheiro Guimarães (1999, 2006), who served as secretary-general (the number two position) in Brazil's foreign ministry during the Lula administration, likewise suggest a shift from "five hundred years of periphery" to "Brazilian challenges in the era of giants." And several prominent North American analysts of Brazilian affairs also identify massive, albeit unfinished, transformations since the 1980s. Lincoln Gordon (2001) argued that Brazil was taking its "second chance" at joining the developed world (the first had come in the late 1950s; Gordon served as U.S. ambassador in Brazil in the 1960s); a decade later, Riordan Roett (2010) observed a "new Brazil," and Albert Fishlow (2011) portrayed Brazil as "starting over" since the democratic transition of 1985. Such claims resonate powerfully in terms of democracy and citizenship, and are useful in terms of sustainable economic development (although they tend to brush over some of the military regime's accomplishments), but they are more questionable in the area of foreign policy, where Brazil has arguably displayed remarkable continuities (Darnton 2014).

Contrasting analyses

Descriptions of change produce concerns about uncertainty. If Brazil has recently transformed, such that prior track records are not a valid guide, then how can we know how it is likely to act? From a U.S. foreign policy standpoint, is Brazil going to be a reliable partner, or is it likely to thwart the United States when it has the opportunity? A useful starting point is the security dilemma, a fundamental concept in international relations (IR), in which uncertainty over an antagonist's intentions, in the context of an anarchic world in which one must provide for one's own security, frequently leads to interpreting even defensive moves as threatening, provoking reciprocal measures that the antagonist likewise finds hostile, leading to an escalating spiral of insecurity (Jervis 1978). However, it is also possible for actors in an anarchic environment to develop reciprocal cooperation, and even create a spiral of mutual security, if they can avoid letting uncertainty turn into fear and mistrust (Wendt 1992; Axelrod 1984).

Recent Brazilian military developments can be interpreted from either of these standpoints. In particular, Brazil is developing more advanced fighter planes (in cooperation with France) and nuclear submarines (with a range of foreign partners, including France and Russia). In terms of doctrine, Brazil is not only enhancing its emphasis on the Amazon (by proposing a new military base and by pledging unconventional warfare in case of invasion), but also labeling its territorial waters and undersea oil resources the 'Blue Amazon,' implying an equally vital security priority and sense of vulnerability (Brazilian Ministry of Defense 2008, 2012). Are these defensive or aggressive measures? What, if anything, do they signal about Brazilian security objectives? To the extent that they indicate a higher likelihood of conflict with the United States, is Brasília taking provocative initiatives, or is it reacting to perceived threats from Washington, such as the reintroduction of the U.S. Fourth Fleet in 2008?

For analysts of Brazilian foreign policy, uncertainty tends to breed an unhelpful dichotomy of optimistic and pessimistic interpretations. For instance, a Council on Foreign Relations task force report (2011) offers a rosy (if somewhat patronizing) view, repeatedly emphasizing Brazil's newfound maturity. This perspective is consistent with a number of Brazil's major, recent foreign policy activities that seem to reflect a determination to participate within the existing international system rather than to transform it. Former Brazilian Foreign Minister Celso Amorim's dedication to achieving a permanent seat for Brazil on the UN Security Council, along with his emphasis on Brazil as a "soft-power power," might underscore status quo intentions (Glasser 2010). Brazil's involvement in peacekeeping missions, most notably its decade-long leadership of the UN's MINUSTAH operation in Haiti, and its diplomatic efforts at conflict resolution, such as between Ecuador and Peru (and, abortively, between Israel and the Palestinians), might also reflect a pacific stance (Silva 2003).

Conversely, a 2010 monograph by Hal Brands for the U.S. Army War College Strategic Studies Institute repeatedly calls Brazil revisionist, and notes the potential for domestic instability and external conflict, short of war, with neighbors and with the United States (Brands 2010). This perspective seems compatible with a number of Brazil's recent activities. Brazil has worked closely with a number of what U.S. leaders often consider rogue regimes. Brazil's participation in UNASUR seemed to bolster former Venezuelan President Hugo Chávez against the United States. Brazil's negotiation of a nuclear deal in Iran, alongside Turkey, may have undermined U.S. policy initiatives in the region. And President Dilma Rousseff's effective cancellation of a planned state visit to Washington, following the September 2013 disclosure of U.S. National Security Agency espionage in Brazil, compounded this image of U.S.-Brazilian opposition. Despite Brazil's longstanding emphasis on sovereignty and nonintervention, it is increasingly involved in its neighbors' political and developmental decisions, strategically wielding development loans and Petrobrás investments. Although the 2013 spiriting of a Bolivian senator, convicted of corruption in his country, across the border into Brazil may have been the sole initiative of one junior diplomat, it may well have escalated the concerns of Brazil's neighbors.

These divergent interpretations are common in security studies conversations about other rising powers, where uncertainty over future behavior produces fraught debates. China offers the most acute example. Arguments about whether China's rise will be peaceful or violent tend to collapse into positive and negative images, with accompanying stereotypes that are patronizing and oversimplified at best, and at worst actively harmful by over-steering policy responses towards either preventive conflict or complacency. If China is either a panda or a dragon, then the policy response is clear, and proponents of one image or the other dismiss their opponents as dragon slayers or panda huggers.[2] North American conversations about Brazil, thankfully, are somewhat more muted, perhaps in part due to less familiarity with Brazilian fauna, but also because Brazil is a democracy and is not a peer competitor, so the perceived stakes are lower.

Broadly, the pessimistic and optimistic interpretations tend to coincide with realist and liberal perspectives on international relations, respectively. Two arguments hopefully illustrate briefly the central debate. First, John Mearsheimer's *Tragedy of Great Power Politics* explains that states strive to maximize power, to achieve hegemony; states that lack regional hegemony are necessarily revisionists, while those that achieve it become, at least regionally, satisfied status quo powers (Mearsheimer 2001). Here, the long-run probability of violent confrontation between an existing Great Power and its rising challenger is quite high. Conversely, G. John Ikenberry's *After Victory* (2001) argues that Great Powers are able to lock in the status quo by establishing an international order with constitutional features and by practicing strategic restraint, reassuring potential future challengers, and obtaining their support for the existing system. In this scenario, the odds of violent clashes between rising and declining powers are much lower. Realism and liberalism each encompass a broad and diverse intellectual terrain; some realists surely see opportunities to accommodate or coopt rising powers nonviolently, while some liberals would note that shifting domestic preferences and coalitions within a rising power might make it more aggressive, irrespective of relative capabilities and superpower policies. However, the central tendency of each school of thought seems to fit only weakly with Brazilian foreign policy and with U.S.-Brazilian relations. Brazil is democratic and capitalist, but hardly subscribes fully to the U.S. vision of regional and global order. Brazil is the largest and most powerful country in South America, but is territorially satisfied. And the United States is a clear regional hegemon, but its recurrent interventions in the affairs of its neighbors suggest a penchant for revisionism rather than system maintenance.

Assessing capabilities

To assess how well the rising power concept fits the Brazilian case, however, a more straightforward starting point would be the question of capabilities. As Paul Kennedy (1989) explains in one of the seminal works on power transitions, achieving and maintaining resource superiority is the sine qua non for Great Power status. Debates on the conceptualization and measurement of power are extensive in security studies, taking into account new forms of leverage and vulnerability during globalization, the quality of troops and weapons, and the mobilization potential of various types of domestic political regimes, among other factors (see Lobell et al. 2009; Baldwin 1989). These are particularly important points for discussing actual war-fighting potential, and for assessing the ability of countries to use their power for particular policy ends, including through coercion. However, for the descriptive question of rising powers, even crude 'bean-counting' metrics of national capabilities, like the size of an economy, population, defense budget, or territory, or the number of troops or tanks or nuclear weapons, offer a valuable first cut (Waltz 1979).

Is Brazil really rising? Since 2011 Brazil's economic progress seems to have stalled, so even if a rising power conversation seemed attractive in the Lula years, it may have outlived its relevance. Massive protests in 2013, triggered by price increases in bus fares and other staples, subsided, but a new wave of demonstrations emerged the following year against heavy government expenditures for the upcoming World Cup (at the expense of domestic social spending, in the eyes of many). Dilma Rousseff won reelection in the fall of 2014, but the ongoing social unrest signals how thin her support base really is, particularly among the middle class rather than among the beneficiaries of the Bolsa Família welfare program, a deeply popular initiative of Lula's government (*The Economist* 2014a, 2014b). Although Brazilian economic growth outpaced market expectations in 2012 and 2013, achieving rates of one per cent and 2.3 per cent, respectively, forecasts had been pessimistic to the point of stagnation (*The Economist* 2014c, 2014d). Although Brazil is not in recession, the high single-digit growth rates of the Lula years are gone, and with them, much of the rationale for discussing Brazil as a rising power. Moreover, inflation too is higher than the government anticipated, suggesting the potential for further protests and calling into question the sustainability of current growth, particularly as Brazil raises interest rates (*The Economist* 2014e). Still, Brazil may very well recover from this lull and attempt to restore its previous growth rates.

Even so, a long-term examination of Brazilian capabilities relative to the United States and to its neighbors in South America suggests that the 'rise' story has been misleading for some time. Not only is Brazil distant from offering a peer competitor challenge to the United States, but also it is not progressively outdistancing its neighbors. Although Brazil now rates as the sixth-largest economy in the world, such rank-order lists can be misleading. An alternative approach, expressing the ratio of Brazil's economy to that of the United States, or to the rest of South America, effectively rebuts the notion of rising power or of new hegemony. Brazil's economy in 2012 was a mere eight per cent of the U.S.'s; although this has nearly doubled since the 1960s (when Brazil stood between 4.3 and 4.6 per cent of the United States), it is actually lower than in the early 1980s on the eve of the Latin American debt crisis, when Brazil reached its historic peak of 8.7 per cent of the United States, in 1980.[3] Turning to the question of South American hegemony, Brazil weighed in at 105 per cent of the combined economies of the rest of South America in 2012. Although this is clearly predominant, it had also remained fairly static, hovering in the 111 to 126 per cent range for more than 20 years (1991 to 2010), and Brazil's ratio in 2012 was actually its lowest since 1974. In fact, Brazil's economy was more predominant in the late 1980s, in the 130 per cent range, peaking at 140 per cent of the rest of South America in 1990. Brazil hit parity with the rest of the continent during 1973–1974; although it has never relinquished this dominance, it has also not demonstrated a recent shift in capabilities that increasingly outpaces its neighbors (and if the 2010 through 2012 trend continues, Brazil might drop below parity with the rest of the continent within two years).

Defense spending and population figures tell a similar story. Since 1990, Brazil has remained around parity with the rest of South America combined in terms of defense expenditure; in the same time period, Brazil's defense spending has generally fallen between 2.5 to four per cent of the United States.[4] In terms of population, Brazil is clearly growing in absolute terms, having doubled since 1972 to today's 200 million inhabitants. Even here, though, growth has been slowing steadily, from more than three per cent a year in the early 1960s to under 0.9 per cent in the early 2010s. Meanwhile, the rest of South America has been growing as well: Brazil's population in 2012 stood at 97.6 per cent of the figure for the rest of the continent, exactly where it did in 1961, more than half a century earlier. Brazil remained between 100 and 103 per cent for nearly four decades (1967 to 2004), but has since lost even that narrow lead. The underlying point is clear: Over the last three decades, it is very hard to argue that Brazil is leaving South America in the dust, let alone catching up to the United States.

Alternative concepts

If 'rising power' is a problematic concept with which to analyze contemporary Brazilian roles in world affairs, how might analysts reframe the conversation? Nine alternatives seem potentially promising. One option would be to discuss Brazil as a *middle power* (Soares de Lima and Hirst 2006). A virtue of this approach is its focus on relative rank, broadly construed rather than short-term momentum – it remains as relevant during a period of economic stagnation as during boom years. However, middle powers are generally understood in niche and multilateral terms (Canada is the paradigmatic case), which fail to capture the scope of Brazil's activity and ambition (Cooper 1997). Moreover, the middle power model was used repeatedly with reference to Brazil, both under Getúlio Vargas during the Second World War and during the military regime in the 1970s, so it may be too broad to offer much guidance about the policy of democratic Brazil under the Workers' Party (the PT, Partido dos Trabalhadores, the party of Lula and Dilma) (Selcher 1981; Fox 1977).

A second alternative is to discuss *emergence rather than rise*. Analysts in the United States and Brazil, however, mean very different things when they label Brazil 'emerging.' Collectively, U.S. policy analysts continue to overlook Brazil, especially regarding security issues; Brazil is more likely to be discussed in *Foreign Affairs* than in *International Security*, and the attention will be predominantly economic. Broadly, U.S. analysts see Brazil as a BRIC, or in the 1990s term, an 'emerging market.' Thus, a Brookings Institution volume in 2009 not only refers to Brazil as an *economic* superpower, but does so with a question mark – in limited areas like energy, agriculture, or the scope of a particular Brazilian multinational company, Brazil perhaps fights above its weight class (Brainard and Martinez-Diaz 2009). An emerging market is potentially a source of crises, but not of threats; it is a destination for exports or investments but is not a central actor or an equal partner. Alternatively, South American analysts – for instance, in the pages of Brazil's leading foreign affairs journal, the *Revista Brasileira de Política Internacional* – tend not to write in terms of rising powers or of emerging markets, but rather of emerging powers or countries (Schenoni 2012; Santos 2011; Barros-Platiau 2010). And emergence, whether of markets or powers, implies an absence of threat (as compared with 'rising'); it also suggests nascence and newness, thus enhancing the uncertainty. But what if Brazil has, in many ways, already emerged?

Setting aside the terms of 'power as capability,' with its focus on rise and decline and tiered rankings, we might turn our attention to four alternative but neighboring concepts. A third option is *hegemony*. This is a particularly rich concept, frequently used to incorporate dimensions of influence beyond coercion, and dimensions of power beyond brute capabilities, and with these, an implication of possible resistance from below. Hegemony may be useful, particularly in terms of Brazil's hemispheric relations, both regarding the United States and regarding South America: Even if the capability ratios of the United States to Brazil to South America remain relatively static, such that rise or decline are unhelpful concepts, the exercise of hegemony may offer more fluctuation and thus more fruitful terrain for analysis. Worthwhile research in this vein includes Sean Burges's monograph on the subtleties of Brazilian regional leadership and Nancy Lapp's chapter on Latin American pushback against Brazil's attempts to exercise that leadership (Burges 2009; Lapp 2012). Attention to hegemony suggests a tiered analysis in which power and influence may vary by issue area and by bilateral relationship, and be different between Brazil and the U.S., and Brazil and its neighbors.

Fourth, drawing from international relations realists like Hans Morgenthau (1948) and Robert Gilpin (1981), analysts might shift their focus from power as such to the relationship between power and prestige, to issues of *status and recognition*. This relates to issues of satisfaction and revisionism, which in the Latin American context have been primarily addressed on the issue of territory, which for Brazil is misleading. Prestige seems particularly apt to capture elements of Brazil's defense strategy such as the call for its "deserved spot in the world" (Brazilian Ministry of Defense 2008). It has proven a useful move in discussions of other rising powers, as with China (Deng 2008). However, too much of a shift to prestige risks losing sight of capabilities altogether, and becoming a description of the pageantry of international relations rather than an analysis of its underlying forces.

Fifth, a particularly promising development in security studies that deserves application to Brazil is David Lake's discussion of *international hierarchy*, with its consideration of suzerains constrained by the need for legitimate authority, and of secondary states subordinating themselves but simultaneously opening economically and lessening their defense burdens by outsourcing them (Lake 2009). Certainly patron-client relations are resonant within Brazil's domestic political system, and such images have frequently appeared in studies of U.S.–Latin American relations. Hierarchy is also helpful by asking scholars to rethink their images of the international system, not merely of Brazil's place within it. However, the model of predominance and acquiescence might fit most of the smaller states of Latin America far better than it does Brazil.

Sixth, we might set aside the coercive or competitive overtones of hegemony, hierarchy, and prestige, by discussing *soft power*. Focusing on the practices of cultural or public diplomacy would explore Brazil's ability to attract rather than to compel international influence. This might fit much of Brazil's African outreach, where both Lusophone and postcolonial ties complement not only trade and investment deals, but also military special forces' training. And it provides a useful template for discussing Brazil's efforts to project a strategic image or national brand on global platforms like the 2014 World Cup and 2016 Olympic Games. However, the spectacle of global sporting events often does not translate into soft-power victories for host countries (Manzenreitor 2010). Global attention could also backfire in the event of protests, violence, or infrastructural problems. North American coverage of the sewage content of Rio de Janeiro's sailing course presages these difficulties, as does International Olympic Committee Vice President John Coates's April 2014 discussion of Brazil's construction progress as "the worst I have experienced" and "not ready in many, many ways" (Romero and Clarey 2014; Barnes 2014). As with hegemony, soft power touches on issues of regional leadership, though with less conflictual notes (Destradi 2010; Nabers 2010). However, in much of the Americas, Brazilian attraction is dubious, particularly if the 'Brazilian model' of development proves less robust and sustainable than it appeared in the 1990s and 2000s. As Leslie Bethell argues, the identity gap between Brazil and its neighbors is broad and centuries old, post–Cold War diplomatic engagement in South America notwithstanding (Bethell 2010). To the extent that Brazil seems like a "leader without followers" in Latin America, soft power might shed little light on its regional interactions (Malamud 2011). Meanwhile, outside the region, Brazilian construction of new partnerships often appears to follow narrowly material or pragmatic interests, hard to couch in soft-power terms.

Three further options bracket, at least initially, the question of power altogether. A seventh move might be to *decouple Brazil's roles by contexts*: Rather than considering Brazil's rise or power across the board, consider separately Brazil's relations with the United States, its interactions with Latin America, and its extraregional activities. This approach allows analysts to discuss Brazil as a global player, unencumbered by the need to rate Brazil's power on some universal scale – creative policies deserve creative analysis. Decoupling is also useful for avoiding the teleological narrative in which the global stage largely supersedes the regional one, let alone stapling that transition to a timeline of either economic or political domestic transitions. However, a decoupling approach risks parochializing even further studies of Brazilian foreign policy – discussion of Brazil in terms of power helps connect it to broader conversations in security studies, while piecemeal analysis of intra–South American relations and Brazilian extraregional diplomacy might be of interest only to specialists. Moreover, unless analysts remained attentive to these other issue areas, they might miss synchronized changes – for instance, are there tradeoffs between Brazilian leadership activity in South America and interactions with the United States, or do these escalate in tandem?

An eighth option turns strictly to *Brazilian aspirations and identity* rather than its capacity or its perception by others. Brazilian statements, including in the 2012 White Book on National Defense, about a global environment of multipolarity might suggest ambition rather than contemporary assessment (Brazilian Ministry of Defense 2012). Although a future orientation makes sense for defense planners, it is a riskier approach for scholars. Comments on the moving target of any country's contemporary foreign policy might drift from research and analysis into punditry and speculation. In the particular case of Brazil, though, the 'country of the future' label, shopworn through generations of political analysis, underscores both the difficulty of accurate prediction and the desirability of newer approaches. Although identity is closely connected to the prestige framework discussed above, considerations of status claims relative to some objective measure of power or prestige seem more firmly grounded than analyses of ambition or self-perception per se. However, a focusing on Brazilian perspectives, on subjective rather than external assessments, would have the significant virtue of turning researchers' attentions to primary sources, to Brazilian texts and contexts, rather than shoehorning Brazil into international relations templates derived from 19th-century Europe.

A ninth and final approach trades in the change implicit in discussions of rise or emergence for a *focus on continuity*. Instead of contemporary Brazil as an unknown quantity, it highlights patterns, recurrent longstanding trends in Brazilian foreign policy behavior. Four themes in particular seem to fit a model of continuity: development, conflict resolution, the U.S.-Brazil relationship (or lack thereof), and the organizational politics of Brazilian foreign policy-making. National economic development has been the paramount goal of Brazilian foreign policy for at least a century – even when coups or presidential handovers produce major policy changes, this bedrock does not change. Development is tightly entwined with national security – Brazil's current defense strategy calls these issues "intimately linked" and "inseparable" (Brazilian Ministry of Defense 2008). The quest for development is unlikely to go away once Brazil hits a particular level of per capita GDP, and is thus likely to remain a lodestone in foreign affairs. Brazil has been recurrently committed to conflict resolution in and beyond Latin America, going back to its own territorial disputes in the 19th century; although a standard Brazilian narrative depicts the country as intrinsically peaceful, an alternative view would see Brazil's mediation and peacekeeping efforts in terms of prestige, as a tool to earn and display influence and status. Regarding the United States, rather than regarding the ebb and flow of cooperation and distancing, a continuity perspective might highlight how the United States and Brazil generally do not see one another as a top priority, and thus tend to make foreign policy almost without regard for the other's preferences. Thus, U.S. and Brazilian policies towards Latin America – and, increasingly, towards extraregional actors, such as Iran – tend to bounce off of one another, creating unintended complications and frustrations for the U.S.-Brazil relationship. Finally, in terms of the process of policy-making, Itamaraty, Brazil's foreign ministry, has been a uniquely steady hand in decision-making for much of the country's independent history, a dominance that extended through periods of both civilian and military rule and which is only now beginning to give way to a greater array of governmental and societal actors, such as congress, individual presidents, public opinion, and the PT (Cason and Power 2009; Danese 1999).

Continuity is a story that fits with several works on specific bilateral relationships and issues in Brazilian foreign policy by sidestepping the question of rising powers (Albuquerque 2003). For instance, on the U.S.-Brazil relationship, both Mônica Hirst and Britta Crandall see long-term patterns, even though they reach different conclusions about the likelihood of cooperation and high-level engagement (Crandall 2011; Hirst 2005). Brazilian leaders and scholars have long touted an underlying postcolonial national identity as a consistent driving force behind foreign policy (Lafer 2000; Rodrigues 1962). The emphasis on autonomy, for instance, is a core component of Brazilian strategy, even though presidents have employed different methods in its pursuit (Vigevani and Cepaluni 2009). Continuity, like the other concepts and reference groups, however, has its drawbacks. As in financial markets or meteorology, the best predictor of tomorrow's conditions is usually those of today. Reliability has a drawback: Although continuity offers precedent and explanation for seemingly puzzling contemporary events, it is likely to underpredict and misperceive major foreign policy change.

Comparisons and conclusions

All of this attention to concepts and framing is not merely semantic: It matters because choices about concepts imply reference groups and outline universes of comparable cases. This is a fundamental issue in comparative politics and international relations, insofar as these are social sciences rather than solely commentary on current events (George and Bennett 2005; Gerring 2001). Brazil's very diversity of bilateral outreach and institutional involvement muddies the waters of comparison – should it be lumped in with India and South Africa as a rising or middle power; with the G-77, as a developing country or emerging market; with its South American neighbors, through UNASUR and MERCOSUR, as a regional hegemon? And yet each is a partial view, since Brazil uses each, and could readily divest from any (Flemes 2013). To analyze Brazil in terms of hegemony, hierarchy, or prestige might require more creative comparisons – perhaps with France during the Cold War, for instance. Sorting by regime type or ideology rather than capabilities might tell us little about Brazilian foreign policy; although Brazil under the PT can be classed among the Latin American 'left turn' governments, and although this comparison group correctly suggests that sovereignty and autonomy will be core concerns in Brazilian foreign policy, it does little to narrow the range of predicted responses to globalization or of agendas in inter-American affairs (Weyland et al. 2010; Remmer 2012; Castañeda and Morales 2008).

Continuity, as a conceptual framework, suggests a particularly intriguing comparison group: Brazil's own diplomatic history. A number of diachronic, rather than synchronic and cross-national, comparisons might be addressed. Focusing only on Brazil's rise since the 1980s debt crisis overlooks several previous Brazilian 'risings:' the apex of empire in the 19th century, the heyday of the Barón of Rio Branco as Brazil's foreign minister in the early 20th, the 1950s–1960s democratic developmentalism of Juscelino Kubitschek and Jânio Quadros, and the height of the bureaucratic-authoritarian Brazilian 'miracle' in the early 1970s. This offers not necessarily predictability, but comprehension of likely future Brazilian roles: There is a great deal of precedent and parallel for contemporary Brazilian actions. For instance, Brazil's push for a permanent seat on the United Nations Security Council predates the UN itself, and essentially goes back to the origins of the League of Nations at the end of the First World War. If some of Brazil's recent actions seem perplexing or unprecedented – public diplomacy through the World Cup and Olympics, mediation with Iran, or Dilma Rousseff's exploitation of a breach with the United States for domestic electoral benefit, for example – they may be neither. Emperor Dom Pedro II and his advisors strove to promote Brazil's image (and soft power, though the term had not been invented yet) through World's Fairs, Brazilian diplomats sought to mediate the rift between the United States and Fidel Castro's Cuba in 1960 and 1961, and Jânio Quadros, as the United States recognized, aimed much of his 'independent foreign policy' (with its overtones of neutralism) at domestic audiences.

This discussion concludes by suggesting directions for future research to better integrate analyses of Brazilian foreign relations and of security studies more broadly. First, we need more extensive dialogue between studies of Brazilian foreign policy and those of international relations – theories, concepts, and cases should not proceed apart from one another. Especially, rather than just looking at Brazil through a favored lens, let alone atheoretically, or assembling a volume on rising powers or on Latin American foreign relations and including a Brazil chapter, more structured comparative analysis of Brazil with other relevant cases would be valuable, as would collections on Brazil from a variety of analytical perspectives. The richness of Brazilian foreign policy studies is unfortunately often divorced from broader conversations in security studies and international relations.[5] This is not to say that Brazilianists have been atheoretical. However, many of the concepts and debates and thinkers they explicitly engage – e.g., dependency, hegemony, and levels of analysis in comparative foreign policy – are far from the contemporary mainstream in (again) North American security studies.[6] Where major IR theories are explicitly and centrally incorporated, the focus is usually on particular relationships of Brazil's (with the United States or Argentina, particularly) rather than on the country's global role.[7] As this discussion has explained, however, some of the predominant security studies frameworks do not fit Brazil that well, or have been applied casually; thus, both sides have much to do.

Second, we need to transcend the easy national and linguistic parochialism of much foreign affairs scholarship. North American analysts would do well to follow Brazil's massive literature (mostly in Portuguese) on its foreign policy and on international relations, not only for case studies but also for concepts. Also, surely much of the ink on Brazil's rise or leadership or hegemony is likely to be spilled in Spanish, and neither analysts in Brazil nor in the United States should overlook these insights.

Third, more should be done to unpack the connections between Brazil's domestic politics and its foreign policy, examining the roles of individual leadership, the rise of congress, federalism and regional diversity, social movements around environmental, racial, and other issues, and the politics of inequality, recession, and growth.

Fourth, beyond bilateralism or Brazil in global perspective, more attention should be paid to triangular relationships. For instance, as Brazil reacts to a crisis-stricken, post-Chávez Venezuela, how is it incorporating its relationship with the rest of South America, with its global ambitions and projected image, and with the United States? To what extent was Brazil's involvement in Iran driven by conflict resolution, by its search for prestige as a global player, or by its relations with the United States?

Fifth, both Brazilian and non-Brazilian scholars alike should scrutinize more intensively and extensively the copious documentation produced by the Brazilian state about its own policy behaviors. From what data should we draw conclusions about Brazilian policy causes, objectives, efforts, and results? For instance, what do Brazil's UN speeches reveal, and not reveal? These texts are important for Brazil, and they are aimed at too many audiences (internal governmental, historical, domestic popular, Great Powers, developing countries, etc.) to dismiss as deception or cheap talk. And how should we untangle the extensive overlap between primary and secondary sources? That is, much research on Brazilian foreign relations has some connection to the Brazilian government (either authored by current or former diplomats, or published by centers like the Alexandre de Gusmão Foundation [FUNAG] or the Instituto de Pesquisa de Relações Internacionais [IPRI]) and is, not entirely coincidentally, often closely concerned with the processes, institutions, and hagiography of Itamaraty and its leading figures.

These suggestions all have a central argument in common: The rising powers framework is initially attractive, but ultimately impoverished. For a clearer understanding of the roots and ramifications of contemporary Brazilian foreign policy, in connection to a broader security studies research agenda, we need to take into account more complexity than just capabilities, while not losing sight of theory and focused comparison.

Notes

1 An earlier version of this chapter was presented at the 2014 International Studies Association conference. I thank Arie Kacowicz, Andrés Malamud, Detlef Nolte, Arturo Sotomayor, and particularly David Mares for constructive criticism.

2 See, for example, Gries (2004: 1–4). Contrast for instance the perspectives on East Asian security in Roy (2013) and Kang (2007). Rhetorically, these labels are actually rather weak taunts, since a greater error would be to apply the wrong strategy to the target – i.e., slaying pandas or hugging dragons.

3 All figures in this paragraph were calculated from the World Bank *World Development Indicators*, retrieved from http://databank.worldbank.org/data/views/variableSelection/selectvariables.aspx?source=world-development-indicators, series on GDP in constant 2005 US$ (1960–2012).

4 Ibid., series on GDP in constant 2005 US$ (1960–2012), military expenditure as a percentage of GDP (1988–2012), and population (1960–2012).

5 This is true more broadly in inter-American relations. See, for example, Mora and Hey (2003: 1–9).

6 On levels of analysis, see Vigevani and Cepaluni (2013: 265–289).

7 On U.S.-Brazilian relations, see Hurrell (2005: 75–90); on MERCOSUR's origins, see Solingen (1998), Brooks (2005), and Kupchan (2010).

References

Albuquerque, J.A.G. (2003) 'Brazil: From Dependency to Globalization' in F. O. Mora and J.A.K. Hey (eds) *Latin American and Caribbean Foreign Policy*, Lanham, MD: Rowman & Littlefield, pp. 267–287.

Axelrod, R. (1984) *The Evolution of Cooperation*, New York: Basic Books.

Baldwin, D. (1989) *Paradoxes of Power*, New York: Basil Blackwell.
Barnes, T. (2014, April 30) 'Olympic Committee Official Calls Rio's Preparations for 2016 Games "the Worst" ', *The New York Times*.
Barros-Platiau, A. F. (2010) 'When Emergent Countries Reform Global Governance of Climate Change: Brazil Under Lula', *Revista Brasileira de Política Internacional*, 53(Special Issue): 73–90.
Bethell, L. (2010) 'Brazil and "Latin America" ', *Journal of Latin American Studies*, 42(3): 457–485.
Brainard L. and Martinez-Diaz, L. (eds) (2009) *Brazil as an Economic Superpower? Understanding Brazil's Changing Role in the Global Economy*, Washington, DC: Brookings Institution Press.
Brands, H. (2010) 'Dilemmas of Brazilian Grand Strategy', US Army War College Strategic Studies Institute. Retrieved from http://www.strategicstudiesinstitute.army.mil/pubs/download.cfm?q=1017.
Brazilian Ministry of Defense (2008) 'National Strategy of Defense'. Retrieved from http://www.defesa.gov.br/projetosweb/estrategia/arquivos/estrategia_defesa_nacional_ingles.pdf, pp. 13–15, 22, 26–27.
——— (2012) 'Livro Branco de Defesa Nacional'. Retrieved from http://www.defesa.gov.br/projetosweb/livrobranco/lbdndigital/#/0, pp. 21, 46–47, 74, 291.
Brooks, S. (2005) *Producing Security*, Princeton, NJ: Princeton University Press.
Burges, S. (2009) *Brazilian Foreign Policy After the Cold War*, Gainesville, FL: University Press of Florida.
Cason, J. and Power, T. (2009) 'Presidentialization, Pluralization, and the Rollback of Itamaraty: Explaining Change in Brazilian Foreign Policy Making in the Cardoso-Lula Era', *International Political Science Review*, 30(2): 117–140.
Castañeda J. and Morales, M. (eds) (2008) *Leftovers: Tales of the Latin American Left*, New York: Routledge.
Cooper, A. (ed) (1997) *Niche Diplomacy: Middle Powers after the Cold War*, New York: St. Martin's Press.
Council on Foreign Relations (2011) 'Global Brazil and US–Brazil Relations', Independent Task Force Report No. 66. Retrieved from http://i.cfr.org/content/publications/attachments/Brazil_TFR_66.pdf, pp. 4, 48–49, 54–55, 76.
Crandall, B. (2011) *Hemispheric Giants: The Misunderstood History of US–Brazilian Relations*, Lanham, MD: Rowman & Littlefield.
Danese, S. F. (1999) *Diplomacia Presidencial*, Rio de Janeiro: Topbooks.
Darnton, C. (2014) 'Whig History, Periodization, and International Cooperation in the Southern Cone', *International Studies Quarterly*, 58(3): 579–590.
de Onis, J. (2008) 'Brazil's Big Moment: A South American Giant Wakes Up', *Foreign Affairs*, 87(6): 110–122.
Deng, Y. (2008) *China's Struggle for Status: The Realignment of International Relations*, New York: Cambridge University Press.
Destradi, S. (2010) 'Regional Powers and Their Strategies: Empire, Hegemony, and Leadership', *Review of International Studies*, 36(4): 903–930.
Fishlow, A. (2011) *Starting Over: Brazil Since 1985*, Washington, DC: Brookings Institution Press.
Flemes, D. (2013) 'Network Powers: Strategies of Change in the Multipolar System', *Third World Quarterly*, 34(6): 1016–1036.
Fox, A. B. (1977) *The Politics of Attraction: Four Middle Powers and the United States*, New York: Columbia University Press.
Fundação Alexandre de Gusmão (2013) *Brazil in the United Nations, 1946–2011*, Brasília, pp. 965–971.
George A. and Bennett, A. (2005) *Case Studies and Theory Development*, Cambridge, MA: MIT Press, pp. 17–20, 77–78
Gerring, J. (2001) *Social Science Methodology: A Criterial Framework*, New York: Cambridge University Press, ch. 3.
Gilpin, R. (1981) *War and Change in World Politics*. New York: Cambridge University Press.
Glasser, S. (2010, November 28) 'The Soft-Power Power', *Foreign Policy*, 183.
Gordon, L. (2001) *Brazil's Second Chance: En Route toward the First World*, Washington, DC: Brookings Institution Press;
Gries, P. H. (2004) *China's New Nationalism: Pride, Politics, and Diplomacy*, Berkeley: University of California Press, pp. 1–4.
Guimarães, S. P. (1999) *Quinhentos Anos de Periferia: Uma Contribuição Ao Estudio Da Política Internacional*, Porto Alegre, BR: Editora da Universidade Federal do Rio Grande do Sul.
——— (2006) *Desafios Brasileiros na Era dos Gigantes*, Rio de Janeiro: Contraponto.

Hirst, M. (2005) *The United States and Brazil: A Long Road of Unmet Expectations*, New York: Routledge.
Hurrell, A. (2005) 'The United States and Brazil: Comparative Reflections', in M. Hirst *The United States and Brazil: A Long Road of Unmet Expectations*, New York: Routledge, pp. 75–90.
Ikenberry, G. J. (2001) *After Victory: Institutions, Strategic Restraint, and the Rebuilding of Order after Major Wars*, Princeton, NJ: Princeton University Press.
Jervis, R. (1978) 'Cooperation Under the Security Dilemma', *World Politics*, 30(2): 167–214.
Kang D. (2007) *China Rising: Peace, Power, and Order in East Asia*, New York: Columbia University Press.
Kennedy, P. (1989) *The Rise and Fall of the Great Powers: Economic Change and Military Conflict from 1500 to 2000*, New York: Vintage Books.
Kupchan C. (2010) *How Enemies Become Friends*, Princeton, NJ: Princeton University Press.
Lafer, C. (2000) 'Brazilian International Identity and Foreign Policy: Past, Present, and Future', *Daedalus*, 129(2): 207–238.
Lake, D. (2009) *Hierarchy in International Relations*, Ithaca, NY: Cornell University Press.
Lapp, N. (2012) 'Resistance is *Útil* (Useful): Responses to Brazilian Hegemony' in K. Williams, S. Lobell and N. Jesse (eds) *Beyond Great Powers and Hegemons: Why Secondary States Support, Follow, or Challenge*, Stanford, CA: Stanford University Press, pp. 145–160.
Lobell, S., Ripsman, N. and Taliaferro J. (eds) (2009) *Neoclassical Realism, the State, and Foreign Policy*, New York: Cambridge University Press.
Malamud, A. (2011) 'A Leader without Followers? The Growing Divergence between the Regional and Global Performance of Brazilian Foreign Policy', *Latin American Politics and Society*, 53(3): 1–24.
Manzenreiter, W. (2010) 'The Beijing Games in the Western Imagination of China: The Weak Power of Soft Power', *Journal of Sport and Social Issues*, 34(1): 29–48.
Mearsheimer, J. (2001) *The Tragedy of Great Power Politics*, New York: W.W. Norton.
Mora F. O. and Hey, J.A.K. (2003) 'Introduction: The Theoretical Challenge to Latin American and Caribbean Foreign Policy Studies' in F. O. Mora and J.A.K. Hey (eds) *Latin American and Caribbean Foreign Policy*, Lanham, MD: Rowman and Littlefield, pp. 1–9.
Morgenthau, H. (1948) *Politics Among Nations: the Struggle for Power and Peace*, New York: Knopf.
Nabers, D. (2010) 'Power, Leadership, and Hegemony in International Politics: The Case of East Asia', *Review of International Studies*, 36(4): 931–949.
Remmer, K. (2012) 'The Rise of Leftist-Populist Governance in Latin America: The Roots of Electoral Change', *Comparative Political Studies*, 45(8): 947–972.
Rodrigues, J.H. (1962) 'The Foundations of Brazil's Foreign Policy', *International Affairs*, 38(3): 324–338.
Roett, R. (2010) *The New Brazil*, Washington, DC: Brookings Institution Press.
Rohter, L. (2010) *Brazil on the Rise: The Story of a Country Transformed*, New York: Palgrave Macmillan.
Romero, S. and Clarey, C. (2014, May 19) 'Note to Olympic Sailors: Don't Fall in Rio's Water', *The New York Times*. Retrieved from http://www.nytimes.com/2014/05/19/world/americas/memo-to-olympic-sailors-in-rio-dont-touch-the-water.html.
Roy, D. (2013) *Return of the Dragon: Rising China and Regional Security*, New York: Columbia University Press.
Santos, S.C. (2011) 'Brasil y la Región: Una Potencia Emergente y la Integración Regional Sudamericana', *Revista Brasileira de Política Internacional*, 54(2): 158–172.
Schenoni, L. (2012) 'Ascenso y Hegemonía: Pensando a las Potencias Emergentes Desde América del Sur', *Revista Brasileira de Política Internacional*, 55(1): 31–48.
Selcher, W. (ed) (1981) *Brazil in the International System: The Rise of a Middle Power*, Boulder, CO: Westview Press.
Silva, R.M. (ed) (2003) *Missões de Paz: A Diplomacia Brasileira nos Conflitos Internacionais*, Rio de Janeiro: Log On Editora Multimídia.
Soares de Lima, M.R. and Hirst, M. (2006) 'Brazil as an Intermediate State and Regional Power: Action, Choice and Responsibilities', *International Affairs*, 82(1): 21–40.
Solingen, E. (1998) *Regional Orders at Century's Dawn*, Princeton, NJ: Princeton University Press.
The Economist (2014a, April 30) 'Dilma's Fragile Lead: Brazil's Election', *The Economist*.
——— (2014b, January 4) 'Kick-off Approaches; Brazil's Big Year', *The Economist*.
——— (2014c, February 28) 'Sunny to a Fault: Brazil's Economy', *The Economist*.
——— (2014d, December 7) 'Brazil's Economy: The Deterioration', *The Economist*.
——— (2014e, January 16) 'The Bugbear of Brazil: Inflation in Brazil', *The Economist*.

Vigevani, T. and Cepaluni, G. (2009) *Brazilian Foreign Policy in Changing Times: The Quest for Autonomy from Sarney to Lula*, Lanham, MD: Lexington Books.
——— (2013) 'Brazil: Global Power-To-Be?', in R. Beasley et al. (eds) *Foreign Policy in Comparative Perspective: Domestic and International Influences on State Behavior* (2nd ed.), Washington, D.C.: CQ Press, pp. 265–289.
Waltz, K. N. (1979) *Theory of International Politics*, Reading, MA: Addison-Wesley Publication Company.
Wendt, A. (1992) 'Anarchy is What States Make of It: The Social Construction of Power Politics', *International Organization*, 46(2): 391–425.
Weyland, K., Madrid, R. and Hunter, W. (eds) (2010) *Leftist Governments in Latin America: Successes and Shortcomings*, New York: Cambridge University Press.

17

GUERRILLAS, TERRORISTS, OR CRIMINALS?

The new face of antistate violence in Latin America

Román D. Ortiz

Since the end of World War II, the logic of security in Latin America has been marked by the confrontation between the states of the region and violent nonstate actors. The latter is a category encompassing groups such as terrorist organizations, guerrillas, militias, and criminal gangs that use violence to capture resources and gain influence over population and territory. Traditional academic analyses of these various violent groups developed with a set of rigid conceptual boundaries that separated groups that exercised violence with criminal purposes (such as drug cartels and criminal gangs) from those who did so for political reasons (revolutionaries or counterrevolutionaries). Subsequently, groups that resorted to arms for political reasons were divided into 'terrorists' and 'guerrillas,' with the latter assumed to have more popular support or a more just cause than the former.

Limitations of the traditional categories

Analytic divisions between criminals or insurgents and guerrillas or terrorists masked a complex and ambiguous reality. Historically, cases of social banditry abounded in the region, and the frequency with which the line between insurgency and criminal was crossed in scenarios such as the Mexican Revolution revealed the weakness of the conceptual barrier between political violence and criminal violence. Similarly, the armed groups that emerged in the region combined terrorist operations, guerrilla campaigns, and urban insurrections in a sufficiently fluid manner that it was difficult to pigeonhole them into one or another category. In the early 20th century the anarchist movement in Argentina combined the use of terrorism with participation in urban uprisings and peasant rebellions (Simon 1946: 38–50). The insurrection led by Sandino in Nicaragua between 1926 and 1933 engaged in a guerrilla war against the National Guard and the U.S. forces aiding them, as well as terrorist acts against civilians intended to discourage cooperation with the authorities and encourage them to boycott elections (Macaulay 1985: 116–117, 128–131; Boot 2002: 242–243).

The evolution of Latin America's strategic scenario in the 1980s highlighted the conceptual ambiguity of the old categories that distinguished among those who violated the law for political or criminal reasons. For example, although the Colombian Movement *M-19 de Abril* (*M-19A*) utilized actions normally classified as terrorism – hostage-taking, kidnappings, selective assassinations – they were often denoted as 'guerrillas' (Villamizar 1995: 79–239). Yet, the armed organizations opposed to the Sandinista regime in Nicaragua – from the Democratic Revolutionary Alliance (*Alianza Democrática Revolucionaria*, ARDE) to the Nicaraguan Resistance (*Resistencia Nicaraguense*, RN) – were frequently considered simply terrorist networks under the control of U.S. intelligence. These groups, nonetheless, also had characteristics of an insurgency with its own social base and an armed wing, and carried out guerrilla operations (Sereseres 1989: 14–23; Pardo-Maurer 1990: 1–70; Brown 2001: 3–108).

Revolutionary armed groups and criminal organizations increased their connections and assumed strategic behaviors with increasing similarities. For example, FARC (*Fuerzas Armadas Revolucionarias de Colombia*) provided security for Medellín Cartel cocaine labs in the 1980s (Gilibert 1989: 175–190), creating links that later gave the FARC organizational control of a thriving, illegal cocaine economy. Concurrently, *Sendero Luminoso* (the Shining Path) in Peru followed a similar roadmap, providing protection for coca crops in the Upper Huallaga (Mason and Campany 1995: 140–170). In turn, drug trafficking organizations began using terrorism to protect their interests. Between the late 1980s and the early 1990s, the Medellín Cartel's armed campaign to force the Colombian government to cancel an extradition agreement with the United States included the assassination of political figures and car bomb attacks (Salazar 2001: 203–334). A few years later, Mexico began to suffer similar strategies, with important political assassinations (Shelley 2001: 213–231) and car bombs used to settle conflicts with rival criminal groups (Bunker and Sullivan 2013).

In the 21st century, the convergence between political and criminal violence accelerated. The FARC and *Sendero Luminoso* integrated global drug trafficking networks at the same time that they widened their economic portfolio with activities such as illegal mining. Smaller groups with a shorter history sought similar criminalization strategies, including Mexico's *Ejército Popular Revolucionario* (EPR) (Revolutionary Popular Army) (Miró 2003: 36–38) and the *Ejército del Pueblo Paraguayo* (EPP, Paraguayan People's Army) (*ABC Color* 2013). Criminal organizations now make propaganda, impose mechanisms of parallel justice, and dispute the control of territories with the state, just as revolutionary armed groups have traditionally done; e.g., the First Commando of the Capital of Brazil (Sullivan and Bunker 2011: 742–763), the Mexican *Zetas* and *Caballeros Templarios* (Zaluar 2004: 139–154), and the Colombian *Urabeños* and the *Nudo de Paramillo* (*El Universal* 2011; *El País* 2014). A group can combine criminal violence and politics so seamlessly that it is difficult to identify the main motivation behind its armed actions. A prime example is the United Self-Defense Forces of Colombia (*Autodefensas Unidas de Colombia,* AUC), a confederation of paramilitary organizations linking different groups closely associated with drug trafficking to fight guerrillas for both ideological reasons and over control of the drug industry (Garzón 2005: 47–135).

Conceptual redefinition: political and criminal violence in Latin America

Given this reality, the question of whether the traditional, compartmentalized view of antistate violence in Latin America retains some analytical potential or if one should discard the old distinctions between political and criminal violence or between terrorists and guerrillas remains very relevant.

The effort to reinvigorate the analytical potential of the concepts of terrorism and guerrilla should begin by addressing their depoliticization. The 'terrorist' and 'guerrilla' labels have been loaded with two different meanings: One is of an operational character, and the other has political connotations. The operational meaning distinguishes between the use of irregular armed actions aimed at destroying the state security apparatus to capture territory and population (guerrilla) from the implementation of specific attacks seeking to create fear among the population and disrupt social life (terrorism) (Reinares 1998: 13–46; Hoffman 2006: 35–41). The political use of these concepts is based on the assumption that the guerrilla applies 'respectable' violence, since it limits its attacks to government forces, respects civilians, and becomes feasible only if it has considerable social support. On the contrary, terrorism is directed against civilians, and it is the weapon of radicalized minorities. Consequently, guerrillas are legitimate actors, whereas terrorists deserve condemnation.

This discrimination between guerrillas and terrorists based on political criteria has two essential weaknesses. First, all groups that practice guerrilla war use terrorism in more or less large doses as an essential component of their strategy to weaken the credibility of the state, intimidate their opponents, and impose their authority over the population (Villalobos 1999: 25). Consequently, one cannot make a rigorous distinction between terrorists and guerrillas. Moreover, the use of guerrilla warfare by a particular armed group has nothing to do with its legitimacy to resort to armed struggle and to the justice of its cause. In fact, many of the actions developed by the FARC during the period 1998–2008 deserve to be called guerrilla actions (Spencer 1997: 474–477 and 1998: 35–40). However, the organization has not gained any legitimacy from the use of this form of irregular warfare, since it acts against a democratically elected government, the source of its power is not popular support but drug money, and its attacks hit indiscriminately the civilian population.

Moreover, the growth of the military capacity of the drug cartels, which, as we already mentioned, occasionally conduct guerrilla operations without changing their criminal nature, complicates matters further. In other words, the use of guerrilla wars as a formula for violence neither grants the group greater legitimacy nor guarantees its political character. That being so, if the analytical relevance of the concepts of terrorism and guerrilla is to be recovered, it seems essential to limit their meanings to the sphere of strategy and relinquish their political connotations. In this light, by analyzing its actions, one could easily identify the operational formula that a group practices. The assessment of the greater or lesser legitimacy of the use of violence should be subject to a debate based on different considerations such as the context where violence occurs, the victims thereof, and the objectives it pursues.

As for the distinction between violent groups of a political and criminal nature, applying such terms to the current strategic Latin American scene demands a change of criteria in order to distinguish one from the other. Traditionally, the distinction between political and criminal violence has been based on two principles: on the one hand, the classification of groups according to the ultimate goal of their armed activity – capturing quotas of political power or income – and on the other, a static view of the group character to the extent that organizations were classified permanently in either category. This division into rigid categories was built according to legal categories that established a clear distinction between common and political offenses, and gave the latter a different and special treatment (Orozco 2006: 37–82). According to this view, *Sendero Luminoso* would deserve the label of a revolutionary armed organization, because its stated objective was to impose a Maoist model in Peru, and would keep such character despite having been progressively involved with drug trafficking. In contrast, the Medellín Cartel should be defined as a criminal structure, because its members were driven by profit, and the *capos*' systematic practice of political corruption and terrorism would not have softened this classification.

Yet the growing trend to overlap criminal and political violence in Latin America requires that analysts reexamine the criteria with which the differentiation has traditionally been established. In that sense, the first change of perspective would be to consider the political or criminal nature of an armed group, not so much for its theoretical goals as for the role it assumes and the functions it performs among the areas and the population in which it is present. Therefore, an armed organization would assume a political role or would remain as a merely criminal group, not so much for what are supposed to be its motives, but rather for what it does in practice. Thereby, when a group controls a territory, provides security services, and keeps a system of parallel justice or, in other words, acts as a para-state structure, one might assume that it is fulfilling political roles. A second perspective would be to consider the political and criminal actions not as static conditions but rather as processes. Therefore, an armed structure could politicize or criminalize over time depending on whether it embarked on criminal activities that sought profit or, on the contrary, assumed political functions.

These reconceptualizations provide insights into the profiles that terrorism and organized crime are gradually assuming in Latin America. Thus FARC was born as a revolutionary armed organization, but gradually underwent a process of criminalization as a result of their ties with drug trafficking and illegal mining to the point that today it could be classified as a political-criminal group (Saskiewicz 2005: 94–101; NIR et al. 2010: 6). Cartels such as the *Zetas* or the *Familia Michoacana* have experienced degrees of politicization insofar as they gained influence over some regions, established mechanisms to control population, and imposed parallel justice systems (Valdés 2013). Certainly, even under such conditions, it is misleading to classify criminal gangs as organizations of a political nature; however, it could be analytically useful to define them as criminal groups with political functions.

Strategic rationale of the convergence between terrorism and organized crime

Although the connections and overlap between political violence and organized crime are quite old, a number of factors speeded up a process of convergence between both phenomena in the 1980s. The key driving force pushing some guerrilla groups towards criminality was a need for funding. This search for funds among leftist guerrillas preceded the disintegration of the Soviet Union and the defeat of the Socialist Bloc. Seeking new financial support was motivated by the ambition of the leadership of certain armed groups to achieve political and strategic independence from their initial state sponsors. For example, FARC and *Sendero Luminoso* began building links with the cartels in the 1980s, long before the fall of the Soviet Union (Jaramillo et al. 1989; Gonzales 1992: 105–125).

Ultimately, these strategic choices turned out to be crucial for the survival of both organizations. Other guerrilla groups that preferred to remain subordinate to the support of foreign powers lost their freedom of action, so that their capacity to make critical decisions was compromised by their dependency upon external patronage. For example, the FMLN in El Salvador was forced to negotiate with the government after Moscow cancelled all its support. By the 1990s the links between political violence and drug trafficking grew stronger, especially in Colombia where guerrilla groups went from receiving payment for the armed protection of coca fields, laboratories, and drug shipments, to producing and dealing narcotics on their own.

Drug cartels in turn saw the acquisition of political power as both a need and an opportunity. As their interests expanded, the mafias realized that the accumulation of influence over government institutions and political elites offered an excellent means to their self-protection. This strategy is quite visible in Colombia, where drug trafficking organizations chose several ways to weaken institutions and build their own parallel power structures. First, they turned to violence with terrorist campaigns such as the one launched by the Medellín Cartel by the end of the 1980s. They engaged in a systematic effort of political corruption whose best example was the penetration of the Cali Cartel in the electoral campaign of President Ernesto Samper in 1994. Finally, they also implemented social programs that garnered popular sector sympathy, such as the *Bogotá sin Tugurios* (Bogotá without hovels) program of Pablo Escobar. This combination of armed pressure, corruption, and populism undermined state control over certain regions and some sectors of population, including in the periphery of Medellín, the second-largest city of Colombia and its industrial heart. Simultaneously, Escobar's partners, such as Rodriguez Gacha, extended their influence to regions like Magdalena Medio, by means of a combination of paramilitary violence, large-scale land acquisitions, and the corruption of local and regional public officials (Medina 1990: 243–287; Grupo de Memoria Histórica 2010: 296–308).

This convergence of criminality and politics has become visible in other countries of the region as well. During the 1990s a number of Brazilian criminal groups used drug money and the weapons it bought to establish parallel governments in the peripheries of large cities. It is estimated that in Rio de Janeiro around 800 communal leaders were murdered, thrown out from their residences, or coopted into the cartels from 1992 to 2001, as part of the establishment of a new criminal order in the *favelas* (Zaluar 2004: 149–153). Similarly, the expansion of drug trafficking in Mexico came together with massive corruption that affected justice, police services, and local and state governments; such growth in criminality would have been impossible without the vast networks of political complicities they built throughout Mexico (Garzón 2008: 106–119; Beith 2011: 786–806). Jamaica's Shower Posse and the Sprangler Posse used drug trafficking and the generalized practice of extortion to control the peripheral districts of Kingston, impose informal justice systems in the zones where they were present, and get involved in local politics by means of pacts with political parties such as the Jamaican Labor Party (JLP) and the Popular National Party (PNP) (Robinson 2008: 2–10; Kilcullen 2013: 89–102).

Changes in the strategic balance between the state and violent nonstate actors

The expansion of the economic autonomy of violent nonstate actors through their involvement in a broad range of illegal business – drug trafficking, illegal mining, extortion – has contributed critically to a change in the strategic balance among governments, criminal, and terrorist organizations. The capacity of many Latin American governments to protect their population and control their territory has been seriously diminished while criminals, terrorists, and guerrillas have gained autonomy and consolidated safe havens in ungoverned spaces (see Trinkunas and Clunan, this volume). To understand this trend, it is fundamental to consider that the consolidation of state institutions in Latin America has suffered several critical restrictions.

Traditionally, governments in the region faced difficulties extending their control over their entire national territory. The natural terrain of countries like Colombia or Peru presents great challenges, since mountains and rainforests make building communication networks, integrating the national economy, and facilitating the movement of the population and projecting security difficult. These physical limitations have been partially overcome by the progressive mitigation of the geographical challenges by a combination of technology, investment of capital, and political will. Other obstacles of a political and social nature, however, have been strengthened. The best examples of these nonphysical barriers are border areas where the legal and illegal flows of people and goods create an environment of overlapping sovereignties that restrict the capability of governments to assert control. Likewise, many Latin American countries have granted a special status to certain regions and restricted the application of the national legal system within them. In these special areas, the provision of state services – from police to education – requires permission from traditional authorities or faces legal challenges and systematic hostility. Finally, a combination of difficult social conditions and 'local patriotism' often creates an invisible fence against the presence of state services and institutions. This is the typical scenario in remote areas connected to illicit economic activities and in the peripheral districts of rapidly growing cities, in which the concentration of population, the absence of infrastructure, and the lack of planning make it difficult for the authorities to effectively regulate social life and prevent the emergence of parallel powers of a criminal character.

Apart from the territorial barriers, the presence of the state in Latin America is also dramatically uneven, depending on socioeconomic conditions. The social segmentation of geographical space and the manner in which the state developed resulted in a greater presence in urban districts with higher income, as compared to poorer or rural areas. In addition, the bonds between state and society are weaker in sectors that have a large, informal economy. Spaces dominated by the black economy – from informal street vendors to illegal mining – instinctively reject public regulations because they impose legal restrictions, administrative controls, and tax burdens. Finally, Latin American states also face serious limitations in the provision of basic social services to the majority of the population. The results of institutional inefficacy are lack of basic infrastructure, fragile social protection, and the impossibility to guarantee minimum levels of security and justice to significant sectors of the society. This scenario creates deep strategic implications, since it erodes the legitimacy of state institutions among broad sectors of the population, creating a demand for parallel state services to fill the gaps left by government incompetence. In this context, violent Latin American nonstate actors have found a key opportunity to gain social support.

Given the fragility of the state, several factors have strengthened the strategic position of illegal organizations. As noted, the economic foundations of terrorist and criminal organizations widened and consolidated. Moreover, the drug industry diversified. Mexican cartels became key suppliers of heroin for the North American market, thanks to the cultivation of opium poppies in the states of Oaxaca and Guerrero. In addition, they turned to the production of synthetic drugs, becoming major suppliers of methamphetamines for the U.S. market.

Concurrently, the economic portfolio of criminals and terrorists expanded substantially. Criminal organizations in Mexico and Central America incorporated kidnapping into their panoply of illegal businesses. The National System for Public Security in Mexico reported an increase from 505 to 1,322 kidnapping cases in 2001 and 2011, respectively. The entire region experienced a dramatic rise in the number of extortions by criminal and terrorist organizations (*El Universal* 2007; *O Globo* 2011; *The New York Times* 2012; *El Tiempo* 2013; *La República* 2013; *The Christian Science Monitor* 2014). In addition, the cartels became involved in trafficking migrants from the south of the continent to the border with the United States. Criminal and terrorist groups also became involved in illegal mining activities to take advantage of the increased price of precious metals. The ELN and FARC guerrillas, for example, promoted the exploitation of gold in areas under their control, with devastating environmental consequences (*InSight Crime* 2013; *El Espectador* 2011; Torres et al. 2013: 58–122; Rettberg and Ortiz-Riomalo 2014: 22–36). Finally, but equally important, terrorists and criminals have assumed state functions among those sectors of the population that live on the margins of official government.

Technology and globalization: force multipliers of terrorism and organized crime

Criminal and terrorist organizations increased their capacity to compete with the state based on two key factors: access to new technology and global projection. Regarding technology, during the past decade illegal groups acquired a series of capabilities that have been, until recently, the monopoly of states (Ortiz 2006: 205–222; Kenney 2007: 25–77). The dissemination of these means – which range from Semi-Submergible Boats (SSBs) to Man-Portable Air Defense Systems (MANPADS) – has resulted from several factors. Part of the criminal and terrorist structures has been formed by, or has incorporated individuals, that formerly belonged to the army or police, and utilizes tactics, techniques, and procedures used by law enforcement and armed forces in activities such as the collection of intelligence and special operations. The most famous example is the Mexican cartel, the *Zetas*, a group of former members of the Airborne Group of Special Forces (*Grupo Aerotransportado de Fuerzas Especiales*, GAFE) who abandoned the Mexican Army to establish one of the most feared mafia structures in the country.

A second source of innovation for criminal and terrorist structures came from the capacity to produce their own technological systems in areas such as weapons and transport. The most widely known cases are the FARC and ELN guerrillas, who have developed the capability to manufacture explosive devices, including land mines and mortar grenades. Likewise, Colombian drug traffickers have established a clandestine naval industry that has built increasingly sophisticated Semi-Submergible Boats. For their part, Mexican cartels have systematically produced armored trucks, known as 'monsters,' for use in transporting drugs or combating rival gangs.

Finally, Latin American criminal and terrorist networks developed closer links with both legal and illegal global technology markets as an additional way to increase the sophistication of their operations. Technologies that are merely civilian may be useful in the development of criminal activities – legal markets offer critical services (e.g., commercial flights) and equipment (e.g., GPS systems, encrypted communication systems of commercial use) for their operations. At the same time, the black markets of military equipment have grown in size and sophistication, providing increasing opportunities to get larger quantities of sophisticated and powerful weapons. An example is the shipment of 3,000 Chinese AK-47 assault rifles acquired by the Colombian criminal gang *Rastrojos* in 2008. Criminal and terrorist groups have had access to antibunker rockets and surface-to-air missiles. Weapons systems with a significant destabilizing potential have been used to commit terrorist attacks (Geibel 2012; Bunker 2012; Kuhn et al. 2013).

Moreover, the capacity of Latin American illegal organizations to compete with the state is strengthened by their ability to globalize by developing strategic alliances and acquiring resources. The key advantages of criminal and terrorist networks have been their facility in crossing borders and their invulnerability to the rule of sovereignty that restricts the ability of governments to act beyond their national borders. This transnational projection follows two strategic rationales. First, affinities of a political character enable terrorist groups of the region to build support networks beyond their countries of origin. Second, the rationality of global, illegal businesses, such as arms and drugs trafficking, has fostered alliances between the Latin American mafias and their counterparts in other countries. Regarding ideological connections, FARC has been critical to the development of a cooperation network among terrorist organizations in the region. To a great extent, their central role stems from their resources and their will to lead an armed campaign of continental dimensions. Two episodes demonstrate their regional reach. First is the cooperation discovered between Colombian terrorists and the Paraguayan People's Army (*Ejército del Pueblo Paraguayo*, EPP) that included advice and training for the kidnapping and murdering of the daughter of ex-President Raúl Cubas. The second was the discovery of the international cooperation networks that FARC was trying to build from the base camp of one of its leaders, Raul Reyes, which was destroyed in an operation by the military and police forces of Colombia.

Beyond ideological ties, criminal groups engaged in drug trafficking, illegal arms trade, and the smuggling of consumer products cooperate in a continental network driven by a desire for profit. Examples highlight the linking of groups that supposedly have very different, even rival, agendas. The Mexican *Zetas* built an alliance with the urban gang *Mara Salvatrucha* from El Salvador, which guarantees security and speed in transporting drugs, weapons, and people from Central America to the U.S. border. In Colombia, FARC, in the region of Nudo de Paramillo, cooperates with a criminal gang, the *Urabeños*, providing them with coca paste that they process into cocaine and export by sea. In the Colombian-Venezuelan border region of Catatumbo, a group of former guerrilla members from the Popular Liberation Army (*Ejército Popular de Liberación*, EPL), led by Victor Ramon Navarro 'Megateo,' acquired the cocaine produced by FARC and ELN to resell it to their contacts in Venezuela. The Brazilian criminal group First Command of the Capital (*Primer Comando de la Capital*) has developed cooperation links with Bolivian and Paraguayan drug trafficking organizations as part of their cocaine and marijuana smuggling.

The landscape has become more complex due to connections between Latin American criminal organizations and the global networks of organized crime and terrorism elsewhere. Most significant is the Islamist penetration in the region (Ortiz 2010: 137–152). For many years there has been increasing evidence that the Lebanese terrorist organization Hezbollah, with the support of the Iranian government, has built links with local Islamist groups. The most dramatic events took place in Buenos Aires in 1992 and 1994, with attacks against the Israeli Embassy and a building of the Jewish community, (*Asociación Mutual Israelita, Argentina*, AMIA). Connections between terrorist organizations from the Middle East and Latin American criminal groups have been detected. In October 2008, the Titan Operation conducted by law enforcement agencies from the United States, Colombia, and Spain dismantled a network that connected the Colombian criminal organization *Oficina de Envigado* with Hezbollah. Subsequently, in October 2011, the FBI discovered an attempt by an agent, linked to the Iranian Islamic Revolutionary Guard Corps, to contact the *Zetas* cartel to hire it to execute terrorist attacks in several countries of the region, including the United States. Beyond the Islamic connection, criminal networks linked to the Chinese Triads, the Japanese, and the Russian mafia have been identified in different countries of the region, trafficking arms, drugs, and people. These overlapping networks provide Latin American drug cartels and terrorist groups with enormous opportunities to expand their global projection.

The new face of political and criminal violence in Latin America

A substantial change in the nature of political violence and organized crime is taking place in Latin America, with both phenomena converging. Revolutionary activists in Latin America have been forced to change their strategic behavior, giving up their maximalist purpose of destroying the state. As they lost their bids to openly defeat the state, the search for economic resources has become a priority, due both to the need for resources to sustain their operations and the change in their leadership that has become more interested in profit than in ideology.

Parallel to the changes in the terrorist and guerrilla organizations, organized crime has gained increasing political influence in the region. Although they are criminal structures whose upper echelons are driven by profit, their multiple and sophisticated capabilities weaken state institutions and become parallel powers in some peripheral urban districts and marginal rural areas. When an organization is capable of defying the state, competing for control over the territory with the government, and maintaining a strong influence on the population, it is very difficult to characterize it as simply a criminal actor and deny its political relevance.

In this context, the historical distinction between organized crime and political violence is creating obstacles for analyzing the security challenges faced by Latin America and designing the strategies required to confront them. In fact, the links between criminals and terrorists are progressively closer, and their behavior similar. Alliances between them have become routine, and groups of a mixed nature, part criminal, part political, are appearing.

The evolution of criminal and political violence in Latin America has not been reflected in scholarly research. Many key questions for scholars, analysts, and policy-makers remain unresolved. More research is needed to develop effective analytical tools to understand these phenomena and the processes that have strengthened the strategic position of violent nonstate actors. The most urgent task is revising the traditional categories in which guerrilla activities, terrorism, and organized crime have been separately classified in order to construct concepts to deal with an increasingly fluid and ambiguous reality. This is the aim of new concepts, such as 'criminal insurgency,' that have begun to be constructed and applied in the strategic reality of Latin America. However, work in this field requires further attention.

In addition to clarifying concepts, it is fundamental to deepen our understanding of the dynamics that allow political and criminal violence to converge, detailing the causes that have led Latin American guerrillas to become criminalized, as well as how mafias and drug cartels have been able to acquire political roles and how far these developments will go in changing their nature. Likewise, it is important to analyze the relation between the rise of illegal power structures and the expansion of criminal economies. Within this context, important steps have been taken to understand the ties that develop between illicit crops and insurgencies. Identifying the equation that connects socioeconomic conditions and antistate violence demands a major analytical effort, especially with respect to how organized crime and the informal economy relate within an urban context.

Finally, changes in the strategic balance between state and violent nonstate actors demand greater study. It is fundamental to determine at what point the balance of power is turning against governments and in favor of illegal actors, as well as the consequences. Furthermore, it is important to analyze how traditional security policies are deficient when confronting guerrilla groups, terrorists, and criminals that operate in an integrated system that makes it all the more difficult to distinguish one from the other. The conclusions should encourage debate on how to design criminal prevention programs, necessary reform within the criminal justice system, strategies to combat illegal economies, ways to act within urban sectors with high crime rates, and operational concepts to use the police and the military in the struggle against threats to domestic security. The final objective will be to encourage a revision of counterterrorist and anticrime policies at a time of increasing violence that threatens institutional stability and economic prosperity in many Latin American countries.

References

ABC Color (2013, August 26) 'Sospechan que narcos proveen armas al EPP'. Retrieved from http://www.abc.com.py/edicion-impresa/politica/sospechan-que-narcos-proveen-armas-al-epp-610765.html.

Beith, M. (2011) 'A Broken Mexico: Allegations of Collusion between the Sinaloa Cartel and Mexican Political Parties', *Small Wars & Insurgencies*, 22(5): 786–806.

Boot, M. (2002) *The Savage Wars of Peace. Small Wars and the Rise of American Power*, New York: Basic Books, pp. 242–243.

Brown, T. (2001) *The Real Contra War: Highlander Peasant Resistance in Nicaragua*, Norman: University of Oklahoma Press, pp. 3–108.

Bunker, R.J. (2012, September 27) 'Mexican Cartel Tactical Note 14: Anti-Aircraft Mounted .50 cal. Machine Gun and Surface-to-Air Missile', *Small Wars Journal*. Retrieved from http://smallwarsjournal.com/blog/mexican-cartel-tactical-note-14.
Bunker, R.J. and Sullivan, J.P. (2013) *Cartel Car Bombings in Mexico*, Carlisle: The Letort Papers, Strategic Studies Institute, pp. 9–13.
El Espectador (2011, September 16) 'La nueva arma financiera de las FARC'. Retrieved from http://www.elespectador.com/noticias/judicial/nueva-arma-financiera-de-farc-articulo-245255.
El País (2014, July 19) 'Autodefensas gaitanistas, la fachada política de "Urabeños"'. Retrieved from http://www.elpais.com.co/elpais/judicial/noticias/autodefensas-gaitanistas-fachada-politica-urabenos.
El Tiempo (2013, March 20) 'En Medellín se paga por cruzar la calle o para usar escalera eléctrica'. Retrieved from http://www.eltiempo.com/archivo/documento/CMS-12703000.
El Universal (2007, August 20) 'Delitos de extorsión registran Franco crecimiento durante 2007'. Retrieved from http://www.eluniversal.com/2007/08/20/sucgc_art_delitos-de-extorsion_413150.
——— (2011, September 8). 'Capturan a alias "chocolate", cabecilla de "los Urabeños" en Córdoba'. Retrieved from http://www.eluniversal.com.co/monteria-y-sincelejo/sucesos/capturan-alias-%E2%80%98chocolate%E2%80%99-cabecilla-de-%E2%80%98los-urabenos%E2%80%99-en-cordoba-42666.
Garzón, J.C. (2005) 'La complejidad paramilitar: Una aproximación estratégica' in A. Rangel (ed) *El poder paramilitar*, Bogotá: Planeta Colombiana, pp. 47–135.
——— (2008) *Mafia & co. La red criminal en Mexico, Brasil y Colombia*, Bogotá: Planeta Colombia, pp. 106–119.
Geibel, A. (2012, June 7) 'Mexican Cartel Tactical Note 12A: Lanzagranadas y Lanzacohetes', *Small Wars Journal*. Retrieved from http://smallwarsjournal.com/blog/mexican-cartel-tactical-note-12a-lanzagranadas-y-lanzacohetes.
Gilibert, L.E. (1989) 'Tranquilandia, primer golpe al cartel de Medellín' in G. Martínez (comp) *Hablan los generales. Las grandes batallas del conflicto Colombiano contadas por sus protagonistas*, Bogotá: Grupo Editorial Norma, pp. 14–23.
Gonzales, J.E. (1992) 'Guerrillas and Coca in the Upper Huallaga Valley' in D. C. Palmer (ed) *Shining Path of Peru*, New York: St Martin's Press, pp. 105–125.
Grupo de Memoria Histórica (2010) *La rochela. Memorias de un crimen contra la justicia*, Buenos Aires: Aguilar, Altea, Taurus, Alfaguara, pp. 296–308.
Hoffman, B. (2006) *Inside Terrorism*, New York: Columbia University Press, pp. 35–41.
InSight Crime (2013, July 26) 'ELN Deepen Involvement in Illegal Mining'. Retrieved from http://www.insightcrime.org/news-briefs/colombias-eln-deepen-involvement-in-illegal-mining.
Jaramillo, J., Mora Riveros, L. and Cubides, F. (1989) *Colonización, coca y guerrilla*, Bogotá: Alianza Editorial Colombiana.
Kenney, M. (2007) *From Pablo to Osama. Trafficking and Terrorist Networks, Government Bureaucracies, and Competitive Adaptation*, University Park: The Pennsylvania State University Press, pp. 25–77.
Kilcullen, D. (2013) *Out of the Mountains. The Coming Age of the Urban Guerrilla*, Oxford: Oxford University Press, pp. 89–102.
Kuhn, D., Wadhawan, A. and Bunker, R.J. (2013, November 30) 'Mexican Cartel Tactical Note #20: RPG-29 Anti-armor Munitions', *Small Wars Journal*. Retrieved from http://smallwarsjournal.com/jrnl/art/mexican-cartel-tactical-note-20-rpg-29-anti-armor-munitions.
La República (2013, June 9) 'Terroristas amenazan a consorcio con cobro de "cupos de guerra"'. Retrieved from http://www.larepublica.pe/09–06–2013/terroristas-amenazan-a-consorcio-con-cobro-de-cupos-de-guerra.
Macaulay, N. (1985) *The Sandino Affair*, Durham: Duke University Press, pp. 116–117.
Mason, T.D. and Campany, C. (1995) 'Guerrillas, Drugs and Peasants: The Rational Peasant and the War on Drugs in Peru', *Terrorism and Political Violence*, 7(4): 140–170.
Medina, C. (1990) *Autodefensas, paramilitares y narcotráfico en Colombia. Origen desarrollo y consolidación. El caso Puerto Boyacá*, Bogotá: Editorial Documentos Periodísticos, pp. 243–287.
Miró, R. (2003) *Organized Crime and Terrorist Activity in Mexico, 1999–2002*, Washington, DC: Federal Research Division, Library of Congress, pp. 36–38.
NIR, ANDI and Fundación Ideas para la Paz (2010) *Entornos complejos: Buenavetura*, Bogotá: Fundación Ideas para la Paz.

O Globo (2011, November 3) 'Milícias se alastram por pelo menos 11 estados'. Retrieved from http://oglobo.globo.com/politica/milicias-se-alastram-por-pelo-menos-11-estados-3079181.

Orozco, I. (2006) *Combatientes, rebeldes y terroristas. Guerra y derecho en Colombia*, Bogotá: Editorial Temis, pp. 37–82.

Ortiz, R. D. (2006) 'Renew to Last: Innovation and Strategy of the Revolutionary Armed Forces of Colombia (FARC)' in J. Forest (ed) *Teaching Terror. Strategic and Tactical Learning in the Terrorist World*, Lanham: Rowman & Littlefield Publishers, pp. 205–222.

——— (2010) 'El terrorismo yihadista en América Latina: ¿La amenaza ignorada' in J. Jordán, P. Pozo and M. G. Guindo (eds) *Terrorismo sin fronteras. Actores, escenarios y respuestas en un mundo global*, Madrid: Aranzadi-Thomson Reuters, pp. 137–152.

Pardo-Maurer, W. (1990) *The Contras, 1980–1989: A Special Kind of Politics (The Washington Papers)*, Washington, DC: Praeger, pp. 1–70.

Reinares, F. (1998) *Terrorismo y antiterrorismo*, Barcelona: Paidos Ibérica, pp. 13–46.

Rettberg, A. and Ortiz-Riomalo, J. (2014) *Golden Conflict: Exploring the Relationship Between Gold Mining, Armed Conflict, and Criminality in Colombia*, Bogotá: Centro de Estudios sobre Seguridad y Drogas (CESED), Los Andes University, pp. 22–36.

Robinson, W. (2008). *Eradicating Organized Criminal Gangs in Jamaica: Can Lessons Be Learnt from a Successful Counterinsurgency?*, Unpublished dissertation, United States Marine Corps, Command and Staff College, Marine Corps University, Quantico, US, pp. 2–10.

Salazar, A. (2001) *La parábola de Pablo: Auge y caída de un gran capo del narcotráfico*, Bogotá: Planeta Colombiana, pp. 203–334.

Saskiewicz, P. (2005) *The Revolutionary Armed Forces of Colombia - People's Army (FARC-EP): Marxist-Leninist Insurgency or Criminal Enterprise?*, Unpublished dissertation, Naval Postgraduate School, Monterey, US, pp. 94–101.

Sereseres, C. (1989) 'The Nicaraguan Resistance and U.S. Policy' in D. Ronfeldt and B. Jenkins (eds) *The Nicaraguan Resistance and U.S. Policy*, Santa Monica: RAND Corporation, pp. 14–23.

Shelley, L. (2001) 'Corruption and Organized Crime in Mexico in the Post-PRI Transition', *Journal of Contemporary Criminal Justice*, 17: 213–231.

Simon, F. (1946) 'Anarchism and Anarcho-Syndicalism in South America', *Hispanic American Historical Review*, 26: 38–50.

Spencer, D. (1997, October) 'A Lesson for Colombia', *Jane's Intelligence Review*, 9(10): 474–477.

——— (1998, November). Bogota continues to bleed as FARC find their military feet. *Jane's Intelligence Review*, 10:11, 35–40.

Sullivan, J. and Bunker, R. (2011) 'Rethinking Insurgency: Criminality, Spirituality, and Societal Warfare in the Americas', *Small Wars & Insurgencies*, 22(5): 742–763.

The Christian Science Monitor (2014, March 19) 'Mexico's Rising Threat: Extortion'. Retrieved from http://www.csmonitor.com/World/Americas/2014/0319/Mexico-s-rising-threat-extortion.

The New York Times (2012, January 9) 'In Brazil, Officers of the Law, Outside the Law'. Retrieved from http://www.nytimes.com/2012/01/10/world/americas/in-parts-of-brazil-militias-operate-outside-the-law.html?pagewanted=all&_r=0.

Torres, J., Menam, J. and Gonzalez, C. (2013) *La explotación ilícita de recursos minerales en Colombia: Casos valle del cauca (Río Dagua)–Chocó (Río San Juan). Efectos sociales y ambientales*, Bogotá: Contraloría General de la República, pp. 58–122.

Valdés, G. (2013, September 1) 'El nacimiento de un ejército criminal', *Nexos*. Retrieved from http://www.nexos.com.mx/?p=15460.

Villalobos, J. (1999) 'Sin vencedores ni vencidos: Pacificación y reconciliación en El Salvador', *FASOC*, 14(3): 23–36.

Villamizar, D. (1995) *Aquel 19 será*, Bogotá: Planeta, pp. 79–239.

Zaluar, A. (2004) 'Urban Violence and Dug Warfare in Brazil' in K. Kooninngs and D. Kruijt (eds) *Armed Actors. Organised Violence and State Failures in Latin America*, London: Zed Books, pp. 49–153, 139–154.

18
WEAPONS OF MASS DESTRUCTION
Will Latin America backtrack?

Carlo Patti

Latin America is usually considered a weapons of mass destruction–free zone. Starting from the mid-1990s and with few exceptions, all the countries of the continent are members of the main regimes of nonproliferation, such as the nuclear, the biological, and the chemical. At the beginning of the 2000s, Cuba was the last country of the region to commit to all the regional and international norms for curbing the spread of weapons of mass destruction (WMDs). The lack of relevant external threats can justify the absence of WMDs in the region. However, in the last few years, because of deteriorating relations between some Latin American countries, and between Venezuela and the United States, many analysts opened a debate about possible new attitudes in the region towards weapons of mass destruction, particularly nuclear weapons.

The revival or launching of both civilian and military nuclear programs in Brazil, Argentina, Venezuela, and very recently Bolivia can justify this international concern. Moreover, the two most *nuclear capable* countries in the region – Brazil and Argentina – strongly criticize the international regime of nuclear nonproliferation. The governments of Brasília and Buenos Aires are particularly concerned with the growing Western pressure to apply stricter safeguards to their nuclear activities through the adoption of an Additional Protocol to the International Atomic Energy Agency (IAEA) safeguards. Despite the ratification of the Tlatelolco regional regime, the acceptance of the Non-Proliferation of Nuclear Weapons Treaty (NPT), the full ratification of the Comprehensive Test Ban Treaty (CTBT), and the establishment of a bilateral system of nuclear mutual inspections, the two countries censure the unfair nature of the regime because of the lack of commitment of the nuclear weapon states (NWS) toward a full atomic disarmament. Moreover, recently in Brazil, key members of the cabinet criticized the decision of the country to adhere to the NPT.

In order to gain a full understanding of the past and recent attitudes of the Latin American countries towards WMDs and, above all, nuclear proliferation, there is a vast array of research projects on the issue in Latin America and elsewhere. Two kinds of scholarly activities on the issue have emerged.[1] First, there is a deep historical research on the roots of the behavior of Latin American countries in the nuclear field (Hurtado de Mendoza 2014; Mallea 2012; Patti 2010, 2014a, 2014b). Second, scholars and analysts are focusing their attention on the current state of nuclear proliferation and nonproliferation in the region. The two research efforts are very much related and open avenues to new research on the proliferation of weapons of mass destruction in Latin America and elsewhere. Theorists, historians, and security studies specialists are already enjoying the fruits of this new generation of research either for supporting new theories or elaborating new analyses (Monteiro and Debbs 2015; Hymans 2015; Wheeler 2009).

There is a strong international attention by nonproliferation scholars towards Latin America (Kassenova 2014; Homan 2013; Hymans 2015; Rublee 2010; Trinkunas 2006; Wheeler 2009). In this context, this chapter deals with the possible change of Latin American attitudes towards nuclear nonproliferation through the analysis of two specific cases: Venezuela and Brazil. Finally, the effectiveness of regional and subregional nuclear nonproliferation regimes will be discussed.

Venezuela: the next nuclear proliferator?

International scholars and U.S. policy-makers consider the spread of nuclear weapons the greatest security threat for global stability. During the Hugo Chávez regime, Venezuela's proposal to set up its own nuclear program raised international, above all U.S., concern over possible nuclear proliferation risks (Garner 2010; Homan 2013; Trinkunas 2006). The declared purpose of the Venezuelan government was to provide the country with nuclear power plants for alternative energy. However, growing tension with the United States could justify the Caracas quest for nuclear weapons to deter any U.S. military threat (Sagan 1996; Homan 2013).

Even if Venezuela owns rich reserves of uranium in the south of the country, it needs foreign cooperation for acquiring technologies, knowledge, and machineries. As noted by Matthew Fuhrmann (2012), technology transfer for peaceful purposes can prompt the spread of nuclear weapons as an unintended consequence. Even if Chávez declared the peaceful nature of the Venezuelan nuclear program, some analysts and policy-makers argued that the government of Caracas was pursuing nuclear weapons (Garner 2010). In order to acquire them, however, Venezuela should rely on the assistance of the 'capable nuclear suppliers,' states that, according to Matthew Kroenig, "have the ability to provide sensitive nuclear assistance" (2010). Capable nuclear suppliers include nuclear weapon states, like Russia, or nonnuclear weapon states, such as Brazil, Argentina, and Iran, that have mastered parts of the nuclear fuel cycle.

Venezuela is a member of the global and regional nuclear nonproliferation regimes, but, like Brazil and Argentina, maintains a critical stance towards the inequities of the regime and decided not to accept the Additional Protocol to the International Atomic Energy Agency (IAEA) safeguards (Kassenova 2014). Thus it increased international suspicions about the diversion of an allegedly civilian nuclear program towards nonpeaceful ends. Venezuela drew further international concern through its support in recent years of Iranian and North Korean claims in the nuclear field.

In order to pursue its nuclear ambitions Venezuela sought the cooperation of possible partners in the region and among non-U.S. aligned countries. For this reason the government of Caracas tried to collaborate both with Argentina and Brazil – partners also in MERCOSUR – as well as with Russia and Iran. After having established cooperation in the defense field with Moscow, in 2010 Venezuela signed a major deal for importing two nuclear power plants and a research reactor (Hirst and Pearl 2010; Homan 2013). It was an ambitious project that strengthened collaboration with Russia, which gained a possible strong ally in Latin America.

Brazil and Argentina were also crucial partners. In the early 1980s Brazil and Venezuela signed an agreement for cooperating in the nuclear research field, but it was never implemented because a few years later Venezuela dismantled their incipient nuclear research program (Patti 2012). Starting in 2005, Venezuela sought to renew this kind of cooperation and to acquire nuclear know-how from its MERCOSUR partners (Trinkunas 2006: 622). The Brazilian government showed great interest in collaborating with Caracas for expanding its presence in the global nuclear market. Argentina, with a traditional program of cooperation towards other Latin American countries, was also available to cooperate by selling research reactors, such as those already transferred to Australia, Peru, and Algeria (Carasales and Ornstein 1998; Hurtado de Mendoza 2014). The most alarming cooperation has involved Iran, which planned to cooperate with Venezuela in locating deposits of uranium – estimated at 50,000 tons – in the South American country (Homan 2013). International analysts and U.S. policy-makers considered such a partnership as a potential channel to provide Iran with forbidden material (Hirst and Pearl 2010). Further suspicions included speculation that Iran might help Venezuela through secret agreements to acquire nuclear capabilities without international verification and in unsafeguarded facilities (Homan 2013: 65). If true, this could represent a case of sensitive nuclear assistance between two states with a common enemy (Kroenig 2010: 52).

Even if it were possible to begin a fruitful cooperation with these countries – especially with Russia, Argentina, and Brazil – Venezuela faced internal and external obstacles. In the domestic realm, Caracas lacks adequate human and technical resources to begin or implement a nuclear project (Trinkunas 2006). Second, given the current economic crisis, the government lacks financial resources for such investments. Furthermore, as a consequence of the incident in the nuclear power plant in Fukushima, Japan, Hugo Chávez in March 2011 froze Venezuela's nuclear projects. In addition, two crucial drivers for starting a nuclear program were lacking: a technical and scientific bureaucracy and, above all, strong political motivations. The main supporter of Venezuela's acquisition of atomic energy was the late President Hugo Chávez. In the current economic and political landscape it is difficult to see nuclear plans in the imminent future of Venezuela.

External obstacles include actions of Brazil and Argentina that aim at preserving the nonproliferation regime and avoiding security threats within the region (Trinkunas 2006: 618). New research should explain the behavior of the two countries in limiting the spread of sensitive nuclear technologies in the region. Moreover, further analyses should also explore the role of Russia. Would Moscow be available to transfer sensitive equipment and knowledge? The attitude of Russia, one of the main promoters of the nuclear nonproliferation regime, and of Argentina and Brazil, supporters of global nuclear disarmament, might avoid such a scenario. Therefore, scholars from different theoretical approaches should use the Venezuelan case for testing the effectiveness of nonproliferation norms in Latin America. Will the action of both Argentina and Brazil restrain any deviance of possible nuclear aspirants such as Venezuela? Homan (2013) proposed that the two countries could push for an extension of the Brazilian-Argentine Agency for Accounting and Control of Nuclear Materials (ABACC – *Agência Brasileiro-Argentina de Contabilidade e Controle de Materiais Nucleares*) system to the rest of Latin America, in order to guarantee the nonproliferation of nuclear weapons in the region.

Brazil: a threat to the nuclear nonproliferation regime?

While Venezuela does not seem to represent a serious threat to the nonproliferation regime in the foreseeable future, Brazil is a "nuclear threshold state" that, according to Rublee, has "chosen nuclear restraint despite having significant nuclear capabilities" (2010). The government of Brasília, in fact, had definitely renounced nuclear weapons in 1990, after having pursued nuclear projects that involved the construction of a peaceful nuclear device and that allowed the country to acquire sensitive nuclear technologies, such as uranium enrichment capability (Barletta 1997; Hibbs 2014; Patti 2012). Furthermore, in 1991 Brazil began a process that led to signing the Non-Proliferation Treaty in 1998, after 30 years of opposition. Given that, why would the largest Latin American country challenge the nonproliferation regime? Following Rublee (2010: 53) three reasons can be identified: the ambiguous stance on nonproliferation norms, especially safeguards, its uranium enrichment program, and Brazil's plan to develop nuclear-powered submarines.

In recent years, international commentators have highlighted ambiguous declarations by key members of the Brazilian government about nuclear weapons. Between 2003 and 2009, in fact, the then Vice-President José Alencar, the Minister of Science and Technology Roberto Amaral, and the Secretary-General of the Foreign Ministry Samuel Pinheiro Guimarães openly contested Brazil's participation in the NPT as an important limitation on the country's aspirations as an emergent global player (Kassenova 2014; Patti 2010). For Alencar, for instance, possessing a nuclear arsenal could improve Brazilian possibilities to gain a permanent seat at the United Nations Security Council. The Brazilian government immediately censured these statements, calling them personal and nonofficial positions, even though a few years earlier former President Luiz Inácio Lula da Silva had also expressed reservations towards joining the NPT (Patti 2012).

Even if Brazil is a full member of all the main nuclear nonproliferation forums and a staunch promoter of nuclear disarmament, several international analysts doubt its commitment to nuclear nonproliferation (Rublee 2010). Since the early 2000s, in fact, Brazil has made important decisions in the nuclear realm, including inaugurating a new facility for enriching uranium for commercial purposes, and taking serious steps towards the construction of a submarine with nuclear propulsion.

The main controversial point consists in Brazil's refusal to accept the IAEA Additional Protocol to the Safeguards Agreement. Brazil, in fact, refuses to allow IAEA inspectors full access to both declared and possible undeclared civilian or military nuclear activities. Above all, under the protocol the IAEA is granted expanded rights of access to information and nuclear sites (Hirsch 2004). Since 1996, both Brazil and Argentina have opposed signing the protocol – considered too intrusive – and including it within the NPT. In 2004 Brasília's opposition became a matter of international concern, when the local authorities denied the international inspectors full visual access to its centrifuges for enriching uranium. These had been developed by the Brazilian Navy during the secret nuclear program in the 1980s and were then transferred in 2004 to a civilian enrichment plant in Resende, in the state of Rio de Janeiro. The main concern was that hiding the centrifuges could also allow Brazil to conceal unsafeguarded enriched uranium. All of this caused growing concern among U.S. and foreign policy analysts, who perceived the opposition to the Additional Protocol as a Brazilian strategy to conceal ambiguous nuclear activities (Palmer and Milhollin 2004).

Nonetheless, after long negotiations, Brazil granted the IAEA access to verify the nuclear material; however, it preserved the centrifuges from visual inspections. As noted by Rublee (2010), there are several reasons behind the Brazilian attitude. First, Brazil considers stricter safeguards unnecessary for a country already covered by international and the bilateral Argentine-Brazilian safeguards. Second, the adoption of the Additional Protocol would cause a financial burden for Brazil and other developing countries. Third, Brazilian authorities declared that they wanted to protect their industrial secrets, since the centrifuges used in the civilian plant were the product of science and technology developed in Brazil. The United States mildly criticized Brazil's stance and continues to request, as other nuclear and nonnuclear powers do, the full acceptance of the protocol. Brazilian authorities declared that the issue was not central to the reform of the NPT and underlined Brazil's right to maintain its industrial secrets.

As already noted, Brazil retains its pre-1997 attitude towards the NPT. Several years ago, Brazilian diplomats proposed to resolve the issue by recognizing the bilateral Brazilian-Argentine

ABACC inspection system as an alternative to the Additional Protocol. In June 2011, after several years of negotiation, Brazil achieved a significant success: The Nuclear Suppliers Group (NSG) accepted the Brazilian proposal, and that decision had several important consequences for Brazil. It put an end, at least temporarily, to the worry of the international community over a supposedly ambiguous Brazilian nuclear attitude. Brazil, in fact, could now be considered a player who accepted the international norms of nonproliferation. The NSG decision also had significant importance for bilateral relations with Argentina. The recognition of the binational agency means international approval of the cooperation between the two countries. Finally, this represents a temporary victory for both Argentina and Brazil, which, thanks to the NSG decision, can now enter the international market for sensitive nuclear material and technologies. The issue, however, is not completely resolved, since in the future Brazil will be asked to make a final decision on the adoption of the Additional Protocol. Not adhering to one of the norms that integrates the international regime of nonproliferation could, in fact, undermine Brazil's credibility as a promoter of global disarmament. Today, as in the recent past, not only Brazilians but also Argentine authorities are discussing internally a possible acceptance of the protocol (Patti 2010).

Another matter of concern for security scholars is the Brazilian plan to develop nuclear-powered submarines. Several analysts question the real drivers of the Brazilian choice, since Brazil lacks significant external security threats (Kassenova 2014; Taylor 2009; Thielmann and Kelleher-Vargantini 2013). In 2008, the Brazilian government provided its official rationale. Brazil's National Defense Strategy, in fact, underlined the necessity to achieve nuclear autonomy for economic development and for building a fleet of nuclear submarines (Patti 2010). Using its traditional rhetoric, Brazilian strategists justified that decision by the need to preserve the country's immense marine and undersea resources from possible enemies and, above all, to defend the oil reserves off the coast of the states of Rio de Janeiro and Espírito Santo. Whatever the actual reason, thanks to an agreement with France signed in December 2008, Brazil will construct submarines using Brazilian nuclear reactors to be built by the navy research center in Iperó (state of São Paulo). By 2025 Brazil should own its first nuclear submarine, and it will be the first nonnuclear weapon state with such a capability.

Analysts do not perceive Brazil as a direct threat to nuclear nonproliferation, but do see it as setting a dangerous precedent for more aggressive countries, such as Iran (Thielmann 2012). This is related to the loopholes present in the NPT. The treaty, in fact, does not ban non-nuclear powers from developing nuclear vessels and does not impose international safeguards for military facilities. The most dangerous loophole, however, is that a country has the right to fuel its nuclear reactors for naval propulsion with weapons-grade material. Consequently, Brazil can represent a negative precedent for several international actors with nuclear ambitions. A country like Iran, a full member of the NPT but considered by many observers to have ambiguous nuclear ambitions, could freely exert its right to produce large amounts of highly enriched uranium for naval purposes and then divert it to other aims, such as the construction of nuclear weapons. However, in contrast to the United States and Russia, several analysts reported that Brazil has opted not to use weapons-grade nuclear material; instead, it plans to use low-enriched uranium (LEU) for fueling its submarines, following the example of China and France (Kassenova 2014; Patti 2015; Philippe 2014).

In the future, a possible solution would be the revision of the NPT for eliminating these dangerous loopholes and, above all, a United States–Russian decision to fuel the reactors of the nuclear fleet through LEU. Brazil, highly advanced in nuclear technology, with the ambition to become a member of the exclusive elite of states with nuclear submarines, and with a safeguarded military nuclear program, could promote the revision of the nuclear nonproliferation normative framework. Given its traditional role in the last 20 years as a vocal player for nuclear disarmament, Brazil could advance a proposal to ban the use of weapons-grade material for naval propulsion (Philippe 2014).

This would be an important move in advancing Brazil's ambition to dispel concerns about Brazilian willingness to develop a nuclear arsenal in the future. Such a proposal would help in supporting Brasília's position favoring a more equitable and effective NPT, in which both nuclear and nonnuclear states would renounce dangerous material. It is not clear if Brasília will take that position, but it would surely represent a less hazardous and more constructive decision than that taken in 2010, when Brazilian diplomacy unsuccessfully promoted the Tehran declaration, facing the opposition of the United States and other Great Powers (Dalaqua 2013; Kassenova 2014; Patti 2010; Viera de Jesus 2011).

Tlatelolco and ABACC: effective regimes for keeping nuclear weapons out of Latin America?

Latin America has a long tradition of promoting nonproliferation and disarmament. Since 1967, with the signing of the Treaty on the Prohibition of Nuclear Weapons in Latin America, also known as the Treaty of Tlatelolco, the region has been the first nuclear-weapons-free zone (NWFZ) of the world. Since then, as all Latin American and Caribbean countries signed the treaty, none has acquired nuclear weapons. The regime has been demonstrated to be effective, including international inspections from its inception, and has inspired the creation of NWFZs in other regions of the world.

Moreover, as noted by Hymans (2015), the Latin American NWFZ has had substantive results in obliging nuclear weapon states – above all France – to follow the rules of the treaty (Appendix 1 and 2 of the treaty), renouncing the production, use, carrying, and placement of atomic devices in the region. From the 1970s, in fact, all the countries of the nuclear club began to accept the rules imposed by the Treaty of Tlatelolco. It represents an important precedent for the future global disarmament proposed by Article IV of the NPT.

The commitment of Latin America against nuclear weapons was strengthened in 1994 with the final full acceptance of the treaty by the two main countries supposed to have nuclear ambitions and to be engaged in a nuclear arms race in the past: Brazil and Argentina. The acceptance is related to the establishment of another and complementary nuclear nonproliferation regime in the Southern Cone: ABACC, the Brazilian-Argentine Agency for Accounting and Control of Nuclear Materials. As noted in recent studies, the Brazilian-Argentine regime resulted from a long period of cooperation between the two countries, which began before the end of the military regime (Mallea 2012; Kutchesfahani 2014; Patti 2012), and above all because of the strong commitment of the two governments towards avoiding a nuclear arms race. Thanks to diplomatic action by Brazil and Argentina, and because of the personal commitment of Presidents Collor de Mello (Brazil) and Menem (Argentina), the two countries renounced their right to explode nuclear devices – even if for peaceful purposes – and above all to set up a bilateral nonproliferation safeguards system, guaranteeing mutual inspections of their nuclear activities. ABACC was created before the agreement of the two countries to join the NPT. Together with a quadripartite IAEA-ABACC-Brazil-Argentina agreement on full-scope safeguards, the system represented a necessary step for joining the Treaty of Tlatelolco by waiving the requirement of universal state agreement. As with the Latin American nuclear-weapons-free zone, the ABACC system has been considered an important precedent for resolving the nuclear rivalries present in the Indian subcontinent, the Korean peninsula, and the Middle East. Almost 25 years after its establishment, researchers should explore the future of the bilateral agency. Will it be expanded to the rest of the region, as discussed in the section on Venezuela? Will it turn into a cooperative agreement for spreading the peaceful use of nuclear energy in Latin America? Moreover, will the system be strengthened or weakened by the action of the two main stakeholders? These remain important issues for a region that is interested in developing nuclear energy.

Conclusions

Latin America figures importantly in the scholarly debate over the spread of weapons of mass destruction. The previous pages provided an analysis of possible threats to Latin America's full renunciation of nuclear weapons and of the existing regimes of nuclear nonproliferation in the region, with special focus on the Venezuelan and Brazilian cases. Venezuela's decision to establish a civilian nuclear program, together with its ambiguous position towards international nonproliferation norms, raises the concerns of international scholars and policy-makers. Similarly, Brazil, a country that renounced nuclear weapons and is a vocal proponent of nuclear disarmament, has recently decided to expand its civilian nuclear program, to build a fleet of nuclear-powered submarines; furthermore, it continues to oppose the adoption of the Additional Protocol to IAEA safeguards.

This chapter provides reasons to believe that Latin American countries will not revise their attitude towards weapons of mass destruction, especially nuclear. Venezuela, in fact, renounced development of its nuclear program, and there are no elements suggesting the resumption of such ambitions in the near future. However, some Latin American countries may exercise influence on the nonproliferation regime, even short of acquiring nuclear weapons. International scholars should pay attention to Venezuela's attitude in the disarmament forums. The support and justification of Iranian and North Korean nuclear ambitions could, in fact, undermine the global efforts for preserving the nuclear nonproliferation regime and curbing the spread of weapons of mass destruction among state and nonstate actors. Similarly, Brazil will not change its position towards nuclear weapons. A global promoter of nuclear disarmament, Brazil has taken relevant steps for resuming its civilian nuclear programs and to acquire nuclear-powered submarines, but has not broken its nonproliferation commitments. After the self-imposition of constitutional limitations against nuclear weapons and the adoption of all the nonproliferation and disarmament norms, Brazil keeps an ambiguous position towards the IAEA Additional Protocol. However, together with Argentina, the government of Brasília found a temporary solution with the recognition of the ABACC system as an alternative to the IAEA Additional Protocol.

The existence of the regional regimes of nuclear nonproliferation and safeguards provides a clear answer to the central question of this essay: Will Latin America backtrack in the WMD realm? All the Latin American countries are parties of the Treaty of Tlatelolco, and the two major nuclear countries, with supposed nuclear weapon ambitions in the past, also established a bilateral system of mutual inspection of their nuclear facilities and material. The existing literature suggests that Latin America could become safer in the future, with the expansion of the ABACC system to the rest of the continent.

Future academic research will confirm if the Latin American countries will accept stricter nonproliferation rules, and if any country will abandon the current position towards nuclear weapons, the worst weapons of mass destruction. A deep analysis of the diplomatic attitude of the main Latin American players, such as Brazil and Argentina, in the debate over nuclear disarmament and nuclear nonproliferation will provide future researchers crucial data for interpreting the behavior of those actors towards stronger nonproliferation norms. While Latin America is currently a region with a firm commitment towards nuclear nonproliferation, the criticism of crucial Latin American countries towards several measures for strengthening the regime could weaken the global efforts for curbing the spread of nuclear weapons.

Note

1 By way of illustration, the William and Flora Hewlett Foundation financed several research initiatives for understanding current Brazilian nuclear ambitions, Brazilian-Argentine nuclear relations, and Latin American regional nuclear governance. Between 2012 and 2015 the Foundation awarded generous grants to the Carnegie Endowment for International Peace, the Getulio Vargas Foundation (*Fundação Getulio Vargas* – FGV), the University of Brasilia, and the Pontifical Catholic University of Rio de Janeiro. All those institutions organized or are currently organizing several workshops and conferences on nonproliferation in Latin America and are publishing the results of their research. The Getulio Vargas Foundation has carried out an outstanding research project on the history of the Brazilian nuclear program and on the roots of the Brazilian-Argentine cooperation in the atomic field. Such an effort has been done thanks to a very generous grant offered by the Brazilian funding authority for studies and projects (*Financiadora de Estudos e Projetos* – FINEP). The FGV is also part of the Nuclear Proliferation International History Project (NPIHIP) – a network based in the Woodrow Wilson Center for International Scholars in Washington – an initiative financed by the Carnegie Corporation of New York. Moreover, several projects are being carried out by the Stanley Foundation, the Konrad Adenauer Stiftung, and the Defense College of the North Atlantic Treaty Organization. Research on the history of Mexican and Argentinean behavior in the nuclear field is being carried out by, among others, prominent scholars such as Edna Suarez, Gisela Mateos, and Diego Hurtado.

References

Barletta, M.A. (1997) 'The Military Nuclear Program in Brazil', Working Paper, Center for International Security and Cooperation, Stanford, CA: Stanford University.

Carasales, J.C. and Ornstein, R.M. (1998) *La cooperación internacional de la Argentina*, Buenos Aires: CARI.

Dalaqua, R.H. (2013) 'Brazil and the Prague Agenda: Convergence and Conflict between Brasilia and Washington's Views on Achieving Nuclear Disarmament and Curbing Nuclear Proliferation', *CEBRI Artigos*, 1(8). Retrieved from midias.cebri.org/Brazil_Prague_Agenda.pdf.

Fuhrmann, M. (2012) *Atomic Assistance: How "Atoms for Peace" Programs Cause Nuclear Insecurity*, Ithaca, NY: Cornell University Press.

Garner, C. (2010) 'Venezuela's Nuclear Program – The Alarmists are Right', *International Affairs Review*. Retrieved from http://www.iar-gwu.org/node/240.

Hibbs, M. (2014) 'Looking Back at Brazil's Boreholes', *Arms Control Wonk*. Retrieved from http://hibbs.armscontrolwonk.com/archive/2670/looking-back-at-brazils-boreholes#comments.

Hirsch, T. (2004) 'The IAEA Additional Protocol. What It Is and Why It Matters', *The Nonproliferation Review*, 11(3): 147–167.

Hirst, J.D. and Pearl, J. (2010) 'Venezuela's Troubling Nuclear Ties', *Council of Foreign Relations*. Retrieved from www.cfr.org/venezuela/venezuelas-troubling-nuclear-ties/p232–67.

Homan, P. (2013) 'Exploring the Next Generation of Proliferators', *The Nonproliferation Review*, 20(1): 63–80.

Hurtado de Mendoza, D. (2014) *El sueño de la Argentina atómica: Política, tecnología nuclear y desarrollo nacional (1945–2006)*, Buenos Aires: Edhasa.

Hymans, J.E.C. (2015) 'The Dynamics of Nuclear Politics: Lessons from Latin America' in A. Covarrubias and J. I. Domínguez (eds) *Routledge Handbook of Latin America in the World*, New York: Routledge, pp. 362–375.

Kassenova, T. (2014) *Brazil's Nuclear Kaleidoskope: An Evolving Identity*, Washington, DC: Carnegie Endowment for International Peace.

Kroenig, M. (2010) *Exporting the Bomb: Technology Transfer and the Spread of Nuclear Weapons*, Ithaca, NY: Cornell University Press.

Kutchesfahani, S.Z. (2014) *Politics and the Bomb: The Role of Experts in the Creation of Cooperative Nuclear Non-Proliferation Agreements*, New York: Routledge.

Mallea, R. (2012) 'La cuestión nuclear en la relación Argentino–Brasileña (1968–1984)', Master's thesis, Universidade do Estado do Rio de Janeiro, Brazil.
Monteiro, N. and Debbs, A. (2015) *Nuclear Politics: The Strategic Logic of Proliferation*, New York: Cambridge University Press.
Palmer, L. and Milhollin, G. (2004) 'Brazil's Nuclear Puzzle', *Science*, 306(696): 617.
Patti, C. (2010) 'Brazil and the Nuclear Issues in the Years of the Luiz Inácio Lula da Silva Government (2003–2010)', *Revista Brasileira de Política Internacional*, 53(2): 178–197.
——— (2012) 'Brazil in Global Nuclear Order', Ph.D. dissertation, Università degli Studi di Firenze, Italy.
——— (2014a) *O programa nuclear Brasileiro: Uma história oral*, Rio de Janeiro: CPDOC/FGV.
——— (2014b) 'The Origins of the Brazilian Nuclear Programme (1951–1955)', *Cold War History*. doi :10.1080/14682745.2014.968557
——— (2015, published online 2014) 'The Origins of the Brazilian Nuclear Programme, 1951–1955', *Cold War History*, 15(1). doi:10.1080/14682745.2014.968557
Philippe, S. (2014) 'Safeguarding the Military Naval Nuclear Fuel Cycle', *Journal of Nuclear Materials Management*, 42(3): 40–52.
Rublee, M. R. (2010) 'The Nuclear Threshold States: Challenges and Opportunities Posed by Brazil and Japan', *The Nonproliferation Review*, 17(1): 49–70.
Sagan, S. (1996) 'Why Do States Build Nuclear Weapons?', *International Security,* 21 (3): 54–86.
Taylor, P. D. (2009) 'Why Does Brazil Need Nuclear Submarines?', *Proceedings Magazine*, 135/6/1,276.
Thielmann, G. (2012) 'Submarine Nuclear Reactors: A Worsening Proliferation Challenge' in *Threat Assessment Brief*. The Arms Control Association. Retrieved from https://www.armscontrol.org/files/TAB_Submarine_Nuclear_Reactors.pdf.
Thielmann, G. and Kelleher-Vergantini, S. (2013) 'The Naval Nuclear Reactor Threat to the NPT', *Arms Control Association*. Retrieved from www.armscontrol.org/files/TAB_Naval_Nuclear_Reactor_Threat_to_the_NPT_2013.pdf.
Trinkunas, H.A. (2006) 'Assessing Potential Nuclear Proliferation Networks in Latin America: 2006–2016', *The Nonproliferation Review*, 13(3): 617–625.
Viera de Jesus, D. S. (2011) 'Building Trust and Flexibility: A Brazilian View of the Fuel Swap with Iran', *The Washington Quarterly*, 34(2): 61–75.
Wheeler, N. J. (2009) 'Beyond Waltz's Nuclear World: More Trust May be Better', *International Relations*, 23(3): 428–445.

19

THE POLITICS OF ARMS ACQUISITIONS IN SOUTH AMERICA

Trends and research agenda[1]

Jorge Battaglino

Arms purchases have greatly increased in South America in recent years, climbing 92 per cent from the 1997–2005 period to the 2005–2013 period (SIPRI 2014).[2] The prior wave of arms purchases developed during the 1970s when the region was undergoing a time of military competition between Argentina, Chile, and Brazil; Chile and Peru; Peru and Ecuador; and Colombia and Venezuela. Up to the early 1990s the region was defined as a zone of negative peace (Hurrell 1998; Kacowicz 1998), characterized by distrust, arms races, and military competition. Furthermore, these zones are characterized by the predominance of nondemocratic regimes and by a low level of economic relations (Martin 2006). The quality of peace is low, since war has not been ruled out (Kacowicz 1998). Since the 1990s, however, the region has increasingly moved towards stable peace. Some significant border differences have been resolved, military cooperation has deepened, and an unprecedented process of building regional institutions is underway. Zones of stable peace are defined by the presence of confidence and trust. States do not prepare for armed conflict with neighboring countries, nor expect neighbors to do so. This context is mostly associated by the presence of democratic rule and strong economic relations between countries. Although the impact of democracy and economic relations on the emergence of a zone of stable peace is still unclear, the presence of these two factors has had a positive impact on the quality of the peace (Kacowicz 1998).

In this process of developing a stable peace, how can one explain major arms purchases? Do they represent the return of interstate conflict in the region? Are they a manifestation of changes in threat perceptions of South American countries? Scholarly work on contemporary arms purchases in South America is scarce and limited to a few case studies. The analysis of the motivations and nature of arms purchases is critical to understanding the dynamics of regional peace and security in a region. This chapter lays out a research agenda for understanding and explaining major arms purchases in an evolving zone of peace.

This chapter has four main sections. The first discusses methodological issues related to researching arms purchases, and the second examines the state of the art regarding the literature on arms acquisitions. A third section examines the central features of arms purchases during the period of 2005–2013, and a fourth forwards the possible motivations of such acquisitions in the cases of Argentina, Brazil, Chile, and Venezuela. The concluding section summarizes a research agenda for the topic.

Defense budget or arms spending?

South American arms purchases are widely reported by the media and, to a lesser extent, by academia. Among the former, there is a tendency to blend the resources allocated to the defense budget with those assigned to the purchase of weapons. In other words, an increase in the defense budget is automatically associated with more weapons purchases. The reality suggests otherwise – e.g., Argentina increased its military budget by 123 per cent from 2004 to 2013, compared to 1997–2004, but reduced purchases of weapons 467 per cent at the same time (SIPRI 2014). In fact, analysis of South American countries' defense budgets reveals no relationship between total defense spending and weapons purchases. The country allocating the most resources to its defense, Brazil, is only the third-largest importer of weapons; whereas Chile, the biggest spender on arms in the region, has a military budget four times smaller than that of Brazil. Similarly, Venezuela is the second-largest importer of weapons, but maintains only the fourth-largest military budget, which is very similar to that of Argentina, the fifth importer.

This chapter focuses on arms purchases through an analysis of variations in *arms imports spending*. Measuring arms spending in South America is a complex task that entails analysis of the defense budgets of all countries, year by year, and identifying items that have been earmarked for the purchase of military equipment. This is a difficult task not only because each country names these items differently (capital expenditures, investments, acquisitions), but also because in many cases there is no discrimination of the budgeted resources.[3] For instance, the subitem 'weapons systems for the Army' may comprise not only the incorporation of different kinds of equipment, from tanks to missiles, but also the maintenance of existing equipment or simply the acquisition of spares. In the case of significant purchases, secret agreements are typically signed without publishing the amounts in official budgets.[4] The same happens when acquisitions are made through loans provided by the selling country. Furthermore, the approved budget is not always entirely spent; therefore, the budgeted number cannot be taken as a literal representation of the amount acquired. These limitations are intrinsic to any comparative study on this topic, but can be partially overcome by using a standardized measure. The only database that collects information on this variable using a standardized methodology is that of the SIPRI arms transfers. While the use of this database can be contested, as it does not include domestic production of weapons, it is also true that South American countries produce small quantities of arms and when they do, as in the cases of Argentina and Brazil, they tend to import the most advanced and expensive components. For this reason, arms import figures will account for almost all of the most important items of military equipment acquired by states in South America during the period analyzed.[5]

Argentina, Brazil, Chile, and Venezuela together account for 84 per cent of the total armament imports of South America between 1997 and 2013. The chapter compares the two periods of 1997–2004 and 2005–2013, as 2005 represents a turning point marking the acceleration in acquisitions of military equipment, coinciding with a period of widespread economic growth that began in 2002.

The arms dynamic literature

This section examines a different theoretical lens used to conceptualize the factors that drive states to acquire weapons. Academic analyses of the motivations for arms acquisitions use the concept of an 'arms dynamic,' which is "the entire set of pressures that makes actors (usually states) both acquire armed forces and change the quantity and quality of the armed forces they already possess" (Buzan and Herring 1998: 790). The voluminous literature on 'arms dynamic' can be grouped into two main blocks: studies that analyze the reasons for acquisitions and those that investigate their impact on interstate security. It is noteworthy that most of the existing research on this topic in South America is dissociated from theoretical approaches to arms purchases. Moving from empirical description to theoretically based analysis is an important step for social scientists working on South American arms issues.

Realism

A substantial part of the theoretical literature and general information on the subject is based on the assumptions of realism. In the realist world perceptions of external threats pose a central role in the decision of a state to acquire weapons. This dynamic is fuelled by the security dilemma that favors a logic of action and reaction in which states check dangerous concentrations of power by building up their own capabilities (internal balancing), or aggregating their capabilities with other states in alliances (external balancing) (Waltz 1979). This interaction can trigger arms races, defined as a dynamic of action and reaction between two countries experiencing an intense security dilemma (Hammond 1993). Some authors have attempted to explain arms purchases in South America using this concept (Calle 2007; Malamud and Garcia Encina 2006). However, the action-reaction pattern is not present in the region. Peru and Colombia, which maintain border and ideological disputes with Chile and Venezuela, respectively, have not acquired weapons in response to purchases made by their neighbors. Moreover, in cases where military spending has increased, it is not apparent that external threat in the region played a role. Brazil and Chile, for instance, do not perceive significant threats to their security from the region, yet have acquired large amounts of weapons. Meanwhile, Argentina has only procured a small amount of weaponry, in spite of being surrounded by the more powerful armed forces of Brazil and Chile (Battaglino 2008). A realist might explain that anomaly using balance of threat theory, which holds that states balance against threats, not the concentration of military capabilities (Walt 1985).

Although Brazil and Venezuela identify extraregional threats to their defense, the automatic application of the action and reaction model does not provide an accurate understanding of the phenomenon. Realist-oriented analysts need to include analyses of the military strategies of the countries of the region, the recent evolution of defense issues, and progress/setbacks in regional relations in the political, economic, and military dimensions to determine more accurately the source of the perceived threat and its relation to the type of weaponry purchased, as well as to anticipate the impact that acquisitions may have on regional security.

Domestic arms dynamics

Some analysts emphasize a 'domestic arms dynamics' that is mainly self-generating and not strongly linked to the external actions of other states. Domestic factors can be broadly subdivided into three types: economic, bureaucratic/organizational, and political.

Economic explanations assume that countries experiencing higher levels of economic growth should buy more weapons (Dunne and Perlo-Freeman 2003; Frederiksen and Looney 1983). This hypothesis could be complemented by the idea that countries with larger GDPs spend more on arms than those with lower GDPs. This argument is fairly intuitive, and the causal chain of high economic growth, rising public spending, and expanded defense budgets is a compelling account of the regional trend of increased spending on arms. However, the argument does not explain why countries with similar rates of economic growth acquire different quantities of weapons. Neither data on average GDP growth nor ranking by nominal

GDP between 2000 and 2013 provide a clear pattern between the size of an economy and the amount of resources allocated to the purchase of weapons. For example, Brazil's GDP is the largest in South America and 10 times larger than that of Chile, yet Brazil is only the third-largest importer of weapons in the region, after Chile and Venezuela.[6] The same applies to Venezuela, whose GDP is twice that of Chile. Argentina has the second-largest GDP and is the state that spends less than Chile, Venezuela, Brazil, Colombia, Peru, and Ecuador. As noted above there is also no correlation between countries with the highest weapons purchases in recent years and those with the highest defense budgets. Although the economic boom of the 2000s in the region created favorable conditions for the purchase of military equipment, the causal mechanisms are not obvious. More research on how economic variables interact with other potential causal variables to produce variations on arms expenditures is needed. A comparison with the domestic dynamics operating in the prior wave of arms acquisitions would be especially helpful.

Other domestic factors could be bureaucratic politics or organizational cultures such as military doctrines (Brzoska 2004; Smith and Tasiran 2005). There are no studies that try to explain the arms purchases in South America from this perspective – only a few mention those issues (Bromley and Guevara 2010). Since bureaucratic and organizational processes are often dissociated from the perception of external threat and even from economic cycles, this could constitute a promising avenue of research on arms acquisitions.

Domestic politics approaches focus mainly on the 'military industrial complex,' although some explain arms purchases in terms of the need for governments to boost the economy in times of economic downturn or to protect jobs. The only work that has analyzed the impact of the military industrial complex in South America is that of Pion-Berlin (2007), who argues that this complex is not sufficiently developed to favor the alliance between congress, politicians, and the defense industry. However, this line of research should not be completely discarded, especially if one takes into account the recent revival and strengthening of the defense industry in several countries in South America.

Liberalism

Liberal approaches are based on the assumption that the presence of certain political features (regime type) and economic conditions (level of economic interaction), among others, influence whether arms purchases are perceived as threats to the countries of a region (Russett 1993). In this sense, this account is 'contextual-centered,' unlike realism that favors an 'arms-centered' explanation (Butfoy 1997).

Among the contextual-centered theories, the 'liberal triad' offers a parsimonious explanation based on the pacifying effect of democracy, trade, and international institutions. Thus, purchases of weapons made in a region where democracies have strong economic relations and where robust regional institutions exist should not increase threat perception. A few studies have analyzed the impact of these variables in South America. Jorge Battaglino (2012) and Brigitte Weiffen et al. (2011) argue that the establishment of regional institutions such as UNASUR has encouraged the development of regional networks of civil and military officials that contribute to the circulation of information, particularly as related to the strategic intentions of its members. This interaction, in turn, plays a key role in generating trust and transforming previous perceptions of rivalry and competition, resulting in a different meaning to arms purchases than that in the 1970s and 1980s (see Malamud and Schenoni, this volume). How much and how adequately these institutions of regional governance ease anarchy remains open to question. However, understanding and explaining the context of regional security in

South America increasingly requires incorporating the role of regional institutions such as UNASUR and the South American Defense Council (SADC).

The literature on the 'democratic peace' has been scarcely developed in the region. One cannot claim that democracy causes peace in South America because peace lasted for much of the 20th century, though democracy was scarce. However, several authors argue that the democratization of the 1980s and 1990s has helped improve the quality of regional peace (Kacowicz 1998; Oelsner 2007). Democratic leaders proved willing and committed not only to cooperate in political, economic, and military matters (especially in the Southern Cone), but also to resolve any pending territorial conflicts peacefully. A number of territorial conflicts have been solved since the return of democracy in the 1980s, though others remain. The advent of democracy may have further strengthened the region's historical predisposition to settling disputes through peaceful means (Kacowicz 1998, 2005). Notably, the strengthening of South American zones of peace in recent years has developed in the context of new forms of democracy that emphasize the participatory dimension more than the liberal tradition. To turn this empirical correlation into a causal argument, however, requires a rethinking of the theory of democratic peace, since it suggests that neither democracy nor economic integration need to be liberal to promote peace or reduce perceptions of threat. Theorizing the mechanisms that promote peace in a region in which the liberal dimension of most of its democracies is attenuated at different levels would constitute a major contribution to international relations theory in general.

Zones of peace

Another contextual approach is the zones of peace theory. This perspective may be useful to explain the motivations of the purchases and their impact on the security of a region. The scarcity of wars during the 20th century led South America to be defined as "the most peaceful region in the world" (Holsti 1996: 155). The main cause of this 'long regional peace' was the shared normative consensus for the peaceful settlement of international disputes that prevailed among South American nations (Kacowicz 1998, 2005).

Although realism and liberalism have their own explanations on the sources of peace and conflict, some authors have argued that the combination of both theories is a promising way to deal with peace foundations (Kacowicz 1998; Miller 2007). These authors propose a series of variables that situate the 'zone of stable peace' as beginning with the return of democracy. Some have gone as far as defining it as an emerging pluralistic security community. In either of these perspectives, the recent wave of arms purchases is not an indicator of the return of conflict scenarios among South American countries. As Kacowicz sustains, "there is a great overlap between stable peace and pluralistic security communities" (1998: 61). An important line of research is not only the improvement of the classifications on regional types of peace, but also the empirical development of indicators of their evolution and, fundamentally, the enrichment of our theoretical understanding on the relations between types of peace and specific patterns of arms purchases.

Constructivism

The constructivist perspective is rarely employed to explain arms purchases in South America. For constructivists, beliefs, expectations, and interpretations are inescapable factors for explaining human behavior. One constructivist explanation of the purchase of weapons utilizes the concept of 'global military culture' to postulate that motivations for the acquisition of defense technology have less to do with objective threats and the military application of technology and more to do with the meanings attached to such technology (Collins 2007: 315). Thus, weapons may more often have been acquired for reasons of national prestige, as symbols of statehood, as both agents of symbols of modernization or as vehicles to cement alliances. Some studies have explained Brazil's arms purchases as symbolic attributes a rising power must necessarily possess (Duarte Villa and Weiffen 2014). More research is needed on what culture of anarchy (Hobbesian, Lockean, or Kantian) prevails in the region, if any actually predominates, or if there is a coexistence of cultures. The analysis of the shared understandings behind these cultures is a line of research of great relevance to account for the impact of arms purchases on regional security (see Thies, this volume).

Who sold, who bought, and what did they buy?

Taken together, weapons purchases in our four cases have seen a 92 per cent increase, from $6.3 billion dollars between 1997 and 2004 to $12.5 billion between 2005 and 2013.[7] Five facts in South American arms purchases during the period of 2005–2013 reveal themselves: (1) a significant increase in the amount of purchases in the region, (2) a reduction in sales from some traditional suppliers, such as France and the United Kingdom, with a significant rise in sales from other established suppliers, including Spain, Italy, and Holland, (3) the emergence of new players in the regional arms trade such as China and Russia, (4) substantial increases in acquisitions in two cases (Chile and Venezuela), a slight reduction in one case (Brazil), and a significant drop in another (Argentina), and (5) the main armaments acquired in most cases are different types of aircrafts, followed by ships.

The top five arms suppliers during the most recent period were Russia with 24.5 per cent of the total, the United States with 13.1 per cent, Germany with 10.4 per cent, The Netherlands with 9.2 per cent, and Spain with 7.9 per cent. This profile represents important changes in relation to the previous period (1997–2004). Traditional suppliers like France, Britain, and the United States reduced their sales by 24.5 per cent ($953 million in 1997–2004 to $719 million in 2005–2012), 20.8 per cent ($719 million to $569 million), and 18.4 per cent ($2 billion to $1.6 billion), respectively. By contrast, other regular suppliers significantly increased their sales: Italy by 533 per cent ($155 million to $982 million), Spain by 516 per cent ($166 million to $1 billion), Holland by 194 per cent ($401 million to $1.1 billion), Israel by 134 per cent ($264 million to $618 million), and Germany by 102 per cent ($664 million to $1.3 billion). Finally, new providers emerged, having had virtually no presence during the previous period: China increased its sales by 5,087 per cent ($8 million to $415 million) and Russia increased by 929 per cent ($305 million to $3.1 billion).

In terms of purchasers, Chile acquired the most weapons between 2005 and 2013, with a total of $3.8 billion dollars, accounting for 31.8 per cent of regional purchases. This reveals an increase of 277 per cent when compared to the previous period. Chile has allocated much of its resources to the acquisition of warships and combat aircrafts and has relied on The Netherlands, Britain, and Germany as its main suppliers.

Venezuela is the second-largest buyer of equipment in the region, with a total of $3.7 billion dollars and a growth rate of 772 per cent. Its main suppliers have been Russia, China, and Spain, with purchases largely consisting of combat aircrafts, armored vehicles, and warships.

In third place is Brazil, showing a slight nine per cent reduction in purchases ($2.2 billion to $2 billion). Brazil acquired 16.9 per cent of all weapons in the region during the period of 2005–2013, with the most important incorporations being combat aircrafts and ships provided by France, Germany, and the United States.

Finally, the case of Argentina reveals an important decline in purchases by 467 per cent ($959 million to $169 million). The United States has been the country's main supplier, followed by Germany and France.

These purchases by the four main buyers in the region were distributed as 42.6 per cent of the regional imports for fighter planes, 26.2 per cent for warships, and 10.9 per cent for armored vehicles. This pattern of spending is related to the higher cost of aerial combat systems and the fact that most of the warships were acquired secondhand. For instance, Chile received a delivery of 10 F16 C/D Block-50 and Venezuela 24 SU30 MKV. Most Latin American navies, nevertheless, are in the process of either procuring frigates on the secondhand market or upgrading their existing frigate and submarine fleets.

Motivations of Argentina, Brazil, Chile, and Venezuela

The following section reviews potential causes and effects of weapons purchases in the cases of Argentina, Brazil, Chile, and Venezuela. The discussion is not exhaustive but seeks to show how to operate some of the theories discussed in the previous section. It is important to note that these are offered explanations, but we lack theoretically informed comparative analyses to evaluate these preferred explanations.

Chile: Analysts often attribute Chile's status as the highest spender on arms in the region to both the ample financial resources derived from the Copper Law and the importance attributed by their elites to the deployment of a modern military organization possessing last-generation weaponry. Chile's traditional image is of a country with strong and efficient institutions, willing to cooperate with the West in the maintenance of international peace and security (Martin 2010). In this context, the military has been a symbol of national prestige and particularly a vehicle to cement alliances through international deployment.

Chile's defense strategy, however, is changing. One can postulate that this process has been driven by the gradual resolution of nearly all of its territorial disputes. The most important territorial conflicts with Argentina were resolved in the 1990s. Current disputes with Bolivia and Peru are expressed in diplomatic negotiations. An additional factor may be a new international stance by Chilean elites, who "have abandoned completely regional isolationism and belligerence as the primary means of effectuating Chilean national and security interests" (Martin 2010).

Chilean politicians and military, alike, have favored the armed forces' adoption of a NATO military standard. In fact, the arms purchases made by Chile during the last eight years have transformed it into the only state in the region to follow NATO standards (Duarte Villa 2008). The most important items acquired by Chile were eight secondhand frigates, two Scorpene submarines, 200 Leopard-2 tanks, and 48 aircraft F-16. In addition, Chile has recently taken another step to organize military capabilities that enable its participation in multilateral missions. In 2012, the first Amphibious Expeditionary Brigade was created, becoming the first of its kind in the history of Latin America. This is a rapid deployment force composed of four battalions of marines and a Strategic Projection Ship. Chile also signed an agreement of association with the Common Security and Defense Policy (CSDP) of the European Union in October of 2013, thereby becoming its first South American member. The agreement will allow for the participation of its armed forces in EU-led international operations.

Chilean arms purchases are among the most challenging for analysts to understand. While the NATO standards make Chile more compatible with NATO-level military forces for international missions, the submarines, battle tanks, and fighter aircraft of the Chileans have not been deployed on extraregional missions, and do not appear to be part of Chile's international peacekeeping profile. The purchases, nevertheless, also increase Chile's abilities within its neighborhood. A question for research, therefore, is how to explain these particular purchases in light of the new defense strategy.

Venezuela: The acquisition of military equipment in the case of Venezuela has been primarily driven by the surge of economic resources flowing from the latest oil boom, as well as by a shift in perceptions of threat, which has identified the United States as the main threat to security. This new scenario of conflict has been functional to legitimize the numerous weapons purchases in recent years. Until the late 1990s, the main mission assigned to the Venezuelan military was the preparation for a conventional conflict with Colombia. However, the perception of threat changed drastically after the 2002 coup attempt, which Chávez accused of being backed by the United States (Jacome 2006, 2011). Although conventional conflict with Colombia has not been completely ruled out, the possibility of a confrontation with the United States has become the main concern for the armed forces. The possibility of a conflict with Colombia is primarily associated with the scenario of an intervention of the United States that uses its territory as a bridgehead. The scenario of a military conflict against the United States has two main components in the Venezuelan military doctrine, one conventional and one asymmetrical. The latter contemplates the implementation of a strategy of national resistance for a prolonged period of time against an invasion from the United States. To this end, in mid-2007 this doctrine led Venezuela to acquire 5,000 sniper rifles from Moscow and 1,800 shoulder-fired antiaircraft missiles (*The Washington Post* 2010). Venezuela has concurrently bought equipment to maintain, at least for a short period of time, a conventional, or symmetrical, conflict with a Great Power while also acquiring material to sustain an asymmetrical resistance.

This combination of missions demands not only the acquisition of light equipment but also of some of the most advanced weapons, such as the Su-30MK combat aircraft or the S-300 air defense systems. Long-term Russian loans have been fundamental for the acquisition of such equipment. Since 2005, Russia replaced the United States and Europe as the main supplier of military equipment to the Bolivarian state. There are two prominent phases discernible in the arms trade between the two countries. Between 2005 and 2007, Venezuela and Russia signed 12 contracts worth a total of between three and 4.4 billion U.S. dollars (Bromley and Guevara 2010). These deals covered the acquisition of 10 Mi-35 combat helicopters, three Mi-26 heavy helicopters, 40 Mi-17 helicopters, 100,000 AK-103 rifles, and 24 Su-30MK combat aircrafts. The second phase began in September 2009, when Russia agreed to loan Venezuela over $2.2 billion to finance the purchase of T-72 tanks and S-300 air defense systems, among other equipment, which was completely delivered in 2014. This material has been displayed in several military parades.

Brazil: The emerging world power is the third-leading buyer of arms in the region, but is also one of the two countries that have reduced its purchases, with a nine per cent decrease between the first period and the second. It should be noted, however, that SIPRI data have yet to incorporate the costs that will reflect recently announced major acquisitions. The most important purchases were acquired from France under the military agreement signed in September of 2009 for $18 billion. Effective through 2020, the agreement includes the provision of four Scorpene submarines, the hull of a nuclear submarine, and 50 EC-725 helicopters. Moreover, it was recently announced that the Swedish aerospace company Saab would provide 36 Saab JAS 39 Gripen fighter aircraft. With these purchases taken into account, Brazil will surpass Chile as the top regional buyer of weapons within the next few years.

The scope of these acquisitions is often linked by analysts to both the implementation of a new defense strategy as a result of the perception of new threats, and the emergence of a shared understanding among Brazilian elites that a rising power must develop proper military capabilities (Duarte Villa and Weiffen 2014). For much of the 20th century, Brazilian defense assessments were determined by the likelihood of a war with Argentina. This scenario was abandoned thanks to an intense process of political, economic, and military cooperation that began in the 1980s and continues today (Kacowicz 1998). This remarkable change in bilateral relations had an inevitable impact on the missions assigned to the armed forces. While Argentina ceased to represent a threat, the Amazonian region began to be identified in the early 1990s as the main security concern. The new edition of the *Defense Policy* (DP), issued in 2005, officially articulated a scenario of conflict that had been debated during the previous decade: the defense of the Amazon against a Great Power invasion.[8] Additionally, the publication of the *National Defense Strategy* (NDS) in 2008 further clarified the mission by establishing the need to mount a hybrid defense strategy to be implemented against an invasion. Accordingly, the military must be prepared "for asymmetrical warfare, especially in the Amazonian region, to resist an enemy of superior military power" (Government of Brazil 2008). Nevertheless, the navy and air force should also have conventional capabilities to "deny the use of the sea to any concentration of enemy forces approaching Brazil by sea" and "secure local air superiority" (Government of Brazil 2008). The recent discovery of offshore oil reserves has been another factor that has significantly influenced the orientation of the NDS. As a direct result, the Brazilian Navy intends to increase its patrol and power projection capabilities considerably, expecting to invest an estimated $70 billion by the mid-2030s. This includes the acquisition of more than 50 ships (Government of Brazil 2012).

In this sense, the significant increase of weapons purchases is directly related to the impact that the defense strategy has had on the missions of the armed forces. It is one thing to pose a conflict scenario with Argentina and quite another to identify Great Powers as potential adversaries; the latter case necessarily entails greater pressure to acquire the latest and most advanced equipment. This modernization process of military hardware, the largest in Brazilian history, has received full support from politicians who believe that defense capabilities are intrinsic to the rise of Brazil as a global power.

Nevertheless, the types of weapons purchased by Brazil, particularly the nuclear submarine, are criticized by some analysts as not the most efficient means of defending Brazil's coastal or deep sea waters (Diniz 2009). This potential gap between military strategy and arms purchases raises another challenge for analysts seeking to explain the overall level of purchases and their makeup.

Argentina: The expenditure on weaponry in Argentina has proved the lowest in the region during the latest period analyzed. Despite the economic boom in the country since 2003, the lack of social and political support for military spending on weapons has been the main obstacle to increasing it. Certainly, politicians and civilians in general have exhibited a remarkable lack of interest in defense issues since 1983. This trend is a product of the political, economic, and military failures of the last military dictatorship (1976–1983). The defeat in the Malvinas War, together with the deep economic crisis and massive human rights violations committed by the regime, finally meant the downfall of a culture of militarism and praetorianism that had characterized the Argentine political system during the previous decades. Since then, the resulting deficit of social interest in defense issues has not favored a scenario of significant weapons purchases (Battaglino 2013; Pion-Berlin and Trinkunas 2007).

Final remarks and agenda for future research

This chapter presented the main theories on the purchases of weapons and their effects on interstate relations. The analysis revealed that studies on this topic in the region are scarce and in most cases are largely based on empirical correlations rather than theoretical argumentation about cause and effect. The research agenda on arms purchases clearly requires greater attention from social scientists.

The literature on arms purchases in the region agrees neither on the causes nor its implications for regional security. Perhaps this is because South America could be going through a transition in security dynamics, where the old coexists with the new. In this way, while some authors see acquisitions as a new indicator of a dynamics of military competition that never disappeared (Mares 2012), others interpret them as irrelevant because the context of rivalry that prevailed during the last century has largely disappeared (Battaglino 2008, 2012). However, the argument that the region is undergoing a new dynamic of regional security qualitatively different from those that existed a few decades ago should not be taken as a fact but as a research question. This line of inquiry should include a discussion of the advantages and disadvantages of contextual and arms-centered approaches.

Moreover, traditional theories hold great explanatory power as long as limitations are taken into account when analyzing the South American experience. For example, the theory of balance of threat may contribute to a less linear and decontextualized realist approach to the phenomenon of purchases. Similarly, the fact that several of these democracies do not manifest the normative or institutional factors that the democratic peace theory sees as causal is a theoretical anomaly that should be investigated; the payoff could be a nonliberal democracy model that can explain peace.[9]

As demonstrated in this chapter, a simple economic model to explain spending on defense and weapons is inadequate. Certainly economic factors will matter, but they must be integrated into a causal explanation with other variables to explain variations in expenditures. Less straightforward but perhaps as promising would be the analysis of bureaucratic/organizational processes that stimulate purchases. In particular, the impact of the intra and inter services disputes and military doctrines in the number and type of weapons purchased could be a fruitful avenue to pursue.

Finally, researchers who consider that the region is undergoing a transformation in its defense orientations should consider the concept of "deficit of threat, in terms of the low probability of intra-regional conflicts."[10] Overcoming this deficit has been one of the main catalysts for the reconfiguration of threats formulated by many of the countries across the region. The most significant evidence of this has been the increasing adoption by South American countries of military missions that envisage extraregional threats or the possibility of extraregional deployment of the armed forces. At least four countries (Argentina, Brazil, Bolivia, and Venezuela) have identified potential scenarios involving military conflict with an extraregional state, and a fifth state, Chile, has oriented its defense strategy toward the international employment of its armed forces. This is an entirely new and exciting trend. More research is needed on how countries are meeting their deficit of threat; this line of research is essential to anticipate whether the political response to this deficit is reinforcing, or weakening, the intraregional peace.

Notes

1 I would like to thank the comments and advice of David Mares and Arie Kacowicz; their insights and ideas contributed decisively to improve the overall quality of this chapter.
2 The four cases selected for this study account for 84 per cent of the arms purchases in Latin America during the period under study; therefore, they can be taken as a sample for the whole region.
3 With the aim of resolving this limitation the South American Defense Spending Record was established in 2012, in the framework of the South American Defense Council of the UNASUR. The main goal of this record is to build a common methodology for measuring defense spending in the region.
4 Since the registry has been recently launched there is still no published data.

5 The most important items of military equipment are combat aircrafts, helicopters, tanks, and capital ships.
6 The data of this paragraph is from SIPRI (2014).
7 All the figures are in constant dollars.
8 Note that both the DP and the NDS makes no reference as to which would be that Great Power.
9 I would like to thank David Mares for this observation.
10 The concept of "deficit of threats" refers to the disappearance, or loss of relevance, of those scenarios – mainly threats of state origin, which had historically oriented the military deployment, organization, and budget (Buzan 2006).

References

Battaglino, J. (2008) 'Palabras mortales ¿Rearme y carrera armamentista en América del Sur?', *Nueva Sociedad*, 215: 23–34.

——— (2012) 'Defence in a Post Hegemonic Regional Agenda: The Case of the South American Defence Council' in R. Riggirozzi and D. Tussie (eds) *The Rise of Post-Hegemonic Regionalism: The Case of Latin America*, London: Springer, pp. 81–100.

——— (2013) 'The Determinants of Arms Spending in South America', *Journal of Politics in Latin America*, 5(1): 71–103.

Bromley, M. and Guevara, I. (2010) 'Arms Modernization in Latin America' in A.T.H. Tan (ed) The Global Arms Trade: A Handbook, London: Routledge, pp. 166–178.

Brzoska, M. (2004) 'The Economic of Arms Imports after the End of the Cold War', *Defence and Peace Economics*, 15(2): 111–123.

Butfoy, A. (1997) 'Offence–Defence Theory and the Security Dilemma: The Problem with Marginalizing the Context', *Contemporary Security Policy*, 18(3): 38–58.

Buzan, B. (2006). 'Will the Global War on Terrorism be the New Cold War?', *International Affairs*, 82(6): 1101–1118.

Buzan, B. and Herring, E. (1998) *The Arms Dynamic in World Politics*, Boulder, CO: Lynne Rienner.

Calle, F. (2007) 'Rambo, versión Sudamericana el impacto regional del rearme de Venezuela y Chile', *Nueva Sociedad*, 211: 13–21.

Collins, A. (2007) *Contemporary Security Studies*, Oxford: Oxford University Press.

Diniz, E. (2009) 'Defesa, orçamento e projeto de força: O Brasil em perspectiva comparada' in M. Cepik (ed) *Segurança internacional: Práticas, tendências e conceitos*, São Paulo: Hucitec, pp. 148–166.

Duarte Villa, R. (2008) 'Corrida armamentista ou modernizacao de Armamentos na America do Sul: Estudo comparativo dos gastos militares'. Retrieved from http://observatorio.iesp.uerj.br/images/pdf/estudos/8_estudosecenarios_2008-12%20-%20Estudos_Villa.pdf.

Duarte Villa, R. and Weiffen, B. (2014) 'South American Re-armament: From Balancing to Symbolizing Power', *Contemporary Security Policy*, 35(1): 138–162.

Dunne, J. and Perlo-Freeman, S. (2003) 'The Demand for Military Spending in Developing Countries', *International Review of Applied Economics*, 17(1): 23–48.

Frederiksen, P. C and Looney, R. E. (1983) 'Defense Expenditures and Economic Growth in Developing Countries', *Armed Forces and Society*, 9(4): 633–645.

Government of Brazil (2008) *National Defence Strategy*, Brasilia: Ministerio de Defensa.

——— (2012) *Libro blanco de la defensa 2012*, Brasilia: Ministerio de Defensa.

Hammond, G.T. (1993) *Plowshares into Swords: Arms Races in International Politics, 1840–1991*, Columbia, SC: University of South Carolina Press.

Holsti, H.J. (1996) *The State, War and the State of the War*, Cambridge: Cambridge University Press.

Hurrell, A. (1998) 'An Emerging Security Community in South America?' in E. Adler and M. Barnett (eds) *Security Communities*, Cambridge: Cambridge University Press, pp. 137–154.

Jacome, F. (2006) *Venezuela frente al contexto andino y hemisférico ¿Cambios en la doctrina de seguridad? 1999–2005*, Caracas: ILDIS.

——— (2011) 'Venezuela: defensa y seguridad. Bolivarianismo y socialismo del siglo XXI' in H. Mathieu and C. Guarnido (eds) *Anuario 2011 de la seguridad regional en América Latina y el Caribe*, Bogotá: Friedrich Ebert Stiftung, pp. 286–309.

Kacowicz, A. (1998) *Zones of Peace in the Third World: South America and West Africa in Comparative Perspective*, Albany: State of New York Press.

——— (2005) *The Impact of Norms in International Society: The Latin American Experience, 1881–2001*, Notre Dame: University of Notre Dame Press.

Malamud, C. and García Encina, C. (2006) '¿Rearme o renovación del equipamiento militar en América Latina?' in Documento de Trabajo No. 31, Madrid: Real Instituto Elcano.

Mares, D. (2012) *Latin America and the Illusion of Peace*, London: International Institute for Strategic Studies/Routledge.

Martin, F. (2006) *Militarist Peace in South America: Conditions for War and Peace*, New York: Palgrave/MacMillan Press.

——— (2010) 'Chilean Strategic Culture' in *Findings Report* 10, Miami: Florida International University.

Miller, B. (2007) *States, Nations, and the Great Powers: The Sources of Regional War and Peace*, Cambridge: Cambridge University Press.

Oelsner, A. (2007) 'Friendship, Mutual Trust and the Evolution of Regional Peace in the International System', *Critical Review of International Social and Political Philosophy*, 10(2): 257–279.

Pion-Berlin, D. and Harold, T. (2007) 'Attention Deficit: Why Politicians Ignore Defense Policy in Latin America', Latin American Research Review, 42(3): 76–100.

Russett, B. (1993) *Grasping the Democratic Peace*, Princeton: Princeton University Press.

SIPRI (2014) 'SIPRI Arms Transfers Data'. Retrieved from http://armstrade.sipri.org/armstrade.

Smith, R. and Tasiran, A. (2005) 'The Demand for Arms Imports', *Journal of Peace Research*, 42(2): 167–181.

Walt, S. (1985) 'Alliance Formation and the Balance of Power', *International Security* 9(4): 3–43.

Waltz, K. (1979) *Theory of International Politics*, New York: McGraw-Hill.

Washington Post (2010) 'Venezuela Acquires 1,800 Antiaircraft Missiles from Russia', *The Washington Post*. Retrieved from http://www.washingtonpost.com/wp-dyn/content/article/2010/12/11/AR2010121102586.html.

Weiffen, B., Dembinski, M., Hasenclever, A., Freistein, K. and Yamauchi, M. (2011) 'Democracy, Regional Security Institutions and Rivalry Mitigation: Evidence From Europe, South America and Asia', *Security Studies*, 20: 378–415.

20

LATIN AMERICAN MILITARIES IN THE 21ST CENTURY

Civil-military relations in the era of disappearing boundaries

Deborah L. Norden

In Latin America, men in uniform rarely govern anymore. This obvious observation highlights what has changed about Latin American political-military relations in the early 21st century. Latin American democracies have aged without necessarily maturing, while security threats have evolved in ways that change what militaries do. This chapter begins by examining the question of control of the armed forces, and the ways in which challenges have changed and concepts have become more nuanced. Specifically, I look at the range from civilian autonomy, to domination, and finally defense and security management. I then turn to three significant challenges to civil-military relations: first, the political context, which in several Latin American countries has strayed significantly from ideals of liberal democracy; second, the security context, which has altered what militaries do, especially given the constraints of limited resources; and third, the ways in which the composition and social bases of the armed forces may have shifted since the wave of democratic transitions. Briefly, patterns of political-military relations have been changing in Latin America because all the major variables determining these patterns have evolved over the past decades. Despite the apparent obsolescence of military regimes, civilian control remains limited and, in some ways, even precarious.

Expanding political control

At the heart of most concerns about civil-military relations in Latin America are political-military relations. Over time, the armed forces have alternately governed, threatened political leaders and governments, interfered with policy-making, and resisted orders. These overriding concerns about precarious political stability and uncertain civilian political control have predominated in the literature on civil-military relations. Yet, understandings of 'civilian political control' have shifted over time, becoming more complex as Latin American militaries have become further removed from direct governing. In the 1980s, as military regimes gradually ceded to civilians, new governments mostly focused on the overwhelming challenge of preventing renewed military rule. Yet, even without directly threatening coups, Latin America's militaries remained disproportionately capable of calling the shots, often determining whether governments would survive or fall, or more subtly hampering their ability to effectively implement policy. Thus, as the likelihood of generals donning presidential sashes diminished, conceptualizations of civilian control shifted from merely preventing military control to more effective civilian oversight.

This expanded understanding of civilian control encompasses at least three different themes. These include, first, *civilian autonomy*, or establishing minimum levels of civilian control by reducing military prerogatives and political meddling; second, challenges to *domination*, especially military decisions to disregard orders; and third, *management* of military affairs, including such issues as defense ministries, civilian expertise, civilian control of budgets and education, and oversight of military activities.

Civilian autonomy: keeping the military out of politics

The first step toward establishing civilian control involves ensuring *civilian autonomy*, or the government's freedom to act without military threat or direct interference. This military abstention from politics could conceivably occur in two very different situations: when the military is politically neutral, or when the armed forces share the government's political views. In either scenario, the military would still be likely to lobby the government for institutional interests – as would any bureaucracy – but would refrain from threats or undue interference in policy decisions.

Even without the pervasive military regimes of the 20th century, militaries have continued to violate civilian governments' autonomy, particularly through excessive military 'prerogatives,' and, more ominously, through moderating military coups (Mares 2014). Military prerogatives refer to entrenched military privileges (Stepan 1988: 93–97). While some essentially involve professional military matters, others stretch well beyond the terrain of military affairs, such as holding cabinet positions, exercising control over police or intelligence, or managing state enterprises, as in contemporary Ecuador and, increasingly, Venezuela. Any of these prerogatives allows the military to either penetrate civilian decision-making or usurp areas of civilian authority and responsibility.

More dramatically, Latin American militaries have continued to organize rebellions and military coups. For example, mid-level Argentine army officers launched a series of military rebellions in the 1980s, in response to human rights trials and other government efforts to punish the armed forces and reduce their prerogatives. These were essentially organized, armed, and public strikes, in which the military sought to force the government to change its policies. While stopping short of demanding the president's removal, these episodes nonetheless interfered with civilian autonomy, successfully compelling the government to alter its policies and even to implement legislation that ended the human rights trials.

Elsewhere, militaries continued to oust governments from office, belying expectations of a definitive democratic triumph. Twenty-first-century cases of military coups include the 2002 coup against Hugo Chávez, which briefly placed businessman Pedro Carmona in the presidency; the 2009 military coup in Honduras, in which the armed forces backed a Supreme Court decision to oust President José Manuel Zelaya after a controversial constitutional reform attempt; and Ecuador's 2000 coup, in which the military joined forces with an indigenous movement to remove President Jamil Mahuad. While none of these events resulted in military rule, they nonetheless constitute 'moderating coups' and demonstrate a lack of civilian autonomy. According to David Mares, Latin America remains vulnerable to these coups since, despite distaste for military rule, support for democracy is "distressingly modest" in comparison to relatively high respect for the military (Mares 2014: 90).

Domination and military 'shirking'

If civilian autonomy remains elusive in Latin America, extending civilian control comprises an even greater challenge. A minimum level of civilian control would entail civilian *domination*, which, following Max Weber's definition, means that those in a subordinate position obey orders, whether or not they consider those orders to be legitimate (Weber 1978: 53). If ordered, will the military repress protests or engage in policing? Will the military follow orders that may conflict with institutional interests?

David Pion-Berlin, along with coauthors Diego Esparza and Kevin Grisham (2012), has called attention to the critical issue of military 'shirking,' demonstrating that militaries – without overtly rebelling – make decisions about whether or not to comply with orders to repress civilian protests. According to these authors, institutional interests such as concerns about legality and institutional integrity, along with military-role beliefs and relations to society, affect military decisions about whether to comply with orders (Pion-Berlin et al. 2012). Surprisingly, they find that "it is rare that the armed forces comply with presidential orders to repress the protesters . . . [T]he dominant pattern of behavior has been defiance" (Pion-Berlin 2014: 72). This *inaction* has major consequences for whether or not a government will survive, although not always in predictable ways. In 2000, the Ecuadorian military's decision to ally with protestors instead of repressing them led to the fall of the government. Yet, the Bolivian military's decision in 2003 to follow orders to repress actually seems to have intensified the conflict, and may even have hastened the government's end.

Militaries engage in less dramatic forms of shirking as well. Maiah Jaskoski notes that militaries have a range of possible responses to military commands: "In response to a civilian command, the military may refuse to do the work (less control), conduct the mission as ordered (more control), or proactively conduct missions more intensively than instructed (less control)" (Jaskoski 2012: 71). In both Ecuador and Peru, Jaskoski has demonstrated that the military's economic interests have led to neglecting higher priority security missions, in order to instead serve the powerful hydrocarbon and mining industries (Jaskoski 2013). This form of shirking may not threaten the government's survival, but certainly indicates fragile political control.

Military management: political oversight of the military

With greater management and oversight of the armed forces, militaries would be much less likely to evade civilian directions. Yet, the necessary institutions and competencies have developed only slowly in this respect. During the initial period of democratization in the late 20th century, governments throughout the region sought to establish civilian-led defense ministries, which served as the focal point for management and oversight of the armed forces. Within a few years though progress in this critical area of civilian control appeared to stall; while civilians led fully 88 per cent of defense ministries in 2003, this declined to only 53 per cent by 2010 (Pion-Berlin 2014: 75).

One major challenge that defense ministries have faced has been a shortage of knowledgeable civilian experts, in large part because of the lack of incentives to attract them. Not only do salaries for civil servants tend to be low, but also, in a region with few external threats, politicians may find that defense expertise wins few votes (Pion-Berlin 2005). Regardless of the cause, without sufficient civilian expertise, civilian leaders cannot easily penetrate military autonomy, especially more specialized areas such as defense budgets and military education.

How much do civilians need to know, and how minutely do they need to oversee military, defense, and security affairs to ensure compliance? In this area there has been some disagreement. Pion-Berlin has taken the position that civilians' failure to develop defense expertise is really not so dire, as long as they remain skilled managers of military affairs and can gain military compliance through those administrative skills (Pion-Berlin 2005: 28). Tom Bruneau, however, argues that while civilians may not need to know as much as military specialists – and, in fact, really cannot, given the scope of their responsibilities – they do need to have enough familiarity with core military issues "to be able to ensure that the armed forces are doing what they are required to do, not only in terms of submitting to civilian control . . . but also in successfully fulfilling the current very wide spectrum of roles and missions" (Bruneau 2005: 113).

As the above discussion demonstrates, civilian control of the armed forces is both elusive and evolving. For decades, the emblematic issue of civil-military relations has been the military coup. Yet the meaning most often given to the term civilian control is a lack of military threat or intrusion into civilian political affairs: In truth, this refers not to civilian *control*, but to civilian *autonomy*. In the post-authoritarian era, moderating coups and rebellions have remained part of the political picture in Latin America, while establishing meaningful civilian control – avoiding military shirking and managing the armed forces well enough to gain effective military compliance – has proven difficult, especially with limited resources and incentives. At the same time, the context of civil-military relations has changed quite a bit from the initial transition moments of the 1980s, redefining how 'control' might be implemented. The remainder of this chapter turns to these issues, exploring how this evolving context influences civil-military relations and Latin American security affairs.

The changing context and content of civil-military relations

In 1989, Francis Fukuyama declared that the "end of history" had arrived (Fukuyama 1989). In Latin America, that truly appeared to be the case: the end of ideologically driven conflicts between armed revolutionary movements and repressive U.S.-supported military regimes, and the beginning of a new liberal democratic era, dominated by consensus around liberal capitalist economic models. Furthermore, with the end of the Cold War, presumably internal security threats would also diminish, reducing the need for militaries to assume domestic roles and allowing a political-military division of labor. As it turned out, however, this was only the first stage in Latin America's post-authoritarian evolution. Instead, an antiliberal political shift, emerging new security issues, and the broadening of military social bases gradually transformed the civil-military nexus in Latin America, leading to a renewed internal focus for many militaries, and a shift *away* from liberal models of civil-military relations.

Alternative political models and alternative political-military relations

At the forefront of the antiliberal response stood former coup leader, Lt. Col. Hugo Chávez, elected and reelected president of Venezuela from 1998 until his death in 2013. Spouting strong nationalist, anti-U.S., and socialist rhetoric, Chávez looked very different than expectations of post–Cold War liberalism. Furthermore, Chávez was not alone; while the left-leaning governments that emerged in the 1990s and early 2000s in Argentina, Brazil, Chile, and Uruguay all stayed largely within the accepted parameters of liberal democracy, the more radical presidents of Bolivia and Ecuador pursued 'Bolivarian' models that more closely resembled Chávez's ambitiously antiliberal agenda. Thus, the political side of the civil-military equation in Latin America proved to be much less predictable than expected.

The liberal democratic assumption and civilian control of the military

The political migration away from liberal democracy creates significant challenges for both civilian autonomy and civilian control, given the essentially liberal democratic assumptions underlying classic formulations about civil-military relations. Both Samuel Huntington and Eric Nordlinger predicated their classic models of democratic civilian control on assumptions of political neutrality and relatively limited civilian management or interference with military affairs. In *Soldier and the State*, Huntington advocates "objective control," which relies on military professionalism to ensure the military's political neutrality and abstention from political intervention (Huntington 1957: 83). Huntington therefore sees the military's professional autonomy as an asset to civilian control, in that by "militarizing the military," the armed forces would be absorbed by their professional duties and consequently would be disinclined to intervene in politics. Under this model, the professional military would be "politically sterile and neutral, ready to carry out the wishes of any civilian group which secures legitimate authority within the state" (Huntington 1957: 84). Nordlinger's "liberal" model similarly rests on "the differentiation of elites according to their expertise and responsibilities," with separate political and military spheres, in which the armed forces unwaveringly accept subordination (Nordlinger 1977: 12).

Yet the Huntington and Nordlinger models of control through specialization presume that no one questions the legitimacy of those holding political office, and that political leaders would have little temptation to seek political converts and allies within the armed forces. Not only the military, but also the *political system* is presumed to be politically neutral. Despite Nordlinger's clarification that leaders may be "elected, appointed, or anointed" (Nordlinger 1977: 12), Huntington and Nordlinger assume a neutral and legitimate political system, with a distinct separation between policy-making and implementation that coincides most strongly with a liberal democratic political model.

Radical regimes and the fusion of civil-military roles

The new 'Bolivarian' governments that emerged in the Andes in the 1990s and early 2000s sought to redefine their countries' political systems in a way that directly conflicted with those assumptions. The new constitutions and constitutional reforms implemented in Venezuela, Bolivia, and Ecuador shifted these electoral regimes toward a greater emphasis on ideology and substantive commitments, such as the right to food, water, housing, and education in Bolivia. With political systems defined more around ends than means, these governments have also approached the military as a potential political partner, rather than the politically neutral instrument envisioned in the liberal model. The Chávez government thus actively sought to politicize the Venezuelan military, demanding that military personnel swear allegiance to "fatherland, socialism or death," incorporating officers into the administration, and utilizing the military for a wide range of nondefense missions directly connected to the government's broader political agenda. In this respect, the Venezuelan model approximated a *fusion* of civil-military roles, with military involvement in everything from distributing food to building schools through the Bolivarian missions. Bolivia's military has similarly cooperated with the Morales government in carrying out the government's political agenda – for example, assisting the government in enforcing the nationalization of oil and gas. In 2010, Bolivia's Army commander in chief, General Antonio Cueto, took the lead in declaring the military "socialist, anti-imperialist and anti-capitalist" (quoted in Pion-Berlin 2014: 70), sentiments reiterated in 2012 by the incoming military commander, General Tito Gandarillos. In several countries, military involvement in such nondefense functions as providing private security for oil companies (Ecuador) or managing state enterprises has also broadened the military presence within society, diffusing military functions and blurring lines between civilian and military organizations.

The Bolivarian countries' approach resembles the penetration model that Nordlinger associated more with revolutionary regimes (Nordlinger 1977: 15), or Huntington's 'subjective control,' in which civilian political leaders seek to 'civilianize' military leaders, rather than differentiate between civilian and military roles. Yet, with sufficient political continuity within the regime, the penetration model can still give the civilian leadership enough recognized authority with the military to secure the latter's compliance with the civilian leaders' political agenda. However, the lack of political neutrality could make it difficult for militaries to adapt to more competitive democratic politics.

Shifting security threats and role expansion

Along with these Andean political shifts, new security threats throughout the region also contributed to changing Latin American civil-military relations, partly by prioritizing new missions outside early democratizers' more narrow constructions of appropriate military roles. As Juan Rial writes, "conventional, localized, border conflicts have practically ended" (2013: 29). Guerrilla warfare has also diminished, with peace accords resolving many internal conflicts, and the Soviet Union's collapse sapping support and revolutionary motivation from the few that remained. Rial argues that this loss of threats has contributed to militaries' shifting attentions, as they seek new missions to replace those that have faded. International peacekeeping became an especially appealing option in some instances, allowing the armed forces to refocus their attentions on internationally respected, external roles, especially in Argentina (Norden 1995; Sotomayor 2014, and his chapter in this volume). However, globalization and postconflict social conditions have also helped generate new and very real security challenges, augmenting the intensity and organization of criminal threats.

International peacekeeping

Following the end of the Cold War, the number of international peacekeeping operations and peacekeepers expanded dramatically, as did Latin American participation. According to Arturo Sotomayor, during the 2000–2010 period Uruguay was among the top 10 contributors to peacekeeping operations, with 20,934 troops, while Brazil and Argentina were among the top 25 contributors, and Chile and Bolivia among the top 50. Peru, Guatemala, Ecuador, Paraguay, El Salvador, and Honduras all fell further down on the list, but still among the top 100 peacekeeping participants (Sotomayor 2014: 26–27).

Notably, all of these countries had experienced some degree of authoritarian rule and/or internal conflict, and the largest contributors had all emerged relatively recently from long-lasting, repressive military regimes. For these countries, participating in international peacekeeping offered various advantages. Most importantly, it allowed governments to redirect military efforts and attentions *outside* the country, in roles acceptable to those traumatized by military repression. Peacekeeping participation was also perceived as potentially supportive of professionalization, given the participants' interactions with highly trained forces from elsewhere. In Argentina, under President Carlos Menem, peacekeeping participation also coincided particularly well with the government's broader, pro-U.S., and internationally oriented foreign policy approach (Norden 1995; see also Escudé, this volume). Despite some continuity in specific military peacekeeping tasks, the specialized and physically external nature of peacekeeping made it a better fit with the liberal model of civilian control than other internal security functions.

Domestic security

In contrast, internal security roles for the armed forces can be problematic, especially in relatively new democracies: Military involvement in policing both violates the liberal concept that a professional military should be narrowly specialized in defense, and creates the risk of renewed human rights violations, given the nature of military training. Nevertheless, maintaining a strict line between police and military roles has become increasingly unrealistic in most Latin American countries. Growing crime – whether narcotics trafficking, other organized crime, gangs, or different street crime – has in many cases far surpassed the capabilities of police forces, and in several instances seriously threatens governability. Increasing threats from transnational terrorism have also expanded military roles beyond traditional defense, despite the greater relevance of this issue elsewhere.

When is the military most likely to be called from the barracks to the streets? In part, this has to do with the extent of the threat. If criminal gangs own towns and ports, if political opponents have defied government authority and wrested rural zones from government control, if the government cannot actually govern due to the scope of the threat, and the police lack the capacity to restore order, then the government will turn to those with the biggest guns – the armed forces. Thus, when Bolivia's autonomy movements began edging toward independence movements in 2008, the government called in the troops. Likewise, when narcotics traffickers had become the true source of power in parts of Mexico and gangs virtually governed the Brazilian favelas, their governments turned to the army.

Administrative structure also helps explain the presence or absence of the military in internal security, however. Countries with strong intermediate or hybrid forces – possibly more appropriate for addressing such challenges as highly organized criminal gangs, narcotics trafficking, or social disruptions – may be less likely to *need* the traditional military for domestic roles. Primarily trained for internal security rather than defense, hybrid forces tend to be more heavily armed and more centralized than traditional police forces, with organization and ranks more closely resembling military forces. Where these forces predated transitions from authoritarianism, civilian governments have often sought to transfer these powerful bodies away from military control, thereby reducing the military's domestic presence through bureaucratic restructuring. For example, Chile's *carabineros* fell under the authority of the ministry of defense during the military regime, but moved to the ministry of interior in 2011. Similarly, Argentina's *Gendarmería* (Border Guard) and *Prefectura Naval (*Coast Guard) were moved, first from the army to the ministry of defense in 1984, shortly after the transition to democracy, and then to the ministry of interior through a couple of steps beginning with the Internal Security Law (24.059) in 1992, and culminating in a formal transfer in 1996; finally, the *Gendarmería* and *Prefectura* moved to the newly created ministry of security in December 2010.

Elsewhere, though, administrative structures preserved or even augmented the military's role in internal security. In Brazil, the confusingly named 'military police' – actually a militarized civilian police force – also functions as an intermediate force, and primarily answers to state governments, rather than to the military or national government. As a reserve force, though, the military police fell under military command during the favela occupations that preceded the 2014 World Cup. Conversely, Venezuela's National Guard remains a branch of the armed forces, joined in 2005 by the Bolivarian Militia, a civilian reserve force designed to support the armed forces in multiple roles, both external and domestic. Thus, despite similarities in these intermediate forces, all of which blend military and police characteristics, the bureaucratic location matters. When the military or defense ministry controls the intermediate forces, behaviors and expectations may be more 'military,' with a potentially easier extension to using traditional armed forces for policing. While this may not directly threaten civilian control, it does, again, counter models that would advocate narrower defense specialization for the armed forces and could increase the risk of human rights violations.

Who wears the uniform? The changing nature of Latin American officer corps

Militaries have evolved in tandem with security threats, political regimes, and military roles. Since the beginning of the third wave of democratization, the composition and culture of Latin America have changed. No longer are military officers necessarily male, separately educated, and elite. These military-society relations undoubtedly influence military-political relations, changing how members of the armed forces respond to different political leaders or missions, and the extent to which they see themselves as similar or distinct from their civilian compatriots.

Beginning in the late 1970s and early 1980s, Latin American militaries began accepting women into the armed forces, until by the turn of the century few all-male militaries remained, even if the percentage of women remained relatively small and advancement limited (Donadio and Mazzotta 2009; see Donadio, this volume). Increasingly, women are even making their way to the helm of the armed forces and the defense ministries. For example, Chilean President Michelle Bachelet served as minister of defense from 2002 to 2004. Argentina also boasted a female minister of defense, Nilda Garré, from 2005 until 2010, when she moved to the position of minister of security. In November 2012, Ecuadorian President Rafael Correa appointed María Fernández Espinosa as defense minister, and in July 2013, Venezuelan President Nicolas Maduro appointed the country's first female admiral, Carmen Teresa Meléndez, as the country's minister of defense.

Depending on the leader's expertise and leadership, and the defense ministry's management capabilities, female leadership may be mostly symbolic. However, the female presence within the armed forces would seem likely to help bridge the gap between military and civilian cultures. In a 1994 study of the U.S. military, Karen Duniven wrote that "a deeply entrenched 'cult of masculinity' (with accompanying masculine norms, values, and lifestyles) pervades military culture" (Duniven 1994: 534). Yet, Duniven's research reveals that while these values remained deeply entrenched in policies and practices, by 1992 three-fourths of military personnel believed that gender should not be a factor in determining combat assignments (Duniven 1994: 539). This would suggest that inclusionary policies may well contribute to transforming military cultures to more closely resemble the societies that surround them.

Educational policies also helped diminish insularity. For example, in Argentina, prior to democratization, the military's education system remained strictly separate from that of civilians. Not only did officers' educational track keep them strictly in military schools for their postsecondary education, but many began their military education much earlier in the *liceos militares*, secondary schools subordinate to the armed forces. The *liceos* remain in existence, but the education in the service academies has been reformed to more closely resemble university standards, as part of the effort to 'civilianize' the armed forces and enhance integration. Thus, beginning in the early 1990s, the University Institutes of the Armed Forces began offering degrees parallel to those in civilian universities – evaluated and accredited by the National Accreditation Committee – and even began including civilians within their student bodies. In

Chile, limited integration has also occurred, at least at the top levels of the military education system, with civilian faculty members teaching at the National Academy of Political and Strategic Studies (ANEPE) and some civilians included in the student body. Like the policies to include more women, education policies that increase similarities between military and civilian education or, even more importantly, encourage civil-military integration in the classroom seem bound to transform military subcultures in Latin America.

Yet, with changing socioeconomic origins, militaries may already be in transition. While most Latin American officer corps have tended to come from primarily middle-class origins, in the Southern Cone – and especially in Argentina – the officer corps historically drew more from the upper range of the middle class than the somewhat more broadly based Andean militaries (Fitch 2009). These differences had an important influence on the kinds of military regimes that emerged in these cases. Notably, the military regimes installed in Peru in 1968, Ecuador in 1972, and, at least initially, in Bolivia in 1964 were reformist or even radical, especially when compared to those implemented by the more elite-dominated Argentine and Chilean military regimes.

In recent years, though, the social origins of even the Southern Cone militaries have changed, partly due to declining status in many countries following military rule, and partly because of the economic challenges that these countries have faced. According to Sam Fitch, the debt crisis of the 1980s initiated a decline in salaries and social status of officers, with a "general trend toward greater recruitment of future officers from the lower-middle and popular classes" (2009: 5). This shifting socioeconomic status could have a significant impact on the military's political attitudes. In what ways might these simultaneous shifts in military status and civil-military integration affect larger patterns of civil-military relations? The implications appear to be mixed. On the one hand, increased integration between the military and civilians would seem likely to protect against the kinds of military repression that occurred in the Southern Cone in the 1970s, when the military elites' insularity led to perceiving civilians as distinctly 'Other,' and alternately corrupting or even dangerous. On the other hand, declining social status and increasing identification with sectors *other* than governing elites could conceivably cause a breach between the military and political leaders, depending on the policies that they pursue. If so, this would imply that the social origins and experiences of the armed forces might themselves be detrimental to the military's political neutrality, particularly if government policies were to exacerbate those tendencies through deliberate politicization.

Emerging challenges and unanswered questions

From the above discussion, a complex picture emerges. Clearly, political leaders in most Latin American countries have not yet achieved decisive control over the armed forces, meaning not only civilian autonomy from military interference, but also dominance and effective management. Is this because of, or despite, the changes in security threats, political regimes, and officer corps composition and orientation? How do these changes impact such critical issues as political stability, human rights, and regional relations?

Overall, the changes that have occurred have led to *civilianizing* the armed forces, diminishing the distinctions between militaries, civil societies, and civilian police forces. This appears to have been the case in all Latin American militaries. The more radical regimes in the Andean region have deliberately politicized their armed forces, and have increasingly utilized them for nondefense and even nonsecurity roles. Military personnel interact daily with civilians through national development issues, and work side by side with civilians in administrative positions. Elsewhere in Latin America, efforts at democratization in some ways have had similar civilianizing consequences, as educational reforms have brought military education more in line with that experienced by civilians, and restrictions on military budget cuts have forced military officers to share economic challenges with less-privileged groups within the society. Throughout the region, furthermore, the most pressing security threats have tended toward transnational and organized crime, which have increasingly been pulling militaries into roles generally considered more appropriate to civilian police forces.

'Civilianizing' militaries, however, is not necessarily the same thing as establishing civilian control, and may not even ensure civilian autonomy. Notably, Huntington considered 'subjective control' – a model in which political leaders seek like-minded military leaders – to be distinctly inferior to objective control in ensuring political stability under democracies. The risk here is that, without political neutrality, the militaries may resist or even threaten political leaders with opposing values and policies. Nor would more working-class or lower-middle-class origins or identifications eliminate the likelihood of military coups. As mentioned, at least some of the military regimes initiated in the 1970s defined themselves as leftist and reformist, with different policy goals than the more conservative military regimes more frequently associated with bureaucratic-authoritarianism. Yet, the reality is that coups *have* become much less common in Latin America, and military regimes virtually obsolete. Thus we can hypothesize that at least some aspects of civilianization and civil-military integration may have supported civilian autonomy, at least to the extent that civilians have rejected military rule as an alternative.[1] However, extending civilian control still requires greater management, including deepening civilian staffing and dealing with the geographic challenges of military personnel posted far from the civilians charged with overseeing them.

With respect to human rights, the developments above would seem to have mixed implications. Bringing military values more in line with those of civilians would certainly seem to be advantageous with respect to defending and promoting human rights. However, the proliferation of military roles – due both to the new Bolivarian political models and the new security threats – raises some concerns. First, the role expansion and concomitantly broad interpretation of 'security' seem far too reminiscent of the national security doctrines, attributed with having justified the military regimes of the 1970s (see Tickner, this volume). Second, when militaries – trained to kill – engage in internal security, excess violence is unavoidably a risk: Bigger guns on the street mean more blood.

Looking at security issues more broadly, how have emerging threats and changing patterns of civil-military relations affected regional relations in Latin America? After the collapse of authoritarianism and the end of the Cold War, in many respects, regional relations in Latin America improved greatly, with deliberate efforts and confidence-building measures designed to diminish interstate conflict. And while a few border skirmishes have occurred – most notably between Peru and Ecuador in 1995 – interstate relations have mostly been peaceful. Yet, much of the violence that does occur is transnational in origin, especially the violence linked to narcotics trafficking.

The transnational nature of threats would appear to call for more international cooperation, or even joint hybrid forces to counter these threats. However, according to Harold Trinkunas (2013), international security cooperation has remained quite limited, despite initial increases in regional economic cooperation, OAS pro-democracy initiatives, and subsequent efforts by UNASUR to develop a shared agenda to counter transnational crime. The problem is that Latin American countries continue to experience different security threats: Mexico's violent narcotics cartels, guerrillas on the Ecuadorian border, and gang violence in Central America all pose very different challenges. Distinctions between newer and older political models, and conservative and radical political ideologies have, to some extent, complicated regional cooperation and weakened earlier integration efforts. As Trinkunas explains, "threat perceptions remain heterogeneous across the region; disagreements over what is a democracy have produced new ideological tensions between states; . . . and the perennial calls to regionalize responses to growing criminal violence have foundered on national interests" (2013: 84). Furthermore, transnational crime – one of the factors that presumably would have encouraged regional cooperation – has, in fact, led to further conflicts, particularly at vulnerable borders.

The picture that emerges of civil-military relations and the security panorama in Latin America thus reveals at least as many questions as findings. First, new security threats and new political models have brought militaries back into internal security in a way that, at the beginning of the third wave of democracy, would have been seen as inherently threatening to the constitutional order. But is it? Perhaps this is merely a step toward a new kind of security force, an evolution toward predominantly hybrid forces, better suited toward the kinds of threats that countries are more likely to face in an increasingly intertwined world system. Second, the linear path toward liberal democracy is clearly a mistaken assumption; given that, how should we rethink models of civilian control of the military? How do, and have, politicized militaries respond when the political leadership changes? How do values and political orientations within the armed forces change over time, and how relevant are they to explaining military subordination and responsiveness to civilian leadership? Both of the above are areas where we have made logical assumptions about military behavior, but have not necessarily tested the questions adequately and empirically. Third, with respect to the issue of management and oversight, to what extent are problems of military autonomy simply extensions of bureaucratic autonomy elsewhere? And if so, who can best ensure political responsiveness – civil servants, equally entrenched in institutional interests, or political appointees, who may or may not have deep knowledge of subject matter and will likely only be in their positions for a few years before the next government comes to office? In many respects, our understandings of what militaries do and how civil-military relations should work have been fossilized from an earlier era, with clearer national boundaries and somewhat stronger distinctions between what constitutes 'defense' and what comprises 'internal security.' This new era, with its proliferation of political alternatives and weakening of state boundaries, calls for a much more ambitious reevaluation of the nature, purpose, and appropriate organization of militaries and civil-military relations.

Note

1 The loss of international support for military rule following the end of the Cold War, and the various regional and subregional mechanisms established to discourage and punish (albeit weakly) military coups have also helped deter the reemergence of military regimes.

References

Bruneau, T. (2005) 'Civil-Military Relations in Latin America: The Hedgehog and the Fox Revisited', *Revista Fuerzas Armadas y Sociedad*, 19(1–2): 111–131.

Donadio, M. and Mazzotta, C. (eds) (2009) 'La mujer en las instituciones armadas y policiales: Resolución 1325 y operaciones de paz en América Latina', *RESDAL*. Retrieved from http://www.resdal.org/genero-y-paz/ebook/Libro-mujer-RESDAL.pdf.

Dunivin, K. (1994) 'Military Culture: Change and Continuity', *Armed Forces & Society*, 20(4): 531–547.

Fitch, J.S. (2009) 'The Armed Forces and Society in South America: How Similar? How Different?', *Universidad de Belgrano Documentos de Trabajo*, No. 236.

Fukuyama, F. (1989, Summer) 'The End of History', *The National Interest*, 16: 3–15.

Huntington, S. (1957) *The Soldier and the State: The Theory and Politics of Civil-Military Relations*, Cambridge, MA: Belknap Press.

Jaskoski, M. (2012) 'Civilian Control of the Armed Forces in Democratic Latin America: Military Prerogatives, Contestation, and Mission Performance in Peru', *Armed Forces and Society*, 38(1): 70–91.
——— (2013) 'Private Financing of the Military: A Local Political Economy Approach', *Studies in Comparative International Development*, 48(2): 172–195.
Mares, D. (2014) 'Citizen Security, Democracy and the Civil-Military Relationship' in D. Mares and R. Martínez (eds.) *Debating Civil-Military Relations in Latin America*, Eastbourne, UK: Sussex Academic Press, pp. 81–100.
Norden, D. (1995) 'Keeping the Peace, Outside and In: Argentina's UN Missions', *International Peacekeeping*, 2(3): 330–349.
Nordlinger, E. (1977) *Soldiers in Politics: Military Coups and Governments*, Upper Saddle River, NJ: Prentice Hall.
Pion-Berlin, D. (2005) 'Political Management of the Military in Latin America', *Military Review*, 85(1): 19–31.
——— (2014) 'Latin American Civil-Military Relations: What Progress Has Been Made?' in D. Mares and R. Martínez (eds) *Debating Civil-Military Relations in Latin America*, Eastbourne, UK: Sussex Academic Press, pp. 61–80.
Pion-Berlin, D., Esparza, D. and Grisham, K. (2012) 'Staying Quartered: Civilian Uprising and Military Disobedience in the Twenty-First Century', *Comparative Political Studies*, 47(2): 230–259.
Rial, J. (2013) 'Las relaciones civiles-militares en sociedades en transformación: América Latina', Documentos CIDOB. América Latina, no. 36, pp. 21–36 (translation is mine). Retrieved from http://diposit.ub.edu/dspace/handle/2445/49223.
Sotomayor, A. C. (2014) *The Myth of the Democratic Peacekeeper: Civil-Military Relations and the United Nations*, Baltimore: Johns Hopkins University Press.
Stepan, A. (1988) *Rethinking Military Politics: Brazil and the Southern Cone*, Princeton: Princeton University Press.
Trinkunas, H. (2013) 'Reordering Regional Security in Latin America', *Journal of International Affairs*, 6(2): 83–99.
Weber, M. (1978) *Economy and Society*, G. Roth and C. Wittich (eds), Berkeley: University of California Press.

21

INTERSTATE DISPUTES

Militarized coercion and 'peaceful settlement'

David R. Mares

The dominant discourse for scholars of Latin American security studies is about interstate peace, trust, and regional institutions that are producing a 'zone of peace' or 'positive security.' Yet living in peace with one's neighbors surely must mean that a state does not expect a verbal threat from a neighbor, much less a threat accompanied by military mobilizations and actual military violence. Indeed, the American Treaty on Pacific Settlement (Pact of Bogotá 1948), one of the region's earliest confidence- and security-building mechanisms (CSBMs), stipulated that signatories "agree to *refrain from the threat or the use of force, or from any other means of coercion* for the settlement of their controversies, and *to have recourse at all times to pacific procedures*" (U.S. Department of State, emphasis added).

The notion that Latin America is a zone of peace (whether negative or positive peace) simply because it has no major wars ignores the militarized disputes spanning a large range of issues and is an inaccurate and misleading standard to declare that the region is peaceful. General IR analysts studying militarized interstate conflict do not equate the lack of 'war' with peace, and discuss recurrent militarized conflict as an absence of peace (Quackenbush and Venteicher 2008). The study of interstate violence in the region, however, has largely been ignored and, when studied, generally lacks theoretical rigor. The research challenge is to understand the use of military force within a regional/subregional context that has some characteristics of peace zones. Battaglino (2012) has offered a corrective, but its theoretical and empirical bases for distinguishing a 'hybrid peace' do not stand up to scrutiny, so the challenge remains.

Interstate violence is a constant empirical reality in Latin America (Mares 2001, 2012b, 2012c). To say "oh, but those incidents don't mean anything" or "they did not lead to further violence, or stopped far short of war, so they don't matter" is to confuse explanation and description. The vast majority did not result in a 'war,' defined as a conflict with at least 1,000 battlefield-related deaths, but they were acts of violence. The experience of interstate violence should lead to a number of important questions for social scientists that study Latin America's international relations, especially with other Latin American countries. Why do they use military force in their relations, especially given the rhetoric of peace? How does the threat of military violence against regional neighbors coexist with institutional and normative frameworks that are widely offered as evidence that Latin America, or some part of it, is moving towards or even has achieved a 'positive peace'? What is the relationship between militarizing a dispute and its settlement?

This chapter sets a research agenda for understanding why any use of force by one Latin American country against another continues to be considered a legitimate, if disagreeable, tool of foreign policy. I open with a discussion of the empirical record of contemporary (2000 to 2011) interstate coercion in the region. The next section examines the place of militarized disputes in the study of Latin American security. A third section proposes a research agenda for the study of coercive diplomacy in intra–Latin American relations.

The empirical record of coercive diplomacy

Empirical reality does not fit well with the rhetoric of peace zones, unless one insists simply on the criterion of 1,000 battlefield-related deaths. There are peaceful regional interactions in the region, but ignoring the empirical record of violent interactions results in a poorly selected dependent variable – 'why peace and settlement' instead of 'why sometimes violence, sometimes peace, and sometimes settlement.' Overall, research on interstate relations in the region reflects a poor research design that suffers from an incomplete and biased description of the dependent variable, independent variables that are poorly specified and that may actually *not* have the causally related characteristics in Latin America that are theorized to produce peace, and little systematic testing of the hypothesis.

The claim that 'Latin (or South) America is the most peaceful region in the world' is empirically incorrect. Latin America is not an outlier in having few wars (using the standard definition of at least 1,000 battlefield-related deaths in a 12-month period). Worldwide, there have only been 38 wars in the 61-year period from 1946 to 2007 in the latest Correlates of War database. Latin America has been the scene of three of those wars (1969 El Salvador and Honduras, 1982 Argentina and Great Britain, and 1995 Ecuador and Peru), which is statistically no different than East Asia or Europe with four each; even the Indian subcontinent has only experienced five wars in this period. Interstate war occurs mainly in Africa and the Middle East (Southeast Asia's six wars all happened before 1990) (Sarkees 2010). War is statistically insignificant as an occurrence everywhere because, by the standard definition, it is so rare, considering the universe of interactions among states.

The use of military force short of war in Latin America's interstate relations is, unfortunately, not rare. Evidence of militarization is easy to find. Colombian forces attacked a guerrilla camp in Ecuador in 2008, with Venezuela mobilizing its military as well. In June 2011, after months of Nicaraguan military operations along the San Juan River that divides Nicaragua and Costa Rica and a complaint about the provocation to the OAS, the Costa Rican foreign ministry claimed that the Nicaraguan army was establishing a permanent presence on the San Juan River to permit easy access for Nicaraguan civilians to occupy disputed marshlands on the Isla Calero. Costa Rican President Laura Chinchilla denounced the "undeserved aggression" by Nicaragua (Zibechi 2009). The Venezuelan military blew up gold mining dredges in an area Venezuela claims, but which is recognized internationally as Guyanese. Using the Militarized Interstate Dispute (MID)[1] standard for classification, there were 47 incidents among Latin American nations from 2000 to 2010 (Correlates of War n.d.).

Some scholars claim that South America experiences a stable peace or is developing a pluralistic security community (Hurrell 1998; Kacowicz 2005). The rest of Latin America (Mexico, Central America, and the Caribbean), however, has not had a war since 1969, while South America has had one intraregional war (1995) and one extraregional war (1982) in this period. In terms of MIDs we see a similar distinction: Since 2004, South America has had more than the rest of Latin America. The empirical fact is simply that South America is not as 'peaceful' as the rest of Latin America, whether one discusses war or violent, coercive diplomacy.

Still, other scholars divide South America into two zones: north and south. In the north, a 'hybrid peace' reigns where military threats exist, although there is no war. In the south, a 'positive peace' exists, given that no one – scholars, policy-makers, and even society – believes that escalation could occur, and the threat of force is ruled out (Battaglino 2012; Kacowicz 1997, 2000).

Empirically, however, these claims do not hold. In the south, Paraguay complained to the OAS in 2008 that Brazil was using live ammunition military exercises with 10,000 soldiers, ships, planes, and tanks close to the border as a means of pressuring it into a new treaty for the joint Itaipú dam. Paraguayans drew no comfort from a quote by the Brazilian general in charge of the exercises: "The time for hiding things is over. Today we have to demonstrate that we are a leader, and it is important that our neighbours understand this. We cannot continue to avoid exercising and demonstrating that we are strong, that we are present, and we have the capacity to confront any threat" (quoted in Zibechi 2009). In 2007, Uruguayan President Tabaré Vazquez consulted with his military chiefs and U.S. President George W. Bush concerning a possible Argentine military action over the disputed pulp paper mill on the Uruguayan side of the Rio de la Plata (*MercoPress* 2011a). In 2007 the number of Chileans who believed that Argentina could attack Chile was more than half (53 per cent), and 7.6 per cent higher than in 1991 (46.1 per cent) (Varas et al. 2008: 67). Chile was not the only state whose citizens believed Argentina could potentially be a threat: The British maintain a naval and air force presence in the Falklands/Malvinas, and sent their most advanced destroyer to the region in 2012 as Argentine rhetoric escalated before the 30th anniversary of the Falklands/Malvinas War (*MercoPress* 2011b).

None of these incidents 'proves' that the Southern Cone is not a zone of positive peace. But analysts who argue that violence in intra–Latin American relations is becoming inconceivable need to address such incidents and indicate how they fit in the argument, rather than simply ignoring them and asserting that no one fears the use of military force by its neighbor.

Militarized interstate disputes and Latin American security studies

The decision to use military force in some fashion (threat, display, confrontation) is a policy choice. As such, it has a rationale and logic, whether that is framed in terms of presidential, bureaucratic, or state interests. MIDs are not simply random events; they are intended to have an impact, though they are not generally intended to be a prelude to war. Comparing the interstate wars and MID databases clearly indicates that most MIDs worldwide do not lead to war. So MIDs cannot be studied merely as preludes to war, nor dismissed because they did not lead to war.

A reasonable assumption for studying interstate conflict and conflict resolution is that a state should not want to be coerced into negotiations by either fear of a war or pressure from third parties who fear regional instability. We can find some quick empirical support for this claim by comparing Costa Rica, Peru, and Chile on the question of appealing to the International Court of Justice (ICJ) to settle their territorial disputes with Nicaragua, Ecuador, and Bolivia, respectively. Costa Rica did not want to go to the ICJ on the Isla Calero question, but once Nicaraguan troops were in the contested area the only way for Costa Rica to get them to leave was to win the case at the ICJ. Peru refused to negotiate a new interpretation of the 1942 treaty with Ecuador, but after a short war failed to dislodge Ecuadorian troops in contested territory, Peru found that it had to negotiate to avoid a costlier war. Chile refuses to allow any third party to rule on its territorial dispute with Bolivia, and Bolivia has been unable to create a situation with Chile in which negotiation or arbitration becomes its preferred option. Once we think about the relationship between militarizing a dispute and coercing behavior, a range of important questions for the study of Latin American security studies emerges.

In previous work (Mares 2001), I have argued that MIDs are part of the diplomatic repertoire a state has and of which it may make use in one of five political-military strategies.

Keep the issue alive – the revisionist state is bilaterally weak and has no international influence, and the other state(s) are in control of the situation (hold the territory, refuse to patrol their side of the border, etc.). The revisionist state is simply concerned that its claim that a dispute exists not be forgotten; it has no timetable for negotiations concerning the issue.

Defend the status quo – the status quo state is not interested in opening negotiations on the issue and wants to demonstrate its commitment to the status quo.

Affect bilateral negotiations – one of the negotiating parties wants to demonstrate its commitment to the status quo or push the other side to reconsider its bargaining strategy.

Attract the support of third parties – one party (not necessarily the weaker one) wants to bring outside pressure on a rival to negotiate or, if already in negotiations, to accept a settlement that is more favorable to the initiator of the violence than preferred by the target of the MID.

Impose a solution – the initiator (status quo or revisionist) seeks to settle the issue unilaterally on its own terms.

The relationship between militarizing a dispute and its resolution has not been theorized or tested, despite the possibility that its militarization in the recent past may have contributed to making the dispute 'ripe for resolution.' Kacowicz (1994: 79–80) found that war experience had no statistically significant impact on peaceful territorial change, but he did not study MIDs. Others who studied the end of rivalry (whether or not territorial change was part of the termination of the rivalry) have found that the way in which a dispute is settled has a significant impact on the likelihood of conflict recurring (Quackenbush and Venteicher 2008). Case studies on conflict resolution suggest that MIDs may contribute by revealing high potential costs associated with their continuation (Mares and Palmer 2012), but the relationship has not been systematically tested, nor have the conditions under which it does and does not help resolution been specified. Considering that the Bolivia-Chile dispute has not experienced many MIDs and is not on the path towards resolution, while the Isla Calero dispute between Costa Rica and Nicaragua experienced serious MIDs and is now at the ICJ, the need for a comparative and historical perspective on the relationship between MIDs and resolution of conflict should be clear.

Note, however, that only three of the five political-military strategies are directed at resolving the dispute, and only two of the three via negotiations. Studying MIDs in the expectation that their use is perceived by the initiator to increase the likelihood of a positive resolution of the dispute (Battaglino 2012: 134) is too narrow an understanding of MIDs. If analysts wish to claim that a region does not use military force in relations with its neighbors and is peacefully settling its disputes, it is more fruitful to engage discussion of MIDs rather than treating them as unimportant aberrations. In addition, because studying Latin American security has long been about institutions and norms, as pointed out in Chapter 1 of this Handbook, scholars also need to relate militarized coercion to the institutional and normative context. In this era of institutional proliferation and democratic assertiveness, how does militarizing a dispute fit in?

We can usefully classify the context in which a government decides to utilize coercive diplomacy in its relations with another state with which it has a disagreement into five categories. For purposes of theoretical discussion, we can assume three relevant actors: a government that initiates the use of force at some level (initiator), a government against whose policies that force was directed (target), and everyone else that might become involved in the dispute, from allies to institutions (third party).

1 An initiator of militarization expects no material response or any negative consequence from either the target or third parties (i.e., Argentina's occupation of the Malvinas in 1982 and Nicaragua's mobilization against Costa Rica in 2010).
2 An initiator begins, or a target responds, with a low level of force, but is ready to escalate to higher levels of force, depending on the response of the other state (i.e., Argentina and Chile in the Beagle dispute in 1977–1978 up to full mobilization).
3 An initiator militarizes, or a target responds with a militarized act, but expects a third party to intervene and lower the probability of escalation, especially to war (i.e., Ecuador as initiator in both 1981 and 1995).
4 An actor militarizes, expecting no escalation, but in the face of escalation finds the cost of backing down to outweigh the expected cost of fighting (i.e., Argentina in the Malvinas).
5 An actor seeks war because it perceives the cost of fighting to be minimal and acceptable (i.e., El Salvador against Honduras in 1969).

In categories one, four, and five, security institutions and norms are too weak to affect the escalation. In the Nicaraguan mobilization against Costa Rica (an example of category one), the Nicaraguans knew Costa Rica had no military capability and simply told the OAS, to whom Costa Rica had appealed, that it had no jurisdiction on the issue, and the OAS accepted that judgment. The weakness of an institution is also seen in the example in category four. The Inter-American Treaty of Reciprocal Assistance ostensibly created to provide a hemispheric, unified front in the face of extrahemispheric military threats could not come to Argentina's aid because the institution's key member (the United States) sided with and provided aid to the British outside of the context of that institution. In category five, El Salvador did not fear OAS sanctions and was unconcerned about a war's impact on the Central American Common Market, which collapsed as a result of the war. In category two, third parties can only play an important role if the militarizing parties have convinced each other that war is likely and its costs would be higher than its benefits (Argentina and Chile were militarily balanced with significant firepower). To interrupt the escalation, a third party may offer the two sides an opportunity and a context in which to negotiate their way down the ladder.

In contemporary Latin America, most uses of force fall into categories one and three. The unequal military balance between rivals in Latin America's current potential conflict dyads make category two incidents unlikely. For example, if relations deteriorated once again between Colombia, Venezuela, and Ecuador, Colombia could reasonably expect the United States to step in and ensure that Venezuela and Ecuador could not ally and impose severe military costs on it. Consequently, thinking about the use of military force in Latin America means explaining why the costs of militarizing are so low for the initiator (category one) and why even a weak state that can reasonably expect a militarized response might initiate or respond with a use of force (category three).

Institutions have their greatest impact in category three, but without some way of imposing costs on militarizing, the institutions may create incentives that make militarization more likely – i.e., a 'moral hazard' phenomenon. A moral hazard results when a party is endowed with an 'insurance policy' that diminishes the risks of a particular activity to a point at which the party perceives such risks to be low enough to engage in the activity; insurance providers seek to minimize moral hazard by excluding such activities from coverage or charging a premium that raises the cost to the insured to a point that dissuades such behavior.

'Moral hazard' possibilities may encourage hard-line positions, even violence, by weaker parties in the dispute in the hope that an interested hemispheric community might increase pressure on a rival to settle (Mares 1996/1997). Although the hemisphere rejoices that Ecuador and

Peru have settled their dispute, we should not ignore the fact that it took a small war in 1995 and the threat of a large one in 1998 to convince the parties to settle. By guaranteeing that conquest would not be recognized and that escalation into a costly and long war would be unlikely, the OAS and the four guarantor countries helped convince Ecuador to engage in the adventurous behavior that developed into the short war of 1995. Ironically, regional security institutions may actually promote this risky behavior (category three). The moral hazard component of regional security institutions is a flaw in their institutional design. We need to understand why the institutions were designed in this manner in order to understand how and whether they can be modified to eliminate or reduce the moral hazard. This is a fundamental research question for Latin American studies, as the institutional context grows broader and denser (Mares 2007, 2012a, 2012b).

The challenge of explaining coercion among Latin Americans

The possibility of a 'moral hazard' incentivizing violence among Latin American countries could be eliminated, were the preparation for the use of violence among countries of the region to become transparent enough that no one need fear its sudden use, costly enough that no rational decision-maker would risk the consequences of militarization, or if its use became illegitimate normatively. The majority of scholars working on Latin American interstate security studies claim that international institutions, domestic institutions, and the evolution of norms and integration in the region provide that firewall to violent conflict. This scholarship confronts important research design challenges. The theoretical arguments regarding the peace-inducing impact of institutions and norms present a logic on how the specific characteristics of particular types of institutions, norms, and economic integration cause actors to evaluate options for behavior in ways that make recourse to violence impossible (in the strongest versions) or significantly less likely (Doyle 1997). The application of theory to empirical events must follow the definitions and logic of the theory being used; if the definitions and logic are different than those developed in a particular theory, then that theory does not provide an explanation for events, even if the pattern of events is as hypothesized. The scholar must look elsewhere for an explanation. Scholars must move beyond correlations (real and illusionary) to arguments that link the characteristics of the hypothesized causal variables to the properly specified outcomes. As this concluding section illustrates, the scholarly challenges are theoretical, methodological, and empirical.

International institutions – International institutions, of which regional are a subset, are theorized to enhance peaceful interstate relations by developing mechanisms that increase transparency, provide dispute resolution capabilities, and 'lengthen the shadow of the future' by increasing states' confidence and trust in each other. All of these measures require that the institution itself have both legitimacy and institutional capability to carry out the tasks. The challenge for Latin American security scholars who argue that regional organizations, other than the OAS, are important actors in building peace and bringing about the peaceful settlement of disputes is to demonstrate how the Unión Sudamericana de Naciones (UNASUR), the South American Defense Council (SADC), the Comunidad Andina de Naciones (CAN), or any other such institution has, and mobilizes, these capabilities. Presidential summits during crises periods are not sufficient to assert influence.

Scholars need to examine the empirical record of conflict and peaceful resolution and the characteristics of Latin American institutions to see if they meet the characteristics in the institutions that create the hypothesized effects. Recourse to international institutions has been a constant in Latin America's history, as noted in Chapter 1 (see also Malamud and Schenoni, this volume). So the mere fact that institutions exist today and we have some settlements cannot be an indication of the causal influence of those institutions, unless we have a causal argument about why the characteristics of those institutions in the past are no longer relevant in the contemporary period and why the current institutions are able to step into the breach. Scholars working on institution and dispute settlements in Latin America today focus on the latter step without addressing the first. The institutions themselves need to be studied to determine whether they are institutionalized sufficiently to perform these roles or are institutional shells that become activated when presidents or ministers meet.

Part of the challenge is that UNASUR, and even more so CELAC, have existed for such a brief time (since 2008 and 2010, respectively). But while that limited life means that they cannot be blamed for the Colombian attack in Ecuador or the Venezuelan attack on a Guyanese barge, by the same token, the claim for their peaceful influence does not yet have empirical support. This limitation is especially relevant given that the regional security environment in general has limited common understanding of threats and competing strategic views. In it, the use of low levels of military force in interstate bargaining is considered a national prerogative (Mares 2012a, 2012b). Rather than insist on a rule of 'no first use' of military force in a dispute between neighbors, the security architecture is designed to become active after a government has militarized. The role of the security structure is restricted to providing a forum for dialogue among sovereign and democratic nations to lower tensions rather than to resolve problems. Even the defense ministerial meetings do not address intra–Latin American disputes that are not currently in a crisis stage, preferring to leave those to bilateral negotiations.

Domestic institutions (democracy) – Battaglino's chapter in this volume notes the importance of examining the impact of 'participatory democracy' on peace and security. An example of the scholarly challenge for proponents of the democratic peace argument is that in the Polity VI database, Venezuela and Ecuador have fallen out of the democratic ranks since 2005 and 2008, respectively (Polity IV Project 2014). Yet Latin American analysts continue to include them in their democratic peace claims.

Until 'participatory democracy' is defined, its key components theorized to affect foreign policy behavior, and those hypotheses tested, one cannot assume that this type of democracy has a positive impact on interstate behavior. There are, in fact, many reasons to hypothesize the opposite. Liberal democratic theory takes limited state power, transparency of governmental processes, internationalism, and the right to dissent as institutional and normative elements that make democrats reject violence against other liberal democrats, while increasing their distrust and fear of nonliberal democratic polities. Participatory democracy, however, is nationalist and majoritarian – leaders and followers assert their defense of the nation against domestic minorities that are seen as obstacles to achieving national goals, and increase state power to limit the claims of opponents and punish them for articulating opposing views. Especially in the case of Venezuela, it would be difficult to claim that the government processes are transparent. If one were to translate the domestic institutional and normative causal logic of participatory democracy into foreign policy behavior, one would expect participatory democrats to take similar views against foreigners that compete for territory or resources or anything that blocks the populist democracy's national development. In particular, the mix of liberal and participatory democracies, given the logic of the argument, should produce mistrust between both sides and increase the likelihood of the use of force.

Analysts that see participatory democracy as a stage in the development of a mature democracy have another challenge. Mansfield and Snyder (2007) have argued that politicians in a new democracy find it easier to mobilize voters on the basis of nationalism, and this leads them to be involved in more international violence than would otherwise be expected given their democratic character. Thus, whether one sees participatory democracies as mature or not, there are arguments to suggest that they may be more prone to violence.

Economic integration – The theoretical claim about how economic integration reduces the incentive to engage in violent relations is fundamentally about the economic costs associated with fighting someone with whom your trade and financial relations are significantly developed (Gartzke 2007). In some formulations, economic integration creates common values among members as well. The causal hypothesis is that political leaders will prefer not to face significant economic disruptions to the economy or the political backlash from important economic sectors that would result from a disruption of those international economic relations.

The existence of economic integration that matters for these peace and conflict theories is not determined simply by the volume of trade and financial exchanges; it has to account for a significant (not specified, however) share of economic activity of both partners. The empirical reality is that, in the current era, there is a proliferation worldwide of regional economic agreements that are rarely implemented (Jupille et al. 2013). Economic integration processes stagnated throughout Latin America after a promising restart in the 1990s, though new ones are again being created (i.e., the Alliance of the Pacific). For some nations, regional integration stagnates because they have opened their economies to the world, thus lessening the attraction of regional integration (Mexico, Costa Rica, Panama, Colombia, Chile, and Peru). For others, protection of the national economy creates obstacles to implementing integration within the group (Argentina and Chile regarding natural gas, MERCOSUR). In fact, failed integration attempts can decrease trust – i.e., Chilean perceptions of Argentina as an 'enemy country' grew after the natural gas agreements were restricted in 2004 and exports halted in 2007 (Varas et al. 2008).

MERCOSUR is a favorite example of economic integration and peaceful relations in Latin America, despite the difficulties in advancing its agenda in the past 15 years. Analysts need to demonstrate the relative intra-MERCOSUR weight of these economic relations and the level of political influence of the beneficiaries and opponents of MERCOSUR within the partnering countries to sustain the argument that it is today an important component of the 'no war' assumption between Brazil and Argentina. One also needs to explain why MERCOSUR is not sufficient to eliminate Paraguayan and Uruguayan worries about being militarily coerced by their giant partners (Brazil and Argentina). In the process, scholars need to demonstrate not only that interrelated networks of social and economic actors were invested in the economic relationship, but also that they have the political clout to influence government decisions on whether or not to militarize a dispute.

Norms – The impact of norms on relations between states is argued to lie in their contribution to identity formation and the definition of interests. Norms that bring states together reduce uncertainty about intentions and make government policies credible to other countries. The content of the norms is thus fundamental in understanding how states respond to each other in specific circumstances. Four norms stand out in arguments about Latin America's approach to international security: peaceful settlement of international disputes, sovereignty, *uti possidetis*, and no wars for conquest. It is interesting that one norm about violence between states does not exist in Latin America, though one can deduce its existence in Western Europe and in the U.S.-Canada and U.S.-Japan relationships: no first use of force.

Peaceful settlement of international disputes – Kacowicz (1998, 2005) has argued that a shared, normative consensus for the peaceful settlement of international disputes has prevailed among South American nations. Taking Kacowicz's perspective, one could argue that history suggests that Mexico, Central America, and the Caribbean share the norm as well. Yet the norm is not specified correctly – it is a norm of no more than 1,000 battlefield-related deaths, but certainly not a norm of 'no use of force' in pursuit of a process that leads to a settlement of a dispute. It is misleading, therefore, to postulate that the region has a norm of peaceful settlement of disputes – that is certainly not how the Latin American diplomats defined 'peaceful settlement' in 1948. An important research question is whether this acceptance of violence below 1,000 battlefield deaths is also what the norm of peaceful settlement of disputes in other regions implies. If so, what does that mean about the way we think of this norm?

A subset of this norm is Martin's (2007) hypothesis about a South American military transnational identity and solidarity explaining negative peace. But this argument runs into significant empirical difficulties. He incorrectly claims that there were no casualties in the militarized disputes between Colombia and Peru in 1932 or between Ecuador and Peru in 1941, 1981, and 1995 (Martin 2007: 8–9); the Peruvian military wanted to resume war with Ecuador in August 1998, and it was a civilian president who stopped it. Chile's laying of 500,000 mines along the Peruvian and Bolivian borders during the 1976–1977 tension indicates that the Chilean military believed it was in a crisis situation, despite the fact that all three countries were under military rule. I have yet to find evidence that the Argentine military pulled back from its 1978 confrontation with Chile at the last minute because of a 'transnational identity and solidarity' with Chile's military.

Sovereignty – Sovereignty is widely defined as the ability to decide to do whatever one wants or to decide oneself whether and how to regulate transnational flows of goods, ideas, and people. Imposing sanctions on a government, and thereby raising costs for its behavior, is thus defined as a violation of sovereignty. Latin American leaders believe, more or less, that respect for a nation's sovereignty is the basis for peace: To cite Mexican statesman Benito Juarez, "*el respeto al derecho ajeno es la paz* [the respect of the rights of others is peace]" (my translation). One can see this in the common approach of Latin American multilateral organizations, which bring rivals to the table to talk about their differences, rather than condemning or sanctioning one party for deciding to use violence.

Norm of uti possidetis – The norm 'as you possess' was initially used to defend Spanish colonial territories undergoing the process of independence from other colonial powers, since they had not previously possessed the territory (Cornell University Law School LII). There are two major problems with using this norm for understanding intra–Latin American relations, however. First, among the newly independent Spanish colonies there was disagreement about which of the three Spanish colonial boundaries (administrative, military, or ecclesiastical, with subsets) were appropriate to use for delimiting the new nations. This meant that the juridical definition of who 'possessed' the territory was not clear. Thus the MIDs, including wars, around territorial issues between Latin American states occur within the boundaries set by *uti possidetis*. Second, Brazil did not accept Spanish colonial borders and argued for the norm of *uti possidetis de facto* – what mattered was who was in physical control of the territory, and *uti possidetis juris* became secondary (Gros Espiell 1986). Brazil convinced international arbitrators to accept this version of the norm. Despite many claims to the contrary, Brazil's efforts were not all peaceful: Bolivians recall the 'Acre War' of 1906 when Brazil sent its troops into disputed territory and claimed *de facto* possession. The challenge for scholars who appeal to this norm is to explain its evolution and its rejection in numerous historical and contemporary cases. For example, how can we explain that Chile refuses to submit its dispute with Bolivia regarding territory seized in a war of conquest to international adjudication?

No wars for conquest – Latin American publics do not sympathize with wars of conquest, despite their nationalistic tendencies. But low levels of militarized bargaining, such as verbal threats and displays of force, often garner public support. For example, in the Isla Calero dispute, Nicaraguans believed that Costa Rica, which has no army, could invade Nicaragua

(Sánchez 2011). This belief helps rationalize the Nicaraguan decision to send troops into a region that Costa Rica believed was settled by arbitration in the 19th century. One only has to recall the spontaneous and massive popular demonstrations supporting the Argentine military government's decision to seize the Falklands/Malvinas Islands, to recognize the importance of gathering empirical data about how citizens view the use of military force to defend national interests.

Why not: No first use of force – Latin America already has norms precluding use of force to conquer territory and overthrow a democracy, so why not against first use of force? Latin America has already accepted limits on 'sovereignty,' so why not limit it regarding the use of violence to coerce one's neighbors? One might hypothesize that, in the absence of significant costs in the militarization of regional relations, this norm could not be developed and accepted by all. The democracy norm was developed only after the horrors of the national security dictatorships, so it is in the immediate self-interest of governments in office. Neither of these conditions holds for low-level use of force. But note that this answer is more about costs and benefits, rather than norms. The sanctioning of first use, no matter the excuse, would eliminate the moral hazard in current regional security institutions.

Some empirical challenges: identifying trust and confidence-building

Virtually every scholar working on contemporary Latin American interstate security claims that confidence-building has proceeded and trust has been achieved, or is developing well. Yet there is no methodological discussion of how one ascertains if the outcome exists and how it has been achieved. To claim proof based on no war is to engage in circular reasoning.

The daily activity of confidence- and security-building continues to be at the bilateral level. Without a methodology to distinguish between mere contact and the actual building of confidence, however, it is difficult to evaluate the impact of activities such as a military ski championship between Chile and Argentina or Brazilian military students taking courses in Mexico. Even the countries that are ostensibly building confidence with each other do not agree on what measures build confidence. Colombia listed five CSBMs of a military nature with Ecuador in 1995, while the latter reported nine such measures between them. Peru did not list Argentina as a country with which it was engaged in such measures, but the latter listed Peru 11 times in its inventory. OAS experts produced five single-spaced pages listing measures that could be considered CSBMs; as guidelines for the analysis of CSBMs they are virtually useless (OEA 1995, 2003). Researchers also need to investigate how much confidence is necessary for it to have an impact on the decision to militarize, what determines those threshold levels, and whether they vary by issue area, country, or time and if so, why.

When scholars argue that countries are 'generating trust,' they provide select empirical evidence of interaction and assume 'trust' is generated. We have no studies of trust, but a few indicators that question whether 'trust' is actually generated. The aforementioned Chilean and Uruguayan concerns about Argentina are intriguing and need to be considered. The fact that Argentina has perhaps the weakest military in the region strongly suggests that 'trust' has both historical and domestic politics elements that need to be integrated into analyses of how, and whether, 'trust' is generated.

Conclusions

Avoiding conflict that produces more than 1,000 battlefield-related deaths is clearly positive. It is not, however, the most fruitful way to think about the role of military force in interstate relations, especially in a region in which 'sovereignty' continues to play as important a rhetorical role in foreign policy as in Latin America. There are important scholarly puzzles in the continued use of military threats and lower-level uses if one recognizes the empirical facts. Deciphering those puzzles will help us better understand Latin America's security situation and will contribute to the general literature on security studies.

Notes

1 The Correlates of War project has usefully categorized the use of military force into five 'hostility levels:' 1 = no use; 2 = threat; 3 = display; 4 = use < 1,000 battlefield-related deaths; 5 = war. Militarized incidents between states do not include accidental cross-border crossings by military that are not protested by the country whose territory has been violated, nor military violence against criminals/illegal migrants who cross into countries and are attacked by the forces there, unless that home country protests. See http://www.correlatesofwar.org/ and Jones et al. (1996).

References

Battaglino, J. M. (2012) 'The Coexistence of Peace and Conflict in South America: Toward a New Conceptualization of Types of Peace', *Revista Brasiliera de Política Internacional*, 55(2): 131–151.

Cornell University School of Law LII. 'Uti Possidetis'. Retrieved from http://www.law.cornell.edu/wex/uti_possidetis_juris.

Correlates of War. (n.d.) Militarized Interstate Disputes Incident Participants, MIDIP 4.01.csv. Retrieved from http://www.correlatesofwar.org/data-sets/MIDs.

Doyle, M. W. (1997) 'Kant, Liberal Legacies, and Foreign Affairs' in M. E. Brown, S. M. Lynn-Jones and S. E. Miller (eds) *Debating the Democratic Peace*, Cambridge: MIT Press.

Gartzke, E. (2007) 'The Capitalist Peace', *American Journal of Political Science*, 51(1): 166–191.

Gros Espiell, H. (1986) *Conflictos territoriales en Iberoamérica y solución pacífica de controversias*, Madrid: Ediciones Cultura Hispánica.

Hurrell, A. (1998) 'An Emerging Security Community in South America?' in E. Adler and M. Barnett (eds) *Security Communities*, Cambridge: Cambridge University Press.

Jones, D. M., Bremer, S. A. and Singer, J. D. (1996) 'Militarized Interstate Disputes, 1816–1992: Rationale, Coding Rules, and Empirical Patterns', *Conflict Management and Peace Studies*, 15(2): 163–212.

Jupille, J., Joliff, B. and Wojcik, S. (2013, March 28) 'Regionalism in the World Polity'. Available at SSRN: http://ssrn.com/abstract=2242500 or http://dx.doi.org/10.2139/ssrn.2242500.

Kacowicz, A. M. (1994) *Peaceful Territorial Change*, Columbia, SC: University of South Carolina Press.

——— (1997) 'The Third World Zones of Peace', *Peace Review: A Journal of Social Justice*, 9(2): 169–176.

——— (1998) *Zones of Peace in the Third World: South America and West Africa in Comparative Perspective*, Albany, NY: State University of New York Press.

——— (2000) 'Geopolitics and Territorial Issues: Relevance for South America', *Geopolitics*, 5(1): 81–100.

——— (2005) *The Impact of Norms in International Society: The Latin American Experience, 1881–2001*, Notre Dame: University of Notre Dame Press.

Mansfield, E. D. and Snyder, J. (2007) *Electing to Fight: Why Emerging Democracies Go to War*, Cambridge: MIT Press.

Mares, D. and Palmer, D. S. (2012) *Power, Institutions, and Leadership in War and Peace: Lessons from Peru and Ecuador, 1995–1998*, Austin: University of Texas Press.

Mares, D. M. (1996/1997) 'Deterrence in the Ecuador-Peru Enduring Rivalry: Designing Around Weakness', *Security Studies* 6(2): 91–123.

——— (2001) *Violent Peace: Militarized Interstate Bargaining in Latin America*, New York: Columbia University Press.

——— (2007) 'Confidence and Security-Building Measures as Inter-American Security Institutions: Relevance and Efficiency' in G. Mace, J-P. Thérien and P. Haslam (eds) *Governing the Americas: Regional Institutions at the Crossroads*, Boulder, CO: Lynne Rienner, pp. 97–109.

——— (2012a) *Latin America and the Illusion of Peace*, London: Routledge.

——— (2012b) 'Por que os Latino-Americanos continuam a se ameaçarem o uso da força militar nas relações intra Latino-Americanas', *Varia Historia*, 28(48): 599–625.
——— (2012c) 'Constructing Real Peace and Security in Latin America: Minimizing the "Moral Hazard" Character of Security Institutions', *Pensamiento Propio*, 17(36/37): 157–174.
Martin, F. E. (2007) *Militarist Peace in South America*, New York: Palgrave.
MercoPress (2011a, October 13) 'Argentina Denies Any "War Hypothesis" with Uruguay Over Controversial Pulp Mill'. Retrieved from http://en.mercopress.com/2011/10/13/argentina-denies-any-war-hypothesis-with-uruguay-over-controversial-pulp-mill.
——— (2011b, June 27) 'UK committed to Falklands in spite of all the 'huff and puff' from Argentine politician'. Retrieved from http://en.mercopress.com/2011/06/27/uk-committed-to-falklands-in-spite-of-all-the-huff-and-puff-from-argentine-politicians.
Organización de Estados Americanos (OEA), Committee on Hemispheric Security, Miami Group of Experts (2003) *Illustrative List of Confidence- and Security-Building Measures for Countries to Consider Adopting on the Bilateral, Sub-Regional and Regional Level.*
Organización de Estados Americanos (OEA), Inter-American Defense Board (1995) *Report of the Inter-American Defense Board on the Draft Inventory of Confidence-Building Measures of a Military Nature that are Being Implemented in the Hemisphere.*
Polity IV Project (2014) Political Regime Characteristics and Transitions, 1800–2013. Retrieved from http://www.systemicpeace.org/polity/polity4.htm.
Quackenbush, S. L. and Venteicher, J. F. (2008) 'Settlements, Outcomes, and the Recurrence of Conflict', *Journal of Peace Research*, 45(6): 723–742.
Sánchez, A. (2011) 'Costa Rica: An Army-Less Nation In A Problem-Prone Region', *Council on Hemispheric Affairs*. Retrieved from http://www.coha.org/costa-rica-an-army-less-nation-in-a-problem-prone-region/.
Sarkees, M. R. (2010) 'The List of Inter-State Wars' in M. R. Sarkees and F. W. Wayman (eds) *Resort to War: A Data Guide to Inter-State, Extra-State, Intra-State, and Non-State Wars, 1816–2007*, Washington, DC: CQ Press.
U.S. Department of State 'American Treaty on Pacific Settlement'. Retrieved from http://www.state.gov/p/wha/rls/70580.htm.
Varas, A., Fuentes, C. and Aguero, F. (2008) 'Instituciones cautivas: Opinión pública y nueva legitimidad social de las fuerzas armadas', Santiago: FLACSO-Catalonia, Santiago de Chile.
Zibechi, R. (2009) 'Is Brazil Creating its Own Backyard?', *Zeibechi Report*, 12.

22
ILLICIT THREATS
Organized crime, drugs, and small arms[1]

Phil Williams

Introduction

Peter Andreas, in his trenchant history of the United States as a 'smuggler nation,' reminds us that smuggling has been around for centuries (Andreas 2013). This kind of historical perspective is particularly relevant to Latin America, which, in the last several decades, has become renowned for both the entrepreneurialism and the violence of its drug trafficking organizations. Lance Grahn, in a study of New Granada (or what is now northern Colombia) in the early 18th century, suggested "the better known representatives of modern Colombian and Caribbean smuggling – narcotraffickers, U.S. Drug Enforcement agents, and inner city cocaine addicts – are current symbols of a dynamic economic informality with a long historical tradition" (1997: 3). Moreover, in a comment that has a very modern ring to it, he noted that smuggling "encouraged venality and deepened political corruption, frustrating the legitimate rule of law" (1997: 6). The echoes of these sentiments in the contemporary discourse about corruption and trafficking in Latin America are, if anything, even stronger than the original articulations.

Before exploring the contemporary manifestations of trafficking and organized crime, it is useful to delineate some definitions and distinctions. Smuggling is a term that has traditionally been used to refer to the act of "secretly importing prohibited goods or goods on which duty is due" (The Free Dictionary n.d.), or more broadly, to the "act of importing and exporting secretly and illegally to avoid paying duties or to evade enforcement of laws (i.e. drug or firearms-control laws)" (*Merriam-Webster* 2014). Although this broader definition explains why smuggling and trafficking are often used as synonyms, the notion of trafficking, at its core, is about circumventing enforcement of laws rather than simply avoiding duties. A handbook on illicit trafficking defined it as "behavior that facilitates the illegal entry of persons or prohibited products into a territory. Such behavior, typically involving transactions that violate laws and statutes, is deemed criminal" (Kelly et al. 2005: xiii). Even this definition needs to be extended, however, to include not just products that are prohibited but those, such as endangered species or cultural property, that are regulated, particularly in relation to their trade across borders (Williams 2001).

The key difference between past and present is that, whereas smuggling for the most part was historically about evasion of duties, much contemporary trafficking involves the movement of goods and even people that are subject to prohibition or regulation. An additional wrinkle is the distinction between human trafficking and human smuggling. Human smuggling occurs when people migrate illegally but voluntarily and commit a crime against the destination state; human trafficking occurs when the persons being moved are themselves victims of crime, and are subject to violence, coercion, or deceit, and sold into sexual slavery or forced labor.

The other important distinction relevant to this analysis is between mafias and transnational organized crime. Mafias, to use the classic definition enunciated by Gambetta, are groups involved in the business of private protection (Gambetta 1983). In practice, they often offer their services after directly or indirectly issuing threats that have made such protection necessary, thereby rendering protection little more than a euphemism for extortion. Organized crime is more amorphous but is used here to refer to organizations or criminal enterprises that, among other things, engage in various forms of trafficking, especially drug trafficking.

The essence of trafficking is logistics, supplemented by secrecy, concealment, bribery, and other techniques to avoid detection and disruption. As Patrick Keefe noted in a brilliant dissection of the Sinaloa Federation, its logistical network is as sophisticated, in some ways, as that of Amazon or the United Parcel Service (UPS) – doubly sophisticated, when you think about it, because traffickers must move both their product and their profits in secret, and constantly maneuver to avoid death or arrest. As a mirror image of a legal commodities business, the Sinaloa Cartel brings to mind that old line about Ginger Rogers doing all the same moves as Fred Astaire, only backwards and in heels (Keefe 2012). Sinaloa remains the most successful drug trafficking organization in Mexico and, perhaps, the world. Yet it is not alone in exhibiting the kinds of skills described by Keefe. Other drug trafficking organizations also display considerable skill, sophistication, and ingenuity in moving their commodities to market with acceptable losses and without serious disruption.

If trafficking is above all about logistics, in Latin America it is closely associated with violence. For several reasons, Latin American drug trafficking involves higher levels of violence than traditional smuggling ventures, and more than drug trafficking elsewhere. Cocaine, in particular, appears to attract violence, both in production and transshipment countries, although the relationship between the business and the violence is not simply unidirectional. In Peru and Colombia, two of the three major coca-producing countries, cultivation occurred in areas controlled by violent left-wing insurgencies – *Sendero Luminoso* in Peru and *Fuerzas Armadas Revolucionarias de Colombia* (FARC) in Colombia.

In the Colombian case, many peasants involved in coca cultivation moved to regions controlled by FARC in order to receive protection against the state. Colombia has also witnessed endemic violence among trafficking organizations, whether Medellín vs. Cali, FARC against rival trafficking organizations, or various criminal bands fighting one another.

Since the end of the Partido Revolucionario Institucional (PRI) monopoly of political power in Mexico in 2000, drug trafficking violence in Mexico has also increased: steadily during the Fox presidency and sharply under his successor, President Calderón. During the Calderón years (2006–2012), violence in the northern triangle of Central America also increased dramatically, as both Sinaloa and its major rival, *Los Zetas*, moved southwards to obtain earlier control of routes into Mexico and to offset the Mexican government's interdiction of cocaine shipments coming directly into Mexico from Colombia.

Other forms of trafficking in and from Latin America are far less significant than drug trafficking. Indeed, trafficking in firearms is driven in part by the prevalence of drug trafficking organizations, as well as by gangs, some of which are becoming more involved in the drug business. Human smuggling and human trafficking are a reflection of poverty and despair, combined with hope and aspirations by those being moved, and criminal opportunism on the part of those involved in the moving business. Illegal migration in particular has sometimes intersected in several ways with the drug business.

If the focus of this chapter were on a region other than Latin America, then various kinds of trafficking would have to be given equal consideration. In Latin America, however, organized crime and illicit trafficking have revolved around the drug trade. Everything else pales when set against the scale, scope, and profitability of drug trafficking, and the power of many of the organizations involved in the business. Against this background, therefore, this chapter seeks to answer several questions:

- What are the conditions in Latin America that have been so conducive to the rise of drug trafficking in particular, but that have also contributed to other forms of trafficking?
- Why is trafficking a threat, and how has this manifested itself in different countries and regions in Latin America?
- What are the recent, current, and likely future trends in trafficking and organized crime?
- What are the priority areas for future research on illicit trafficking and the threats it poses to national security?

Conditions in Latin America

Latin America has mostly been spared the large-scale interstate wars that for so long characterized Europe and Asia. While this has been a blessing, it has also had some undesirable consequences. As Charles Tilly pointed out, in Europe in particular, war-making and state-making typically went hand in hand (Tilly 1985: 186). In Latin America, in contrast, states did not need to mobilize their populations, enhance their capacity for resource extraction and taxation, develop a large and complex state apparatus, or engage in extensive social welfare. In effect, the Latin American state remained underdeveloped and subject to the vagaries of a political elite that placed more emphasis on self-interest than the public interest. As a result, states in Latin America have often exhibited a curious and even puzzling combination of repression and weakness. Moreover, as military dictatorship and one party rule have given way to more democratic forms of government, state weaknesses have often become more obvious. These include low levels of state legitimacy, high distrust of state institutions among the population, highly permeable borders with inadequate controls, ineffective laws and norms, rent-seeking politicians and corrupt officials, little economic or social provision for the citizenry, underdeveloped social control mechanisms, and unfair and antiquated criminal justice systems. Few state functions are carried out with efficiency, let alone effectiveness. Not surprisingly, these weaknesses and deficiencies provide fertile breeding grounds for lawlessness and criminality that have found perhaps the perfect expression in drug trafficking organizations.

Within these broad-brush characterizations, there are differences among the countries of Latin America. Chile, for example, has never had to confront the kinds of challenges that have faced Colombia and its Andean neighbors. This brings in an important regional factor, which is the long tradition of coca cultivation in the Andes (Clawson and Lee 1998). Traditionally coca leaf was chewed for altitude sickness and used in various rituals. This tradition, along with geographical conditions and an ideal climate, facilitated the large-scale cultivation of coca and production of cocaine when the drug first became fashionable in the United States. As demand increased, trafficking organizations coalesced, particularly in Medellín where Pablo Escobar worked with the Ochoa brothers and Carlos Lehder, and in Cali where the Orejuela brothers and Santa Cruz Londono emerged as the key players. With a large neighbor to the north with an almost insatiable appetite for the drugs produced in Latin America, the stakes increased considerably, and the organizations in Medellín and Cali not only developed high levels of market share but also vertically integrated the business, controlling the import of raw materials, the processing of cocaine, and the transportation and distribution to and within the United States (Zaitch 2002). They also industrialized the business by using boats, planes, and containers to move their product, sometimes via small Caribbean island countries where they were able to buy acquiescence. Cocaine was to prove far more lucrative than marijuana, and "in the hands of more audacious, rational and organized businessmen soon acquired great dimensions" (López-Restrepo and Camacho-Guizado 2003: 14). Not only did this lead to more sophisticated organizations but also "the close support of managers, lawyers, economists and other experts in dealing with large sums" (López-Restrepo and Camacho-Guizado 2003: 15).

Colombia became the central node in the cocaine trade, even though initially coca cultivation was far higher in Peru and Bolivia. Thoumi explains this partly in terms of the competitive advantage provided by state weakness: The Colombian state was weak because Colombian society was both divided along ideological lines and very violent (Thoumi 1995). While this is important, it was a necessary but not sufficient condition (Thoumi 2009). An additional factor explaining the rise of Colombian drug trafficking organizations was that Colombians made up the largest émigré population from South America living in the United States (Zaitch 2002: 38). If the Colombians had the resources and opportunity to exploit the growing demand for cocaine, they also had the expertise – Colombian cocaine trafficking was informed and facilitated by long traditions of contraband smuggling.

Colombia's domination of the cocaine business was consolidated when a fungus damaged the Peruvian coca crop in the Upper Huallaga Valley in the early 1990s, and interdiction efforts hampered the supply air bridge between Peru and Colombia. Consequently, for a decade from 1995 or 1996 onwards, Colombia led the Andean nations in both coca cultivation and cocaine production. In recent years, the trend has reversed, with both Peru and Bolivia increasing cultivation and cocaine production while Colombian output has declined precipitously. The 2012 World Drug Report highlighted

> . . . a major decline in cocaine manufacture in Colombia in the five-year period 2006–2010. A sizeable shift has taken place as coca bush cultivation and coca production increased in the same period in the other two coca-producing countries, Bolivia and Peru, which are becoming increasingly important producers.
>
> *(UNODC 2012: 2)*

It appears, however, that Colombian traffickers remain critical in the trafficking process to both the United States and Europe.

An important factor keeping Colombia at the forefront of cocaine trafficking is the disregard for the rule of law. Francisco Thoumi has increasingly placed emphasis on the dependence of drug export industries on "complex illegal organizations that can grow only in countries where there are groups whose social or informal behavior rules and norms differ substantially from the formal rules and norms formulated by the government prohibiting drug production and trafficking" (2009: 106). As he has noted, this gap has been particularly prevalent in Colombia, largely because government has relied on a form of clientelism that "turns the state into a bounty and undermines the rule of law and the ability of the state to enforce its norms" (Thoumi 2009: 123).

While Colombia might exhibit a particularly pronounced case of the gaps between formal norms and lawlessness, the extent to which other countries in Latin America have become an integral part of the trafficking process suggests that this gap is far from unique. In this connection, the two most noteworthy developments have been the rise of Mexican drug trafficking organizations and the growing involvement of Central America as a major transshipment region.

Although Mexico has long been a supplier of marijuana and black tar heroin to the United States, during the last two decades Mexican drug trafficking expanded enormously: The marijuana business increased significantly, Mexican drug organizations replaced Colombians as the dominant cocaine traffickers in the United States, and Mexicans became major suppliers to the U.S. methamphetamine market, a market largely created by entrepreneurial Mexican traffickers.

Mexican involvement in the cocaine business, in particular, illustrates the law of unintended consequences. One result of the United States clampdown on trafficking into Florida in the early 1990s was increased reliance on trafficking through Mexico. U.S. and Colombian successes in dismantling the Medellín and Cali drug trafficking organizations followed soon after. The main lesson for Colombian drug trafficking organizations was the need to truncate operations to avoid direct confrontation with the United States. At the same time, Mexican organizations, which already had the responsibility for moving the cocaine into the United States, increasingly demanded payment in cocaine. As a result they graduated from transportation services to traffickers in their own right, and soon achieved primacy in the U.S. market. The cast of Mexican trafficking organizations varied over time as a result of government efforts and internecine warfare. Among the key organizations with staying power, however, were the Sinaloa Federation, the Gulf, *Los Zetas*, and the Carrillo Fuentes Organization in Juárez. All these organizations developed a significant presence in U.S. cities (NDIC 2010). Significantly, their rise coincided with the loss of the political monopoly of the PRI, which had hitherto controlled and constrained the traffickers. The elite-exploitation model broke down, placing the Mexican state and the trafficking organizations on a major collision course (Pimentel 2003: 180).

The other key development is the involvement of Central America as both a transshipment region and an area where some of the rivalries among the Mexican groups are played out. The 'northern triangle' of Guatemala, El Salvador, and Honduras has been particularly impacted. This reflects the geopolitical imperatives of the trafficking business, or more simply the location curse of being between drug producers and the most profitable consumer market – the United States. Moreover, as Steven Dudley has noted, these countries have

> . . . vast coastlines, large ungoverned spaces and the greatest proximity to Mexico. However, geography is only part of the problem. Armed conflicts in Guatemala, El Salvador and parts of Honduras between 1960 and the mid-1990s laid the foundations for the weapons trafficking, money laundering and contraband traffic that we are witnessing today. Peace accords in Guatemala and El Salvador, and police and military reform, only partially resolved deep-seeded socio-economic and security issues, and, in some cases, may have accelerated a process by which drug traffickers could penetrate relatively new, untested government institutions.
>
> *(2010: 3)*

Dudley's assessment leads very naturally to consideration of why drug trafficking in Latin America is a security threat.

Drug trafficking and national security

As suggested above, trafficking, in its essence, is little more than a highly specialized and covert form of logistics. The traffickers' toolkit involves deception, concealment, facilitation through corruption, and circumvention of control points (for example, through the tunnels under the Mexican-U.S. border). Apart from corruption, however, there is little inherent threat in trafficking as such. Many trafficking organizations are small, decentralized, and nonviolent, and pose little threat to public or national security. In the final analysis, however, at least five dimensions of drug trafficking organizations in Latin America create national security threats.

First, major drug trafficking organizations wield inordinate power. Somewhat paradoxically, drug trafficking organizations exhibit tendencies both towards expansion and concentration of power and towards fragmentation and dissolution. The challenge, however, is that some trafficking organizations start small, but through a process of Darwinian evolution become large and powerful, before eventually going into decline. As such, they represent a concentration of illicit power in the society and one that can challenge state authority and behave with a high degree of impunity. Moreover, what differentiates these organizations from corporations is that they are, in effect, outside the law and behave according to a different set of rules and norms. Trafficking organizations represent a ruthless entrepreneurialism that is not only unconstrained by laws and regulations but is also underpinned by a willingness to use violence against both rivals and the state. They sometimes become so large and powerful that they challenge the state's monopoly of force. In this sense, the challenge of drug trafficking is related to fundamental issues of state fragility, governance and corruption, and erosion of the rule of law. Drug trafficking, particularly by larger organizations, not only undermines national sovereignty and exploits seams and weakness in national border control, but also corrodes the effectiveness and integrity of law enforcement, and provides opportunities for violent, armed groups to fund campaigns of terror and intimidation. While drug trafficking is not necessarily a fundamental source of state weakness, traffickers certainly exploit such weaknesses and often seek to perpetuate them. This is particularly easy in Latin America, because of the nature of the state.

A second and closely related threat is that trafficking organizations – in a few cases through deliberate intent, but more often than not through incrementalism – provide alternative forms of governance (see Trinkunas and Clunan, this volume). Sometimes this reflects an intense resentment towards central government, as is the case in Michoacán where both La Familia and its successor, Los Templarios Caballeros, blended criminality with a cult-like approach and tapped into a deep vein of resentment regarding the neglect of the federal government in Mexico City. Yet, in this case, the groups became so predatory that they galvanized an upsurge of vigilantism. In other cases, however, the alternative forms of governance are based on a calculated paternalism in which the traffickers extend the benefits to local populations rendered sympathetic by patronage and the provision of public goods. Where government provision has not been adequate, trafficking organizations provide forms of governance that are local and organic, bottom-up rather than top-down, and that pose a challenge to state governance. Although these forms of alternative governance are predatory, this might count for less in Latin America, where the state itself has often been the most predatory of all.

Following directly from this is a third form of threat: Trafficking organizations pose a threat to security because they are often seeking, in a highly competitive manner, if not monopoly control then a larger market share. The world of Latin America drug trafficking exhibits many of the qualities of Hobbes's state of nature in which life is nasty, brutish, and, for those that are unsuccessful, relatively short. Ironically, this competitive environment provides both challenges and opportunities for the state. The challenges come from the fact that when criminal enterprises compete overtly they often create "politically inconvenient levels of violence" (Bailey and Taylor 2009: 9) that undermine government legitimacy (Carreras 2013). The opportunities arise from the ability of governments to exploit the competition through a variation of balance of power strategies. Balancing is particularly useful where a major trafficking organization is particularly violent or is directly confronting the state. By allying with other criminal organizations the major threat can be neutralized – after which the former partners themselves become targets of government enforcement efforts. This occurred in Colombia, where the government tacitly and temporarily allied with the Cali organizations to bring down their more violent rivals operating out of Medellín before turning on Cali. Something similar occurred in Mexico, where there are persistent claims that the Calderón government gave preferential treatment to the Sinaloa Federation while targeting its rivals, whether *Los Zetas* or the Beltran Leyva Organization (BLO). The dynamic seems to have been the same: Tacitly ally with one drug trafficking organization to take out more violent and dangerous organizations, and then turn on that organization. Moreover, although it is often argued that the capture of Guzman will make no difference to Sinaloa's capacity to move drugs to the United States, it could make a difference to the level of violence. Under Guzman's leadership, Sinaloa became what can only be described as a "revisionist power" (Morgenthau 1948: 40–44), in turn challenging the Arellano Felix Organization in Tijuana, the Gulf in Nuevo Laredo, and the Carrillo-Fuentes Organization in Ciudad Juárez for control of key crossing points into the United States. Partly because Sinaloa has had significant success with this strategy, and partly because it was so closely associated with Guzman, it is conceivable that, with his incarceration, Mexican drug trafficking organizations might be able to establish a new equilibrium characterized by lower levels of violence.

The problem, however, is that Sinaloa and the *Zetas* have already made serious inroads into Central America, bringing with them increased levels of violence. This is an example of both the balloon effect – when squeezed or stifled in one area, whether city block, city, or country, the trafficking balloon simply pops up elsewhere – and the cockroach effect – when the light is turned on, the cockroaches scatter (Bagley 2013: 2). Yet this does not provide the whole story. The geographical expansion from Mexico into Central America resulted, in part, from a competitive dynamic in which the two organizations sought advantage by obtaining both allies and territorial control earlier in the transshipment process. The spillover in Guatemala certainly seems to have this characteristic and belies the notion that these organizations were simply seeking safe havens outside Mexico.

Although the future trajectory of Mexican drug trafficking organizations is not entirely clear, it is possible that it will follow the earlier Colombian pattern in that the large drug trafficking organizations will gradually be replaced by a larger number of smaller groups. Yet this is not preordained. The dialectic between trends towards centralization and consolidation and trends towards fragmentation and diffusion is constant. In Colombia, by early 2013, the Urabeños organization had emerged as the dominant player, and once again a predominant group wielded enormous power. In the final analysis, it is difficult to determine whether the most challenging arrangement from a security perspective is virulent competition among drug trafficking organizations or hegemony by one – or, indeed, the process whereby one of these conditions shifts into the other.

A fourth threat stems from the propensity of large trafficking organizations to develop sophisticated risk management strategies, using a mix of corruption and violence to encourage state complicity or, at the very least, compel state acquiescence in their activities. Bailey and Taylor identified three kinds of strategy for criminal organizations in dealing with government: evasion, corruption, and confrontation (2009). While the preference might be for evasion – as it is less costly than the alternatives – when an organization becomes large, powerful, and highly visible, it almost invariably has to resort to corruption, confrontation, or, more likely than not, some combination of the two. Silver is more attractive to judges and officials when the alternative is lead. For traffickers, the targets of corruption vary according to where in the trafficking process they are, and can be either systemic (Nadelmann 1993: 269–270) or operational. In the home base of the trafficking organization, corruption will typically be directed at government, the judiciary, and law enforcement agencies to ensure that the organization can act with impunity. In these circumstances, corruption often becomes systemic or institutional. In transshipment and destination states corruption has traditionally been more operational, with customs personnel and border guards as primary targets. In Mexico and Central America, however, corruption has become even more extensive and has reached into the police forces, the military, and local and central government institutions. Corruption linked to organized crime and trafficking is particularly pernicious, as it seeks to neutralize and circumvent the powers of the state, to coopt the servants of the state, to eliminate social and territorial controls, and to erode the criminal justice system. Trafficking organizations develop corrupt and collusive relations with political and military elites, bureaucrats, and law enforcement and customs officials. As a result members of these elites become major beneficiaries of the trafficking process and other criminal activities. In some cases, they even play a key role in organizing these activities; in others they simply provide a degree of protection that enables trafficking to continue with little or no interference. Whatever the exact role of corrupt political elites, however, they exacerbate the trafficking problem and undermine the state. Moreover, once these criminal corruption networks are in place they are difficult to dislodge – not least because they develop strong interests in both perpetuating and protecting themselves.

A fifth threat stems from another form of trafficking – arms trafficking. Although the arms trafficking business is subordinate to, and serves the interests of, drug trafficking organizations and the gangs concentrated in Central America and in Brazilian prisons and favelas, the flow of weapons feeds directly into the armed violence that has been characterized as "a defining problem for contemporary Latin America and the Caribbean" (Davis 2006: 178). Such a characterization is not an exaggeration. As one observer has pointed out, "South America has 14 percent of the global population, and roughly 3.5 to 4 percent of the world's civilian firearms, but it suffers from roughly 40 percent of all homicides committed with firearms" (Karp 2009: 15).

Much attention in recent years has focused on the trafficking of firearms from the United States to Mexico, and sometimes even further south into Central America. The sources for these firearms include: gun stores, pawnshops, private owners, and perhaps most important of all gun shows. Although such smuggling is extensive, it is not clear if it operates through an atomistic market with a large number of small suppliers, or a more organized supply chain with a limited number of larger suppliers. In November 2008, a report submitted to the Mexican president described the process as 'ant trafficking' (*Excelsior* 2009). Some of the weapons smuggling, however, seems to have been orchestrated by drug trafficking organizations using intermediaries to buy and move weapons (Williams 2009).

Contemporary arms trafficking in Latin America also reflects Brazil's status as a major weapons producer, and the inability of military and police forces throughout Latin America to maintain control of the weapons arsenals. Karp, for example, has noted that in Brazil poor stockpile security and corruption leads to widespread firearms diversion from law enforcement agencies into criminal hands, and trafficking of guns remains a major problem, particularly in the Triple Frontier (Karp 2009: 31). Colombia, too, has a large and dynamic internal weapons market that has been driven by the conflicts among drug trafficking organizations and the criminal bands. Central America is also awash with arms, some of which are a legacy of the civil wars, while others are stolen from police and military forces in the region.

In sum, it is clear that organized crime and drug trafficking pose major threats throughout Latin America, particularly to Central America, where several nations suffer from weak institutions, and are bedeviled by high levels of corruption and violence. Moreover, trends towards greater transparency and accountability are undermined by trafficking organizations that kill journalists, intimidate media outlets, and are as repressive of a free press as any authoritarian government.

Current trends and priorities for research

In an extremely stimulating analysis, Garzón has argued that illicit trafficking in Latin America has moved into a new phase. He has characterized this phase as the 'era of the rebellion of criminal networks' characterized by

> . . . disputes between criminal factions that . . . compete rather than . . . reach agreements; reprisals of criminal groups against the state; the search of "legal" actors for greater involvement in criminal activities; the violent expression of criminal density and social accumulation of violence and illegality; and the replacement of capos (bosses) with "brokers."
>
> *(Garzón 2012: 1)*

This is a persuasive argument. Yet it is important not to overlook patterns of continuity and to avoid exaggerating the novelty. Both competition and violence against the state are more widespread than in the past, but are not unprecedented. In fact, nothing in the current assaults on the state compares with the terrorist campaign in Colombia initiated by Pablo Escobar in response to the extradition agreement between Bogotá and Washington. Moreover, as Peter Lupsha pointed out some years ago, in the drug business the players change but the game continues (Lupsha 1991).

One area of change is that drug trafficking organizations were traditionally businesses run by extended families and friends; yet in both Colombia and Mexico this has altered dramatically. The rise of the Urabeños, for example, exemplifies Thoumi's thesis that, in Colombia, warlords more concerned with the internal competition for power and territory replaced traditional drug lords who focused exclusively on the narcotics business, and in turn were replaced by paramilitary forces (Thoumi 2012). Something similar is true in Mexico, where organizations such as the *Zetas* or La Linea in Cuidad Juárez are primarily 'entrepreneurs of violence' rather than drug entrepreneurs (Volkov 2002).

Not surprisingly, the change in players has also meant the game itself is evolving in several directions. The first and perhaps most striking is the broadening of criminal portfolios. During the last 50 years, organized crime in Latin America has revolved around the drug business. Yet this is changing. Extortion has become much more widespread. Whether extorting school teachers and shopkeepers or engaging in large-scale killings of illegal immigrants to demonstrate to the coyotes moving people that they have to pay for safe passage, *Los Zetas* has established major new revenue streams. Perhaps even more striking has been the move into the exploitation of natural resources: FARC involvement in illegal gold mining, the Knights Templar involvement in the mining and sale of iron ore, and the *Zetas* control of much of the coal mining in Coahuila are just three examples.

The drug business itself has been characterized by diffusion to more countries in Latin America, especially Venezuela, Brazil, and Argentina. This reflects the increased importance of the cocaine market in Europe, which has become almost as lucrative as that in the United States, and the resulting diversity of transshipment routes, including those through West Africa. But it is also linked to the growing importance throughout Latin America of local drug markets, or as they are sometimes known, 'micro-markets.' One result of this is that the old distinction between supplier and consumer countries has broken down. The coincidence of this with increased understanding of the pernicious "circuit in which a 'victory' in one country becomes a problem for another" (Garzón 2013) has led to growing calls to rethink the war on drugs and consider alternatives to outright prohibition.

Against this background, there are several areas of research that are critical to both understanding and the development of more effective policy responses. The first is a more sustained examination of the relationship between trafficking and violence and the extent to which they can be decoupled by more refined government policies and strategies. A second concerns the relationship between the shape of the drug trafficking industry and the nature of the threats posed to security. Third, more attention needs to be paid to what appear to be growing linkages between drug trafficking organizations and the *maras* in Central America. Perhaps most important of all, however, is a sustained analysis of how the deficiencies and weakness of governance mechanisms throughout much of Latin America can be overcome in ways that help to contain the security threats posed by drug trafficking yet avoid reverting to past patterns of authoritarianism. That perhaps is the single greatest challenge for the future.

Note

1 The author would like to thank Alexander Halman for his assistance in the research for this chapter.

References

Andreas, P. (2013) *Smuggler Nation*, New York: Oxford University Press.

Bagley, B. (2013) *Drug Trafficking and Organized Crime in Latin America and the Caribbean in the Twenty First Century: Challenges To Democracy*, Bogotá: Universidad de los Andes.

Bailey, J. and Taylor, M. M. (2009) 'Evade, Corrupt, or Confront? Organized Crime and the State in Brazil and Mexico', *Journal of Politics in Latin America*, 1(2): 3–29.

Carreras, M. (2013) 'The Impact of Criminal Violence on Regime Legitimacy in Latin America', *Latin American Research Review*, 48(3): 85–107.

Clawson, P. L and Lee, R.W. (1998) *The Andean Cocaine Industry*, New York: St. Martin's.

Davis, D. (2006) 'The Age of Insecurity: Violence and Social Disorder in the New Latin America', *Latin American Research Review*, 41(1): 178–197.

Dudley, S. S. (2010) 'Drug Trafficking Organizations in Central America: Transportistas, Mexican Cartels and Maras', Working Paper Series on U.S.-Mexico Security Collaboration, Washington, DC: Wilson Center.

Excelsior (2009, January 5) 'Gulf Cartel Top Arms Smuggler in Mexico'.

Gambetta, D. (1983) *The Sicilian Mafia*, Cambridge: Harvard University Press.

Garzón, J. C. (2012) *The Rebellion of Criminal Networks: Organized Crime in Latin America And the Dynamics of Change*, Washington, DC: Woodrow Wilson Center Update on the Americas.

——— (2013) *The Criminal Diaspora: The Spread of Transnational Organized Crime and How to Contain its Expansion*, Washington, DC: Wilson Center.

Grahn, L. (1997) *The Political Economy of Smuggling: Regional Informal Economies in Early Bourbon New Granada*, Boulder: Westview Press.

Karp, A. (2009) *Surplus Arms in South America: A Survey*, Geneva: Small Arms Survey, Graduate Institute of International and Development.

Keefe, P. R. (2012, June 15) 'Cocaine Incorporated', *The New York Times Magazine*. Retrieved from http://www.nytimes.com/2012/06/17/magazine/how-a-mexican-drug-cartel-makes-its-billions.html?pagewanted=all&_r=0.
Kelly, R. J., Maghan, J. and Serio, J. D. (2005) *Illicit Trafficking*, Santa Barbara: ABC-CLIO.
López-Restrepo, A. and Camacho-Guizado, A. (2003) 'From Smugglers to Warlords: Twentieth Century Colombian Drug Traffickers', *Canadian Journal of Latin American and Caribbean Studies*, 28(55/56): 249–275.
Lupsha, P. A. (1991) 'Drug Lords and Narco-corruption: The Players Change but the Game Continues', *Crime, Law and Social Change*, 16(1): 41–58.
Merriam-Webster (2014) 'Smuggling'. Retrieved from http://www.merriam-webster.com/dictionary/hacker.
Morgenthau, H. J. (1948) *Politics Among Nations: The Struggle for Power and Peace*, New York: Knopf.
Nadelmann, E. (1993) *Cops Across Borders*, University Park: Penn State University Press.
NDIC (2010) *Cities Where Mexican Drug Trafficking Organizations Operate Within the United States*, Washington, DC: National Drug Intelligence Center.
Pimentel, S. (2003) 'Mexico's Legacy of Corruption' in R. Godson (ed) *Menace to Society: Political-Criminal Collaboration Around the World*, New Brunswick: Transaction, pp. 175–197.
The Free Dictionary (n.d.) 'Smuggling'. Retrieved from http://www.thefreedictionary.com/smuggling.
Thoumi, F. E. (1995) *Political Economy and Illegal Drugs in Colombia*, Boulder: Lynne Rienner.
——— (2009) 'Necessary, Sufficient and Contributory Factors Generating Illegal Economic Activity, and Specifically Drug-Related Activity, in Colombia', *Iberoamericana*, IX(35): 105–126.
——— (2012) 'Colombian Organized Crime: From Drug Trafficking to Parastatal Bands and Widespread Corruption' in D. Siegel and H. van de Bunt (eds) *Traditional Organized Crime in the Modern World: Responses to Socioeconomic Change*, New York: Springer, pp. 131–149.
Tilly, C. (1985) 'War Making and State Making as Organized Crime' in P. B. Evans, D. Rueschemeyer and T. Skocpol (eds) *Bringing the State Back In*, Cambridge: Cambridge University Press, pp. 169–171.
UNODC (2012) *World Drug Report 2012*, Vienna.
Volkov, V. (2002) *Violent Entrepreneurs: The Use of Force in the Making of Russian Capitalism*, Ithaca: Cornell University Press.
Williams, P. (ed) (2001) 'Transnational Organized Crime, Illicit Markets, and Money Laundering' in P. J. Simmons and C. Ouderen *Challenges in International Governance*, Washington, DC: Carnegie Endowment, pp. 106–150.
——— (2009) 'Illicit Markets, Weak States and Violence: Iraq and Mexico', *Crime Law and Social Change*, 52: 323–336.
Zaitch, D. (2002) *Trafficking Cocaine: Colombian Drug Entrepreneurs in the Netherlands*, The Hague: Kluwer.

23

ENVIRONMENTAL SECURITY AND DISASTERS IN LATIN AMERICA AND THE CARIBBEAN

A blind spot in research

Gavin O'Toole

Introduction

The devastating earthquake that struck Haiti in 2010, killing hundreds of thousands of people, illustrates the risks posed by natural disasters in Latin America and the Caribbean, a part of the world that has also been prominent in debates about environmental change. Yet the region represents a blind spot within discussions on environmental and human security, and English-language scholarship continues to be dominated by traditional U.S. security concerns, despite evidence that Latin American militaries have been engaging with notions of environmental and human security for some time. A comprehensive research agenda that throws light on changing conceptions of security in a context of growing cooperation within the region – but which also explains why scholarship is missing the boat – is required.

Disasters and climate change

Natural disasters, events triggered by natural hazards that overwhelm local response capacity and seriously affect a region's development, are classified as biological, geophysical, climate-related, and meteorological (Leaning and Guha-Sapir 2013). At an aggregate level, they can have serious effects on economies and extract an obvious human cost (Charvériat 2000). Between 2002 and 2011 the annual average number of people killed globally by natural disasters was 107,000, and the annual average number of those affected was 124.5 million (Guha-Sapir et al. 2013). There is a growing body of evidence to suggest that the number of casualties and the economic impact of disasters are increasing (Zapata and Madrigal 2009: 9; Dalby 2009: 111). Climate change helps to explain this, and for many years has been generating alarm (World Bank/GFDRR 2011).

Disasters are common in Latin America and the Caribbean, which is exposed to a wide variety of hazards, and have had considerable impact upon the region's development (World Bank/GFDRR 2011; Khamis and Osorio 2013: 10–11). Significant disasters that have occurred in the region include, most recently, the Haitian earthquake (222,570 deaths) (World Bank/GFDRR: xviii–xix). Between 1990 and 2011, on average 24 intensive disasters occurred in the region per year, each costing 39 lives and affecting 22,000 people (UNISDR/OSSO 2013: 45).

The *Annual Disaster Statistical Review* suggests that in 2012 the Americas endured the most disaster damages of any region (Guha-Sapir et al. 2013: 2).

Yet the impact of disasters is uneven, and levels of damage are directly related to levels of vulnerability and resilience (Zapata and Madrigal 2009: 14). For example, the Chilean mega-earthquake on February 27, 2010 had a magnitude (Mw) approaching nine and caused 577 deaths (Medina et al. 2010: v). This can be compared with the impact of the Haiti quake the previous month, which measured 7.0 Mw.

There is a general consensus that development patterns in Latin America and the Caribbean create risk factors that are likely to increase the human and economic cost of disasters (World Bank/GFDRR 2011: 9). The region is exposed to a wide variety of hazards, including earthquakes, volcanoes, storms, extreme temperatures, droughts, floods, and landslides, many of which are aggravated by the recurrent El Niño phenomenon (World Bank/GFDRR 2011; Khamis and Osorio 2013: 10–11). Many of its main cities are located close to or on top of seismic faults; population growth and rapid urbanization means that many cities are expanding into floodplains or on hillsides susceptible to landslides and other hazards; and territorial planning, building standards, and other risk mitigation measures are often inadequate.

Climate change will only reinforce these trends, and the World Bank estimates that the annual cost in the region of adapting by 2050 could reach US$21 billion (World Bank 2010). The risk of natural disasters makes preparedness an important theme in multilateral, regional, and national policy-making (SELA 2010: 57–68; Fernandez and Sanahuj 2012; Poncelet 1997; World Bank/GFDRR 2011; Rocha and Christoplos 2001). Military forces are frequently called upon to respond to disasters, and some countries, such as Mexico, maintain dedicated units for this (Foster 2005; Smith 2007). The obvious question this raises in Latin America is to what extent, if at all, has the response to disasters been based upon a security perspective that is theoretically grounded.

Disasters and security

Mandel (2002) argues that natural disasters can help to reveal the actual scope and meaning of a state's security doctrine because of its underlying goal to return stability to a society in crisis. Although the relationship between disasters and security has been undertheorized, it has increasingly been examined through the lens of development, building on Cold War perspectives that linked security concerns to aid (McNeish and Sande Lie 2010). Securitization of underdevelopment in recent years has often been expressed in terms of the notion of the 'failed state' (Duffield 2001, 2007; Vannoni 2012; Buzan et al. 1998; Kaldor 2001; McNeish and Sande Lie 2010: 10).

McNeish and Sande Lie (2010) attribute the growing prominence of the relationship between security and development, among other things, to the growing use of "states of exception," referred to by Agamben (2005) as the normalization of situations of danger or threats to the state – including environmental collapse – that legally justify the suspension of rights and the rule of law. Inevitably, such arguments have prompted debates about the moral criteria that justify humanitarian intervention and what this means for sovereignty (Pape 2012: 41; McNeish and Sande Lie 2010: 2, 10; Ignatieff 2003).

An example of an intervention with humanitarian aims that generated debates about sovereignty within Latin America and the Caribbean was Brazil's military deployment in Haiti in 2004 to command a UN-mandated peacekeeping operation, which President Luiz Inácio Lula da Silva characterized not in terms of a new doctrine but in terms of continuity with Brazil's traditional commitment to national sovereignty (Spektor 2012).

The developmental link between natural disasters and security can be further explored through notions of *environmental security*, which in the late 1970s became part of the language of national security (Floyd and Matthew 2013: 4). The end of the Cold War and its implications for realism further widened security studies to include broader environmental and other threats (Mastanduno 1997; Dalby 2009: 39). In their most extreme form, natural disasters pose the ultimate security risk – an existential threat (Diamond 2006; Linden 2007).

A number of authors explicitly began to suggest that the structure of military forces built up during the Cold War now seemed useless in face of environmental change (Myers 1998; Tuchman Matthews 1989; Renner 1989; Dalby 2009: 24). Most research in this area concerns the relationship between environmental change and conflict (Matthew et al. 2010: 11–12; Dalby 1992; Deudney and Matthew 1999; Homer-Dixon 1999; Kaplan 1994; Kahl 2006). These scholarly debates have tended to conclude that claims about conflict are alarmist, and environmental scarcity by itself is not considered a causal factor of hostilities (Homer-Dixon 1999; Lonergan 2001; Gleditsch et al. 2006; Barnett 2000; Dalby 2009: 27; Matthew et al. 2010: 14). It has been argued that literature that links the environment to conflict is theoretically rather than empirically driven and is a product of a northern security agenda (Floyd and Matthew 2013: 8).

Perhaps more importantly, natural resources have also been identified as important to peacebuilding and conflict resolution (Ali 2007; Srinivas 2001). Writing on natural disasters also sheds light on how the environment can be as much a source of cooperation as it is of confrontation (Dalby 2009: 129, 145; Barkdull and Harris 2002; Tiefenbacher and Hagelman III 2008). Cooperation in the face of disasters is now becoming standard in international thinking (Dalby 2009: 129, 145; Barkdull and Harris 2002; Kelman 2007; Tiefenbacher and Hagelman III 2008). While some traditional sovereign security issues persist, these often derive from disputes over resources (Domínguez et al. 2003). Yet at the same time resources such as energy and water are now the focus of considerable cooperation throughout the region (Luft and Korin 2009; UNEP/OSA/UNA 2007). Indeed, cooperation has become the key motif of security policy (Resende-Santos 2002; Sotomayor Velázquez 2004).

The most important recent theme in debates on environmental security concerns climate change (Floyd and Matthew 2013: 11; Helmer and Hilhorst 2006). Early environmentalists labelled environmental changes as risks to national security, and today many label climate change as a security issue (Brown 1977: 8). The U.S. armed forces were among the first to raise concerns about the prospect of conflict in a climate-changed world (Floyd and Matthew 2013: 11; Matthew 2013: 267). A prominent theme within national security literature on climate change is migration, and concerns that this could fuel tensions and spread terrorism (Doty 1998: 264). Yet writers such as Dalby (2009: 132) insist that the priority given by states to military preparations has little to offer by way of policy guidance for dealing with climate change itself.

During the 1990s the notion of human security also developed within post-Cold War debates on international relations and development (UNDP 1994; Matthew et al. 2010: 8). By this notion, security is no longer just about conflict but addresses risks to stability posed by social, political, and economic factors (Dalby 2009: 7; Matthew et al. 2010: 9, 18; Lonergan 1999). Environmental security and human security have inevitably been linked, not least because global environmental change poses risks to human security (UNISDR 2012: 17; Matthew et al. 2010: 15–20; Dodds and Pippard 2005). Just as environmental change poses pressing questions for such traditional concepts as state sovereignty, so too do the concepts of human security and military interventions that have a humanitarian objective (Bain 2001; Robinson 2007; Matejkova 2008; Eckersley 2007). The concepts of environmental and human security invite consideration of the many contextual factors that can undermine security, and their relationship is often a function of the dependence of people on natural resources, coupled with their degree of social power. In the literature, the emphasis on context focuses attention on the concept of vulnerability and how social and economic factors develop during and in the aftermath of an event (Fussel 2007; Turner et al. 2003). Levels of vulnerability are associated with a country's size, state of development, social and economic disparities, and quality of infrastructure (Zapata and Madrigal 2009: 14). Debate about vulnerability focuses on the context in which disasters happen and how social and economic factors influence impacts (Turner et al. 2003; Dalby 2009: 109). Disaster preparedness is heavily dependent on institutional and social capacity. The assessment of vulnerability has been enhanced by risk analysis, and much of the work that has been done on natural disasters has been on behalf of the insurance and risk analysis industries (Von Winterfeldt 2009: 177, 181). Governments, intergovernmental, and nongovernmental organizations have shifted their focus towards ex-ante approaches to disaster risk management and reducing vulnerability (World Bank/GFDRR 2011).

Security in Latin America and the Caribbean

Security perspectives within Latin America and the Caribbean have been heavily shaped by the position of the military in politics and society, proximity to the United States, and the divisions created by the Cold War. Conspicuous by their absence in scholarship are discussions about either the military's relationship with environmental issues or its role in responding to natural disasters. In the absence of scholarly work, one can only speculate as to why this is the case, though the answer almost certainly lies in the hitherto dominant influence of a U.S. agenda in security studies – a point that comes across elsewhere in this Handbook. Yet there is little doubt that the traditional security context in Latin America and the Caribbean has influenced the way in which states have responded to disasters. The region has, for example, been the destination for many relief operations by U.S. forces, which have invariably generated questions about sovereignty (Kingsley and Rimsky Vernon 2011; Cecchine et al. 2013). It also seems likely that geopolitical relationships have shaped the distribution of disaster aid (Associated Press 2005). Yet natural disasters in Latin America and the Caribbean have mostly been ignored in post–Cold War security scholarship. In 1995, Pettiford argued that recognition of the political importance of disasters in Central America requires us to question traditional notions of security, and suggested that the analysis of disasters should inform debates about redefining this concept. His call has been all but ignored.

Where attention has grown to the relationship in Latin America between some traditional security issues and the broader implications of climate change, this agenda has arguably been superimposed upon the region from outside and has focused on the potential to influence migration across the U.S. border (Deheza and Mora 2013; McGrady, Kingsley and Stewart 2010). Research has looked almost solely at Mexico and Central America and has, implicitly, assumed a failed state model (Deheza and Mora 2013; Guerrero 2013). In a similar vein, while Revolution in Military Affairs (RMA) debates have clear relevance to the relationship between security and disasters, the very few studies that have examined the application of RMA approaches to Latin America and the Caribbean have done so solely on the basis of its applicability to traditional security concerns, such as the tactical positions taken by the Colombian and U.S. governments towards the FARC (Rochlin 2011).

What is most striking about this apparent blind spot in scholarship is that it is out of step with Latin American security perspectives themselves, which *have* engaged with issues of environmental and human security. This can be demonstrated empirically. Chile offers a case study in which disasters pose major risks, the military has been an important actor, and security doctrine has since the 1990s been under review. The armed forces have long played an active role in responding to natural disasters and in recent years have given explicit attention to improving capabilities in this area (Arancibia Ramírez 2010: 41; Gobierno de Chile 2010).

Since 1997, the Chilean Centro de Estudios y Investigaciones Militares (CESIM) has published the journal *Escenarios Actuales* that provides an insight, albeit limited, into military thinking. An examination of this journal reveals, first, that there has been an ongoing recognition of new, nontraditional threats to Chilean security that include environmental factors (CESIM 1997). There is acknowledgment that security planning should extend beyond geopolitical and strategic thinking to take into account political, social, cultural, and environmental dimensions (Arellano Gramunt 2002: 18; Villagrán Calderón 2003: 14; Concha Pantoja 2003: 41). Second, there has been a clear theoretical evolution in the discussion of security that has extended beyond the notion of conflict to incorporate environmental and human security perspectives (Ramírez Beiza 1998: 11; Neira Hernández 2004: 13; González Aninat 2005: 16; CESIM 2005, 2007, 2009). Lastly, environmental hazards are interpreted as hemispheric challenges to security that demand cooperation and require, among other things, the adoption of global regimes that accept limitations on sovereignty (Van Klaveren Stork 2000: 31). The role of Chile's armed forces in responding to disasters is seen primarily in terms of the extension of military cooperation as regional security initiatives to this end have proliferated (Pradenas Wilson and Villagra Massera 2006: 12; Fernández Amunátegui 2009: 42; Bartolomé Inglese 2011: 14; Arancibia Ramírez 2010: 42).

In the absence of empirical research it is not possible to say whether Chile is exceptional in terms of the extent to which its armed forces have engaged with environmental and human security, although the extension of cooperation clearly suggests similar perspectives in neighboring Argentina. In 2002, for example, the militaries of Chile and Argentina conducted joint exercises aimed at enhancing their mutual responses to natural disasters in border areas (Arancibia Ramírez 2010: 42). One outcome of this was the establishment by Argentine forces of field hospitals in 2010 to help communities affected by the Chilean earthquake. In keeping with this perspective, in 2006 MERCOSUR's Committee of Army Commanders agreed to develop a joint response to natural disasters, and similar initiatives have since been taken by the Conferencia de Ejércitos Americanos (CEA) and the Consejo de Defensa Suramericano (CDS) established by UNASUR (O'Ryan Burotto and Placencia Rodríguez 2007: 26–27; Salas Kurte 2007: 38; Guarda Barros 2011: 57).

Despite empirical evidence demonstrating that environmental and human security have been addressed in Latin America, English-language scholarship on these themes has been lacking. This failure might appear to confirm how, since the end of the Cold War, conceptualizations of security continue to be shaped by political order and state power. Above all, it fails to recognize how in any discussion of environmental and human security Latin America and the Caribbean offer rich examples.

First, the state of exception thesis is of clear relevance to the region, where many states of emergency have been imposed to confront instability. McNeish (2010: 68–71) has gone further, arguing that the refinement of techniques of exception may have taken place in Latin America itself. The fear of disorder in the aftermath of natural disasters is likely to make states of exception easier to proclaim and hence more frequent. Chile's military, for example, has a duty to respond to disasters under constitutional articles setting out states of exception that specify an *Estado de Catástrofe* (catastrophic case) gravely affecting the functioning of the state (Arancibia Ramírez 2010: 41; Gobierno de Chile 2010: 247).

Second, Latin America has been a prominent actor in the global evolution of environmental governance, and a plausible case can be made that the relationship between the environment and security originated in the threat discourses and agenda that coalesced at the Rio Earth Summit in 1992 (Floyd and Matthew 2013: 1; Hecht and Cockburn 1990; Dalby 2009: 23). The region is prominent in debates about climate change and, in particular, its potential impact on extreme weather events (Van Aalstm 2006; Warner and Oré 2006; Dilley and Heyman 1995). Glacial melting in the Andes linked to the impact of climate change offers one example of the potential for resulting natural disasters. Catastrophic glacier floods and mudflows have occurred in the Cordillera Blanca in Peru and at the Copiapó River and the Villarrica Volcano in Chile, claiming thousands of lives.

Third, historically the Latin American and Caribbean region has provided dramatic examples of the existential challenges posed by natural disasters and environmental change to societies (Diamond 2006: 10; Crosby 1986). According to UNEP (2010), various phenomena indicate that the impact of global warming in the region includes increased intensity and frequency of hurricanes in the Caribbean, changes in precipitation distribution and intensity, changes in temperature levels, and more droughts.

Extreme weather and ecological crises have also been used to explain major historical shifts in development (Johnson 2011). There are examples of disasters that have had important long-term implications for security in countries such as Guatemala (Gawronskil and Olson 2013).

Fourth, Latin America has been the subject of research into the relationship between natural resources and conflict, especially in Amazonia and Central America (Little 2001; Timura 2001; Bobrow-Swain 2001; Matthew et al. 2010: 13). At the same time, the region provides many examples of resources such as water and biodiversity that enhance cooperation (Floyd and Matthew 2013: 9; Tiefenbacher and Hagelman III 2008; López 2010). It also provides a valuable focus for how discussions of migration frequently invoke geopolitical security narratives (Dalby 2009: 144).

Finally, contextual factors that help to explain the differential impacts of disasters are much in evidence in the region and official responses to these (Wisner 2001; Tobin and Whiteford 2002; Saldaña-Zorrilla and Sandberg 2009). In the Caribbean subregion, for example, ECLAC has employed an environmental vulnerability index to measure these (Khamis and Osorio 2013: 44–45; Charvériat 2000). Latin America also provides many examples of initiatives that seek to address resilience to disasters, and of how gender has been prominent in the study of disaster responses (Sims and Vogelmann 2002; Dalby 2009: 153; Miles et al. 2012; Warner and Oré 2006; Detraz 2009; Cupples 2007; Bosmans et al. 2012; Meertens 2010; Alzate 2008). Latin America also provides a source of innovative, community-led initiatives that seek to address vulnerability and resilience to disasters. In Cuba, noteworthy developments include community-based shelters and emergency planning to minimize loss of life in hurricanes (Sims and Vogelmann 2002; Dalby 2009: 155). In Guatemala, analysis has focused on measures to reduce urban disaster risk for informal settlements (Miles et al. 2012). Finally, in Peru participatory approaches to disaster management have been experimented with in Ica and Ayacucho (Warner and Oré 2006).

Conclusions

For half a century Latin American and Caribbean military ties with the United States were forged upon a Cold War national security template. However, regional cooperation is gathering force, and armed forces have been engaging with ideas about environmental and human security. Security scholars have signally failed to catch up, and the turrets of research need to be turned. The potential benefits to the discipline are great: This region, with its many environmental and human challenges, as well as a history that has mostly avoided the violent interstate conflicts of other parts of the world, offers the prospect for taking the definition of security in entirely new directions. At the top of any research agenda has to be a *mea culpa* – an explanation for why scholarship has persisted in following Cold War themes within the (limited) study of security in the region. Other areas of research should then fall into place: the main threat narratives and how are they represented, and how and why militaries are engaging with environmental and human security challenges and climate change. Unless scholarship can engage with Latin American and Caribbean security narratives on these themes, it will remain blind to the possibilities the region has to offer it.

References

Agamben, G. (2005) *State of Exception*, London: University of Chicago Press.
Ali, S. H. (ed) (2007) *Peace Parks: Conservation and Conflict Resolution*, Cambridge: MIT Press.
Alzate, M. M. (2008) 'The Sexual and Reproductive Rights of Internally Displaced Women: The Embodiment of Colombia's Crisis', *Disasters*, 32(1): 131–148.
Arancibia Ramírez, F. (2010) 'Contribución histórica del ejército frente a las catástrofes naturales', *Escenarios Actuales*, 15(3): 41.
Arellano Gramunt, J. (2002) 'Globalización, mundialización y amenazas; El complejo escenario se avecina', *Escenarios Actuales*, 7(2): 3–23.
Associated Press (2005) 'Castro: Cuban Death Toll from Hurricane Dennis Raised to 16', Havana. Retrieved rom http://usatoday30.usatoday.com/weather/stormcenter/2005-07-12-dennis-cuba_x.htm?POE=WEAISVA.
Bain, W. (2001) 'The Tyranny of Benevolence: National Security, Human Security and the Practice of Statecraft', *Global Society*, 15(3): 277–294.
Barnett, J. (2000) 'Destabilizing the Environment-Conflict Thesis', *Review of International Studies*, 26(2): 271–288.
Barkdull, J. and Harris, P. G. (2002) 'Environmental Change and Foreign Policy: A Survey of Theory', *Global Environmental Politics*, 2(2): 63–91.
Bartolomé Inglese, M. C. (2011) 'Convergencias y divergencias entre los conceptos de seguridad y defensa en el siglo XXI', *Escenarios Actuales*, 16(3): 5–18.
Bobrow-Swain, A. (2001) 'Between a Ranch and a Hard Place' in N. L. Peluso and M. Watts (eds) *Violent Environments*, London: Cornell University Press.
Bosmans, M., Gonzalez, F., Brems, E. and Temmerman, M. (2012) 'Dignity and the Right of Internally Displaced Adolescents in Colombia to Sexual and Reproductive Health', *Disasters*, 36(4): 617–634.
Brown, L. R. (1977) *Redefining National Security*, Washington, DC: Worldwatch Institute.
Buzan, B., Waever, O. and De Wilde, J. (1998) *Security: A New Framework for Analysis*, Boulder: Lynne Rienner.
Cecchine, G., Morgan, F. E., Wermuth, M. A., Jackson, T., Gereben Schaefer, A. and Stafford, M. (2013) *The US Military Response to the 2010 Haiti Earthquake: Considerations for Army Leaders*, Santa Monica: RAND Corporation.
CESIM (1997) 'Nuevas amenazas, globales y locales', *Escenarios Actuales*, 2(5): 3–9.
——— (2005) 'Seminario ejército y derechos humanos: Compromiso para el siglo XXI', *Escenarios Actuales*, 10(4): 1–60.
——— (2007) 'Seguridad, desarollo y recursos naturales', *Escenarios Actuales*, 12(3): 30–38.
——— (2009) 'Quinta sesión plenaria: Recursos naturales, cambio climático y seguridad', *Escenarios Actuales*, 14(3): 121–141.
Charvériat, C. (2000) *Natural Disasters in Latin America and the Caribbean: An Overview of Risk*, New York: Inter-American Development Bank (IDB).
Concha Pantoja, J. (2003) 'Tendencia futura de los conflicto', *Escenarios Actuales*, 8(4): 34–41.
Crosby, A. (1986) *Ecological Imperialism: The Biological Expansion of Europe 900–1900*, Cambridge: Cambridge University Press.
Cupples, J. (2007) 'Gender and Hurricane Mitch: Reconstructing Subjectivities after Disaster', *Disasters*, 31(2): 155–175.

Dalby, S. (1992) 'Ecopolitical Discourse: "Environmental Security" and Political Geography', *Progress in Human Geography*, 16(4): 503–524.
——— (2009) *Security and Environmental Change*, Cambridge: Polity Press.
Deheza, E. and Mora, J. (2013) *Climate Change, Migration and Security: Best-Practice Policy and Operational Options for Mexico*, London: Royal United Services Institute (RUSI).
Detraz, N. (2009) 'Environmental Security and Gender: Necessary Shifts in an Evolving Debate', *Security Studies*, 18(2): 345–369.
Deudney, D. and Matthew, R. (eds) (1999) *Contested Grounds: Security and Conflict in the New Environmental Politics*, Binghampton: State University of New York Press.
Diamond, J. (2006) *Collapse: How Societies Choose to Fail or Survive*, London: Penguin.
Dilley, M. and Heyman, B. N. (1995) 'ENSO and Disaster: Droughts, Floods and El Niño/Southern Oscillation Warm Events', *Disasters*, 19(3): 181–193.
Dodds, F. and Pippard, T. (eds) (2005) *Human and Environmental Security: An Agenda for Change*, London: Earthscan.
Domínguez, J., Mares, D., Orozco, M., Scott Palmer, D., Rojas Aravena, F. and Serbin, A. (2003) *Boundary Disputes in Latin America*, Peaceworks 50, Washington, DC: United States Institute of Peace (USIP).
Doty, R. L. (1998) 'Immigration and the Politics of Security', *Security Studies*, 8(2–3): 71–93.
Duffield, M. (2001) *Global Governance and the New Wars: The Merging of Development and Security*, London: Zed.
——— (2007) *Development, Security and the Unending War*, Cambridge: Polity.
Eckersley, R. (2007) 'Ecological Intervention: Prospects and Limits', *Ethics and International Affairs*, 21(3): 293–316.
Fernandez, R. and Sanahuj, H. (2012) *Linkages Between Population Dynamics, Urbanization Processes And Disaster Risks: A Regional Vision Of Latin America*, Panama City: UN Office for Disaster Risk Reduction, Regional Office for the Americas (UNISDR-AM)
Fernández Amunátegui, M. (2009) 'Relaciones internacionales en América Latina', *Escenarios Actuales*, 14(3): 35–43.
Floyd, R. and Matthew, R. A. (eds) (2013) *Environmental Security: Approaches and Issues*, London: Routledge.
Foster, G. D. (2005) 'A New Security Paradigm', *Worldwatch Magazine*, 18(1): 36–46.
Fussel, H. M. (2007) 'Vulnerability: A Generally Applicable Conceptual Framework for Climate Change Research', *Global Environmental Change*, 17: 155–167.
Gawronskil, V. T. and Olson, R. S. (2013) 'Disasters as Crisis Triggers for Critical Junctures? The 1976 Guatemala Case', *Latin American Politics and Society*, 55(2): 133–149.
Gleditsch, N. P., Furlong, K., Hegre, H., Lacina, B. and Owen, T. (2006) 'Conflicts over Shared Rivers: Resource Scarcity or Fuzzy Boundaries?', *Political Geography*, 25: 361–382.
Gobierno de Chile (2010) *Libro de la defensa nacional*, Santiago de Chile: Ministerio Defensa Nacional.
González Aninat, R. (2005) 'Los nuevos desafíos para la paz mundial que presenta el siglo XXI', *Escenarios Actuales*, 10(3): 10–19.
Guarda Barros, E. (2011) 'El centro de estudios estratégicos de la defensa de UNASUR: Fundamentos, objetivos y desafíos de una propuesta regional', *Escenarios Actuales*, 16(2): 55–59.
Guerrero, E. (2013) 'Towards a Transformation of Mexico's Security Strategy', *The RUSI Journal*, 158(3): 6–12.
Guha-Sapir, D., Hoyois, P. and Below, R. (2013) *Annual Disaster Statistical Review 2012: The Numbers and Trends*, Brussels: Centre for Research on the Epidemiology of Disasters (CRED), University of Louvain.
Hecht, S. and Cockburn, A. (1990) *The Fate of the Forest: Developers, Destroyers, and Defenders of the Amazon*, New York: Harper Collins.
Helmer, M. and Hilhorst, D. (2006) 'Introduction: Natural Disasters and Climate Change', *Disasters*, 30(1): 1–4.
Homer-Dixon, T. F. (1999) *Environment, Scarcity, and Violence*, Princeton: Princeton University Press.
Ignatieff, M. (2003) *Empire Lite: Nation-Building in Bosnia, Kosovo and Afghanistan*, London: Vintage.
Johnson, S. (2011) *Climate and Catastrophe in Cuba and the Atlantic World in the Age of Revolution*, Chapel Hill: University of North Carolina Press.
Kahl, C. (2006) *States, Scarcity and Civil Strife in the Developing World*, Princeton: Princeton University Press.

Kaldor, M. (2001) *New and Old Wars: Organised Violence in a Global Era*, Cambridge: Polity.
Kaplan, R. D. (1994) 'The Coming Anarchy', *Atlantic Monthly*, 273(2): 44–76.
Kelman, I. (2007) 'Hurricane Katrina Disaster Diplomacy', *Disasters*, 31(3): 288–309.
Khamis, M. and Osorio, C. (2013) *América del Sur: Una visión regional de la situación de riesgo de desastres*, Panama City: The United Nations Office for Disaster Risk Reduction (UNISDR).
Kingsley, M. and Rimsky Vernon, A. (2011) *Disaster Relief and Engagement Operations, 1990–2010: A Synthesis of CNA Analyses*, Alexandria: CNA.
Leaning, J. and Guha-Sapir, D. (2013) 'Natural Disasters, Armed Conflict, and Public Health', *The New England Journal of Medicine*, 369: 1836–1842.
Linden, E. (2007) *The Winds of Change: Climate, Weather, and the Destruction of Civilizations*, London: Simon & Schuster.
Little, P. E. (2001) *Amazonia: Territorial Struggles on Perennial Frontiers*, Baltimore: The Johns Hopkins University Press.
Lonergan, S. (1999) *Global Environmental Change and Human Security: GECHS Science Plan*, Bonn: International Human Dimensions Programme on Global Environmental Change (IHDP).
——— (2001) 'Water and Conflict: Rhetoric and Reality' in P. F. Diehl and N. P. Gleditsch (eds) *Environmental Conflict*, Boulder: Westview Press.
López, A. (2010) 'Environmental Transborder Co-operation in Latin America: Challenges to the Westphalia Order' in R. A Matthew, J. Barnett, B. McDonald and K. L. O'Brien (eds) *Global Environmental Change and Human Security*, London: MIT Press.
Luft, G. and Korin, A. (eds) (2009) *Energy Security Challenges for the 21st Century: A Reference Handbook*, Santa Barbara: Praeger.
Mandel, R. (2002) 'Security and Natural Disasters', *Journal of Conflict Studies*, 22(2): 118–143.
Mastanduno, M. (1997) 'Preserving the Unipolar Moment: Realist Theories and US Grand Strategy after the Cold War', *International Security*, 21(4): 49–88.
Matejkova, S. (2008) 'Establishing the Norm of Humanitarian Intervention in International Relations', *Central European Journal of International and Security Studies*, 2(2): 76–91.
Matthew, R. A. (2013) 'Climate Change and Security' in R. Floyd and R. A. Matthew (eds) *Environmental Security: Approaches and Issues*, London: Routledge.
Matthew, R. A., Barnett, J., McDonald, B. and O'Brien, K. L. (eds) (2010) *Global Environmental Change and Human Security*, London: MIT Press.
McGrady, E., Kingsley, M. and Stewart, J. (2010) *Climate Change: Potential Effects on Demands for US Military Humanitarian Assistance and Disaster Response*, Alexandria: CNA.
McNeish, J. A. (2010) 'Securing Resources through Exceptional Means in the Americas' in J. A. McNeish and J. H. Sande Lie (eds) *Security and Development*, Oxford: Berghahn Books.
McNeish, J. A. and Sande Lie, J. H. (2010) 'Introduction' in J. A. McNeish and J. H. Sande Lie (eds) *Security and Development*, Oxford: Berghahn Books.
Medina, F., Yanev, P. I. and Yanev, A. P. (2010) *The Magnitude 8.8 Offshore Maule Region Chile Earthquake of February 27, 2010: Preliminary Summary of Damage and Engineering Recommendations*, Santiago de Chile: World Bank.
Meertens, D. (2010) 'Forced Displacement and Women's Security in Colombia', *Disasters*, 34(S2): S147–S164.
Miles, S. B., Green, R. A. and Svekla, W. (2012) 'Disaster Risk Reduction Capacity Assessment for Precarious Settlements in Guatemala City', *Disasters*, 36(3): 365–381.
Myers, N. (1998) 'Environment and Security', *Foreign Policy*, 47: 23–41.
Neira Hernández, A. (2004) 'Hacia un nuevo concepto de seguridad de las Américas', *Escenarios Actuales*, 9(1): 9–14.
O'Ryan Burotto, C. and Placencia Rodríguez, R. (2007) 'MERCOSUR y cooperación militar', *Escenarios Actuales*, 12(1): 23–27.
Pape, R. A. (2012) 'When Duty Calls: A Pragmatic Standard of Humanitarian Intervention', *International Security*, 37(1): 41–80.
Pettiford, L. (1995) 'Towards a Redefinition of Security in Central America: The Case of Natural Disasters', *Disasters*, 19(2): 148–155.
Poncelet, J. L. (1997) 'Disaster Management in the Caribbean', *Disasters*, 21(3): 267–279.
Pradenas Wilson, D. and Villagra Massera, H. (2006) 'El desafío de operacionalizar la cooperación y la integración regional', *Escenarios Actuales*, 11(3): 8–14.
Ramírez Beiza, H. (1998) '¿Que ocurre en materia ambiental', *Escenarios Actuales*, 3(6): 10–17.

Renner, M. (1989) *National Security: The Economic and Environmental Dimensions*, Washington, DC: Worldwatch Institute.
Resende-Santos, J. (2002) 'The Origins of Security Cooperation in the Southern Cone', *Latin American Politics and Society*, 44(4): 89–126.
Robinson, C. A. (2007) 'Humanitarian Intervention, Dirty Hands, and Deliberation', *Central European Journal of International and Security Studies*, 1(1): 85–99.
Rocha, J. L. and Christoplos, I. (2001) 'Disaster Mitigation and Preparedness on the Nicaraguan Post-Mitch Agenda', *Disasters*, 25(3): 240–250.
Rochlin, J. (2011) 'Plan Colombia and the Revolution in Military Affairs: The Demise of the FARC', *Review of International Studies*, 37(2): 715–740.
Salas Kurte, J. (2007) 'Visiones. Discurso ceremonia 121° aniversario de la Academia de Guerra del Ejército', *Escenarios Actuales*, 12(2): 35–39.
Saldaña-Zorrilla, S. O. and Sandberg, K. (2009) 'Spatial Econometric Model of Natural Disaster Impacts on Human Migration in Vulnerable Regions of Mexico', *Disasters*, 33(4): 591–607.
SELA (Latin American and Caribbean Economic System) (2010) *Meeting on the Institutional Framework for Disaster Risk Reduction in Latin America and the Caribbean, Asia and Africa: Conclusions and Recommendations*, Panama City, Panama 13 and 14 Caracas.
Sims, H. and Vogelmann, K. (2002) 'Popular Mobilisation and Disaster Management in Cuba', *Public Administration and Development*, 22(5): 389–400.
Smith, P. J. (2007) 'Climate Change, Mass Migration and the Military Response', *Orbis*, 51(4): 617–633.
Sotomayor Velázquez, A. C. (2004) 'Civil-Military Affairs and Security Institutions in the Southern Cone: The Sources of Argentine-Brazilian Nuclear Cooperation', *Latin American Politics and Society*, 46(4): 29–60.
Spektor, M. (2012) 'Humanitarian Interventionism Brazilian Style?', *Americas Quarterly*, 6(3): 54–55.
Srinivas, R. K. (2001) 'Profile – Demystifying Dams and Development: The World Commission on Dams and Development', *Environmental Politics*, 10(3): 135.
Tiefenbacher, J. P. and Hagelman III, R. R. (2008) 'Emergency Cooperation Between the USA and Mexico in Disaster Management: Co-dependency and Geopolitics', *International Journal of Emergency Management*, 5(3–4): 261–274.
Timura, C. T. (2001) ' "Environmental Conflict" and the Social Life of Environmental Security Discourse', *Anthropological Quarterly*, 74(3): 104–113.
Tobin, G. A. and Whiteford, L. M. (2002) 'Community Resilience and Volcano Hazard: The Eruption of Tungurahua and Evacuation of the Faldas in Ecuador', *Disasters*, 26(1): 28–48.
Tuchman Matthews, J. (1989) 'Redefining Security', *Foreign Affairs*, 68(2): 162–177.
Turner, B. L., Kasperson, R. E., Matson, P. A., McCarthy, J. J., Corell, R. W., Christensen, L., . . . and Schiller, A. (2003) 'A Framework for Vulnerability Analysis in Sustainability Science', *Proceedings of the National Academy of Sciences*, 100(14): 8074–8079.
United Nations Development Program (UNDP) (1994) *Human Development Report 1994*, New York.
United Nations Environment Programme (UNEP) (2010) *Latin America and the Caribbean: Environment Outlook GEO LAC 3*, Panama City.
United Nations Environment Programme (UNEP)/Oregon State University (OSA)/Universidad Nacional de Costa Rica (UNA) (2007) *Hydropolitical Vulnerability and Resilience along International Waters: Latin America and the Caribbean*, Nairobi.
United Nations International Strategy for Disaster Reduction (UNISDR) (2012) *Disaster Risk Reduction in the Americas in 2011: UNISDR Regional Office for the Americas Annual Report 2011*, Panama City.
United Nations International Strategy for Disaster Reduction (UNISDR)/Corporación OSSO (2013) *Impacto de los desastres en América Latina y el Caribe, 1990–2011. Tendencias y estadísticas para 16 países. Informe*, Panama City.
Van Aalstm, M. K. (2006) 'The Impacts of Climate Change on the Risk of Natural Disasters', *Disasters*, 30(1): 5–18.
Van Klaveren Stork, A. (2000) 'Areas críticas en la cooperación regional: Alternativas de solución', *Escenarios Actuales*, 5(3): 27–32.
Vannoni, M. (2012) 'Failed States and Theories: The (Re)Securitisation of Underdevelopment', *Central European Journal of International and Security Studies*, 6(3–4): 27–45.
Villagrán Calderón, J. (2003) 'Dilemas de la situación mundial', *Escenarios Actuales*, 8(2): 12–22.

Von Winterfeldt, D. (2009) 'Lessons from Risk Analysis: Terrorism, Natural Disasters and Technological Accidents' in H. Kunreuther and M. Useem (eds) *Learning from Catastrophes: Strategies for Reaction and Response*, Upper Saddle River: Pearson/Wharton School Publishing.

Warner, J. and Oré, M. T. (2006) 'El Niño Platforms: Participatory Disaster Response in Peru', *Disasters*, 30(1): 102–117.

Wisner, B. (2001) 'Risk and the Neoliberal State: Why Post-Mitch Lessons Didn't Reduce El Salvador's Earthquake Losses', *Disasters*, 25(3): 251–268.

World Bank (2010) *The Economics of Adaptation to Climate Change: A Synthesis Report*, Washington, DC.

World Bank/Global Facility for Disaster Reduction and Recovery (GFDRR) (2011) *Disaster Risk Management in Latin America and the Caribbean Region: GFDRR Country Notes*, Washington, DC.

Zapata, R. and Madrigal, B. (2009) *Economic Impact of Disasters: Evidence from DALA Assessments by ECLAC in Latin America and the Caribbean*, Mexico City: ECLAC Subregional Office in Mexico.

PART V

Latin America and contemporary international security challenges

24

THE IMPACT OF CHINA ON THE SECURITY ENVIRONMENT OF LATIN AMERICA AND THE CARIBBEAN

R. Evan Ellis

Introduction

When the Panamanian government assumed control over that nation's canal from the United States on December 31, 1999, one of its first major decisions was to award port concessions at both the Atlantic and Pacific entrances to the Hong Kong–based firm Hutchison-Whampoa, prompting conservative U.S. politicians to warn that a waterway vital to the movement of U.S. military forces was falling into the hands of 'red China' (Garvin 1999; *BBC News* 1999).

The People's Republic of China (P.R.C.) seeking commercial inroads in Latin America and the Caribbean at the turn of the millennium was dramatically, if not completely, different from the revisionist power that had broadcasted revolutionary messages in Quechua to indigenous peoples of the Andean highlands a generation before (Rothwell 2013). Within the span of a few short years, the sustained high rates of economic growth that began with China's opening to the world economic system in 1978 transformed the P.R.C. from an impoverished Cold War menace to a pragmatic, economic juggernaut. For Latin America and the Caribbean, from the takeoff of trade with the P.R.C. in 2003, overall trade expanded almost tenfold, from $29 billion to $270 billion by 2012 (IMF 2009: 28).

Political leaders from the late Venezuelan leader Hugo Chávez (*El Universal* 2008) to U.S. Secretary of State Hillary Clinton (Keyes 2009) have noted the geopolitical significance of expanding Chinese engagement with the region. An array of scholarly works has emerged to document what was happening in both economic and political terms (Dumbaugh and Sullivan 2005; Ellis 2009; Jubany and Poon 2006). This includes numerous compiled volumes containing generally independent, country-specific studies of the economic, political, and social dimension of the phenomenon (Aranson et al. 2008; Roett and Paz 2008; Fernández and Hogenboom 2010; Hearn and Márquez 2011; Strauss and Armony 2012) and, recently, those of Chinese scholars publishing in English (Shuangrong 2012).

Consistent with the dominance of commercial activities in the engagement, the new literature principally focuses on economic issues, including the characteristics of Chinese trade with and investment in Latin America and the Caribbean, and how such activities are impacting the region (Blázquez-Lidoy et al. 2006; Devlin et al. 2006; Jenkins and Peters 2009; Gallagher and Porzecanski 2010).

A more modest body of scholarship has also emerged, addressing security military issues related to Chinese engagement in the region. These works focus primarily on two areas: (1) China–Latin America military relations, and (2) the impact on the strategic position of the United States. The consensus of such analyses in general is that, while potentially significant, P.R.C. military engagement is not the most important facet of China's relationship with the region (Ellis 2013c; Marcella 2012; Watson 2013).

Beyond purely military issues, various authors have noted that the advance of the P.R.C. impacts the dominant position that the United States has enjoyed in the region for more than a century (Paz 2012; Ellis 2013c). From a relatively early point, scholars referred to a 'triangle' between China, the United States, and Latin America (Tokatlian 2007; Stallings 2008; Woodrow Wilson Center 2011), although authors such as Ellis (2012b) have noted that the activities of other actors in the region, such as Russia, India, and Iran, also contribute to Latin America's increasing independence from the U.S. sphere of influence, even if those same actors also, at times, compete with each other there in commercial and other matters.

The purpose of this chapter is to analyze the impact of Chinese engagement on the security environment of the region, including the indirect effects of economic engagement on political, social, and other dynamics that impact the security of the region and the United States. I do not argue that the security implications of China's activities in the region are more important than the economic ones, or that such activities present a threat to the United States or the region, which must be resisted. Rather, I analyze ways in which, however inadvertently, the activities of the P.R.C. government, Chinese companies, and other Chinese actors significantly impact the Latin American and Caribbean security environment.

The nature of China's impact on the Latin American security environment

To date, the P.R.C. has not shown intent to establish military bases, or political alliances and client state relationships of an anti-U.S. character in the region. Indeed, Chinese officials have been careful to distance themselves from the anti-U.S. rhetoric of populist leaders such as Venezuela's late President Hugo Chávez (*El Universal* 2008). Similarly, the P.R.C. has repeatedly emphasized respect for the right of each country to conduct their internal affairs as they choose (Government of the People's Republic of China 2008), and has generally deferred from taking positions on the actions of those countries within their own borders (Ellis 2014a).

In general, the most significant impacts of Chinese engagement on the security environment of Latin America and the Caribbean come through indirect effects of its economic activity on the region's social and political dynamics, although the P.R.C. also impacts the region through arms sales, military training and education, and its sporadic military presence there, more than is commonly realized.

The core of this chapter considers 10 direct and indirect effects of China's engagement on the strategic environment of the region:

- Changes to port and transportation infrastructure
- Expanding transpacific criminal activity
- Participation of Chinese companies as local actors
- Crime and violence involving Chinese communities
- Extended life of populist regimes
- Changing imperatives in relations between Latin American states
- Expanded arms market options

- Expanded P.L.A. military education and training activities with the region
- Expanded P.L.A. military presence in the region
- The disposition of Chinese-U.S. relations

Changes to port and transportation infrastructure

Growing trade with the P.R.C. and other countries of Asia is driving the expansion of ports and facilities supporting transpacific commerce. In some cases, such as Machala, Ecuador and Paita, Peru, the expansion is being done by Chinese companies, which have established themselves in the extractive sector, as part of exporting metals and mineral ores to Asia. In other cases, the work is being done by Chinese companies such as SinoHydro, China Water and Electric, or China Harbour (in the case of the new port at Goat Island, Jamaica). In cases such as the expansion of the ports of Buenaventura (Colombia), Callao (Peru), Iquique (Chile), or the Mariel (Cuba) port and free trade zone, the work is being done by others, but driven by commerce with Asia.

Such expanding trade is also driving new road and rail connections linking Pacific coast ports to the interior of the continent, including 'bi-oceanic' corridors from the Peruvian ports of Paita, Callao, Tacna, and Ilo to Manaus, Brazil; the 'inter-oceanic' corridor linking the ports of Arica and Iquique in Chile to Santos and Matto Grosso on the southeast coast of Brazil; or the 'Manta-Manaus' corridor projected to link the Brazilian interior to the Pacific coast of Ecuador. The widening of the Panama Canal is similarly driven by the new transpacific trade, as is the possible second canal across Nicaragua.

Such changes in infrastructure alter the patterns of interstate commerce in the region, giving new importance to previously low volume ports such as Machala in Ecuador (future outlet for the El Mirador mine), or Puerto Morelos in Mexico (the port for the Chinese 'Dragon Mart' retail/distribution center being built near Cancún). In the process, they change sea lines of communication and create new port security requirements around the newly busy facilities. Such changes also increase policing requirements in the surrounding areas as people gravitate to the new sources of employment.

Finally, the new road and rail infrastructure opens up areas such as Madre de Dios in Peru, the Orellana and Sucumbíos provinces in Ecuador, and the Brazilian Amazon, expanding both legitimate commerce and illicit activities, such as drug labs and illegal logging, while also stimulating social conflict as migrants entering the area in search of opportunity clash with its previously isolated residents.

Expanding transpacific criminal activity

Beyond crime associated with new ports and roads, growing transpacific trade also creates new opportunities for criminal activities. These include human trafficking by P.R.C.-based groups such as Red Dragon and the 'snakehead' gangs through Latin America and the Caribbean to the United States and Canada, using Chinese communities in the region as intermediate stops (Ellis 2012a).

Expanding transpacific criminal activity also includes sales of precursor chemicals such as ephedrine and pseudoephedrine from China and India to Latin America–based criminal organizations such as *Los Zetas* and the Sinaloa Cartel in Mexico (*La Prensa* 2009; Ellis 2012a), and reciprocally, flows of cocaine from Colombia and other source zone countries to the P.R.C. through ports such as Hong Kong (*Milenio* 2011; *La Prensa* 2011), which have historically served as points of access to China for the West.

The trade in contraband merchandise produced in China is also a growing problem, as is the illicit metal trade, with stolen scrap metal and ore informally mined in areas such as Michoacán, Mexico or Madre de Dios, Peru (Ruvulcaba 2013), 'taxed' by organized crime groups as it passes through the hands of intermediate buyers and eventually goes to 'legitimate' purchasers in the P.R.C.

Transpacific money laundering is also an increasing problem, fueled by the proliferation of Chinese businesses, financial institutions, and the flow of goods through the region – particularly contraband. Even Chinese-operated casinos in countries such as Panama and Suriname have become sources of concern as vehicles for such activities (Ellis 2012a).

In facing such challenges, Latin American security forces are arguably at a disadvantage, lacking personnel capable of speaking Chinese dialects such as Mandarin, Cantonese, and Hakka to question suspects or collect information from witnesses. Security forces typically have neither ethnically Chinese personnel to operate in Chinese communities nor technical contacts in the P.R.C. to follow leads involving China-based businesses, gangs, or other entities (Ellis 2012a).

Participation of Chinese companies as local actors

Since approximately 2009, as detailed elsewhere (Ellis 2012b, 2013a, 2014a), an increasing number of Chinese companies have established operations within Latin America and the Caribbean. The sectors in which they operate include petroleum, mining, fisheries, timber, construction, manufacturing, telecommunications, banking, and logistics services, among others.

Such physical presence is a highly significant development for P.R.C. relations with the region, since it makes the Chinese companies an inherent part of the security environment, and changes its dynamic, as those companies both face the crime and violence endemic to parts of the region, and in the pursuit of their business objectives occasionally generate unrest with local labor forces, subcontractors, and surrounding communities, and generate protests (sometimes violent) from environmentalists, competitors, and others who oppose their projects (Guthrie 2013).

Problems confronted by Chinese companies operating in the region include strikes, such as those seen in the Marcona mine in Peru (*El Comercio* 2011a) and Sierra Grande in Argentina (*La Nación* 2010), contractors disputing payments (*La Voz de la Selva* 2011), and communities complaining over Chinese businesses not hiring the expected number of workers (opposition pickets – Stabroek News 2013; Matthews 2010). In Orellana, Ecuador, in 2007, such protests against the Chinese company Petroriental led to the death of 30 persons and the declaration of a state of emergency in the province (*El Universo* 2007).

The Chinese focus on mining, petroleum, and large-scale construction projects increases opportunities for violent encounters with groups who oppose their presence. Incidents include the November 2006 takeover of a Chinese-operated oilfield in Tarapoa, Ecuador (*El Universo* 2006), the June 2012 occupation of the Colquiri mine in Bolivia (*Los Tiempos* 2012), and the November 2012 forcible expulsion of Chinese workers from a mine near Puebla, Mexico. Violent protests also temporarily blocked access to the Chinese-owned Bosai mine in Linden, Guyana, the Rio Blanco mine in Piura, Perú (*El Comercio* 2011b), and the Cerro Dragon mine in Chubut, Argentina (*Clarín* 2012).

Security threats against Chinese operations have also included extortion and kidnapping. In June 2013, the Chinese firm Sinohydro temporarily ceased work on the Patuca III hydroelectric project because of threats against its workers (*La Prensa* 2013). In Caquetá, Colombia, FARC guerillas repeatedly attacked assets of the Chinese-owned firm Emerald Energy to force the firm to pay 'protection,' eventually taking three Chinese workers hostage in June 2011(*Colombia Reports* 2012).

While such security challenges are not unlike those faced by Chinese companies in Africa, they have two effects potentially problematic in the Latin American and Caribbean context. On one hand, they induce closer collaboration between the P.R.C. and the region's public security forces, potentially raising concerns within the United States. On the other hand, they induce Chinese companies to contract with private security firms, a market which is not well regulated in some countries of the region, creating the risk of indirectly implicating Chinese entities in politically charged incidents involving the killing of local persons.

Crime and violence involving Chinese communities

Beyond incidents involving companies and personnel from the P.R.C., expanding commercial engagement indirectly impacts ethnic Chinese communities that have lived in Latin America and the Caribbean since the late 19th century. Expanding trade and commercial projects both increases the visibility of such communities and facilitates their expansion through both legal and other means, as Chinese construction workers are brought into the region on temporary visas, and as Chinese criminal groups such as Red Dragon expand their human trafficking networks. The corresponding growth of Chinese communities in recent years, particularly within the smaller countries of the Caribbean basin, has fueled suspicions and resentment among non-Chinese populations (Ellis 2013b), contributing to anti-Chinese demonstrations such as those in Santo Domingo in July 2013 (Santana 2013), ethnic violence against Chinese shops and their owners, including incidents in Papitam and Maripaston, Suriname (Ellis 2012c), and in Buenos Aires in December 2013 (Li 2013).

Such incidents have prompted the Chinese government to become increasingly active in efforts to protect ethnic Chinese living in the region. Following violence against the Chinese community in Maripaston, Suriname in October 2011, the Chinese ambassador to the country, Yuan Nansheng, made a particularly forceful statement, with overtones critical toward the Surinamese government for not having adequately protected ethnic Chinese in the country (*NaSpang* 2011). Similarly, when Jamaican Prime Minister Portia Simpson-Miller traveled to the P.R.C. in August 2013, Chinese Premier Li Keqiang raised the issue of crime against Chinese Jamaicans, inducing the Jamaican government to expand efforts to protect them (*The Gleaner* 2013). As Chinese engagement with the region continues to grow and raise the profile of ethnic Chinese communities there, the associated difficulties faced by those communities are likely to increase, as well as efforts by the P.R.C. government to protect them, forcing the P.R.C. to consider the limits of its frequently proclaimed policy of respect for the domestic affairs of other countries (Government of the People's Republic of China 2008).

Extended life of populist regimes

For Latin American regimes hostile to the U.S. and Western institutions, including Venezuela, Ecuador, and Bolivia, the P.R.C. has become a source of financing, exports, and investment that has allowed those regimes to maintain economic solvency, while turning away from the U.S. and other Western companies and financial institutions. As of March 2014, the socialist regime in Venezuela has received over $45 billion in loans from the P.R.C., including a $4 billion disbursement during the run-up to the 2012 presidential election (*El Universal* 2012), while Ecuador has received $10.8 billion, including $1.4 billion in the months prior to its own February 2013 national elections (Gill 2013).

While, as noted previously, the P.R.C. has been careful not to associate itself with the political projects of such regimes, the capital that it has provided has made it easier for them to continue domestic programs that reward supporters, as well as initiatives such as ALBA, Petrocaribe, and TeleSur, which project influence beyond their borders.

Thus, overall, the most significant security impact of P.R.C. economic support for the regimes of ALBA is not the creation of an anti-U.S. block of Chinese client states, but rather the sustainment of poorly governed spaces in which criminality, terrorism, and other threats to the region can flourish, and the heightened risk of interstate conflict or civil war when such regimes collapse from their own internal contradictions.

Changing imperatives in relations between Latin American states

The increasing importance of commerce with the P.R.C. and other parts of Asia is changing the imperatives regarding how states in Latin America and the Caribbean relate to each other.

For Brazil, the expansion of transpacific commerce has increased the importance of Pacific-facing neighbors such as Peru and Chile, as well as countries in the middle of the continent such as Bolivia and Paraguay, which are key to strategically important routes connecting the interior of Brazil to Pacific coast ports.

For Atlantic-facing states, the new transpacific commerce has also increased the importance of the Panama Canal and contemplated alternatives such as the Nicaragua Canal, as well as current or contemplated hub ports for consolidating and redistributing transpacific cargo, including Freeport (The Bahamas), Goat Island (Jamaica), and Mariel (Cuba), making internal political matters, such as the possible delay in completing the expansion of the Panama Canal (Kriel 2014), of interest to a broader set of actors than would have been the case in a prior era.

Expanded arms market options

Chinese arms companies, like producers of commercial goods, have gradually expanded their product offering, their Latin American and Caribbean client base, and the sophistication of their behavior. Prior to 2005, with limited exceptions, such as the sale of small arms to Bolivia (*Terra* 2008), the Chinese role in the Latin American and Caribbean defense market was principally the sale or donation of simple, nonlethal goods such as military clothing and gear. Venezuela provided Chinese defense manufacturers their first opportunity to sell sophisticated end items to the region, purchasing JYL-1 mobile radars, K-8 fighters, and Y-8 and Y-12 transport aircraft. Ecuador then followed Venezuela's lead, buying four JYL-2 radars, while Bolivia bought six of its own K-8s (Ellis 2013c).

Initial P.R.C. attempts to sell end items outside of the ALBA countries fell short, including a canceled sale of T-2000 main battle tanks to Peru, a failed bid to sell the X-11 helicopter to Argentina, and the truncated purchase of WMZ-551 armored personnel carriers after the delivery of only four units.

Despite such difficulties, Chinese defense companies such as AVIC, CEIEC, NORINCO, and Poly Technologies have become sophisticated players in the Latin American arms market. The vendors are consistently represented at major arms expositions in the region, such as LAAD in Brazil, SITDEF in Peru, and FIDAE in Chile, and have exhibited increasingly sophisticated tactics, such as Poly Technologies's protest of a losing bid for a Peruvian air defense system contract in 2012 (Hearn 2012), and Chengdu Aircraft Corporation's offer to codevelop and produce a version of its FC-1 fighter to Argentina in order to sell it the aircraft (Fisher 2013).

While Chinese arms generally lag behind those of Russia and the West in quality, sophistication, and aftermarket support, they are frequently cheaper, with more readily available financing, thus creating new options for military modernization for all countries in the region. As the Chinese market share expands, it will not only reshape military inventories in the region, but will also lay the groundwork for long-term relationships with the P.R.C. to support and maintain those arms.

Expanded P.L.A. military education and training activities with the region

Beyond arms sales, the People's Liberation Army (P.L.A.) is gradually expanding its education and training interactions with Latin American and Caribbean militaries. The Chinese government has, for some years, brought Latin American and Caribbean military officers to the P.R.C. for strategic level education, including courses at the P.L.A. Defense Studies Institute in Champing and P.L.A. Army and Navy Command and Staff schools near Nanjing (Ellis 2013c). In addition, as the P.R.C. has sold more weapons to the militaries of the region, more personnel have gone to the P.R.C. for training on those systems. Reciprocally, a small number of Chinese soldiers have gone to the region for training (*ABC* 2010).

Such expanding ties are building closer institutional relationships between the P.L.A. and Latin American and Caribbean armed forces, and with it, greater understanding and influence. By contrast to engagement in the region by the Soviet military during the Cold War, however, Chinese personnel have not yet been publicly integrated into those armed forces in positions of authority to 'advise' units or military leaders.

Expanded P.L.A. military presence in the region

The presence of the P.L.A. in Latin America and the Caribbean, while limited, has been evolving from multilateral to bilateral engagements, and from a humanitarian focus to include combat exercises. The first and longest ongoing Chinese military presence in the region was the deployment of P.L.A. military police to support the MINUSTAH peacekeeping force in Haiti from September 2004 through October 2012. The next major advance occurred in November 2010, when the P.L.A. conducted its first bilateral exercise in the region, with the Peruvian military, focused on the use of a mobile field hospital donated by the P.L.A. The next major deployment was similarly focused on a humanitarian theme; in December 2011, the P.R.C. sent its newly commissioned hospital ship 'Peace Ark' to the Caribbean, making port calls in Cuba, Jamaica, Trinidad and Tobago, and Costa Rica, conducting goodwill-building medical treatments for the local populations.

When active duty P.L.A. forces reengaged with the region, the engagement was a leap forward over previous activities; in October 2013, a P.L.A. naval flotilla including the guided missile frigates Lanzhou and Liuzhou sailed to South America, where it conducted exercises with the Chilean military before transiting the straits of Magellan to make port calls in Argentina and Brazil (*Global Times* 2013). By contrast to previous humanitarian or navigation-focused engagements, the exercise with the Chileans was a combat simulation, with the P.L.A. Navy ships coordinating with their Chilean counterparts to defend against a simulated attack by hostile aircraft (*People's Daily Online* 2013).

While such military engagements are not threatening in themselves, they gradually establish the normalcy and legitimacy of a P.L.A. military presence in the hemisphere, while increasing

Chinese awareness of the operating environment and procedures of the armed forces of the region, facilitating other military deployments to the region in the future if invited, or required to do so.

The disposition of Chinese-U.S. relations

As Chinese engagement with Latin America and the Caribbean has expanded, U.S. public officials have sought to avoid actions or rhetoric that would lead to a new 'superpower competition' between the P.R.C. and the United States in the region (Ellis 2012b), with administration officials regularly noting that the United States does not view Chinese engagement in Latin America and the Caribbean as a threat (Noriega 2005; Ting 2011; Jacobson 2013).

For its part, the P.R.C. government has not shown a willingness, to date, to intervene militarily in the hemisphere to protect its nationals, the interests of its companies, or overseas Chinese. Nonetheless, it has used its growing influence in subtle, yet heavy-handed ways to advance its objectives. In 2010, for example, it suspended acceptance of soy oil shipments from Argentina, worth $1.4 billion in annual revenues, letting it informally be known as retaliation for Argentine anti-dumping measures against Chinese products (*Bloomberg* 2010). Similarly, in January 2014, the P.R.C. refused to guarantee a $4.7 billion loan for an important Argentine hydroelectric project, informally linking the action to delays by the Argentine government in taking forward a major railway modernization project in which the Chinese premier, Wen Jiabao, had publicly invested his attention (Ellis 2014b).

While the Chinese preference for such indirect approaches may reflect cultural differences with the United States and other Western actors, the P.R.C.'s caution arguably also reflects its perception that the country's dependence on Western markets, technology, and the dollar-denominated U.S. financial system makes avoiding actions that might provoke the United States a strategic imperative, particularly in the Western Hemisphere where the P.R.C. is at a geographic and material disadvantage to the United States militarily. Nonetheless, the P.R.C's use of its military forces to support its territorial claims closer to home in the South and East China seas suggests that its caution to date in Latin America and the Caribbean is not an inherent attribute of its diplomacy.

Avenues for further research

As this chapter has also shown, much work remains to be done to understand the security dimension of the P.R.C.'s primarily economic engagement with Latin America and the Caribbean, even as those dynamics continue to evolve. At a basic level, more data and analysis is required for virtually all of the relationships discussed in this chapter, including:

- How rapidly are Pacific coast port areas actually growing? Are there correlations between the growth of port cities and road connections to the interior of the continent, and observed patterns of social unrest?
- What is the actual relationship between P.R.C. loans, trade, and other assistance, and the survival and behavior of populist regimes?
- Under what circumstances do Chinese companies operating in the region experience difficulties with labor and subcontractors, communities, governments, project opponents, and security threats? Are there relevant differences between Chinese and non-Chinese companies in this regard?

- How, at the institutional level, is engagement with the P.L.A. and Chinese equipment impacting the capabilities, doctrine, and general orientation of Latin American and Caribbean militaries?
- What are the relationships between Chinese criminal groups, Chinese businesses, and Chinese communities in the region? Similarly, what is the nature of the relationship between Chinese criminal entities and their Latin American and Caribbean counterparts, and how is it shifting with time?
- How do perceptions, cultural differences, and other 'intangible factors' impact the performance of Chinese military, business, and political actors in the region, and how their counterparts in Latin America and the Caribbean relate to them? How is this evolving over time with the entry of new actors into the region, and the accumulation of experience by others?

Finally, there is a need to understand how the possibilities arising from the dynamics described in this chapter could play out over time in individual countries, as expanding Chinese engagement in the region simultaneously fuels greater conflict, influence, and learning and adaptation. The use of gaming, simulation, and scenario-based analysis might be useful in this regard, with a focus on the interaction between multiple, goal-seeking Chinese, Latin American, and other entities that could give rise to particular crises that decision-makers should anticipate and begin to prepare for sooner, rather than later.

References

ABC (2010, September 6) 'China dona US$1 millón a Colombia para armamentos', http://www.abc.com.py.

Aranson, C., Mohr, M. and Roett, R. R. (2008) *Enter the Dragon: China's Presence in Latin America*, Washington, DC: Woodrow Wilson International Center for Scholars.

BBC News (1999, December 8) 'Panama Canal: America's strategic artery', http://news.bbc.co.uk/2/hi/americas/553979.stm.

Blázquez-Lidoy, J., Rodríguez J. and Santiso, J. (2006) *Angel or Devil? Chinese Trade Impacts on Latin America*, Paris: OECD Development Center.

Bloomberg (2010, October 11) 'China agrees to reopen market to Argentine soybean oil imports, people say', http://www.bloomberg.com/news/2010-10-11/china-agrees-to-reopen-market-to-argentine-soybean-oil-imports-people-say.html.

Clarín (2012, July 5) 'Chubut: Pan American Energy dijo que acudirá a la conciliación con los "Dragones"', http://www.ieco.clarin.com/economia/pan-american-encuentro-conciliacion-dragones_0_731327021.html.

Colombia Reports (2012, March 6) 'Emerald Energy suspends operations in southern Colombia following rebel attacks', http://colombiareports.co/emerald-energy-suspends-operations-due-to-farc-attacks/.

Devlin, R., Estevadeoral, A. and Rodríguez-Clare, A. (2006) *The Emergence of China: Opportunities and Challenges for Latin America and the Caribbean*, Cambridge: Harvard University Press.

Dumbaugh, K. and Sullivan, M. P. (2005) *China's Growing Interest in Latin America*, Washington, DC: Congressional Research Service Library of Congress.

El Comercio (2011a, September 8) 'Protestan fuera del Coliseo de Ica mientras congresistas debaten', http://elcomercio.pe/politica/gobierno/protestan-fuera-coliseo-ica-mientras-congresistas-debaten-noticia-1281597.

——— (2011b, November 16) 'Piura: Pobladores agredidos en protesta antiminera exigen justicia', http://elcomercio.pe/peru/lima/piura-pobladores-agredidos-protesta-antiminera-exigen-justicia-noticia-1334617.

El Universal (2008, September 23) 'Pekín se desmarca de vínculo ideológicos con Venezuela a la llegada de Chávez', http://www.eluniversal.com/2008/09/23/pol_ava_pekin-se-desmarca-de_23A2007487.

——— (2012, February 7) 'Programa Mi Casa Bien Equipada ha vendido 850 mil equipos', http://www.eluniversal.com/economia/120207/programa-mi-casa-bien-equipada-ha-vendido-850-mil-equipos.

El Universo (2006, November 14) 'Petrolera china desestima que protesta en Tarapoa haya afectado sus intereses', http://www.eluniverso.com/2006/11/14/0001/9/DDDBC2F740814980A-854CA2B3B92CB18.html.

——— (2007, July 5) 'Heridos 24 militares en incidentes en protestas en Orellana', http://www.eluniverso.com/2007/07/05/0001/12/A97CCA96EE414C7EAB96E4835A1C62D3.html.

Ellis, R. E. (2009) *China in Latin America: The What's and Wherefores*, Boulder: Lynne Rienner Publishers .

——— (2012a) 'Chinese Organized Crime in Latin America', *Prism*, 4(1): 67–77.

——— (2012b) 'The Expanding Chinese Footprint in Latin America: New Challenges for China, and Dilemmas for the US', *French Institute of International Relations (IFRI)*.

——— (2012c) 'Suriname and the Chinese: Timber, Migration, and the Less-Told Stories of Globalization', *SAIS Review*, 32(2): 85–97.

——— (2013a) 'China, S.A. as a Local Company in Latin America', *Regional Insights*, 1: 1–4.

——— (2013b) 'Chinese Commercial Engagement with Guyana: The Challenges of Physical Presence and Political Change', *China Brief*, 13(19): 13.

——— (2013c) *The Strategic Dimension of China's Engagement with Latin America*, Washington, DC: William J. Perry Center for Hemispheric Defense Studies.

——— (2014a) *China on the Ground in Latin America: Challenges for the Chinese and Impacts on the Region*, New York: Palgrave-Macmillan.

——— (2014b) 'Chinese "Face" and Soft Power in Argentina', *The Manzella Report*: 1–2.

Fernández Jilberto, A. E. and Hogenboom, B., eds., *Latin America Facing China: South-South Relations beyond the Washington Consensus.* New York: Berghahn, 2010

Fisher, R. D. (2013, June 23) 'Argentine officials confirm joint-production talks over China's FC-1 fighter', *HIS Jane's 360*, http://www.janes.com/article/23497/argentine-officials-confirm-joint-production-talks-over-china-s-fc-1-fighter.

Gallagher, K. and Porzecanski, R. (2010) *The Dragon in the Room*, Stanford: Stanford University Press.

Garvin, G. (1999, August 25) 'Canal deal gives strategic edge to China, critics charge', *The Miami Herald*, http://www.latinamericanstudies.org/canal/china.htm.

Gill, N. (2013, August 26) 'Ecuador receives $1.2 billion loan from China for budget', *Bloomberg*, http://www.bloomberg.com/news/2013–08–26/ecuador-receives-1–2-billion-loan-from-china-for-budget.html.

Global Times (2013, October 29) 'China, Brazil hold joint naval drill', http://www.globaltimes.cn/NEWS/tabid/99/ID/821136/China-Brazil-holds-joint-naval-drill.aspx.

Government of the People's Republic of China (2008) *China's Policy Paper on Latin America on Latin America and the Caribbean.*

Guthrie, A. (2013, January 17) 'China plan raises ire in Mexico', *The Wall Street Journal*, http://online.wsj.com/news/articles/SB10001424127887324595704578243880802729850.

Hearn, A. and Márquez, J.L.L. (eds) (2011) *China Engages Latin America: Tracing the Trajectory*, Boulder: Lynne Rienner Publishers.

Hearn, K. (2012, May 27) 'China-Peru military ties growing stronger', *The Washington Times*, http://www.washingtontimes.com/news/2012/may/27/china-peru-military-ties-grow-stronger/?page=all.

IMF (2009) *Direction of Trade Statistics Yearbook*, Washington, DC: International Monetary Fund.

Jacobson, R. S. (2013) *The Americas: Our Shared Challenges*, Miami: Remarks at the University of Miami Center for Hemispheric Policy.

Jenkins, R. and Peters, E. D. (2009) *China and Latin America: Economic Relations in the 21st Century*, Bonn: German Development Institute.

Jubany, F. and Poon, D. (2006, March) 'Recent Chinese Engagement in Latin America', Canadian Foundation for the Americas. Retrieved from http://www.focal.ca/pdf/china_latam.pdf.

Keyes, C. (2009, May 1) 'Clinton warns of Iranian, Chinese gains in Latin America', *CNN*, http://edition.cnn.com/2009/POLITICS/05/01/clinton.latin.america.

Kriel, L. (2014, January 23) 'Detener trabajos en Canal de Panamá podría causar grandes demoras: Arbitros', *Reuters*, http://mx.reuters.com/article/topNews/idMXL2N0KX08N20140123.

La Nación (2010, March 21) 'La difícil experiencia China en la mina de Sierra Grande', http://www.lanacion.com.ar/1245513-la-dificil-experiencia-china-en-la-mina-de-sierra-grande.

La Prensa (2009, December 15) 'Cárteles Mexicanos insisten en fabricación de droga, pese a limitantes', http://www.oem.com.mx/elmexicano/notas/n1441531.htm.

——— (2011, April 24) 'Los hermanos González, juzgados en Malasia por "narcotráfico" ', http://www.oem.com.mx/elmexicano/notas/n2052932.htm.

——— (2013, June 10) 'Estancadas las obras en la represa hidroeléctrica Patuca III en Honduras', http://www.laprensa.hn/csp/mediapool/sites/LaPrensa/Honduras/Apertura/story.csp?cid=328490&sid=267&fid=98.

La Voz de la Selva (2011, January 11) 'Empresarios loretanos paralizan obra de alcantarillado de Iquitos por abuso de empresa China', radiolvs.cnr.org.pe/ninterna.html?x=10229.

Li, A. (2013, December 13) 'Chinese shop owners in Argentina arm themselves with guns amid violent looting', *South China Morning Post*, http://www.scmp.com.

Los Tiempos (2012, June 9) 'Colquiri aún dialoga y denuncian más tomas', http://www.lostiempos.com/diario/actualidad/economia/20120906/colquiri-aun-dialoga-y-denuncian-mas-tomas_184554_391189.html.

Marcella, G. (2012) 'What is the Chinese Military Doing in Latin America?', *America's Quarterly*, 6(1): 67–69.

Matthews, K. (2010, September 22) 'Angry protesters demand jobs on Palisadoes Project', *Jamaica Observer*, http://www.jamaicaobserver.com/latestnews/Angry-protesters-demand-jobs-on-Palisadoes-project.

Milenio (2011, September 19) 'Arrestan a 5 Mexicanos en Hong Kong por tráfico de droga'. Retrieved from https://twitter.com/mileniojalisco/status/115814002264780800.

NaSpang (2011, October 25) 'Chinese ambassade steunt landgenote Maripaston', http://www.nospang.net/index.php?option=com_content&view=article&id=13788%3Achinese-ambassade-steuntlandgenotenmaripaston&catid=73%3Abinnenland&Itemid=65.

Noriega, R. (2005, April 6) 'Statement before the House Subcommittee on the Western Hemisphere', http://2001–2009.state.gov/p/wha/rls/rm/2005/q2/44375.htm.

Paz, G. S. (2012) 'China, the United States and Hegemonic Challenge in Latin America: An Overview and Some Lessons from Previous Instances of Hegemonic Challenge in the Region' in J. C. Straus and A. C. Armony (eds) *From the Great Wall to the New World: China and Latin America in the 21st Century*, Cambridge: Cambridge University Press, pp. 18–34.

People's Daily Online (2013, October 14) 'PLAN's taskforce conducts maritime joint exercise with Chilean Navy', http://english.people.com.cn/90786/8434317.html.

Roett, R. and Paz, G. (2008) *China's Expansion into the Western Hemisphere*, Washington, DC: Brookings Institution Press.

Rothwell, M. (2013) *Transpacific Revolutionaries: The Chinese Revolution in Latin America*, New York: Routledge.

Ruvalcaba, H. (2013, August 20) 'Asían mafias in Baja California', *Insight Crime*, http://www.insightcrime.org/news-analysis/asian-mafia-in-mexico.

Santana, O. (2013, July 30) 'Protestan contra "nuevos comerciantes chinos" ', *Diario Libre*, http://www.diariolibre.com/noticias/2013/07/30/i395212_protestan-contra-nuevos-comerciantes-chinos.html.

Shuangrong, H. (ed) (2012) *China-Latin America Relations: Review and Analysis* (vol. 1), Beijing: Paths International.

Stabroek News (2013, February 14) 'Opposition pickets Marriott over hiring practices', http://www.stabroeknews.com/2013/news/stories/02/14/opposition-pickets-marriott-over-hiring-practices/.

Stallings, B. (2008) *The US-China-Latin America Triangle: Implications for the Future*, Washington, DC: Brookings Institution Press.

Strauss, J. C. and Armony, A. C. (2012) *From the Great Wall to the New World: China and Latin America in the 21st Century*, Cambridge, MA: Cambridge University Press.

Terra (2008, June 26) 'Bolivia aclara que 10.000 fusiles fueron donados por China y no por Venezuela', http://noticias.terra.es/2008/espana/0626/actualidad/bolivia-aclara-que-10000-fusiles-fueron-donados-por-china-y-no-por-venezuela.aspx.

The Gleaner (2013, August 27) 'Police to ramp up security measures for Chinese community in Jamaica', http://jamaica-gleaner.com/latest/article.php?id=47538.

Ting, Z. (2011, August 19) 'China "not a threat" in Latin America', http://www.china.org.cn/world/2010–08/19/content_20742146.htm.

Tokatlian, J. G. (2007, February 9) 'Latin America, China, and the United States: A Hopeful Triangle', *Open Democracy*.

Watson, C.A. (2013) 'China's Use of the Military Instrument in Latin America: Not Yet the Biggest Stick', *Journal of International Affairs*, 66(2): 101.

Woodrow Wilson Center (2011) *China, Latin America, and the United States: The New Triangle*, Washington, DC.

25

THE UNITED STATES' IMPACT ON LATIN AMERICA'S SECURITY ENVIRONMENT

The complexities of power disparity[1]

David R. Mares

Latin America and the United States share a long historical relationship in which, from the Latin American perspective, the drawbacks have often outweighed the benefits. Of course, there were many times, perhaps less well remembered, when the 'good' outweighed the 'bad.' The predominant metaphors for understanding the U.S. relationship with Latin America have been either 'the bull in the china shop' or Porfirio Diaz's lament – 'so far from God, so near to the United States.' In the contemporary era, however, there is a sense of a fundamental change in the relationship, due to the combination of global challenges to U.S. leadership and a diversification of Latin America's international relations (Lowenthal and Mostajo 2010; Domínguez and Covarrubias 2014).

As a global power, the United States plays in the world arena, while Latin American countries play in their own region, having little influence outside of it. What the United States chooses to do in Latin America is thus influenced by its commitments and outlay of resources in other regions, which means that analysts must be careful to distinguish between what irritates the United States, but does not rise to the level of justifying investment; what threatens the United States, and therefore requires the expenditure of U.S. resources; and that which is irrelevant to the United States, despite the importance it may carry in the region.

The relationship is influenced by the interaction, not only by the power asymmetry, between the United States and Latin American countries, and also by the global context. For example, when the global environment is threatening to the United States, as in World War II, or when Latin American countries reflect global tensions, as in Latin American communist movements during the Cold War, the United States will make use of the power disparity to structure a security context favorable to itself in the region. Conversely, when the United States faces serious threats that are largely nonregional, as with the current issue over Islamic fundamentalist terrorism or Russian military adventurism in Eastern Europe, it will concentrate its security resources outside of the region, leaving Latin America to largely design its own security environment. Moreover, U.S. opportunities for low-cost involvement in the region are also affected by Latin American options. For example, when commodity prices are high, or alternative sources of financing are readily available, the ability of the United States to influence the region at a low cost to itself shrinks. When commodity prices or alternative sources of financing decline, Latin America must please it more in order to gain U.S. resources, thereby increasing its ability to impact the region. When Latin American economies are well run and growth is sustainable, as in Chile over the last few decades, the United States has less influence (Lowenthal 2010). But when countercyclical funding reaches its noninflationary limits (i.e., Brazil), when macroeconomic policies lead to economic collapse (i.e., Venezuela and Argentina), or economic growth is anemic with compounding problems of crime and corruption (i.e., Mexico), Latin America's need for U.S. resources increases, and with it, the potential for U.S. influence.

Nowadays, it is clear to everyone that U.S. leadership in the international order is under challenge, and that the United States is having a difficult time organizing its own response and convincing a number of key allies to follow its lead. Hence, the availability of resources to address Latin America is necessarily limited. However, if Latin America remains on the margins of what threatens the United States, the need to devote resources to Latin America is also reduced. Thus, the existence of power disparities does not always mean that the greater power must be actively engaged in structuring the security context of the lesser powers.

What is not clear is how contemporary challenges to U.S. global leadership will impact U.S. behavior towards Latin America. Some scholars see a United States that willingly engages less with the region, while others see a region that is actively diversifying its international relationships away from the United States, giving it little room in which to act. Still others see a United States that is working closely with some Latin American countries, keeping its distance from a few others, and remaining engaged bi- and multilaterally across the region.

Understanding these competing perspectives requires comprehensive comparative study, with recognition of the empirical variation of the outcome – e.g., sometimes the United States will sanction anti-U.S. behavior in the region, and sometimes it will not; sometimes it will demand respect for indigenous rights and sometimes it will not. The explanation for that variation in U.S. behavior must look to variables ranging across the U.S. domestic and the Latin American domestic contexts (Pastor 2001; Lowenthal 2010). Though edited volumes demonstrate the variation in U.S. policy and explain it in multiple ways (i.e., Domínguez and Fernández de Castro 2010), we need an explanation that integrates that variation into one argument. For example, in a masterful work Blasier (1976) explained why the United States attempted to overthrow some revolutions (Guatemala, Cuba) but came to an understanding with others (Mexico, Bolivia).

The question of Latin American agency in this relationship is not adequately addressed in the literature. Some studies posit Latin America as merely a recipient of whatever the United States happens to desire for it at a historical moment, with domestic elites sometimes benefiting but often losing out to U.S. insistence on reforms under the Alliance for Progress or the 'need' for military government. Others are overly generous in attributing agency to Latin America, postulating that certain Latin American countries have successfully stymied U.S. capitalist interests and are building socialism (Perla and Cruz-Feliciano 2013). The challenge is to understand how and when the internal dynamics of the national challenges facing Latin American governments and societies (i.e., corruption, crime, authoritarianism, poverty, development, etc.) influence a government's choices for engaging the United States.

The body of this chapter has two parts. I begin with a discussion of the different theoretical lenses that inform scholarship on U.S. relations with Latin America. Realism, liberal internationalism, constructivism, and Marxism each present variations on the causal logic for understanding U.S. international behavior. These theories argue that some international behaviors matter more than others, tell us where to look for causal factors, and how those causal factors are expected to produce the variation on the outcomes that interest us. The second section turns to the context within which U.S.–Latin American relations are currently taking place, and develops a research agenda for future work. Although where we look for context is partly informed by our theories of international behavior, certain empirical events at the international, regional, and national levels will be important across theories. The section stresses the importance of the empirical evaluation of context – defining what we are witnessing and measuring it. These are not easy or clearly objective tasks, but that does not obviate the need to get the context correct, since the values that a theory's causal variable takes in a specific instance will be determined by context.

Theoretical lenses

Realism. Realists are not surprised that the United States has shifted its focus away from the region after the end of the Cold War. For realists, international anarchy means that nations are constantly pushed in the direction of emphasizing their strategic interests, defined above all in terms of maintaining their sovereignty and territorial integrity. Sovereignty is defined as the ability to choose what costs and benefits a state will face in responding to international challenges and opportunities; it is not the ability to choose not to confront any costs. Any government that chooses a policy inconsistent with its interest will exacerbate the international challenges it faces. Successful states recognize this fact and act prudently in using their power resources. Power is defined in terms of the ability to coerce and attract other nations through influencing the costs and benefits associated with the options for behavior facing them. Relative power is therefore the key determinant in a realist analysis of how states relate to each other on matters of security.

Though realists agree on the basic elements of the drivers of international behavior, there is disagreement regarding how those play out in specific historical contexts. Some realists never thought that the United States should care about Latin America during the Cold War (Waltz 1979), though others believed that communist advances in the region would ultimately threaten the United States and thus should be nipped in the bud (Kissinger 1979). Drug trafficking does not rise to the level of realist concerns, and Latin America is on the margins of international terrorism, WMD concerns, and of little strategic interest to China or Russia given the continued superiority of the U.S. Navy in the Western Hemisphere. Realists would expect the United States not to pay too much attention to Latin America, or to become concerned about the region's diversification of international relations as they are progressing at this point. For example, none of the Latin American countries has a military alliance against the United States, and while it is true that Russian warships visit some ports, there is no new naval base established in Latin America for Russia or the Chinese. The fact that a few congressmen might articulate a demand for the United States to get involved in addressing these efforts at diversification and translating them as direct threats is irrelevant to realists; neither Republican (George H. W. Bush and George W. Bush) nor Democractic presidents (William Clinton and Barack Obama) made policy toward the region from that perspective. U.S. policy towards Venezuela from 2002 to the present, in which the government recognized a short-lived coup against President Hugo Chávez but also rejected the notion of embargoing imports of oil from Venezuela, is quite understandable: The former entailed minor costs for potentially getting rid of an irritant, while the latter choice recognized the value of Venezuelan oil for prices and supply of oil on the world market. In short, most realists do not see a prudent reason to divert attention and resources away from the major challenges to U.S. interests in the international system towards the region (for an opposing view, see Desch 1996).

From a realist perspective, Latin American countries should be expected to seek out room to maneuver as the only Great Power in the Western Hemisphere focuses its attention elsewhere. Prudent behavior on the part of Latin American countries would mean diversifying their relations up to the point at which their ability to become a threat to the U.S. process of addressing its international challenges is affected (i.e., if Venezuela had signed an agreement to supply Iran with uranium). In addition, realists would expect that a Latin American country would not seek to become so irrelevant to the U.S. that the U.S. would not find it at all in its interests to support a Latin American country as it addresses its international challenges (i.e., when Argentina engaged in a massive default in 2002). Realists, nevertheless, cannot explain why Venezuela and Argentina seem to gratuitously insult the United States when the parties they expect to help them through difficult times brought on by their economic policies (i.e., Russia, Iran, Syria) will be unable to help them, and China does not require such anti-U.S. behavior to trade or invest in a Latin American country (see Escudé, this volume). Since realism is a theory about how power affects international relations, realists cannot simply claim that their theory has nothing to say about how weaker states behave. Paul's (1994) general work on weak powers and my own early work on Latin American middle powers (Mares 1988a, 1988b) provide examples of the theoretical and empirical work to be done, but the potential insights of realism for understanding Latin American relations with the United States remain understudied.

Liberal internationalism. Liberal internationalists see the creation of international institutions as a means of increasing the level of cooperation among states within international anarchy (Keohane 1984). These institutions provide a means by which states can significantly mitigate the mistrust and competitive relationships that realists see as inherent under anarchy. Institutions create mechanisms that increase the transparency of state behavior and thus provide states with reasonable expectations for cooperation in the future, or alert them to potential cheating by others. To accomplish this function, institutions need to be not merely paper documents but have credibility in terms of longevity, relevance to state interests, and bureaucratic means to provide transparency of state behavior. In their strongest version, liberal institutions spill over into society, creating space for societal groups to reach across borders and develop ties that lead governments (especially democratic ones) to cooperate more with each other (see Malamud and Schenoni, this volume).

From a liberal internationalist perspective, the United States would be expected to address its current international challenges by trying to strengthen international institutions' ability to bring potential threats into their own reach. In the contemporary context, we can see this in the discussion about the need to socialize China into the liberal international order (Economy and Oksenberg 1999). In terms of Latin America, a liberal internationalist would expect that the United States would promote continued Latin American socialization into that liberal international order, including the development of regional institutions that are complementary to that international order. Following this logic, one should expect the United States to encourage Latin American countries to play active roles in international institutions such as the IMF without seeing that activity as threatening to U.S. interests. From a liberal internationalist perspective, the fact that some members of the U.S. Congress make it difficult for the country to accept reforms of these international institutions – e.g., in the IMF – is shortsighted, because even if it loses its veto power over IMF decisions, the IMF regime is predicated on a liberal international economic order. Similarly the development of an institution like UNASUR, since its goal is to promote cooperative political relations among Latin American countries, should not be seen as a threat by the United States, but should be understood to constitute a means of ensuring/promoting that South America not become an unstable and threatening region to the international system. Thus, the United States benefits because it does not have to devote scarce resources to the region. Similarly, the Latin American/Chinese relationship can be a benefit rather than a challenge to the United States (Arnson and Davidow 2011). China is a member of the World Trade Organization (WTO), IMF, and the World Bank, and they are beginning to lend money internationally in support of infrastructure development and productive processes that contribute to the integration of the developing world into a globalizing economy. Recognizing Latin America's fundamentally Western, capitalist, and democratic nature and permitting those countries to develop strong relations with China is an important means of convincing China that it can benefit by becoming socialized into the international order.

From a liberal internationalist perspective, therefore, Latin American efforts to reform international institutions are beneficial to the United States as long as the reforms move in the direction of greater transparency and more international integration (on this general point, see Bradford 2008). The diversity within Latin America between the groups that oppose globalization (e.g., Bolivarians within ALBA) and those who favor globalization (e.g., the Pacific Alliance countries) should give liberal internationalists confidence. Because of that diversity, if a new regional organization (e.g., UNASUR or CELAC) decides to oppose globalization, members who favor globalization (e.g., Colombia, Chile, Peru, Uruguay, and Mexico) will not accept giving the organization the means to block globalization. The antiglobalization organization will exist and protest globalization, but it will have little independent impact on the overall globalization process in the region itself.

The United States and Latin America are tied together by multiple international institutions, a number of which have a long history, bureaucratic infrastructure, and spill over into civil society. The OAS has the Inter-American Commission on Human Rights, which not only investigates accusations of human rights violations but also is a catalyst to Latin American and U.S. NGOs. The Summit of the Americas has a longer history and counts on significant bureaucratic support from the U.S. State Department and multiple Latin American foreign ministries to develop agendas, propose programs, and evaluate progress; despite these institutional advantages, many Latin American international institutionalists see the newer and significantly less institutionalized UNASUR as having a greater impact on U.S.–South American relations than those tying South America to the United States. Explaining this hypothesis that some Latin American institutions matter more than others, however, has not yet been done in terms of the theory of international institutions.

Constructivism. From a constructivist perspective, empirical facts require interpretation to ascertain their meaning, which will vary across audiences. In addition, agents and structures are mutually constitutive (Wendt 1987). In the case of international relations, constructivists deny that anarchy creates a structure that pushes states into competition; rather, "anarchy is what states make of it" (Wendt 1992; Finnemore 1996). For constructivists, the fact that the international order is shifting away from U.S. dominance can lead U.S. elites and citizens to perceive an opportunity to move away from the competitive and militarized perception that the United States must govern the international order to one in which it recognizes the benefits of shared leadership. Alternatively, an international environment with reduced U.S. influence could be perceived as a threat rising to near existential proportions and therefore requiring a U.S. response to undermine all elements that contribute to that new international context. Constructivists believe that moral entrepreneurs mediate the flow of competing ideas and play a fundamental role in determining which ideas gain traction among elites and other citizens (Krebs and Lobasz 2007).

To understand contemporary U.S. relations with Latin America, constructivists would look for moral entrepreneurs in the United States and in Latin American countries who speak not only to their own citizens, but to those of the other country as well. The discourse of these political entrepreneurs would then be evaluated to determine whether they see Latin America as supporting the development of a peaceful and cooperative international order in which the United States and Latin America can coexist without threatening each other, or articulate contrasting visions identifying the other as a threat. The point in constructivism is not just that the ideas are out there floating and being articulated by multiple people, but that their ability to influence policy depends on the leadership capabilities of the moral entrepreneur. Therefore, analysts should not focus on whether Hugo Chávez or Evo Morales attacks the United States as imperialist, or whether Barack Obama articulates a vision of hemispheric cooperation; the question is how those messages create policy coalitions in favor of one or the other vision.

Marxism. In the United States there is a perception that Marxism died with the collapse of the Soviet Union and the turn to state capitalism in China. But Marxist theory continues to have great sway in Latin America. We can see evidence of this vibrancy in the discussion among Latin Americans and some U.S. academics about socialism in the 21st century and how this affects U.S.–Latin American relations (Muhr 2012; French 2009). For Marxists, the underlying focus of analysis has to be on the state of the historical progress of the development of capitalism. But Marxists disagree on whether capitalism is still in the process of creatively destroying precapitalist formations or whether it has reached the stage at which it is no longer a creative destructive force, and thus is ready to collapse in the process leading to communism.

From one perspective, Marxists could evaluate the current manifestations of state capitalism in China, Russia, and the BRICS as steps backward in historical progression because they limit the power of the market to develop the contradictions between capital and labor that will drive progress towards communism. This interpretation expects capitalism to continue progressing, leading to a clash between the advanced capitalist productive formations in the United States, Western Europe, and Japan, and these rising new powers. The clash would be destructive, but, from a Marxist perspective, capitalist nations would emerge victorious only to sow the seeds of their own destruction as the new stage of history moves toward communism. From this perspective, U.S. relations would focus on the more advanced forms of state capitalism in Latin America (Brazil and Argentina), and be more antagonistic towards them than towards the less-developed ALBA states.

For Marxists who think that capitalist progression has eliminated all other modes of production, the articulation of socialism of the 21st century represents the transitional stage between capitalism in decline and the establishment of the communist mode of production (Handal 1993). We have been through this discussion before in the 1970s, when the rise of OPEC and the establishment of the developing countries in the Group of 77 antagonistic to the leading capitalist nations were foreseen as indicating the final demise of the capitalist system. The fact that U.S. capitalism proved more resistant is not proof that the Marxist paradigm was wrong, but that Marxists incorrectly interpreted the signals indicating in which stage of the historical development of capitalism we find ourselves. Marxist scholars articulating this line of reasoning today should address why such analyses were wrong 40 years ago but may be correct now.

The contemporary Marxist analysis of the U.S. response to the pink tide ('new Left') in Latin America depends a great deal upon the interpretation of the Marxist legitimacy of socialism of the 21st century. For Marxists who are appalled by the theoretical eclecticism of socialism of the 21st century, the response of the United States will lead to a situation in which these pink tide leaders confront insurmountable international and domestic obstacles to the development of their national projects and the capitalists emerge stronger, thereby setting the stage for future legitimately Marxist movements to develop and oppose capitalism. For Marxists who interpret socialism of the 21st century as combining variations in national historic experiences with the global progress of forces of production, modern socialism will provoke the advanced industrialized countries into a fruitless opposition to the next stage of history represented by the pink tide. In this case we should see increasingly aggressive U.S. behavior towards the region, and an increasingly frustrated United States (Perla, Mojica and Bibler 2013).

U.S.–Latin American relations: a research agenda

The research agenda for scholars investigating the impact of the United States on Latin America's security, however defined, is going to vary by theoretical paradigm. No matter the paradigm, however, the research challenge begins by stating clearly what the theoretical argument is about how the causal factors lead to variation on the outcome – i.e., the impact of the United States on Latin America's security. That impact is going to vary across issue areas and paradigmatic lenses. We want to know how it varies and why it varies, be able to measure the variation so we can see that empirically it is correct that there is variation and that it is in the hypothesized direction. Each one of these paradigms has to be able to stipulate what a disconfirming event would look like. For social science a paradigm must include the possibility of falsification.

Scholarly analysis must have the richness of the empirical experience in order to find patterns and variations, but not let that empirical richness undermine analytic rigor (Snyder 1984/1985). In that empirical record what we should see is that in some cases the United States is successful in getting what it wants, in others cases it does not care, and in still others it opposes what is happening and cannot stop it. A methodological challenge for each of the theoretical approaches is to devise clear and credible means to distinguish the characteristics of these outcomes so that we can categorize empirical outcomes across the cases to test the hypotheses regarding the determinants of U.S. behavior. Scholars cannot simply ignore the cases where the United States is getting its way to focus on when it does not. Nor can we have confidence in an argument that tells us why the U.S. cannot get its way with particular Latin American countries if one does not distinguish between cases where it does not care and those where it sees the need for a different outcome but cannot achieve it.

Another empirical challenge is to ascertain the degrees of freedom in Latin America's international relations, since that will have an impact on both how the United States sees its relationship with Latin America and the likely outcome of a U.S. policy towards the region as a whole, and vis-à-vis specific countries. Latin American countries today tend to overestimate their ability to distance themselves from U.S. influence: They look at material indicators of trade and finance and assume their own vulnerabilities have been solved.

One should not downplay the theoretical, methodological, and empirical challenges in understanding the U.S.–Latin American relationship in the security realm. These challenges are not peculiar to the study of U.S.–Latin American relations, but are general to the field of international security studies (Johnston 2003). To appreciate the challenges, one only needs to remember the international crisis of the 1970s, the domestic turmoil of the United States, the heady days of the New International Economic Order euphoria, and then the unexpected and dramatic recovery of the United States. Key questions in play are: How much relative power has the United States actually lost, is the international capitalist system in crisis, are Latin American regional institutions going to become institutionalized and effective, have Latin American countries finally turned the corner on the democracy and development factors that undermined their stability and thus international behavior in the past? How does one measure the key factors that permit one to answer these questions – i.e., does a decade of high growth, a rising middle class, and poverty reduction that coincides with high international commodity prices mean that a country is well on its way to stable national development and increased international influence?

In addition to these general questions, specific empirical events require rigorous analysis if we are to think about the likely future policy of the United States towards Latin America. The following examples are illustrative of key challenges facing analysts.

U.S. military exercises with some Latin American countries indicate continuing cooperative security relations. The facts that UNASUR has developed a concept of South American peacekeeping forces and that South American militaries exercise with each other need to be related to the continued U.S. naval presence in the area, as well as what it means for the British deterrent to Argentine claims on the Falklands/Malvinas Islands. Despite Argentine insistence that British military presence represents a threat to the security of the region, and South American diplomatic support for Argentine claims to the islands, no South American countries have joined Argentina in rhetorically and diplomatically harassing British naval presence in the region. Were Argentina to once again test the British deterrent, what hypothesis would one draw regarding U.S. behavior or that of Argentina's South American neighbors? Would UNASUR's defense council be deemed irrelevant if they did not come to Argentina's aid, as many Latin Americans have been wont to claim regarding the OAS after the 1982 war?

The failure of the 2002 coup against Chávez in Venezuela was clearly not the favored outcome for the George W. Bush administration. But, whether the failure of the coup represented a defeat for U.S. policy in the region is not self-evident, just as the fact that Venezuela has diversified its export market away from the United States does not mean that the United States has paid a price for its cold relations with the *Chavista* government. The fact that the United States is importing more oil from Canada and Mexico, which are more reliable partners, and the fact that it is engaged in the shale revolution, and hence has to import less oil in general, positively impacts U.S. energy security. Diversification of economic partners cuts both ways as well. In the short term, Venezuela's collaboration with other OPEC nations to help push up the price of oil had a negative impact on the U.S. economy, but it also made it more profitable to invest in shale and the tar sands in the United States and Canada, respectively, and thus contributed to the developing self-sufficiency in oil and gas of the two nations, as well as the undermining of OPEC itself. Venezuela's economic collapse, as represented by 60 per cent plus inflation, food shortages, and food rationing, might enable the *Chavistas* in Venezuela to radicalize their revolution and survive, but it is unlikely to be a model for export to other Latin American nations. And it will always be a model that is dependent on the export of oil to the world market. Consequently, its survival is unlikely to be a challenge to the U.S.-favored view of a Latin America integrated into a globalizing capitalist economy.

ALBA and CELAC were heralded as indicators of significantly decreased U.S. influence, since they both exclude the United States and utilize anti-U.S. and antiliberal international order rhetoric (Angosto Ferrández 2014). It is not clear, however, what ALBA represents today, given that not only is Hugo Chávez deceased, but Venezuela's ability to finance ALBA has been destroyed by falling international oil prices and economic mismanagement at home. While the United States had poor relations with Venezuela and Bolivia, it maintained cordial relations with Ecuador and even more so with Nicaragua. Therefore, the simple existence of ALBA, while not desirable from a U.S. perspective, does not constitute an intrinsic threat to the United States. In terms of CELAC, while it does not include the United States and Canada, it does include nations who see the presence of the United States in the region as important (Mexico, Guatemala, Costa Rica, Panama, Colombia, and Peru) and therefore cannot be taken at face value as an organization that will automatically oppose or undermine the United States or replace the OAS. The OAS continues to function, and its bureaucratic and institutionalized characteristics continue to play an important role in the region, despite past claims of 'the OAS is dead.'

Latin America has rejected the war on drugs strategy of the United States as regards consumption. Yet only Uruguay has legalized the production and sale of even marijuana, and no country in Latin America has legalized the production and sale of any other drug that the U.S.

and the UN conventions define as illegal. Calls for legalization do not seem likely to drive drug policy in Latin America. The U.S. Drug Enforcement Agency has been thrown out of a number of Latin American countries, but those countries have not established themselves as safe havens for the international drug trade. Venezuela may be the exception, but there is no evidence to support the claim that either Bolivia or Ecuador has become an open venue for the drug trade. Evo Morales is trying a different tact for fighting the production of coca that combines crop eradication with legalization for traditional uses and crop substitution, and the area devoted to coca has declined. But coca crops in U.S. allies Colombia and Peru have also declined (UNODC 2014), so the United States can justify its continued emphasis on aggressive crop eradication. Ultimately, however, what the United States will care about is that coca production be decreased.

Latin American countries' growing concern about crime is pushing them at the same time into a strategy that looks suspiciously like the war on drugs, without the name. Brazil not only periodically mobilizes its military to help domestic police in favelas, but they, like other Latin American militaries and police involved in fighting crime, have been accused of gross violations of human rights on a scale that mirrors accusations against the U.S. war on drugs efforts. For example, Brazilian police are allegedly responsible for the extrajudicial killing of 11,000 people in their pursuit of drug-fed crime (*The New York Times* 2014). The Brazilian military and police are also developing cooperative efforts with Colombian and Peruvian militaries to combat the drug trade corridors through the Andes into Brazil, utilizing drones, radar, and even crossing the border to help neighboring countries fight the traffickers (Lyons 2012). Argentines are becoming increasingly concerned about crime as the number one issue, and Argentina has become a major hub of drug trafficking; the Argentine government will have to formulate a response. Even in Uruguay, where the president pushed through the total legalization of marijuana, public opinion shows that Uruguayans did not support that act, and thus it may be subject to change now that the president's term is up.

The Pacific Alliance develops out of a frustration of some Latin American countries with the speed of the Trans-Pacific Partnership (TPP) to incorporate their perspectives on open trade between the Western Hemisphere and Asia, and to incorporate China. So the Alliance can be seen as a group of Latin American countries that do not reject the U.S. perspective on globalization, but rather wish to speed up the process in direct contradiction to the protectionist bias of MERCOSUR or ALBA.

It is difficult to distinguish reality from rhetoric in Latin America's relations with Iran, Russia, and China, particularly given the lack of transparency. Latin American relations with China may not be a problem for the United States, assuming that the Chinese are interested in developing the supply of Latin American products into the world market. To the degree that these products go into the world market, prices for these products will be stabilized and may even decline. That will integrate more people into the world market. If the Chinese can lend money and help Latin American economies not to fall into crises, that can also benefit the United States. In addition, private oil companies diversify their risk by taking on partners, so it is not clear whether a Chinese entity taking a 10 per cent investment in an entity where the U.S. multinational has a 40 per cent investment and the local SOE has a 50 per cent investment represents a loss to the United States.

In the case of Iran, President Mahmoud Ahmadinejad got a lot of political rhetoric from visiting Latin American capitals, and there may have been some covert and black market dealings in flights between Latin America and Tehran. But Ahmadinejad is no longer in office, and the new Iranian leader, Hassan Rouhani, is less interested in stirring the diplomatic waters in Latin America. The region's intelligence forces are on the trail of uninvited Iranian influence through legitimate commercial contact (see Velez de Berliner, this volume; Ferraz 2013). The Iranian offensive in Latin America may simply represent a minor irritant in U.S. relations with Latin American. In addition, Russian naval visits in Latin American ports make for good press, but Russia is unlikely to want to confront the direct challenge to the United States that establishing a new Russian naval base in the Western Hemisphere (outside of Cuba) would entail. So they will visit and show the flag, but in and of itself, it's not clear how that presence represents a threat to the U.S.

Conclusions

The world has changed in ways that are challenging to U.S. leadership. But how would we know that these changes have occurred in ways that provide Latin America with significantly greater latitude in structuring its own security environment? In the last decade the region has progressed in developing a middle class, raising millions out of poverty, and continuing a pattern of selecting governments through elections. Yet the current slowdown in growth rates for even countries that did not embark on risky, high-growth strategies, like Venezuela and Argentina did, (e.g., Brazil, Chile, Peru, and Mexico) as commodity prices decline and Chinese growth rates slow suggests a new dependency for the region on volatile external stimuli. What must Latin America do to avoid the political and economic chaos that in the past increased U.S. leverage, because a country needed help to overcome domestic social and political crises or economic meltdown and international creditors at the door?

If Latin America cannot avoid these recurring crises, they can lead to a situation in which the relative strengths of the United States in economics, policing, institution-building, and, yes, even military mobilization can once again become attractive to Latin American governments and societies. And that would increase the interest and ability of the United States to once again have more direct influence in the region.

Note

1 I thank Arie Kacowicz for comments and Sofia Lana and Exequiel Lacovsky for research assistance. Responsibility for views herein is mine alone.

References

Angosto Ferrández, L. F. (ed) (2014) *Democracy, Revolution and Geopolitics in Latin America. Venezuela and the International Politics of Discontent*, London: Routledge.

Arnson, C. J. and Davidow, J. (eds) (2011) *China, Latin America, and the United States: The New Triangle*, Washington, DC: Latin American Program, The Woodrow Wilson Center for International Scholars.

Blasier, C. (1976) *The Hovering Giant: U.S. Responses to Revolutionary Change in Latin America*, Pittsburgh: University of Pittsburgh Press.

Bradford, C. I., Linn, J. F. and Martin, P. (2008) 'Global Governance Breakthrough: The G20 Summit and the Future Agenda', *Brookings Policy Brief*, No. 168. Washington, DC: Brookings Institute.

Desch, M. C. (1996) 'Why Realists Disagree About the Third World (and Why They Shouldn't)' *Security Studies*, 5(3): 358–384.

Domínguez, J. I. and Covarrubias, A. (eds) (2014) *Routledge Handbook of Latin America in the World*, New York: Routledge

Domínguez, J. I. and Fernández de Castro, R. (2010) *Contemporary U.S.-Latin American Relations*, New York: Routledge.

Economy, E. C. and Oksenberg, M. (1999) *China Joins the World: Progress and Prospects*, New York: Council on Foreign Relations.

Ferraz, L. (2013, April 11) 'Agencia Brasileira espionou funcionários estrangeiros', *Folho de Sao Paulo*. Retrieved from http://www.folhapolitica.org/2013/11/agencia-brasileira-espionou.html.

Finnemore, M. (1996) *National Interest and International Society*, Ithaca: Cornell University Press.
French, J. (2009) 'Understanding the Politics of Latin America's Plural Lefts (Chávez/Lula): Social Democracy, Populism, and Convergence on the Path to a Post-Neoliberal World', *Third World Quarterly*, 30: 349–370.
Handal, S. J. (1993) 'Socialism: An Alternative for Latin America? Socialism in the Underdeveloped Countries and a Proposal for El Salvador' in J. H. Shafick and C. M. Vilas (eds) *The Socialist Option in Central America*, New York: Monthly Review Press.
Johnston, A. I. (2003) 'Is China a Status Quo Power?', *International Security*, 27(4): 5–56.
Keohane, R. O. (1984) *After Hegemony*, New Jersey: Princeton University Press.
Kissinger, H. (1979) *White House Years*, Boston: Little, Brown.
Krebs, R. R. and Lobasz, J. K. (2007) 'Fixing the Meaning of 9/11: Hegemony, Coercion and the Road to War in Iraq', *Security Studies*, 16(3): 409–451.
Lowenthal, A. F. (2010) 'Obama and the Americas: Promise, Disappointment, Opportunity', *Foreign Affairs*, 89(4): 110–124.
Lowenthal, A. F. and Mostajo, F. G. (2010) 'Estados Unidos y América Latina, 1960–2010: De la pretensión hegemónica a las relaciones diversas y complejas', *Foro Internacional*, 50(3/4): 552–626.
Lyons, J. (2012, December 3) 'Brazil Reaches Across Border to Battle Source of Cocaine', *Wall Street Journal*. Retrieved from http://www.wsj.com/articles/SB10000872396390443624204578060602681774138.
Mares, D. R. (1988a) 'Middle Powers Under Regional Hegemony: To Challenge or Acquiesce in Hegemonic Enforcement', *International Studies Quarterly*, 32(4): 453–471.
——— (1988b) 'Mexico's Foreign Policy as a Middle Power: The Nicaragua Connection 1884–1986', *Latin American Research Review*, 3: 81–107.
Muhr, T. (2012) '(Re)constructing Popular Power in Our America: Venezuela and the Regionalisation of "Revolutionary Democracy" in the ALBA-TCP Space', *Third World Quarterly*, 33(2): 225–241.
Pastor, R. (2001) *Exiting The Whirlpool: U.S. Foreign Policy Toward Latin America And The Caribbean*, Boulder: Westview.
Paul, T. V. (1994) *Asymmetric Conflicts: War Initiation by Weaker Powers*, Cambridge: Cambridge University Press.
Perla, H. and Cruz-Feliciano, H. (2013) 'The Twenty-First-Century Left in El Salvador and Nicaragua: Understanding Apparent Contradictions and Criticisms', *Latin American Perspectives*, 40: 83–106.
Perla, H., Mojica, M. and Bibler, J. (2013) 'From Guerrillas to Government: The Continued Relevance of the Central American Left' in J. Webber and B. Carr (eds) *The New Latin American Left: Cracks in the Empire*, Lanham, MD: Rowman and Littlefield.
Snyder, J. (1984/1985) 'Richness, Rigor and Relevance in the Study of Soviet Foreign Policy', *International Security*, 9(3): 89–108.
The New York Times (2014, November 11) 'Brazil: Police Killed 11,000 People Over Five-Year Period, Report Says'. Retrieved from http://www.nytimes.com/2014/11/12/world/americas/brazil-police-killed-11000-people-over-five-year-period-report-says.html?module=Search&mabReward=relbias%3Ar%2C%7B%222%22%3A%22RI%3A13%22%7D.
United Nations Office on Drugs and Crime (2014) *World Drug Report*, Vienna: KeoUNODC.
Waltz, K. (1979) *Theory of International Politics*, New York: McGraw Hill.
Wendt, A. (1987) 'The Agent-Structure Problem in International Relations Theory', *International Organization*, 41(3): 335–370.
——— (1992) 'Anarchy is What States Make of it: The Social Construction of Power Politics', *International Organization*, 46(2): 391–425.

26

THE MIDDLE EAST AND LATIN AMERICA

Implications for Latin America's security

Maria Velez de Berliner

The security implications for Latin America of its relations with the Middle East are best understood if they are analyzed from the perspective of the long history the Middle East has in Latin America. The presence of Iran in the region since 2005, when Mahmoud Ahmadinejad was elected president of Iran, is particularly relevant, since Iran and a number of Latin American countries share some interests: economic relations, anti-U.S. sentiment, and diversification of trade and foreign relations (Woodrow Wilson Center Reports on the Americas 2010). Except for an undercurrent of anti-Semitism prevalent in the region, particularly as it relates to Israel's actions in Palestine, Latin America sees its relations with the Middle East as an economic opportunity rather than political cooperation.

Those interested in issues of security in Latin America might want to consider the security concerns the United States has had in the region since the terrorist attacks of September 11, 2001. These concerns are based on the fear some security analysts in the United States have of a Middle Eastern, Islamist, radical terrorist movement, particularly from Iran, utilizing the porous borders of South and Central America to enter Mexico, and from there the United States, to conduct nefarious activities. According to the U.S. Department of State (Taylor 2013) these concerns have decreased. However, were such actions to occur, they would have serious consequences in the region. The United States would move to retaliate against the country or countries involved decisively and lethally, thus altering the security environment of the region.

Historical background of the Middle East presence in Latin America

Middle Easterners, including Persians from Iran, are called 'Arabs' in Latin America. Jews are collectively known as *Israelitas*. It is important to note that *Israelitas* does not mean Israelis, the residents of Israel. The scholarly literature on this subject is mostly descriptive and colored by personal assumptions and conclusions drawn from broadly described associations. Journalists have contributed to the discussion by reporting on specific issues, such as the attacks against the Israeli Embassy (1992) and the *Asociación Mutual Israelita-Argentina* (AMIA) (1994), both in Buenos Aires, and the presence of Middle Eastern groups in the Tri-Border Area (TBA). This is a challenge for further study, which would require *in situ* testing of hypotheses.

The ethnic, demographic, and religious distinctions that exist in the Middle East are often blurred in censuses, entry and exit visas, and other population measures in Latin America.

Middle Easterners and their descendants have been assimilated into countries they consider their own. Most are Christians. Sunnis, Shi'as, Maronites, Coptic, Muslims, and other denominations are free to practice their religion without state or cultural constraints.

Three significant migratory waves from the Middle East led to the existence of well-established diasporas throughout the region, the largest in Argentina, Brazil, and Mexico (DeShazo and Mendelson-Forman 2010). Some descendants of these migrants achieved high political office (presidents of Argentina, Ecuador, and Colombia). Many are members of the legislative and judicial branches, and their number includes academics, industrialists, and entrepreneurs in every country. They are part of the educated class, and belong to the middle to the upper rungs of the economic ladder. Mexico's Carlos Slim Helú (of Lebanese descent) is the world's richest man, according to Forbes (Kroll 2013). "There are around ten to twelve million Brazilians of Arab descent. The largest populations of Lebanese and Syrian origin outside those countries reside in Brazil" (Amorim n.d.).

Trade has grown since 2005 as both regions seek diversification from their traditional trading partners: the United States (for Latin America) and the European Union (for the Middle East). Whether this trend will continue, how, and at which levels of participation depends on the as yet unresolved instability in the Middle East, the relations between the United States and Iran, and the actions of Israel in the Middle East, particularly vis-à-vis the Palestinian territories.

There are trade agreements, legal accords, memoranda of understanding (MoU), and institutional frameworks such as the South American–Arab Countries (ASPA) Summits (2005, 2009, and 2013) that tie the two regions together. There are also bilateral agreements with Iran, of which Brazil has more than 30, and Venezuela more than 100. But there appears to be more image than reality regarding the promised, or actual, investments by Iran in Venezuela, Ecuador, Bolivia, and Nicaragua. These investments are shrouded in secrecy and, at best, opacity.

Latin America's bilateral trade agreements with the United States, regional agreements with the European Union, the Pacific Alliance, and the proposed Trans-Pacific Partnership have greater potential for affecting the activities of Middle Eastern countries, including Iran, Israel, and Saudi Arabia, among others, in Latin America. Therefore, it would be misleading to assume relations between the two regions will, of necessity, create a security threat in Latin America, let alone threaten the relations of Latin America with the United States.

Iran–Latin American relations

No other Middle Eastern country attracts as much attention regarding the security of Latin America as Iran, because of its presence in the region, close relationship with Venezuela prior to the death of Hugo Chávez, and Iran's alleged participation in two foreign-inspired terrorist attacks in Argentina in 1992 and 1994. Few scholars and analysts, if any, believed the Middle East had, or could have, significant impact on the security of Latin America prior to 9/11. After 9/11, security concerns focused on the large Middle Eastern diaspora in the Tri-Border Area and the expansion of Iran into Latin America under Chávez's patronage.

An unsuccessful plot to kill the ambassador of Saudi Arabia in the United States in 2012 was thwarted when an Iranian-American, who wanted Mexico's *Los Zetas* drug cartel to contract for the killing, contacted a confidential informant of the U.S. Drug Enforcement Administration. The U.S. attorney general indicated the plot "was directed and approved by elements of the Iranian government and, specifically, senior members of [Iran's] Quds force" (Weiser

2013). The failed attempt to blow up the terminal fuel lines at JFK International Airport was to be carried out by "members of the fundamentalist group *Jamaat al-Muslimeen*, which was behind a bloody coup attempt in Trinidad in 1990" (Buckley and Rashbaum 2007) and received training in Iran (Zambelis 2007). Unlike the strategic attacks against Israel in Argentina, the Saudi and JFK airport cases illustrate the opportunistic threats hostile, nonstate actors might create by taking advantage of the presence of Iran in the region. The attacks in Argentina sought to alter Argentina's relations with Israel, while the other attacks used Iran's presence in Latin America as a cover for those actions. Therefore, the presence of Iran in the region could serve as cover for actions against the United States by groups who might, or might not be, related to Iran.

The assumed Iran-Venezuela threat deserved valid concern during the concurrent presidencies of Hugo Chávez in Venezuela (1999–2013) and Mahmoud Ahmadinejad in Iran (2005–2012). Both men were viscerally hostile toward the United States and acted as facilitators of the presence of transnational terrorist organizations, such as the *Fuerzas Armadas Revolucionarias de Colombia* (FARC) and Iran's Quds Force in Venezuela. During his 14 years in power, Chávez visited Iran 14 times, and Ahmadinejad visited Venezuela, Nicaragua, Bolivia, Ecuador, and Cuba four times since 2005 (Sabo and Orozco 2012).

The potential threat to security in the hemisphere posed by this relationship might have decreased because the thaw of relations between the Unites States and Iran seems to have changed Iran's calculus in Latin America, if there was one beyond Ahmadinejad and Chávez's. It seems that Iran's current president, Hassan Rouhani, is interested in "a constructive dialogue with the United States and the United Kingdom" (Goodman 2013), and will relegate Latin America to a category that includes other states with which Iran seeks to have good relations – for its own sake rather than a strategic purpose (Goodman 2013).

Some security experts in the United States see Iran as a real and significant threat to the security of the region (Noriega 2012), especially those who believe Iran has a plot to establish terrorist beachheads through Hezbollah's Islamic Jihad (Arnson et al. 2010). The United States appears to be adopting a 'wait and see' attitude after the change of government in Iran. By contrast, security analysts in Latin America see Iran nowadays more as an unreliable economic partner than a continuation of Chávez and Ahmadinejad's open challenge to the hegemony and influence of the United States.

A review of the current literature on Latin America–Middle East security relations, with its emphasis on Iran, can be grouped under three general themes: (1) foreign policy and diplomatic relations, (2) military and intelligence links, and (3) planning and abetting terrorist activities.

Foreign policy and diplomatic relations

The internal, interregional, and extraregional differences among Latin America's countries inform their foreign policies, diplomatic relations, and the positive or negative opinion they hold of the Arab Middle East and Iran, as well as the role they play in the region's security. Latin America's internal differences are demonstrated by the fact that regional and subregional organizations muddle along, or perform poorly, as their member countries fail to reach a common agreement, even regarding security. Drug trafficking is considered a region-wide security threat. However, there is no intraregional agreement on which areas of trafficking create the greatest threat. Even when they agree that criminality is the region's paramount security threat, each country has its own idea of who the criminals are and which countercrime policies are needed.

Hence, the existence of Middle Eastern security threats in Latin America requires they should be disaggregated by country. However, this does not preclude that, in some cases, two or more countries might be involved because the region has 11 tri-border areas (Velez de Berliner 2013), where state control or influence are significantly challenged by nonstate actors. One of the largest concentrations of Middle Easterners resides in the Tri-Border Area of Argentina, Brazil, and Paraguay, in which it is generally considered that state control is significantly challenged by a variety of nonstate actors.

Neither Latin America nor the Middle East depends on the other economically, politically, or militarily. The United States, the European Union, and China are the major trading partners of Latin America, including military exchanges and weapons sales.

Despite their constitutional mandates for the separation of powers in Latin America, direct experience demonstrates that the legislative and judicial branches are subservient to the executive branch (presidency) and its occupant of record. For instance, the late Hugo Chávez (from Venezuela) defined his foreign policy with the Middle East using Iran as his point of reference and in open defiance of policies implemented by the United States, the United Nations, and the European Union. Presidents Daniel Ortega (from Nicaragua), Rafael Correa (from Ecuador), and Evo Morales (from Bolivia) chose to fall within Chávez's orbit and followed his lead regarding their countries' relations with Iran. Brazil followed a more pragmatic line in its reach to the Middle East and in its relationship with Iran. Mexico openly distanced itself from Iran. Those interested in in-depth analysis of why these countries pursued individual policies regarding the Middle East would want to conduct *in situ* studies of the drivers of those policies.

Some analysts see the outreach of Latin America to the Middle East not as a long-term pivot from the United States toward the Middle East, but as an expression of Latin America's expansion into the global economy and a symptom of Latin America's desire to move beyond its historical dependence on the United States, without breaking away from it. The following examples show how this outreach has evolved with the changing of president in Brazil and a wealthier trading partner taking over projects Iran had promised to undertake (Nicaragua's Transoceanic Canal). Brazil, under President Luis Inâcio 'Lula' da Silva (2003–2011), sought to expand its reach into the world, and Iran is part of that world. However, Lula and Ahmadinejad encountered strong rejection of their relationship by a majority of Brazil's political and economic establishment. Lula's successor, Dilma Rousseff, has openly retrenched from pursuing relations with Iran. As Evan Ellis indicates, the most significant loss to Iran in Latin America is Brazil under Rousseff (Ellis 2013), which will probably continue under her successors unless the United States fully normalizes relations with Iran, opening the way for reluctant Latin American countries to follow. Despite its distance from Iran, Brazil retains its observer status in the Arab League. In Nicaragua's case, a Chinese company (HK Nicaragua Canal Development Investment Co. Ltd.) undertook the construction of the transoceanic canal Iran pledged to build (see Ellis, this volume).

The most important activity in foreign policy and economic diplomacy has been the establishment of the South American–Arab Countries Summit (ASPA by its Spanish acronym), the idea of Brazil's Lula da Silva. ASPA met in Brazil in 2005, in Qatar in 2009, and in Lima in 2013.

Relations between Venezuela and Iran

The relationship between Venezuela and Iran is longstanding, with significant cooperation beginning in 1960 when the two, plus Iraq, Kuwait, and Saudi Arabia, founded the Organization of Petroleum Exporting Countries (OPEC). Venezuela and Iran have since focused on collaborating in keeping oil prices high to support the government of record. Venezuela's President Carlos Andrés Pérez (1974–1979 and 1989–1993) visited Iran in 1977.

Opportunism, a 'we vs. them' approach buttressed by anti-imperialist ideology, led Chávez's Venezuela to expand into the Middle East and embrace Iran more strongly than Venezuela had done in the past.

Increased ties between Venezuela and Iran came at an opportune point: Iran was isolated by the international community, particularly by the United States, and needed to reach out to find new suppliers and customers, and create a sense of relevance in the world at large. Chávez came to power with the ideology of 21st-century socialism (national resources' nationalism coupled with power to the poor and the dispossessed), bent on unifying Latin America against the hegemonic power of the United States in the region, and creating a multipolar world focused on South-South relations.

Although there is ingrained, but seldom openly discussed, anti-Semitism in Latin America, Chávez was careful not to openly antagonize Israel's interests or the Jewish community in Venezuela, marking probably the only ideological point of departure from Ahmadinejad, an unrepentant Holocaust denier and Israel hater. Anti-Semitism in Latin America remains a matter of controversy and merits further research to determine its influence on Latin America's relations with Israel and possible ramifications in the region's Middle East relations.

Relations between Ecuador and Iran

Iran rode on Chávez's coattails to expand its presence in Ecuador. The election of Rafael Correa as Ecuadorian president helped to strengthen those ties. It is ironic that two countries that harbor and abet recognized terrorist organizations (Hezbollah in Iran and Colombia's FARC in Ecuador) have an agreement to combat international terrorism, money laundering, and cross-border refugees (*LaInfo* 2014).

The relationship between Iran and Ecuador is more opportunistic than strategic. Ecuador is a poor country with a president who relishes going against the United States, but keeps the United States as its largest trading partner. After Chávez's death it was thought Correa could be a successor to Chávez and therefore strengthen Iran's position in Latin America. However, after the departure of Ahmadinejad from power it does not appear that Correa holds a special attraction for Iran. Analysis of the response of the Correa administration to the new Iranian administration could help scholars sort out the relative influence of geopolitics and economics in contemporary Ecuador.

Relations between Bolivia and Iran

Bolivia's association with Venezuela, and consequently with Iran, was part of the political strategy of President Evo Morales for ensuring his ability to continue his constitutionally mandated terms of office (three of his predecessors had been forced from office early). To retain the allegiance of the military and security forces, Venezuela and Iran provided the Bolivian government with weapons, military training, and the professionalization of its security apparatus (Walser 2012; Prudencio 2009–2013).

The world's rush for the natural resources of Latin America, particularly China, lifted Bolivia from an undeveloped to a developing country (see Ellis, this volume). In 2010 Iran and Bolivia signed a free trade agreement. Under it, Iran was to help Bolivia develop its vast lithium reserves. Some analysts in the United States saw the agreement as a way for Iran to circumvent international restrictions on its access to fissile material. Lithium

> . . . can be used as an alternative or as an enhancer to uranium, a key component needed to develop nuclear weapons. In particular, lithium-6 is an internationally controlled substance because of its "booster" role in smaller, highly efficient thermonuclear devices.
>
> *(Jorisch 2011)*

However, Iran's investments in Bolivia's lithium are miniscule and, like those of other countries, have been caught in the legal intricacies of Comibol, Bolivia's agency in charge of lithium (Romero 2009). Iran's influence in the country is thus limited to intelligence gathering and security of the executive branch. A large part of Bolivia's security and intelligence is outsourced to Venezuela, and it is through the work Iran does in these areas in Venezuela that Iran becomes an actor in Bolivia's security of the executive branch and in Bolivia's intelligence corps (Prudencio 2009–2013).

Relations between Nicaragua and Iran

Daniel Ortega called the Sandinista and the Iranian revolutions twins, devoted to justice, freedom, and against imperialism (*BBC Mundo* 2007). Nicaragua's relations with Iran have focused on economic cooperation and Iran's investments, particularly in infrastructure (Farrar-Wellman 2010). However, most of these investments did not materialize as promised. The centerpiece of those expected investments, development of the Nicaraguan Canal, went to China's HK Nicaragua Canal Development Investment Co. Ltd., not to Iran (*The Asahi Shimbun* 2014).

Ortega, like Chávez and his successor, Nicolas Maduro, also supports Iran's right to develop nuclear energy for peaceful purposes; in this they are no different from other Latin American countries. And, like other Latin American countries, Nicaragua does not wish to become involved in creating or participating in any mechanisms to monitor whether Iran develops a secret nuclear weapons program.

Military and intelligence links

In the comprehensive analysis that appears in *Iran in Latin America: Threat or "Axis of Annoyance"?* (Arnson et al. 2010: 29) Farideh Farhi calls the Iran/Venezuela relationship "the axis of unity." However, this unity should be viewed as the product of the personalities of Chávez and Ahmadinejad more than a rational calculus of the long-term international relations objectives of the two countries and, especially, the rational calculus of other countries in the region.

According to Tony Capaccio, the U.S. Department of Defense claims "Venezuela has spent more on arms purchases since 2005 than China, Pakistan or Iran" (Capaccio 2007). The United States stopped selling military technology, arms, and spare parts for F-16s (that were sold to Venezuela in 1989), claiming Venezuela was remiss in helping to fight the United States' Global War on Terror. Consequently, Chávez turned to other suppliers to upgrade his stock and to defend Venezuela, which he believed would be attacked by the United States, which would use Colombia as a staging ground.

Some security analysts focus on the relationship between Iran's National Revolutionary Guard Corps and its Quds Force, and their relationship with Venezuela's military as a serious threat to the security of Latin America and, by reasons of geography and alliances, the

United States. The participation of both militaries in drug trafficking and their association with Colombia's FARC adds to the analysts' concerns (O'Grady 2014). This issue is controversial and remains a critical area of research, particularly with the demobilization of the FARC being negotiated in Havana in 2014 and the security consequences such demobilization might have in the Andean region and the rest of Latin America.

The military under Chávez built a significant intelligence machine to ensure the survival and perpetuation of the 21st-century revolution. Iran's military collaborated closely with Chávez in the training and enhancement of the capacity of an intelligence and security apparatus, whose operatives are welcome in Bolivia, Ecuador, and Nicaragua. These operatives help local militaries protect the executive branch and augment and support the security apparatus in those countries. The connections of high-ranking officers in the Venezuelan armed forces with trafficking networks that operate in the Middle East, Colombia, and the rest of Latin America were documented by Alberto Nisman (Brice 2013) in his investigation of the attacks in Argentina in 1992 and 1994 and their aftermath, until his killing in early 2015.

The U.S. Department of the Treasury claims that large sectors in Venezuela's active and inactive military and some of its leadership are involved in drug trafficking (U.S. Department of the Treasury 2008) and in the protection of FARC. For example, Walid Makled was accused by the United States of involvement in the drug trade, and when arrested in Colombia claimed that he was associated with high officials of Chávez's government, including people in the military. Though the United States requested his extradition, Colombia claimed that Venezuela's extradition request preceded that of the U.S. and sent him to Venezuela. Conversely, Chávez allowed the extrication by Colombia of the FARC's leader Rodrigo Granda (Wagner 2005), who was residing in Venezuela. These two situations point to a complex reality that merits more research regarding the security relations of Venezuela with the United States and other countries in the region.

Venezuela's Bolivarian National Armed Forces have an "active frontline personnel of 155,000 with active reserves of 787,000" (Staff Writer 2014). Contained within them is the Bolivarian National Militia formed by *colectivos*, armed groups embedded in each community and whose members come from inside the community. The *colectivos* are similar to the IRGC – according to "Article 150 of the Constitution of Iran, the Iran Revolutionary Guard Corps (IRGC) operates as a 'guarantor of the Revolution and of its achievements'" (Dumitrescu 2010). The *colectivos* have played a crucial role in suppressing antigovernment protests across Venezuela, as "the self-appointed guardians of Venezuelan's revolution" (Minaya 2014). In this way the *colectivos* act in ways similar to those used by the IRGC in suppressing dissent within Iran.

Some analysts claim the *Cartel de Los Soles* (Cartel of the Suns) is a significant security threat, not only in Venezuela but throughout Latin America, through its connections with other armed forces in the region. *Los Soles* is allegedly composed of units within the national guard, national militia, army, navy, and air force that participate in the cocaine trade that flows from Colombia through Venezuela on its way to Europe, China, Africa, and Central Asia. Due to its association with FARC, *Los Soles* concentrates its operations in the states of Táchira, Zulia, and Apure, across from the Colombian border. *Los Soles* gained power after Chávez ended antinarcotics cooperation with the United States Drug Enforcement Administration (DEA). The DEA's departure left Puerto Cabello without dependable screening capabilities to stop drug shipments. This issue came to the fore with the warrant against retired Venezuelan General Hugo Carvajal for his detention in Aruba in July 2014 to be extradited to the United States on drug trafficking charges and connections with the FARC (*BBC News* 2014). Venezuela protested his arrest, and there were concerns about the Maduro government's economic retaliation against the island. Carvajal was subsequently released to Venezuela by the Dutch government on grounds of diplomatic immunity. The Carvajal case suggests that the role of the Venezuelan government and its armed forces in narco-trafficking can have significant security implications in the region and merits careful scholarly study.

The presence of the Quds Force in Venezuela, and in Venezuelan and Iranian embassies in other countries, is largely taken for granted by some analysts in the United States. As with many diplomatic personnel, it is assumed some Iranian and Venezuelan diplomats are Quds members acting under the veil of commerce, trade, and cultural attachés. However, what the Quds Force is doing, where, and how remains a mystery. Though scholars are not undercover agents and cannot assume the role of intelligence officials, they can contribute to an understanding of the patterns, limits, and successes of using diplomatic missions for intelligence activities.

Planning and abetting terrorist activities

Latin America does not consider the Middle East a threat. Jews in Argentina are the exception based on their experience of the attacks against them there. Argentina is the only Latin American country with an empirical reason to fear terrorist attacks originating in Iran, since it is widely suspected that the IRGC or the Quds Force, and/or its affiliate criminal organization Hezbollah, committed these acts against Jewish community sites (Defend Democracy Organization 2013). But the presence (permanent, temporary, or transient) in the region of a radical, Islamist terrorist is of concern to Latin America to the extent of potentially nefarious, terrorist activities in the United States territory and subsequent retaliation of the United States against Latin America.

As indicated before, of all the countries in the Middle East, Iran is the only one to be closely tied to two successful terrorist attacks in the region. Therefore, Iran is the country assumed to be able to again carry out a terrorist attack in Latin America. As a countermeasure against the possibility of an attack against U.S. interests in Latin America or coming into the United States through Latin America, the United States' House of Representatives enacted a list of the countermeasures to be taken against the possibility of an attack against U.S. interests in Latin America or coming into the U.S. through Latin America. This list can be found in H.R. 3783 (112th), *Countering Iran in the Western Hemisphere Act of 2012* (U.S. House of Representatives, Public Law 112–220).

Some analysts fear that Iran's ultimate aim for its presence in the region is to use Latin America as a path for deploying weapons of mass destruction in the United States. However, no evidence to sustain this concern has been provided. If anything, Iran's unfulfilled promises to states in the region are decreasing its credibility as a partner for Latin America. In addition, given the high stakes Iran has in its efforts to reestablish good relations with the United States, it is unlikely Iran would support or abet an attack on the United States.

Iran and the terrorist attacks in Argentina (1992 and 1994)

Argentina suffered terrorist attacks against the Israeli Embassy in 1992 and the *Asociación Mutual Israelita-Argentina* (AMIA by its Spanish acronym) in 1994, both in Buenos Aires. The attacks were credited by many to Iran's Hezbollah and its armed wing, the Islamic Jihad, and their associates in the Tri-Border Area. In 2008, Israel's embassy in Buenos Aires claimed an attempt by the Islamic Jihad against its facilities. The Argentine Supreme Court vacated the case for lack of proof (Argentina Supreme Court 2008).

In 2006 Argentina's Supreme Court filed to continue the investigation of the 1992 attack on the Israeli Embassy and reiterated the lack of precedent in the case of the statute of limitations. It therefore reinstated the order to continue with the investigation and arrest order of the presumed perpetrators (Defend Democracy Organization 2013).

In 2013, Alberto Nisman, an Argentine prosecutor, issued a 500-page indictment accusing Iran of establishing "local clandestine intelligence stations designed to sponsor, foster and execute terrorist attacks to export the Islamic revolution" (Defend Democracy Organization 2013). Nisman was the only Argentine official who had directly accused Iran of direct participation in the AMIA attack. He claimed he could "corroborate and strengthen [the case against Iran] with new evidence" (Defend Democracy Organization 2013) that the perpetrators of the attack on AMIA received protection and cover from Hezbollah operatives in the Tri-Border Area (TBA) and in Argentina.

According to Nisman, Iran had set up intelligence bases in a number of South American countries, including, but not limited to, Brazil, Paraguay, Uruguay, Chile, Colombia, Guyana, Trinidad and Tobago, and Suriname. However, no one has been able to uncover these cells, their operatives, motives, or objectives. What does appear to exist in Latin America are radical Islamist extremists, alone or in small groups, who have been accused of attempting unsuccessful attacks against JFK International Airport (Muslim extremists from Guyana) and Fort Dixon (Muslim extremists from Albania), or the failed plot against the ambassador of Saudi Arabia in the United States.

Nisman indicated that there continue to be front organizations, such as mosques, cultural and trade centers, charity organizations, and embassies, that give cover to illicit and/or criminal activities carried out by Iran in Latin America. However, no one seems to be certain what these activities are, because houses of worship are protected by the separation of church and state that exists in every country in Latin America, and embassies are foreign territory protected by diplomatic immunity.

The government of Cristina Fernández de Kirchner entered into a controversial memorandum of understanding (MoU) with the Iranian government in 2013 to investigate the two bombings. The credibility of such an agreement was seriously questioned by Argentines outside of the president's cabinet. Argentina rescinded the MoU on May 16, 2014 when Argentina's Supreme Court declared it unconstitutional (*World Jewish Congress* 2014).

This unresolved issue of the Argentine attacks represents an important opportunity for the study of the country's relations with Iran, the impact of President Fernández de Kirchner's general foreign policy goals on Argentina's commitment to fight terrorism, the strange silence of other Latin American countries in the search for why a country in the region was vulnerable to such an attack, and how the region can decrease the likelihood of such attacks in the future.

Research agenda and conclusions

Political volatility is a constant in the Middle East and, to a lesser degree, in Latin America. The future political, ethnic, religious, and economic evolution and organization of the Middle East, including Iran, and its relations with Latin America will remain an area of investigation for scholars of comparative politics and international security relations. Also, given the security concerns the United States has about Iran and the Middle East's presence in Latin America, the United States cannot be excluded from the scholarly inquiry suggested here.

For scholars interested in the potential impact of the Middle East on Latin America's security environment, a number of questions merit study. I have mentioned some specific issues in the relevant sections of this chapter, but overall scholars need to draw on the relevant international relations theories to understand how to conceptualize a trilateral relationship in which a Great Power (the United States) fears the use of neutral territory (Latin America) by non-conventional adversaries fighting the Great Power in their home territory. Many claims about this relationship have been made by policy-makers, pundits, and even academics, but we do not yet have a theoretical structure that can be used to develop hypotheses subject to rigorous empirical testing.

References

Amorim, C. (n.d.) *Brazil and the Middle East*, Cairo: The Cairo Review of Global Affairs, American University Cairo.

Argentina Supreme Court, in Embajada de Israel s/ intim. pública – causa. N° 208/2008- S.C.E. 6, L. XLIV.- O.P. Retrieved from http://www.csjn.gov.ar/confal/ConsultaCompletaFallos.do;jsessionid=0a81010830f5bad6f27c0c5941c289bfb2e94ff27c66.e38Ob3aLaxuKay0LbxaObxmObh4Se6fznA5Pp7ftolbGmkTy?method=realizaConsulta.

Arnson, C., Esfandiari, H. and Stubits, A. (eds) (2010) *Iran in Latin America: Threat or "Axis of Annoyance"?*, Washington, DC: Woodrow Wilson International Center for Scholars.

BBC Mundo (2007, June 11) 'Nicaragua e Iran, "union invencible"'. Retrieved from http://news.bbc.co.uk/hi/spanish/latin_america/newsid_6741000/6741829.stm.

BBC News Latin America & Caribbean (2014, July 28) 'Venezuela Gives "Hero's Welcome" to Freed General Carvajal'. Retrieved from http://www.bbc.com/news/world-latin-america-28520775.

Brice, A. (2013, June 3) 'Iran, Hezbollah Mine Latin America for Revenue, Recruits, Analysts Say', *NCC*. Retrieved from http://www.cnn.com/2013/06/03/world/americas/iran-latin-america/.

Buckley, C. and Rashbaum, W. K. (2007, June 3) 'Men Accused of Plot to Blow Up Kennedy Airport Terminals and Fuel Lines', *The New York Times*. Retrieved from http://www.nytimes.com/2007/06/03/nyregion/03plot.html?pagewanted=all.

Capaccio, T. (2007, July 22) 'Venezuela's Arms Purchases Since 2005 Top China, Iran, Pakistan', *Bloomberg News*. Retrieved from http://www.bloomberg.com/apps/news?pid=newsarchive&sid=a1yScHOQvMm8.

Defend Democracy Organization (2013) 'Amia Case'. Retrieved from http://www.defenddemocracy.org/stuff/uploads/documents/summary_(31_pages).pdf.

DeShazo, P. and Mendelson-Forman, J. (2010, April) *Latin America and the Middle East: The Dynamic and Evolving Relationship*, Miami: Applied Research Center, Latin American and Caribbean Center, Florida International University.

Dumitrescu, O. (2010, November 20) 'The Intelligence and Security Services of Iran', *World Security Network*. Retrieved from http://www.worldsecuritynetwork.com/Iran/Dumitrescu-Octavian/The-Intelligence-and-Security-Services-of-Iran.

Ellis, R.E. (2013) 'Russia, Iran and China in Latin America: Evaluating the Threat', *American Foreign Policy Journal*, 9: 7–10.

Farrar-Wellman, A. (2010) *Nicaragua-Iran Foreign Relations*, Washington, DC: American Enterprise Institute.

Goodman, J. (2013, June 26) 'Iran Influence in Latin America Waning, U.S. Report Says', *Bloomberg News*. Retrieved from http://www.bloomberg.com/news/2013–06–26/iran-influence-in-latin-america-waning-u-s-report-says.html.

Jorisch, A. (2011, May 10) 'Why Iran and Bolivia are in Business', *UPI Analysis*. Retrieved from http://www.upi.com/Top_News/Analysis/Outside-View/2011/05/10/Why-Iran-and-Bolivia-are-in-business/UPI-29341305022140/#ixzz2tyg5dknI.

Kroll, L. (2013, March 4) 'Inside the 2013 Billionaires List: Facts and Figures', *Forbes*. Retrieved from http://www.forbes.com/sites/luisakroll/2013/03/04/inside-the-2013-billionaires-list-facts-and-figures/.

LaInfo (2014, July 22) 'Colombia and Ecuador Have Signed Agreements in Various Areas'. Retrieved from http://lainfo.es/en/2014/07/22/colombia-and-ecuador-have-signed-agreements-in-various-areas/.

Minaya, E. (2014, May 5) 'Armed Civilians Fight Venezuela Protesters, Government Goads Self-Appointed Guardians of Revolution to Counter Unrest', *The Wall Street Journal*. Retrieved from http://online.wsj.com/news/articles/SB10001424052702303948104579537963099935756.

Noriega, R.F. (2012) *Hezbollah's Strategic Shift: A Global Terrorist Threat*, Washington, DC: Rayburn House Office Building Testimony of Ambassador Roger F. Noriega, United States House of Representatives, Committee on Foreign Affairs, Subcommittee on Terrorism, Non-Proliferation and Trade.

O'Grady, M. A. (2014, August 10) 'A Terrorist Big Fish Gets Away', *The Wall Street Journal: The Americas*. Retrieved from http://online.wsj.com/articles/mary-anastasia-ogrady-a-terrorist-big-fish-gets-away-1407710225.

Prudencio, G. (2009–2013) *Personal Interviews, Retired Colonel Bolivia's Army*, Washington, DC.

Romero, S. (2009, February 2) 'In Bolivia, Untapped Bounty Meets Nationalism', *The New York Times Americas*. Retrieved from http://www.nytimes.com/2009/02/03/world/americas/03lithium.html?pagewanted=all&_r=0.

Sabo, E. and Orozco, J. (2012, June 9) 'Ahmadinajed Woos Chavez-Led Allies in Latin America', *Bloomberg News*. Retrieved from http://www.businessweek.com/news/2012-06-19/ahmadinejad-woos-chavez-led-allies-in-latin-america.

Staff Writer (2014) 'The Venezuela Military Showcases Six Major Branches of Service and is Favorably Aligned with Several Regional Powers', *Global FirePower*. Retrieved from http://www.globalfirepower.com/country-military-strength-detail.asp?country_id=Venezuela.

Taylor, G. (2013, June 23) 'State Secrets: Kerry's Department Downplays Iran's Role in Latin America; Likely to Anger Congress', *The Washington Times*. Retrieved from http://m.washingtontimes.com/news/2013/jun/23/state-department-downplays-iran-role-in-latin-amer/?page=all#pagebreak.

The Asahi Shimbun (2014, August 7) 'Nicaragua Sets Sights on Building Rival to Panama Canal with Chinese Backing'. Retrieved from http://ajw.asahi.com/article/asia/china/AJ201408070001.

United States Department of the Treasury (2008) *Treasury Targets Venezuelan Government Officials Supporting the FARC*, Washington, DC: Press Office, HP-1132.

United States Government House of Representatives (2012) *Countering Iran in the Western Hemisphere Act of 2012, Public Law 112–220*, Washington, DC: U.S. Congress.

Velez de Berliner, M. (2013) *Tri-Border Areas in Latin America*, Unpublished lecture, Hurlburt Field, FL: U.S. Special Operations Command, Special Operations School.

Wagner, S. (2005, May 17) 'Venezuelan Authorities Honor Colombian Extradition Request', *Venezuelanalysis*. Retrieved from https://venezuelanalysis.com/news/1132.

Walser, R. (2012) 'The Future of Iran's Influence in Latin America', *inFocus Quarterly*, 6(2). Retrieved from http://www.jewishpolicycenter.org/3233/iran-influence-latin-america.

Weiser, B. (2013, May 30) 'Man Sentenced in Plot to Kill Saudi Ambassador', *The New York Times*. Retrieved from http://www.nytimes.com/2013/05/31/nyregion/mansour-arbabsiar-sentenced-for-plot-to-kill-saudi-ambassador.html?_r=0&pagewanted=print.

Woodrow Wilson Center for Scholars (2010) *A New Trade Policy for the United States: Lessons from Latin America*, Washington, DC.

World Jewish Congress (2014, May 16) 'Argentine Court Says Agreement with Iran to Probe AMIA Bombing is Unconstitutional'. Retrieved from http://www.worldjewishcongress.org/en/news/14735/argentine_court_says_agreement_with_iran_to_probe_amia_bombing_is_unconstitutional.

Zambelis, C. (2007) 'Spotlight on Trinidad and Tobago's Jamaat al-Muslimeen', *The Jamestown Foundation*, 5(12): 1–3.

27

LATIN AMERICA'S EXPERIENCE WITH PEACE SUPPORT OPERATIONS

From peacekeeping recipients to peace exporters

Arturo C. Sotomayor

In recent years Latin America as a region has become an active participant of multilateral sponsored peace and humanitarian operations. Latin American peacekeepers are currently deployed in various UN missions in Haiti, Africa, and Asia. This picture contrasts markedly from past decades, when military institutions were more widely known for intervening in domestic affairs via coups than for promoting human rights and democracy abroad. Historically, the region has been a recipient of foreign troops. To date, Latin America has become an exporter of peace, not because instability and violence have diminished, but because governments across the region have gradually increased their commitment to peace efforts. Peace commitments from Latin America have instituted what might be termed as military diplomacy in the region, in which international security coordination efforts have been put in place by the region's defense and military establishments. The expansion of Latin America's contributions to peacekeeping efforts is notable, but not without controversy. Political, structural, and military challenges persist. This chapter will thus address the following questions: What conditions explain Latin America's increased role in peacekeeping operations? What lessons have been learned? What are the region's most serious challenges?

A working definition of peacekeeping is certainly necessary. I refer to it as the "deployment of international personnel to help maintain peace and security in the aftermath of war" (Fortna 2008: 5). This chapter proceeds in three sections. I will first identify Latin America's contribution to UN peace operations. The second section analyzes the motivations for participation. The third and final section provides a critical assessment of Latin America's engagement in peacekeeping operations.

Latin America's role in UN peacekeeping operations

During the Cold War era, Latin America played a mostly tangential role in peace operations. Few UN blue helmets were from Latin America, and no major UN peace operation ever took place in the Western Hemisphere between 1947 and 1990. Larger South American states, such as Brazil and Argentina, provided regular military observers for missions in the Middle East

(Sinai) and South Asia (Kashmir), but did little to finance or command them (Bobrow and Boyer 1997: 742; Sotomayor 2009: 367). Furthermore, the wave of authoritarian regimes that spread across the region during the 1970s and 1980s increased Latin America's isolation from major world trends, including peacekeeping. Military juntas across South America decided not to commit troops and eventually withdrew all their military observers from UN-sponsored missions. Even Brazil, Latin America's largest and perhaps most influential country in the UN system, reverted towards isolationism during the dictatorship era. By 1967, the Brazilian army abstained from sending troops to the UN, mostly to silence international criticism for a poor human rights record (Ubiraci 2000: 91).

Peacekeeping changed with the end of the Cold War, and the third wave of democratization swept the region. Since the early 1990s, the UN system has witnessed a sea of change in its nature and purposes. Troop levels have increased considerably, and more than half of the top 20 UN troop contributors now come from the third or developing world (Sotomayor 2010: 165–166).

Interestingly, it is in the post–Cold War era that the Latin American region has become more actively engaged in UN peacekeeping affairs and is increasingly seen as a trendsetter in troop recruitment processes. Comparatively speaking, Latin America is not the region with the largest troop deployment rate in the UN system to date; Asia and Africa, as a whole, deploy more than 70 per cent of all UN military personnel in the field, while Latin America provides close to nine per cent of all blue helmets. But these numbers must be put in perspective. South Asia has a critical mass of soldiers, mostly infantrymen, who can be committed for missions overseas. Pakistan, Bangladesh, and India are the top three UN troop–contributing countries; yet, their contribution represents only a small part of the army's force at home, which, in the case of India, totals close to a million men. What is interesting about Latin America is that in spite of these force disparities, some South American states, such as Uruguay, are already ranked among the top 10 troop contributors to UN missions (see Table 27.2). In 2000, Latin America barely contributed, with less than three per cent of all UN troops. In less than a decade, it increased its troop contribution by more than eight percentage points, and it is now the world's third-largest regional UN troop contributor, after Asia and Africa (see Table 27.1).

Furthermore, the UN Stabilization Mission in Haiti (MINUSTAH) has become the testing ground for a joint peacekeeping model, developed by Latin American states, in which troops, development aid, and political support are mostly provided by South American states through joint consultation and regional institutional mechanisms. Indeed, Latin America contributes 48 per cent of all UN troops in Haiti, with Brazil commanding the overall mission since 2004 (Kenkel 2010a: 589).

Table 27.1 Troop contributions to UN peacekeeping by region, 2000 and 2010

Region	*2000*	*2010*
Asia	33.9%	47.6%
Africa	26.6%	34.1%
Western Europe	16.6%	7%
Oceania	10.3%	0.3%
East Europe	8.5%	2%
Latin America and Caribbean	**2.5%**	**8.9%**
North America	1.6%	0.1%

Source: Resdal (2011: 103).

Table 27.2 Latin America's contributions to UN peacekeeping operations, 2000–2010

Ranking in LA	*Country*	*Committed troops*	*World ranking*
1	Uruguay	20,934	8
2	Brazil	9,614	20
3	Argentina	8,633	22
4	Chile	3,688	42
5	Bolivia	2,950	49
6	Peru	1,642	59
7	Guatemala	1,503	61
8	Ecuador	550	78
9	Paraguay	532	79
10	El Salvador	440	82
11	Honduras	131	99
12	Colombia	54	105
13	Dominican Republic	46	106
14	Venezuela	11	120

Source: Adapted from Sotomayor (2014: 26–27).

Certainly, troop contributions vary substantially from country to country. Uruguay stands out: Over 20,000 of the country's soldiers have been involved in at least one UN peacekeeping mission in the past two decades. In relation to its population (less than four million people), there is one Uruguayan peacekeeper for every 280 citizens, making Uruguay the world's largest UN troop contributor per capita. The top ranking of Latin American UN troop suppliers also includes Brazil, Argentina, and Chile. Even former peacekeeping recipient states, such as El Salvador and Guatemala, are now engaging their armies in UN missions (see Table 27.3). By early 2014, 11 Latin American countries had almost 7,000 soldiers in 13 UN operations worldwide (see Table 27.3). Paradoxically, three Latin American states have been notoriously absent from the peacekeeping wave, namely Cuba, Mexico, and Venezuela. These countries are major development aid donors (especially in Haiti), but have yet to commit troops to UN operations. Colombia supports UN efforts with police forces, but not with military personnel.

Explaining the trend: why Latin America participates in UN peace operations

Although states' motivations to participate in UN peace operations vary substantially from case to case, we can identify three general reasons why Latin American states participate in peacekeeping:[1] (1) democratization and impetus for military reform, (2) international prestige and status, and (3) evolving regional norms about intervention.

Democratization and military reform

The region's engagement in Haiti, predominantly through the United Nations Stabilization Mission (MINUSTAH), has been hailed as a 'coming-out party' for the Latin American community. Through MINUSTAH, 11 Latin American nations have broadened their military and diplomatic cooperation, all while contributing to the effort of constructing a difficult peace in Haiti. Yet, strictly speaking, Latin America is not a newcomer to peacekeeping trends. Many of

Table 27.3 Latin American troop and police contributions to UN peace operations, February 2014

UN Mission/ Country	*Uruguay*	*Brazil*	*Argentina*	*Chile*	*Peru*	*Guatemala*	*Bolivia*	*Paraguay*	*El Salvador*	*Ecuador*	*Honduras*
Western Sahara (MINURSO)	1	10	3		1			5	3		11
Haiti (MINUSTAH)	939	1,443	576	424	374	135	207	115	35	53	38
Liberia (UNMIL)	4	4	7		4		3	4	5	3	
Ivory Coast (UNOCI)	7	7			3	5	2	9	3	2	
Congo DRC (MONUSCO)	1,204	6			12	152	10	17			
Darfur (UNAMID)					4		2			2	
South Sudan (UNMISS)		13	4		2	5	3	3	3	4	
Israel-Palestine (UNTSO)			3	3							
Lebanon (UNIFIL)		267				1			51		
India-Pakistan (UNMOGIP)	1			2							
Afghanistan											
Cyprus (UNFICYP)		1	266	14	2			13			
Abyei (UNISFA)	1	4			4		4	4	1	2	
Total/month	**2,157**	**1,775**	**859**	**443**	**404**	**298**	**231**	**170**	**101**	**66**	**49**

Source: These numbers represent monthly average troop contributions as reported by the UN Department of Peacekeeping Operations. UNDPKO (2014)

these Latin American countries increased their troop contributions in the early 1990s. Specifically, Argentina, Uruguay, and Brazil began deploying large contingents, involving at times full battalions of 800 soldiers, almost 25 years ago. Although these countries vary in terms of size and capabilities, they all seemed to share one intrinsic quality: They were in the process of democratic consolidation when they engaged in major UN troop deployments.

Indeed, the desire to reform the military and to shape their roles in a post-authoritarian age encouraged Argentina, Uruguay, and, to a lesser extent, Brazil to join peacekeeping efforts. In all three cases, engagement in peacekeeping provided juicy economic enticements for uniformed personnel and for the armed forces (mostly individual salaries), especially when military budgets were subject to drastic cuts imposed by newly established legislatures (Norden 1995; Palá 1998).

Peacekeeping not only provided needed resources to a debilitating military, but also enabled the government to rehabilitate its armed forces by exposing large numbers of its troops to out-of-area missions conducted by multinational forces. Argentina, Brazil, and Uruguay soon began deploying observers, units, and even full battalions to various UN peace missions in Central America (such as the missions in El Salvador and Guatemala), Europe (Cyprus), and Africa (Angola and Mozambique). Peacekeeping thus provided an opportunity to reorient the militaries away from their traditional internal roles and toward external ones. Hence, transferring soldiers abroad was part of a diversionary strategy to reshape and identify new military roles and missions more suitable for these emerging democracies.

Full engagement in UN peace operations started with Argentina and Uruguay (in 1991 and 1992, respectively), which were part of the early wave of democratization in South America. Within a decade, the wave was followed by Brazil, Bolivia, Ecuador, Peru, Chile, and Paraguay, in that order. The wave of democratization then expanded to and crested with Central America – El Salvador, Guatemala, and Honduras. Interestingly, all of these countries now participate in UN peacekeeping activities in one form or another.

This trend supports the theoretical notion that political transitions towards democracy create strong incentives to commit internationally. As Edward D. Mansfield and Jon C. Pevehouse (2006) argue, democratization is an especially potent impetus for states to join international institutions, especially since these types of states have a difficult time sustaining the liberal reforms needed to consolidate their own democracies. By committing to international organizations, political leaders in transitional states can deliberately tie their hands in such a way that domestic actors are forced to comply with external demands while also increasing the costs of reverting to previous policies. From this perspective, reform can take place by transferring some degree of policy-making to an international institution that is insulated from domestic influence (Martin and Simmons 1998). Empirical studies on Latin American civil-military relations seem to support this thesis; that is, peacekeeping participation has been explicitly linked to military reform efforts in South and Central America. However, the extent to which civil-military reform has been effectively achieved varies substantially from country to country.[2]

Status and prestige

Coupled with the democratization process, a small number of South American countries have also used their peacekeeping commitments to signal international influence and status. In this context, peacekeeping participation became a prime way for countries such as Argentina (in the 1990s) and Brazil (in the 2000s) to send clear and far-reaching signals of their foreign policy commitments and regional leadership. The Argentine and Brazilian governments in particular tried to participate in various UN missions in order to secure greater international exposure. For

Argentina, the move towards increased participation in UN operations (especially in Haiti and Iraq-Kuwait) expressed a tacit alignment with Washington. Indeed, during the administration of President Carlos Menem, Buenos Aires tried to position itself as Washington's most influential partner in the Western Hemisphere. In 1994, the Clinton administration granted Argentina the status of major non-NATO ally in recognition of its peacekeeping contribution, which made it possible to buy outmoded equipment from NATO states, to participate in interoperability exercises, and to obtain credit to buy military gear for UN peace operations (Norden 1995; Mani 2011). However, by 2002, the number of Argentine blue helmets dropped worldwide. The devaluation and subsequent collapse of the Argentine peso in December 2001 drastically affected the country's armed forces and its tacit alignment with Washington. Argentina dropped in the UN troop ranking from first to third place, after Uruguay and Brazil.

International prestige has been notably present in Brazil, especially in the years between 2004 and 2010. The South American giant committed almost 6,000 soldiers to Haiti in six years, making it Brazil's largest foreign military commitment since the Suez mission in the 1950s and World War II. Also for the first time, Brazil was given the general command of the UN mission in Haiti. In particular, the government of President Luiz Inacio da Silva diverged from previous administrations in that he used Brazil's military might to accomplish foreign policy objectives in UN peacekeeping operations. Peacekeeping symbolized a new willingness on the side of Brazil to assert itself in a more proactive way on the international stage. This country used its peacekeeping contribution to demonstrate commanding and leadership skills to be considered a so-called emerging power (Kenkel 2010b). MINUSTAH coincided with the UN reform process of late 2005, in which Brazil publicly reiterated its aspirations to have a permanent seat on the Security Council. Participation in MINUSTAH thus gave Brazil a political platform to support its long-standing request for a seat on the Security Council (Sotomayor 2009: 372).

Increasingly, countries such as Chile, Peru, and Uruguay are relying on sending peacekeeping forces to accomplish political goals in the UN. Like Brazil, these South American countries are using their peacekeeping contributions to support their respective candidacy bids for a nonpermanent seat in the UN Security Council. Chile has already achieved this goal, having been elected as a nonpermanent member for the 2014–2016 term. While troop commitments to peace operations have not shifted the overall regional balance of power, they have effectively altered the way Latin American states relate diplomatically and militarily to the world. As the shadow of democratization evades in the region, foreign policy status is taking precedence to sustain Latin American UN troop commitments.

Evolving regional norms on nonintervention

Historically, Latin America had developed a highly complex system of regional international law, which included norms that regulated domestic and international behavior. Legal and normative aspects about nonintervention and sovereignty were traditionally considered as a *sine qua non* condition for any foreign policy initiative in the region (Kacowicz 2005).

Interestingly, peacekeeping participation has shifted the debate and gradually altered Latin America's narrow definition of international intervention and sovereignty. In 1991 Argentina was the only Latin American state to provide military assistance to enforce a UN-sanctioned embargo, when Iraq invaded Kuwait. In 1994, Buenos Aires was, once again, the only capital in the region that provided ground troops in support of the multinational force led by the United States to depose the Haitian military junta. A decade later, in 2004, nine Latin American states committed troops to enforce peace through the UN Stabilization Force in Haiti (MINUSTAH).

What accounts for this change? Increasingly, Latin American states are beginning to accept certain forms of military intervention as legitimate, provided they are multilaterally justified within the UN framework.

MINUSTAH reflects the new normative and regional understanding about military intervention in two ways. First, unlike the previous UN troop requests, the decision to deploy South American soldiers to Haiti took place through intense diplomatic consultation with the ABC countries (Argentina, Brazil, and Chile). In fact, there was a concerted effort from the UN Security Council to get political support from Latin America in the aftermath of Jean Bertrand Aristide's controversial resignation as president of Haiti. Second, once the support of Brazil and Chile was guaranteed, an agreement was reached to ensure that the troops would come mostly from South American countries. For analysts such as Rut Diamint (2010), the MERCOSUR countries had been outspoken critics of the American invasion and occupation of Iraq, but in Haiti they hoped to be able to export their own democratic model and thus establish themselves credibly as legitimate mediators.

Since then, there have been increasing levels of military coordination between South American countries. What began as an informal consultation mechanism, known as the 2×3, which regularly gathered the two deputy ministries (foreign affairs and defense) from the ABC, eventually grew to the so-called 2×9, involving Argentina, Brazil, Chile, Bolivia, Ecuador, Guatemala, Paraguay, Peru, and Uruguay.[3] The emerging policy convergence and defense coordination amongst South American peacekeepers have led scholars to believe that the region has now become an exporter of peace through military means (Hirst 2009).

The unusually high levels of military cooperation eventually led Brazil to convene the defense ministers of the region to a meeting in Brasilia in 2008 to create the Defense Council of the Union of South American Nations (UNASUR). The Council included the nine South American states involved in MINUSTAH and has the explicit purpose of strengthening regional defense and military cooperation (Mendelson Forman 2011). Together, these initiatives have instituted what might be termed as military diplomacy in South America, which effectively legitimizes certain forms of military intervention for peacekeeping and humanitarian purposes. This has had profound implications for the conception of sovereignty in Latin America. Military intervention, in the form of peacekeeping, is becoming more widely accepted by some states. This certainly does not mean that all Latin American countries have bandwagoned with the ABC. Mexico, Cuba, and Venezuela remain ambivalent, if not openly opposed, to military diplomacy in the Western Hemisphere. Still, an altered sense of sovereignty now allows for some form of military intervention in what used to be considered an issue of strict noninterference in domestic affairs.

Lessons learned: the Latin American record on peace operations . . . thus far

In the remaining sections of this chapter I identify and discuss three problematic issue areas for Latin America's increased role in peacekeeping missions, including the erosion of regional organizations, failure in peace-building missions, and growing challenges in training practices.

Peacekeeping in Latin America: pro-UN and antiregional organizations

International peacekeeping has become a multilateral policy often associated with the UN system. The UN, however, does not have a monopoly on the operation and doctrine of peace missions. To some extent peacekeeping has become a decentralized activity, with other regional organizations now performing various forms of peace operations. In recent years the UN has teamed up with various regional organizations, including the African Union, the Economic Community of West African States (ECOWAS), and the European Union, to conduct peacekeeping operations. Yet, no similar joint peacekeeping ventures exist in Latin America.

In terms of peacekeeping practices, Latin American states tend to overlook or underuse their own regional organizations. Indeed, the overwhelming majority of peacekeeping operations undertaken in the Western Hemisphere have been conducted exclusively by the UN, without the assistance of the existing regional organizations. Since the 1990s, all Central American and Caribbean peace missions were delegated to UN blue helmets, including ONUSAL (UN Mission in El Salvador in 1992), ONUCA (UN Observer Mission in Central America in 1988), MINUGUA (UN Verification Mission in Guatemala in 1997), UNMIH in 1993, and MINUSTAH in 2004. Latin America has experimented with regional peacekeeping only once, when a group of four regional powers – also known as the Rio Protocol guarantor countries, which included Argentina, Brazil, Chile, and the United States – mediated and negotiated a peace settlement between Ecuador and Peru in 1995. Although this regional peace process succeeded in demilitarizing the Cenepa Valley in the Ecuadorean-Peruvian border, the *ad hoc* mediation effort explicitly avoided the participation of the Organization of American States (OAS) (Mares and Palmer 2012; Herz and Nogueira 2002). No other similar *ad hoc* regional peacekeeping efforts have been replicated elsewhere. The OAS, which is a formal regional collective security organization mandated with specific peaceful settlement attributes, has been *de facto* relegated to an electoral monitoring agency (Santa Cruz 2005). Reflecting on the role of regional organizations, Jorge I. Domínguez argues that "each and every Latin American organization has been 'flexible' to the point of ineffectiveness" (2007: 122).

Unlike Africa, where a network of regional organizations has been put to the service of peacekeeping, Latin Americans seem skeptical of their own regional organizations. Yes, there is increased mutual consultation on peacekeeping matters through the 2×9 and UNASUR mechanisms, but when a serious and bloody political crisis erupts, as in Honduras during the Zelaya crisis in 2010 or in Venezuela in the post-Chávez era, these regional fora appear irrelevant for keeping the peace. The OAS and other similar regional organizations, like UNASUR, have lost so much prestige and power that questions have arisen throughout the hemisphere about their overall relevance.[4]

Latin American peacekeepers: good peace observers, suboptimal peace-builders

Although the peacekeeping literature is voluminous and internally disparate, most analysts conclude that the UN has had a mixed record of success at implementing its own peace missions. Empirical findings from these studies reveal that the UN has been more successful at observing cease-fire agreements in interstate conflicts than at building peace in war-torn states (Fortna 2003; Greig and Diehl 2005; Werner and Yuen 2005; Howard 2008; Autesserre 2010). Moreover, UN peacekeepers have struggled with peace enforcement missions and required the assistance of Great Powers or military alliances (such as NATO) to successfully enforce UN mandates (Walter 2002; Doyle and Sambanis 2006).

Given what we know about UN peacekeeping, how different is the record of success for Latin American blue helmets? Sadly, the studies available on Latin American contributions to peacekeeping efforts have paid little attention to measuring and assessing performance. Comparative analyses between South American contingents show that peacekeepers are predominantly present in peace-observing and peace-building missions. Between 1990 and 2003 Argentina mostly deployed soldiers to observational missions (35 per cent) and peace enforcement operations

(62 per cent), whereas Brazil and Uruguay tended to deploy its peacekeepers to peace-building missions (Sotomayor 2014: 104).

As argued before, we lack comparative and systematic assessments of troop performance. The few studies available on Latin American peacekeeping do seem to suggest that peacekeepers from the region have a relatively good record at observing peace agreements. Blue helmets from South America were able to separate belligerent parties in places like El Salvador and Ecuador-Peru and then monitor cease-fire agreements with relative ease. ONUSAL, where troops from Argentina, Venezuela, and even Canada participated, has been hailed as one of the most successful UN peace-observing missions. Peacekeepers successfully separated the two rival forces (the national army and the Farabundo Martí National Liberation Front, now in power) and monitored the implementation of the cease-fire agreements signed in New York and Mexico City (Doyle et al. 1997; Arnson 1999). Similarly, the Military Observer Mission for Ecuador and Peru, consisting mostly of Argentine, Brazilian, and Chilean peace soldiers, effectively monitored troop movement in the border area and created buffer zones, which helped put an end to one of the longest territorial disputes in South America (Mares and Palmer 2012; Herz and Nogueira 2002).

By contrast, the Latin American peace-building record is not so outstanding. Brazil and Uruguay, which have mostly deployed soldiers to UN peace-building missions, have been remarkably unsuccessful at building peace in Cambodia, Angola, and the Democratic Republic of Congo. In all these three cases there have been reports of abuse allegations, troop withdrawals, and conflict renewal (Sotomayor 2014: 99–126). The peace-building operations in Central America, including ONUSAL, utterly failed at disarming, demobilizing, and reintegrating crucial components of the armed forces and combatants (Paris 2004: 112–134).

Most recently, Latin American peacekeepers have struggled to sustain peace-building endeavors in Haiti, especially in the aftermath of the 2010 earthquake. A health crisis hit the island in 2010, when a cholera outbreak debilitated some 300,000 Haitians and killed over 6,000 people between 2010 and 2011. To make matters worse for the Brazilian-led UN mission, the disease seemingly originated from a peacekeeping camp north of the capital, which spilled raw sewage into a tributary of the Artibonite River.[5] A sexual abuse scandal involving Uruguayan peacekeepers also erupted in the fall of 2011, leading to yet another crisis within the mission (*BBC* 2011). MINUSTAH, which was once acclaimed as a 'new way' of conducting peace-building operations by Latin American countries, has thus faced challenges on several fronts. Latin American peace-building initiatives in Haiti have been remarkably unsuccessful at monitoring human rights, strengthening law enforcement, and consolidating democracy (Heine and Thompson 2011). In light of these suboptimal outcomes, South American UN troop contributors to MINUSTAH announced their gradual withdrawal from Haiti, beginning in 2011. It is safe to assert that Latin American peace-building measures have not met the expectations of locals in Haiti, international NGOs, and diplomats in UN circles.

Training for peacekeeping: quantity vs. quality

In recent years, there has been a proliferation of regional peacekeeping training centers, whereby almost every Latin American country involved in peace operations has now established a formal structure to prepare and train soldiers. This has substantially increased military contacts, leading to the creation of the Latin American Association of Peacekeeping Training Centers (ALCOPAZ), which includes Argentina, Brazil, Chile, Colombia, Ecuador, Guatemala, Paraguay, Peru, and Uruguay. Through this mechanism, Latin American soldiers meet every six months to exchange knowledge, lessons learned, and discuss how to better prepare peacekeepers for missions such as MINUSTAH. Recently, Argentina was selected by the UN to develop a nationwide pilot plan to prepare and train the first cadre of female UN force commanders (Sotomayor 2014: 79).

All these national peacekeeping training centers are certainly innovative in the region, but they varied substantially in terms of integration and doctrine. The UN certainly plays a role in this outcome, since the absence of clear doctrinal and unified guidelines allows troop-lending states to train their blue helmets on the basis of national doctrines. As a result, with the exception of Argentina, peacekeeping training had very few positive effects on the military and on civilian control. In most cases, the armed forces have responded to training incentives by simply replicating or reinforcing their conventional security doctrines.

For instance, in Brazil, peacekeeping serves as a training ground for developing the military's urban operations skills, with a view to using the forces for the 'pacification' of *favelas* (slums). In this case, the emphasis is not on developing new professional skills to help reorient the armed forces toward external missions; rather, the focus is on developing militarized policing skills. This has certainly raised a few eyebrows. The international NGO community has harshly criticized the Brazilian peacekeeping doctrine for overlooking human rights and for failing to incorporate civilian components into its practices (Harvard Report 2005). Indeed, Brazil's peacekeeping tactics have suffered from collateral damage in Port-au-Prince (Sotomayor 2014: 127–159).

Training procedures have also raised questions in Uruguay. In the Democratic Republic of Congo, Uruguayan peacekeepers were accused of corrupting and torturing civilians (*El Clarín* 2003). Together, these incidents suggest that military training in Latin America is still suboptimal for peacekeeping operations. Training continues to be an essentially military endeavor, with little civilian oversight or input. Latin American regional peacekeeping training centers thus require substantial improvements. Military institutions across the region need to incorporate international humanitarian law courses and human rights training practices. Moreover, civilian integration (incorporating civilian faculty and staff) varies substantially from country to country, but it is notoriously absent in Brazil and Uruguay (the largest troop contributors in the region).

Conclusions

Latin America, as a region, has slowly but surely become a more active participant of international peace operations. After decades of relative isolation, the armed forces of these countries are now engaged in positive operations other than insurgency and drug trafficking. To some extent, the first challenge has now been met: Latin America has successfully crafted a new mission for the armed forces in a democratic context. In so doing, the region has broadened its previously narrow definitions of sovereignty and intervention. This has also created incentives for increased security coordination between Latin American states, in which the military has become an agent of regional diplomacy.

The 'military diplomacy' in Latin America is not necessarily a bad trend, provided the appropriate mechanisms for accountability are in place. Here is where the challenges persist. Efforts to place Latin America on the center of global politics will fail if the countries continue to undermine their own regional security organizations, which could play a role at improving regional peacekeeping capabilities. Moreover, the focus of attention has been placed exclusively on building military assets for peace operations. If anything, Latin American governments need to learn how to be more effective at implementing peace-building mandates, for which development aid and civilian contributions are more widely needed. Finally, if Latin Americans do not wish to be continuously embarrassed by scandals and corruption accusations in peacekeeping missions, then they should focus on improving military training and best practices. In particular, the top troop-lending contributors, Uruguay and Brazil, should perhaps lead by example. This could involve a gradual shift in approach, focusing more on qualitative peacekeeping contributions instead of massively exporting unskilled and unprofessional soldiers.

Notes

1 For a detailed analysis of motivations for participation across different regions and countries, see Bellamy and Williams (2013) and Cunliffe (2014).
2 For a recent study on Latin America's civil-military relations, see Mares and Martínez (2014).
3 On the 2×9 initiative, see Diamint (2007), Marconedes de Souza Neto (2009), and Mendelson Forman (2011).
4 See De Palma (2011).
5 For a critical view of MINUSTAH, see *NYT* Editorial (2011).

References

Arnson, C. J. (ed) (1999) *Comparative Peace Processes in Latin America*, Palo Alto: Stanford University Press.
Autesserre, S. (2010) *The Trouble with the Congo: Local Violence and the Failure of International Peacebuilding*, New York: Cambridge University Press.
BBC News (2011, September 4) 'Uruguayan Peacekeepers in Haiti Accused of Abuse'. Retrieved from http://www.bbc.co.uk/news/world-latin-america-14783538.
Bellamy, A. J. and Williams, P. D. (eds) (2013) *Providing Peacekeepers: The Politics, Challenges, and Future of United Nations Peacekeeping Contributions*, New York: Oxford University Press.
Bobrow, D. and Boyer, M. A. (1997) 'Maintaining System Stability: Contributions to Peacekeeping Operations', *Journal of Conflict Resolution*, 41(6): 723–748.
Cunliffe, P. (2014) *Legions of Peace: UN Peacekeepers from the Global South*, London: Hurst.
DePalma, A. (2011) 'Is the OAS Irrelevant?', *Americas Quarterly*. Retrieved from http://www.americasquarterly.org/node/2756.
Diamint, R. (2007) 'El 2×9 una incipiente comunidad de seguridad em América Latina?', Policy Paper no. 18 of the Friedrich Ebert Stiftung Foundation, Santiago de Chile. Retrieved from http://library.fes.de/pdf-files/bueros/la-seguridad/50501.pdf.
——— (2010) 'Security Communities: Defense Policy Integration and Peace Operations in the Southern Cone, An Argentine Perspective', *International Peacekeeping*, 17(5): 662–677.
Domínguez, J. (2007) 'International Cooperation in Latin America: The Design of Regional Institutions by Slow Accretion' in A. Acharya and A. I. Johnston (eds) *Crafting Cooperation: Regional International Institutions in Comparative Perspective*, New York: Cambridge University Press, pp. 83–128.
Doyle, M, Johnstone, I. and Orr, R. C. (eds) (1997) *Keeping the Peace: Multidimensional UN Operations in Cambodia and El Salvador*, New York: Cambridge University Press.
Doyle, M. W. and Sambanis, N. (2006) *Making War and Building Peace: United Peace Operations*, Princeton: Princeton University Press.
Editorial (2011, May 10) 'Haiti's Continuing Cholera Outbreak', *The New York Times*. Retrieved from http://www.nytimes.com/2011/05/11/opinion/11wed3.html.
El Clarin (2003, September 21) 'Acusan a cascos azules de Uruguay por torturas en África'. Retrieved from http://old.clarin.com/diario/2003/09/21/i-02201.htm.
Fortna, V. P. (2003) 'Scraps of Paper? Agreements and the Durability of Peace', *International Organization*, 57(2): 337–372.
——— (2008) *Does Peacekeeping Work? Shaping Belligerents' Choices after Civil War*, Princeton: Princeton University Press.
Greig, M. J. and Diehl, P. L. (2005) 'The Peacekeeping-Peacemaking Dilemma', *International Studies Quarterly*, 49(4): 621–645.
Harvard Report (2005, March) *Keeping the Peace in Haiti? An Assessment of the United Nations Stabilization Mission in Haiti, Using Compliance with its Prescribed Mandate as a Barometer for Success*, Cambridge, MA: Harvard Law Student Advocates for Human Rights. Retrieved from http://www.law.harvard.edu/programs/hrp/documents/haitireport.pdf.

Heine, J. and Thompson, A.S. (eds) (2011) *Fixing Haiti: MINUSTAH and Beyond*, New York: United Nations University Press.
Herz, M. and Nogueira, J.P. (2002) *Ecuador vs. Peru*, New York: International Peace Academy.
Hirst, M. (2009) 'La intervención Sudamericana en Haití' in M. Hirst (ed) *Crisis del estado e intervención internacional: Una mirada desde el sur*, Buenos Aires: Edhasa, pp. 338–357.
Howard, L.M. (2008) *UN Peacekeeping in Civil Wars*, New York: Cambridge University Press.
Kacowicz, A. M. (2005) *The Impact of Norms in International Society: The Latin American Experience, 1881–2001*, Notre Dame, IN: University of Notre Dame Press.
Kenkel, K.M. (2010a) 'Stepping out of the Shadow: South America and Peace Operations', *International Peacekeeping*, 17(5): 584–597.
——— (2010b) 'South America's Emerging Power: Brazil as a Peacekeeper', *International Peacekeeping*, 17(5): 644–661.
Mani, K. (2011) *Democratization and Military Transformation in Argentina and Chile: Rethinking Rivalry*, Boulder: Lynne Rienner Publishers.
Mansfield, E.D. and Pevehouse, J.C. (2006) 'Democratization and International Organizations', *International Organization*, 60(1): 137–167.
Marconedes de Souza Neto, D. (2009) 'A participaçâo e a cooperaçâo entre os países de Cone Sul em operaçôes de paz: O caso da MINUSTAH' in E. Svartman, M. C. D'Araujo and S. A. Soares (eds) *Defesa, segurança internacional e forças armadas: II encontro da abed*, Campinas: Mercado Letras, pp. 169–196.
Mares, D.R. and Martínez, R. (eds) (2014) *Debating Civil–Military Relations in Latin America*, Sussex: Sussex University Press.
Mares, D.R. and Palmer, D.S. (2012) *Power, Institutions, and Leadership in War and Peace: Lessons from Peru and Ecuador, 1995–1998*, Austin: University of Texas–Austin Press.
Martin, L.L. and Simmons, B. (1998) 'Theories and Empirical Studies of International Institutions', *International Organization*, 52(4): 729–757.
Mendelson Forman, J. (2011) 'Latin American Peacekeeping: A New Era of Regional Cooperation' in J. Heine and A. S. Thompson (eds) *Fixing Haiti: Minustah and Beyond*, New York: UN University Press.
Norden, D. (1995) 'Keeping the Peace, Outside and In: Argentina's UN Missions', *International Peacekeeping*, 2(3): 330–349.
Palá, A. (1998) 'Peacekeeping and its Effects on Civil–Military Relations' in J. I. Domínguez (ed) *International Security and Democracy: Latin America and the Caribbean in the Post–Cold War Era*, Pittsburgh: University of Pittsburgh Press, pp. 130–150.
Paris, R. (2004) *At War's End: Building Peace after Civil Conflict*, New York: Cambridge University Press.
Red de Seguridad y Defensa Latinoamericana (Resdal) (2011) *Comparative Atlas of Defence in Latin America and Caribbean 2010 Edition*, Buenos Aires: SER.
Santa Cruz, A. (2005) *International Election Monitoring, Sovereignty, and the Western Hemisphere: The Emergence of an International Norm*, New York: Routledge.
Sotomayor, A.C. (2009) 'Different Paths and Divergent Policies in the UN Security System: Brazil and Mexico in Comparative Perspective', *International Peacekeeping*, 16(3): 371–373.
——— (2010) 'Why Some States Participate in UN Peace Missions While Others Do Not', *Security Studies*, 19(1): 160–195.
——— (2014) *The Myth of the Democratic Peacekeeper: Civil–Military Relations and the United Nations*, Baltimore: Johns Hopkins University Press.
Ubiraci, S.R. (2000) 'Intermediate Countries and the Multilateral Arenas: Brazil in the General Assembly and UN Security Council Between 1980–1995' in A. Hurrell (ed) *Paths to Power: Foreign Policy Strategies of Intermediate States, Working Paper 224*, Washington, DC: Woodrow Wilson International Center for Scholars.
UN Department of Peacekeeping Operations (UNDPKO) (2014, February) *Country Contributions Detailed by Post*, New York: United Nations. Retrieved from http://www.un.org/en/peacekeeping/resources/statistics/contributors.shtml.
Walter, B. (2002) *Committing to Peace: The Successful Settlement of Civil Wars*, Princeton: Princeton University Press.
Werner, S. and Yuen, A. (2005) 'Making and Keeping the Peace', *International Organization*, 59(2): 261–292.

28

LATIN AMERICA IN THE NEW WORLD SECURITY ARCHITECTURE

Arie M. Kacowicz[1]

Introduction

With the exception of the United States and Canada, the American continent is, in general, a region that remains on the fringe of the most significant international conflicts. In this chapter, I ask the question: What role does Latin America play in the contemporary world security architecture (WSA)[2] since the end of the Cold War? The short answer is: not much of a role. The longer answer establishes a taxonomy regarding Latin American insertion in the WSA by differentiating among active, passive, and potential roles.

Why does Latin America not fulfill a significant role in the new WSA? There are several explanations to be offered. First, the participation of Latin America in the WSA has been traditionally a function of the intertwining dynamics of U.S.–Latin American relations and the continental hegemony of the United States in the Western Hemisphere. Since the United States has been the paramount power and the 'colossus of the North,' to some extent the participation of Latin America in the world security architecture has been perceived as redundant and insignificant. Furthermore, when and if the United States neglects Latin America, the region is marginalized in terms of its relevance to the WSA, perhaps with the exception of the negative externalities stemming from the internal conflicts and violence situations in the region (especially in Colombia, Mexico, Central America, and Haiti).

Second, one of the essential problems Latin American nations confront in their relations with the rest of the world is that of *asymmetrical significance* (Smith 2008) – that means that the rest of the world (for instance, North America, Europe, Asia) is more important to Latin America than Latin America is to other regions within the international system. Third, in geopolitical terms, the region is far away from hosting the hottest issues of global security. Finally, in normative terms, the Latin American nations might be reluctant to actively participate in the WSA due to ideological reasons; i.e., their critical concern and respect for the norms of sovereignty and nonintervention (Merke 2011: 6).

In theoretical terms, I examine in this chapter the possible links between regional governance (RG) and global governance (GG), focusing on the security realm. Such examination stems from the premise that the Latin American insertion in the WSA is a function of the combined impact of globalization, regionalization, and nationalism on the region (Kacowicz 1999). When we refer to the world economy, it is possible to identify overlapping processes of regional governance and global governance in several domains, such as trade, investment, migration regimes, and the regulation of multinational corporations. By contrast, in the international global security arena, it seems more difficult to assess the coexistence of regional security frameworks with broader dimensions of global security. At the same time, both the United Nations (as the embodiment of GG) and regional bodies seem to need each other and should assume shared responsibilities for resolving security problems, so there is room for cooperation between schemes of GG and RG (Hettne and Soderbaum 2006: 213).

The following section refers to the characteristics of the new WSA since the end of the Cold War, and especially after 9/11. After examining the changing landscape of the WSA I turn to a brief analysis of the Latin American regional security landscape. Paradoxically, and in relative terms vis-à-vis the rest of the world, Latin America stands out as an island of pluralism and relative international peace (Vargas Llosa 2014).

The third and main section refers to the different roles that can be ascribed to Latin America in the WSA: (1) active and cooperative role (in the form of peacekeeping operations and arms control agreements), (2) active and challenging role (in the form of the revisionist approach adopted by ALBA), (3) active and subversive role (in the form of transnational threats), (4) passive role (through lack of intervention and rule-taking instead of rule-making), and (5) potential (and ambiguous) role, as in the case of Brazil. Finally, the last section of the chapter introduces several research questions and an agenda for future research.

The changing landscape of the world security architecture

The contemporary WSA entails: (1) shifting meanings and conceptualizations of security and security threats, (2) a movement from the post–Cold War 'new world order' to the current 'world disorder' of unclear polarity, and (3) the conceptualization of the world as a "world of regions" (Katzenstein 2005), with regions becoming more autonomous as relevant structures through mechanisms of regional security governance.

1. Shifting meanings and conceptualizations of security and of security threats

In the first part of the 21st century, despite important changes taking place in world politics, the traditional ambiguity about international security remains. On the one hand, the world is a much safer and peaceful place to live in as a result of the end of the Cold War and processes of globalization and institutionalization that have reduced some of the competitive aspects of the security dilemma among states. Yet, on the other hand, the same processes of globalization, associated with destabilizing traditional identities and constructing security anomies among states, have simultaneously increased individual and societal insecurity (Baylis 2011: 242–243).

Moreover, the security context after the Cold War brought about a metamorphosis in the characteristics and definitions of threats, moving away from 'traditional' security to a focus on human security, including issue areas of urban criminality, drug trafficking, environmental degradation, and pandemics. Thus, we can identify new types of security threats, which have both domestic and transnational dimensions. The threats of transnational crime, terrorism, drug trafficking, and human trafficking have created new rationales for the demand of regional security governance, especially due to their dual or *intermestic* nature, which requires greater coordination among states and the involvement of new actors. This growing 'intermesticity' of issues challenges policy-makers across the globe (Kirchner and Domínguez 2011; Tavares 2014: 1; Tulchin and Espach 2001: 17–18).

Indeed, the expansion and variation of security threats and risks since the end of the Cold War, the proliferation of actors and mechanisms to address them, and the complexity of contemporary security arrangements imply that the concept of *security governance* can provide a valuable tool for explaining and understanding the development and functioning of security provisions above, beyond, and below the nation-state. At the global level of *security governance*, the basic frame of reference is the United Nations system, which provides the most universal structures for dealing with security issues, ranging from arms control, disarmament, and nonproliferation of weapons, to conflict prevention, peace-making, peace enforcement, peacekeeping, and postconflict peace-building.

2. From a 'new world order' to a new 'world disorder'

The 'new world order' of the post–Cold War era and the "unipolar moment" of the 1990s (Krauthammer 1990–1991) were characterized by U.S. preponderance. It had been transcended after 9/11, and especially in recent years, by an increasing 'world disorder,' a sense of uncertainty and disarray regarding polarity, and the rise of what Kupchan defines as "no one's world." In the new WSA, no country, region, or political model necessarily dominates the world order. Instead, we are witnessing a striking variety and plurality of alternative conceptions of domestic and international orders competing among themselves (Kupchan 2012). For instance, a possible and growing alliance of the BRICS countries, UNASUR, ASEAN, and SCO members in Asia might challenge and oppose the current confrontation with Russia from the standpoint of the United States, NATO, the United Kingdom, and the EU (Zepp-La Rouche 2014), but without offering a viable alternative world order.

Many analysts agree that the planet is in disarray in terms of the current WSA. Not much is left from the optimist thesis suggested by Fukuyama (1992) regarding the new democratic age after the end of the Cold War. The disintegration of Libya, Syria, and Iraq; the renewed Russian threat in Eastern Europe and the Ukrainian crisis; the barbaric surge of the ISIS; the rise and decline of the Arab Spring – all point to the crisis of the world order and the emergence of a new 'world disorder' (Vargas Llosa 2014; Kissinger 2014). Moreover, as Kissinger (2014) points out, despite a myriad of multilateral institutions, there is an absence of an effective mechanism for the Great Powers to cooperate in security issues.

3. World of regions: globalization, regionalism, and the relevance of regional security governance

Since decolonization after World War II, and especially since the end of the Cold War, the regional level of security has become more autonomous and more prominent in international politics (Buzan and Waever 2003: 3; Boerzel 2012). Thus, the contemporary quest for world order requires a coherent strategy to establish a concept of order *within* the various regions and to relate these regional orders to one another (Kissinger 2014). Thus, to make sense of the new WSA we have to disaggregate the global security governance into different and specific schemes of regional security governance, like in the Latin American case.

According to the 'new regionalism' approaches, globalization and regionalism are intimately connected. Globalization promotes regionalism through various causal mechanisms, whereas regionalism facilitates states' integration into the global economy, thus allowing and enforcing the logic of globalization; however, at times the two processes might differ and collide. At the same time, regional integration and regional governance can offer a middle way that preserves the notion (or better, the illusion) that states and citizens are still in control of events facing the deterministic forces of globalization. This might be also evident in the security issue area where schemes of regional security governance might be considered more feasible, realistic, and useful than more general and abstract security schemes at the UN, global level.

The changing landscape of the Latin American security architecture[3]

Security priorities in Latin America have been influenced by the changing patterns of the global security agenda, as well as by the political changes experienced by the region since the end of the Cold War. In terms of regionalism and *regional security governance*, an extensive multilateral regional network has expanded in Latin America in the post–Cold War era, enhancing an already sophisticated and highly developed system of regional international law, including regional norms that had regulated the international and domestic behavior of Latin American states (Kacowicz 2000: 143). This increased 'multilateral density,' including a broad spectrum of regional organizations with overlapping mechanisms of governance, focuses on economic and functional issue areas, but also spillovers into the security dimension. In addition to the impact of the end of the Cold War, the twin pressures of globalization and regionalization have put a premium on regional cooperation in Latin America (Heine 2006: 482–484).

Patterns of regional security cooperation are institutionalized through different and overlapping institutions. There is the OAS as an overarching Western Hemispheric organization that somehow competes with UNASUR and the recent South American Defense Council (created in 2008), as well as with CELAC (created in 2011). While three Pacific Alliance countries (Chile, Colombia, and Peru) are part of UNASUR, Mexico is not. Instead, Mexico maintains close security cooperation links with the United States and the Central American countries, which have also created a security framework in the Central American Regional Security Initiative. Moreover, the cooperation in the different security-related organizations reflects both common and divergent security threats and interests. For instance, despite sharing basic UNASUR goals, Bolivia, Ecuador, and Venezuela, as part of ALBA, ideologically challenge the U.S. hegemony in the Americas (Nolte 2013: 11).

With the end of the Cold War and the resolution of conflicts in Central America, Latin America as a whole has become progressively one of the most peaceful regions in the world, and not only South America (Kacowicz 1998; Oelsner 2005). In comparison to other areas of the Third World, Latin American militarism never represented a danger to the peace of the world, or even to the peace of the region and to the territorial integrity of its nations. It is the region with the lowest number of interstate wars and one with the lowest defense expenditures (Heine 2006: 481). Except for the Chaco War of 1932–1935, one cannot point to a major, violent, international conflict involving Latin American countries in the 20th century and the early decades of the 21st century. Hence, Latin American states have enjoyed a respectable (though qualified) tradition of moderation in military affairs, at least at the international level, through peaceful management and resolution of international conflicts.

Yet, this 'zone of peace' is at best an imperfect peace, related only to the international dimension, and disputed by scholars like David Mares as an 'illusionary' or 'violent' peace due to the persistence of interstate militarized disputes, as well as unsettled border disputes and lingering arms races (Mares 2001, 2012). Although many South American heads of state are eager to portray the region as peaceful and secure, this might be true, at best, only in interstate, and not intrastate, terms (Tavares 2014: 5). Thus, Latin America presents an odd paradox nowadays. While it is one of the most peaceful regions in the world in terms of cross-border violence, nonstate violence in various forms is widespread, ranging from that generated by drug trafficking organizations and transnational criminal cartels to petty local crime rings and gangs. Today's intrastate violence is responsible for as many deaths in Central America as during its brutal civil wars, stemming from crime, organized and unorganized, from the response of criminal cartels to redoubled efforts by governments to destroy or badly wound them, and from the incapacity of weak states to protect citizen security. This violence is also notably high in Venezuela, Mexico, Brazil, Colombia, and parts of the Caribbean basin (Lowenthal 2013: 4–5; O'Neill 2008: 25; Domínguez 1998: 27–28).

The dramatic changes in international relations brought about by the end of the Cold War led to a focus on non- or extramilitary threats. Topics already identified in the 1970s as examples of an emergent global agenda – often *intermestic*, at the intersection of domestic and international dimensions – are taking center stage in the context of international security. This is particularly relevant in the case of Latin America, which traditionally linked issues of security to those of economic and political development (Hirst and Rico 1992: 42–44). Thus, the Latin American countries confront new types of security challenges that they have been hard-pressed to tackle effectively, rendering traditional issues of war and peace irrelevant to cope with *intermestic* problems of national and international security.

This changing landscape of Latin American regional security is also characterized by transnational threats, such as drug trafficking, illegal migration flows, organized international (or rather transnational) crime, guerrilla organizations, transnational terrorism, and arms trafficking. Especially in Latin American cities, new and armed actors have taken over social-territorial spaces where formal or effective governance is by and large absent (Kruijt and Koomings 2013: 100–101). Terrorism and illicit transnational drug trafficking have posed new challenges to subregional security cooperation schemes, such as those existing in MERCOSUR. A case in point is the so-called Tri-Border Area, a duty-free zone where the borders of Paraguay, Brazil, and Argentina converge, which has been suspected as a terrorist 'hotspot' for Islamic groups (Pion-Berlin 2005: 216; Tickner 2007: 7; Flemes and Radseck 2009: 13; Tavares 2014: 63–83; Malamud and Alcañiz 2014: 2).

To sum up, how does the current security environment affect the trajectories of Latin American relations vis-à-vis the rest of the world, and its insertion in the new WSA in specific terms? First, there is a relatively benign environment in terms of geopolitics and traditional international security (absence of international wars), which nowadays includes Central America, as compared to other regions in the developing world. Second, the United States sustains specific, focused, and differentiated security interests in the region, such as the concern with drug trafficking and terrorism vis-à-vis Colombia and Mexico, or the border triangle of Argentina, Paraguay, and Brazil. Third, since the concept of *security* nowadays refers also (or even mainly) to the domestic scene, it is important to understand the political economy context, in order to grasp the contours of the available options and the potential impact and role of Latin America in the WSA. Hence, to a large extent, international, external, but also domestic and socioeconomic problems shape Latin America's strategies and insertion in the world, rather than 'conventional' security concerns vis-à-vis external threats.

What role does Latin America play in the contemporary world security architecture?

In this section, I question the role Latin America fulfills in the contemporary world security architecture by presenting a role taxonomy that includes: (1) active and cooperative vis-à-vis the WSA, (2) active and challenging the status quo, (3) active and subversive of the existing structure of the WSA, (4) passive role, and (5) potential role, especially with reference to Brazil.

Active role: contribution, collaboration, and cooperation within the WSA

Federico Merke aptly summarizes the active, though relatively marginal, role that Latin America plays in the WSA as follows:

> There is a perception in the region that, when it comes to global security, [Latin America] is more part of the solution than of the problem. The script is already known and follows predictable lines. It is known that the region is peaceful in terms of wars between states . . . [Moreover], the region was the first to declare a region free of nuclear weapons. . . . There are no rogue states or failed states (with the exception of Haiti, AK) . . . Some states in the region, including Argentina, Brazil, Chile, and Uruguay contribute regularly to UN peacekeeping operations. Most states are working (albeit moderately) with the United States in the fight against terrorism.
>
> *(Merke 2011: 5)*

In more specific terms, there has been a substantial Latin American participation in the United Nations peacekeeping missions around the world, especially in MINUSTAH, the UN peacekeeping operation in Haiti initiated in March 2004 (Heine 2006: 495–496; Domínguez 1998: 18; Sotomayor 2014). Thus, MINUSTAH is a positive example of overlap and cooperation between global security governance and regional security governance, as illustrated by the functioning of UN peacekeeping forces under the joint cooperation between Argentina, Brazil, and Chile, under the leadership of Brazil.

As for the issue area of arms control in international security, within the WSA, modern Latin American history includes many calls for disarmament, and even some limited success in achieving demilitarized frontiers or zones. In the past, Latin American governments set forth a variety of arms limitations, proposals, and agreements, including: the demilitarization of the Straits of Magellan between Argentina and Chile (1881); the Mayo Pacts of 1902 calling for comprehensive naval arms control between Argentina and Chile; the Treaty of Tlatelolco in 1967, establishing a nuclear free–zone in Latin America, the first of its kind in the world; the Argentine-Brazilian nuclear cooperation in the 1980s and 1990s, including bilateral and multilateral agreements on nuclear arms control and disarmament, leading to their joint ratification (together with Chile) of the Tlatelolco regional regime in 1992. Moreover, Brazil, as an advanced nuclear energy state, has had a significant presence in the nuclear nonproliferation regime since its origins in the 1960s, although it fully joined the Tlatelolco regime only in 1992 (Malamud and Alcañiz 2014: 11).

Thus, regional international treaties and declarations, as well as adherence to international treaties in the area of arms control and nonproliferation, are the clearest multilateral expression of the emphasis on the peaceful nature of international relations in the region (Herz 2010: 602). Significantly, the most important contribution of Latin America to the implementation of norms of disarmament and nonproliferation has been the establishment of the Latin American nuclear-weapons-free zone (NWFZ) through the Treaty of Tlatelolco, a regime that could set a precedent to be 'exported' to other regions of the world (Lacovsky 2014; Kacowicz 2005). Moreover, the ABACC could also be envisioned as a model to be adopted by other regions of the world, due to its potential to address nonproliferation risks similar to those that occurred in the Southern Cone of Latin America until the mid-1980s.

Active role and challenging the status quo of the WSA: the ALBA alternative

Following the end of the Cold War and the disappearance of the Soviet Union, there has been no significant challenge to the U.S. hegemony in the Western Hemisphere. The challenges posed by countries such as Cuba, Venezuela, Bolivia, Ecuador, Nicaragua, and perhaps Argentina to the U.S. paramountcy are first and foremost rhetorical, since they do not suggest a practical alternative to the existing WSA, but rather a diluted form of 'soft balancing,' given the distribution of power in the international system in general, and in the Americas in particular (Lowenthal 2013: 6; Skidmore and Smith 1992: 376).

By launching ALBA in 2005, Venezuela and Cuba have attempted to develop an alternative regional scheme in opposition to neoliberalism and economic globalization, and particularly to the idea (that never came to fruition) of establishing an FTAA, by promoting a nationalistic and alternative regional path of integration. Thus, ALBA should be understood as a counterhegemonic globalization project that operates through international and transnational processes, ranging from the local to the global (Muhr 2012: 768). According to this logic, member-states of ALBA have established 'strategic alliances' with Iran and Syria, as well as with rising powers such as China and Russia, in a kind of 'soft balancing' against the United States.

Challenging the United States has had a strong ideological component, as in practice it rests on the ability of the Cuban and Venezuelan governments to mobilize political, economic, or symbolic resources to resist direct actions from the United States (Russell and Calle 2009). Moreover, some analysts perceive Venezuela as a security threat to the United States, due to its strong links with Iran and its prominent role as a primary transit country for cocaine flowing from Colombia to the United States, Europe, and West Africa. Furthermore, Venezuela has also had a significant effect upon the foreign policy of countries like Argentina, leading to its rapprochement with Iran and against the United States, and it has supported the FARC against Colombia (Walser 2010: 2; Morales Solá 2013).

Active and subversive of the existing structure of the WSA

In the specific context of U.S.–Latin American relations, Latin America might – sporadically and eventually – draw high-level attention from Washington due to geopolitical reasons, due to its neighboring position and proximity. For instance, terrorists from any part of the world might try to enter U.S. territory from Latin America (Smith 2008: 375–376). Moreover, although Latin America may have no weapons of mass destruction, it has one of the richest sources of drugs that fuel much of the U.S. and European markets, and the largest source of U.S. immigrants, both documented and not. The drug trade flourishes from a volatile combination of negative socioeconomic conditions in Latin America and high demand for narcotics in the United States and in Europe. In addition, and as a more immediate and urgent threat, transnational criminal gangs such as the M-18 and the MS-13 have been flagged as a serious emerging threat to hemispheric security (Smith 2008: 376–377; O'Neill 2008: 29–37; Merke 2011: 6).

All of the 'new' security threats the United States perceives as coming from Latin America – drugs, migration, environmental degradation, insurgents, transnational crime – reinforces the U.S. security interest focused upon Mexico, Central America, the Caribbean, Colombia, and Venezuela, which are perceived as the "turbulent periphery" (Russell and Calle 2009; Buzan and Waever 2003: 336–337). In this sense, these security threats perform an active and subversive role of the existing structure of the new WSA, first and foremost vis-à-vis the United States, but also by extension, with reference also to Europe and to other regions of the world.

Passive role vis-à-vis the WSA

The Latin American views on global security are very much affected by their states' strong adherence to the norms of sovereignty and nonintervention. There is a common perception, both in Latin America and vis-à-vis Latin America, that the region is far away from the most pressing global security issues, including terrorism, rogue states, failed states, and the proliferation of weapons of mass destruction. Therefore, it seems that Latin American countries, broadly speaking, are reluctant to take upon international responsibilities 'out of their area' and in the more general context of the new WSA (Merke 2011: 4; Heine 2006: 485–487). This reluctance has a strong ideological basis; most of the Latin American nations are reluctant to actively cooperate with the United States, since they would prefer a more multilateral and multipolar world to the 'unipolar moment' under the aegis of the United States, and opt for a world in which the new WSA would not sanction countries for any actions.

As mostly small or middle-sized powers in a region that is considered traditionally at the margins of global security, Latin America has historically placed a strong emphasis upon a legal international order and its participation in international organizations such as the United Nations (Heine 2006: 481). And yet, by and large, Latin American nations have adopted a rather passive role in the WSA.

A case in point referred to the discussion at the United Nations regarding a possible military action against Iraq in 2003. Mexico and Chile at the UN Security Council, in addition to Cuba and Venezuela, opposed the U.S. invasion. Several Central American countries (including Honduras, El Salvador, Nicaragua, Costa Rica, Panama, and the Dominican Republic) and Colombia supported the United States, whereas most of the South American countries adopted an intermediate, ambiguous, and reluctant position. Similarly in the Libyan case, despite their rhetorical support for the new humanitarian intervention doctrine of 'responsibility to protect,' many Latin American countries opposed the UN actions in Libya.

Broadly speaking, one might suggest that the region has been (and it still is) largely neglected, since it is perceived as posing no significant traditional threats to the countries that dominate international affairs, first and foremost the United States (Smith 2008: 377; Tulchin and Espach 2001: 2). This tendency of irrelevance and marginalization was exacerbated even with the end of the Cold War, and with the 'War on Terror' following the 9/11 attacks upon the United States (Castañeda 1994: 45–48). As Keohane argues, Latin American countries "are takers, instead of makers, of international policy" (Keohane 2001: 211). Similarly, as Escudé suggests in this volume, according to the theory of peripheral realism, there is a clear division between the rule-makers and the rule-takers, so that most of the Latin American countries, with the possible exception of Brazil, belong to the latter category, either passively or actively recognizing that role (Escudé 2012).

Potential role: Brazil as a global player?

Among the Latin American countries, Brazil might be the exception to the rule in terms of its *potential* role as an emergent global player in international relations in general, and in the WSA architecture in particular, despite its lack of significant military power. And yet, as Darnton argues in his chapter in this volume, it is not evident whether one can make a strong argument about Brazil (or for that case, other members of the BRICS constellation) playing a paramount role in the new WSA. True, Brazil leads MINUSTAH, and it is a global leader in the fight against AIDS pandemics; it has also recently moved to play a diplomatic (though unsuccessful) role in the Middle Eastern conundrum (both in the Palestinian and Iranian nuclear questions), and it seeks a permanent seat in the United Nations Security Council. And yet, despite its enhanced international image in terms of global governance, Brazil has not even fulfilled its role as the leader of Latin America in general, and of South America in particular, so its role in the WSA can be described as a potential or ambiguous one (Malamud and Alcañiz 2014; Malamud 2011; Sweig 2011).

In lieu of conclusions: questions for further research

In lieu of conclusions, I offer several questions to articulate a research agenda about the complex issue of the role of Latin America in the new WSA, as follows:

Which role should *Latin America in general, and Brazil in particular, play in the new WSA?*

Unlike the previous questions posed throughout this chapter, this is a normative question. For instance, can Latin America serve as an example and as a model to other regions of the world, in terms of international (but not domestic) peace?

As Merke (2011) and Smith (2008) suggest, the different roles adopted by Latin America in the new WSA are a function of: (1) the distribution of power in the international system in general, and in the Western Hemisphere in particular; (2) the normative framework, identities, and ideologies sustained by the Latin American nations, with a particular emphasis upon their strong adherence to the norm of sovereignty and its corollaries of nonintervention and territorial integrity; and (3) the structure of the international political economic system, through the effects of economic globalization and the traditional relations of dependency in terms of North-South relations (Kacowicz 2005, 2013). Thus, a relevant research agenda in this context would be to develop a theoretically informed model of how the three factors might work together and test it empirically, either within Latin America or cross-regionally.

In the particular case of Brazil, the question remains whether Brazil does not want to or cannot fulfill its potentialities as a great emerging power. Yet, Brazil does not perceive that its international standing depends upon its playing an active leadership in Latin America. Thus, an interesting research question would be whether the major powers in the WSA see it that way too.

What is the role of U.S.–Latin American relations (and to a lesser extent, of Chinese–Latin American relations) in shaping the position of Latin America in the new WSA?

Traditionally, the insertion of Latin America in the WSA has taken place through the prism of the continental hegemony of the United States, since the Monroe Doctrine until the age of globalization. Although the era of the U.S. hegemony in the world might be coming to an end, it is not clear whether China can or will replace the paramount role of the United States in the Western Hemisphere, at least in security terms.

What is the role of Latin American relations with other regions of the world in shaping its position in the new WSA?

That is also a fascinating question that at this stage remains moot. There are increasing instances and possibilities for South-South cooperation – for instance, an increased role for Brazil in

Africa and in the Middle East – and even enhanced security relations with Russia (not only by Cuba). And yet, it is not clear how the Latin American position in the new WSA will be enhanced or changed, if we adopt Kupchan's theory that we live in "nobody's world."

By the end of the day, an enhanced role for Latin America in the new WSA will be dependent not only on external factors to the region (such as the global distribution of power and the rules of the game), but first and foremost upon the willingness and capabilities of Latin American countries to embark on a significant integration project that will increase their bargaining power vis-à-vis the rest of the world, beyond their rhetorical utterances of good Bolivarian intentions. Yet, if Latin America integrates but still retains its normative emphasis upon nonintervention and sovereign equality, how will other actors respond? Even integrating in an effective way, Latin America will remain a supplier of raw materials in the international economic system, so where will an integrated Latin America get its leverage?

Most of the Latin American countries, even the 12 South American members of UNASUR, still do not share a common security policy or a clear IR strategy. If we add to their relative lack of initiative the basic and lingering asymmetrical relationships between Latin America and the rest of the world, then it becomes easier to understand why the United States, Europe, and, increasingly, other powers like China and India remain more proactive in their involvement in the region than the other way around.

Notes

1 This chapter has been written under the auspices and the sponsorship of the Thyssen Foundation in a grant that refers to the linkage between global governance and regional governance in the Latin American context. I would like to thank Keren Sasson, Daniel Wajner, and Exequiel Lacovsky for their research assistance and wonderful insights, as well as the incisive comments of Andreas Feldmann, David Mares, Andrea Oelsner, and Galia Press-Barnathan.

2 By new 'world security architecture' I refer to the contemporary structure of the international system defined in security terms (alliances and polarity, institutions and norms, stability, war and peace, security threats and issues). A related concept is that of *global security governance* as a system of rules conceived by individual and corporate actors through concerted efforts, coordinated management, and regulation of security issues (Kacowicz and Press-Barnathan 2015).

3 A more detailed examination of the Latin American regional security governance and its changing landscape can be found in most of the chapters of this Handbook, especially in Parts II and III.

References

Baylis, J. (2011) 'International and Global Security' in J. Baylis, S. Smith and P. Owens (eds) *The Globalization of World Politics*, 5th edition, Oxford: Oxford University Press.

Boerzel, T. A. (2012) 'Do All Roads Lead to Regionalism?' in T. A. Boerzel, L. Goltermann, M. Lohaus and K. Striebinger (eds) *Roads to Regionalism: Genesis, Design, and Effects of Regional Organizations*, Farnahm: Ashgate.

Buzan, B. and Waever, O. (2003) *Regions and Powers: The Structure of International Security*, Cambridge: Cambridge University Press.

Castañeda, J. G. (1994) 'Latin America and the End of the Cold War: An Essay in Frustration' in A. F. Lowenthal (ed) *Latin America in the New World*, Boulder: Westview.

Domínguez, J. I. (1998) 'Security, Peace, and Democracy in Latin America and the Caribbean: Challenges for the Post-Cold War Era' in J. I. Domínguez (ed) *International Security and Democracy: Latin America and the Caribbean in the Post-Cold War Era*, Pittsburgh: Pittsburgh University Press.

Escudé, C. (2012) *Principios de realismo periférico: Una teoría Argentina y su vigencia ante el ascenso de China*, Buenos Aires: Lumiere.

Flemes, D. and Radseck, M. (2009) 'Creating Multilevel Security Governance in South America', *GIGA Working Papers*, 117.

Fukuyama, F. (1992) *The End of History and the Last Man*, New York: Free Press.

Heine, J. (2006) 'Between a Rock and a Hard Place: Latin America and Multlateralism after 9/11' in E. Newman, R. Thakur and J. Tirman (eds) *Multilateralism under Challenge? Power, International Order, and Structural Change*, Tokyo: United Nations University Press.
Herz, M. (2010) 'Concepts of Security in South America', *International Peacekeeping*, 17(5): 598–612.
Hettne, B. and Soderbaum, F. (2006) 'The United Nations and Regional Organizations in Global Security: Competing or Complementary Logics?', *Global Governance*, 12(3): 227–232.
Hirst, M. and Rico, C. (1992) 'Regional Security Perceptions in Latin America', *Documentos e Informes de Investigación, FLACSO*, 129: 1–74.
Kacowicz, A. M. (1998) *Zones of Peace in the Third World: South America and West Africa in Comparative Perspective*, Albany: SUNY Press.
——— (1999) 'Regionalization, Globalization, and Nationalism: Convergent, Divergent, or Overlapping?', *Alternatives*, 24: 527–556.
——— (2000) 'Latin America as an International Society', *International Politics*, 37: 143–162.
——— (2005) *The Impact of Norms in International Society: The Latin American Experience, 1881–2001*, Notre Dame: University of Notre Dame Press.
——— (2013) *Globalization and the Distribution of Wealth: The Latin American Experience, 1982–2008*, Cambridge: Cambridge University Press.
Kacowicz, A. M. and Press-Barnathan, G. (2015) 'Regional Security Governance' in T. Boerjel and T. Risse (eds) *Oxford Handbook of Comparative Regionalism*, Oxford: Oxford University Press.
Katzenstein, P. J. (2005) *A World of Regions: Asia and Europe in the American Imperium*, Ithaca: Cornell University Press.
Keohane, R. O. (2001) 'Between Vision and Reality: Variables in Latin American Foreign Policy' in J. S. Tulchin and R. H. Espach (eds) *Latin America in the New International System*, Boulder: Lynne Rienner.
Kirchner, E. J. and Domínguez, R. E. (eds) (2011) *The Security Governance of Regional Institutions*, London: Routledge.
Kissinger, H. (2014, August 29) 'The Assembly of a New Global Order', *Wall Street Journal*. Retrieved from http://www.wsj.com/articles/henry-kissinger-on-the-assembly-of-a-new-world-order-1409328075.
Krauthammer, C. (1990–1991) 'The Unipolar Moment', *Foreign Affairs*, 70(1): 23–33.
Kruijt, D. and Koomings, K. (2013) 'From Political Armies to the "War against Crime": The Transformation of Militarism in Latin America' in A. Staurianakis and J. Selby (eds) *Militarism in International Relations: Political Economy, Security, Theory*, London: Routledge.
Kupchan, C. A. (2012) *No One's World: The West, The Rising Rest, and the Coming Global Turn*, Oxford: Oxford University Press.
Lacovsky, E. (2014) *Nuclear Weapons Free Zones: Between Regional and Global Governance*, Jerusalem: 10th Annual Graduate Conference in Political Science, International Relations, and Public Policy, The Hebrew University.
Lowenthal, A. F. (2013) 'Rethinking U.S.-Latin American Relations: Thirty Years of Transformation' in *The Americas in Motion: Looking Ahead*, Washington, DC: Inter-American Dialogue.
Malamud, A. (2011) 'A Leader without Followers? The Growing Divergence between the Regional and Global Performance of Brazilian Foreign Policy', *Latin American Politics and Society*, 53(3): 1–24.
Malamud, A. and Alcañiz, I. (2014) 'Managing Security in a Zone of Peace: Brazil's Soft Approach to Regional Governance', *RSCAS EUI Working Papers*.
Mares, D. R. (2001) *Violent Peace: Militarized Interstate Bargaining in Latin America*, New York: Columbia University Press.
——— (2012) *Latin America and the Illusion of Peace*, London: Routledge.
Merke, F. (2011) 'Framing Global Security in South America', Rio de Janeiro: Paper presented at the workshop on Global Security Regimes in the Making.
Morales Solá, J. (2013, February 3) 'Una foto del aislamiento Argentino', *La Nación*. Retrieved from http://www.lanacion.com.ar/1551395-una-foto-del-aislamiento-argentino.
Muhr, T. (2012) 'The Politics of Space in the Boliviarian Alliance for the Peoples of Our America – Peoples' Trade Agreement (ALBA-TCP): Transnationalism, the Organized Society, and Counter-Hegemonic Governance', *Globalizations*, 9(6): 767–782.
Nolte, D. (2013) 'Latin America's New Regional Architecture: Segmented Regionalism or Cooperative Regional Governance?', Washington, DC: Paper presented at the 31st International Congress of LASA.
Oelsner, A. (2005) *International Relations in Latin America: Peace and Security in the Southern Cone*, New York: Routledge.

O'Neill, S. K. (ed) (2008) *U.S.-Latin American Relations: A New Direction for a New Reality*, New York: Council on Foreign Relations.
Pion-Berlin, D. (2005) 'Sub-regional Cooperation, Hemispheric Threat: Security in the Southern Cone' in L. Fawcett and M. Serrano (eds) *Regionalism and Governance in the Americas: Continental Drift*, New York: Palgrave.
Russell, R., and Calle, F. (2009) 'La periferia turbulenta como factor de la expansión de los intereses de seguridad de EEUU en América Latina' in M. Hirst (ed) *Crisis de estado e intervención internacional: Una mirada desde el sur*, Buenos Aires: Edhasa.
Skidmore, T. E. and Smith, P. H. (1992) *Modern Latin America*, New York: Oxford University Press.
Smith, P. H. (2008) *Talons of the Eagle: Latin America, the United States, and the World*, New York: Oxford University Press.
Sotomayor, A. C. (2014) *The Myth of the Democratic Peacekeeper: Civil-Military Relations and the United Nations*, Baltimore: Johns Hopkins University Press.
Sweig, J. (ed) (2011) *Global Brazil and U.S.-Brazil Relations*, New York: Council on Foreign Relations.
Tavares, R. (2014) *Security in South America: The Role of States and Regional Organizations*, Boulder: Lynne Rienner.
Tickner, A. B. (2007) 'Latin America and the Caribbean: Domestic and Transnational Insecurity', *Coping with Crises: Working Paper Series*.
Tulchin, J. T. and Espach, R. H. (2001) 'Latin America in the New International System: A Call for Strategic Thinking' in J. S. Tulchin and R. H. Espach (eds) *Latin America in the New International System*, Boulder: Lynne Rienner.
Vargas Llosa, M. (2014, September 8) 'Las guerras del fin del mundo', *La Nación*. Retrieved from http://www.lanacion.com.ar/1725347-las-guerras-del-fin-del-mundo.
Walser, R. (2010) 'State Sponsors of Terrorism: Time to Add Venezuela to the List', *Backgrounder*, 2362.
Zepp-La Rouche, H. (2014, September 24) 'We Need a New, Inclusive World Security Architecture', *La RouchePac*. Retrieved from http://larouchepac.com/node/31801.

INDEX

Note: Page numbers with *t* indicate tables.

For Product Safety Concerns and Information please contact our EU
representative GPSR@taylorandfrancis.com
Taylor & Francis Verlag GmbH, Kaufingerstraße 24, 80331 München, Germany

www.ingramcontent.com/pod-product-compliance
Ingram Content Group UK Ltd.
Pitfield, Milton Keynes, MK11 3LW, UK
UKHW050053200926
475702UK00019B/2819
* 9 7 8 0 3 6 7 5 8 1 7 4 9 *